JOSEPHINE BAKER

Dedicated to the memory of Benoîte Groult, journalist, writer and feminist activist. Niece to the fashion designer Paul Poiret, who from 1925 onwards was Josephine Baker's couturier, Benoîte kept pace with this book as it came into being. She insisted on a cameo for her parents, Nicole and André Groult, who were friends of the American starlet. The couple appear with Paul on page 168.

Thank you:
To Jean-Claude Bouillon-Baker for his invitation to journey through his mother's life.
To Akio Bouillon, Luis Bouillon, Brian Bouillon-Baker and Marianne Zinzen for their hospitality.

To Marie-Anne Didierjean, Francine Vergeaux and Christelle Pourrot for their artistic and graphics support. To Stevan Roudaut for arranging the typography, and Catelnéo and Nicolas Sécheret for implementing it. To Lætitia Bocquet for all translations from English.

To all those who guided our steps when we were researching locations:

In St. Louis, Missouri, to Jean-Louis Pautrot, Professor of French and International Studies at St. Louis University, his family and his colleagues at the university, Emily Lutenski and Stephen Casmier. Anne Woodhouse, Shoenberg Curator at the Missouri Historical Society. Jane Roberts, vice-chair of American Friends of the Musée d'Orsay. Frederick Johnson, Josephine's great-nephew. Left Bank Books.

In New York, to Jean-Claude Rouzaud, aka "Baker".

At Le Beau-Chêne, the mansion in Vésinet, to Philippe Baudry, Henri Lanthonie and the members of the Vésinet Historical Society.

In Morocco, to Odile Nublat and Guénaël Borg in the Book Department of the French Institute of Morocco, to Nour-Eddine Bakhouch and Alexandre Pajon from the French Institute in Tangier; to Rachid Taferssiti, Hubert de Chanville, Albrecht Jerrentrup from the El Minzah Hotel in Tangier; to Alban Corbier-Labasse and Magali Laigne from the French Institute in Casablanca; to Dr. El-Haiba Azeddine from the Mers-Sultan Clinic in Casablanca; to Kamal Moueddene from the French Institute in in Marrakesh.

At the Château des Milandes, to Angélique de Saint-Exupery and the team at the Josephine Baker museum.

In Istanbul, to Julie Scheibling.

In Roquebrune-Cap-Martin, to Michèle Bouillon and Caroline Aldrin.

To Brigitte Bardot, Corinne Baret-Idatte, Basile Béguerie, Danielle Bocquet, Emmanuel Bodein, Claire Bouilhac, Brigitte Boujassy, André Bernard, Caroline and Thierry Briez, Christine Cam, Elsa Daillencourt, Blandine de Caunes, Kathy Degreef, Mylène Demongeot, Sabine Desforges, Anne Dive, Céline du Chéné, Laurence Caracalla, Jean-Paul Caracalla, Jocelyne Coffre, Charlotte Gallimard, Stanislas Gaudry, Philippe Ghielmetti, Benoîte Groult, Lætitia Lehmann, Violette Mazza, Benoît Mouchart, Christiane and Jean Muller, Jean-Philippe Muller, Philippe Pierre-Adolphe, Pronto, Pascal Quignard, Nathalie Rocher, Delphine Ribouchon, Estelle Vermer, Marité Vieira, Jean-Pierre Vincenot, Martine Saada, Annie and François Samuelson, Line Scheibling and the entire crew at our publisher, Casterman, for their help.

To Marc Ganem, who first inspired in us the desire to create this book.

And to our three daughters: Lætitia, Julie and Line, without whom all would be impossible.

Lettering and layout for the French edition of this book were created by Nicolas Sécheret.

JOSEPHINE BAKER

CATEL & BOCQUET

Art by Catel Muller
Written by José-Louis Bocquet

Historical consultant:
Jean-Claude Bouillon-Baker

Josephine Baker tells the story of a woman's battle against racism in the first half of the twentieth century, and therefore includes some language and attitudes which modern readers may find offensive.

SELF MADE HERO

First published in English in 2017
by SelfMadeHero
139–141 Pancras Road
London NW1 1UN
www.selfmadehero.com

Written and illustrated by Catel & Bocquet
Pages 1–460 translated from French by Edward Gauvin
Pages 461–568 translated from French by Mercedes Claire Gilliom

INSTITUT FRANÇAIS
ROYAUME-UNI

This book is supported by the Institut français (Royaume-Uni) as part of the Burgess programme.

English edition
Publishing Director: Emma Hayley
Sales & Marketing Manager: Sam Humphrey
Editorial & Production Manager: Guillaume Rater
UK Publicist: Paul Smith
US Publicist: Maya Bradford
Designer: Txabi Jones
With thanks to Dan Lockwood and Nick de Somogyi

A CIP record for this book is available from the British Library

ISBN: 978-1-910593-29-5

10 9 8 7 6 5 4 3 2 1

Printed and bound in Slovenia

1906 : Female Hospital, St. Louis, Missouri, USA

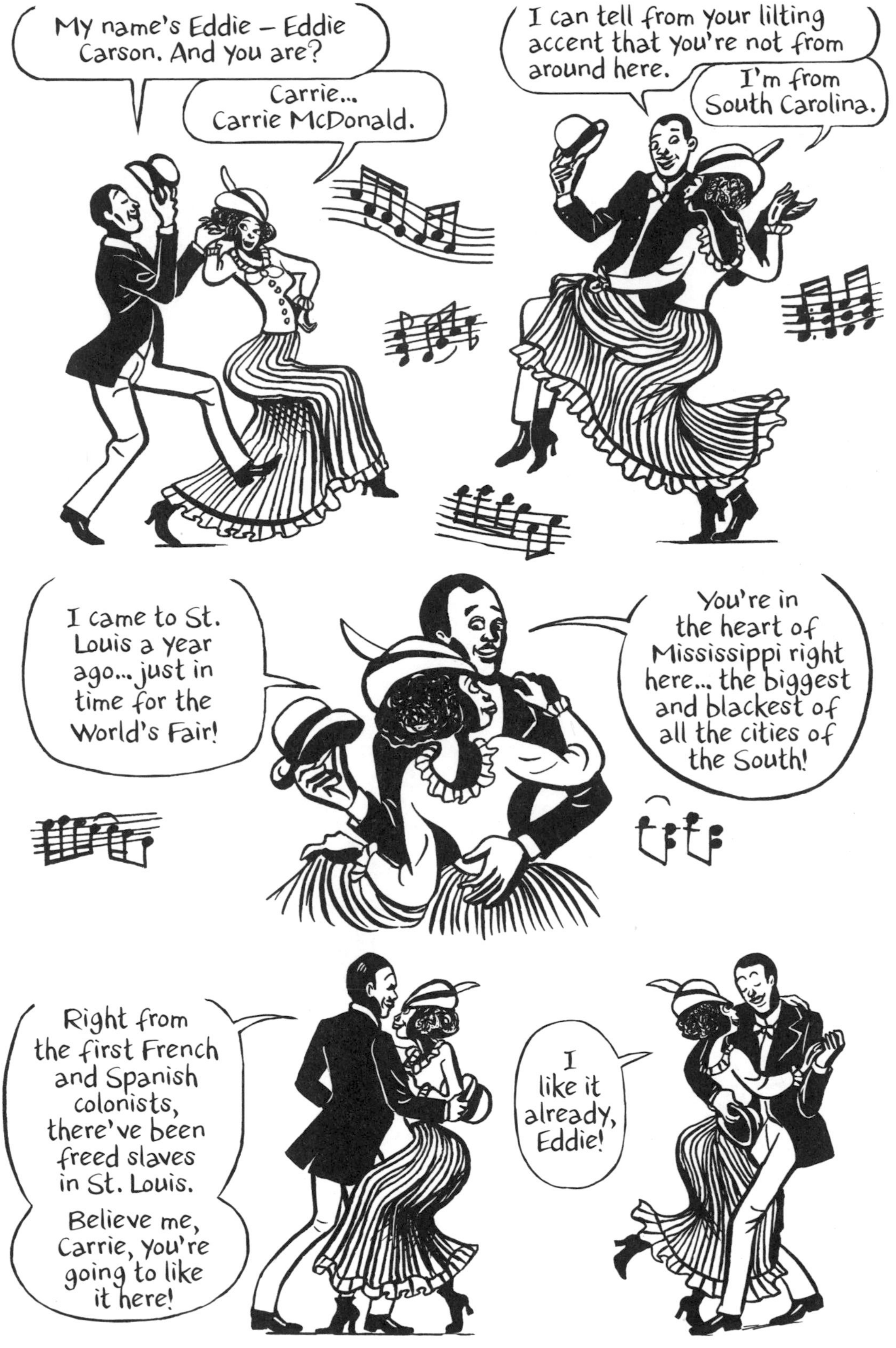

My name's Eddie – Eddie Carson. And you are?
Carrie... Carrie McDonald.
I can tell from your lilting accent that you're not from around here.
I'm from South Carolina.
I came to St. Louis a year ago... just in time for the World's Fair!
You're in the heart of Mississippi right here... the biggest and blackest of all the cities of the South!
Right from the first French and Spanish colonists, there've been freed slaves in St. Louis.
Believe me, Carrie, you're going to like it here!
I like it already, Eddie!

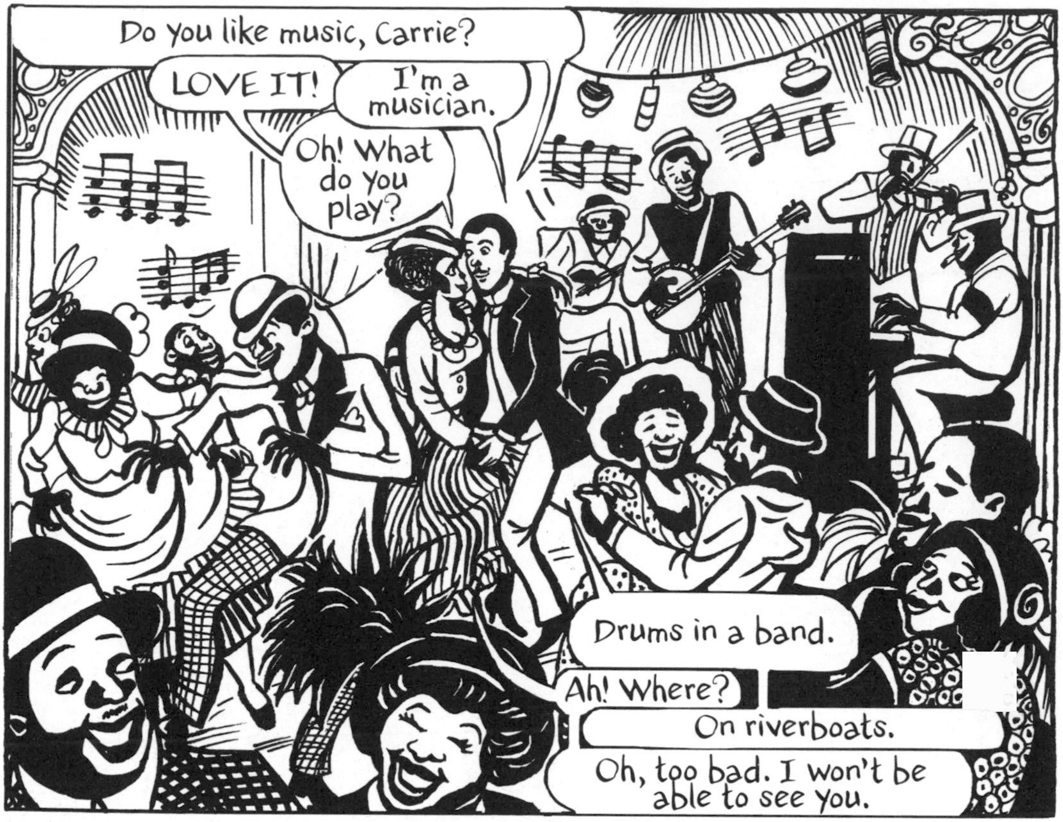
Do you like music, Carrie?
LOVE IT!
I'm a musician.
Oh! What do you play?
Drums in a band.
Ah! Where?
On riverboats.
Oh, too bad. I won't be able to see you.

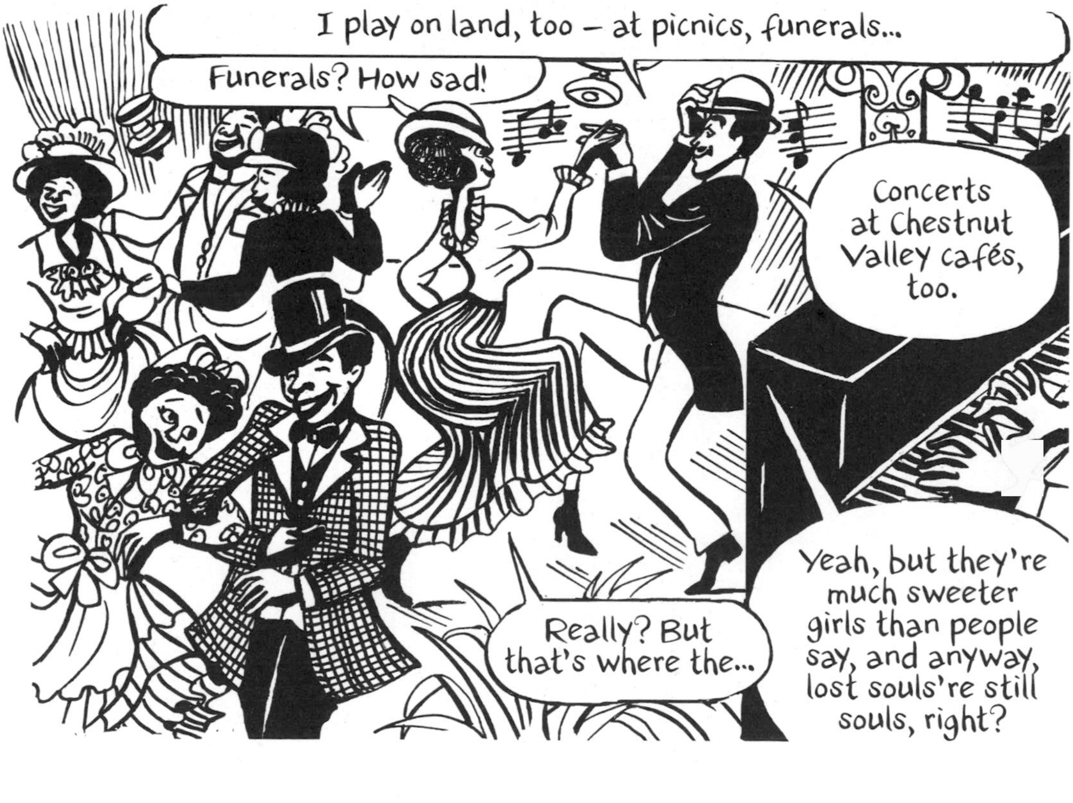
I play on land, too – at picnics, funerals...
Funerals? How sad!
Concerts at Chestnut Valley cafés, too.
Really? But that's where the...
Yeah, but they're much sweeter girls than people say, and anyway, lost souls're still souls, right?

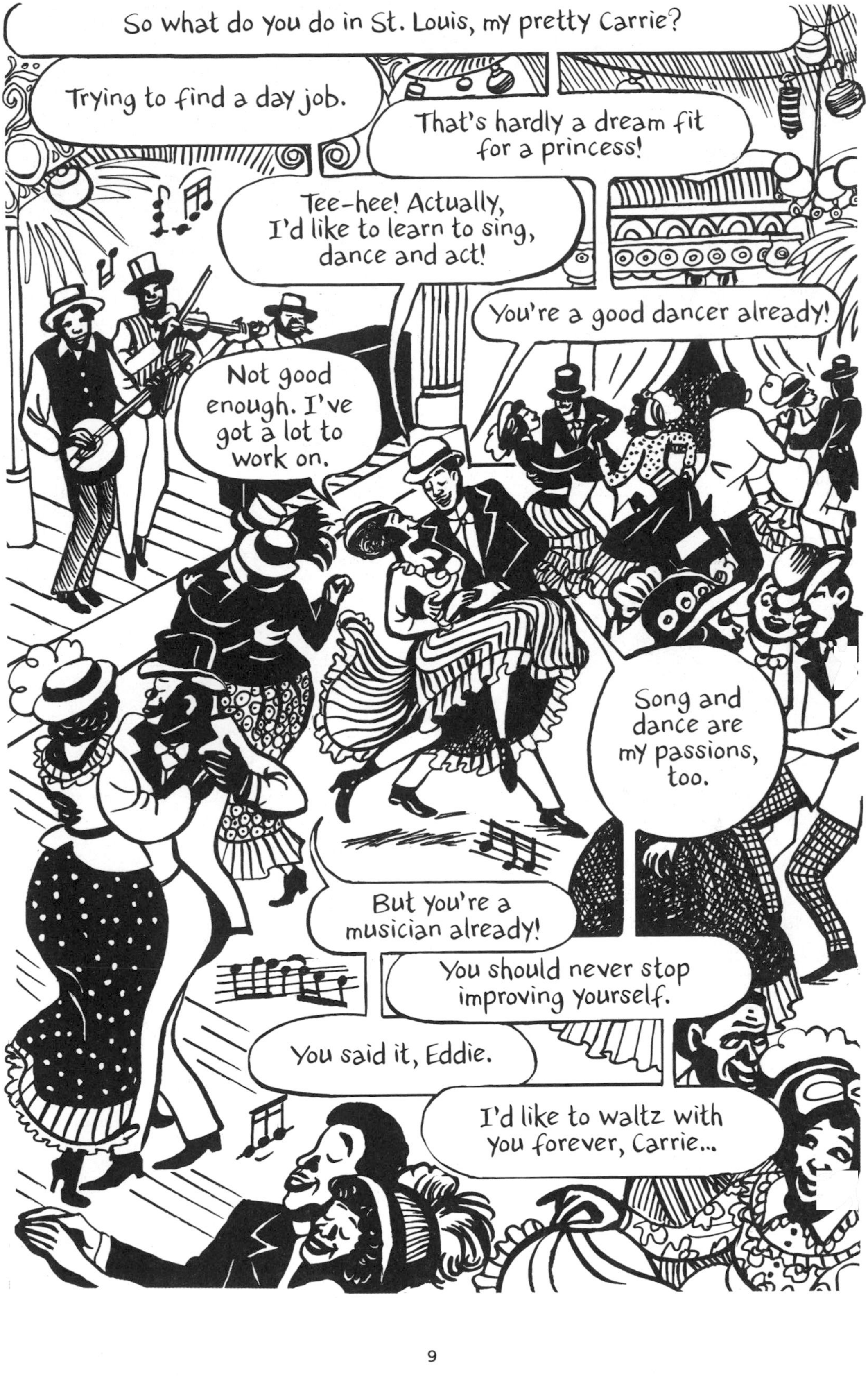
So what do you do in St. Louis, my pretty Carrie?
Trying to find a day job.
That's hardly a dream fit for a princess!
Tee-hee! Actually, I'd like to learn to sing, dance and act!
You're a good dancer already!
Not good enough. I've got a lot to work on.
Song and dance are my passions, too.
But you're a musician already!
You should never stop improving yourself.
You said it, Eddie.
I'd like to waltz with you forever, Carrie...

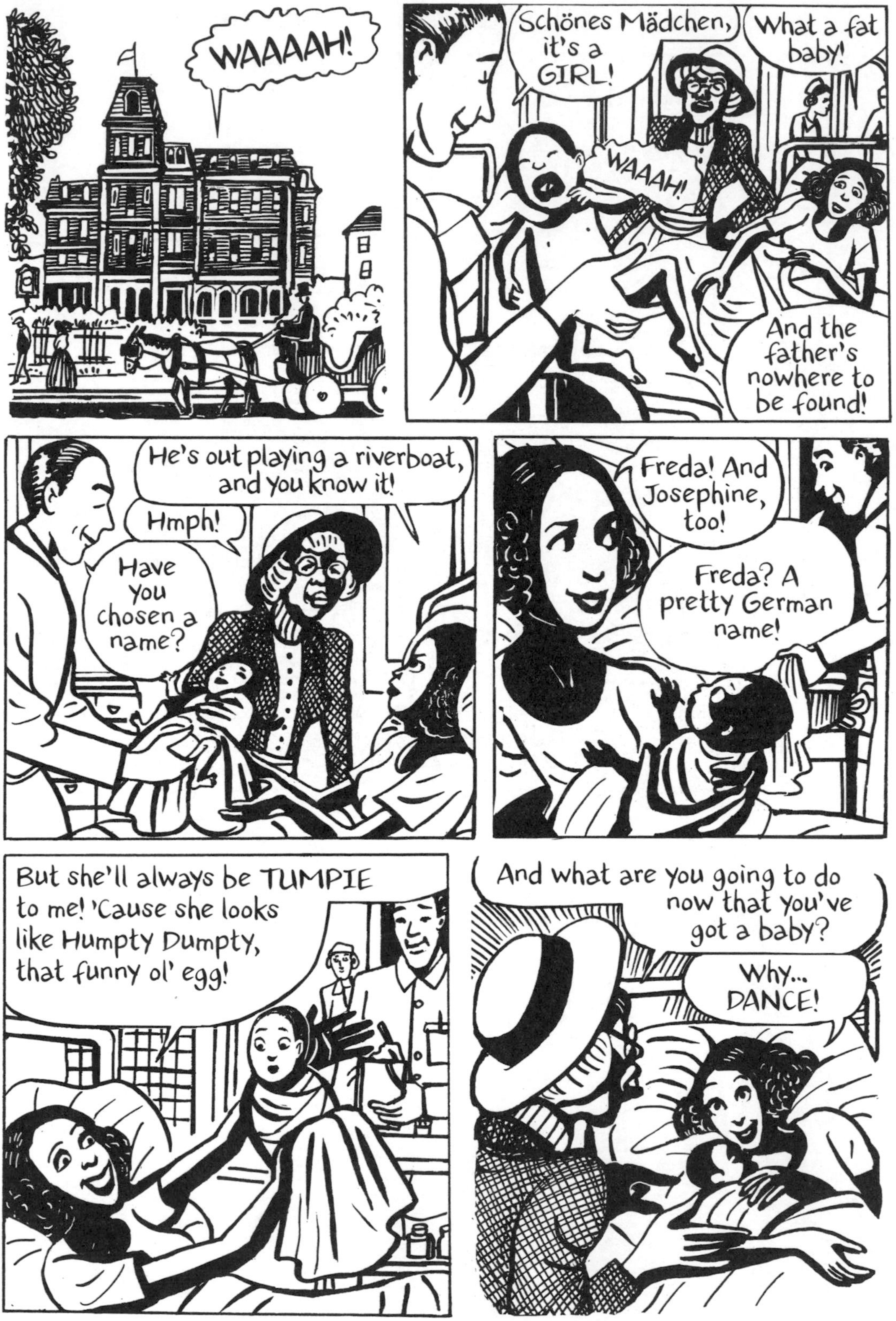
WAAAAH!
Schönes Mädchen, it's a GIRL!
What a fat baby!
WAAAH!
And the father's nowhere to be found!
He's out playing a riverboat, and you know it!
Hmph!
Have you chosen a name?
Freda! And Josephine, too!
Freda? A pretty German name!
But she'll always be TUMPIE to me! 'Cause she looks like Humpty Dumpty, that funny ol' egg!
And what are you going to do now that you've got a baby?
Why... DANCE!

1907: Papin Street, St. Louis, Missouri, USA

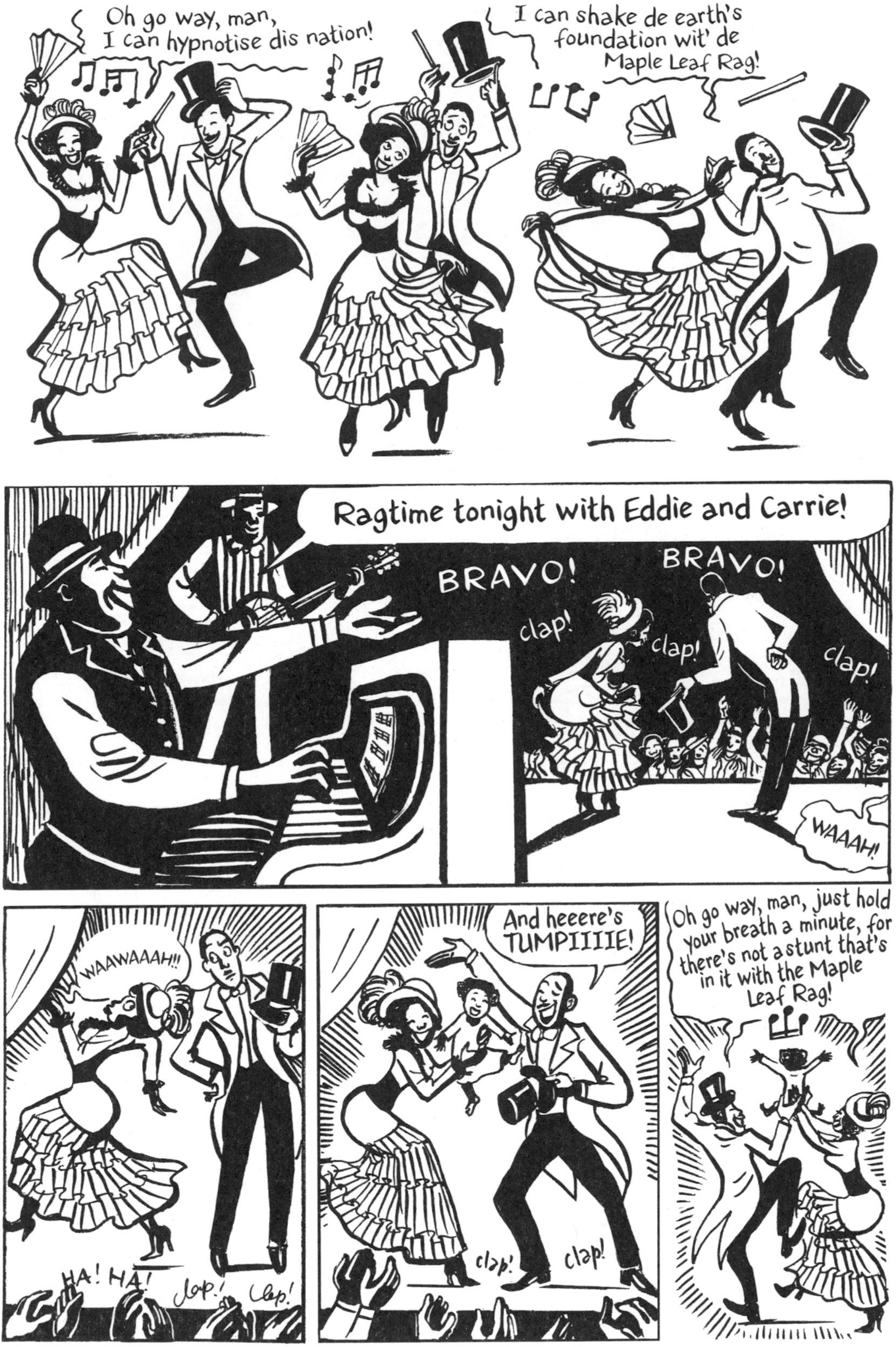

Oh go way, man, I can hypnotise dis nation!
I can shake de earth's foundation wit' de Maple Leaf Rag!
Ragtime tonight with Eddie and Carrie!
BRAVO!
BRAVO!
clap!
clap!
clap!
WAAAH!
WAAWAAAH!!
HA! HA!
clap!
clap!
And heeere's TUMPIIIIE!
clap!
clap!
Oh go way, man, just hold your breath a minute, for there's not a stunt that's in it with the Maple Leaf Rag!

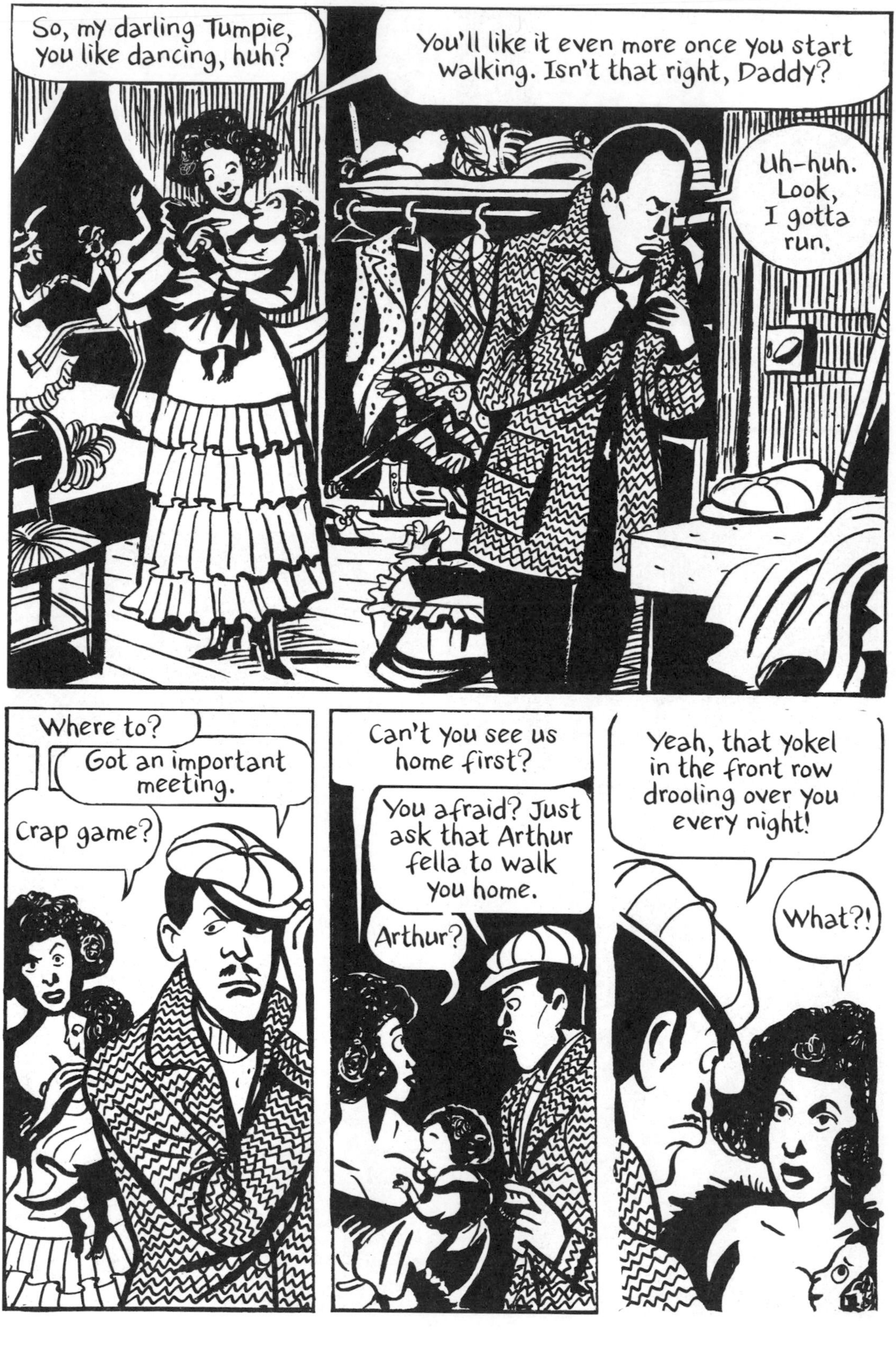
So, my darling Tumpie, you like dancing, huh?
You'll like it even more once you start walking. Isn't that right, Daddy?
Uh-huh. Look, I gotta run.
Where to?
Got an important meeting.
Crap game?
Can't you see us home first?
You afraid? Just ask that Arthur fella to walk you home.
Arthur?
Yeah, that yokel in the front row drooling over you every night!
What?!

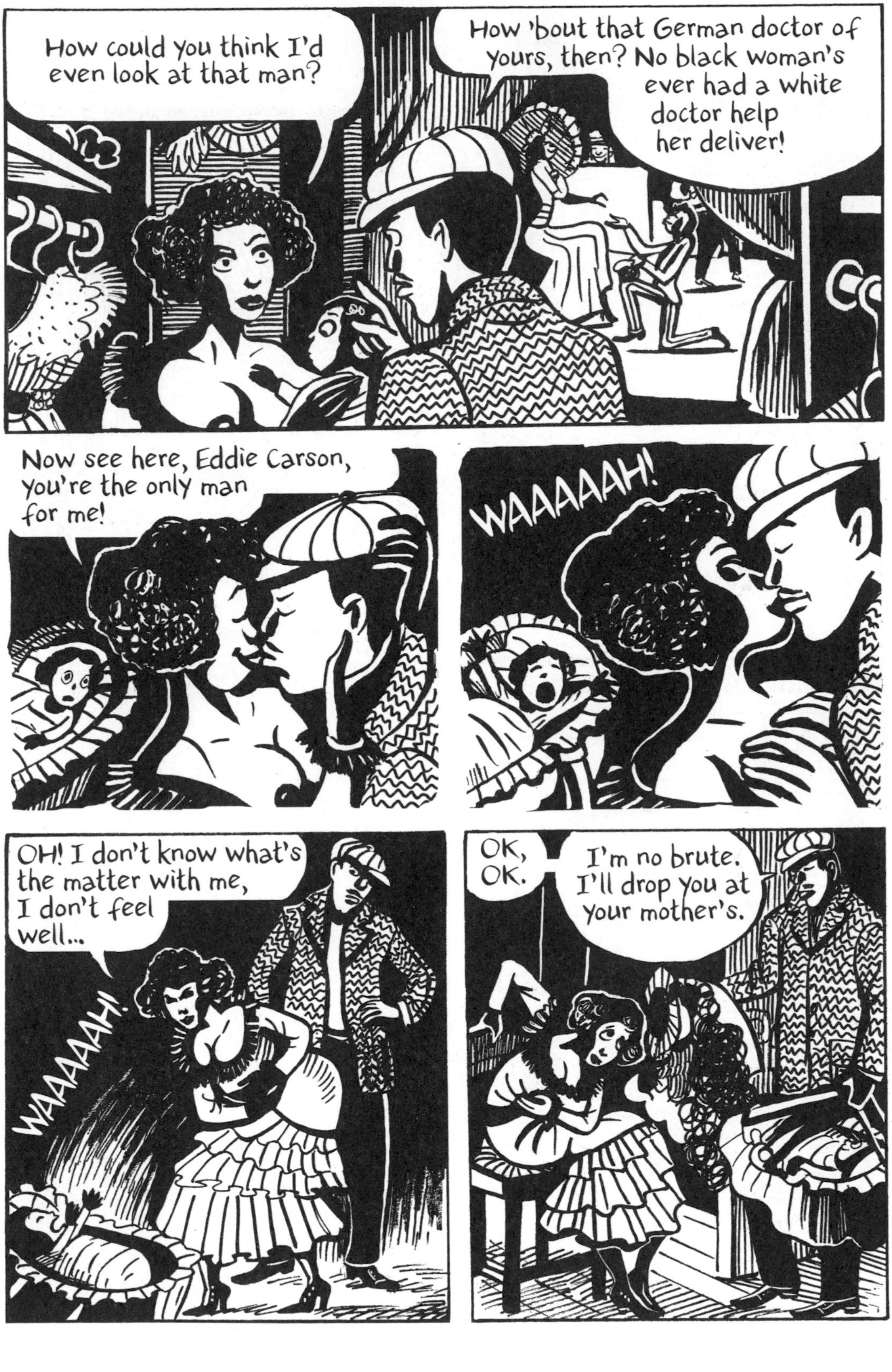
How could you think I'd even look at that man?
How 'bout that German doctor of yours, then? No black woman's ever had a white doctor help her deliver!
Now see here, Eddie Carson, you're the only man for me!
WAAAAAH!
OH! I don't know what's the matter with me, I don't feel well...
WAAAAAH!
OK, OK.
I'm no brute. I'll drop you at your mother's.

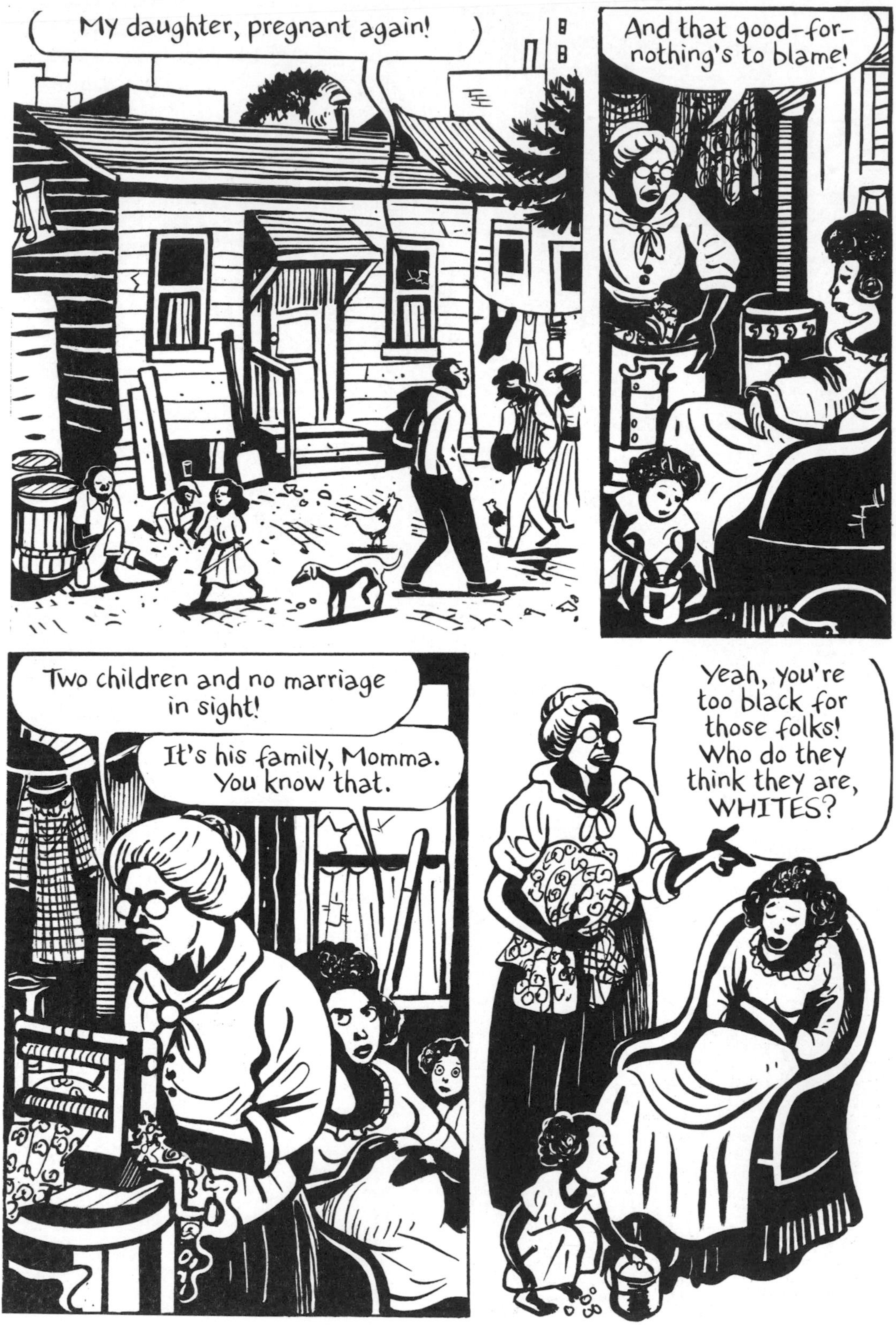
My daughter, pregnant again!
And that good-for-nothing's to blame!
Two children and no marriage in sight!
It's his family, Momma. You know that.
Yeah, you're too black for those folks! Who do they think they are, WHITES?

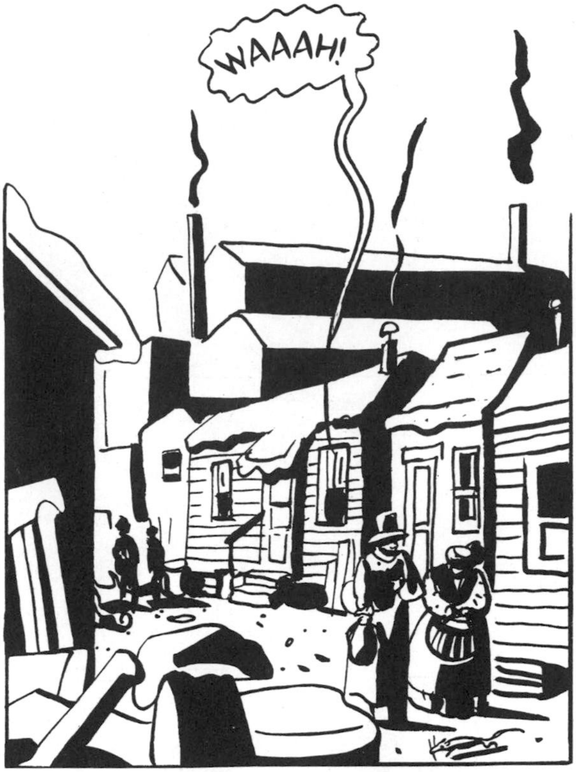
WAAAH!

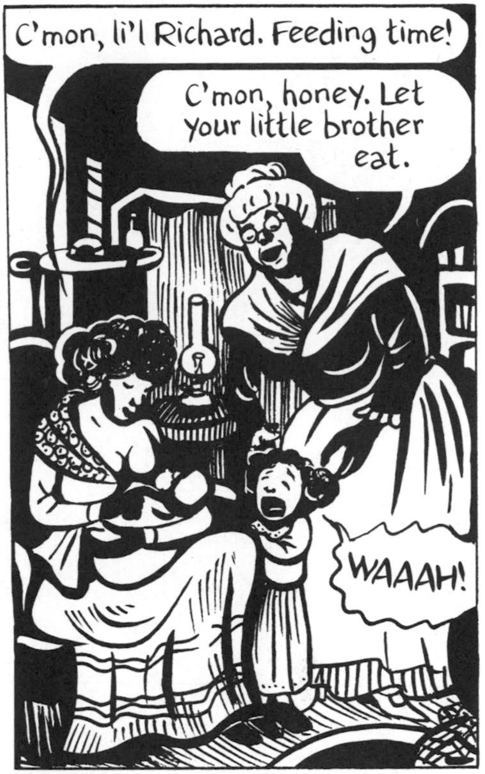
C'mon, li'l Richard. Feeding time!
C'mon, honey. Let your little brother eat.
WAAAH!

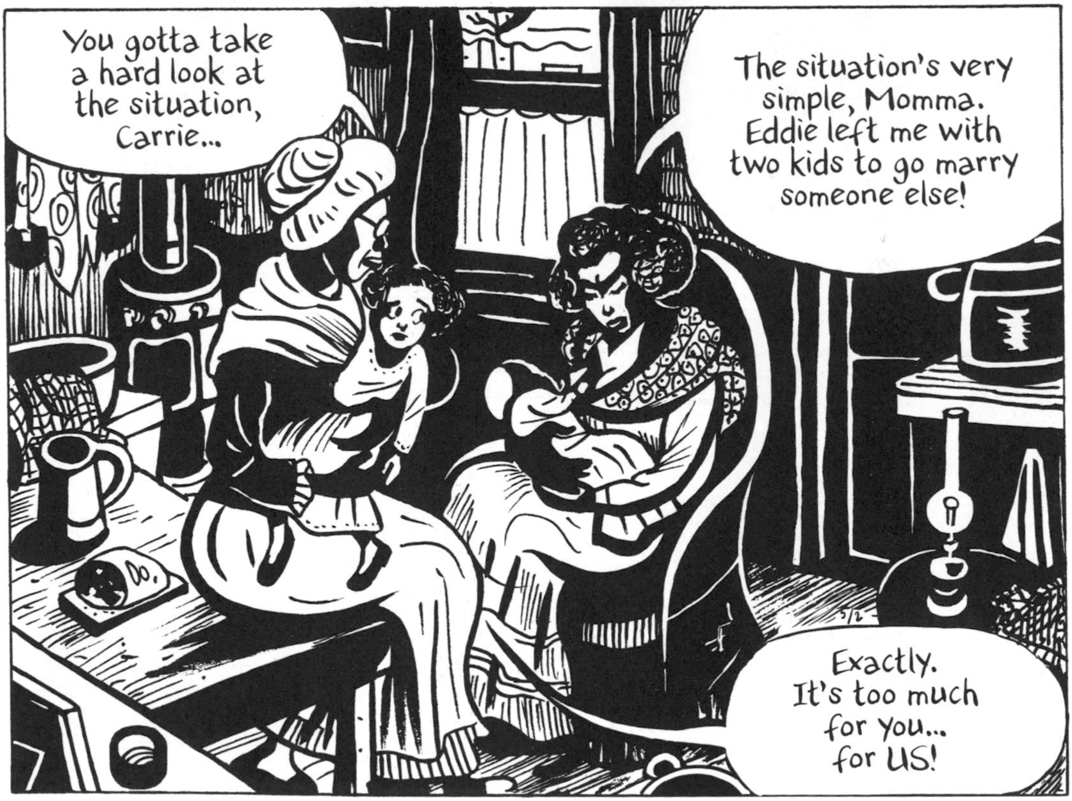
You gotta take a hard look at the situation, Carrie...
The situation's very simple, Momma. Eddie left me with two kids to go marry someone else!
Exactly. It's too much for you... for US!

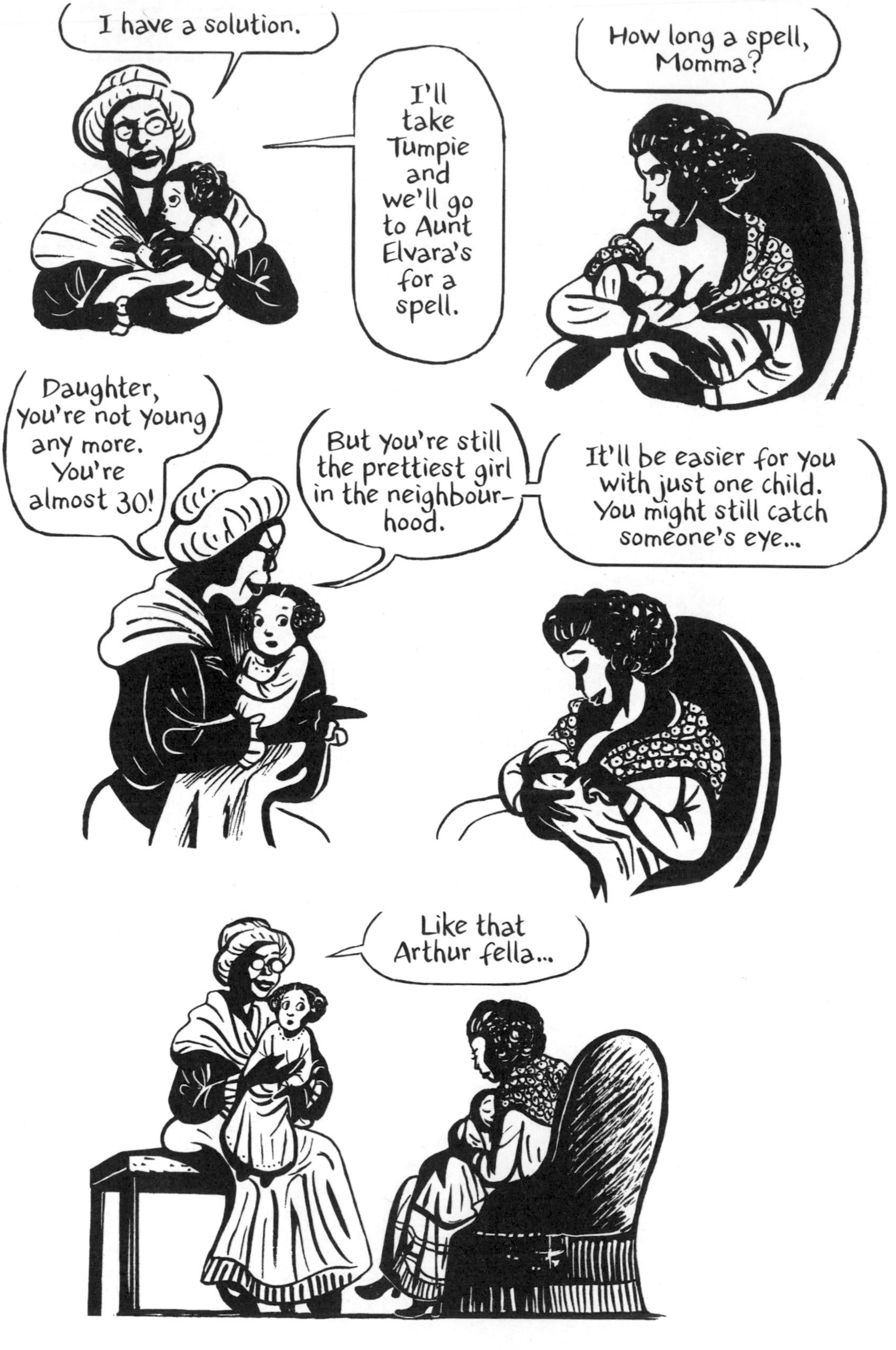
I have a solution.
I'll take Tumpie and we'll go to Aunt Elvara's for a spell.
How long a spell, Momma?
Daughter, you're not young any more. You're almost 30!
But you're still the prettiest girl in the neighbour-hood.
It'll be easier for you with just one child. You might still catch someone's eye...
Like that Arthur fella...

1911: Gratiot Street, St. Louis, Missouri, USA

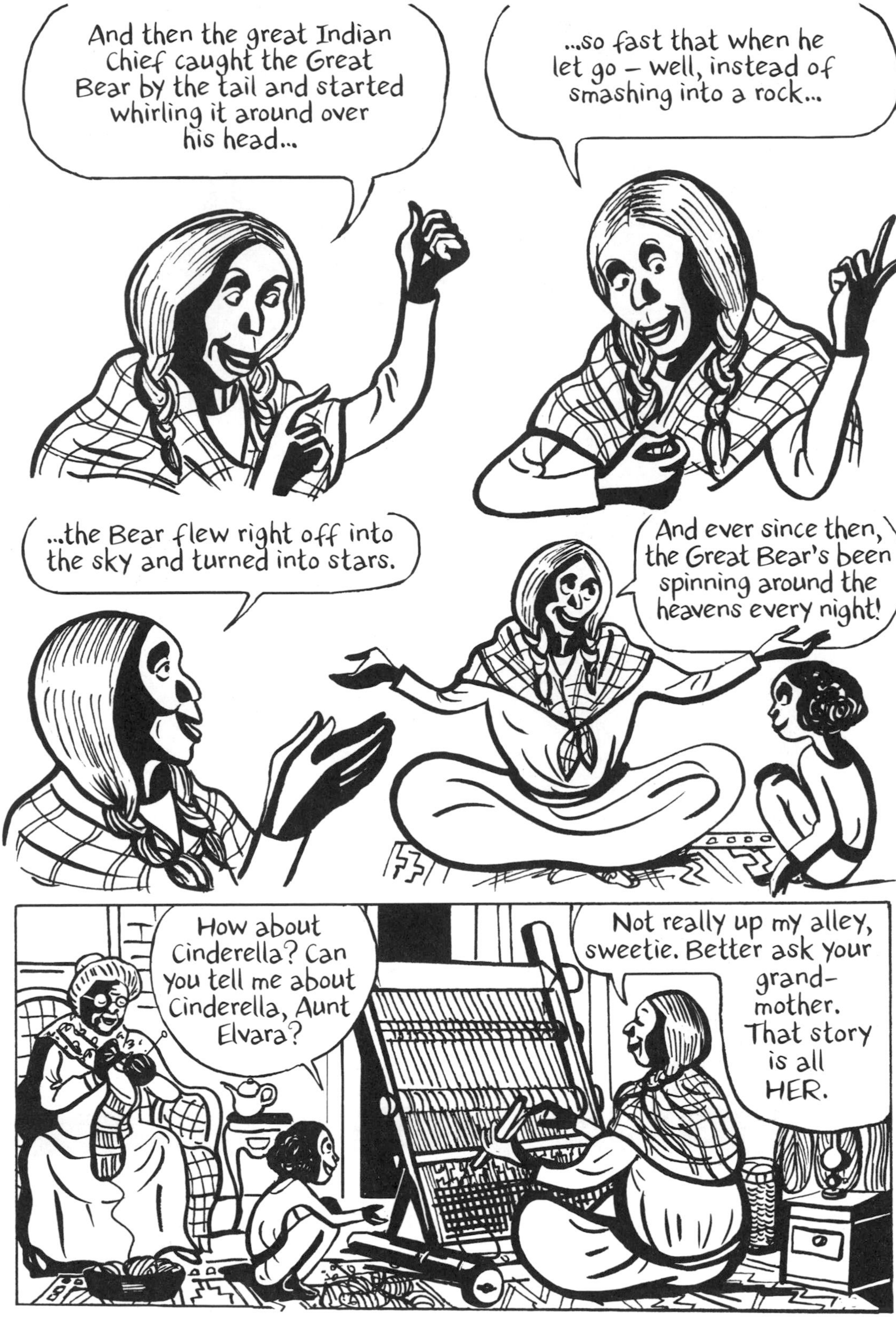
And then the great Indian Chief caught the Great Bear by the tail and started whirling it around over his head...
...so fast that when he let go – well, instead of smashing into a rock...
...the Bear flew right off into the sky and turned into stars.
And ever since then, the Great Bear's been spinning around the heavens every night!
How about Cinderella? Can you tell me about Cinderella, Aunt Elvara?
Not really up my alley, sweetie. Better ask your grand-mother. That story is all HER.

OUCH! Dumb needle!
What was it doing in my cotton?
Did you get a boo-boo, Auntie?
It's nothing, Tumpie – just got pricked!
But you're BLEEDING!
Your blood's all red!
Don't worry, Tumpie. It's not serious.
Oh go way, man
HEY! Stop wriggling around like that!
But I'm dancing!

Well, stop dancing like that! You're distracting me!

I'm just dancing to get warm!

Oh, let her dance, Elvara. It gives her something to do.

Tralala!

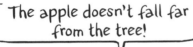

You know where it got her mother!

But you dance, too!

la la la

That's not the same thing at all! I dance to commune with the spirits of our ancestors!

The apple doesn't fall far from the tree!

You and Tumpie are from the same tree!

Hmph! In part, in part!

23

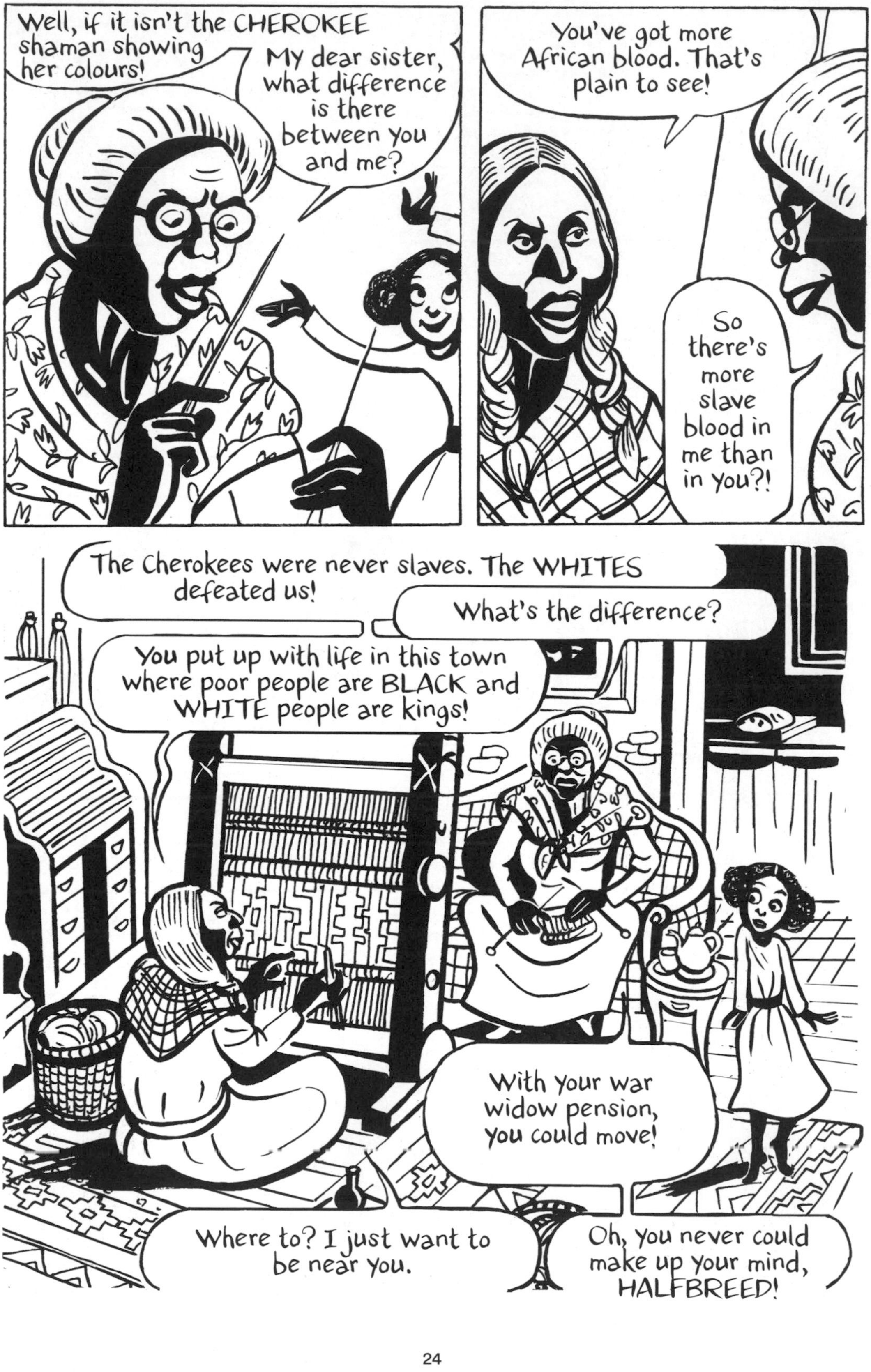
Well, if it isn't the CHEROKEE shaman showing her colours!
My dear sister, what difference is there between you and me?
You've got more African blood. That's plain to see!
So there's more slave blood in me than in you?!
The Cherokees were never slaves. The WHITES defeated us!
What's the difference?
You put up with life in this town where poor people are BLACK and WHITE people are kings!
With your war widow pension, you could move!
Where to? I just want to be near you.
Oh, you never could make up your mind, HALFBREED!

Gramma, you and Aunt Elvara don't have the same momma or daddy?

That doesn't matter. What matters is that we're truly sisters.

Yes. Even if we don't really share the same blood.

OW!

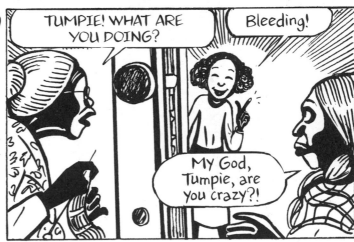

TUMPIE! WHAT ARE YOU DOING?

Bleeding!

My God, Tumpie, are you crazy?!

Look, Aunt Elvara! My blood's the same colour as yours!

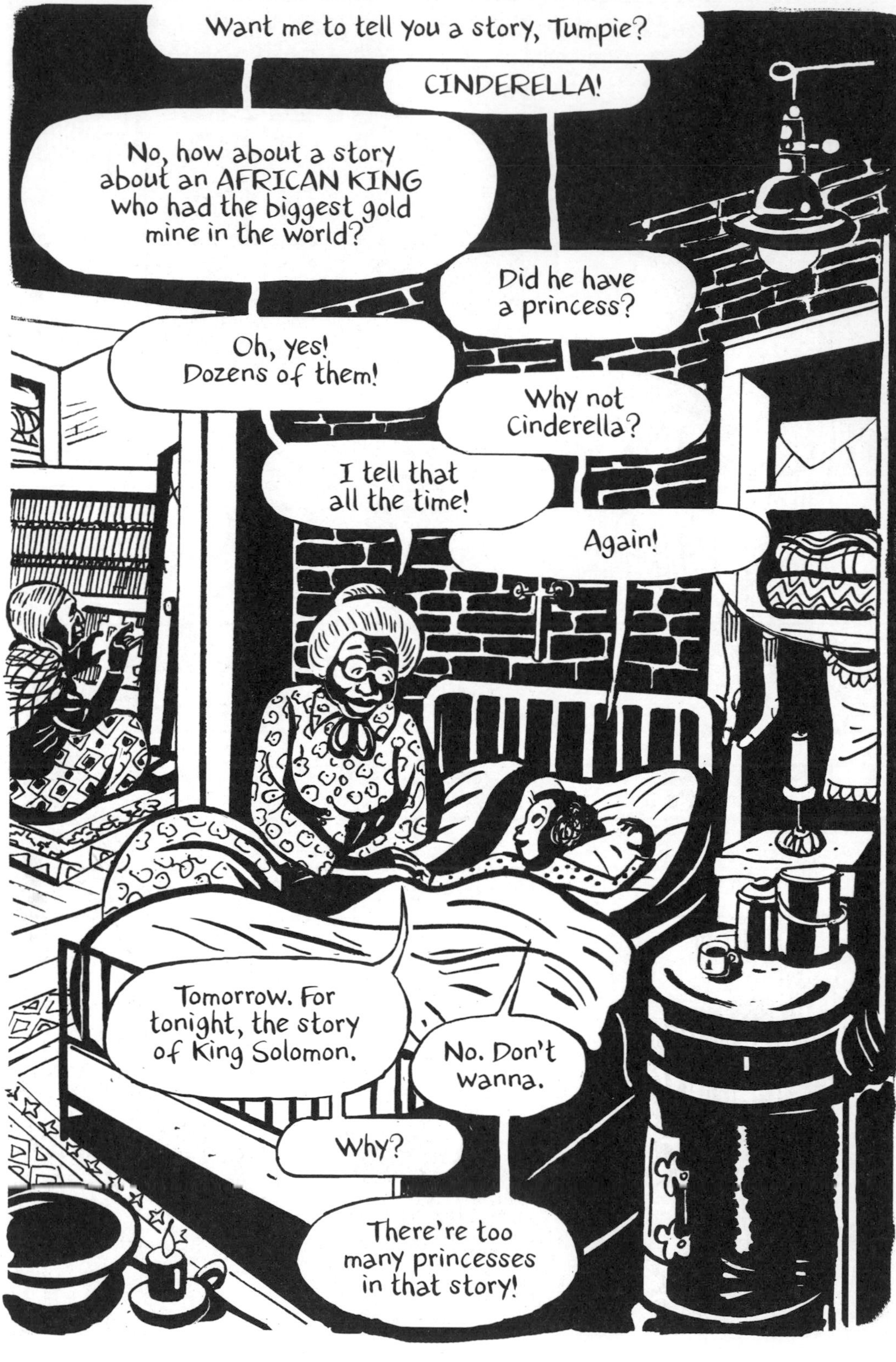
Want me to tell you a story, Tumpie?
CINDERELLA!
No, how about a story about an AFRICAN KING who had the biggest gold mine in the world?
Did he have a princess?
Oh, yes! Dozens of them!
Why not Cinderella?
I tell that all the time!
Again!
Tomorrow. For tonight, the story of King Solomon.
No. Don't wanna.
Why?
There're too many princesses in that story!

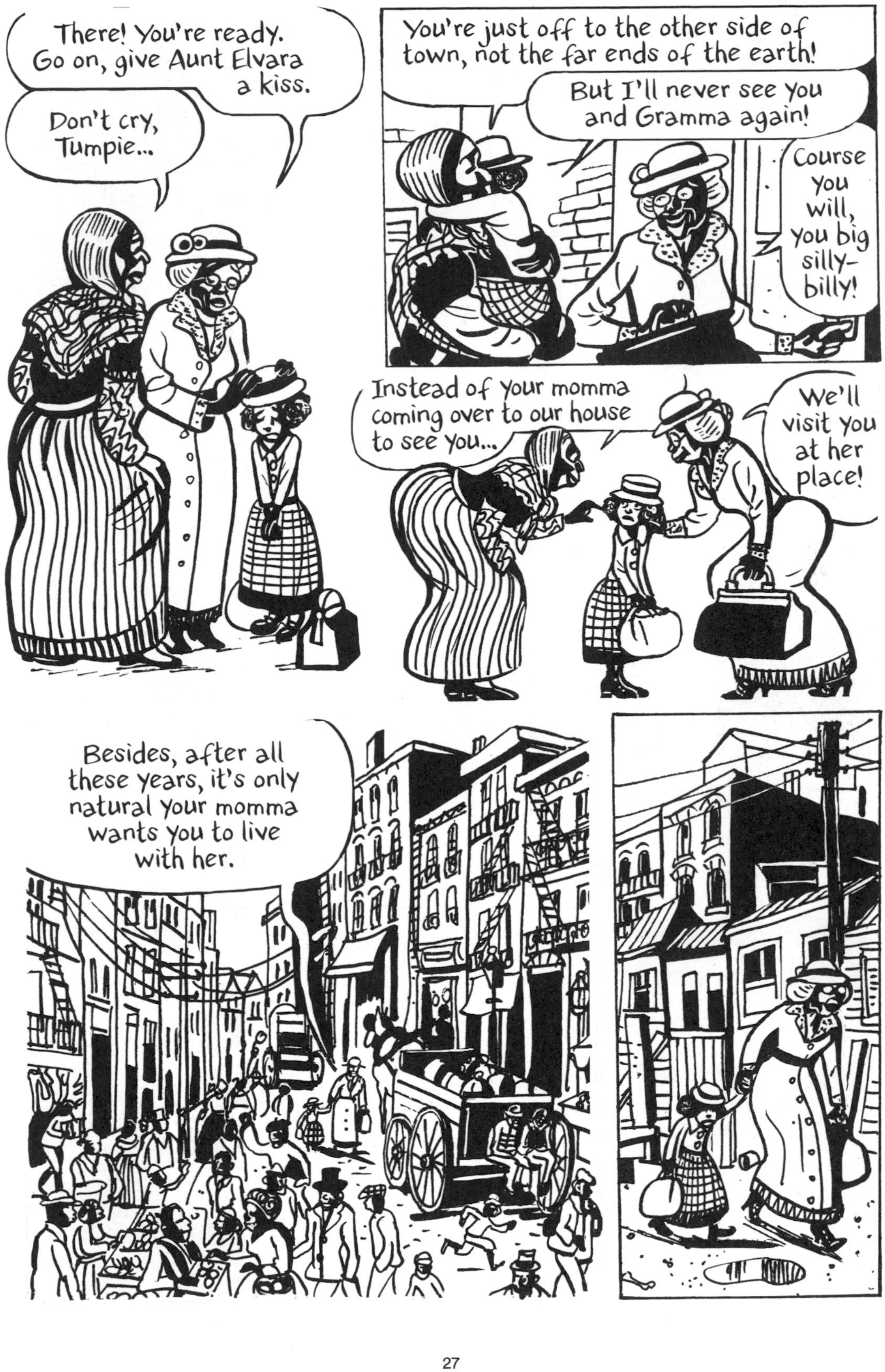

There! You're ready. Go on, give Aunt Elvara a kiss.
Don't cry, Tumpie...
You're just off to the other side of town, not the far ends of the earth!
But I'll never see you and Gramma again!
Course you will, you big silly-billy!
Instead of your momma coming over to our house to see you...
We'll visit you at her place!
Besides, after all these years, it's only natural your momma wants you to live with her.

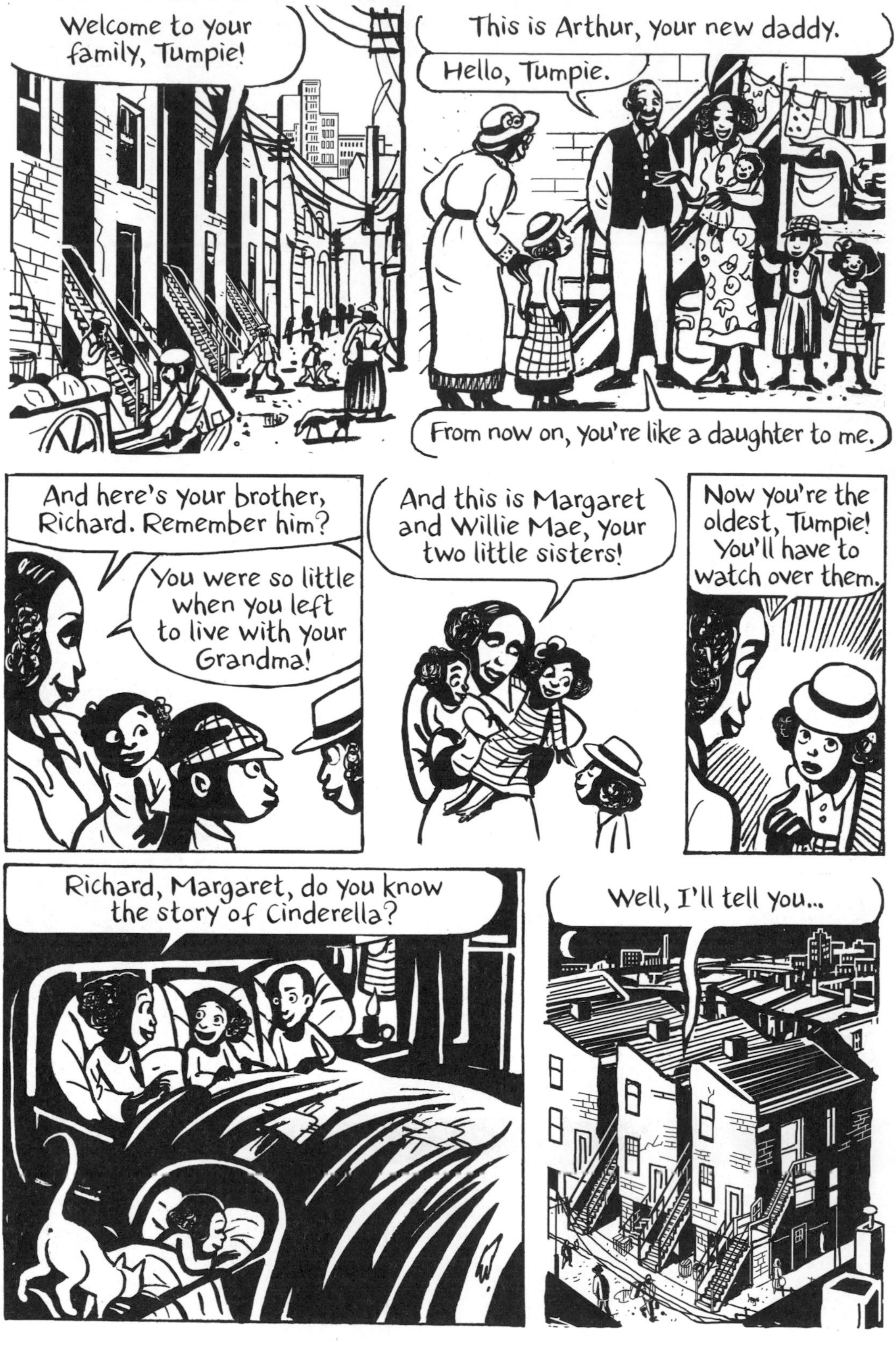
Welcome to your family, Tumpie!
This is Arthur, your new daddy.
Hello, Tumpie.
From now on, you're like a daughter to me.
And here's your brother, Richard. Remember him?
You were so little when you left to live with your Grandma!
And this is Margaret and Willie Mae, your two little sisters!
Now you're the oldest, Tumpie! You'll have to watch over them.
Richard, Margaret, do you know the story of Cinderella?
Well, I'll tell you...

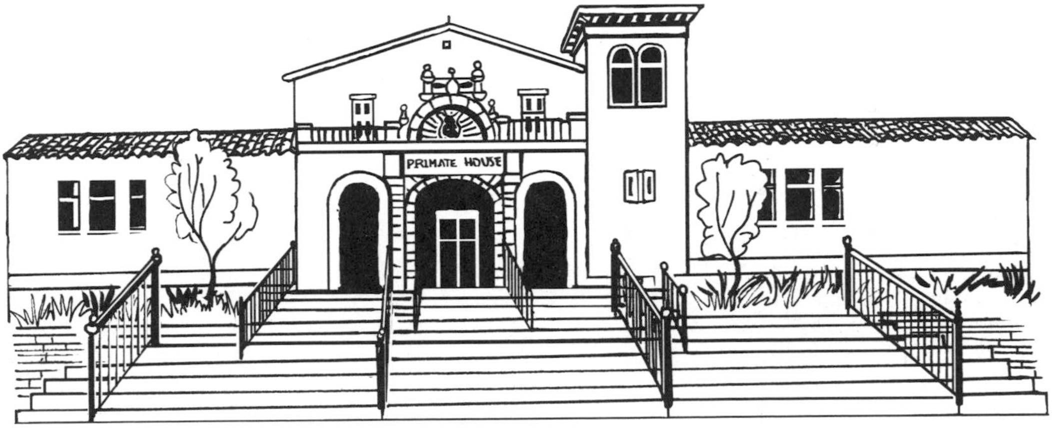
PRIMATE HOUSE

1913: St. Louis Zoo, Missouri, USA

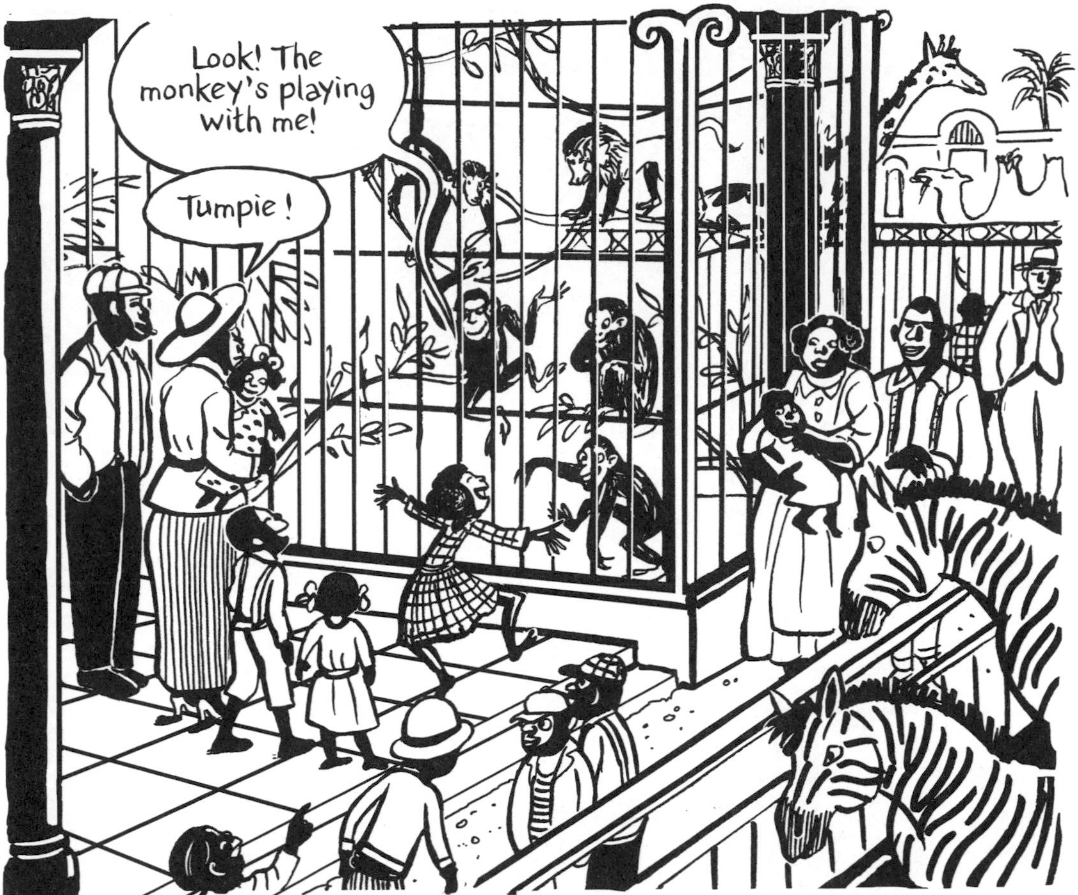
Look! The monkey's playing with me!
Tumpie !

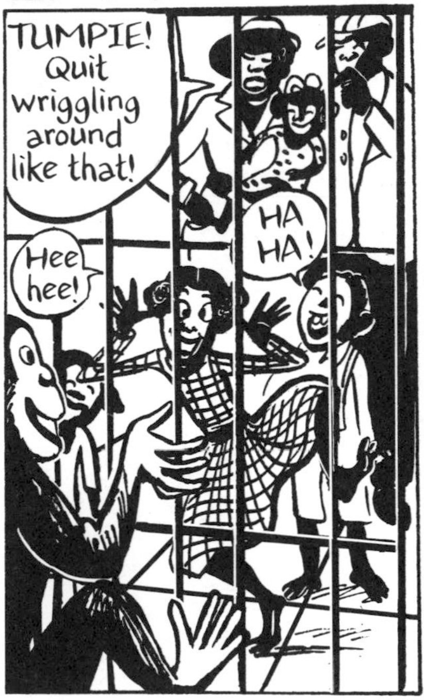
TUMPIE! Quit wriggling around like that!
HA HA!
Hee hee!

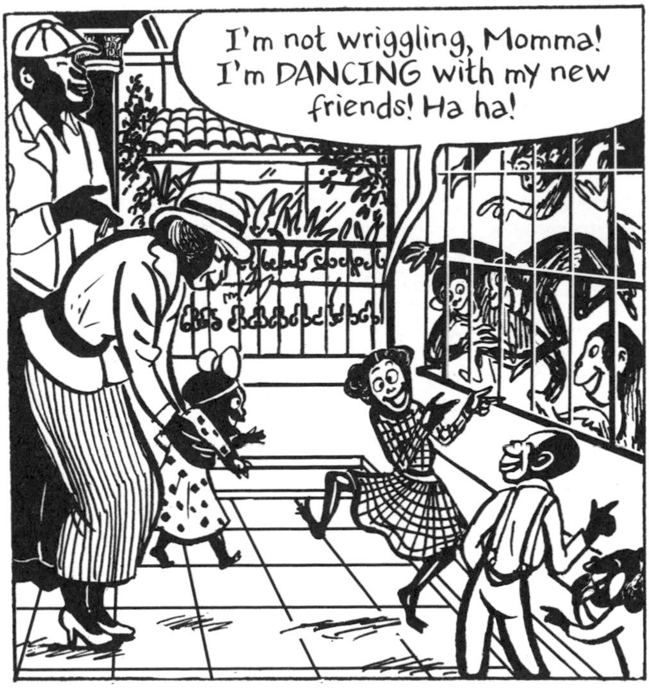
I'm not wriggling, Momma! I'm DANCING with my new friends! Ha ha!

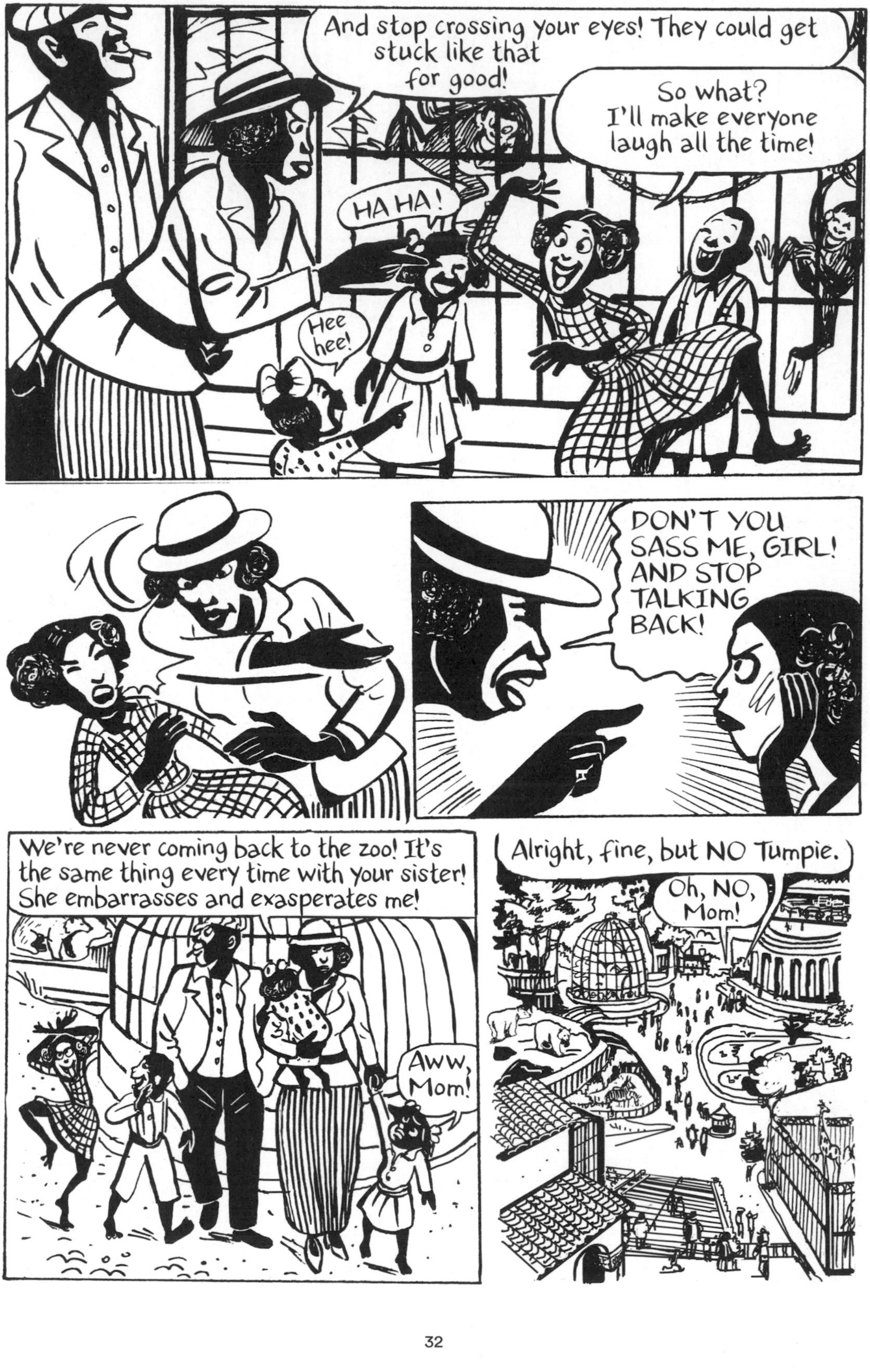
And stop crossing your eyes! They could get stuck like that for good!
So what? I'll make everyone laugh all the time!
HA HA!
Hee hee!
DON'T YOU SASS ME, GIRL! AND STOP TALKING BACK!
We're never coming back to the zoo! It's the same thing every time with your sister! She embarrasses and exasperates me!
Aww, Mom!
Alright, fine, but NO Tumpie.
Oh, NO, Mom!

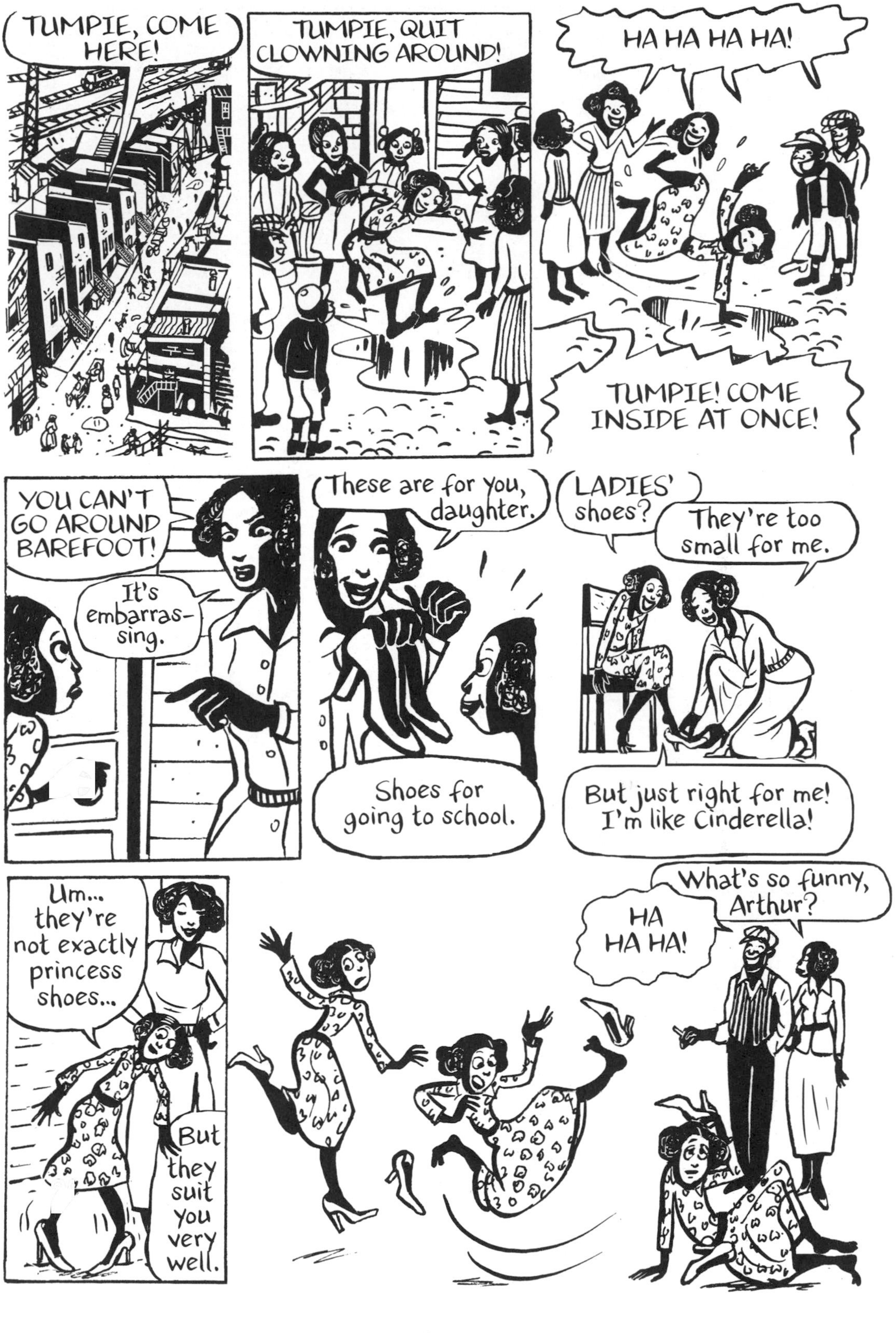
TUMPIE, COME HERE!
TUMPIE, QUIT CLOWNING AROUND!
HA HA HA HA!
TUMPIE! COME INSIDE AT ONCE!
YOU CAN'T GO AROUND BAREFOOT!
It's embarras-sing.
These are for you, daughter.
Shoes for going to school.
LADIES' shoes?
They're too small for me.
But just right for me! I'm like Cinderella!
Um... they're not exactly princess shoes...
But they suit you very well.
HA HA HA!
What's so funny, Arthur?

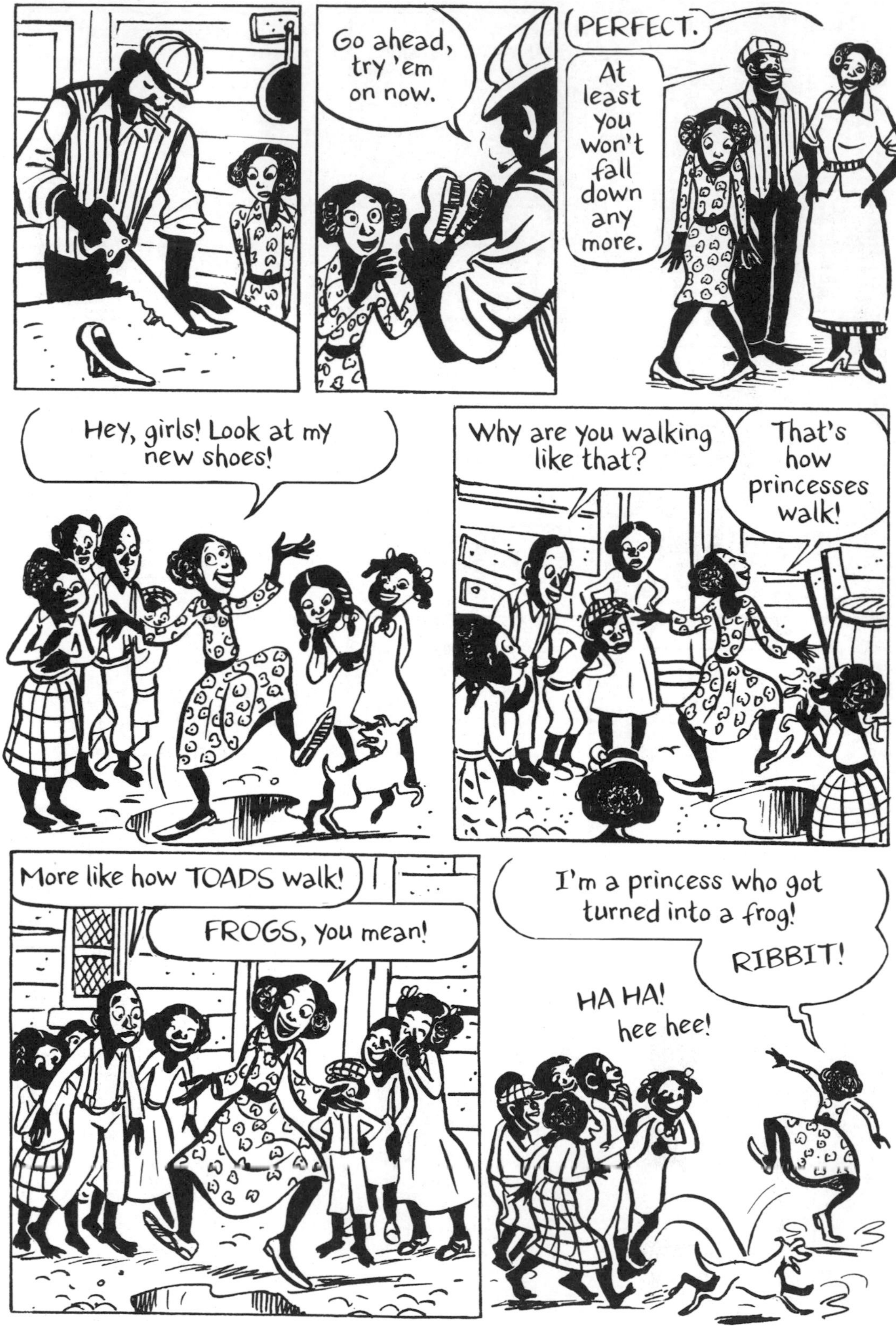
Go ahead, try 'em on now.
PERFECT.
At least you won't fall down any more.
Hey, girls! Look at my new shoes!
Why are you walking like that?
That's how princesses walk!
More like how TOADS walk!
FROGS, you mean!
I'm a princess who got turned into a frog!
RIBBIT!
HA HA! hee hee!

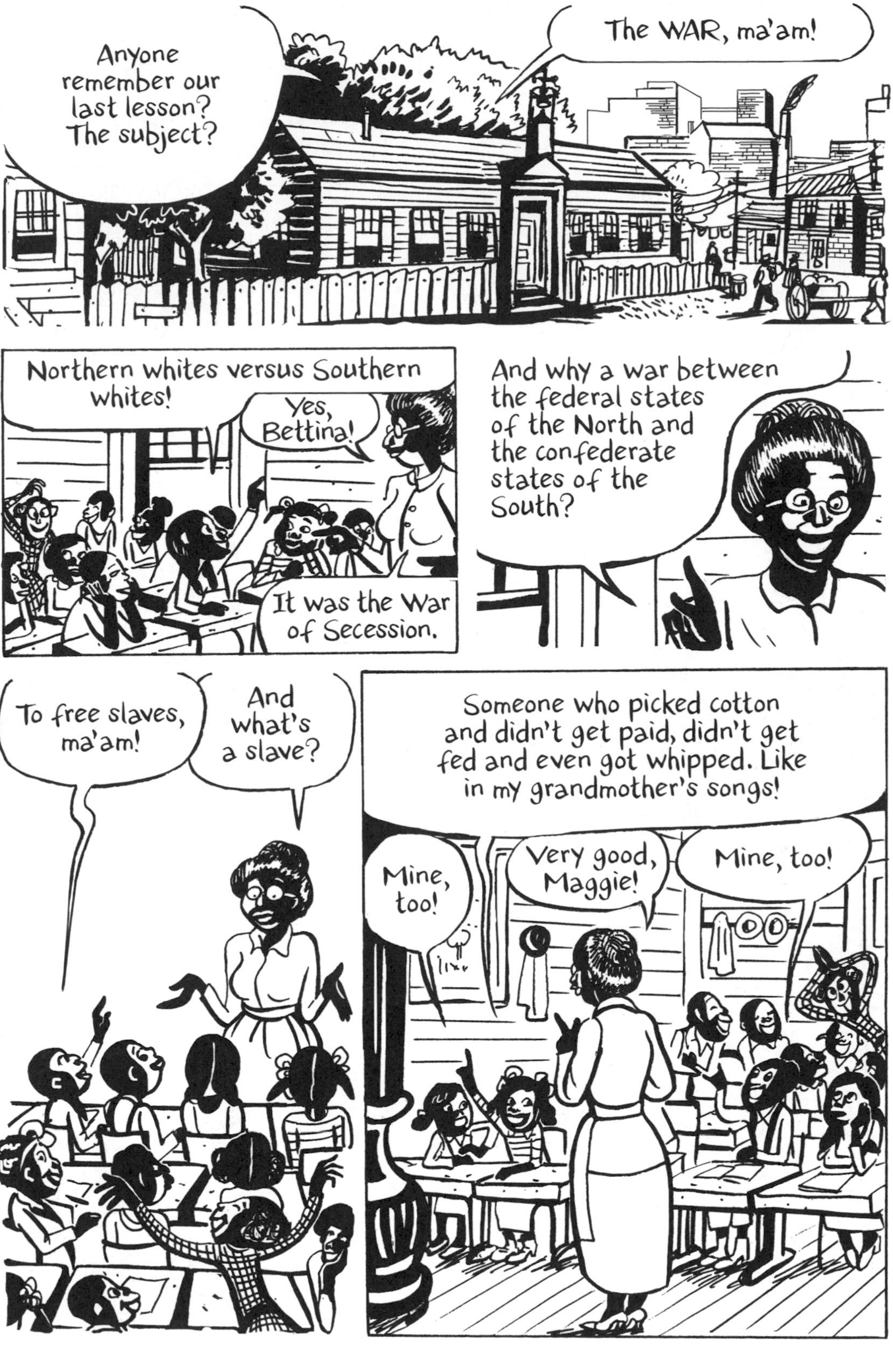
Anyone remember our last lesson? The subject?
The WAR, ma'am!
Northern whites versus Southern whites!
Yes, Bettina!
It was the War of Secession.
And why a war between the federal states of the North and the confederate states of the South?
To free slaves, ma'am!
And what's a slave?
Someone who picked cotton and didn't get paid, didn't get fed and even got whipped. Like in my grandmother's songs!
Mine, too!
Very good, Maggie!
Mine, too!

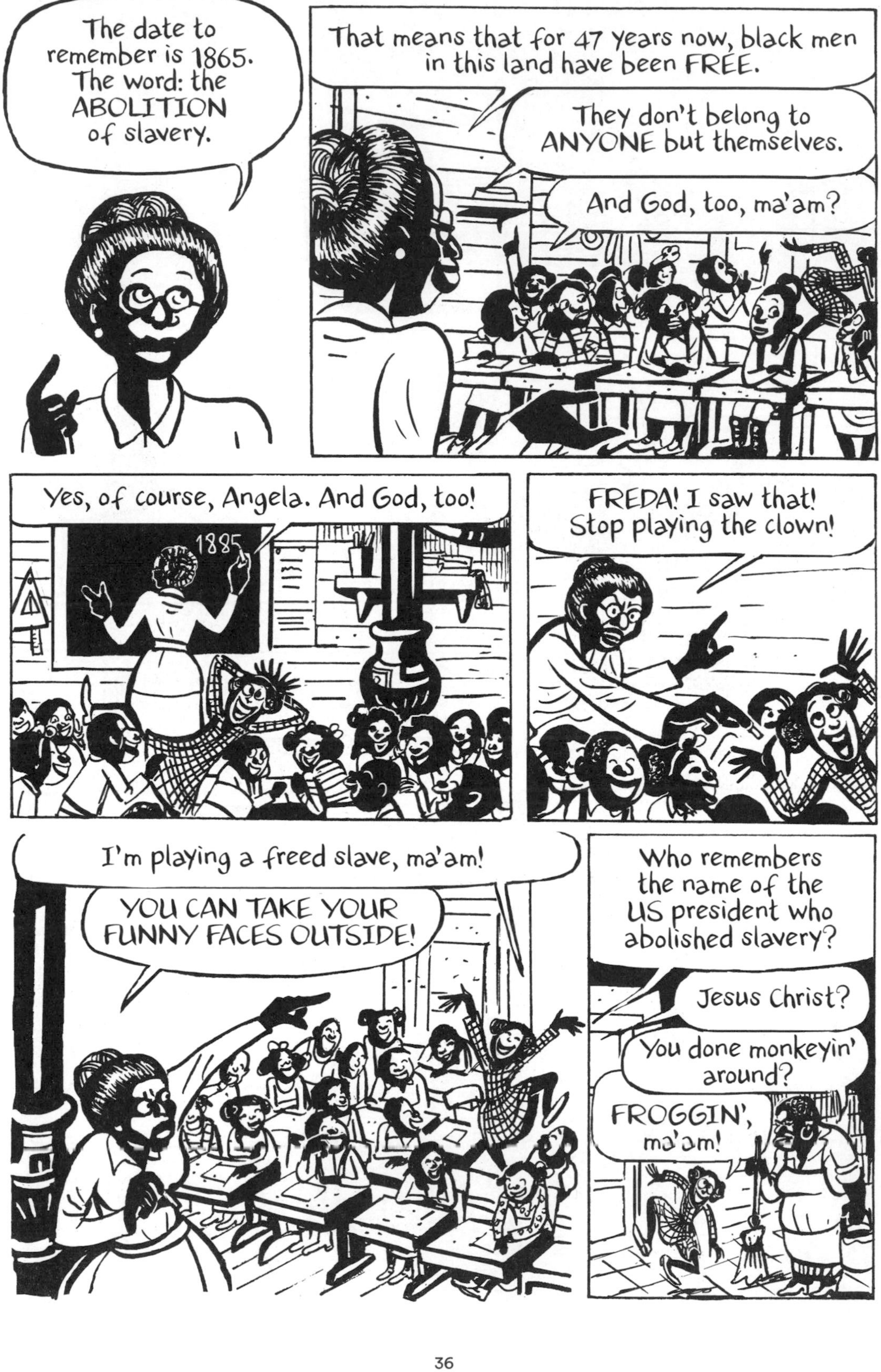

The date to remember is 1865. The word: the ABOLITION of slavery.
That means that for 47 years now, black men in this land have been FREE.
They don't belong to ANYONE but themselves.
And God, too, ma'am?
Yes, of course, Angela. And God, too!
1885
FREDA! I saw that! Stop playing the clown!
I'm playing a freed slave, ma'am!
YOU CAN TAKE YOUR FUNNY FACES OUTSIDE!
Who remembers the name of the US president who abolished slavery?
Jesus Christ?
You done monkeyin' around?
FROGGIN', ma'am!

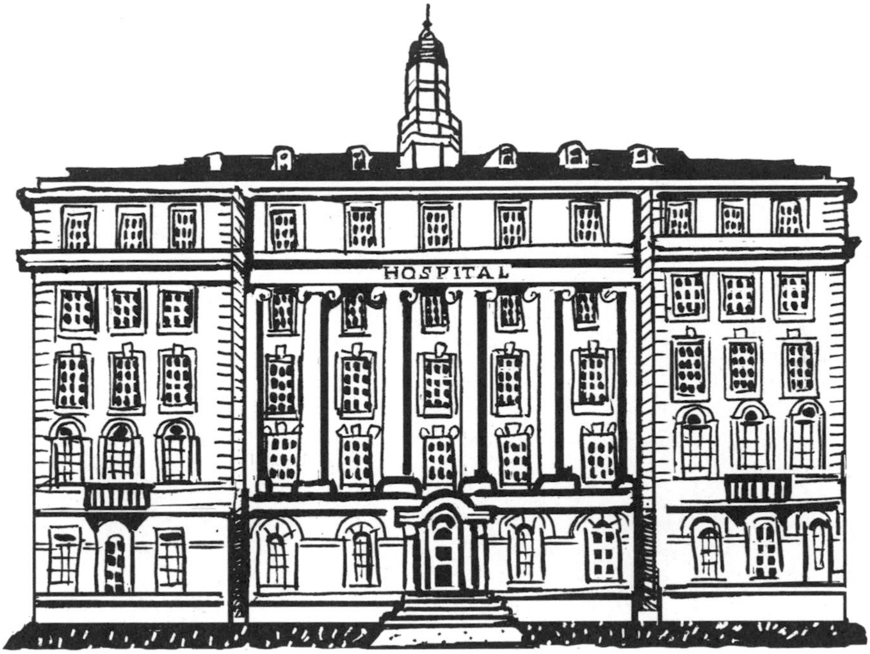
HOSPITAL

1914: St. Louis Hospital, Missouri, USA

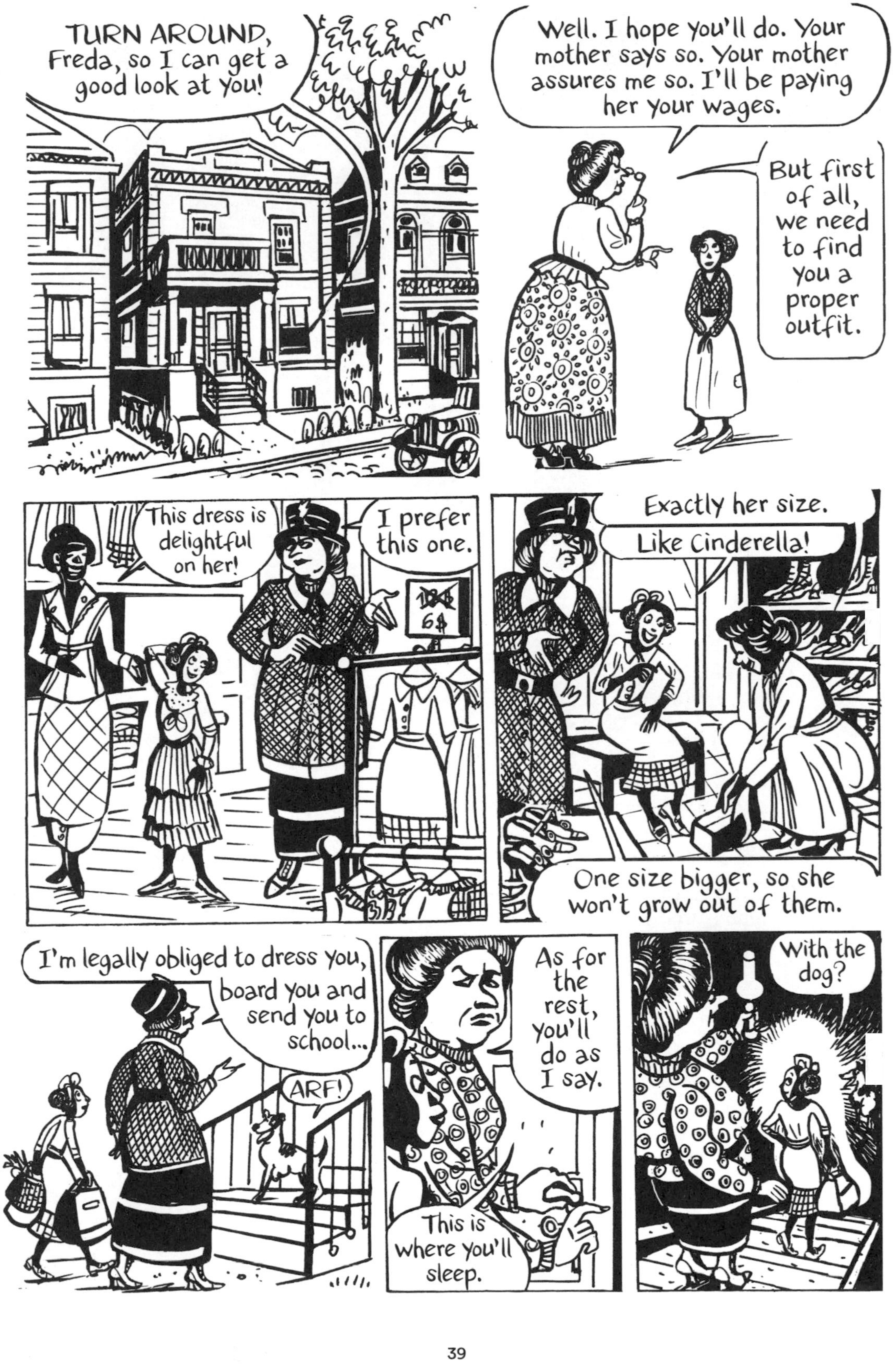
TURN AROUND, Freda, so I can get a good look at you!
Well. I hope you'll do. Your mother says so. Your mother assures me so. I'll be paying her your wages.
But first of all, we need to find you a proper outfit.
This dress is delightful on her!
I prefer this one.
6$
Exactly her size.
Like Cinderella!
One size bigger, so she won't grow out of them.
I'm legally obliged to dress you, board you and send you to school...
ARF!
As for the rest, you'll do as I say.
This is where you'll sleep.
With the dog?

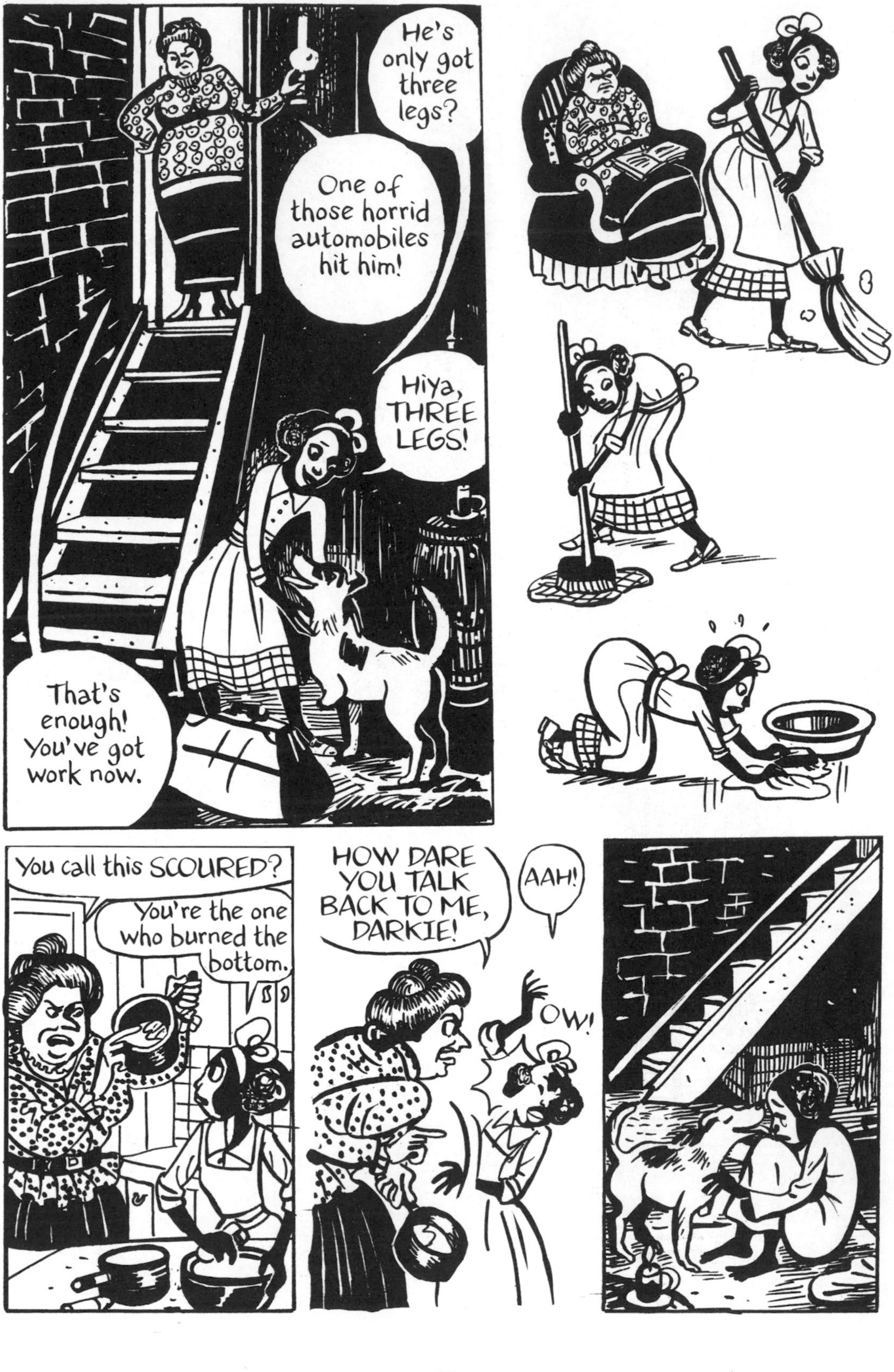
He's only got three legs?
One of those horrid automobiles hit him!
Hiya, THREE LEGS!
That's enough! You've got work now.
You call this SCOURED?
You're the one who burned the bottom.
HOW DARE YOU TALK BACK TO ME, DARKIE!
AAH!
OW!

DING DONG!

Very good, Freda. For once, you haven't fidgeted or fallen asleep. I even felt like you were listening in class.

Hey! Don't you dream of living in a castle like princesses in France, England and Spain?

Meh.

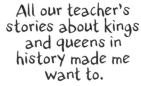

All our teacher's stories about kings and queens in history made me want to.

But those kings kept getting beheaded!

Yeah, but as a result those castles now belong to everyone. Teacher says that's what a republic is.

Not here! You're not about to live in a castle here any day soon! Ha ha!

41

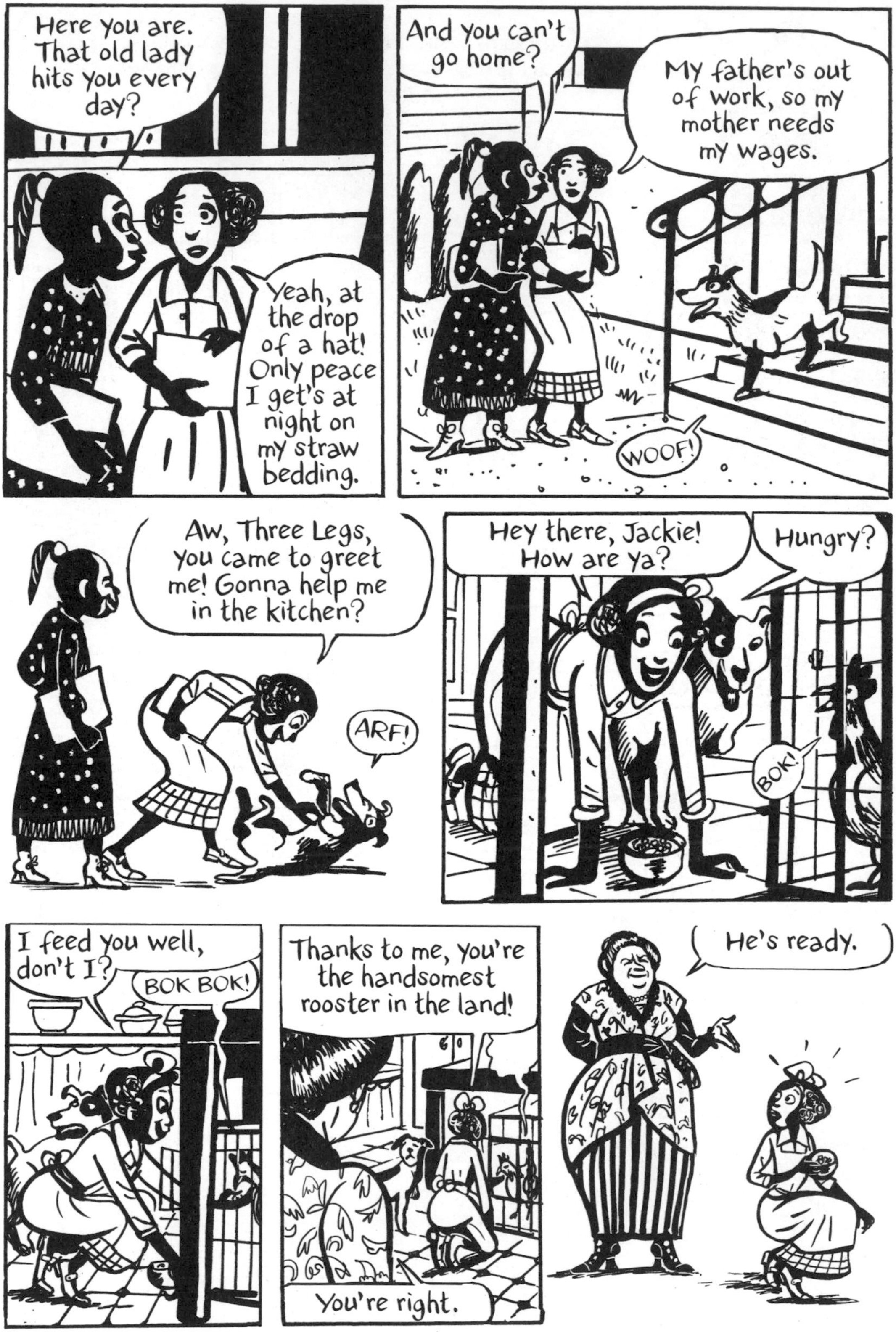
Here you are. That old lady hits you every day?
Yeah, at the drop of a hat! Only peace I get's at night on my straw bedding.
And you can't go home?
My father's out of work, so my mother needs my wages.
WOOF!
Aw, Three Legs, you came to greet me! Gonna help me in the kitchen?
ARF!
Hey there, Jackie! How are ya?
Hungry?
BOK!
I feed you well, don't I?
BOK BOK!
Thanks to me, you're the handsomest rooster in the land!
You're right.
He's ready.

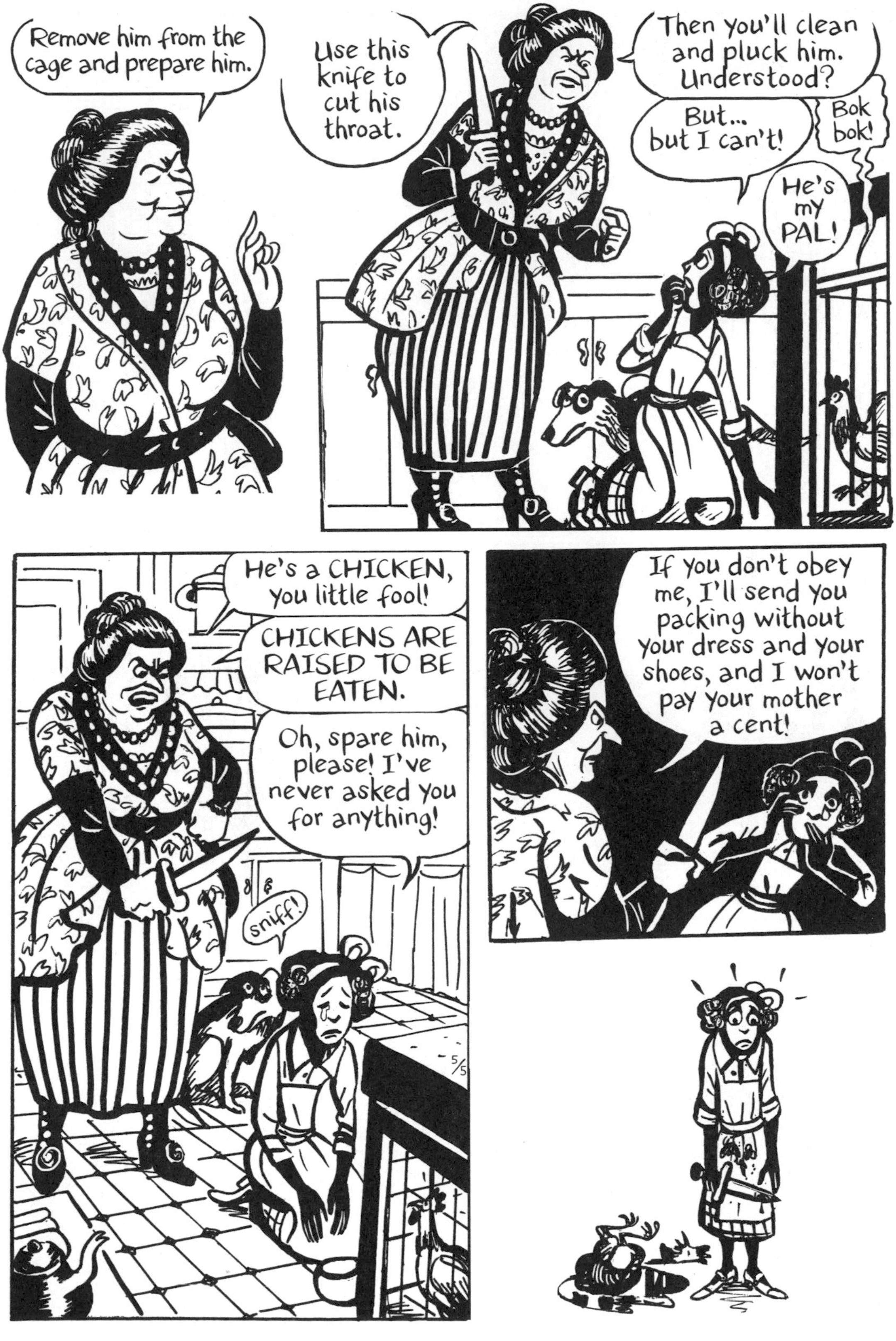
Remove him from the cage and prepare him.
Use this knife to cut his throat.
Then you'll clean and pluck him. Understood?
Bok bok!
But... but I can't!
He's my PAL!
He's a CHICKEN, you little fool!
CHICKENS ARE RAISED TO BE EATEN.
Oh, spare him, please! I've never asked you for anything!
sniff!
If you don't obey me, I'll send you packing without your dress and your shoes, and I won't pay your mother a cent!

LOOK AT THIS, YOU IMBECILE!

This plate... Do you know why it broke?

Because the dishwater's too hot!

And why is the dishwater too hot?

BECAUSE YOU WEREN'T WATCHING THE FIRE!

Get it, you stupid creature? IT'S YOUR FAULT!

Uh... yes, ma'am.

NO! You never understand a THING!

Well, you'll understand NOW!

AAAAHHH!

ARF! ARF!

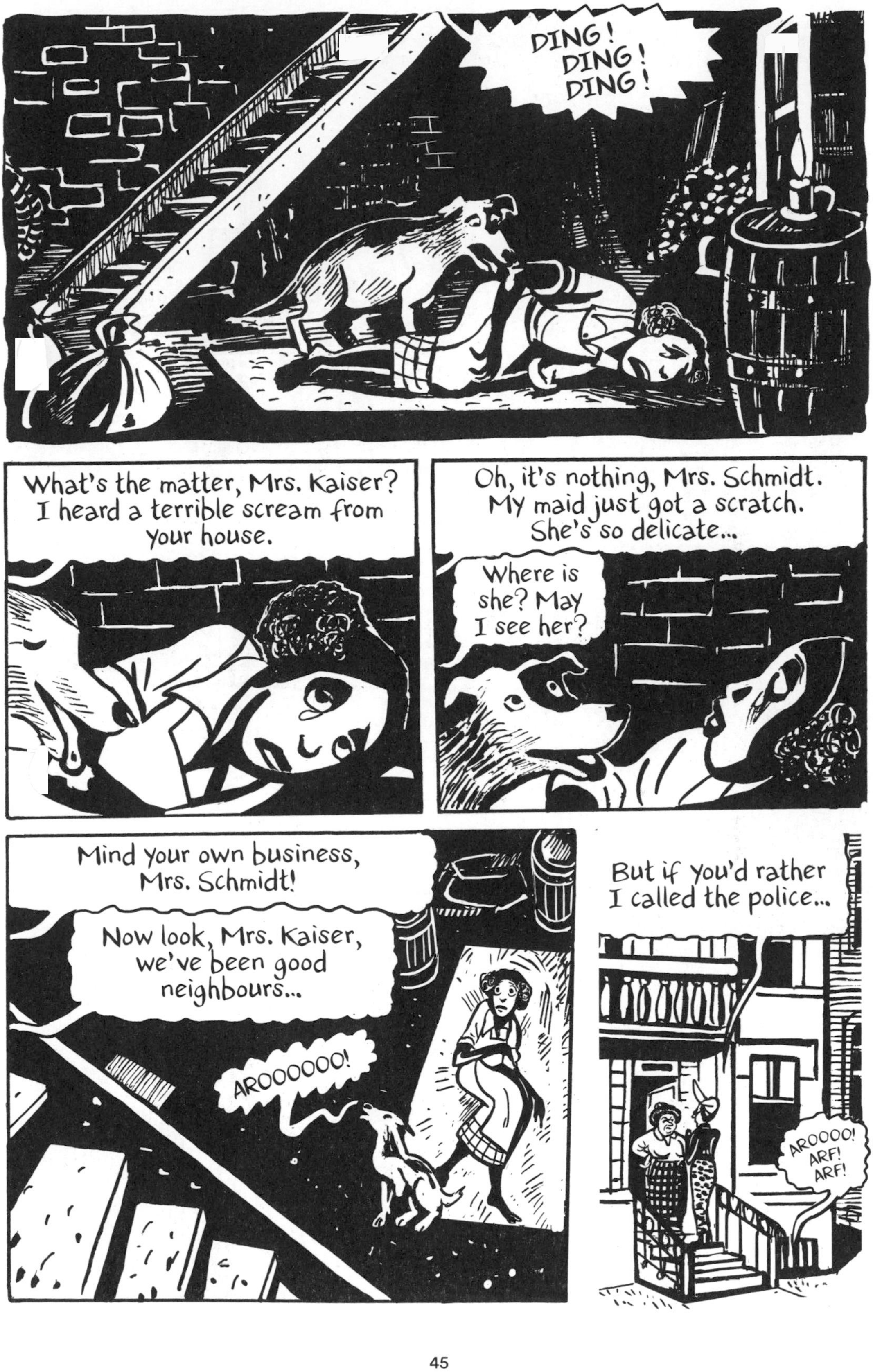
DING! DING! DING!
What's the matter, Mrs. Kaiser? I heard a terrible scream from your house.
Oh, it's nothing, Mrs. Schmidt. My maid just got a scratch. She's so delicate...
Where is she? May I see her?
Mind your own business, Mrs. Schmidt!
Now look, Mrs. Kaiser, we've been good neighbours...
AROOOOOO!
But if you'd rather I called the police...
AROOOO! ARF! ARF!

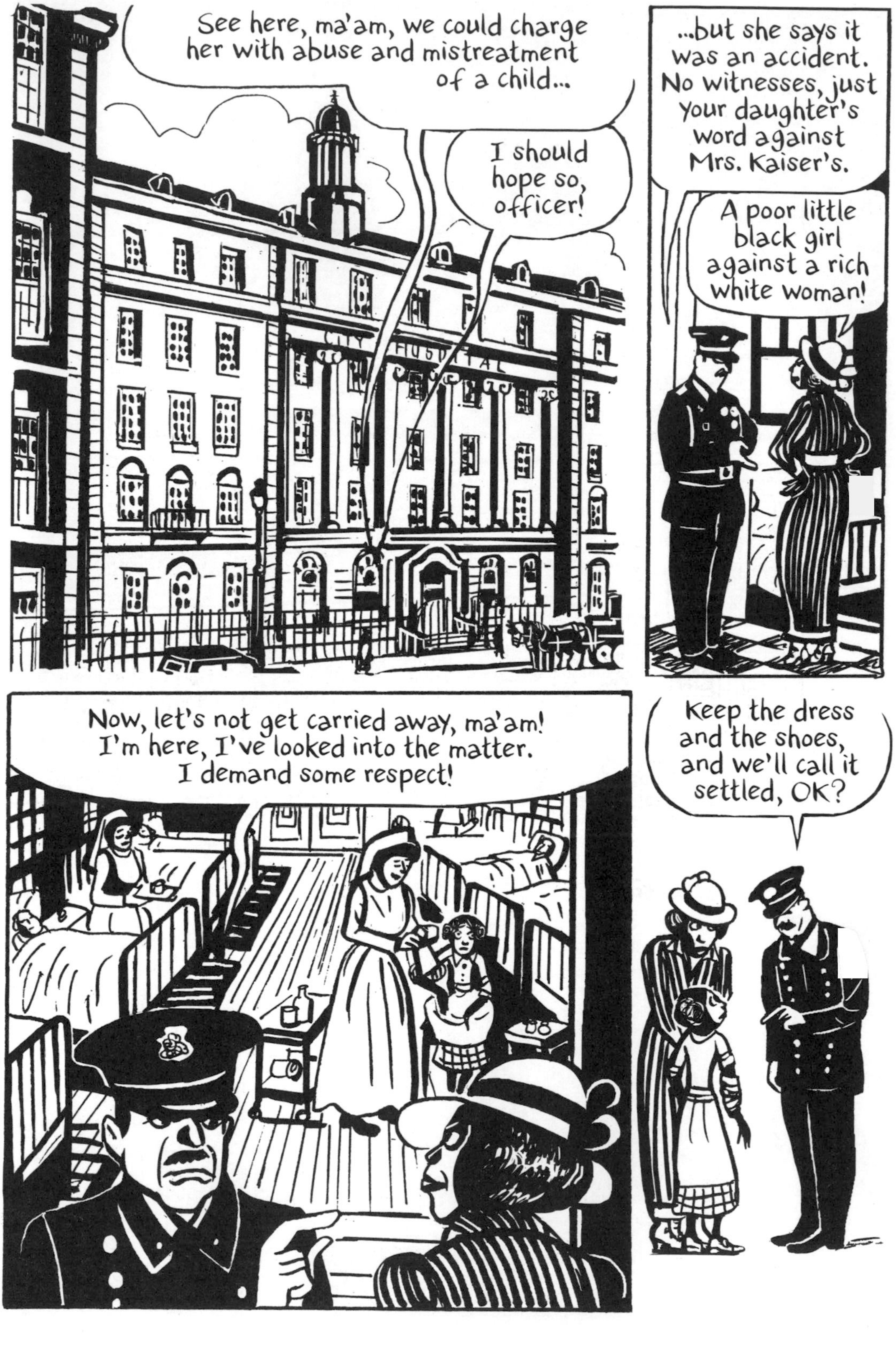
See here, ma'am, we could charge her with abuse and mistreatment of a child...
I should hope so, officer!
...but she says it was an accident. No witnesses, just your daughter's word against Mrs. Kaiser's.
A poor little black girl against a rich white woman!
Now, let's not get carried away, ma'am! I'm here, I've looked into the matter. I demand some respect!
Keep the dress and the shoes, and we'll call it settled, OK?

1916: Lafayette Square, St. Louis, Missouri, USA

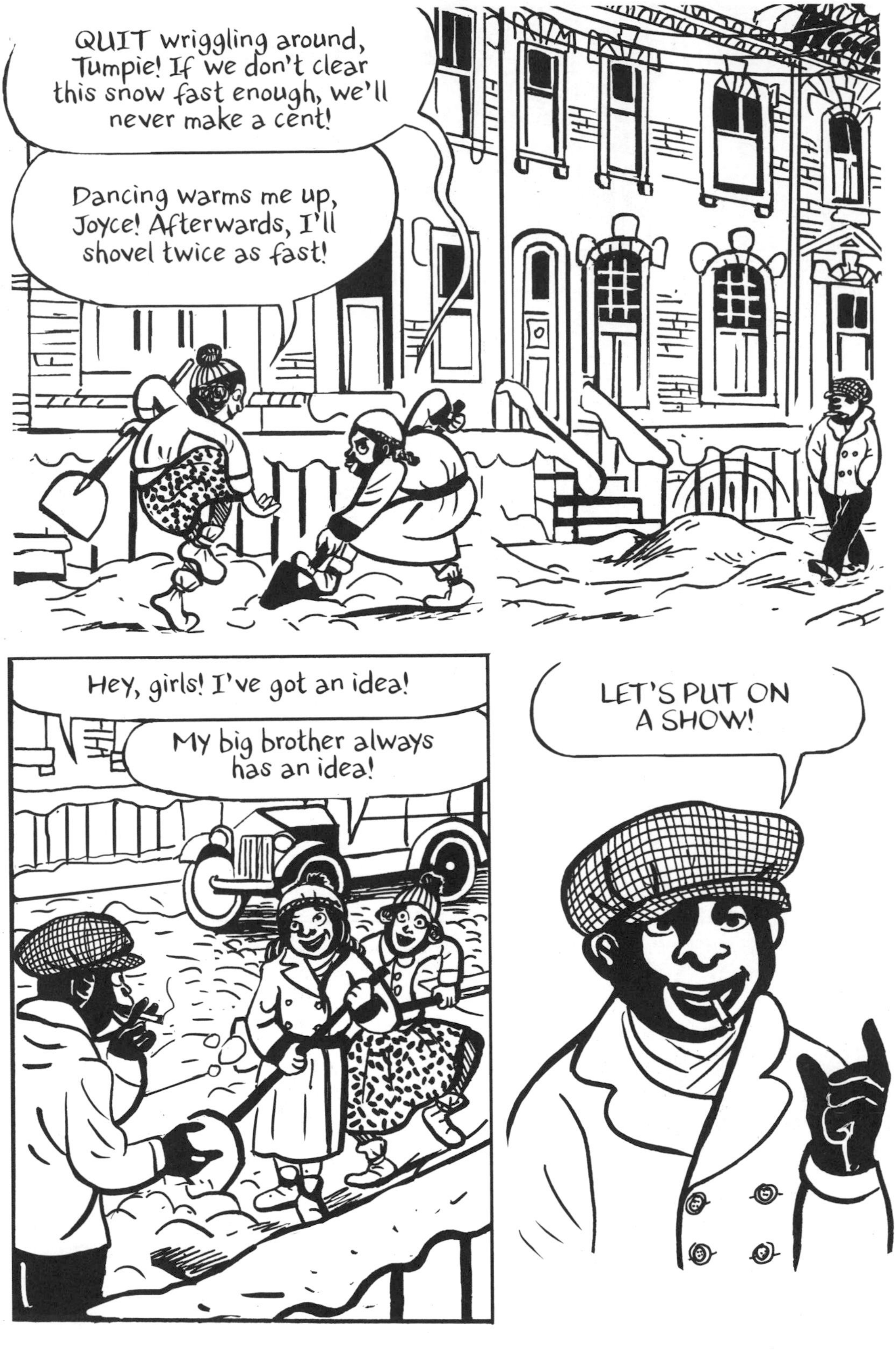
QUIT wriggling around, Tumpie! If we don't clear this snow fast enough, we'll never make a cent!
Dancing warms me up, Joyce! Afterwards, I'll shovel twice as fast!
Hey, girls! I've got an idea!
My big brother always has an idea!
LET'S PUT ON A SHOW!

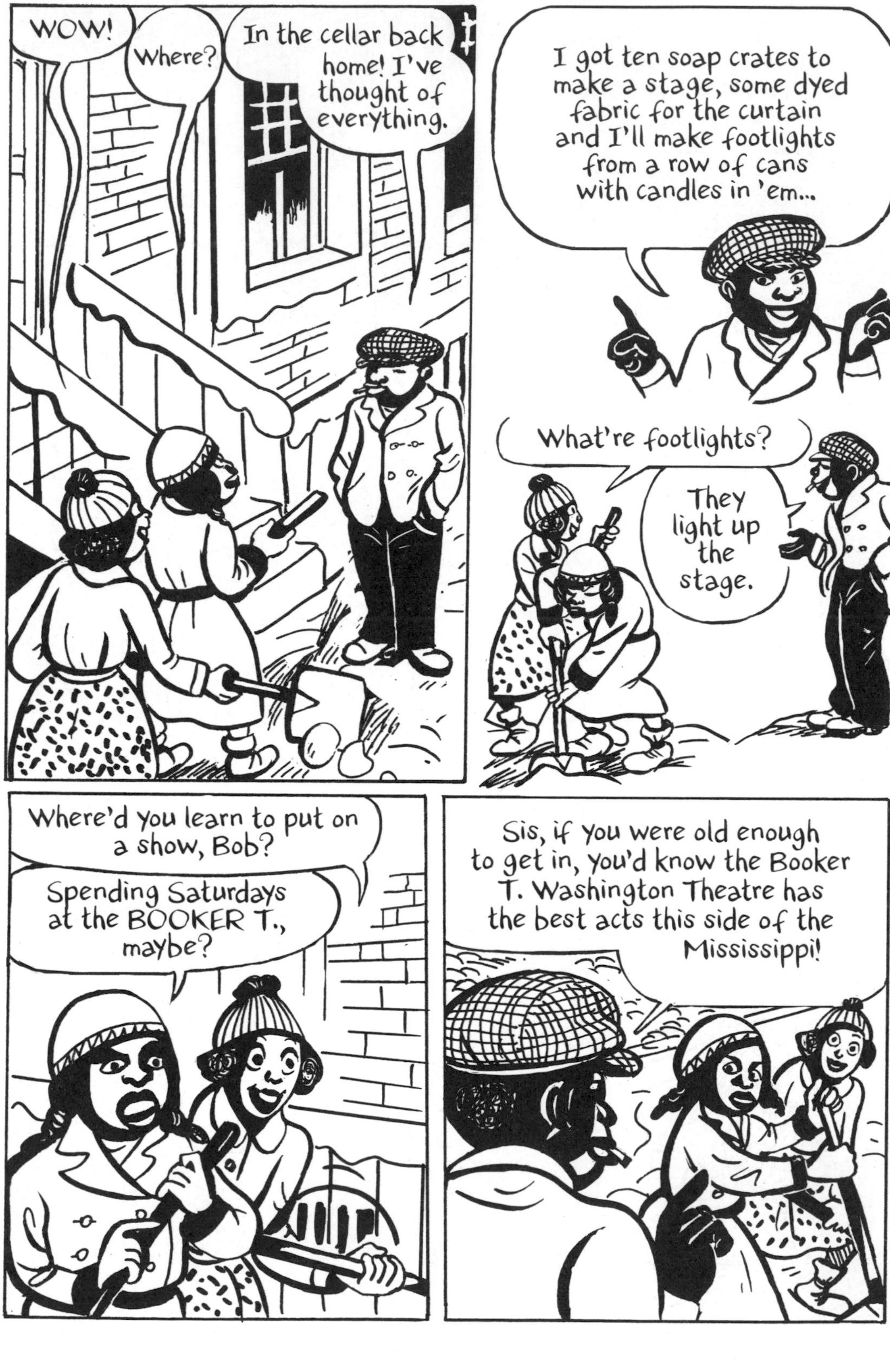
WOW!
Where?
In the cellar back home! I've thought of everything.
I got ten soap crates to make a stage, some dyed fabric for the curtain and I'll make footlights from a row of cans with candles in 'em...
What're footlights?
They light up the stage.
Where'd you learn to put on a show, Bob?
Spending Saturdays at the BOOKER T., maybe?
Sis, if you were old enough to get in, you'd know the Booker T. Washington Theatre has the best acts this side of the Mississippi!

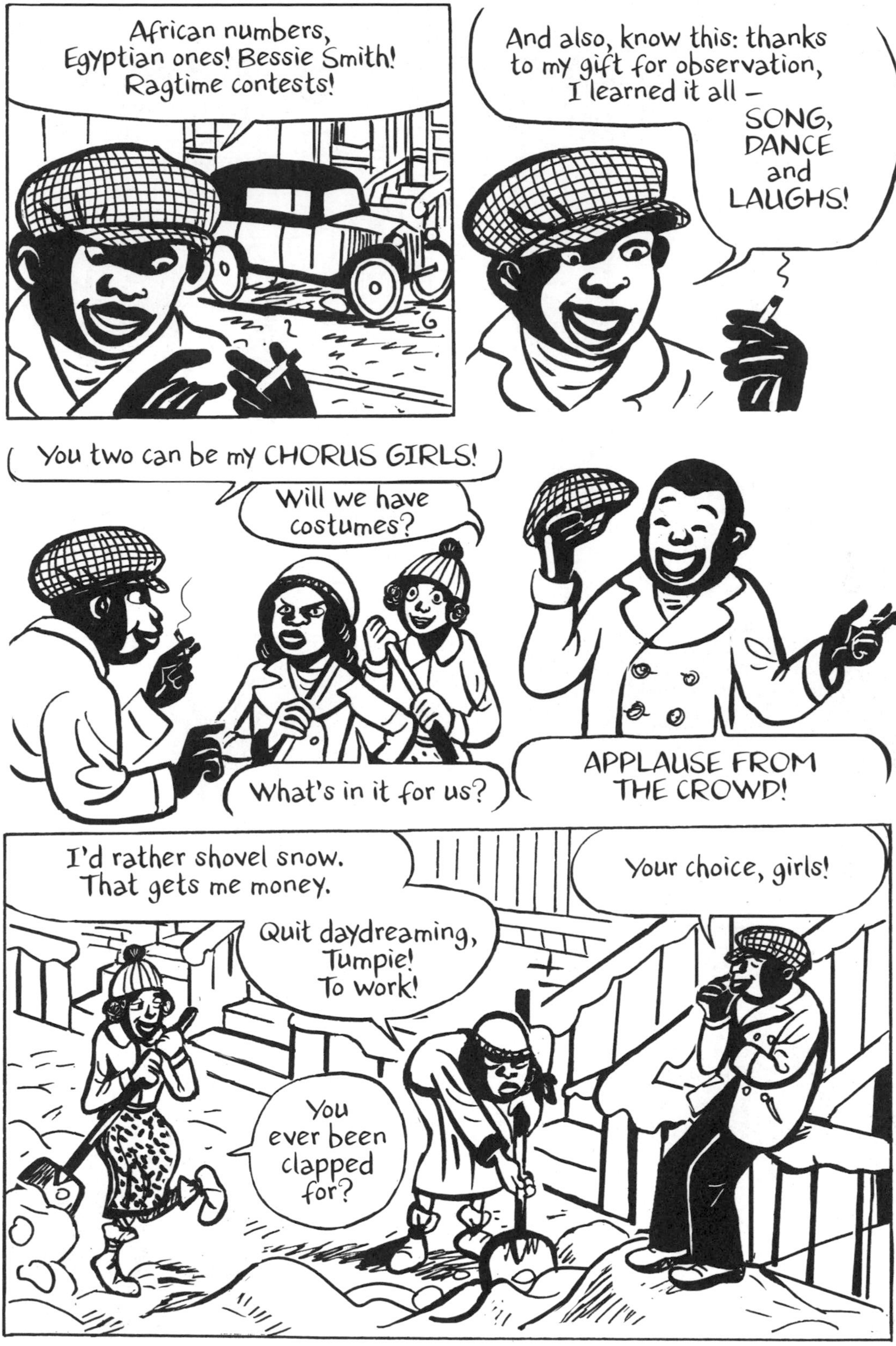
African numbers, Egyptian ones! Bessie Smith! Ragtime contests!
And also, know this: thanks to my gift for observation, I learned it all –
SONG, DANCE and LAUGHS!
You two can be my CHORUS GIRLS!
Will we have costumes?
What's in it for us?
APPLAUSE FROM THE CROWD!
I'd rather shovel snow. That gets me money.
Your choice, girls!
Quit daydreaming, Tumpie! To work!
You ever been clapped for?

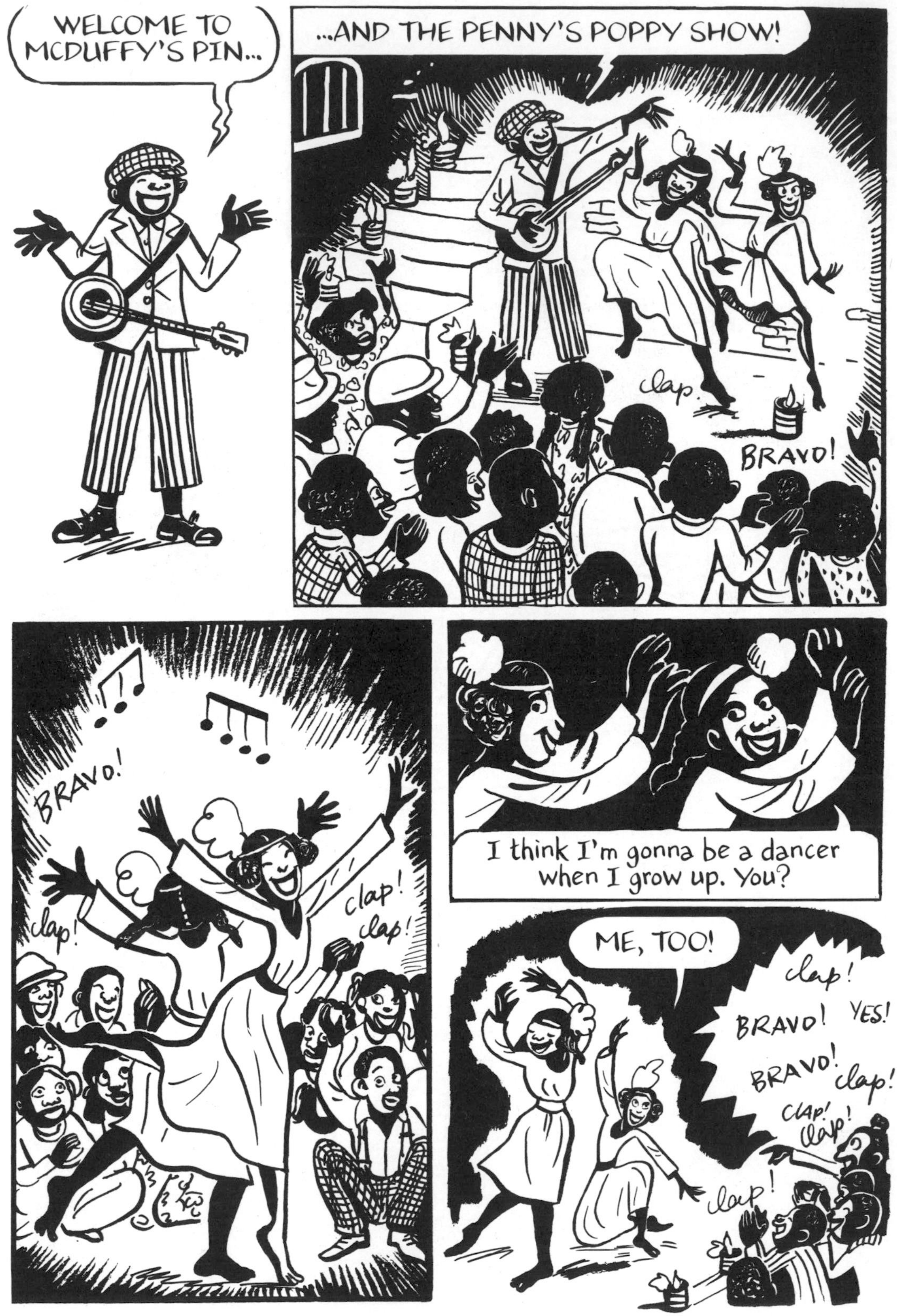
WELCOME TO MCDUFFY'S PIN...
...AND THE PENNY'S POPPY SHOW!
clap.
BRAVO!
BRAVO!
clap!
clap!
clap!
I think I'm gonna be a dancer when I grow up. You?
ME, TOO!
clap!
BRAVO!
YES!
BRAVO!
clap!
clap!
clap!
clap!

1917: Eads Bridge, St. Louis, Missouri, USA

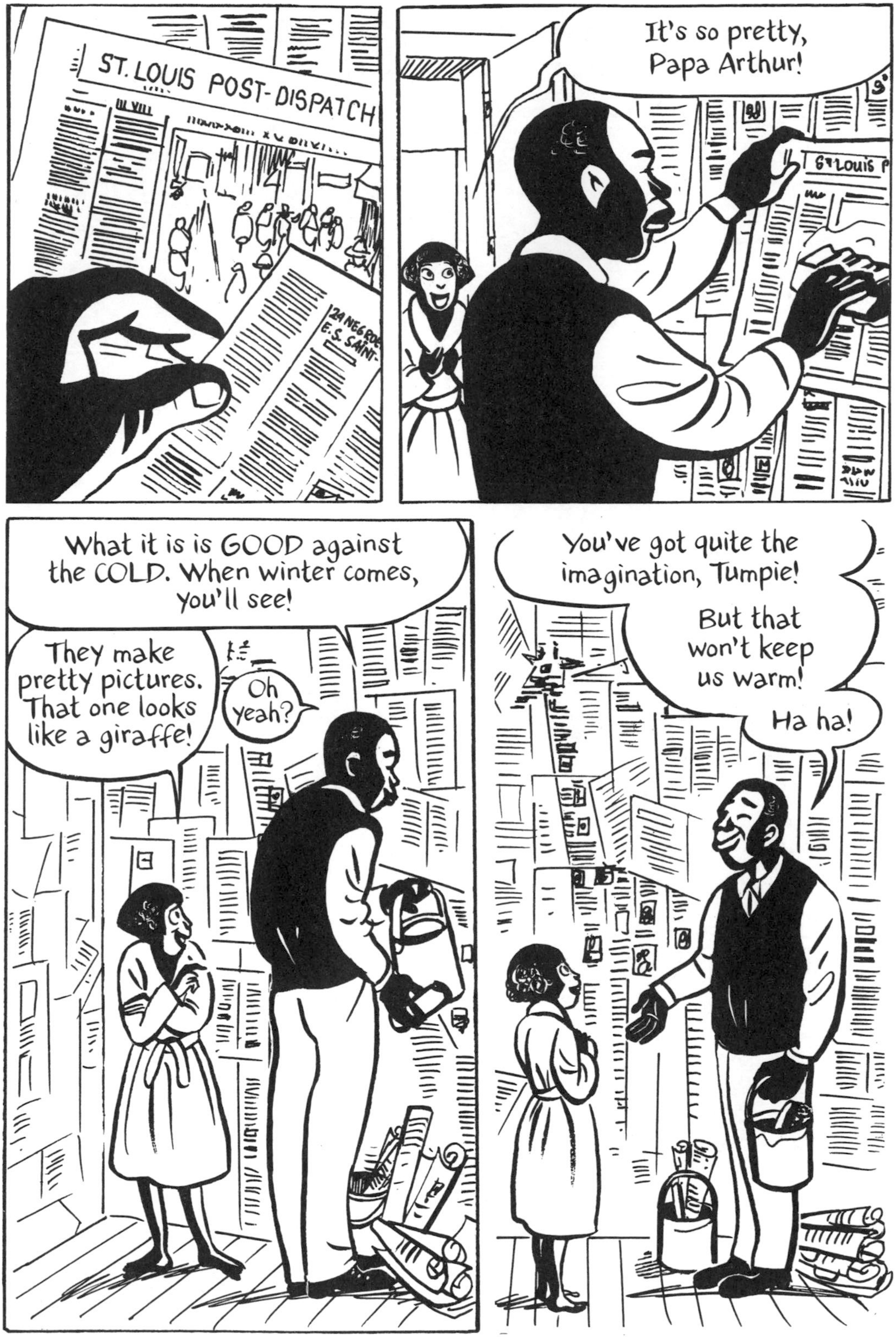
ST. LOUIS POST-DISPATCH
It's so pretty, Papa Arthur!
What it is is GOOD against the COLD. When winter comes, you'll see!
They make pretty pictures. That one looks like a giraffe!
Oh yeah?
You've got quite the imagination, Tumpie!
But that won't keep us warm!
Ha ha!

All clear, Papa Arthur? You'll keep an eye out?
Go ahead! No guards in sight!
Look, Richard! They're way bigger up top!
But Papa Arthur told us only to gather the fallen ones!
But still, they're bigger!
Tumpie, you're crazy!
You're gonna fall!
I won't fall, but the coal will!

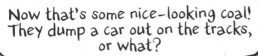

Now that's some nice-looking coal! They dump a car out on the tracks, or what?

Tumpie climbed up top and kicked off some pieces.

She wasn't allowed to, right?

No, they fell by themselves.

Did you really climb up there?

I just wanted to see the station from up high. I even saw our house!

You got that right, Tumpie! The higher you are, the better view you have of life!

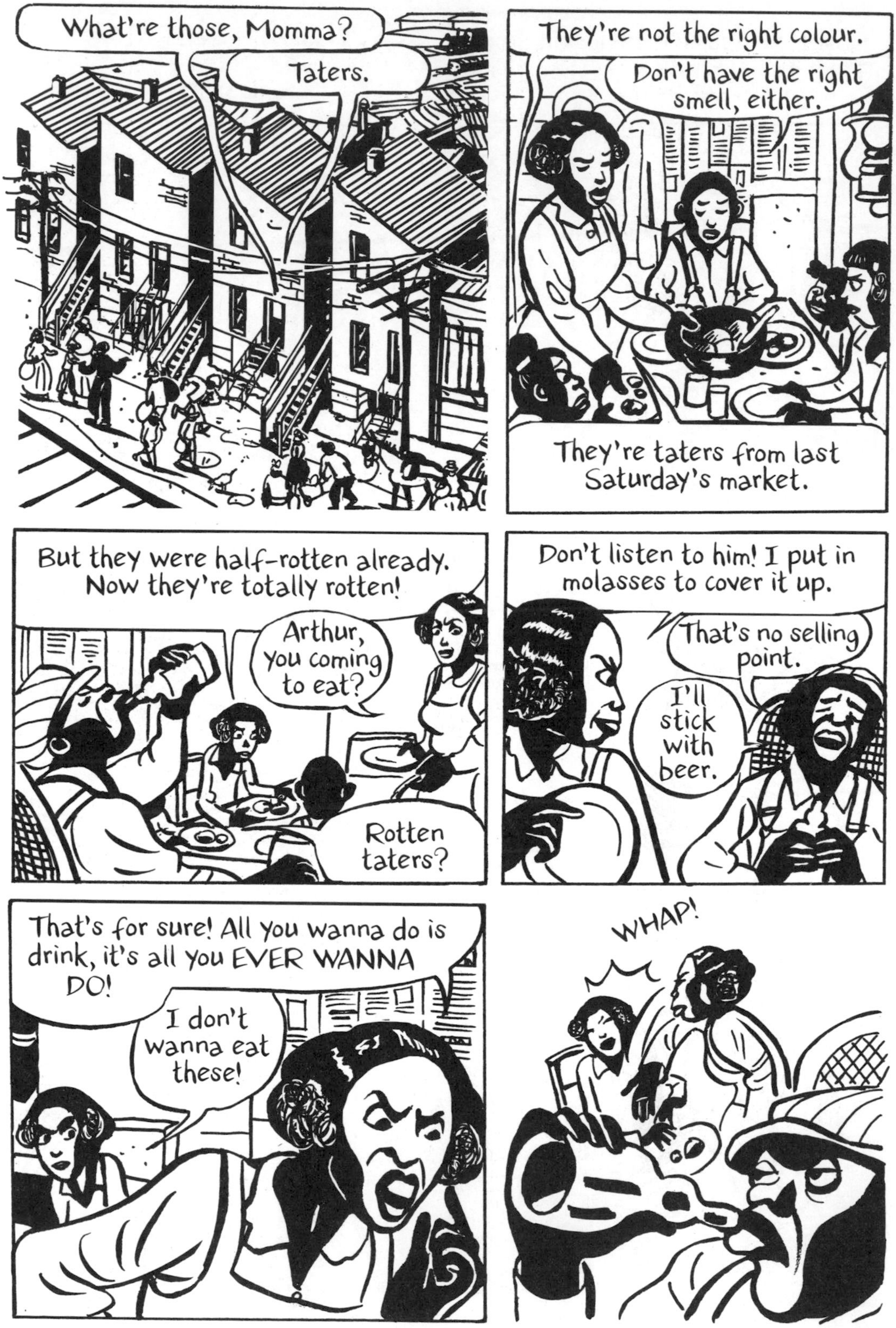
What're those, Momma?
Taters.
They're not the right colour.
Don't have the right smell, either.
They're taters from last Saturday's market.
But they were half-rotten already. Now they're totally rotten!
Arthur, you coming to eat?
Rotten taters?
Don't listen to him! I put in molasses to cover it up.
That's no selling point.
I'll stick with beer.
That's for sure! All you wanna do is drink, it's all you EVER WANNA DO!
I don't wanna eat these!
WHAP!

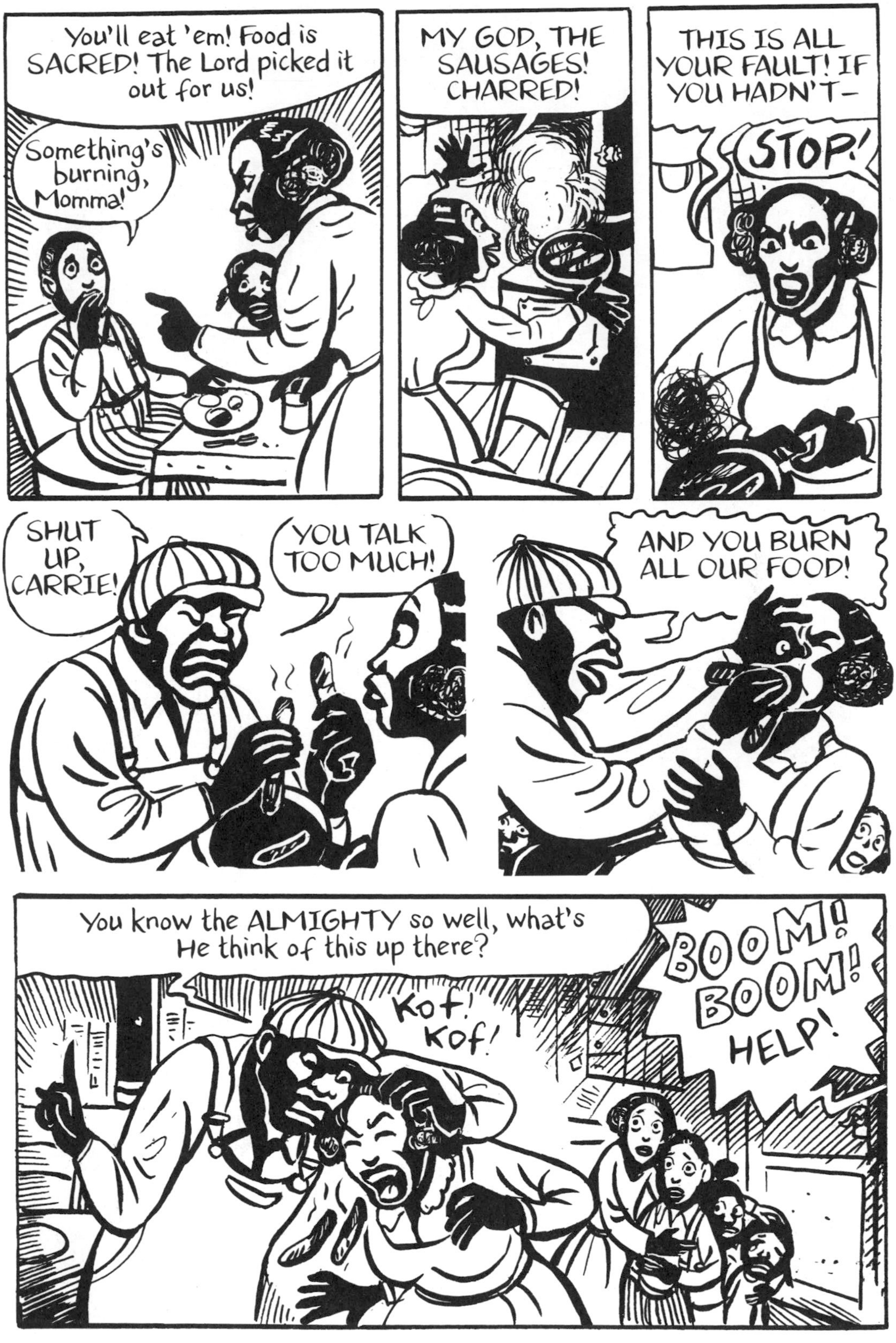
You'll eat 'em! Food is SACRED! The Lord picked it out for us!
Something's burning, Momma!
MY GOD, THE SAUSAGES! CHARRED!
THIS IS ALL YOUR FAULT! IF YOU HADN'T-
STOP!
SHUT UP, CARRIE!
YOU TALK TOO MUCH!
AND YOU BURN ALL OUR FOOD!
You know the ALMIGHTY so well, what's He think of this up there?
Kof! Kof!
BOOM! BOOM! HELP!

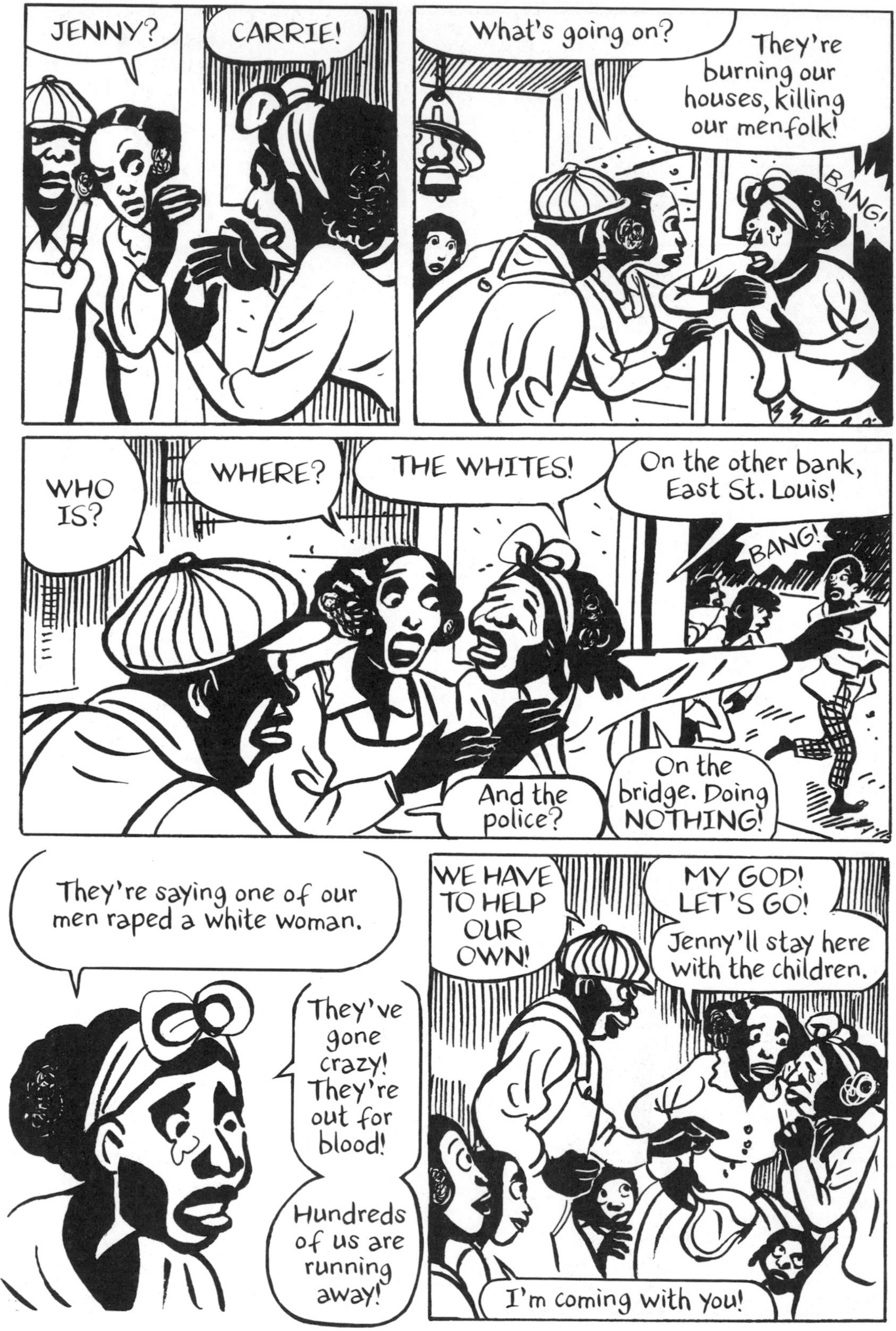
JENNY?
CARRIE!
What's going on?
They're burning our houses, killing our menfolk!
BANG!
WHO IS?
WHERE?
THE WHITES!
On the other bank, East St. Louis!
BANG!
And the police?
On the bridge. Doing NOTHING!
They're saying one of our men raped a white woman.
They've gone crazy! They're out for blood!
Hundreds of us are running away!
WE HAVE TO HELP OUR OWN!
MY GOD! LET'S GO!
Jenny'll stay here with the children.
I'm coming with you!

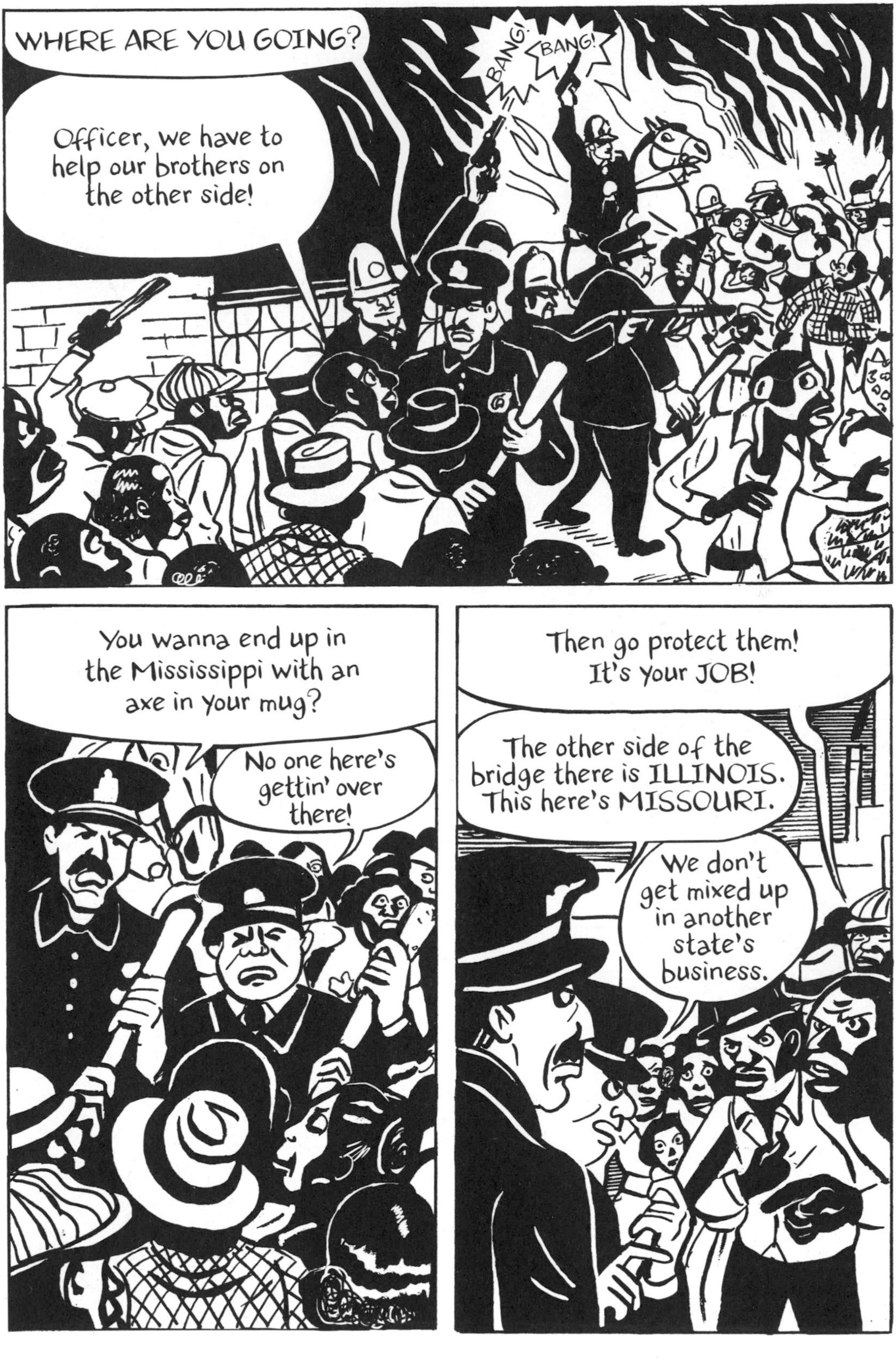
WHERE ARE YOU GOING?
Officer, we have to help our brothers on the other side!
BANG!
BANG!
You wanna end up in the Mississippi with an axe in your mug?
No one here's gettin' over there!
Then go protect them! It's your JOB!
The other side of the bridge there is ILLINOIS. This here's MISSOURI.
We don't get mixed up in another state's business.

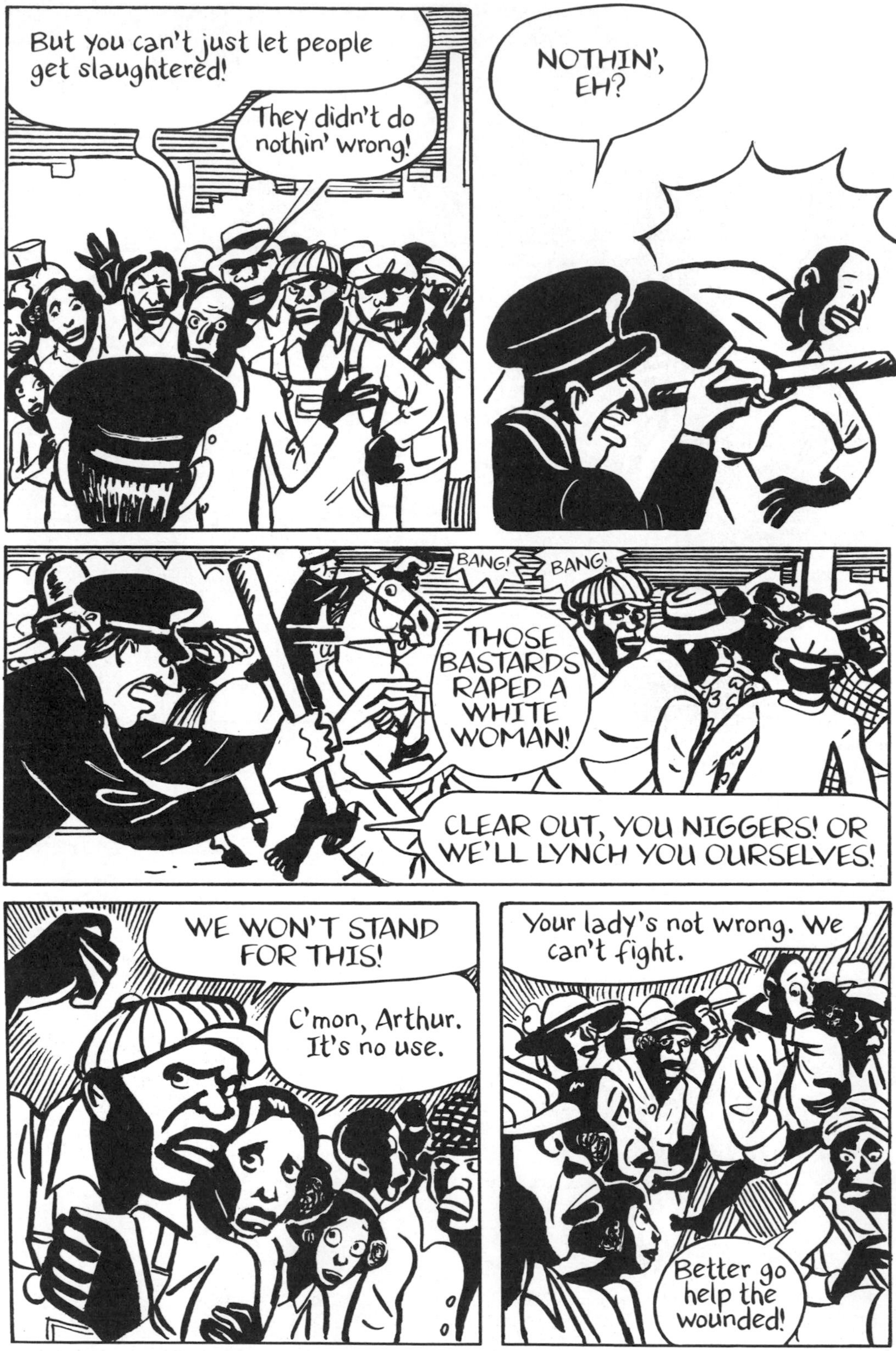
But you can't just let people get slaughtered!
They didn't do nothin' wrong!
NOTHIN', EH?
BANG!
BANG!
THOSE BASTARDS RAPED A WHITE WOMAN!
CLEAR OUT, YOU NIGGERS! OR WE'LL LYNCH YOU OURSELVES!
WE WON'T STAND FOR THIS!
C'mon, Arthur. It's no use.
Your lady's not wrong. We can't fight.
Better go help the wounded!

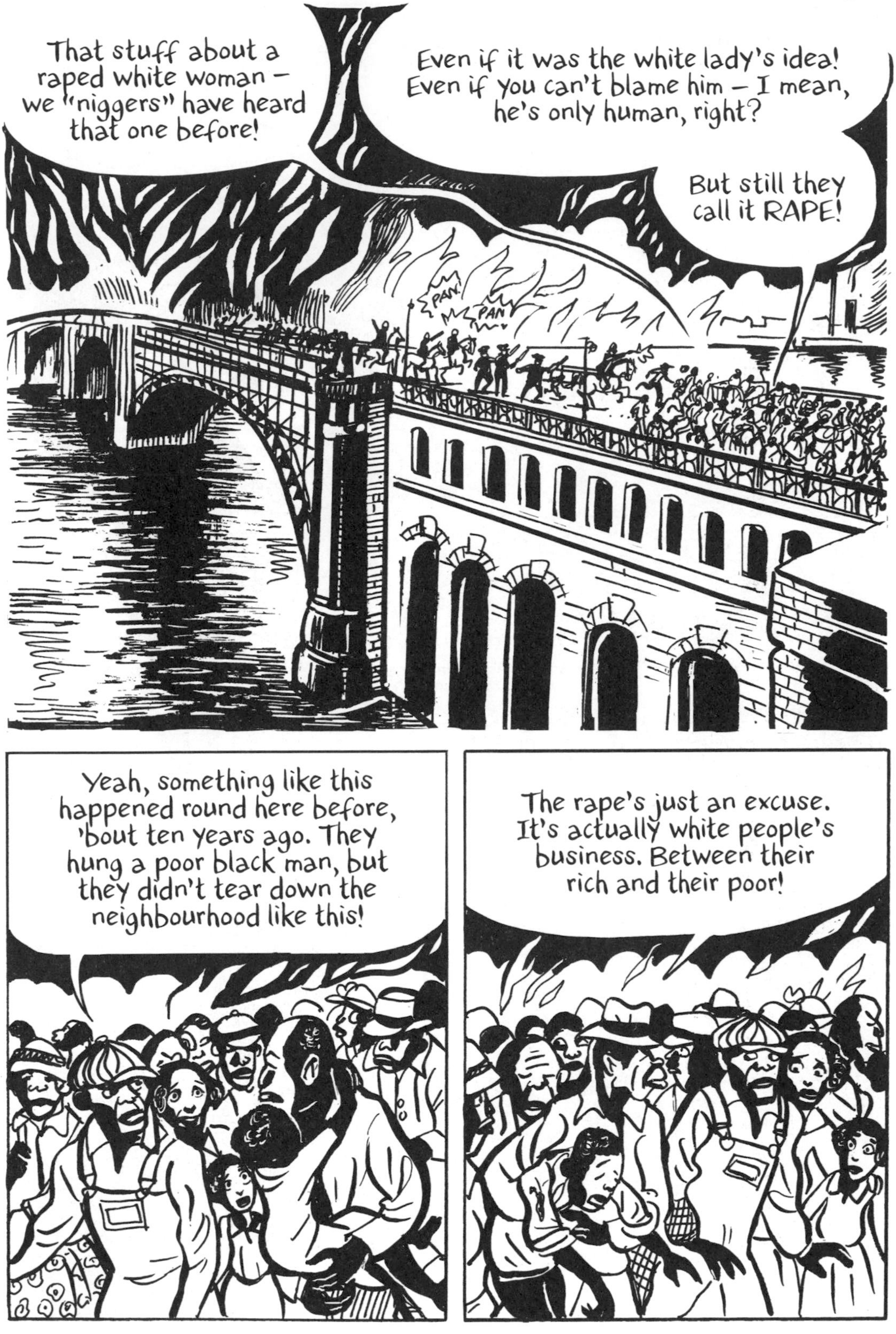
That stuff about a raped white woman – we "niggers" have heard that one before!
Even if it was the white lady's idea! Even if you can't blame him – I mean, he's only human, right?
But still they call it RAPE!
PAN!
PAN
Yeah, something like this happened round here before, 'bout ten years ago. They hung a poor black man, but they didn't tear down the neighbourhood like this!
The rape's just an excuse. It's actually white people's business. Between their rich and their poor!

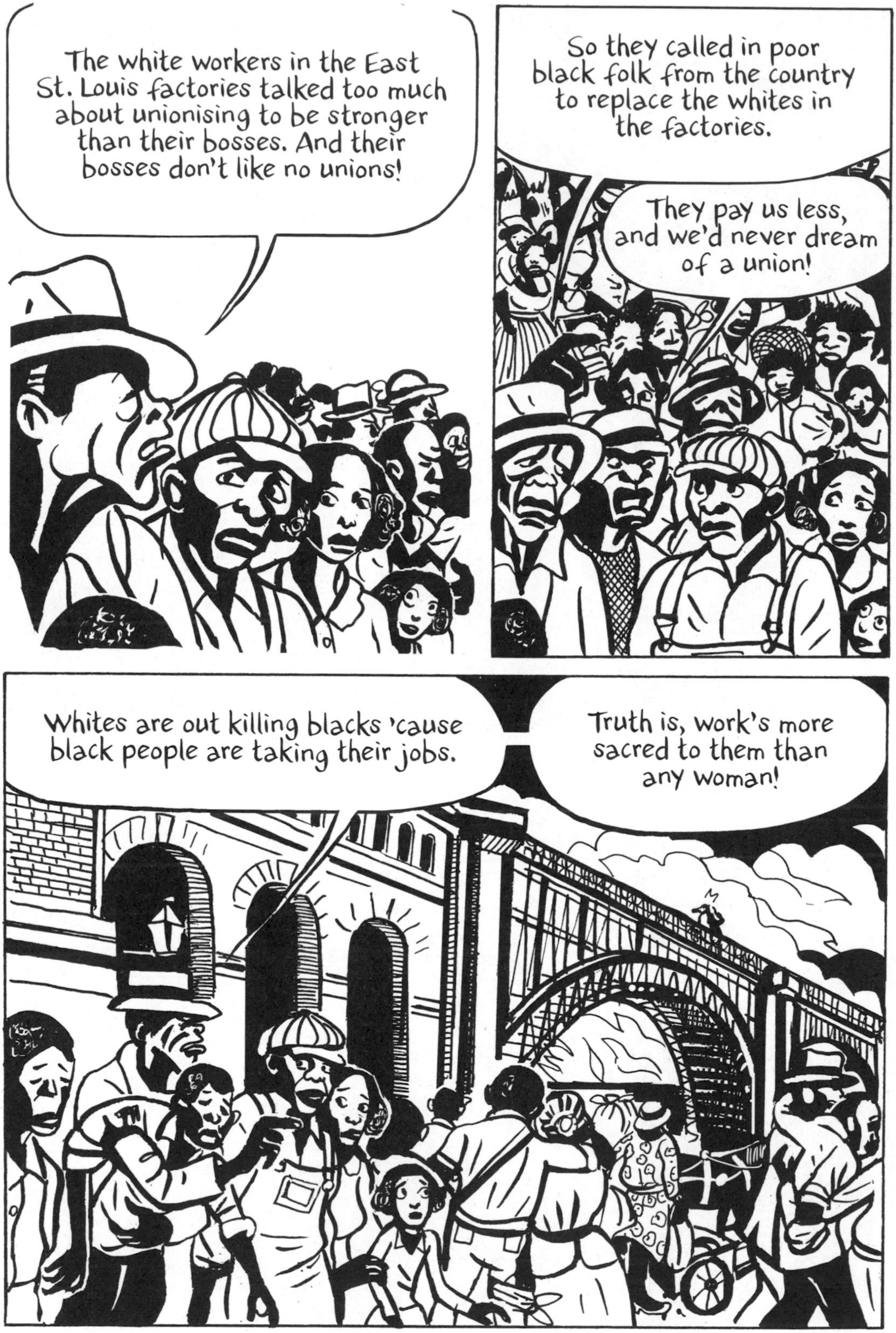
The white workers in the East St. Louis factories talked too much about unionising to be stronger than their bosses. And their bosses don't like no unions!
So they called in poor black folk from the country to replace the whites in the factories.
They pay us less, and we'd never dream of a union!
Whites are out killing blacks 'cause black people are taking their jobs.
Truth is, work's more sacred to them than any woman!

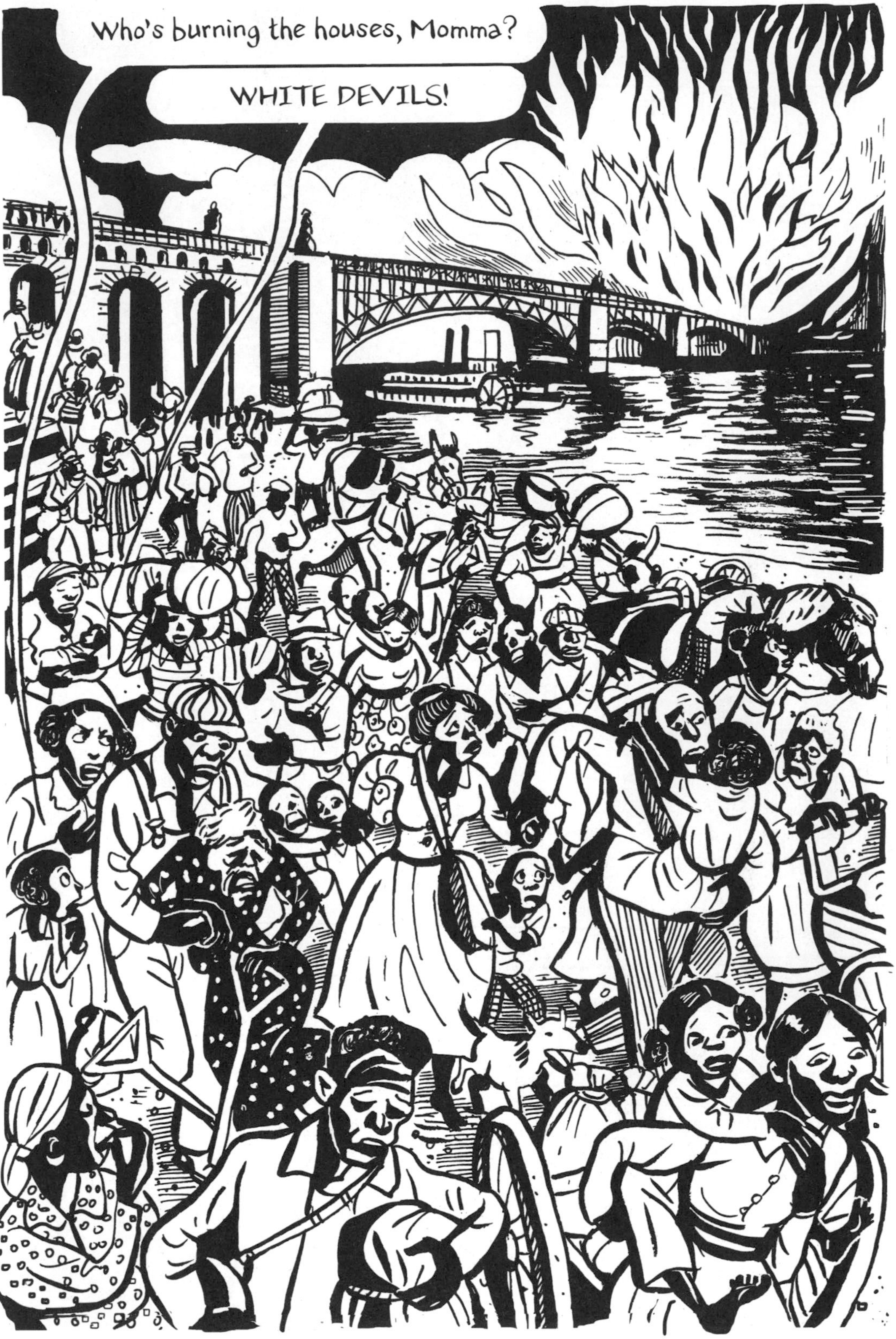
Who's burning the houses, Momma?
WHITE DEVILS!

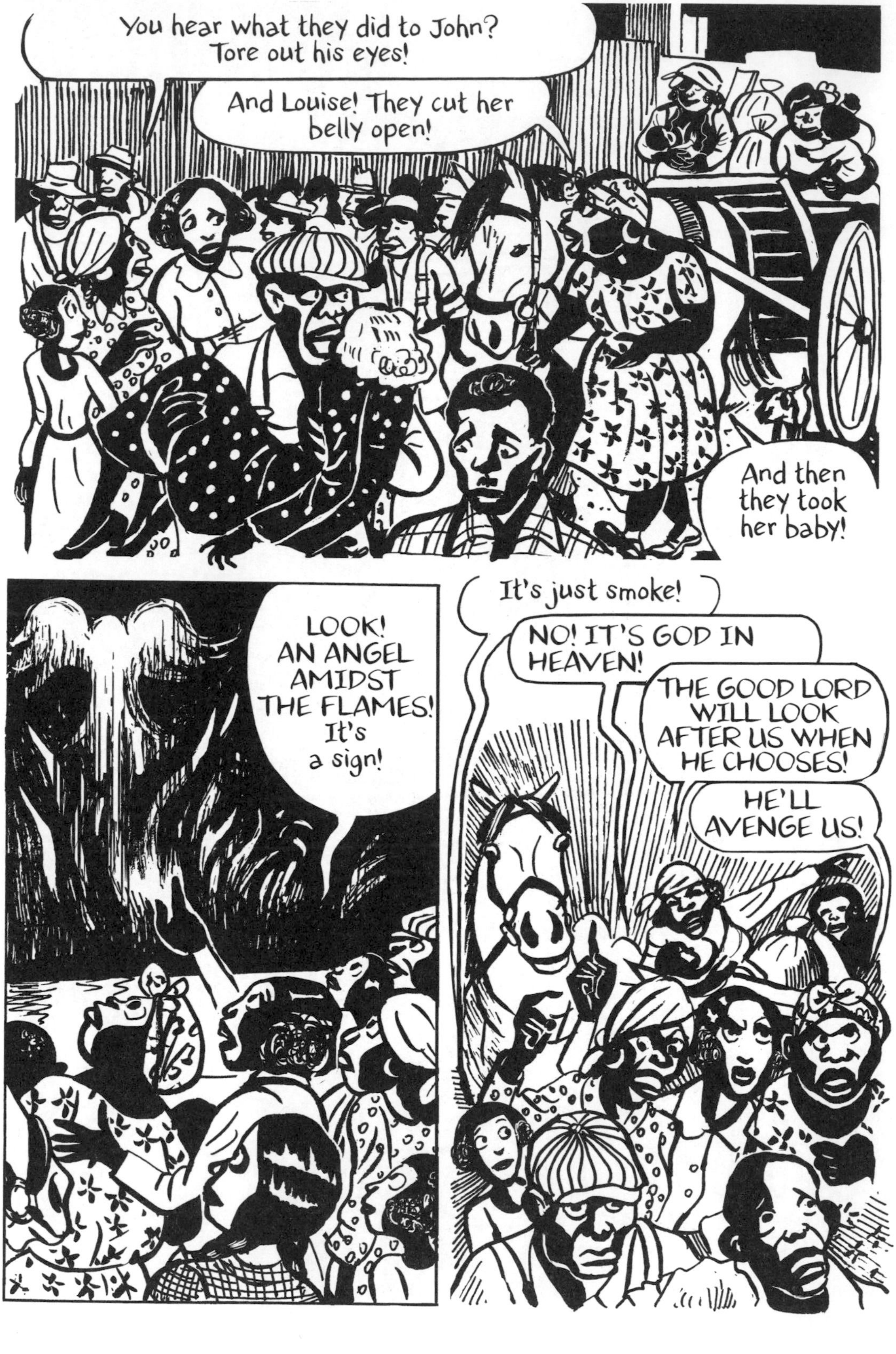
You hear what they did to John? Tore out his eyes!
And Louise! They cut her belly open!
And then they took her baby!
LOOK! AN ANGEL AMIDST THE FLAMES! It's a sign!
It's just smoke!
NO! IT'S GOD IN HEAVEN!
THE GOOD LORD WILL LOOK AFTER US WHEN HE CHOOSES!
HE'LL AVENGE US!

1918: Downtown West, St. Louis, Missouri, USA

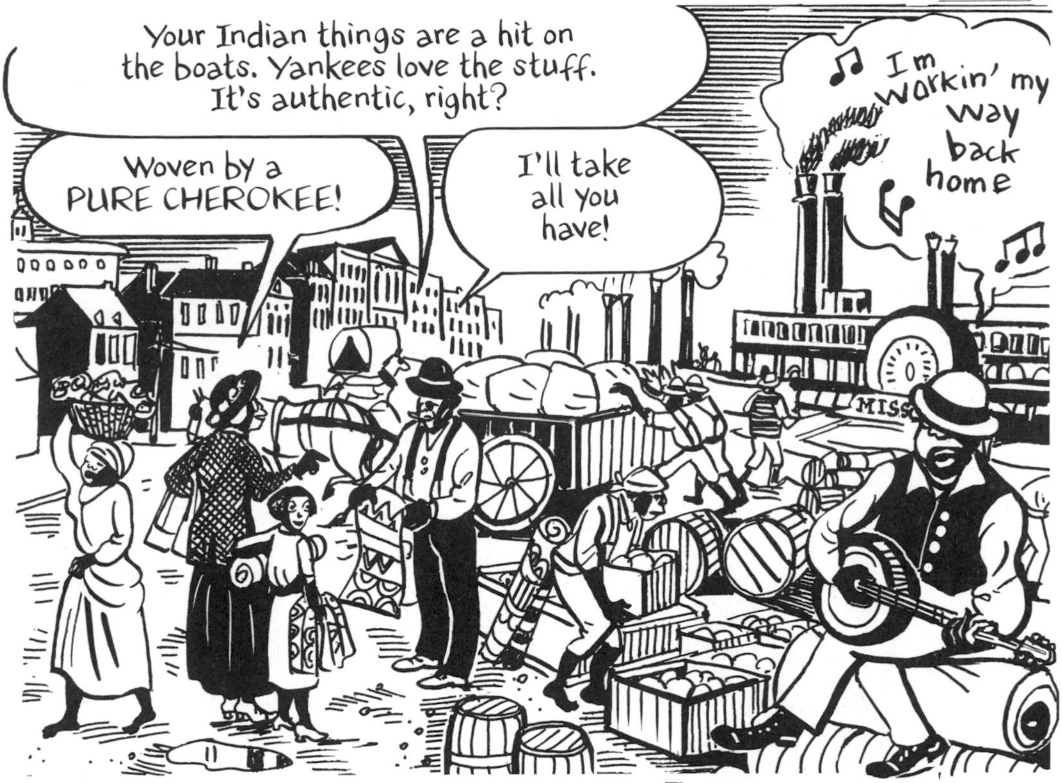
Your Indian things are a hit on the boats. Yankees love the stuff. It's authentic, right?
Woven by a PURE CHEROKEE!
I'll take all you have!
I'm workin' my way back home
MISS

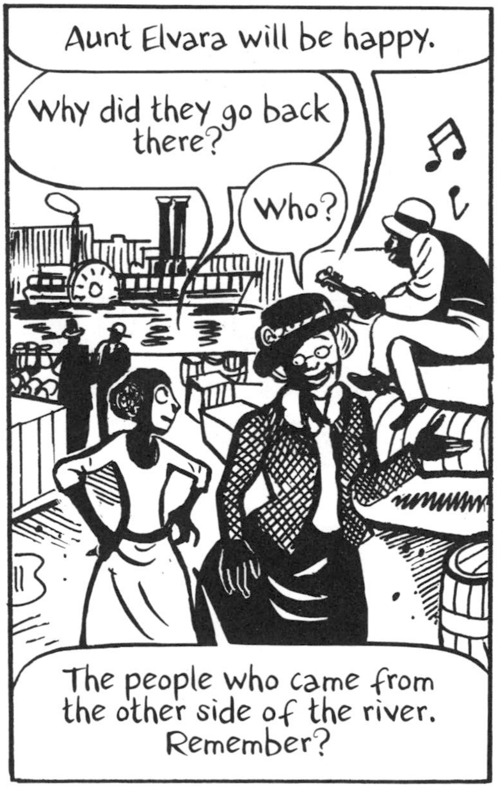
Aunt Elvara will be happy.
Why did they go back there?
Who?
The people who came from the other side of the river. Remember?

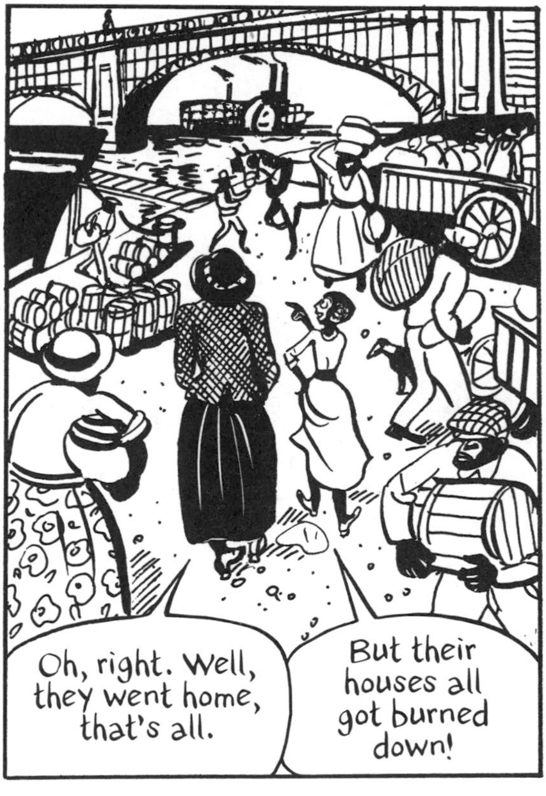
Oh, right. Well, they went home, that's all.
But their houses all got burned down!

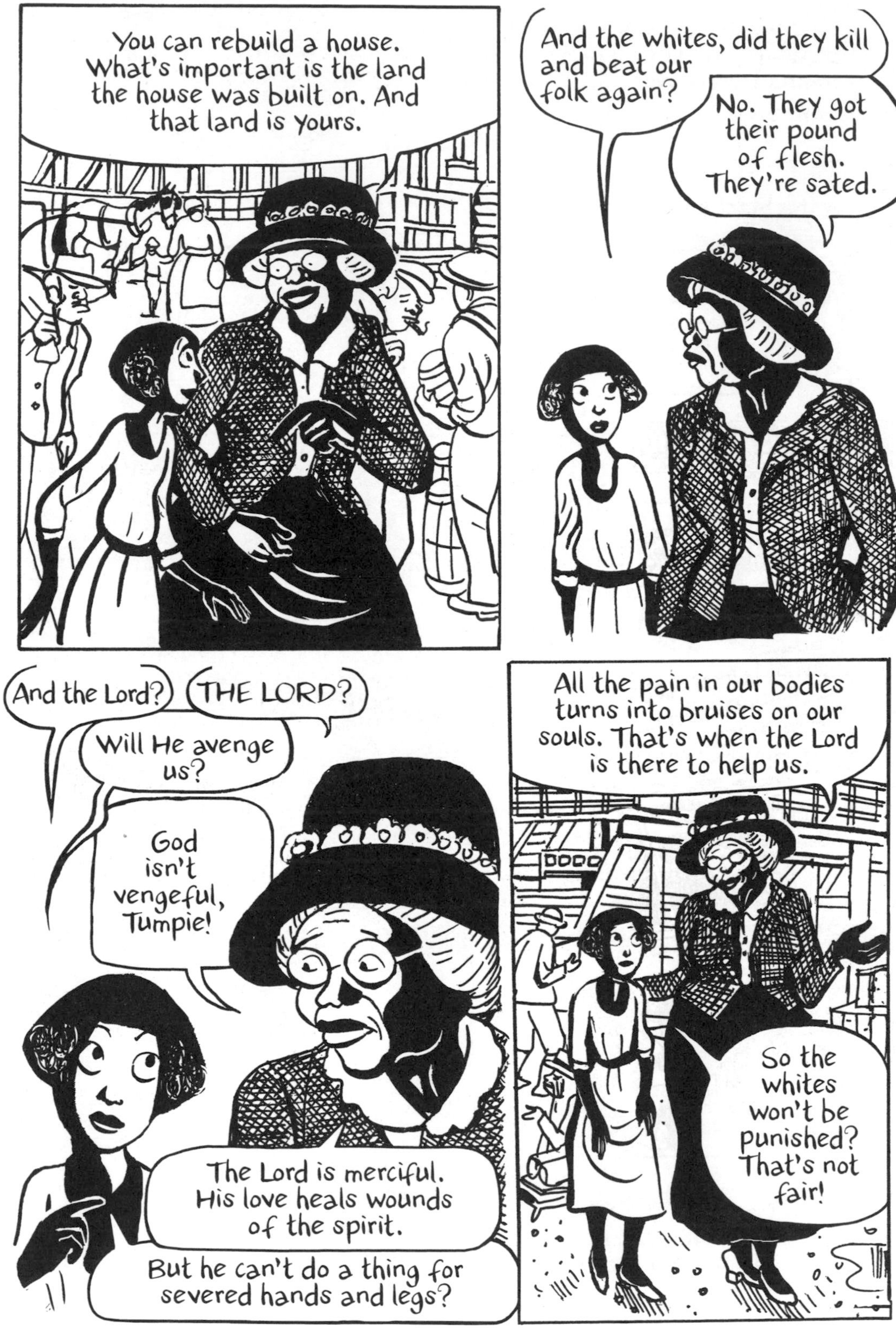
You can rebuild a house. What's important is the land the house was built on. And that land is yours.
And the whites, did they kill and beat our folk again?
No. They got their pound of flesh. They're sated.
And the Lord?
THE LORD?
Will He avenge us?
God isn't vengeful, Tumpie!
The Lord is merciful. His love heals wounds of the spirit.
But he can't do a thing for severed hands and legs?
All the pain in our bodies turns into bruises on our souls. That's when the Lord is there to help us.
So the whites won't be punished? That's not fair!

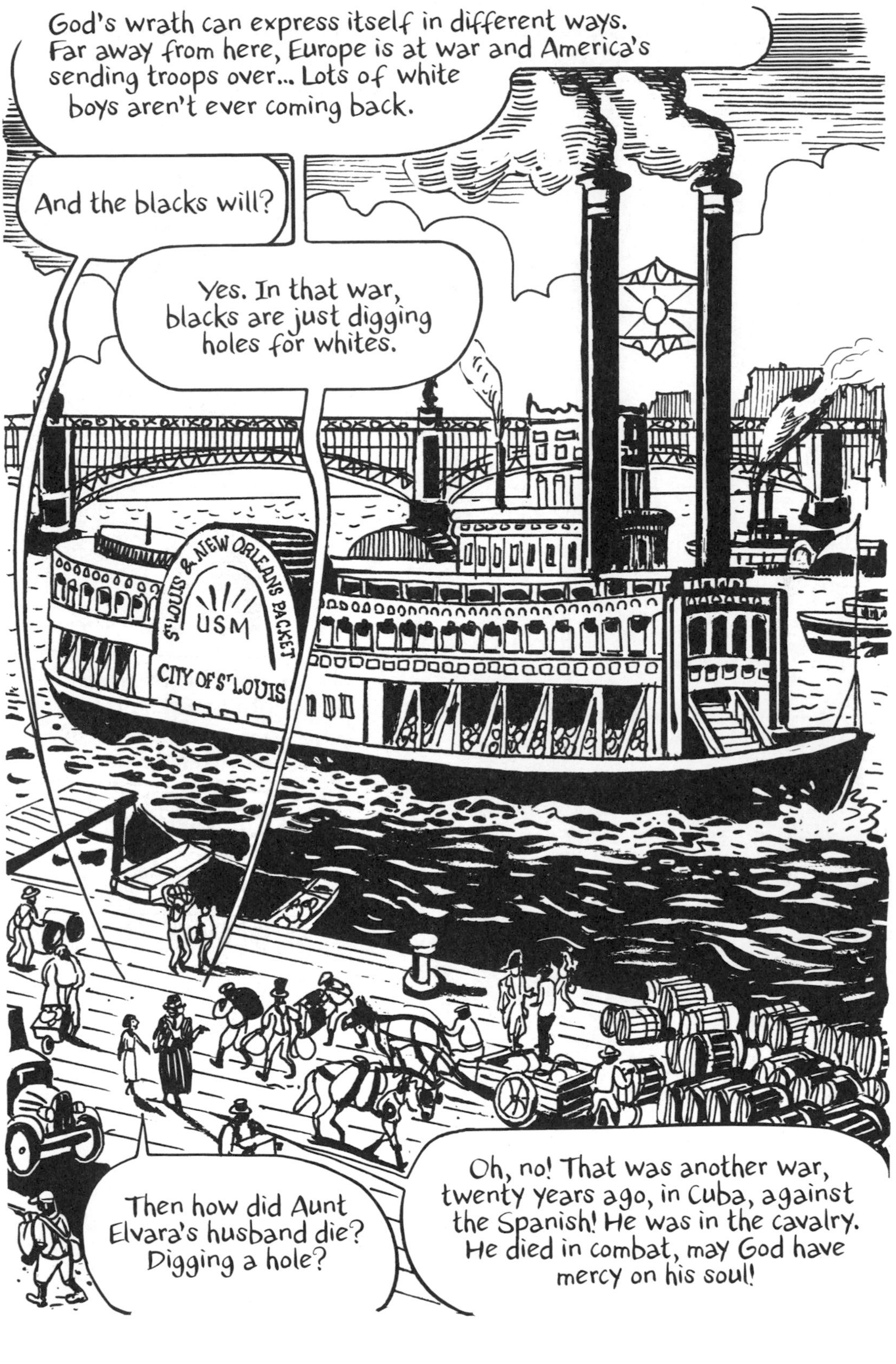
God's wrath can express itself in different ways. Far away from here, Europe is at war and America's sending troops over... Lots of white boys aren't ever coming back.
And the blacks will?
Yes. In that war, blacks are just digging holes for whites.
ST LOUIS & NEW ORLEANS PACKET
USM
CITY OF ST LOUIS
Then how did Aunt Elvara's husband die? Digging a hole?
Oh, no! That was another war, twenty years ago, in Cuba, against the Spanish! He was in the cavalry. He died in combat, may God have mercy on his soul!

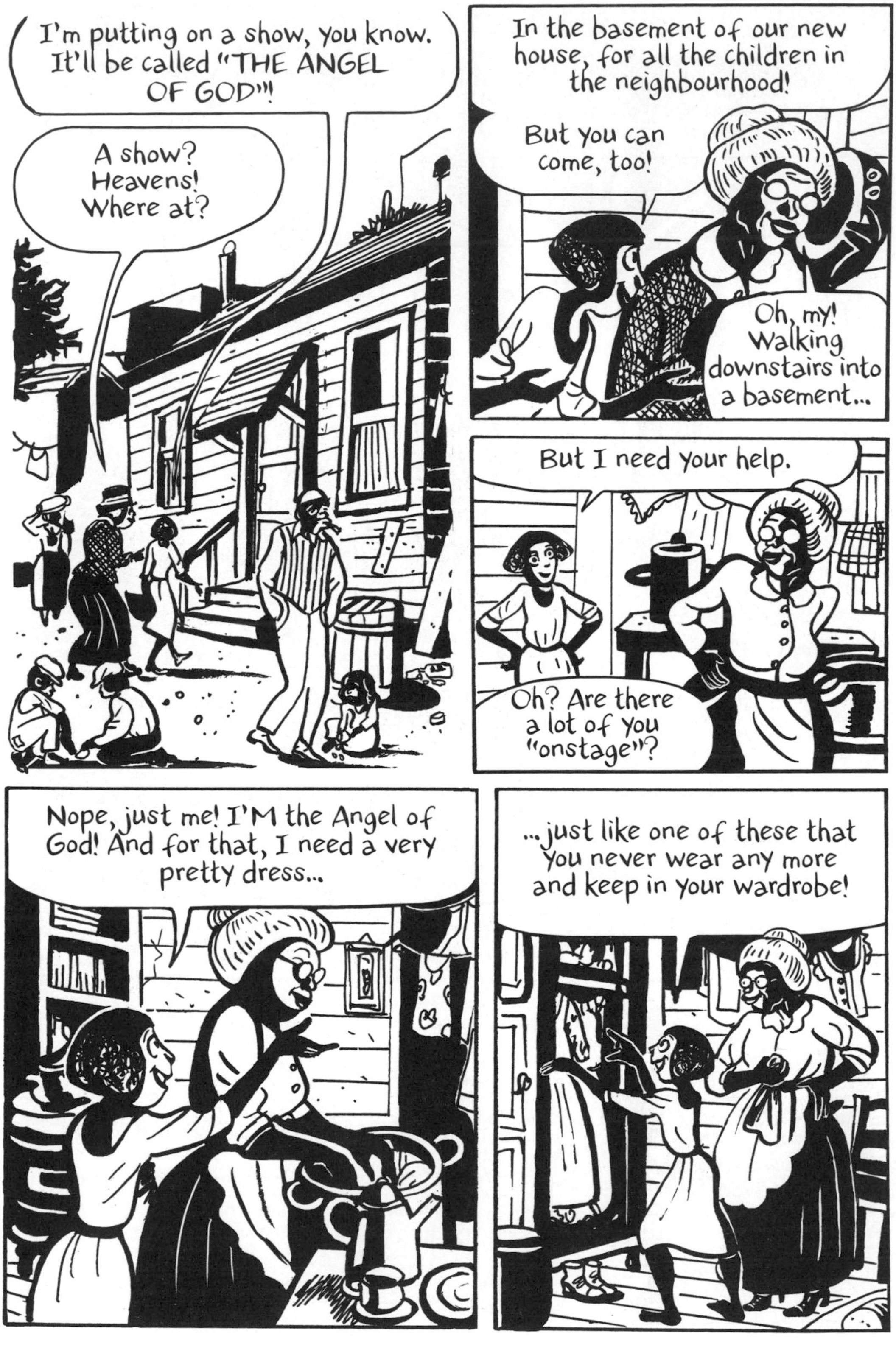
I'm putting on a show, you know. It'll be called "THE ANGEL OF GOD"!
A show? Heavens! Where at?
In the basement of our new house, for all the children in the neighbourhood!
But you can come, too!
Oh, my! Walking downstairs into a basement...
But I need your help.
Oh? Are there a lot of you "onstage"?
Nope, just me! I'M the Angel of God! And for that, I need a very pretty dress...
...just like one of these that you never wear any more and keep in your wardrobe!

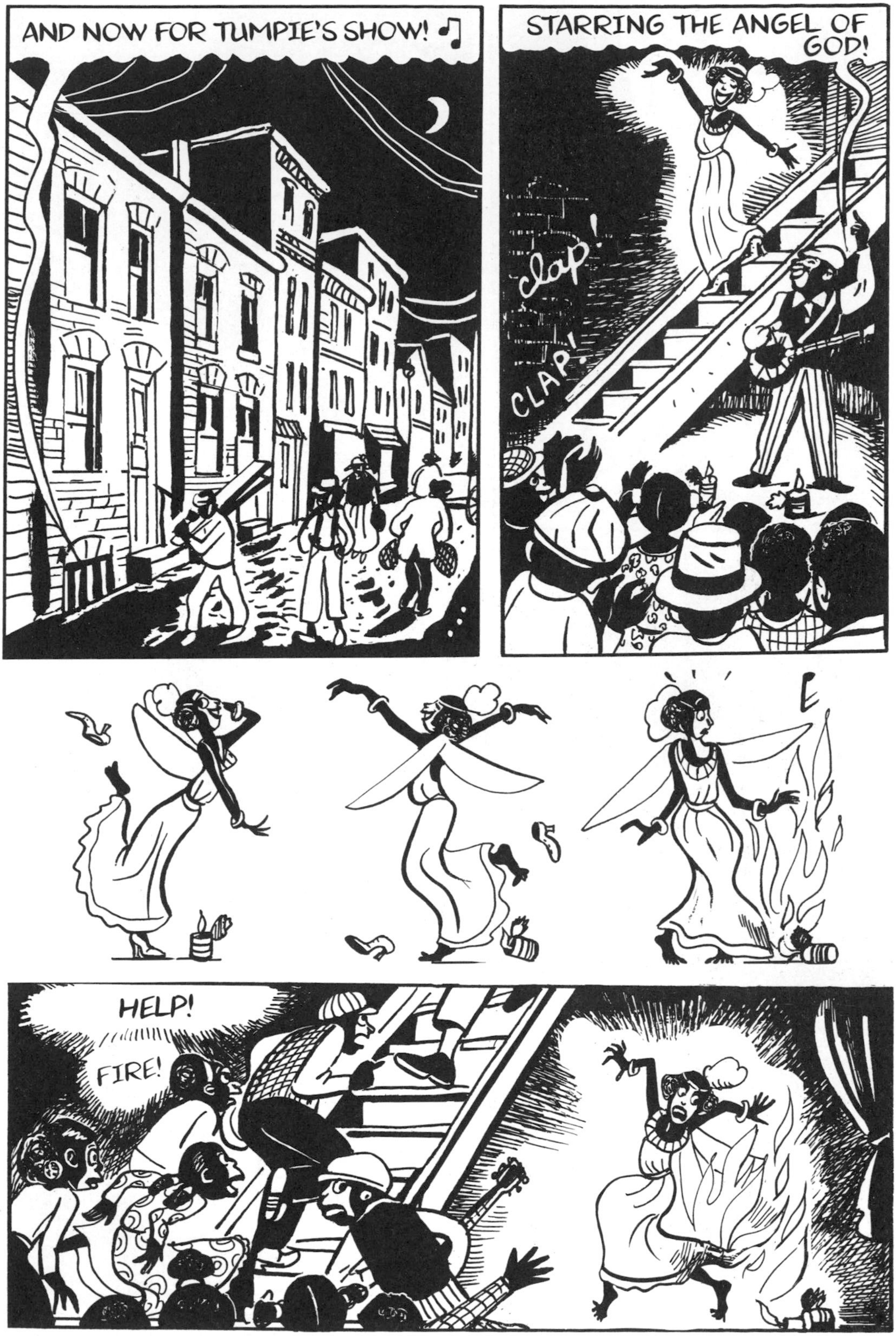

AND NOW FOR TUMPIE'S SHOW! ♫
STARRING THE ANGEL OF GOD!
clap!
CLAP!
HELP!
FIRE!

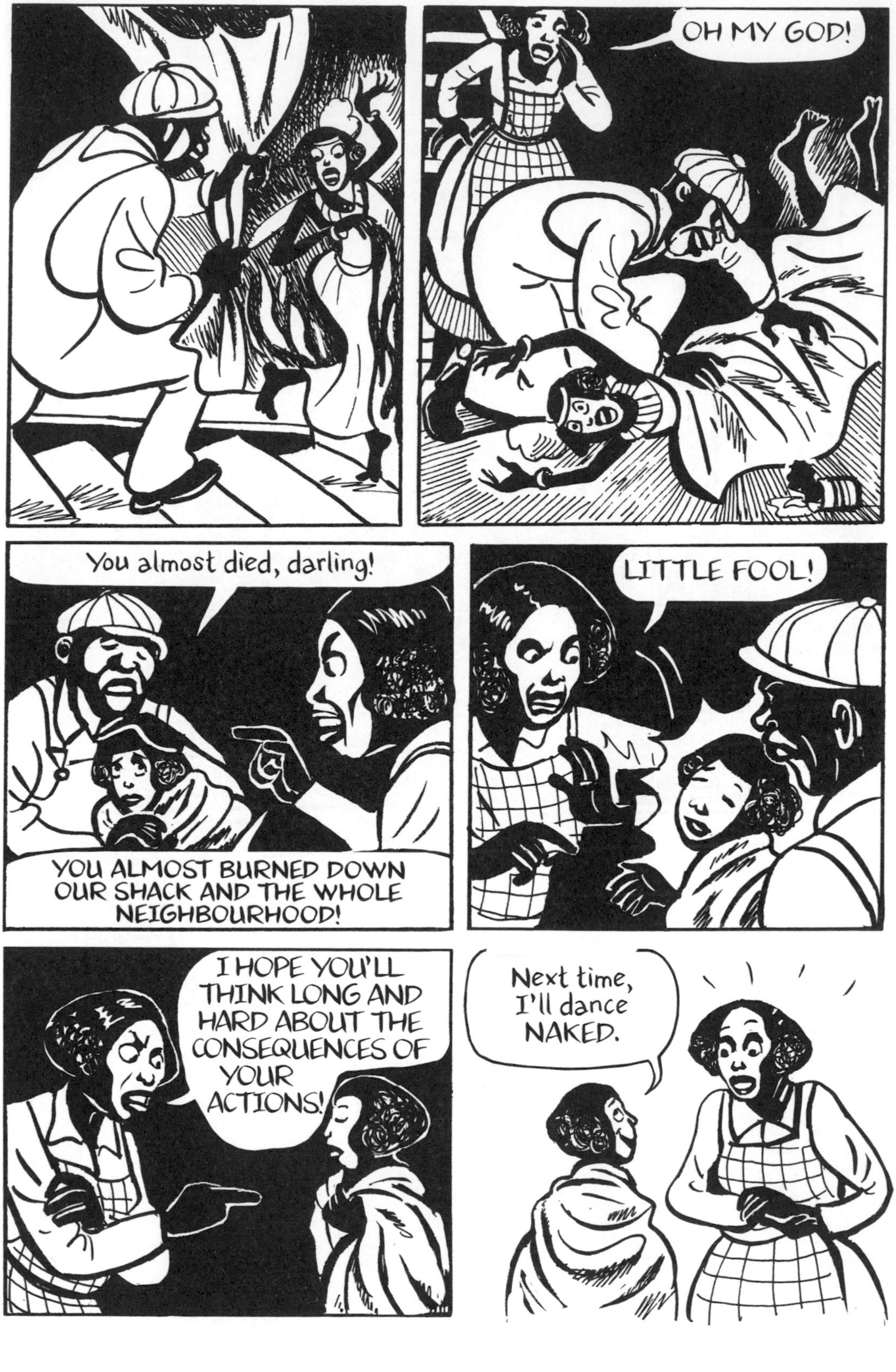
OH MY GOD!
You almost died, darling!
YOU ALMOST BURNED DOWN OUR SHACK AND THE WHOLE NEIGHBOURHOOD!
LITTLE FOOL!
I HOPE YOU'LL THINK LONG AND HARD ABOUT THE CONSEQUENCES OF YOUR ACTIONS!
Next time, I'll dance NAKED.

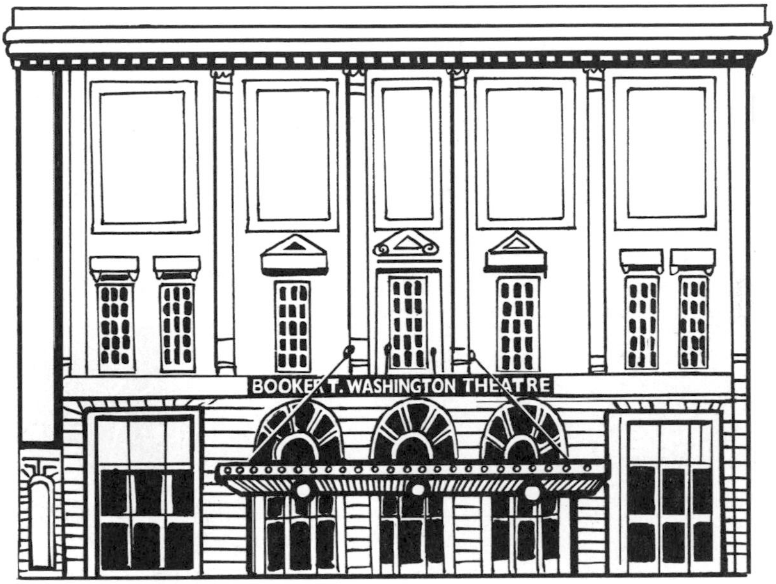
BOOKER T. WASHINGTON THEATRE

1919: Booker T. Washington Theatre,
St. Louis, Missouri, USA

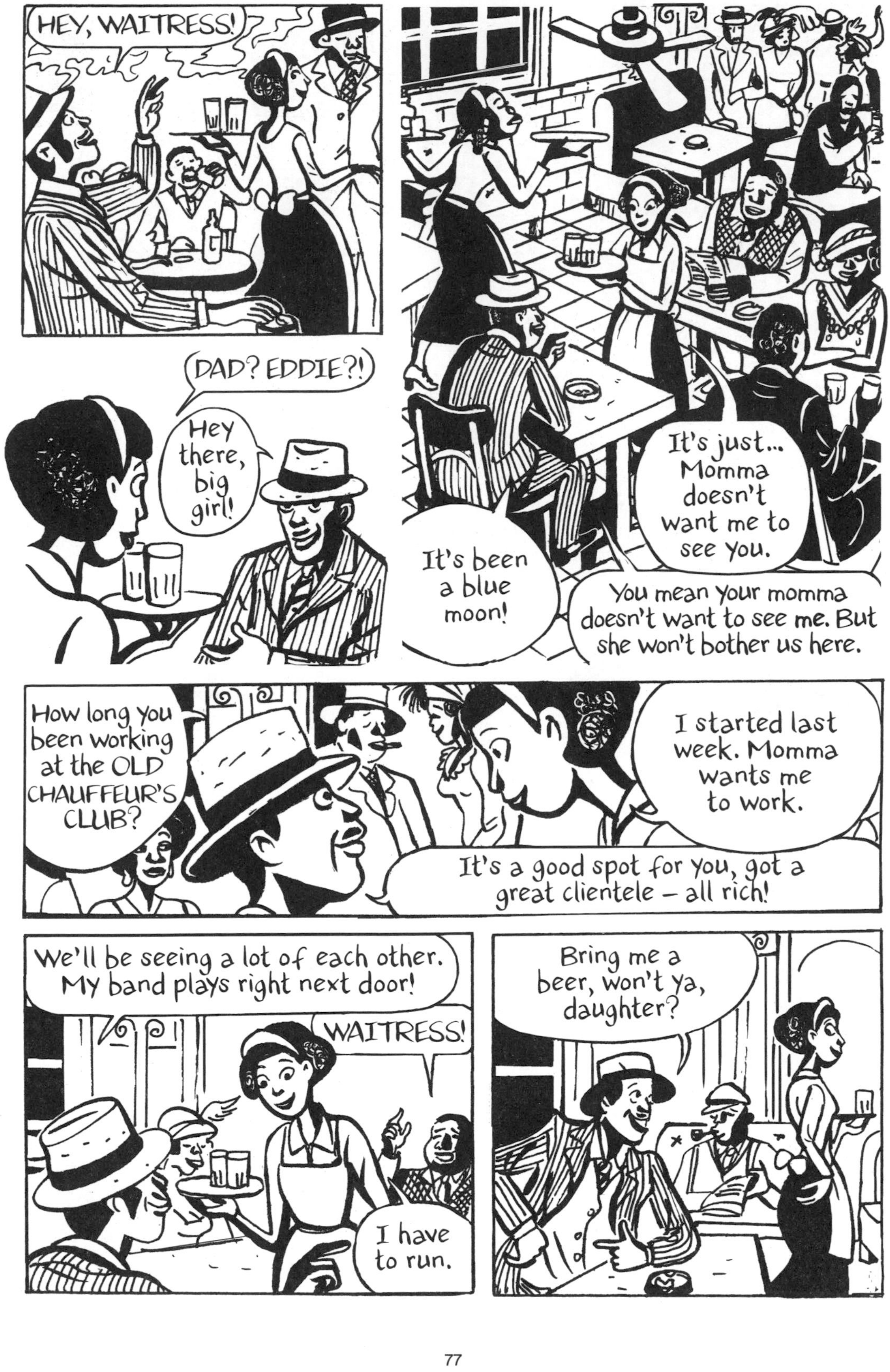
HEY, WAITRESS!
DAD? EDDIE?!
Hey there, big girl!
It's been a blue moon!
It's just... Momma doesn't want me to see you.
You mean your momma doesn't want to see me. But she won't bother us here.
How long you been working at the OLD CHAUFFEUR'S CLUB?
I started last week. Momma wants me to work.
It's a good spot for you, got a great clientele – all rich!
We'll be seeing a lot of each other. My band plays right next door!
WAITRESS!
I have to run.
Bring me a beer, won't ya, daughter?

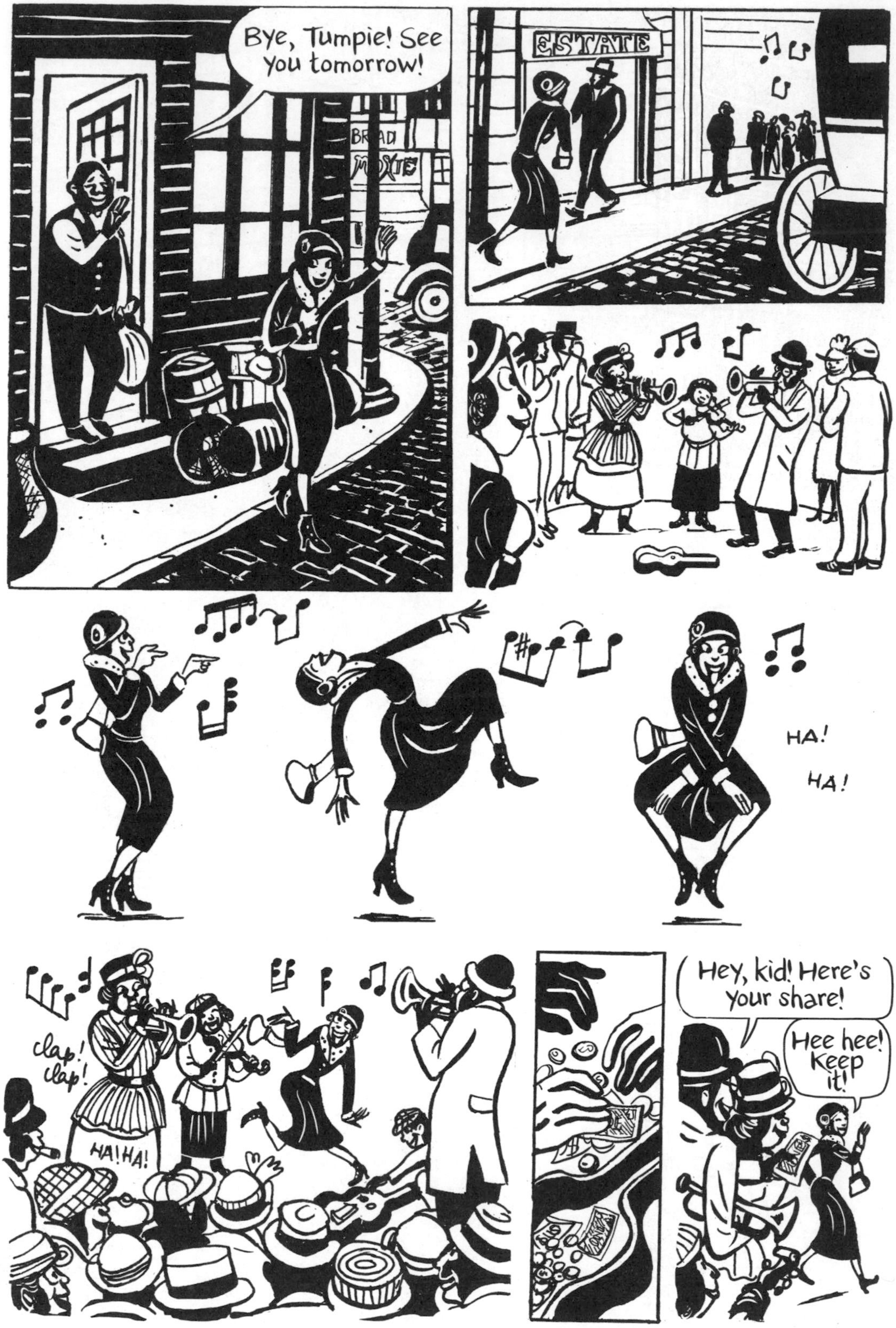
Bye, Tumpie! See you tomorrow!
BREAD
ESTATE
HA!
HA!
clap! clap!
HA! HA!
Hey, kid! Here's your share!
Hee hee! Keep it!

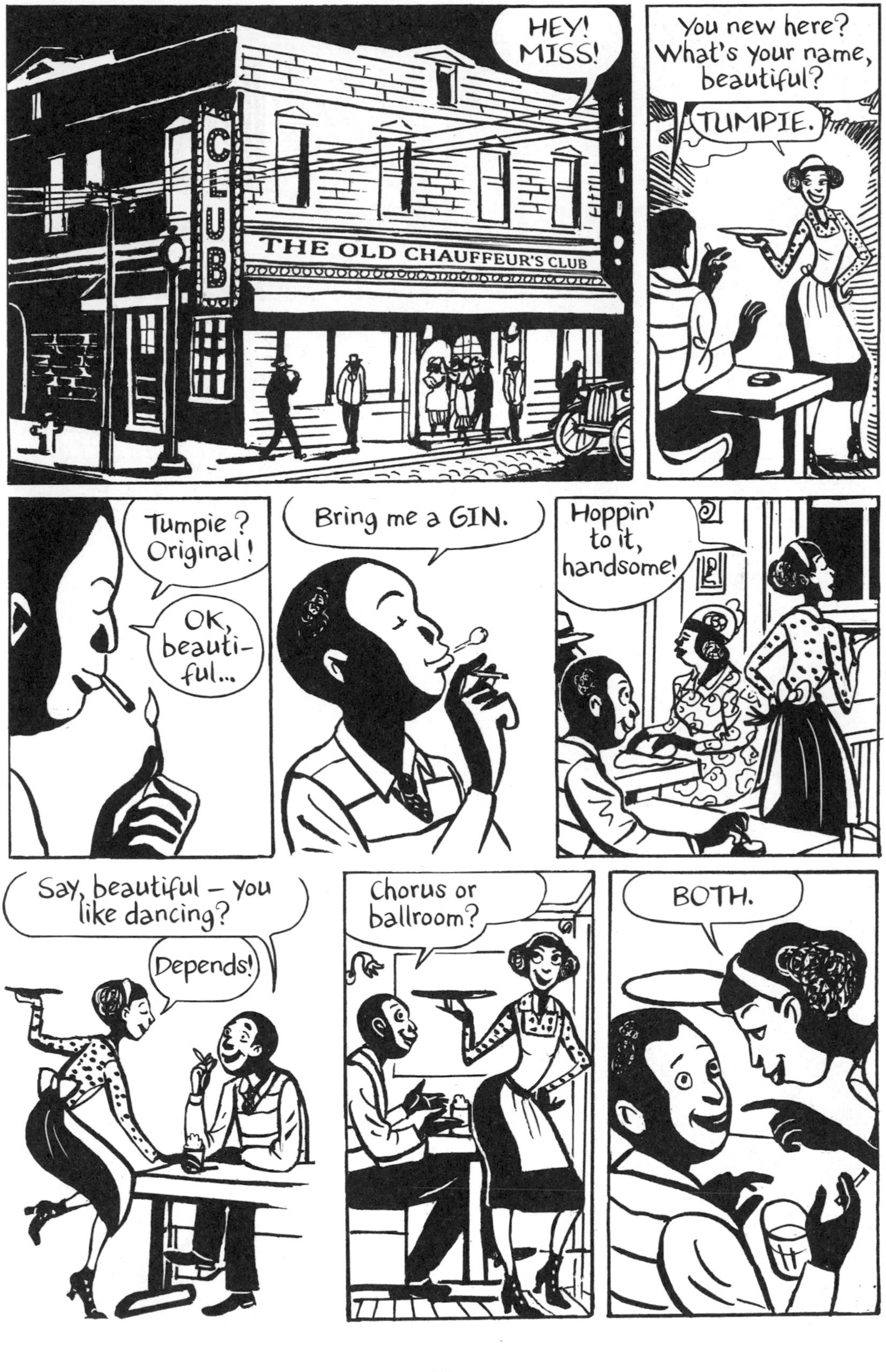
HEY! MISS!
CLUB
THE OLD CHAUFFEUR'S CLUB
You new here? What's your name, beautiful?
TUMPIE.
Tumpie? Original!
OK, beauti-ful...
Bring me a GIN.
Hoppin' to it, handsome!
Say, beautiful – you like dancing?
Depends!
Chorus or ballroom?
BOTH.

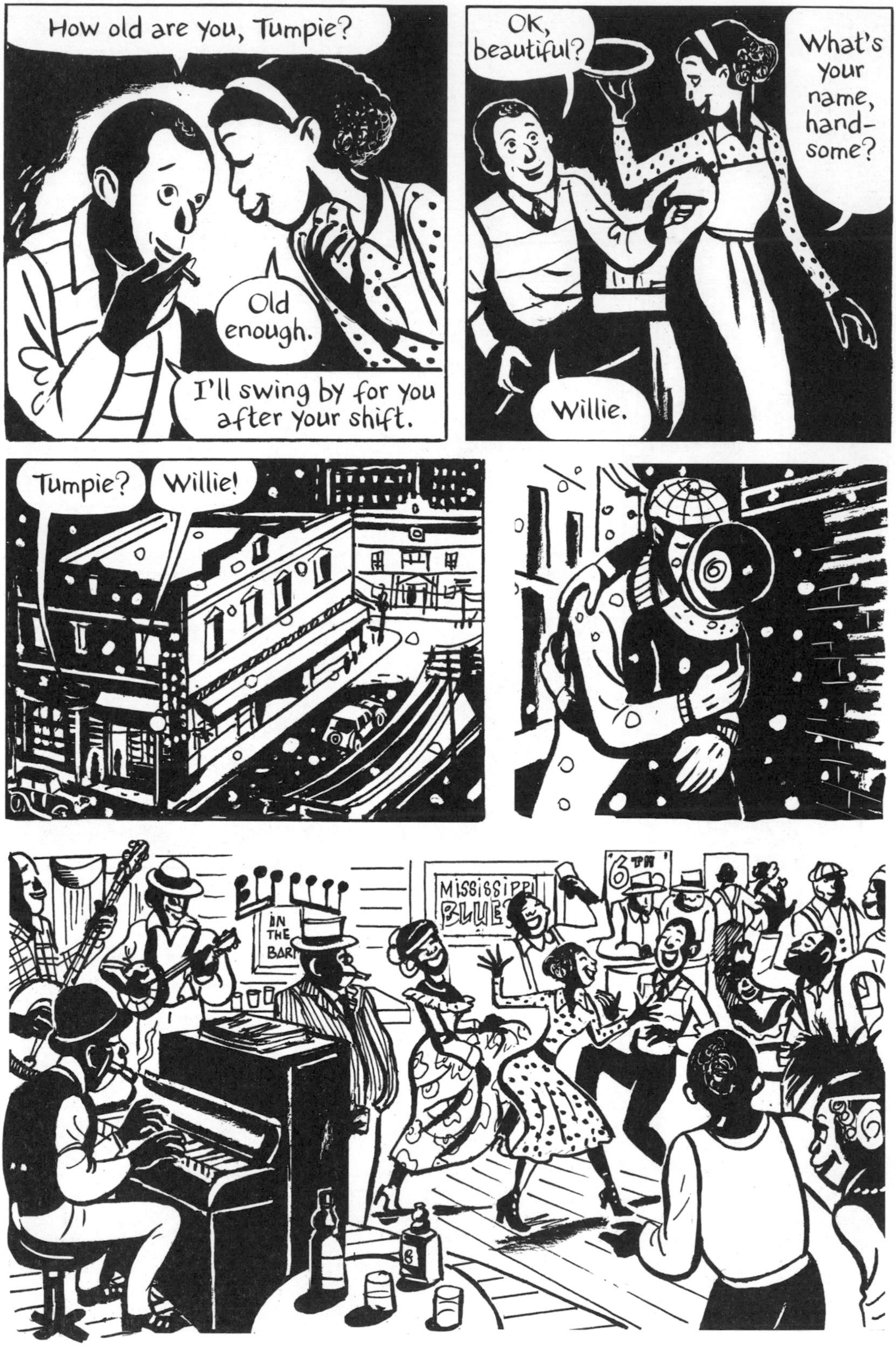
How old are you, Tumpie?
Old enough.
I'll swing by for you after your shift.
OK, beautiful?
What's your name, hand-some?
Willie.
Tumpie?
Willie!
MISSISSIPPI BLUES
IN THE BAR
6TH

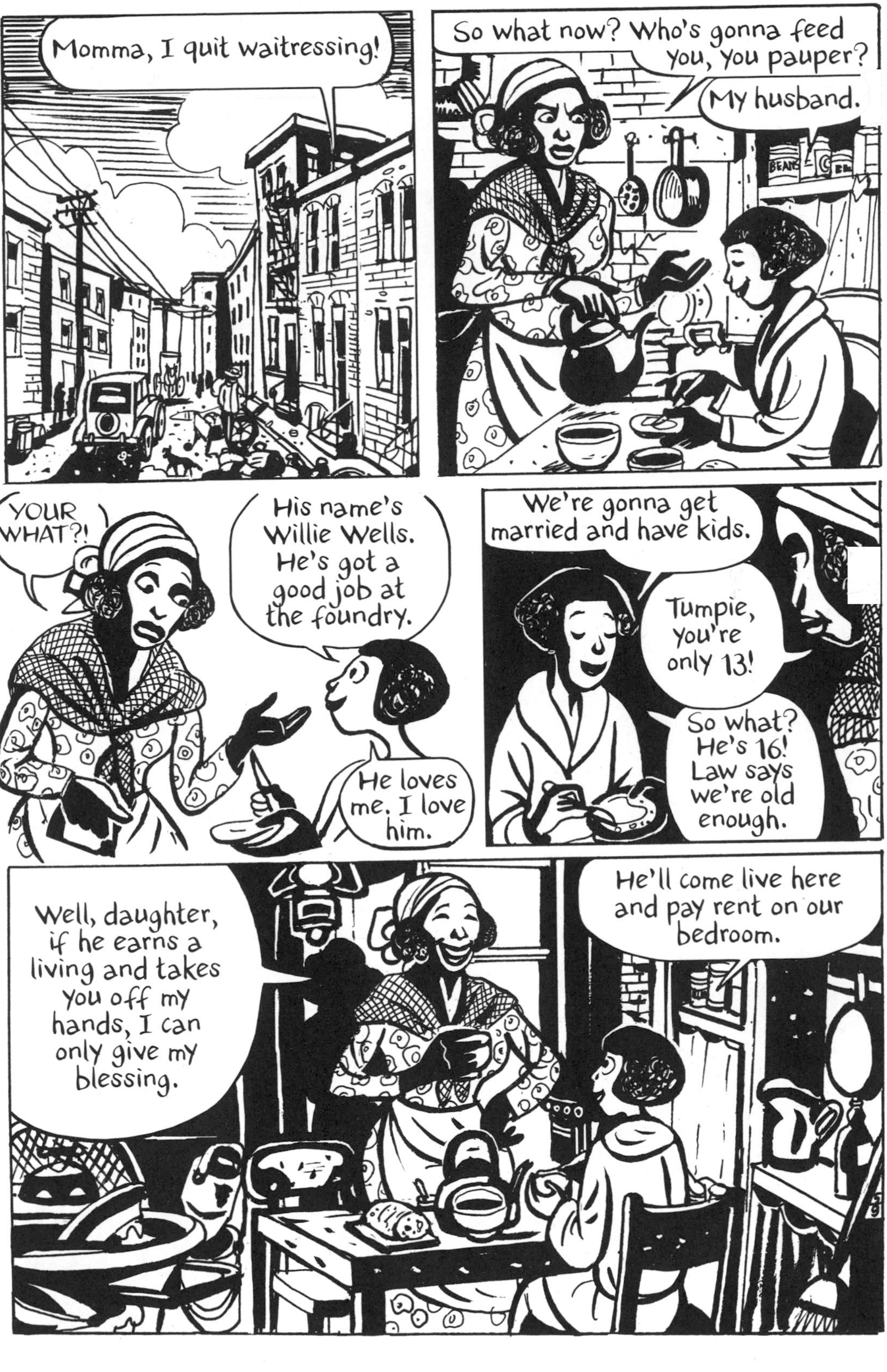
Momma, I quit waitressing!
So what now? Who's gonna feed you, you pauper?
My husband.
YOUR WHAT?!
His name's Willie Wells. He's got a good job at the foundry.
He loves me. I love him.
We're gonna get married and have kids.
Tumpie, you're only 13!
So what? He's 16! Law says we're old enough.
Well, daughter, if he earns a living and takes you off my hands, I can only give my blessing.
He'll come live here and pay rent on our bedroom.

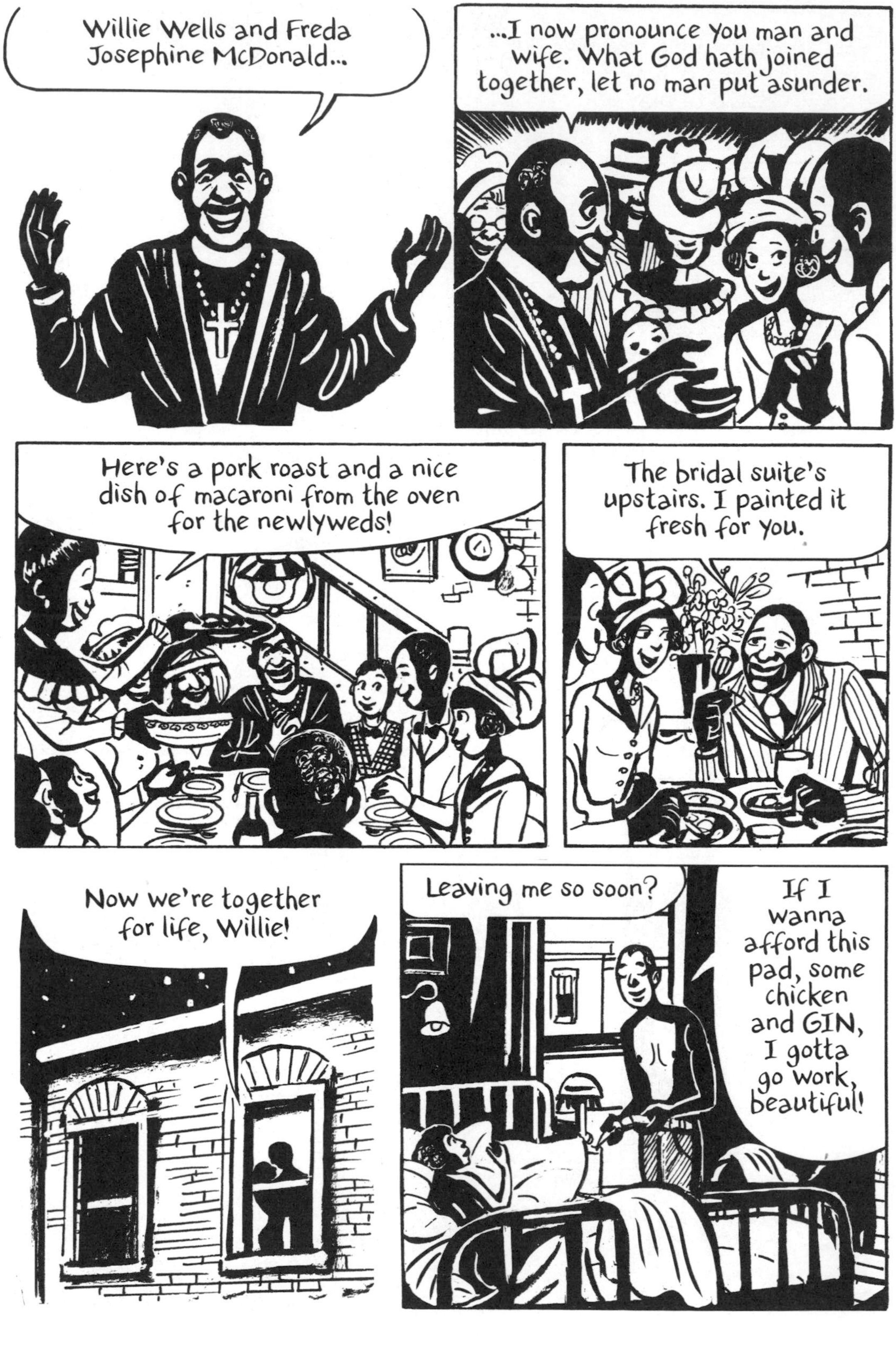
Willie Wells and Freda Josephine McDonald...
...I now pronounce you man and wife. What God hath joined together, let no man put asunder.
Here's a pork roast and a nice dish of macaroni from the oven for the newlyweds!
The bridal suite's upstairs. I painted it fresh for you.
Now we're together for life, Willie!
Leaving me so soon?
If I wanna afford this pad, some chicken and GIN, I gotta go work, beautiful!

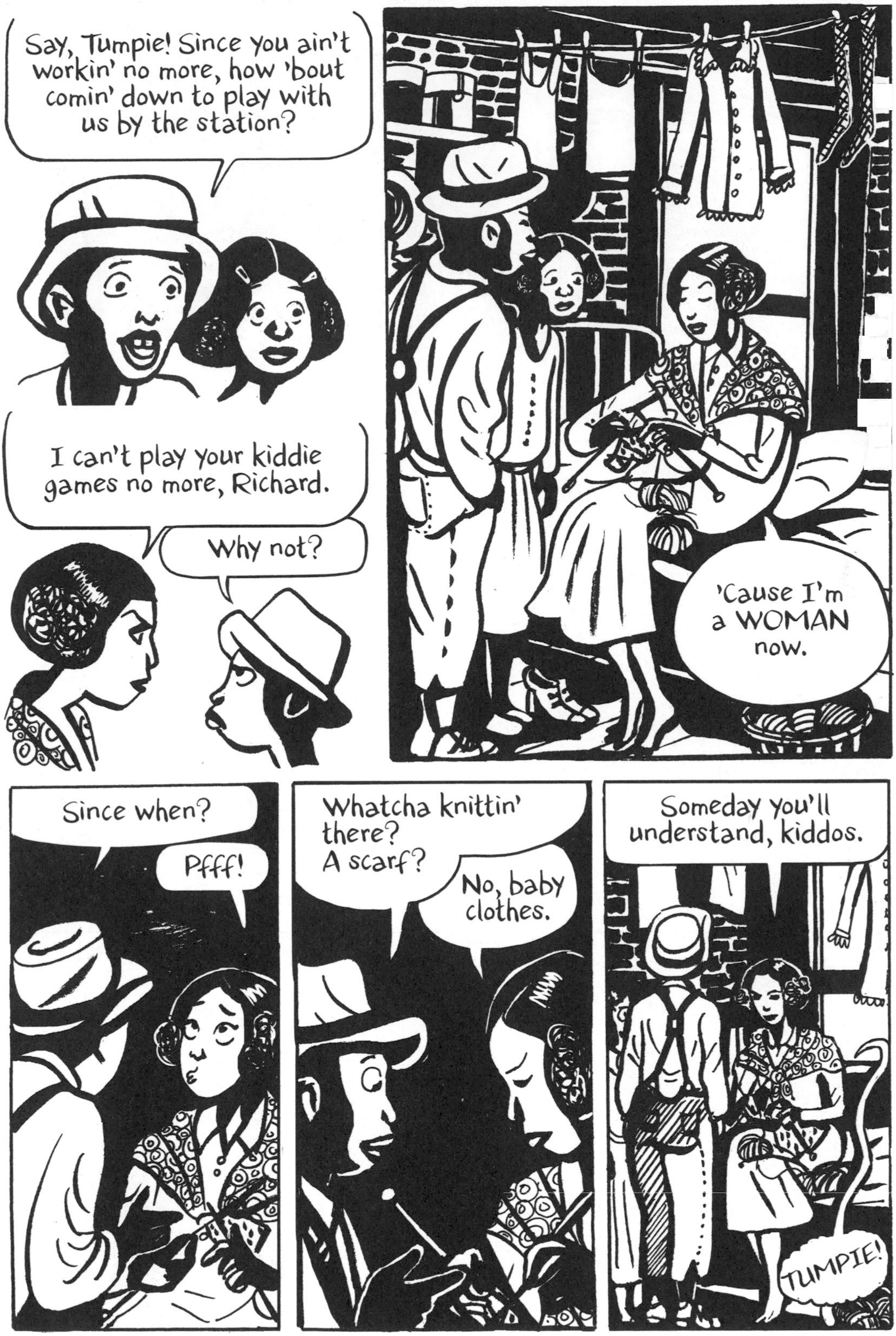

Say, Tumpie! Since you ain't workin' no more, how 'bout comin' down to play with us by the station?
I can't play your kiddie games no more, Richard.
Why not?
'Cause I'm a WOMAN now.
Since when?
Pfff!
Whatcha knittin' there? A scarf?
No, baby clothes.
Someday you'll understand, kiddos.
TUMPIE!

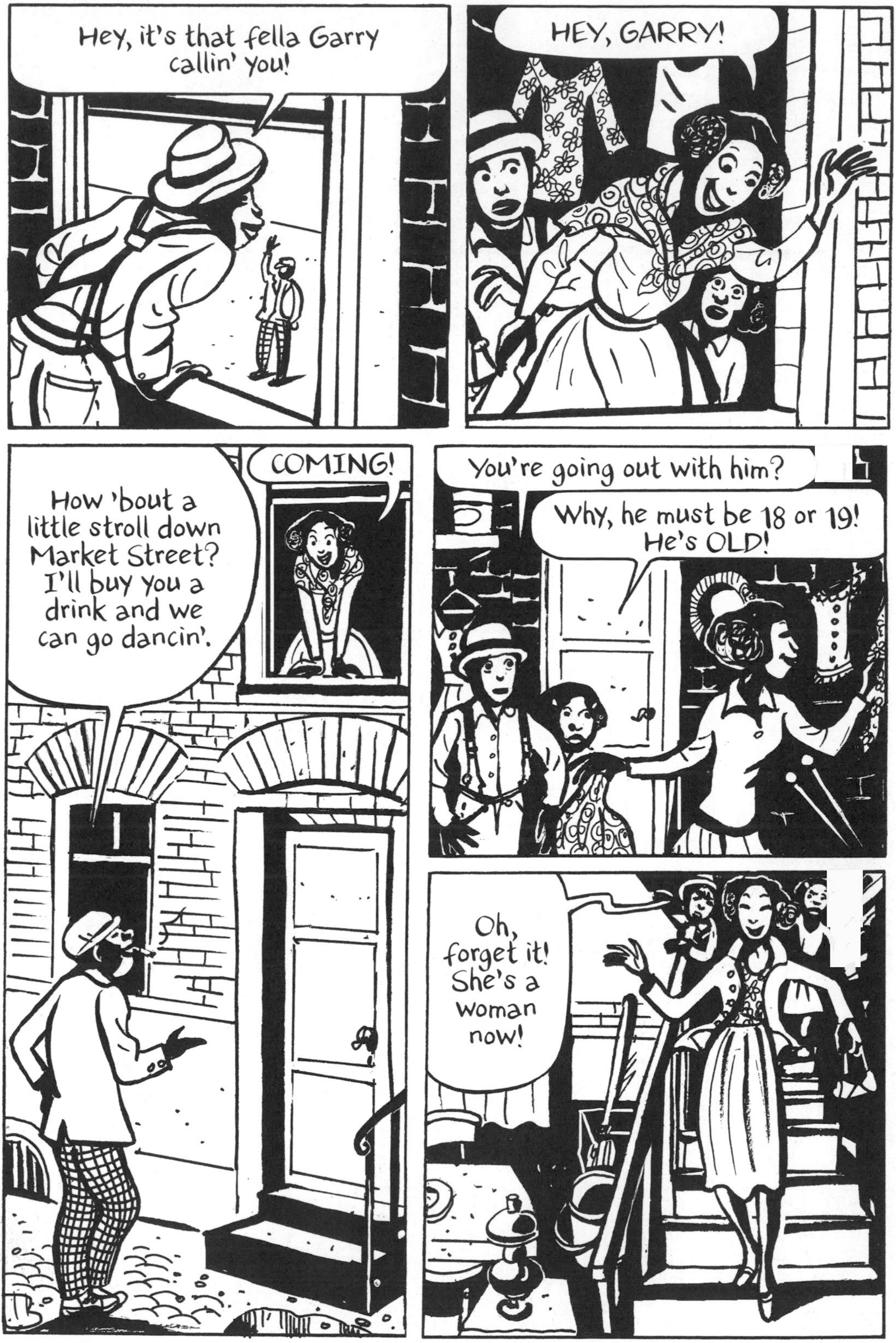

Hey, it's that fella Garry callin' you!
HEY, GARRY!
How 'bout a little stroll down Market Street? I'll buy you a drink and we can go dancin'.
COMING!
You're going out with him?
Why, he must be 18 or 19! He's OLD!
Oh, forget it! She's a woman now!

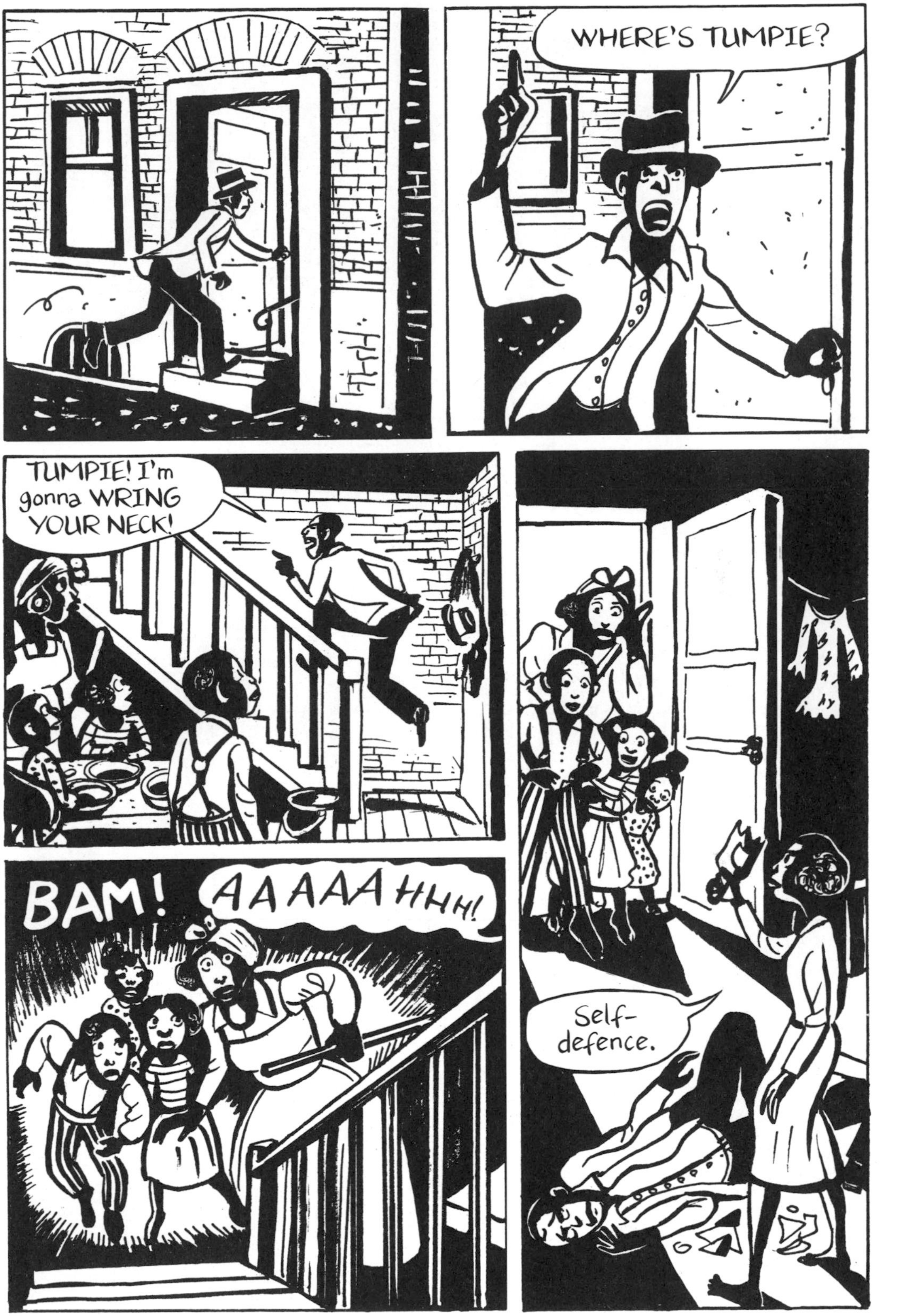
WHERE'S TUMPIE?
TUMPIE! I'm gonna WRING YOUR NECK!
BAM!
AAAAAHHH!
Self-defence.

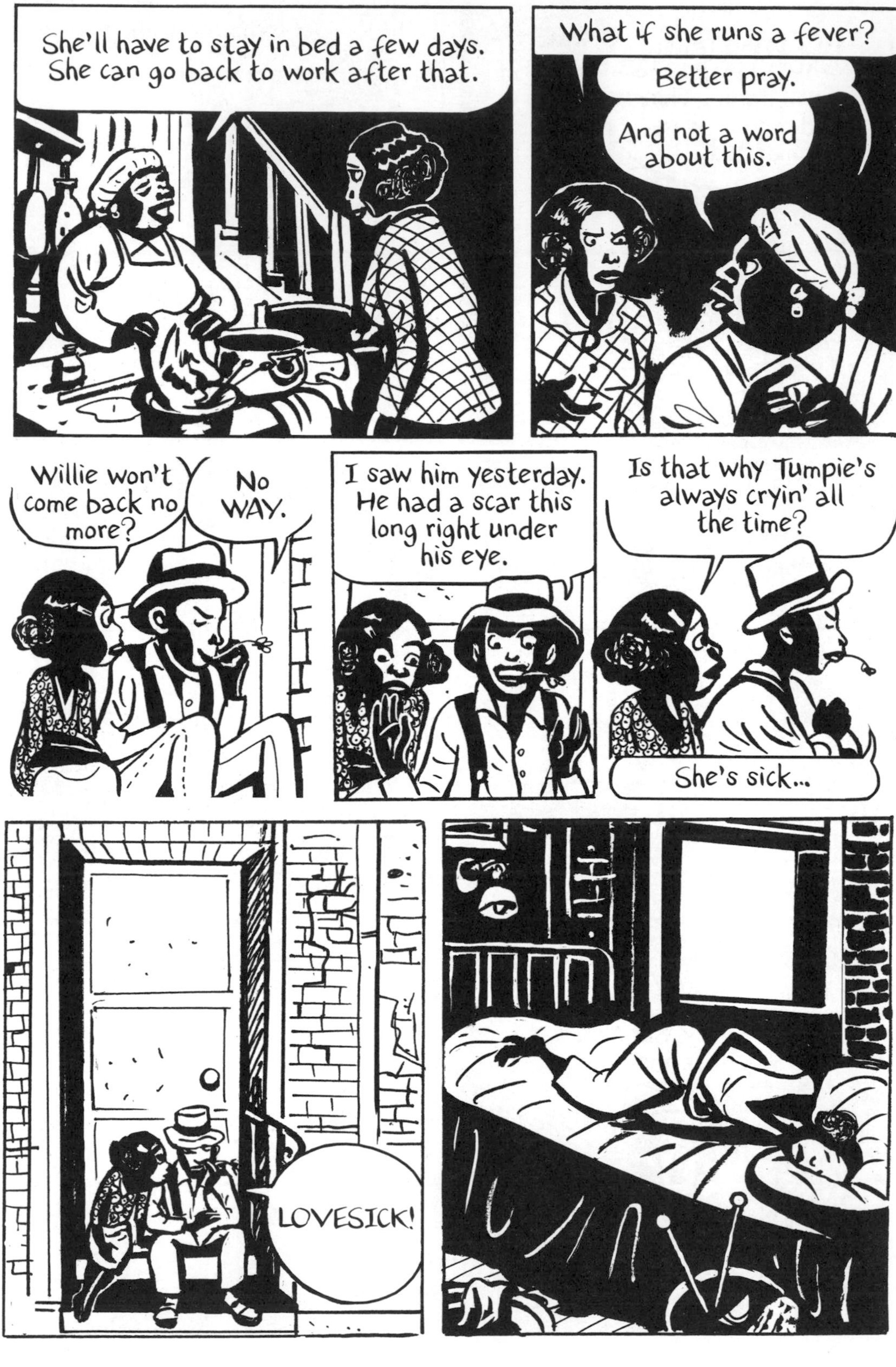
She'll have to stay in bed a few days. She can go back to work after that.
What if she runs a fever?
Better pray.
And not a word about this.
Willie won't come back no more?
No WAY.
I saw him yesterday. He had a scar this long right under his eye.
Is that why Tumpie's always cryin' all the time?
She's sick...
LOVESICK!

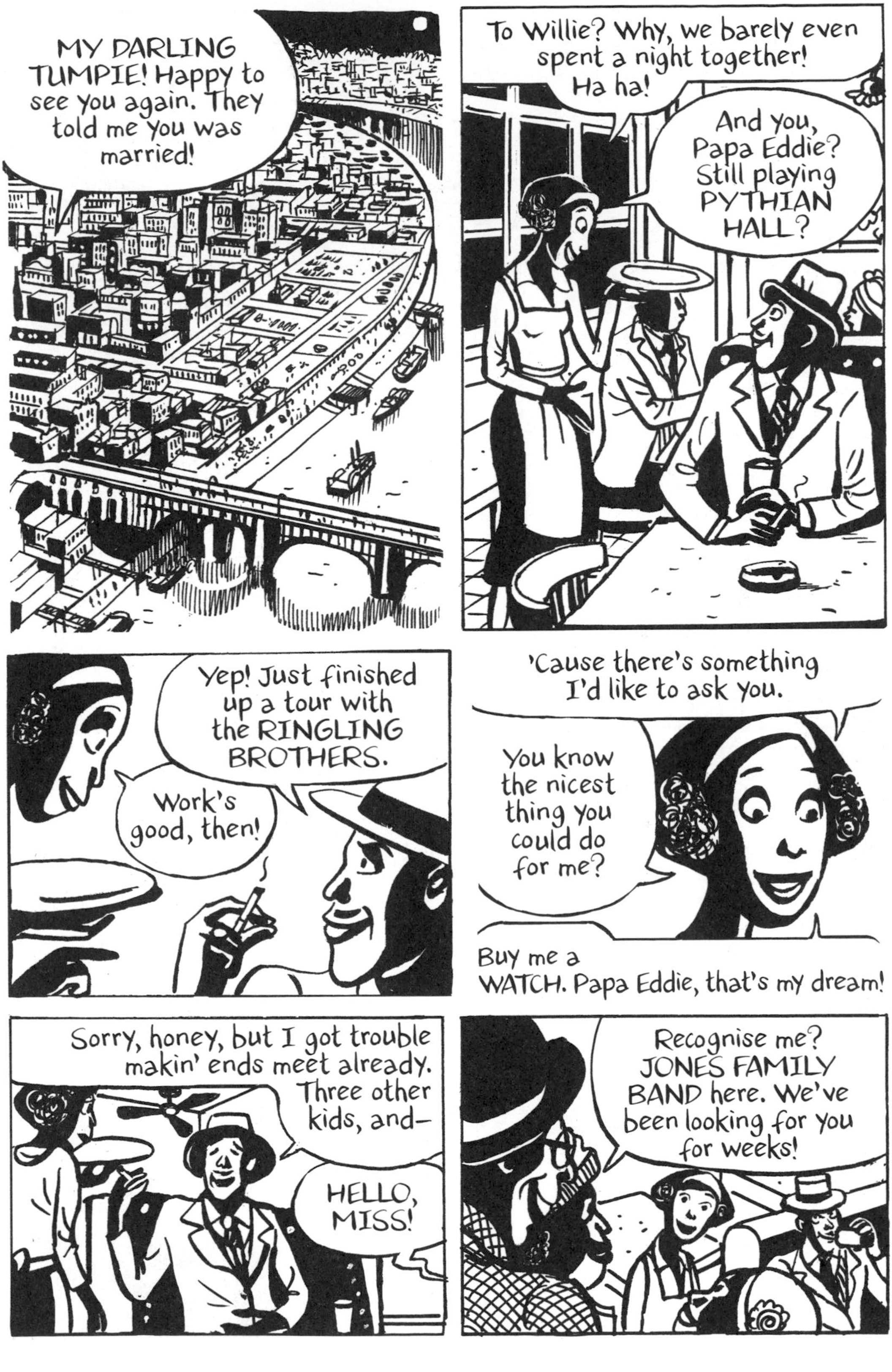
MY DARLING TUMPIE! Happy to see you again. They told me you was married!
To Willie? Why, we barely even spent a night together! Ha ha!
And you, Papa Eddie? Still playing PYTHIAN HALL?
Yep! Just finished up a tour with the RINGLING BROTHERS.
Work's good, then!
'Cause there's something I'd like to ask you.
You know the nicest thing you could do for me?
Buy me a WATCH. Papa Eddie, that's my dream!
Sorry, honey, but I got trouble makin' ends meet already. Three other kids, and–
HELLO, MISS!
Recognise me? JONES FAMILY BAND here. We've been looking for you for weeks!

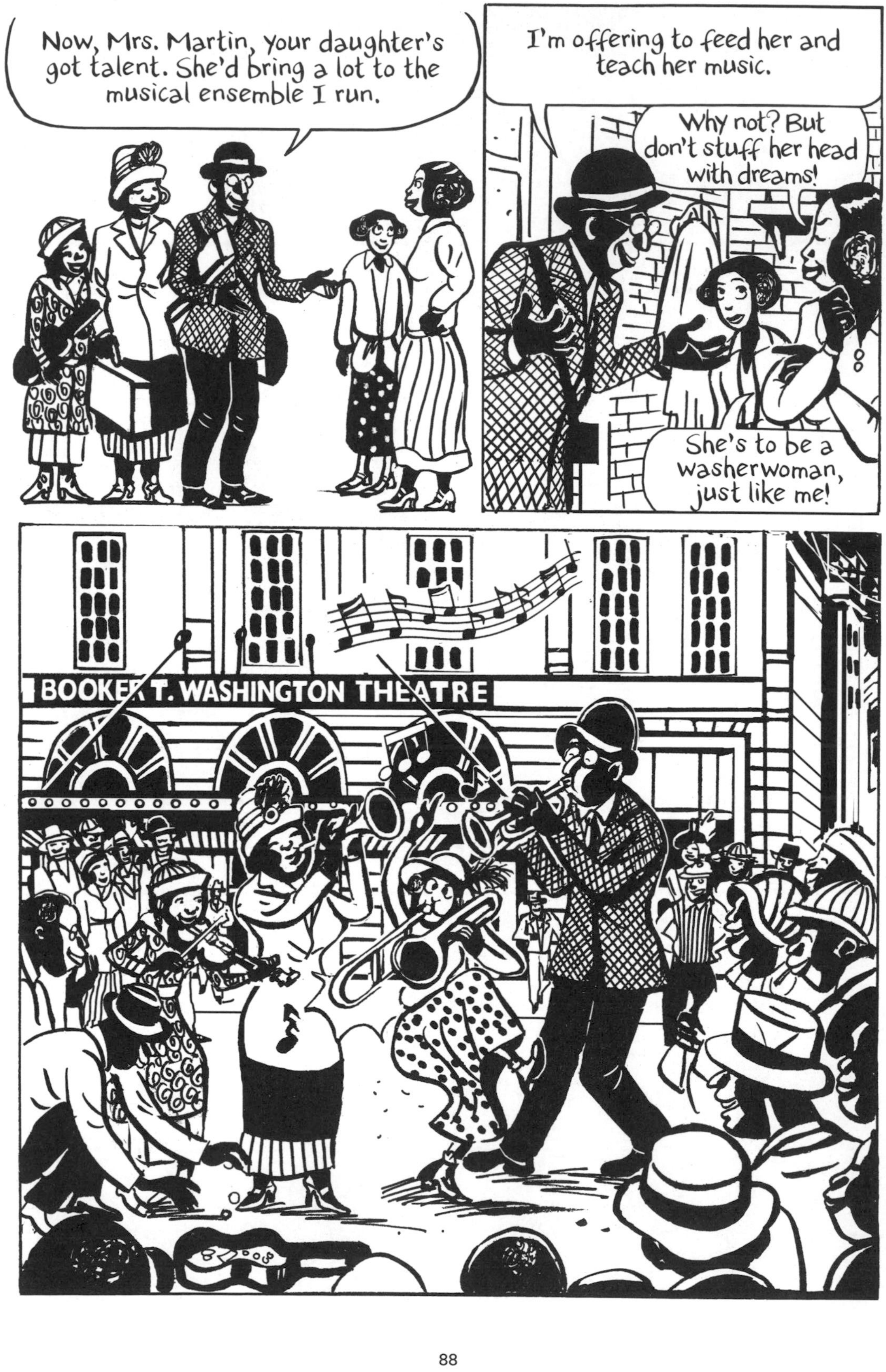
Now, Mrs. Martin, your daughter's got talent. She'd bring a lot to the musical ensemble I run.
I'm offering to feed her and teach her music.
Why not? But don't stuff her head with dreams!
She's to be a washerwoman, just like me!
BOOKER T. WASHINGTON THEATRE

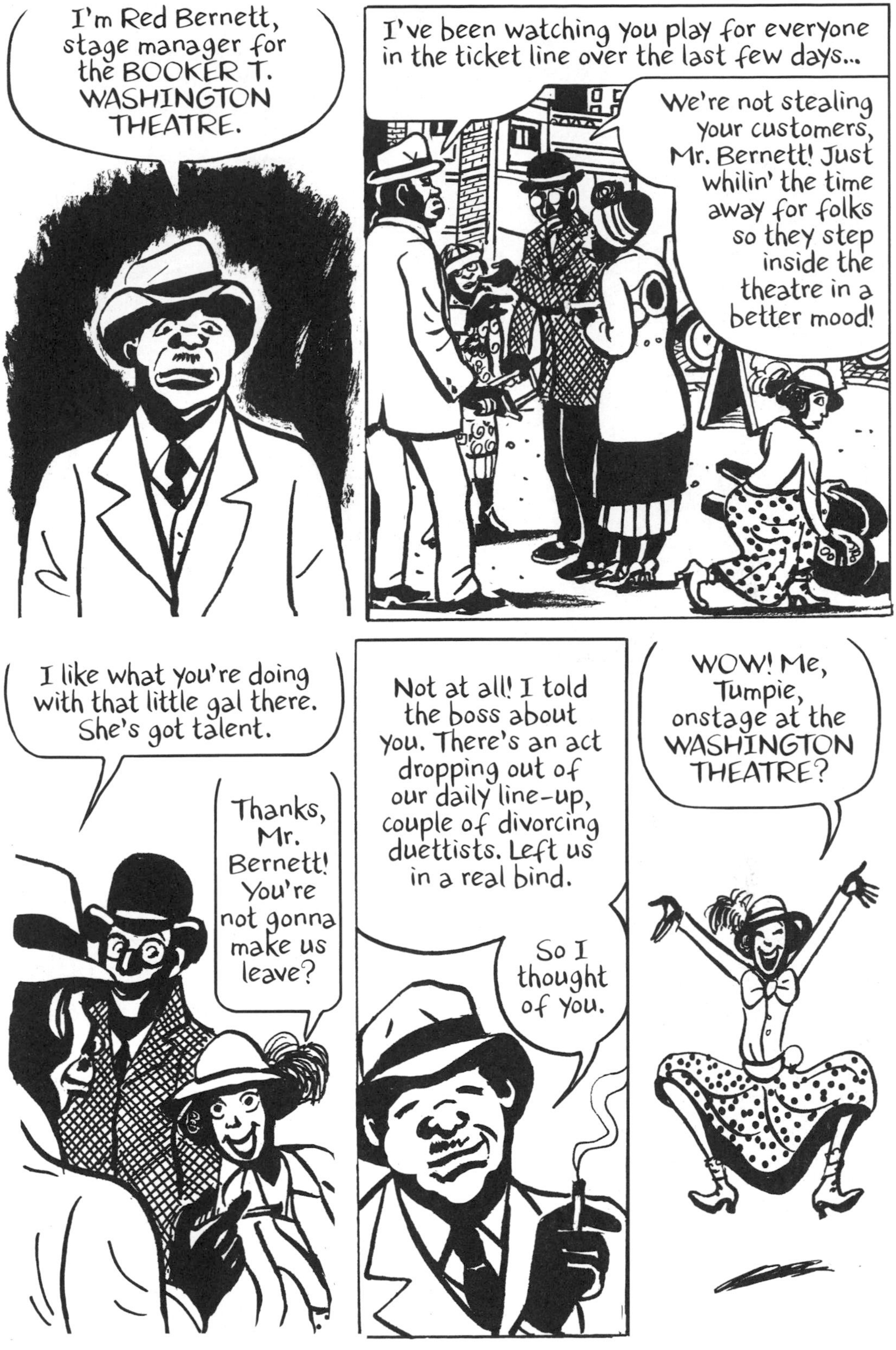
I'm Red Bernett, stage manager for the BOOKER T. WASHINGTON THEATRE.
I've been watching you play for everyone in the ticket line over the last few days...
We're not stealing your customers, Mr. Bernett! Just whilin' the time away for folks so they step inside the theatre in a better mood!
I like what you're doing with that little gal there. She's got talent.
Thanks, Mr. Bernett! You're not gonna make us leave?
Not at all! I told the boss about you. There's an act dropping out of our daily line-up, couple of divorcing duettists. Left us in a real bind.
So I thought of you.
WOW! Me, Tumpie, onstage at the WASHINGTON THEATRE?

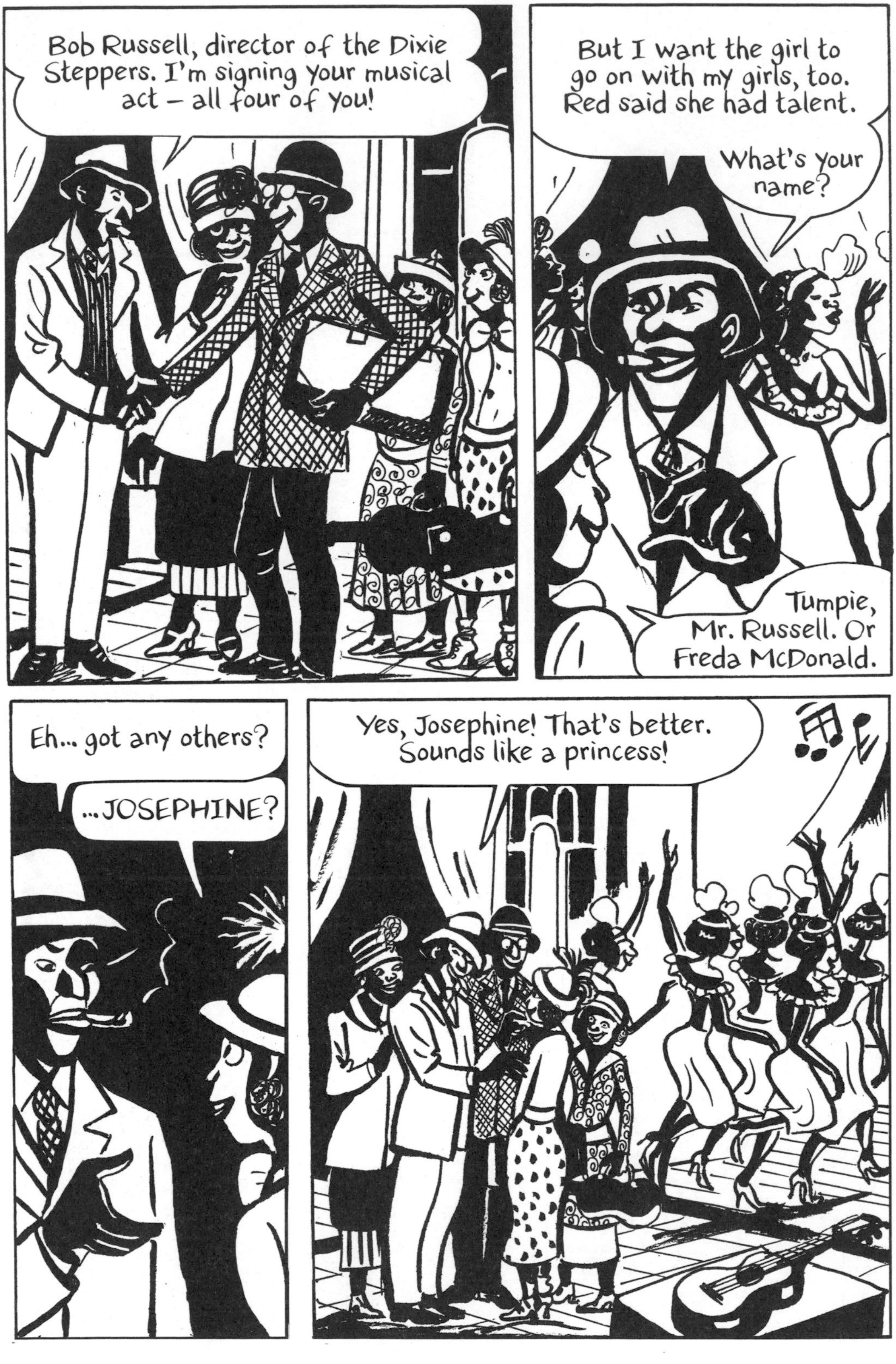
Bob Russell, director of the Dixie Steppers. I'm signing your musical act – all four of you!
But I want the girl to go on with my girls, too. Red said she had talent.
What's your name?
Tumpie, Mr. Russell. Or Freda McDonald.
Eh... got any others?
...JOSEPHINE?
Yes, Josephine! That's better. Sounds like a princess!

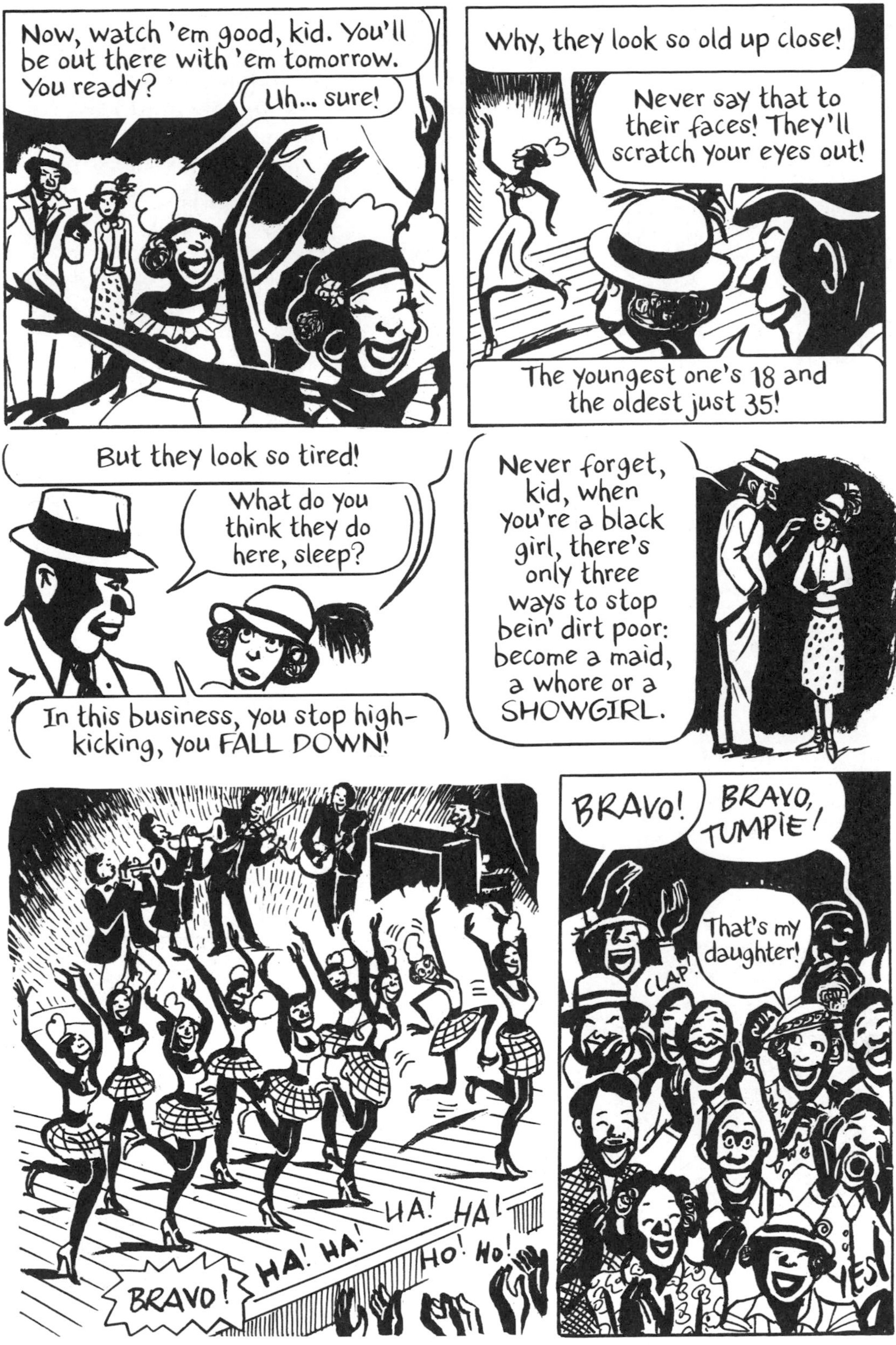
Now, watch 'em good, kid. You'll be out there with 'em tomorrow. You ready?
Uh... sure!
Why, they look so old up close!
Never say that to their faces! They'll scratch your eyes out!
The youngest one's 18 and the oldest just 35!
But they look so tired!
What do you think they do here, sleep?
In this business, you stop high-kicking, you FALL DOWN!
Never forget, kid, when you're a black girl, there's only three ways to stop bein' dirt poor: become a maid, a whore or a SHOWGIRL.
BRAVO!
HA! HA!
HA! HA!
HO! HO!
BRAVO!
BRAVO, TUMPIE!
That's my daughter!
CLAP!
YES!

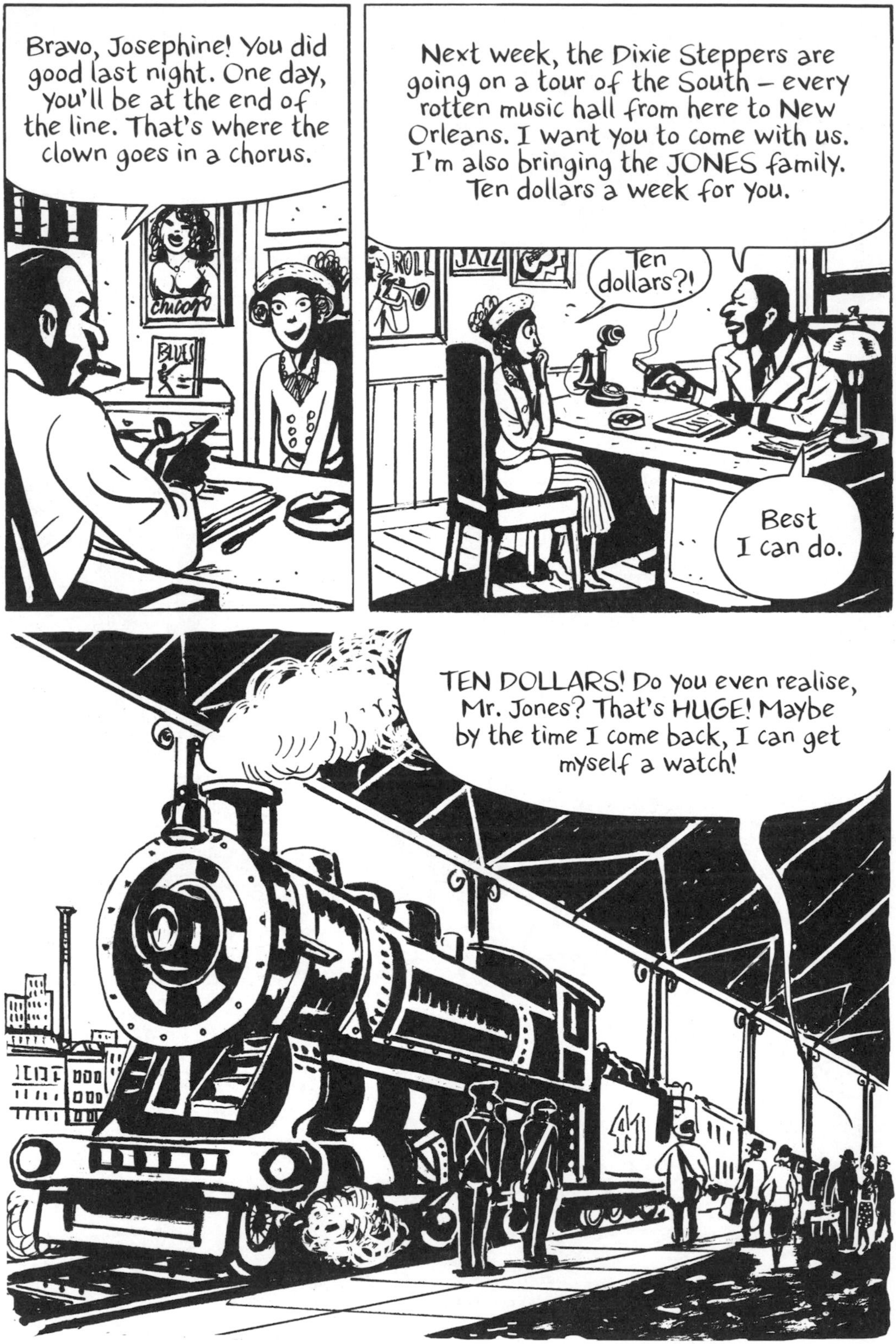
Bravo, Josephine! You did good last night. One day, you'll be at the end of the line. That's where the clown goes in a chorus.
BLUES
Next week, the Dixie Steppers are going on a tour of the South – every rotten music hall from here to New Orleans. I want you to come with us. I'm also bringing the JONES family. Ten dollars a week for you.
ROLL
JAZZ
Ten dollars?!
Best I can do.
TEN DOLLARS! Do you even realise, Mr. Jones? That's HUGE! Maybe by the time I come back, I can get myself a watch!

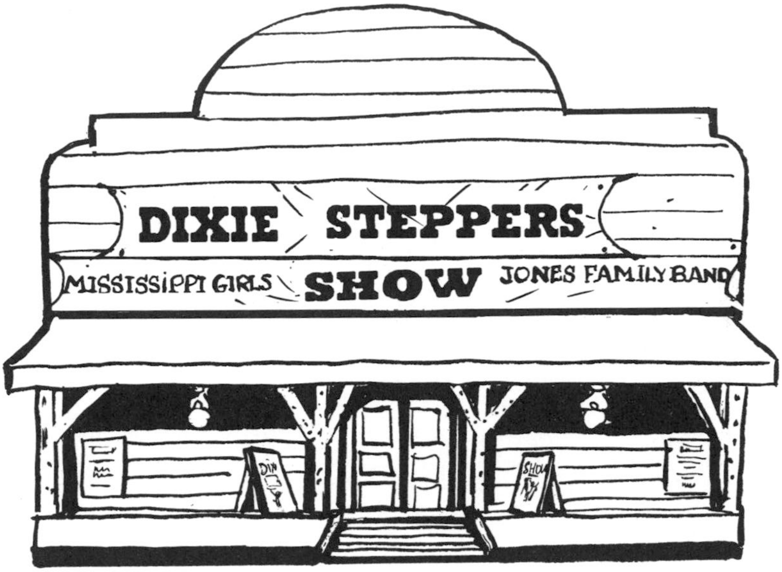
DIXIE STEPPERS
MISSISSIPPI GIRLS
SHOW
JONES FAMILY BAND

1920: Rayne, Louisiana, USA

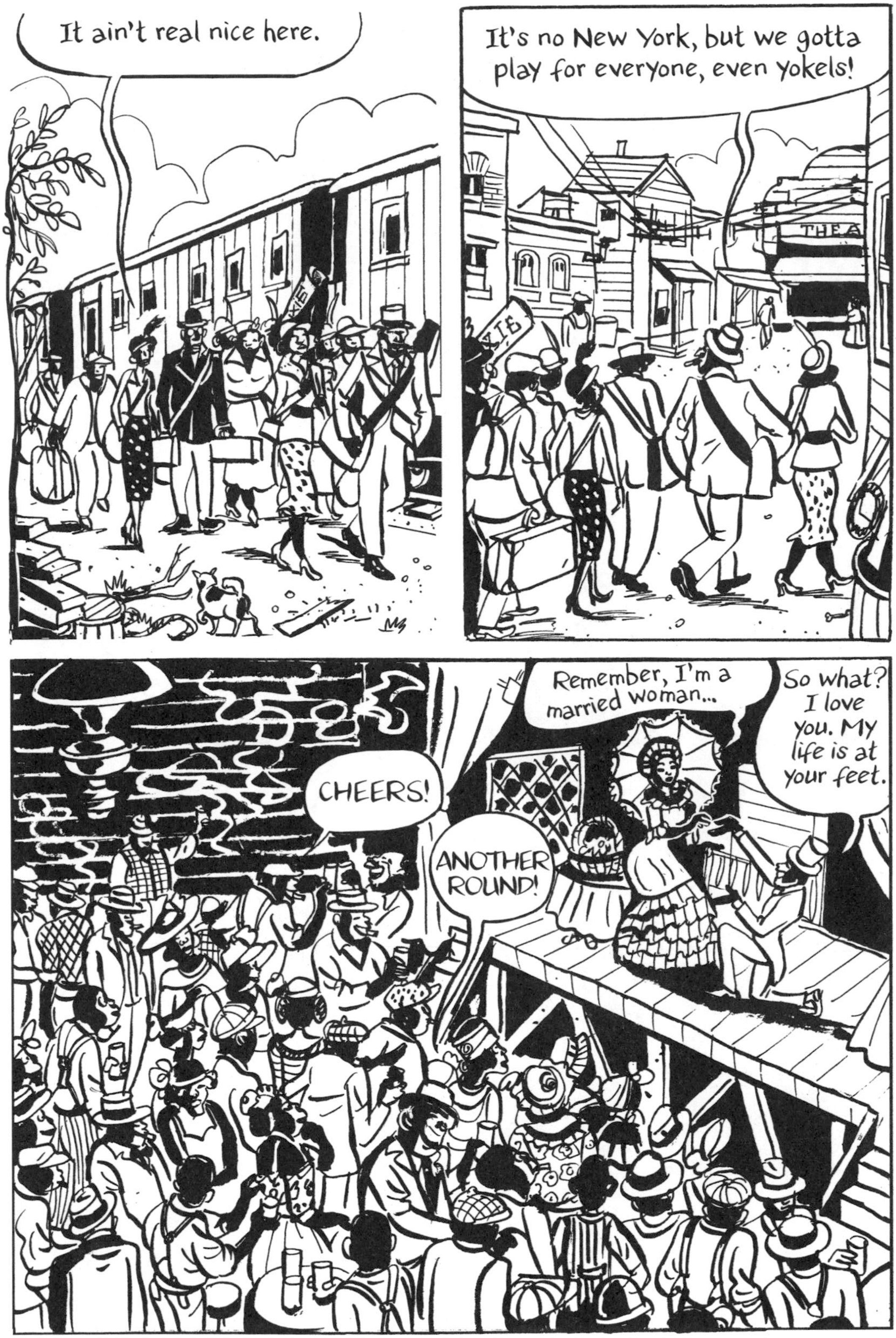
It ain't real nice here.
It's no New York, but we gotta play for everyone, even yokels!
THEA
CHEERS!
ANOTHER ROUND!
Remember, I'm a married woman...
So what? I love you. My life is at your feet.

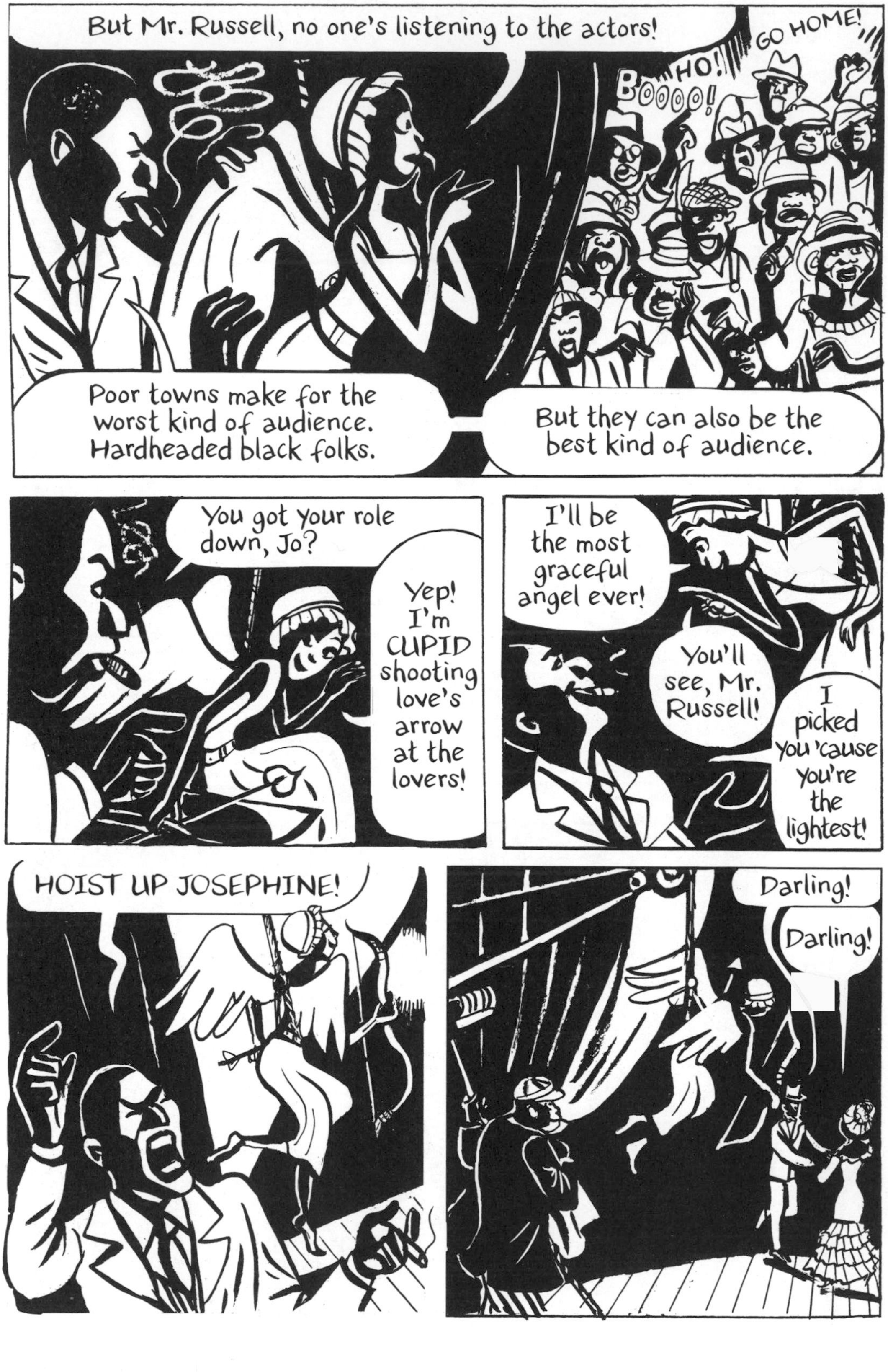
But Mr. Russell, no one's listening to the actors!
GO HOME!
HO!
BOOOOO!
Poor towns make for the worst kind of audience. Hardheaded black folks.
But they can also be the best kind of audience.
You got your role down, Jo?
Yep! I'm CUPID shooting love's arrow at the lovers!
I'll be the most graceful angel ever!
You'll see, Mr. Russell!
I picked you 'cause you're the lightest!
HOIST UP JOSEPHINE!
Darling!
Darling!

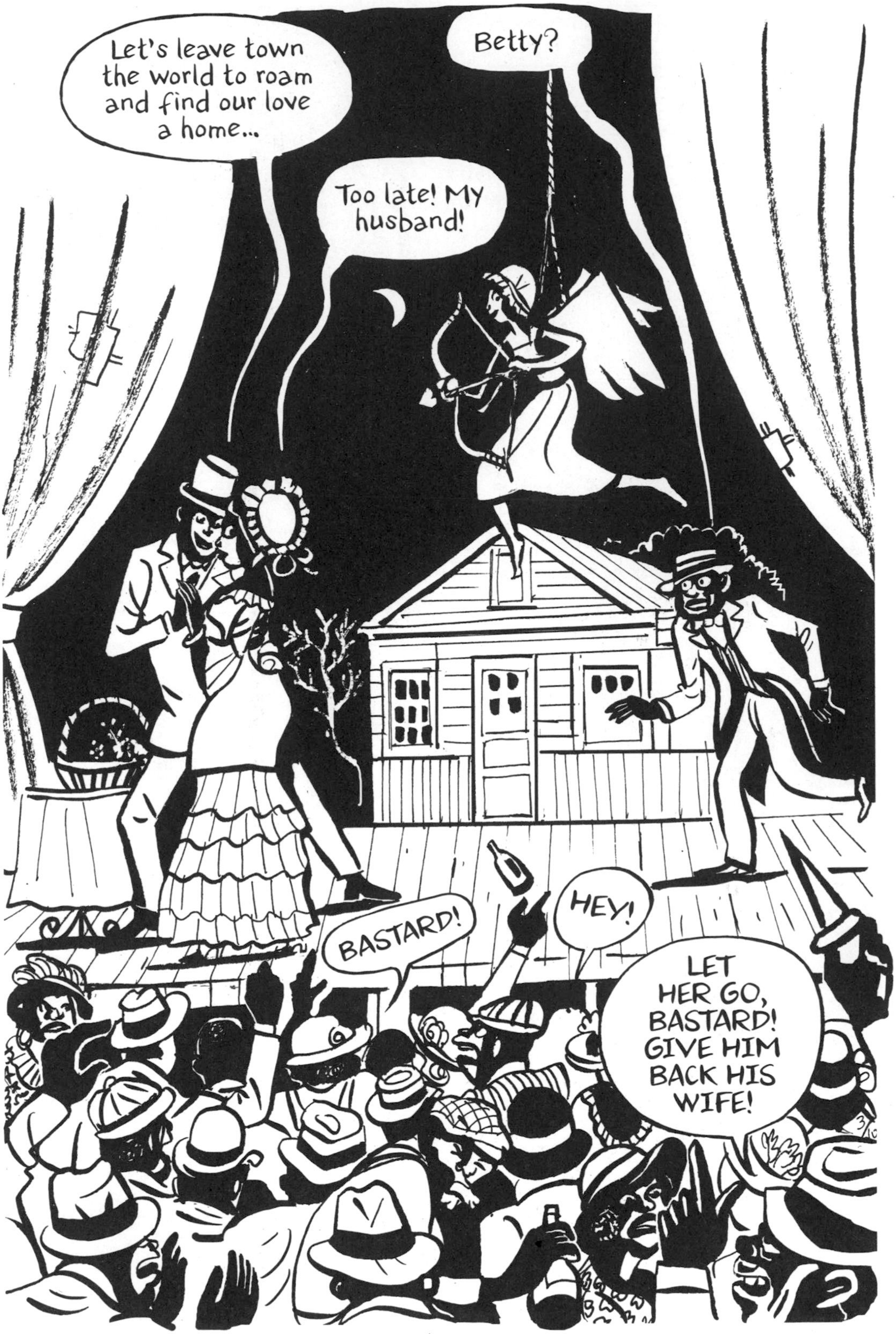
Let's leave town the world to roam and find our love a home...
Betty?
Too late! My husband!
BASTARD!
HEY!
LET HER GO, BASTARD! GIVE HIM BACK HIS WIFE!

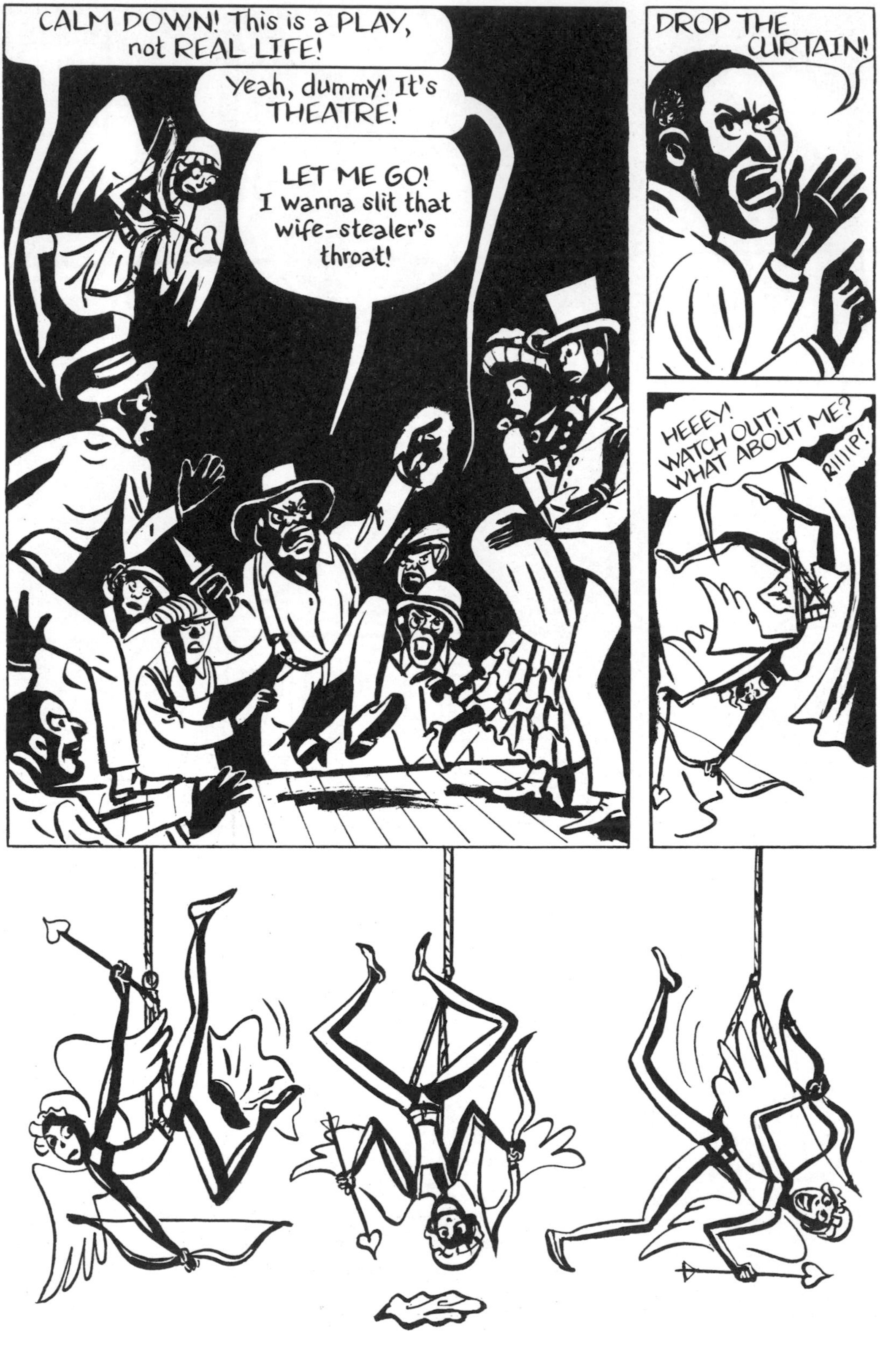
CALM DOWN! This is a PLAY, not REAL LIFE!
Yeah, dummy! It's THEATRE!
LET ME GO! I wanna slit that wife-stealer's throat!
DROP THE CURTAIN!
HEEEY! WATCH OUT! WHAT ABOUT ME?
RIIIIP!

HA! HA!
HO! HO!
HA! HO! HO!
CLAP! CLAP!
BRAVO!
HA! HA!
...THE BEST KIND OF AUDIENCE!

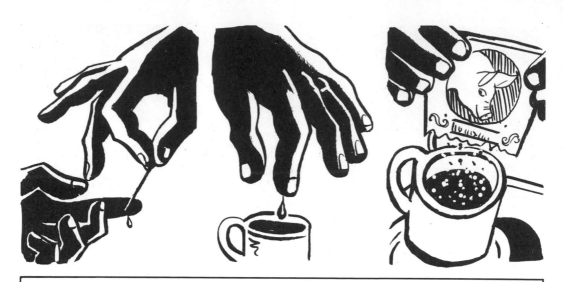

Blood, flea powder from a sow and coffee — a voodoo remedy to give you strength and vigour.

You can have some, too, Josephine.

Thanks, Mr. Jones, but coffee makes me sick!

You're wrong. You need it. In a few days, we'll be in New Orleans.

To us black musicians, New Orleans is our capital, Josephine!

You know, this world is a living hell for black folks. Sometimes I think music is all we've got.

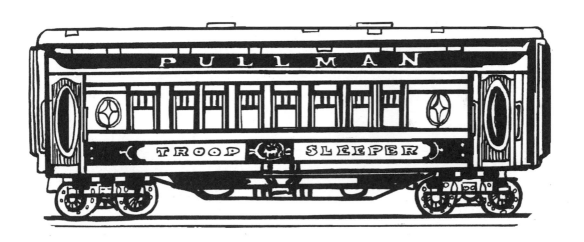

1921: 30th Street Station, Philadelphia, Pennsylvania, USA

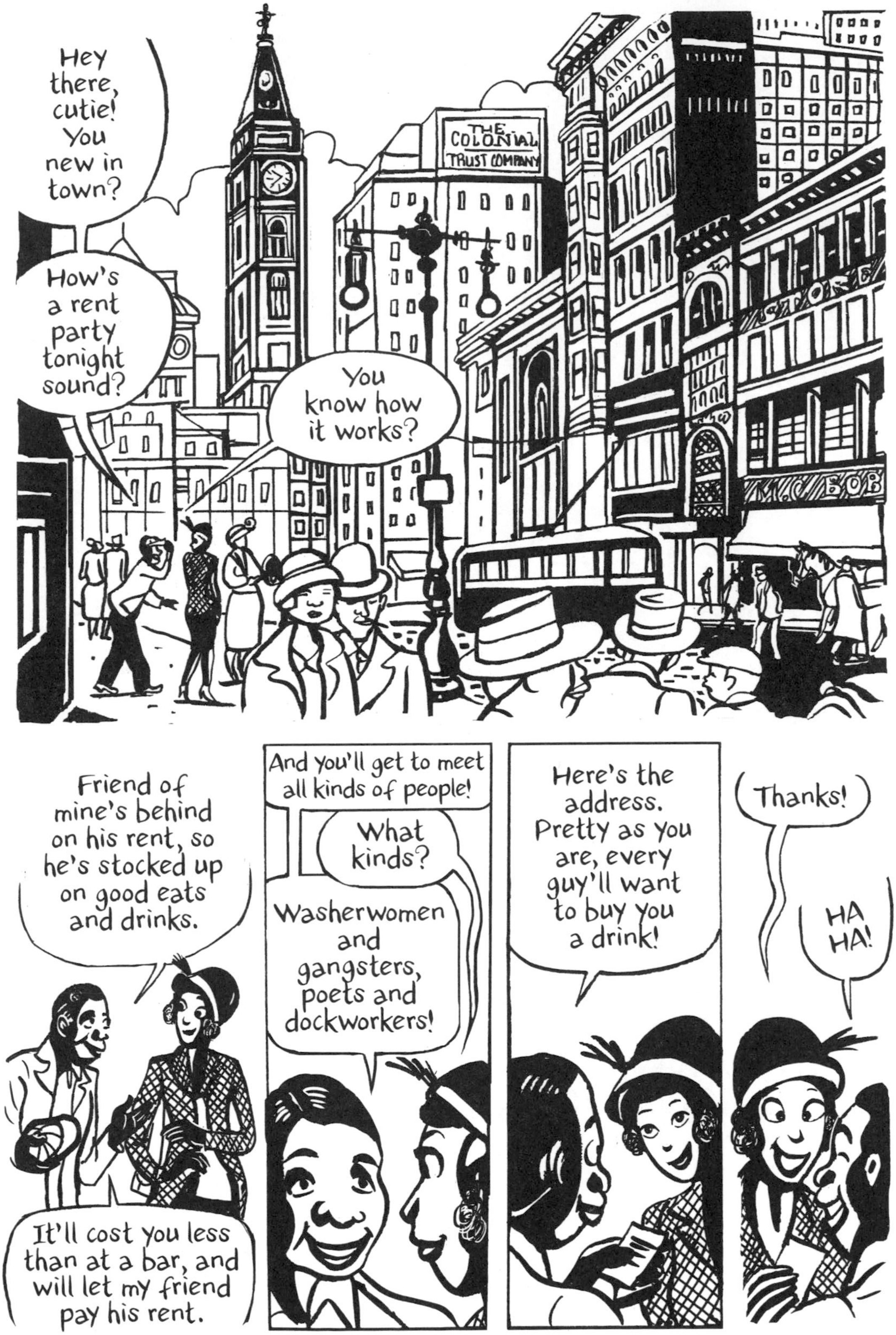
THE COLONIAL TRUST COMPANY
Hey there, cutie! You new in town?
How's a rent party tonight sound?
You know how it works?
Friend of mine's behind on his rent, so he's stocked up on good eats and drinks.
It'll cost you less than at a bar, and will let my friend pay his rent.
And you'll get to meet all kinds of people!
What kinds?
Washerwomen and gangsters, poets and dockworkers!
Here's the address. Pretty as you are, every guy'll want to buy you a drink!
Thanks!
HA HA!

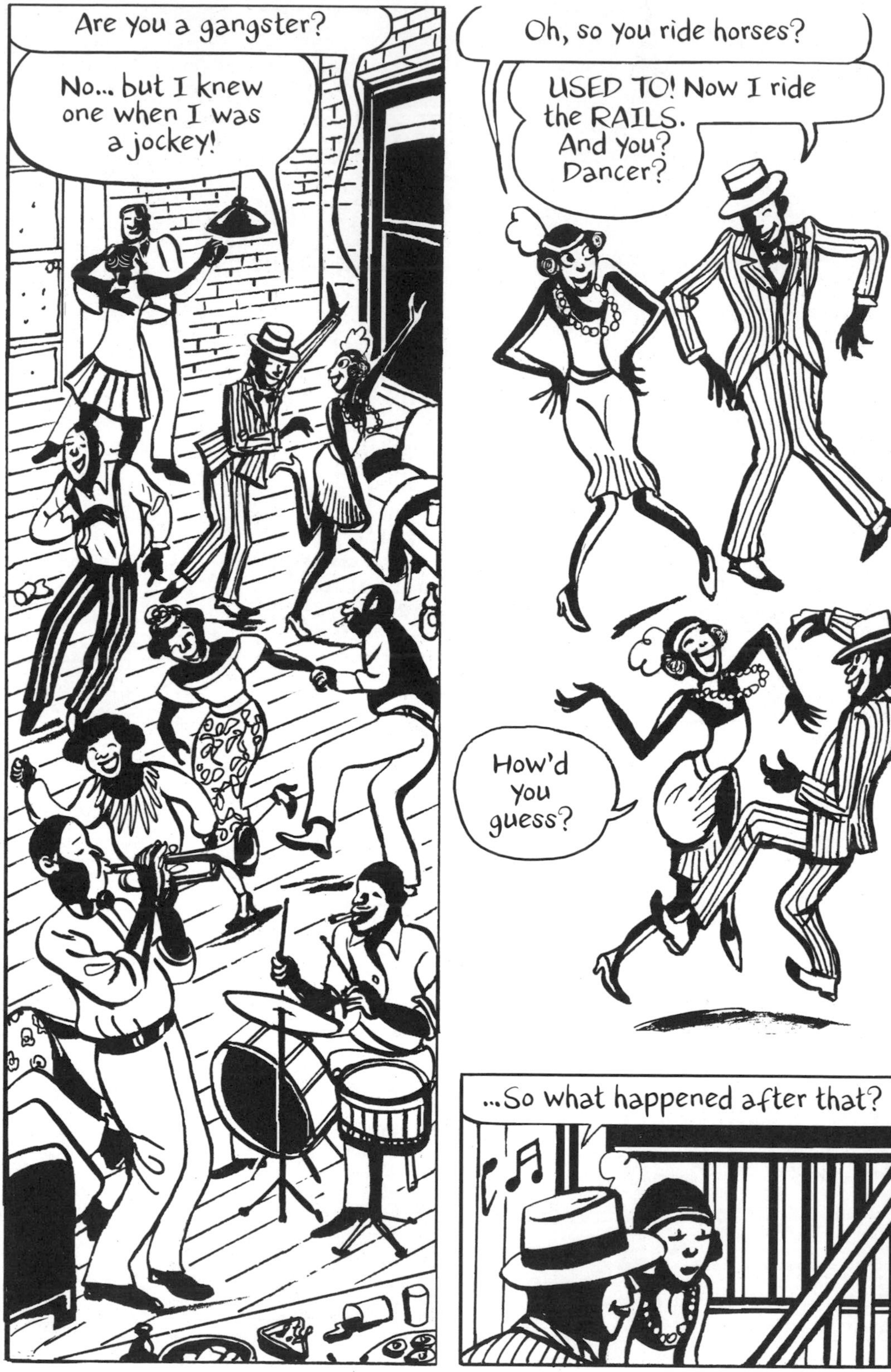
Are you a gangster?
No... but I knew one when I was a jockey!
Oh, so you ride horses?
USED TO! Now I ride the RAILS. And you? Dancer?
How'd you guess?
...So what happened after that?

The Joneses stayed in New Orleans and I left the Dixie Steppers here.

Wasn't no more work for me.

You didn't want to join the chorus girls?

Yeah, but Mr. Russell said I wasn't the right colour. I'd be a big ol' pale spot in the line-up.

So that's why I'm stuck in Philly. I'm looking for auditions. You just passing through, too?

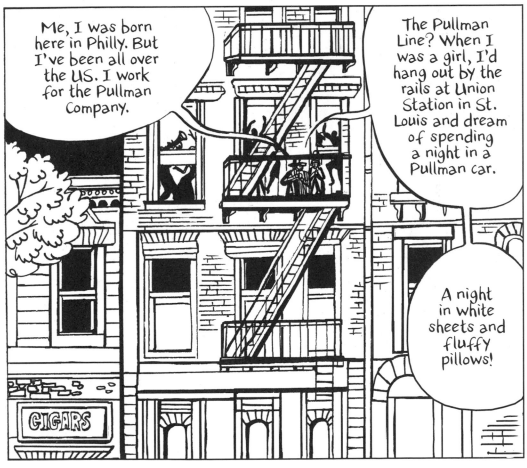

Me, I was born here in Philly. But I've been all over the US. I work for the Pullman Company.

The Pullman Line? When I was a girl, I'd hang out by the rails at Union Station in St. Louis and dream of spending a night in a Pullman car.

A night in white sheets and fluffy pillows!

CIGARS

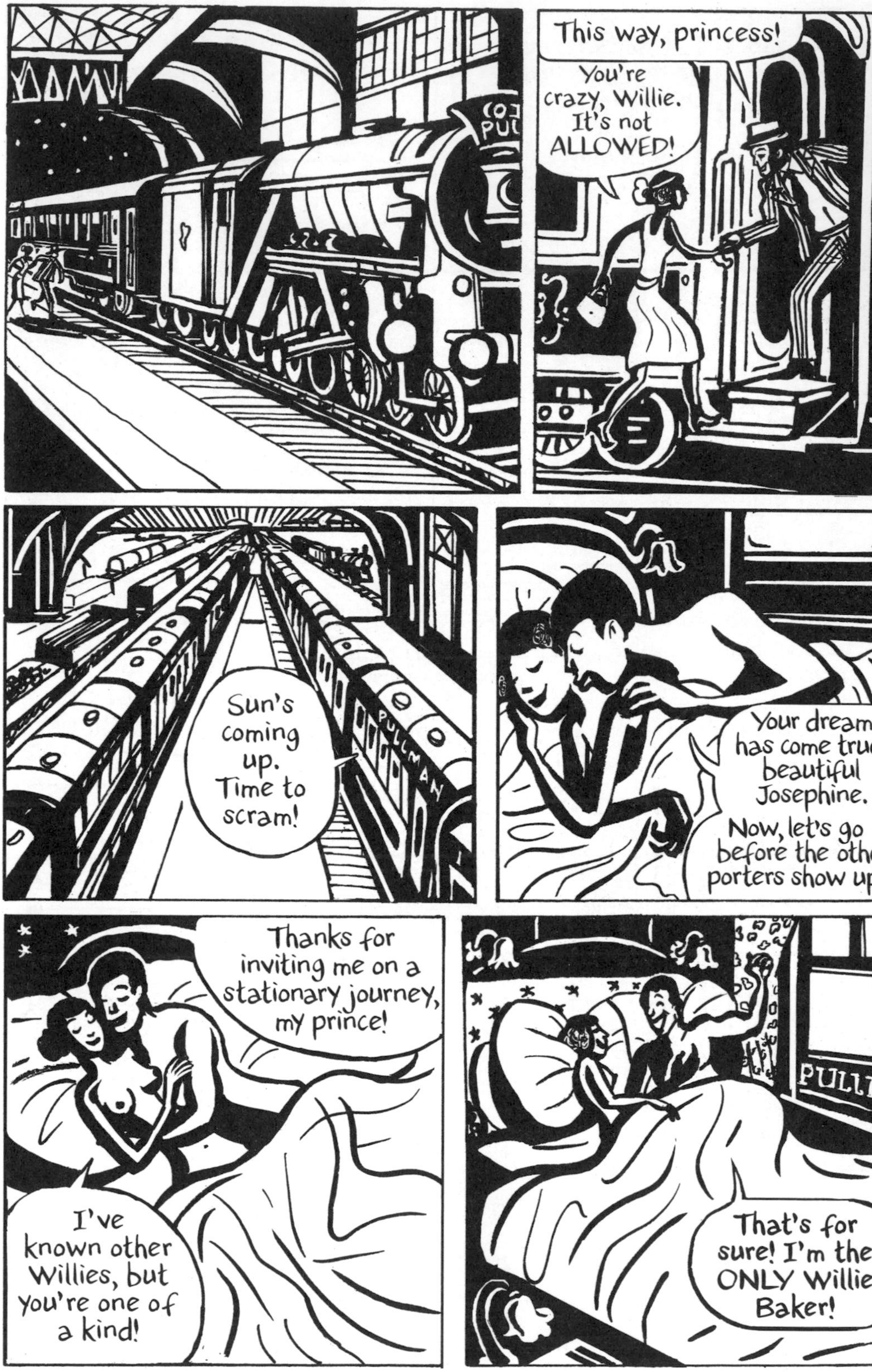
COI
PUL
This way, princess!
You're crazy, Willie. It's not ALLOWED!
PULLMAN
Sun's coming up. Time to scram!
Your dream has come true, beautiful Josephine.
Now, let's go before the other porters show up!
Thanks for inviting me on a stationary journey, my prince!
I've known other Willies, but you're one of a kind!
PULLMA
That's for sure! I'm the ONLY Willie Baker!

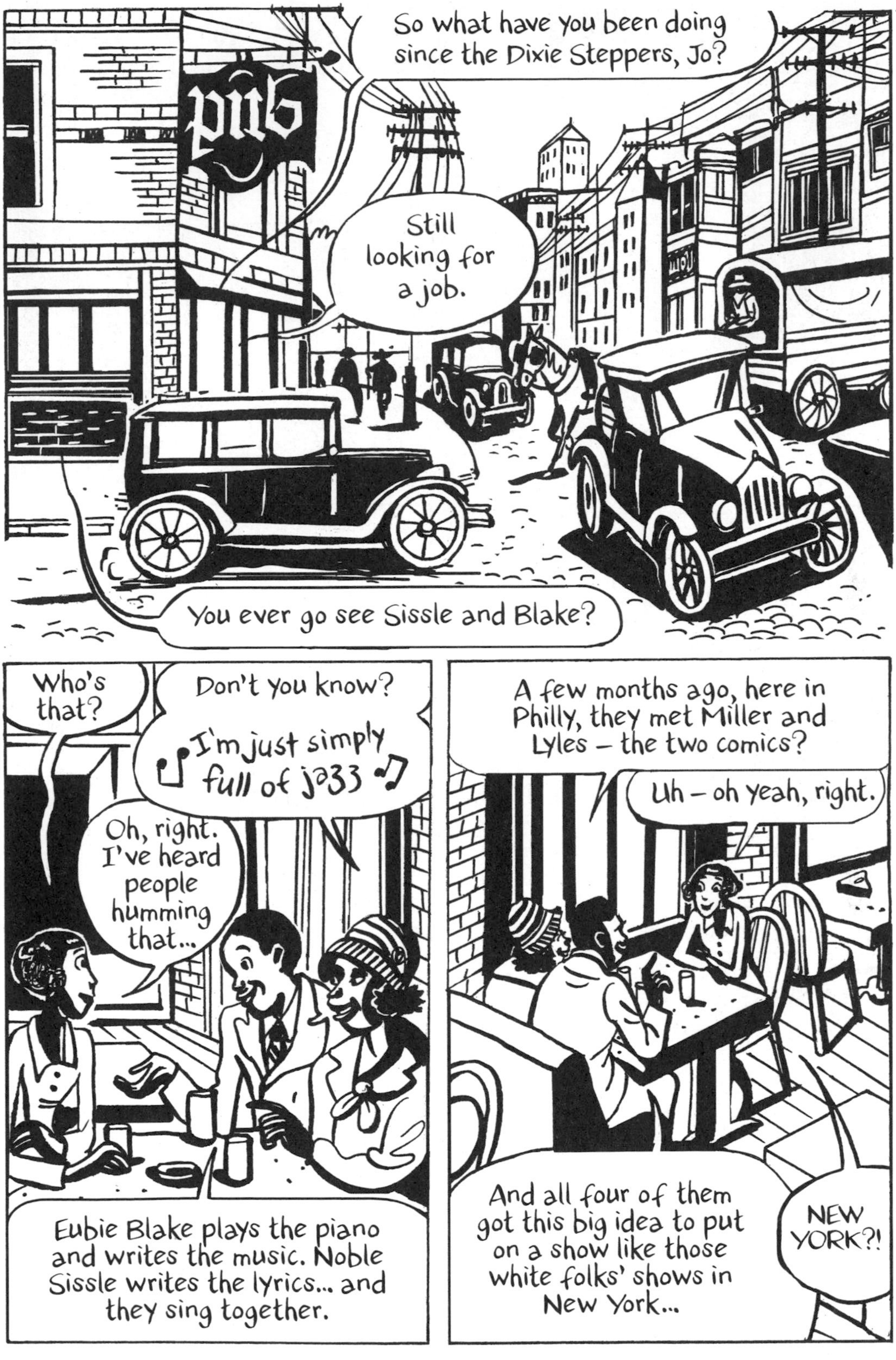

So what have you been doing since the Dixie Steppers, Jo?
Still looking for a job.
pub
You ever go see Sissle and Blake?
Who's that?
Don't you know?
I'm just simply full of jazz
Oh, right. I've heard people humming that...
Eubie Blake plays the piano and writes the music. Noble Sissle writes the lyrics... and they sing together.
A few months ago, here in Philly, they met Miller and Lyles – the two comics?
Uh – oh yeah, right.
And all four of them got this big idea to put on a show like those white folks' shows in New York...
NEW YORK?!

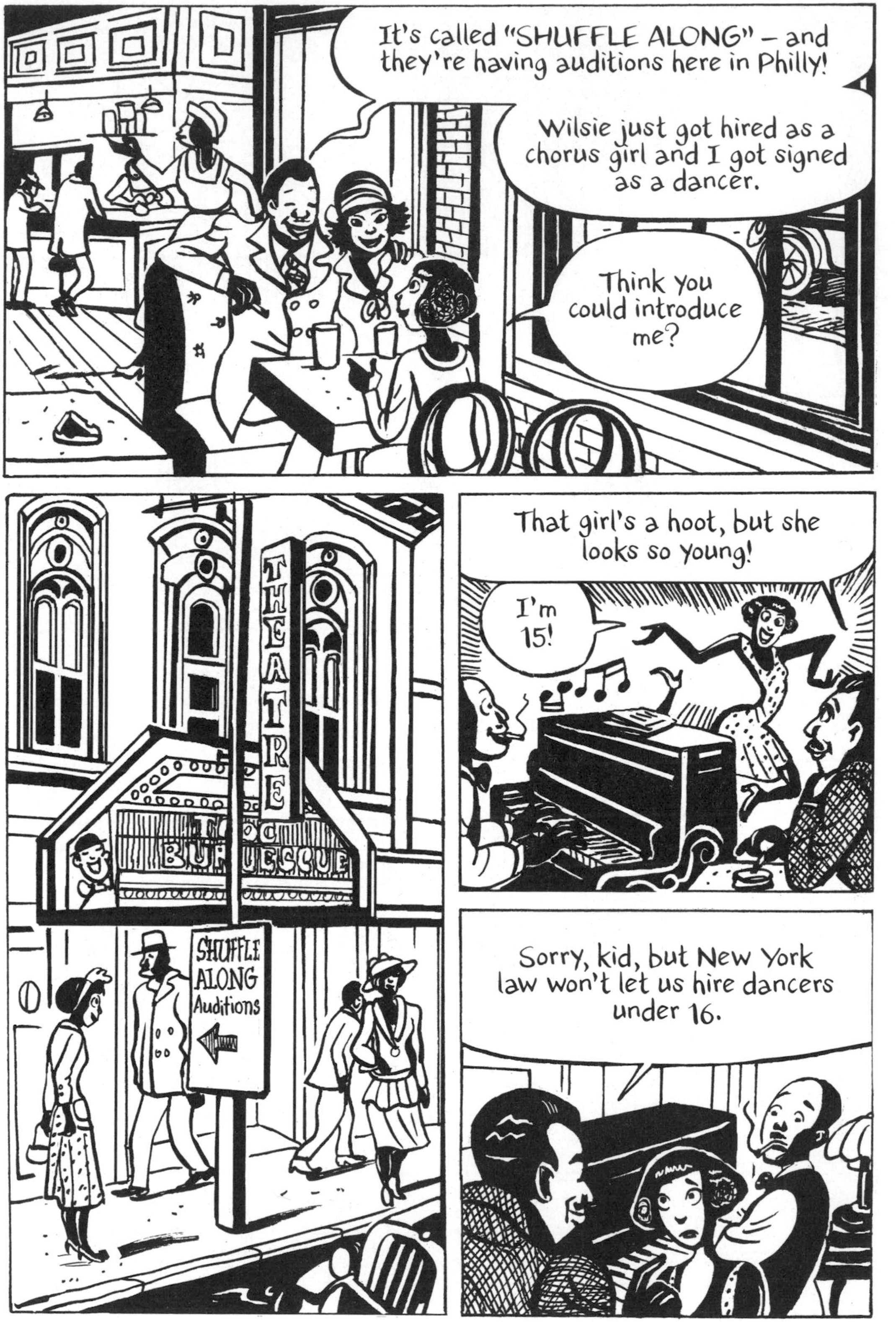
It's called "SHUFFLE ALONG" – and they're having auditions here in Philly!
Wilsie just got hired as a chorus girl and I got signed as a dancer.
Think you could introduce me?
THEATRE
BURLESQUE
SHUFFLE ALONG Auditions
That girl's a hoot, but she looks so young!
I'm 15!
Sorry, kid, but New York law won't let us hire dancers under 16.

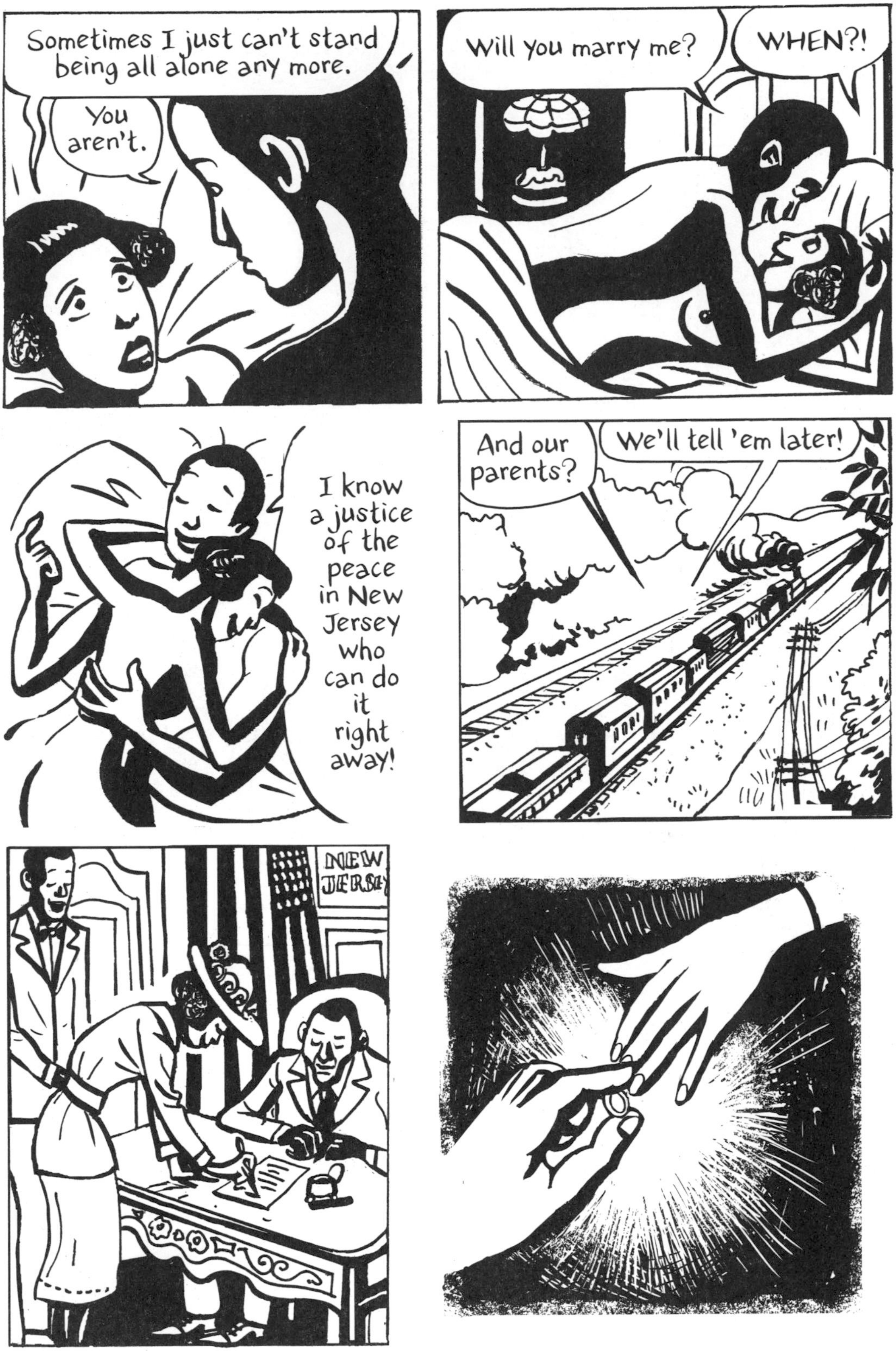

Sometimes I just can't stand being all alone any more.
You aren't.
Will you marry me?
WHEN?!
I know a justice of the peace in New Jersey who can do it right away!
And our parents?
We'll tell 'em later!
NEW JERSEY

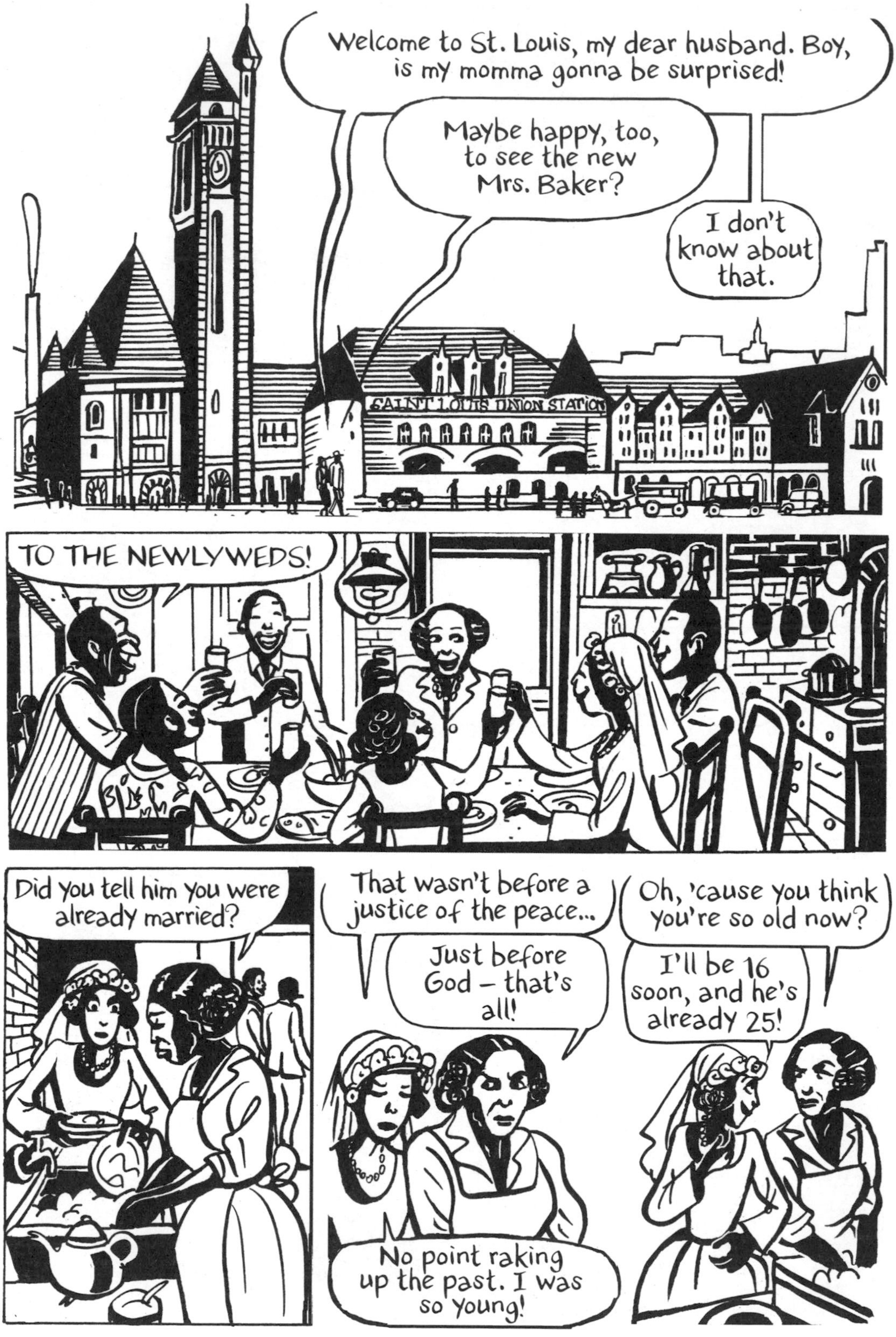
Welcome to St. Louis, my dear husband. Boy, is my momma gonna be surprised!
Maybe happy, too, to see the new Mrs. Baker?
I don't know about that.
SAINT LOUIS UNION STATION
TO THE NEWLYWEDS!
Did you tell him you were already married?
That wasn't before a justice of the peace...
Just before God – that's all!
No point raking up the past. I was so young!
Oh, 'cause you think you're so old now?
I'll be 16 soon, and he's already 25!

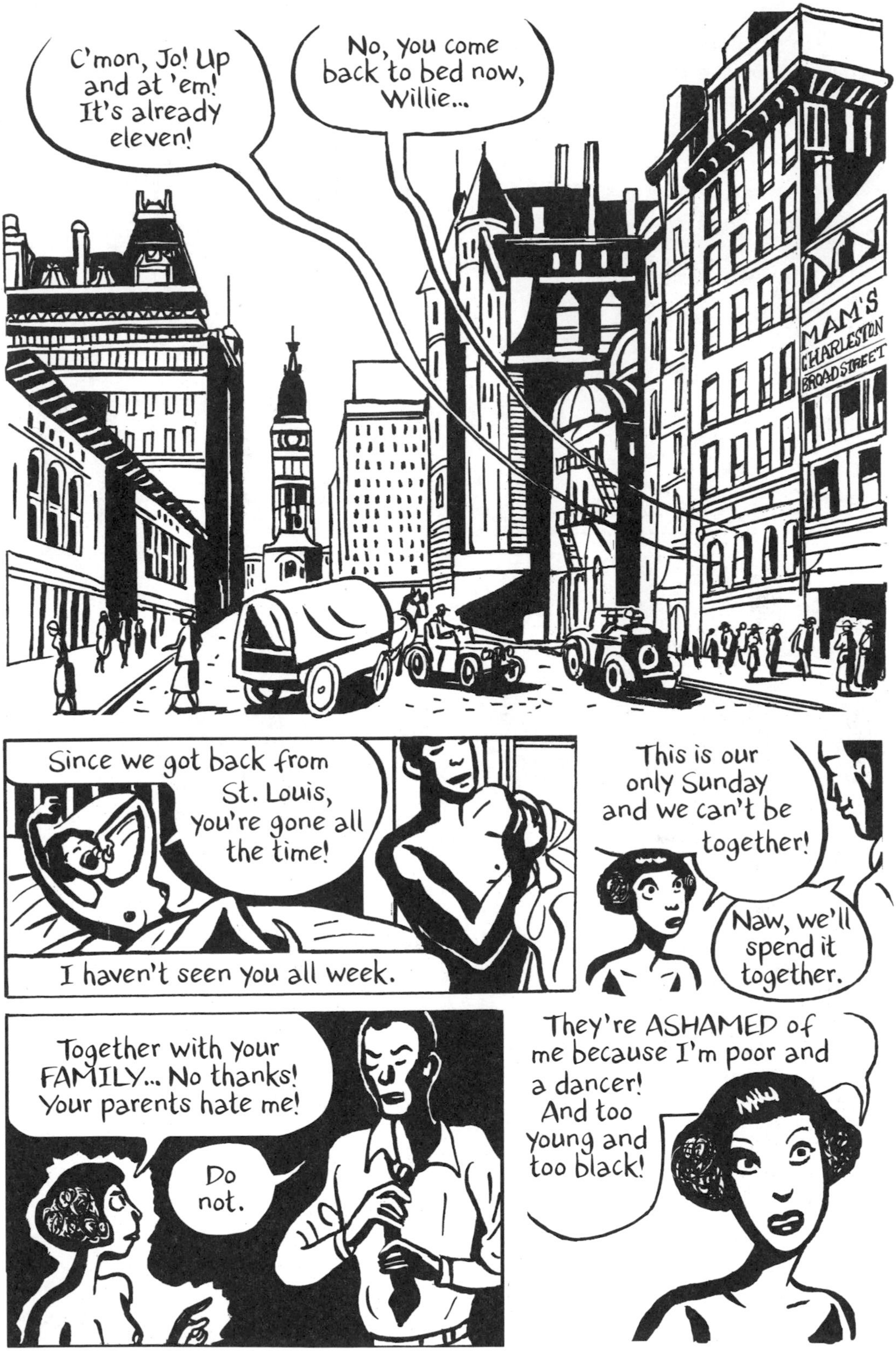

C'mon, Jo! Up and at 'em! It's already eleven!
No, you come back to bed now, Willie...
MAM'S
CHARLESTON
BROAD STREET
Since we got back from St. Louis, you're gone all the time!
I haven't seen you all week.
This is our only Sunday and we can't be together!
Naw, we'll spend it together.
Together with your FAMILY... No thanks! Your parents hate me!
Do not.
They're ASHAMED of me because I'm poor and a dancer! And too young and too black!

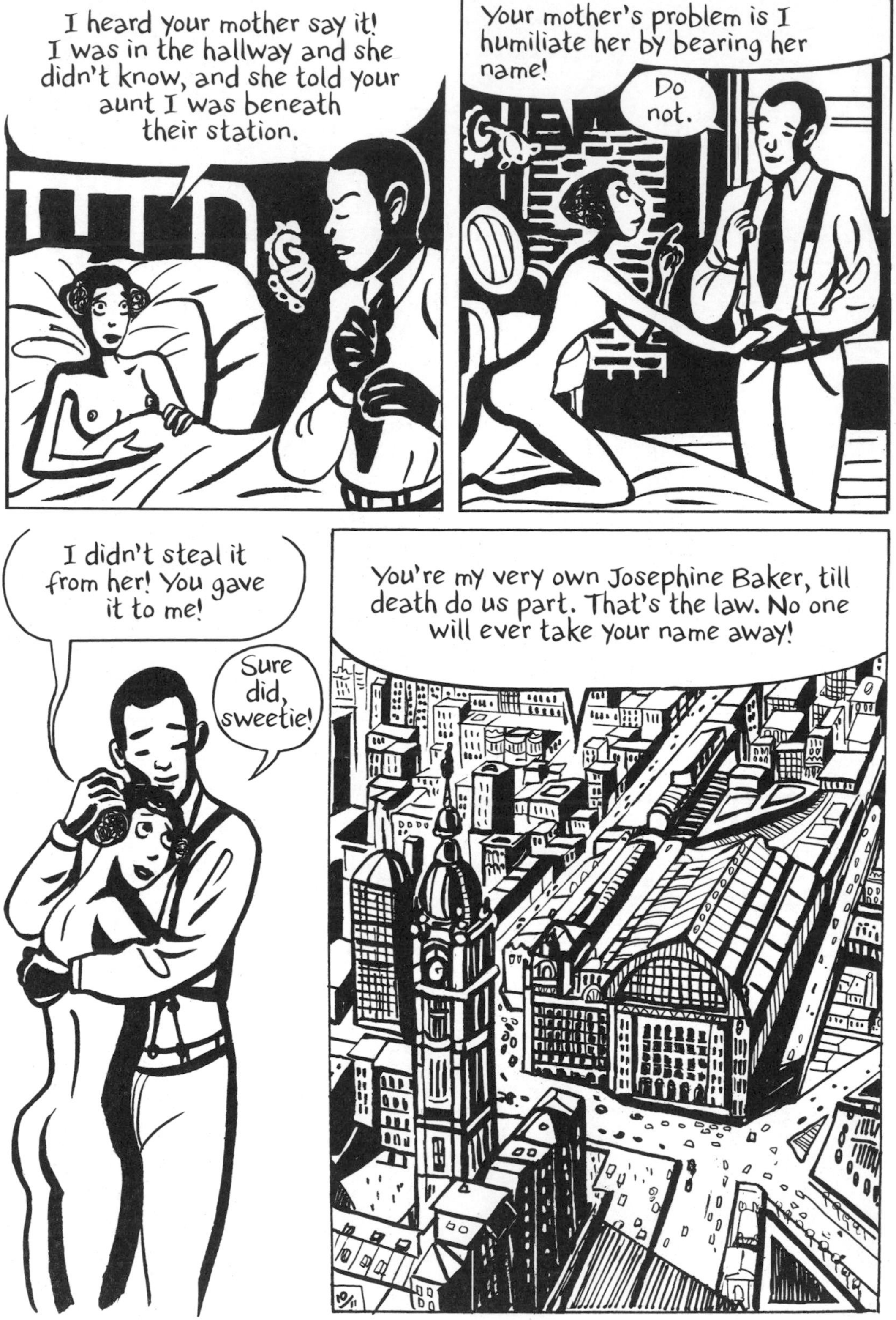
I heard your mother say it! I was in the hallway and she didn't know, and she told your aunt I was beneath their station.
Your mother's problem is I humiliate her by bearing her name!
Do not.
I didn't steal it from her! You gave it to me!
Sure did, sweetie!
You're my very own Josephine Baker, till death do us part. That's the law. No one will ever take your name away!

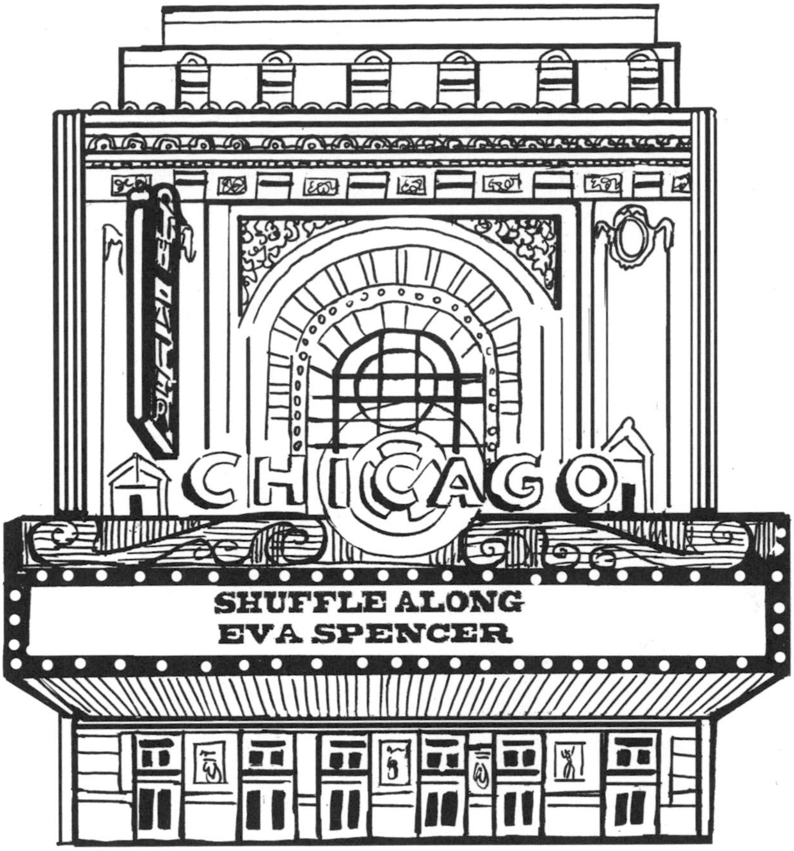
CHICAGO
SHUFFLE ALONG
EVA SPENCER

1923: North State Street, Chicago, Illinois, USA

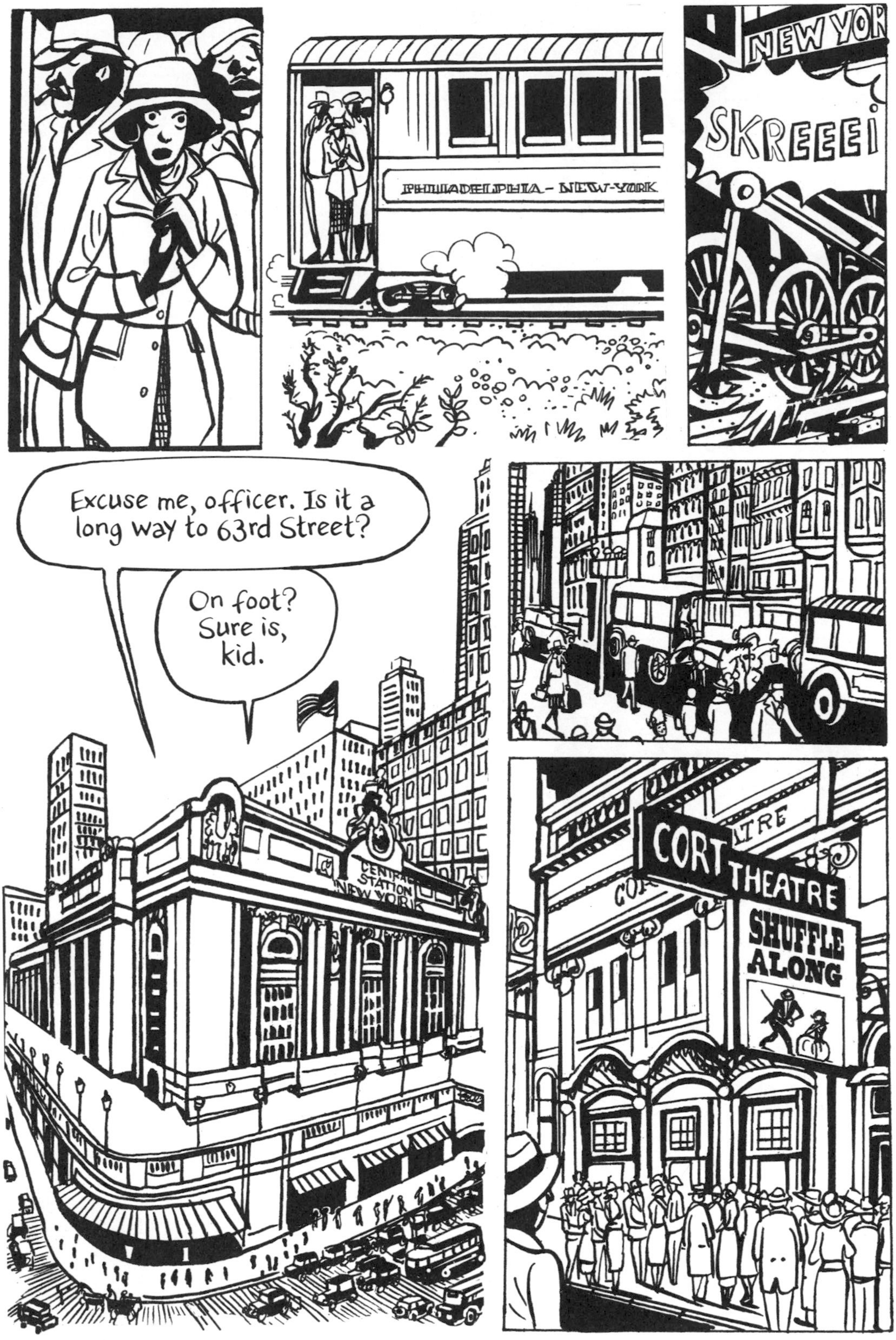
PHILADELPHIA - NEW-YORK
NEW YOR
SKREEEI
Excuse me, officer. Is it a long way to 63rd Street?
On foot? Sure is, kid.
CORT THEATRE
SHUFFLE ALONG

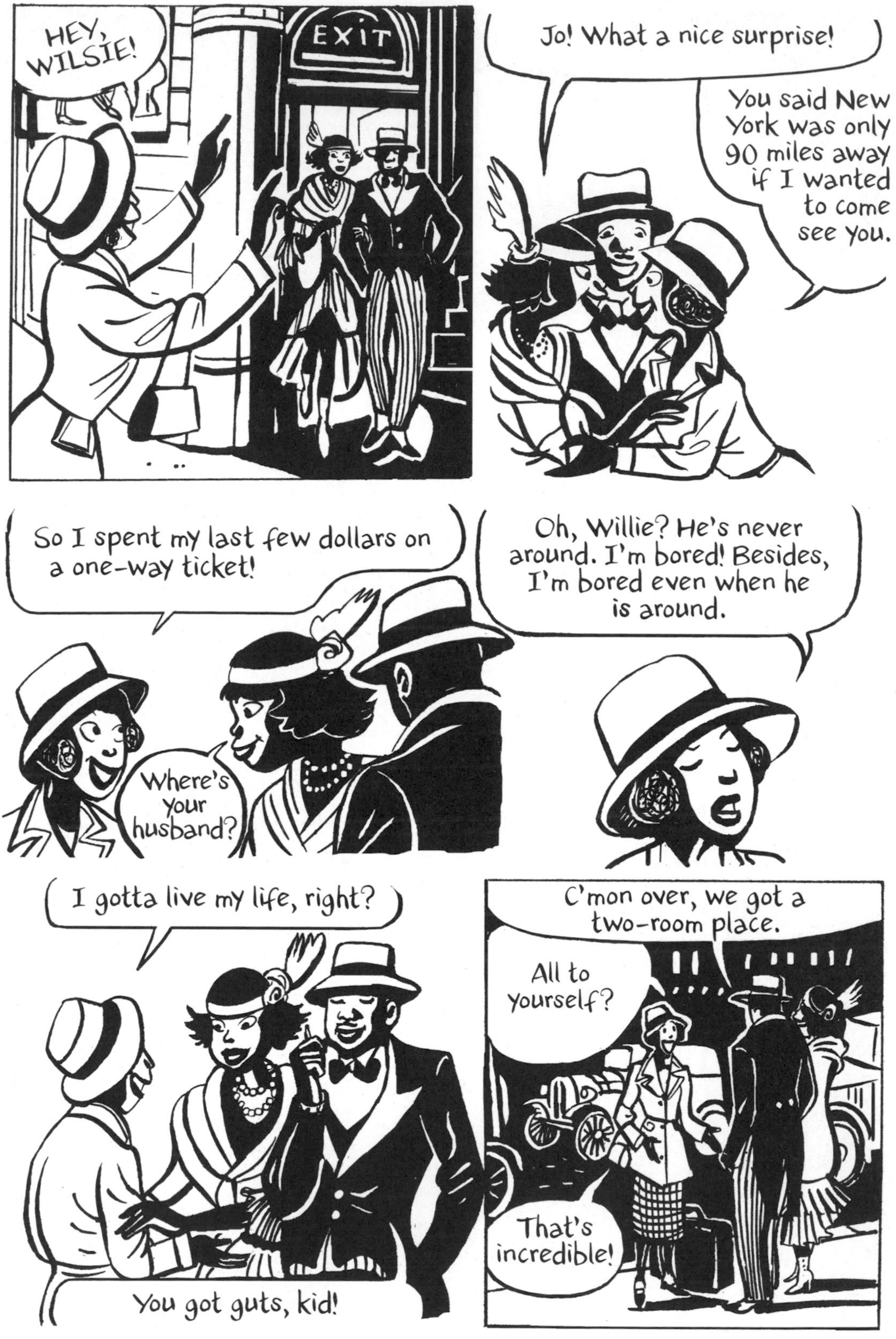
HEY, WILSIE!
EXIT
Jo! What a nice surprise!
You said New York was only 90 miles away if I wanted to come see you.
So I spent my last few dollars on a one-way ticket!
Where's your husband?
Oh, Willie? He's never around. I'm bored! Besides, I'm bored even when he is around.
I gotta live my life, right?
You got guts, kid!
C'mon over, we got a two-room place.
All to yourself?
That's incredible!

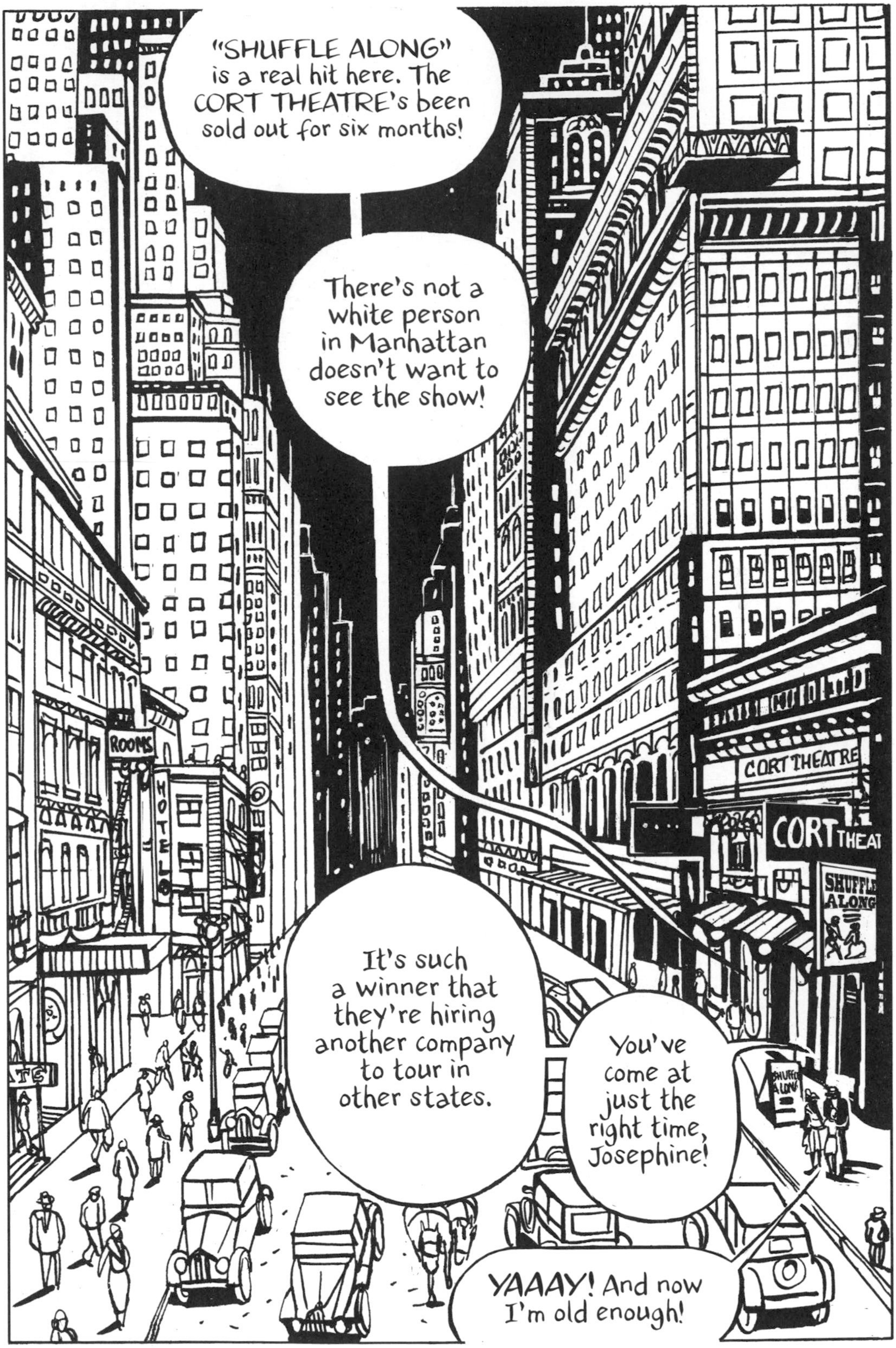
"SHUFFLE ALONG" is a real hit here. The CORT THEATRE's been sold out for six months!
There's not a white person in Manhattan doesn't want to see the show!
It's such a winner that they're hiring another company to tour in other states.
You've come at just the right time, Josephine!
YAAAY! And now I'm old enough!
ROOMS
HOTEL
CORT THEATRE
CORT THEAT
SHUFFLE ALONG

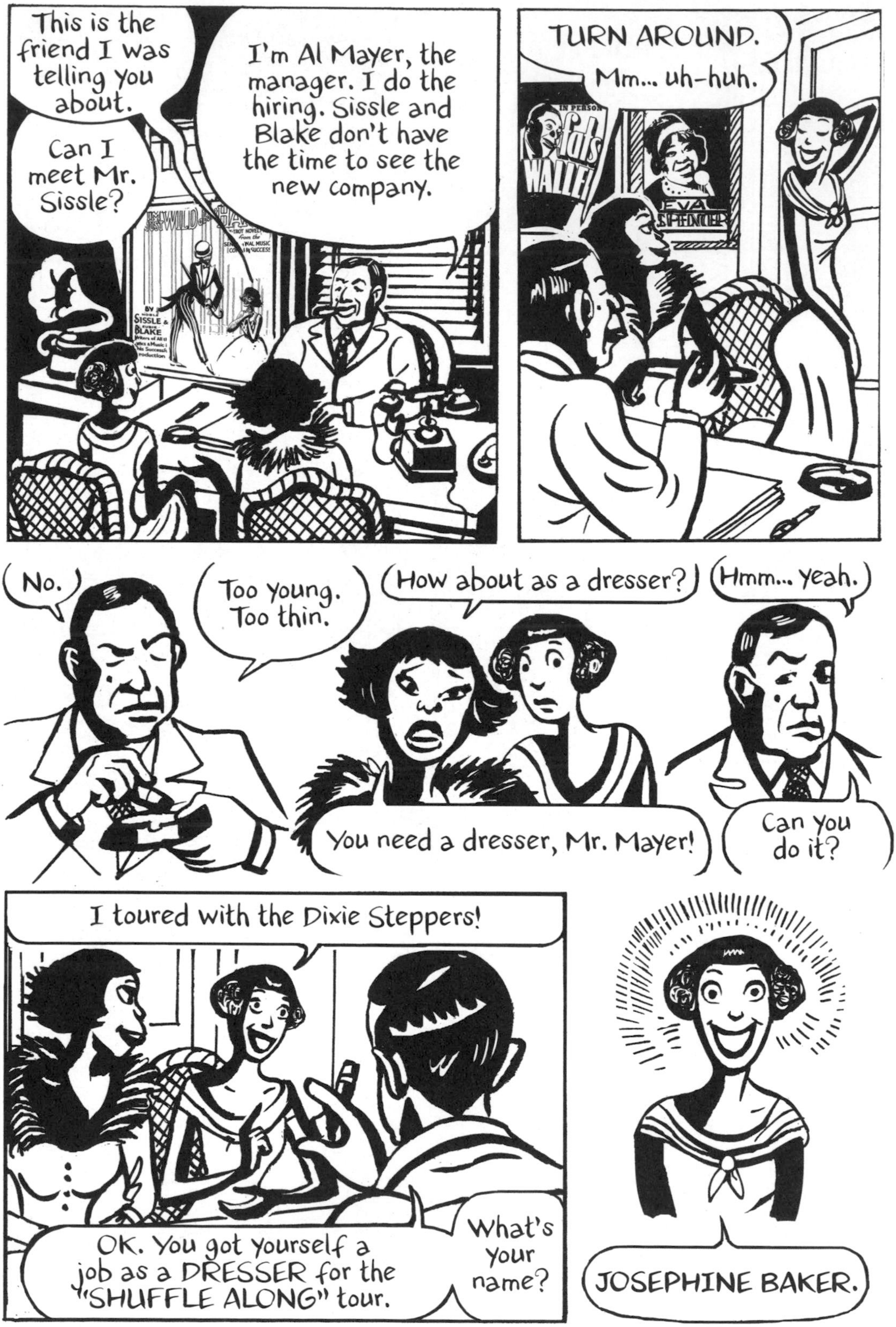
This is the friend I was telling you about.
Can I meet Mr. Sissle?
I'm Al Mayer, the manager. I do the hiring. Sissle and Blake don't have the time to see the new company.
TURN AROUND.
Mm... uh-huh.
No.
Too young. Too thin.
How about as a dresser?
You need a dresser, Mr. Mayer!
Hmm... yeah.
Can you do it?
I toured with the Dixie Steppers!
OK. You got yourself a job as a DRESSER for the "SHUFFLE ALONG" tour.
What's your name?
JOSEPHINE BAKER.

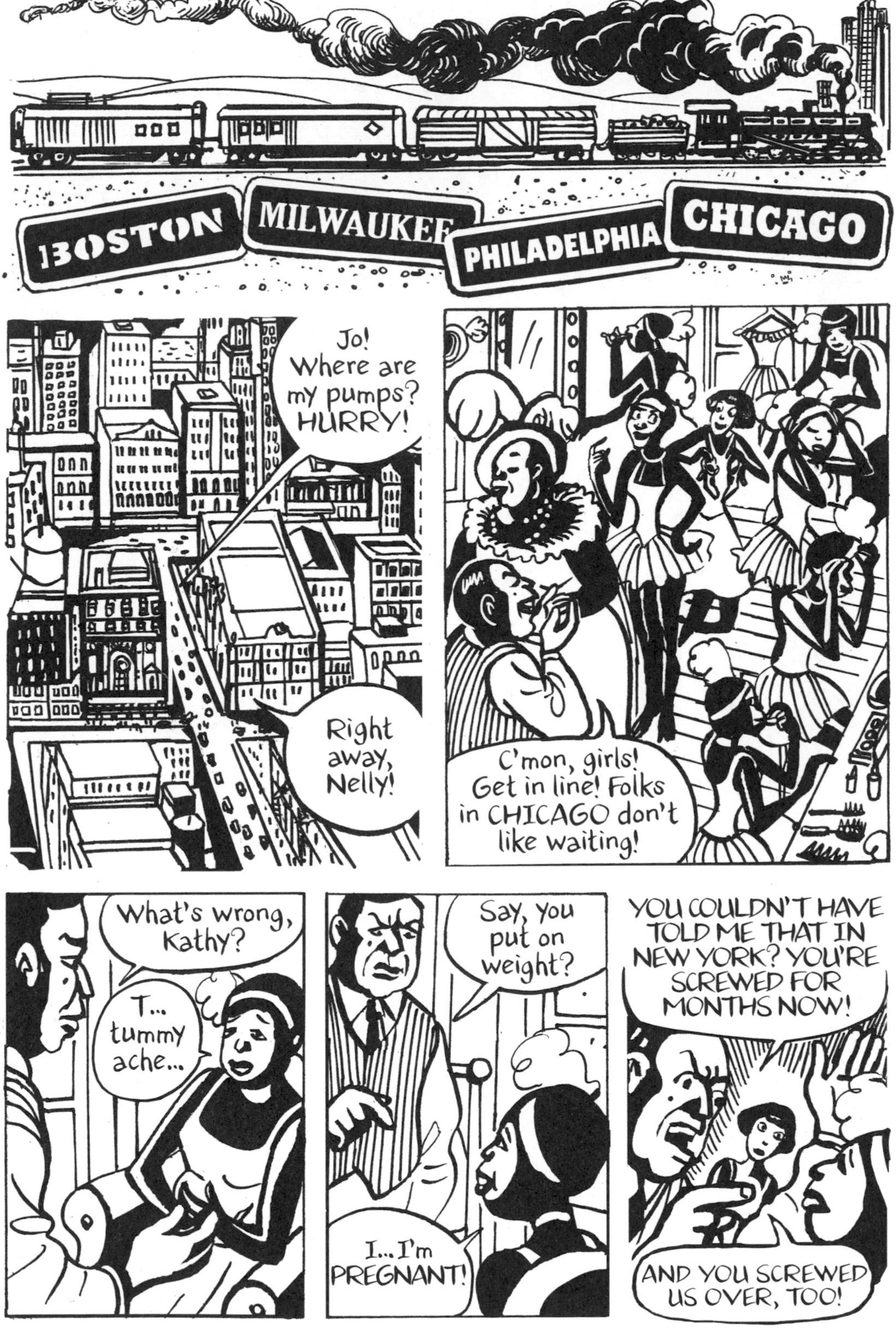
BOSTON
MILWAUKEE
PHILADELPHIA
CHICAGO
Jo! Where are my pumps? HURRY!
Right away, Nelly!
C'mon, girls! Get in line! Folks in CHICAGO don't like waiting!
What's wrong, Kathy?
T... tummy ache...
Say, you put on weight?
I... I'm PREGNANT!
YOU COULDN'T HAVE TOLD ME THAT IN NEW YORK? YOU'RE SCREWED FOR MONTHS NOW!
AND YOU SCREWED US OVER, TOO!

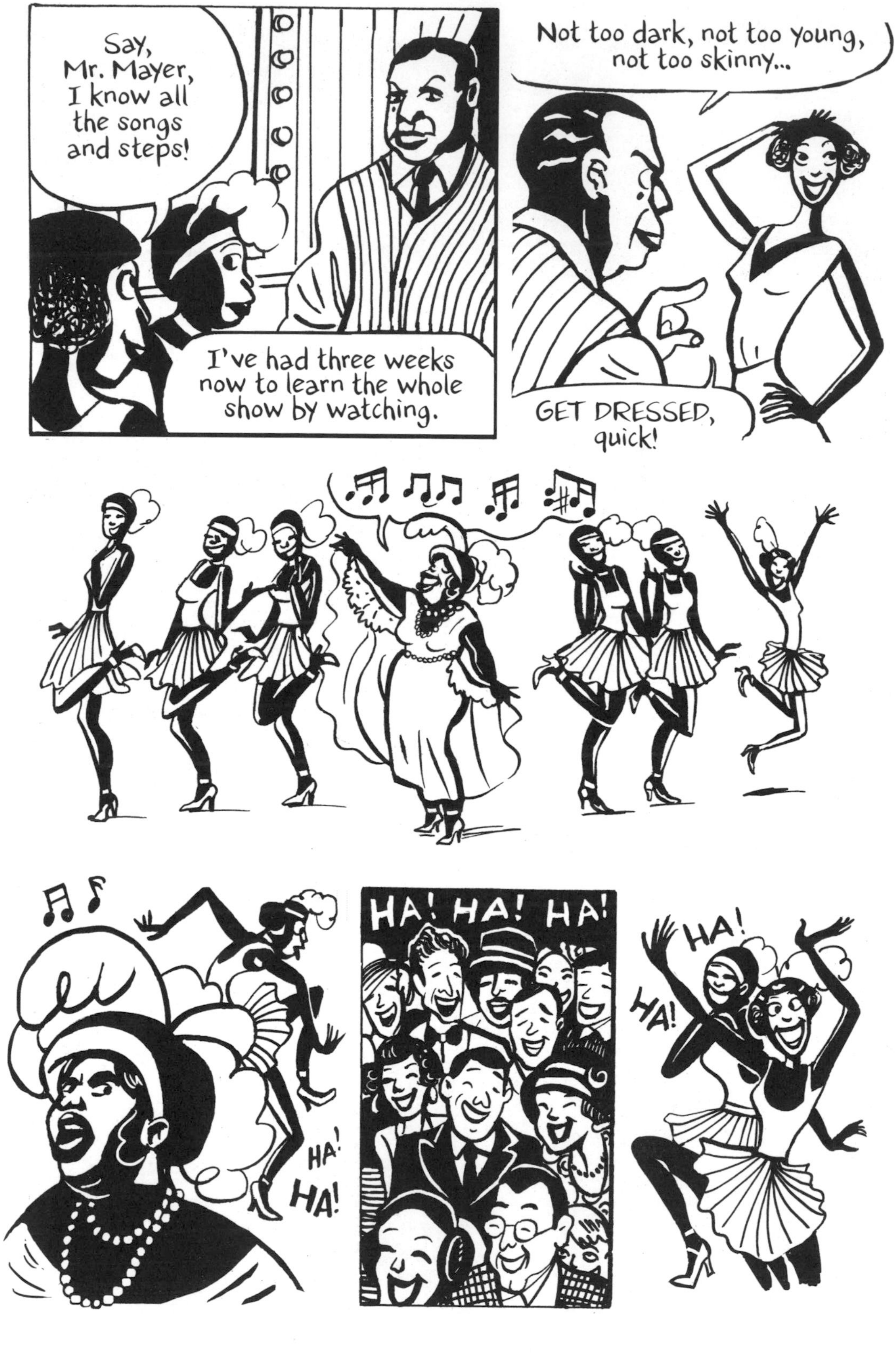
Say, Mr. Mayer, I know all the songs and steps!
I've had three weeks now to learn the whole show by watching.
Not too dark, not too young, not too skinny...
GET DRESSED, quick!
HA! HA!
HA! HA! HA!
HA!
HA!

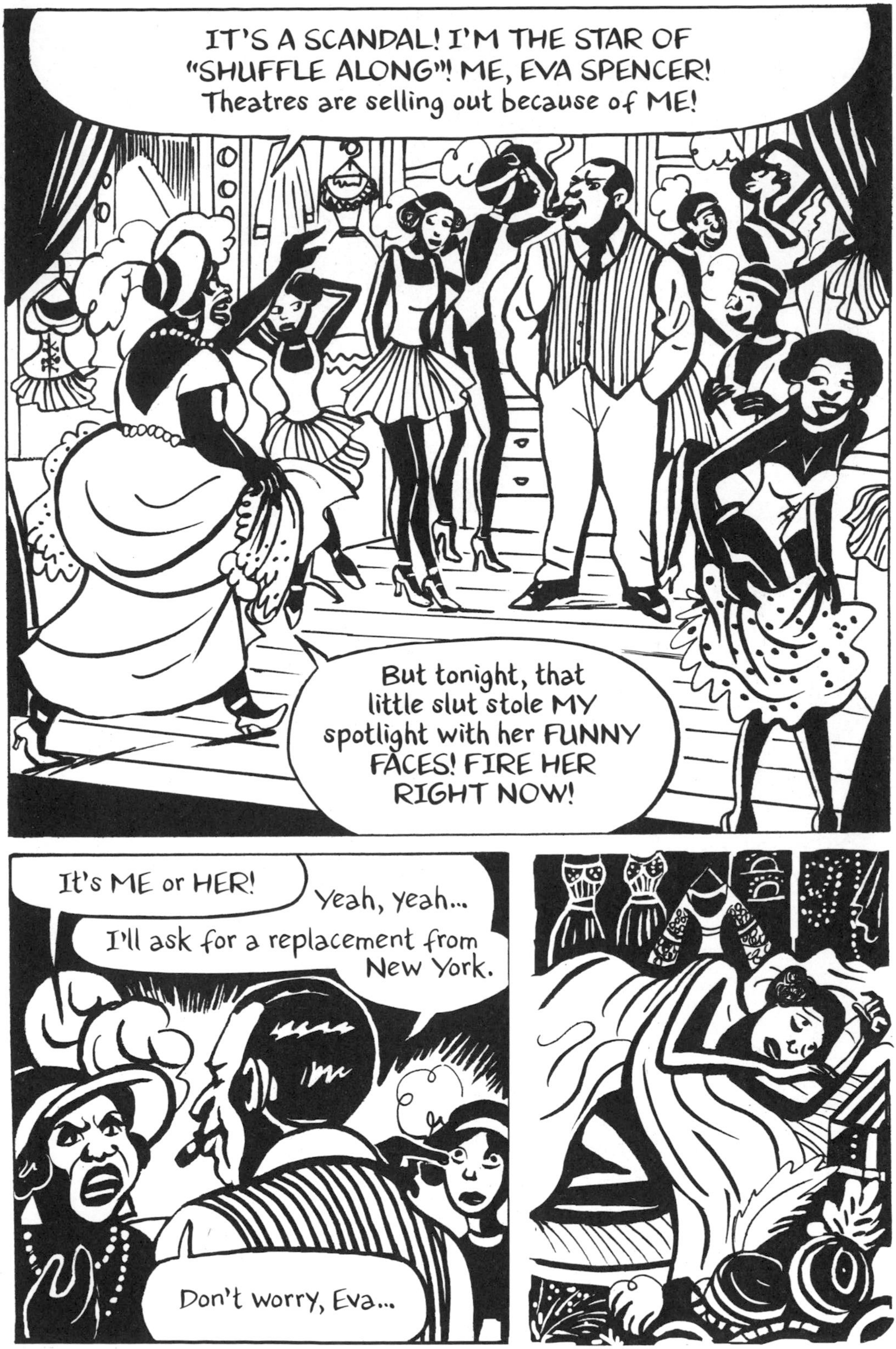
IT'S A SCANDAL! I'M THE STAR OF "SHUFFLE ALONG"! ME, EVA SPENCER! Theatres are selling out because of ME!
But tonight, that little slut stole MY spotlight with her FUNNY FACES! FIRE HER RIGHT NOW!
It's ME or HER!
Yeah, yeah...
I'll ask for a replacement from New York.
Don't worry, Eva...

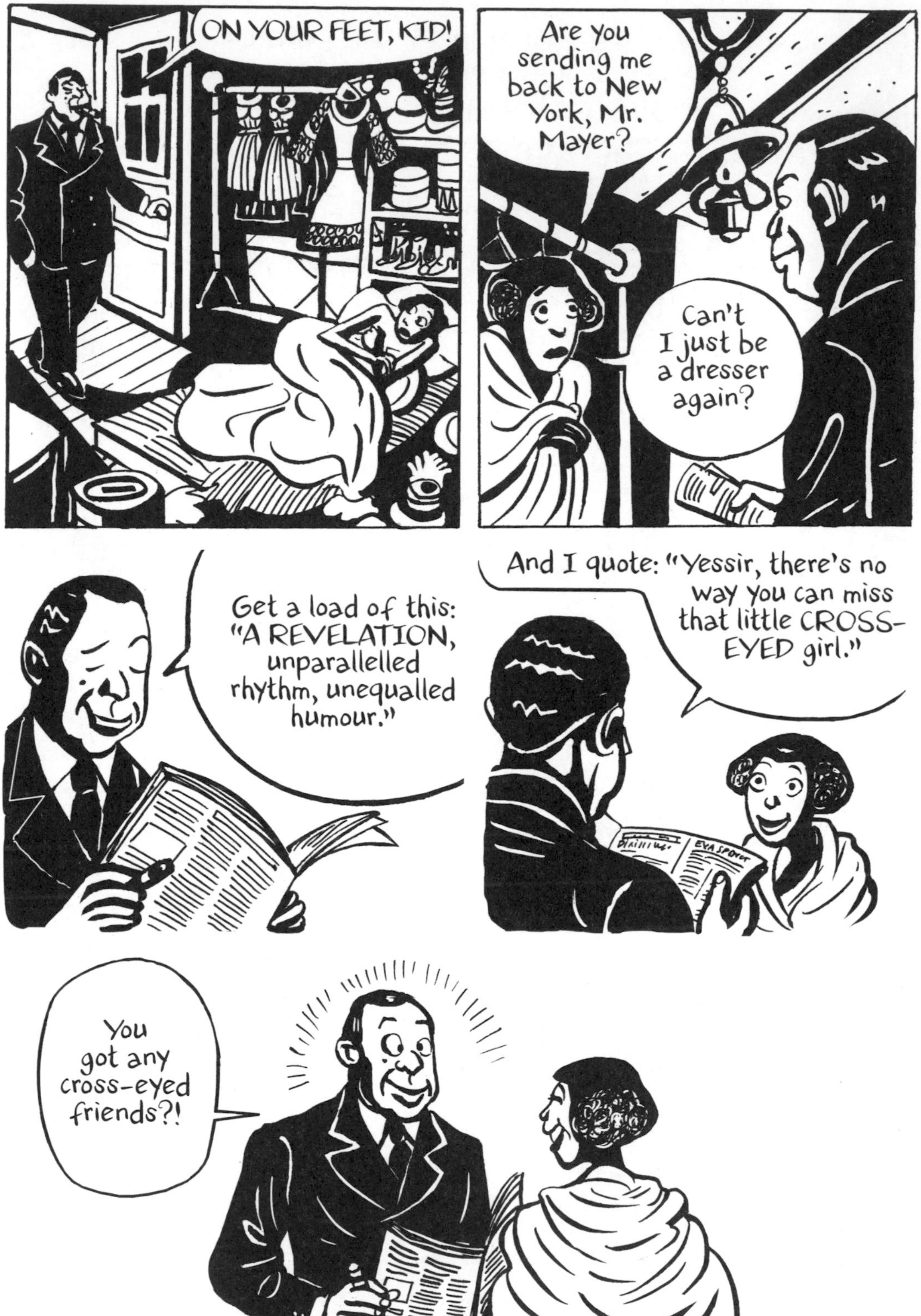
ON YOUR FEET, KID!
Are you sending me back to New York, Mr. Mayer?
Can't I just be a dresser again?
Get a load of this: "A REVELATION, unparallelled rhythm, unequalled humour."
And I quote: "Yessir, there's no way you can miss that little CROSS-EYED girl."
You got any cross-eyed friends?!

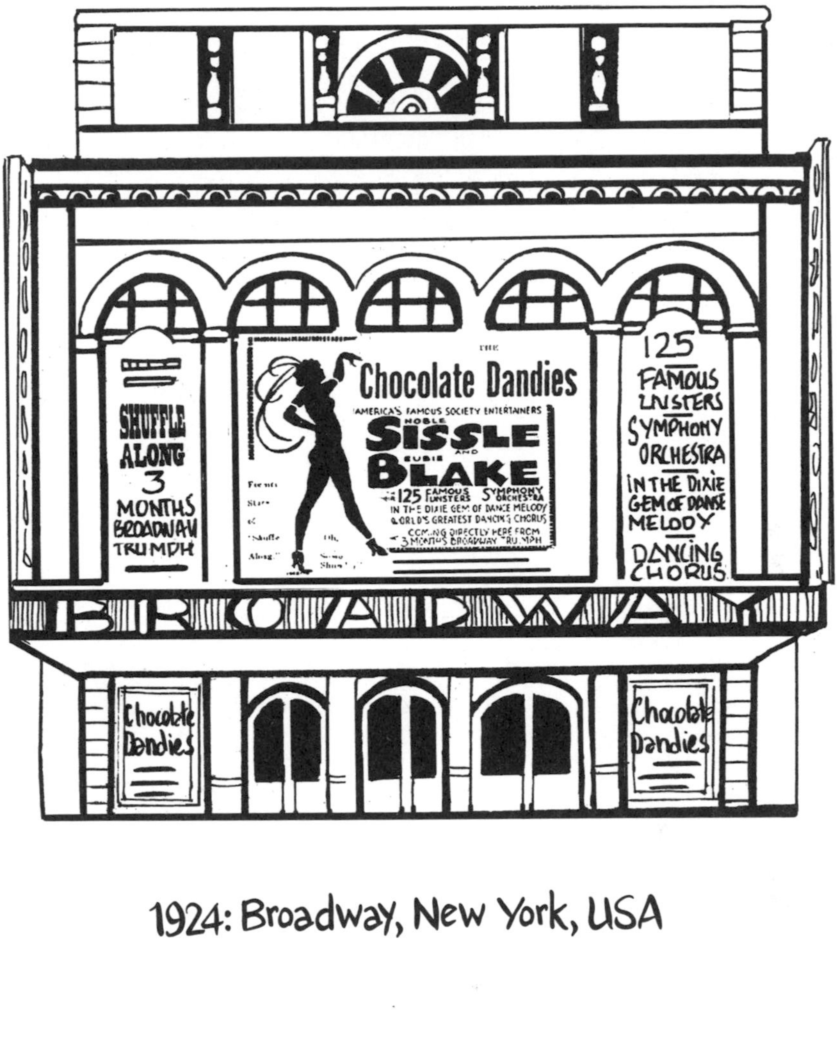
Chocolate Dandies
AMERICA'S FAMOUS SOCIETY ENTERTAINERS
SISSLE
BLAKE
125 FAMOUS FUNSTERS
SYMPHONY ORCHESTRA
IN THE DIXIE GEM OF DANCE MELODY
SHUFFLE ALONG
3
MONTHS
125
FAMOUS
SYMPHONY
ORCHESTRA
IN THE DIXIE
GEM OF DANSE
MELODY
DANCING
CHORUS
BROADWAY
Chocolate Dandies
Chocolate Dandies

1924: Broadway, New York, USA

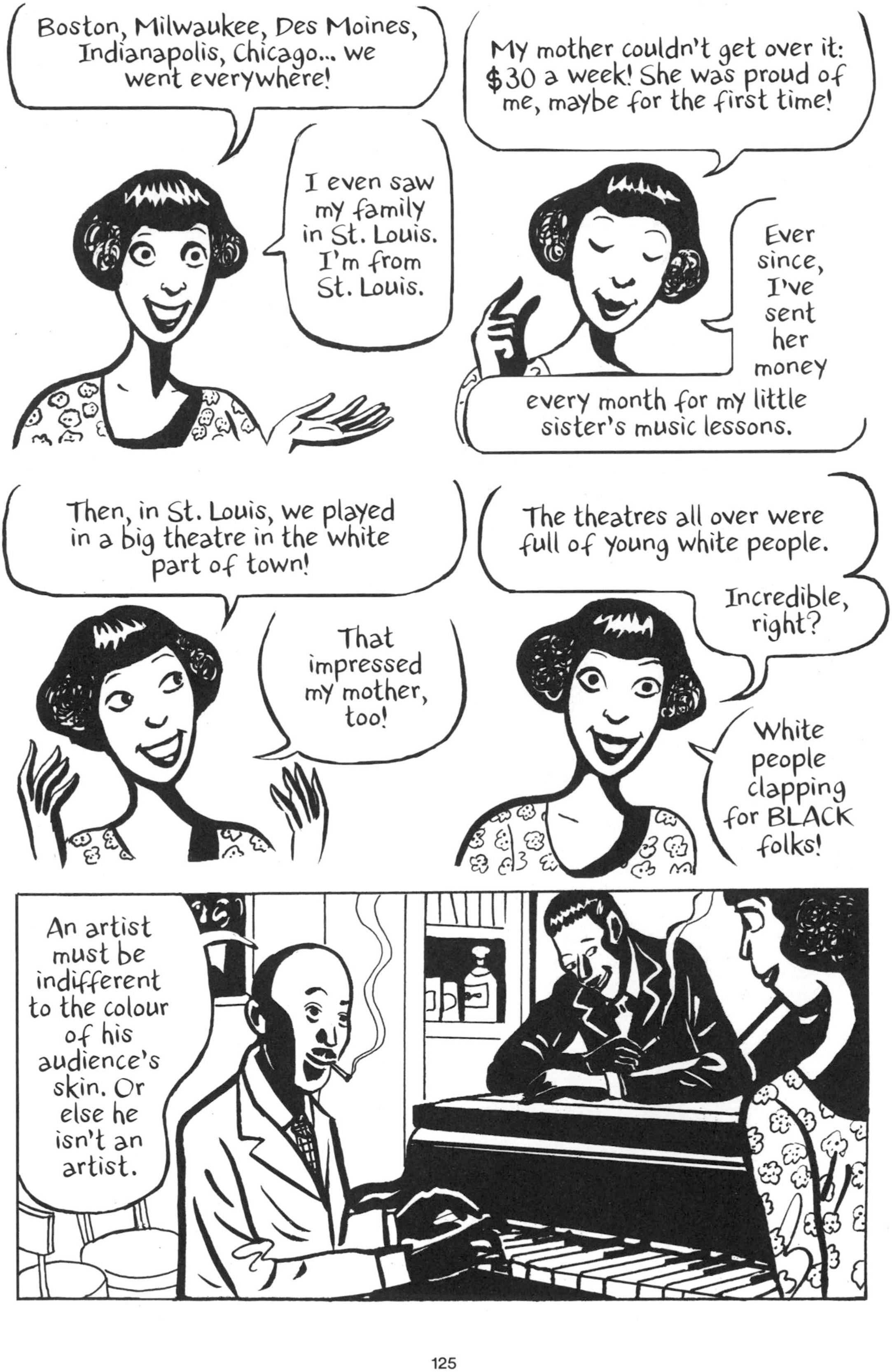
Boston, Milwaukee, Des Moines, Indianapolis, Chicago... we went everywhere!
I even saw my family in St. Louis. I'm from St. Louis.
My mother couldn't get over it: $30 a week! She was proud of me, maybe for the first time!
Ever since, I've sent her money
every month for my little sister's music lessons.
Then, in St. Louis, we played in a big theatre in the white part of town!
That impressed my mother, too!
The theatres all over were full of young white people.
Incredible, right?
White people clapping for BLACK folks!
An artist must be indifferent to the colour of his audience's skin. Or else he isn't an artist.

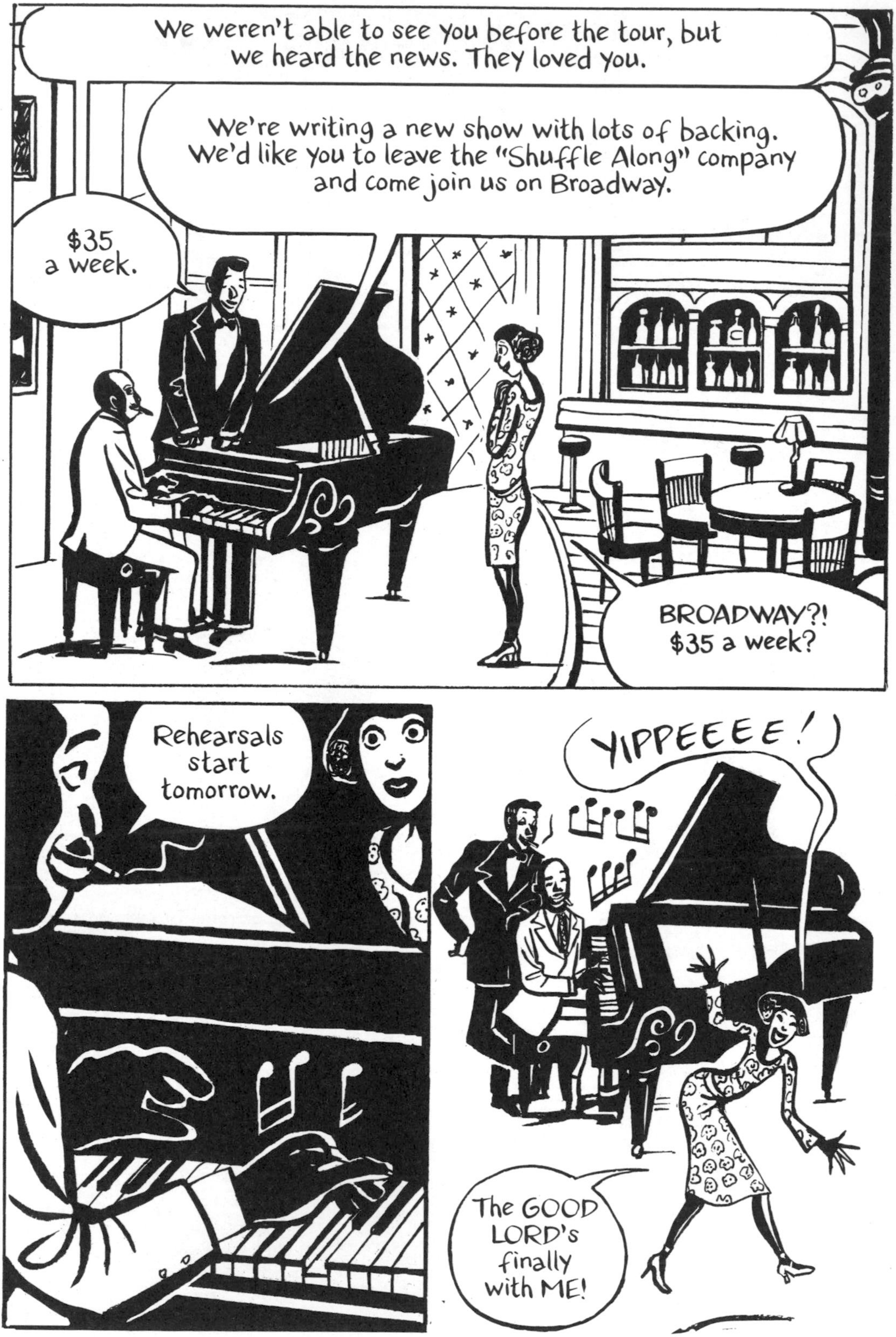
We weren't able to see you before the tour, but we heard the news. They loved you.
We're writing a new show with lots of backing. We'd like you to leave the "Shuffle Along" company and come join us on Broadway.
$35 a week.
BROADWAY?! $35 a week?
Rehearsals start tomorrow.
YIPPEEEE!
The GOOD LORD's finally with ME!

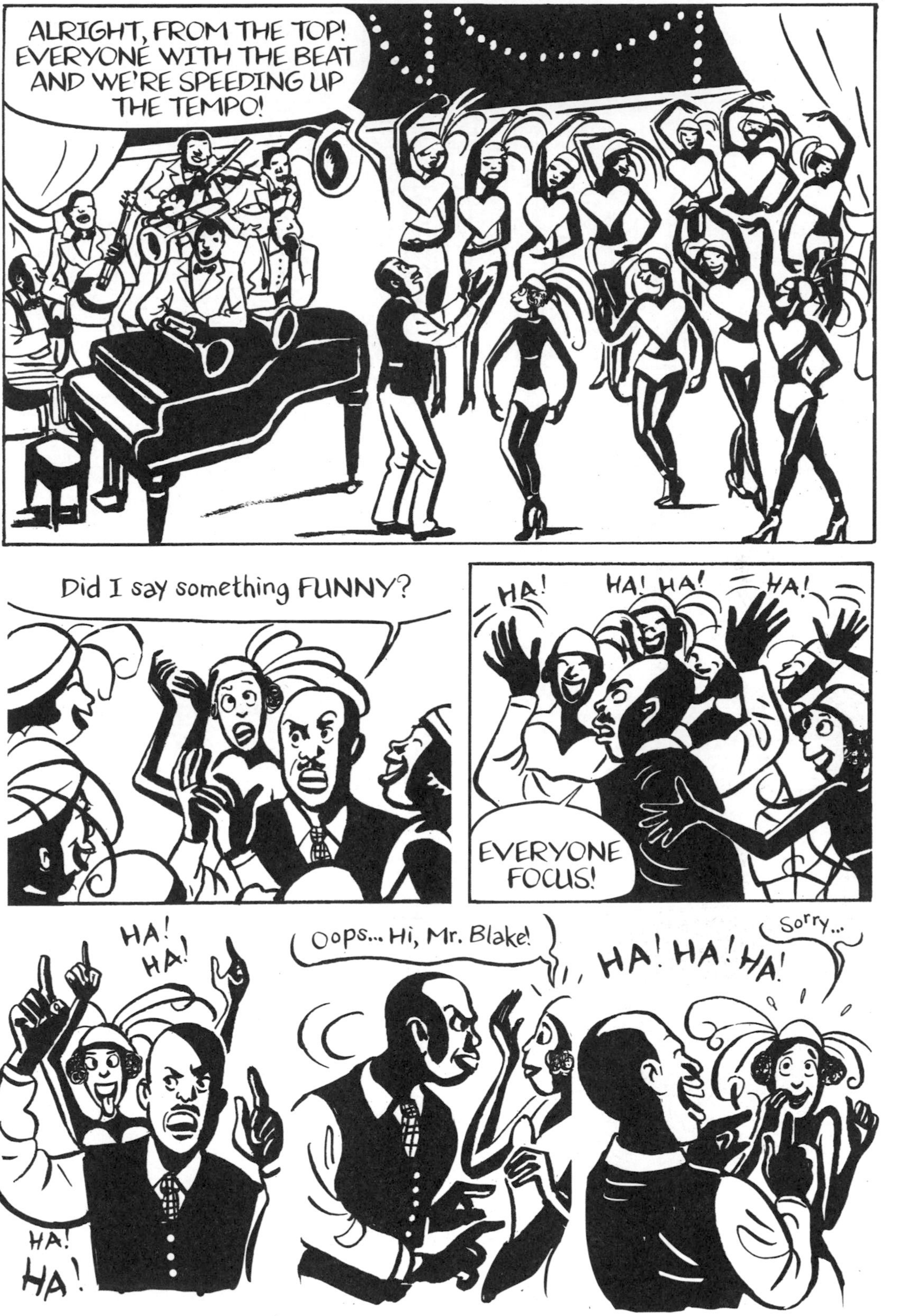
ALRIGHT, FROM THE TOP! EVERYONE WITH THE BEAT AND WE'RE SPEEDING UP THE TEMPO!
Did I say something FUNNY?
HA!
HA! HA!
HA!
EVERYONE FOCUS!
HA! HA!
HA! HA!
Oops... Hi, Mr. Blake!
HA! HA! HA!
Sorry...

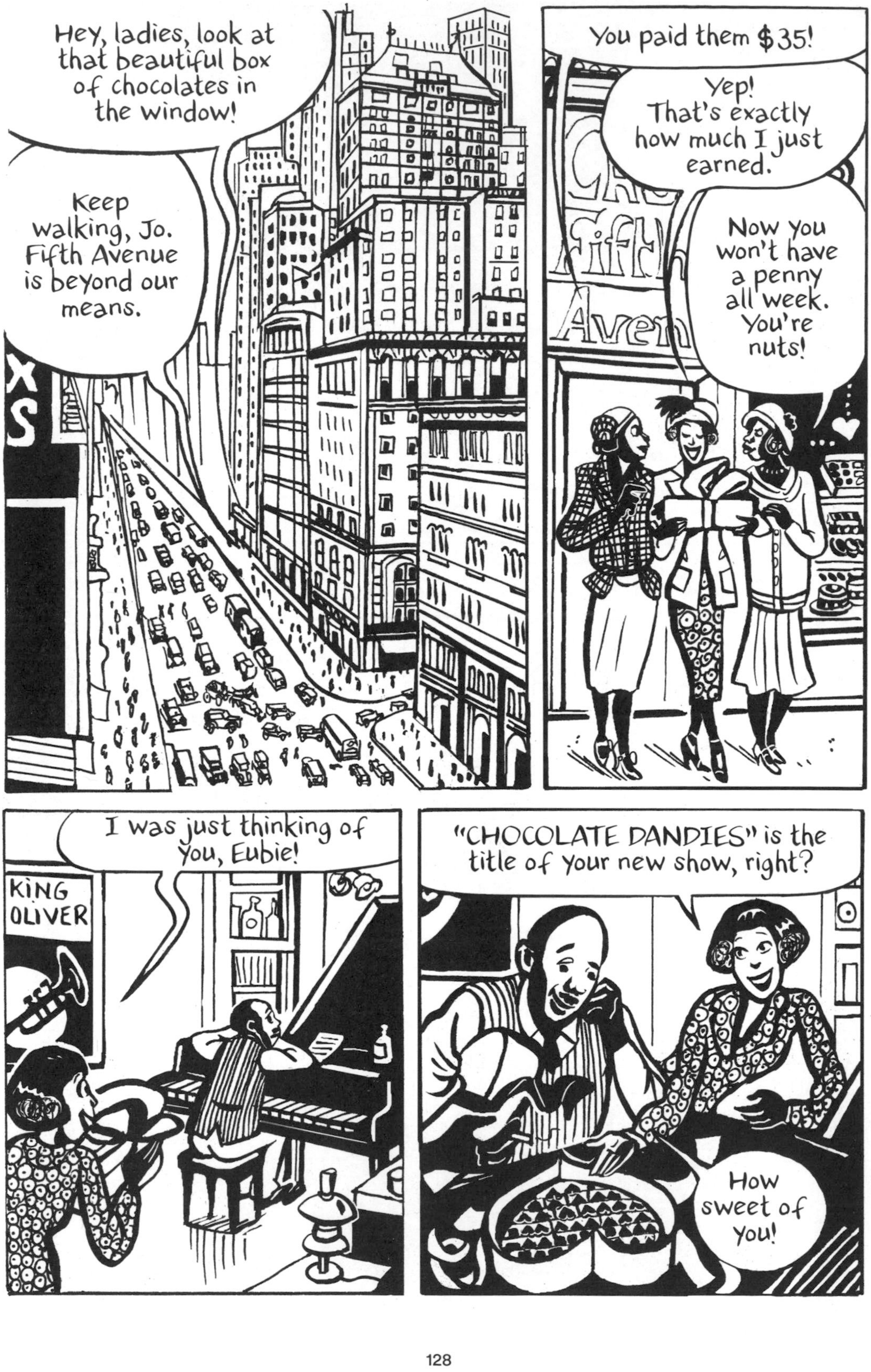

Hey, ladies, look at that beautiful box of chocolates in the window!
Keep walking, Jo. Fifth Avenue is beyond our means.
You paid them $35!
Yep! That's exactly how much I just earned.
Now you won't have a penny all week. You're nuts!
KING OLIVER
I was just thinking of you, Eubie!
"CHOCOLATE DANDIES" is the title of your new show, right?
How sweet of you!

Aren't things going well, Eubie? You got troubles?

Oh, a few worries.

You afraid? Of what? You're the man who's not afraid of anything — not even white folks!

Here, have a little heart!

You know how we put on "Shuffle Along"?

Noble and I were already famous, but when we made the rounds with our idea, the answer was always no.

Then one day, old John Cort believed in us. In our eyes, Cort was a whole chain of theatres.

But he was washed out, ruined. And he put us in his worst theatre.

When we got there, rain was leaking onstage.

Our only costumes were from all the theatre's previous flops!

There were oriental robes, so I wrote some oriental blues...

There were clothes of cotton, so we wrote "Bandana Days".

And all over the phone! With Noble in Boston and me in New York.

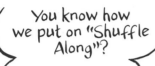

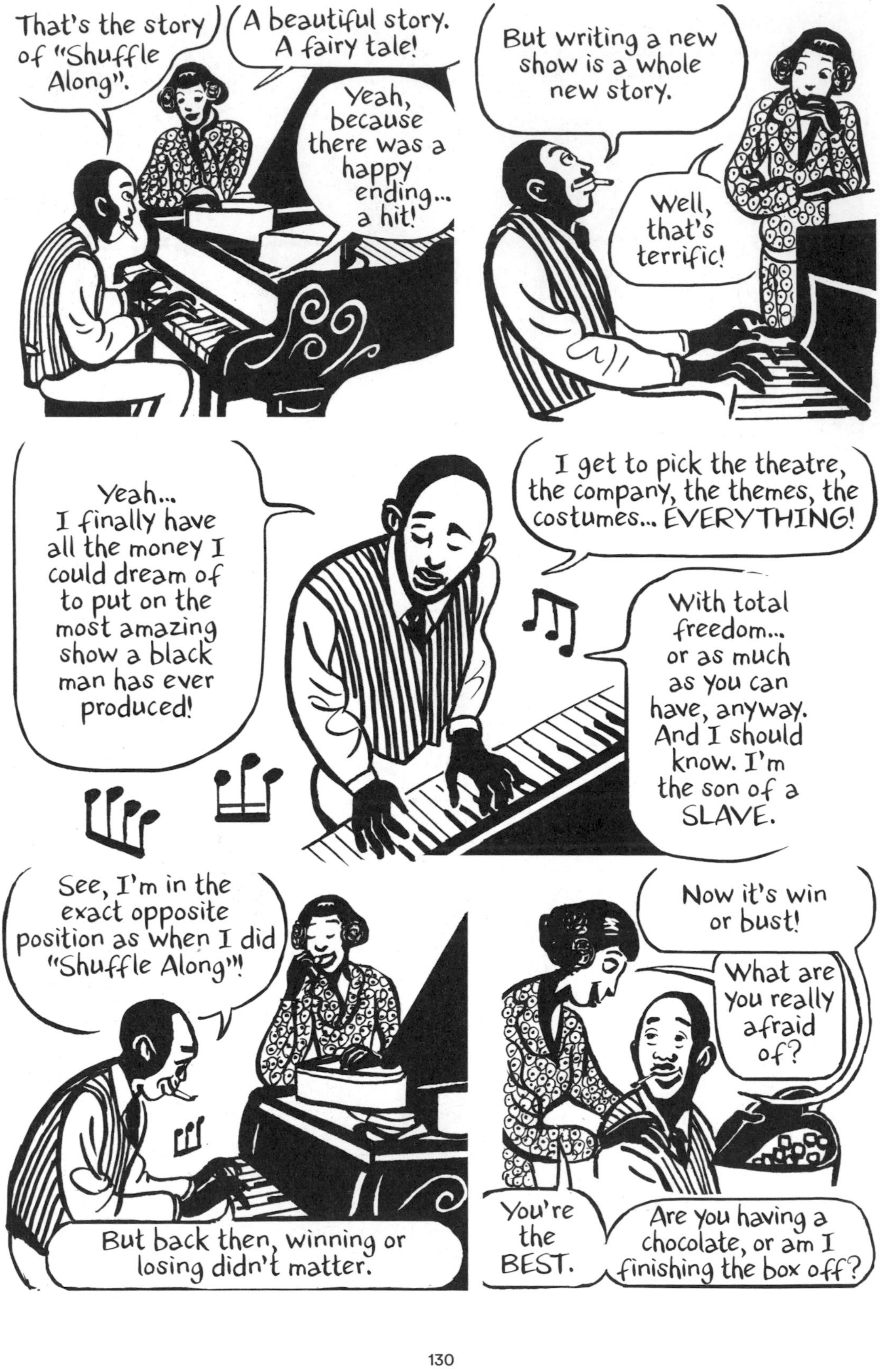

That's the story of "Shuffle Along".
A beautiful story. A fairy tale!
Yeah, because there was a happy ending... a hit!
But writing a new show is a whole new story.
Well, that's terrific!
Yeah... I finally have all the money I could dream of to put on the most amazing show a black man has ever produced!
I get to pick the theatre, the company, the themes, the costumes... EVERYTHING!
With total freedom... or as much as you can have, anyway. And I should know. I'm the son of a SLAVE.
See, I'm in the exact opposite position as when I did "Shuffle Along"!
But back then, winning or losing didn't matter.
Now it's win or bust!
What are you really afraid of?
You're the BEST.
Are you having a chocolate, or am I finishing the box off?

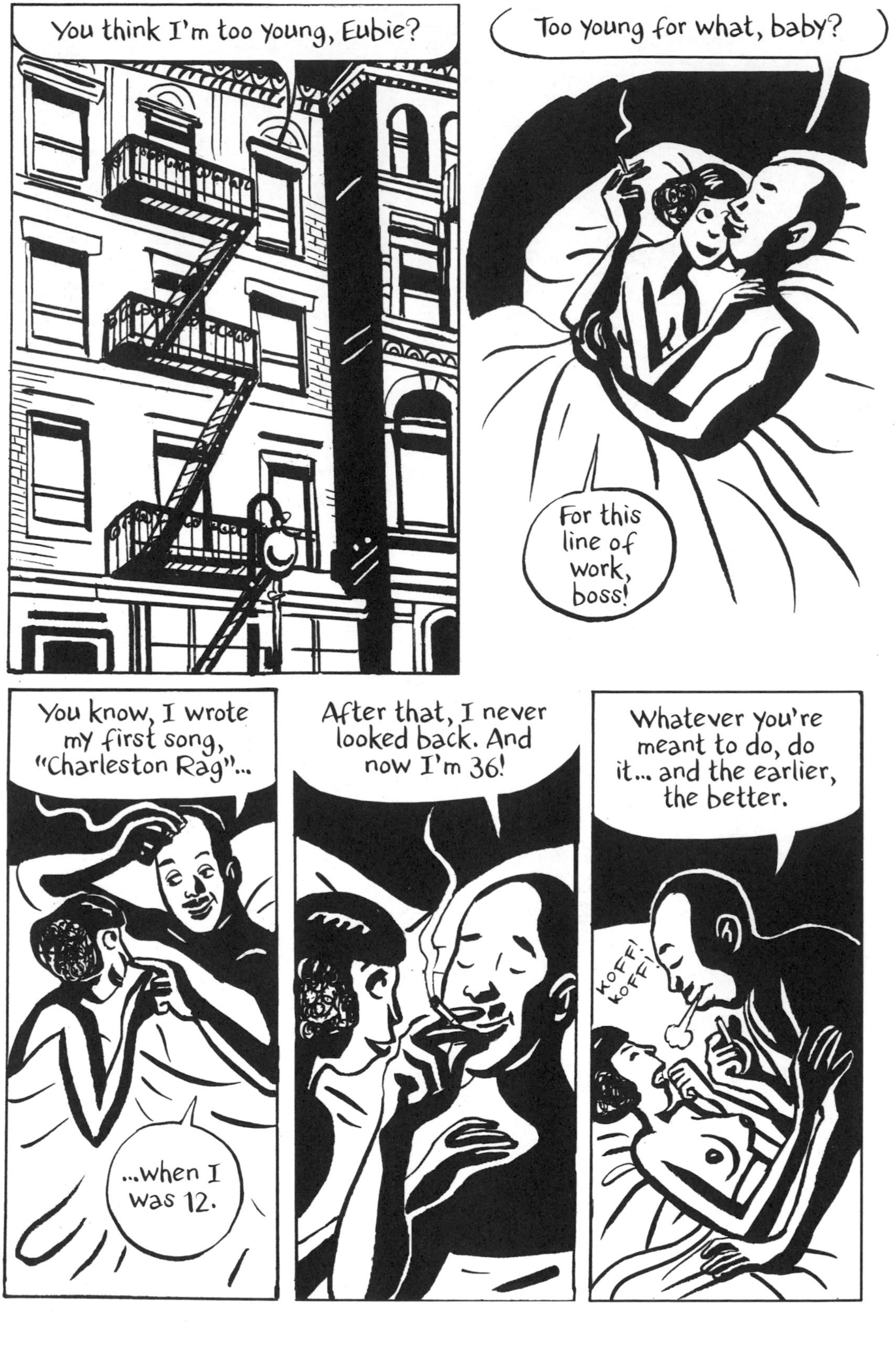
You think I'm too young, Eubie?
Too young for what, baby?
For this line of work, boss!
You know, I wrote my first song, "Charleston Rag"...
...when I was 12.
After that, I never looked back. And now I'm 36!
Whatever you're meant to do, do it... and the earlier, the better.
KOFF! KOFF!

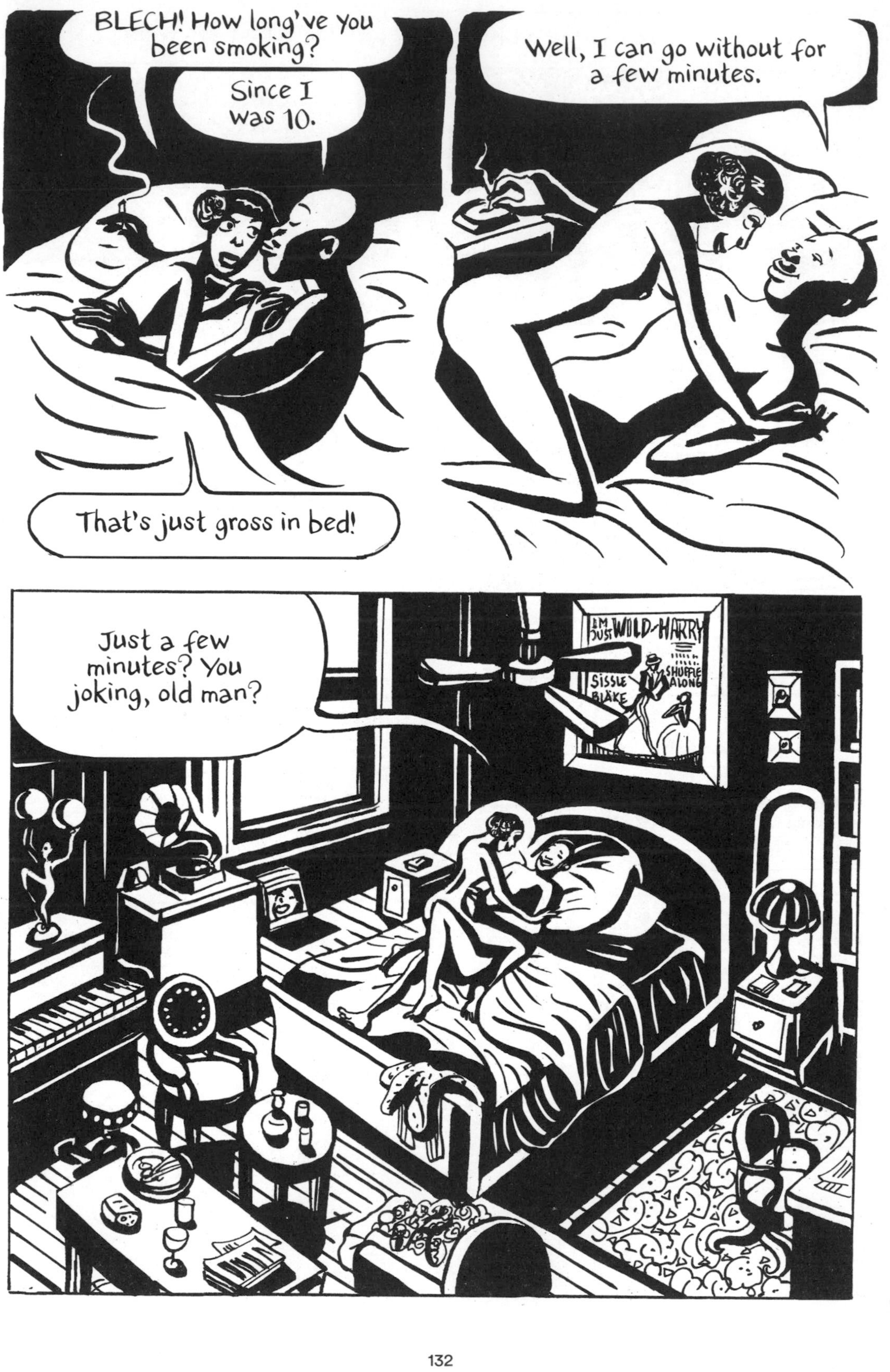
BLECH! How long've you been smoking?
Since I was 10.
That's just gross in bed!
Well, I can go without for a few minutes.
Just a few minutes? You joking, old man?
SISSLE BLAKE
SHUFFLE ALONG

The WORLD FAMOUS
DINNER 150,
50 COPPER COLOURED GIRLS
NEVER COVER CHARGE
SAM LEVIN'S PLANTATION CLUB
CLUB PARADE 50
Broadway
SHOWS NIGHTLY 7 12 22
FRANK SEBASTI
HERE NOW

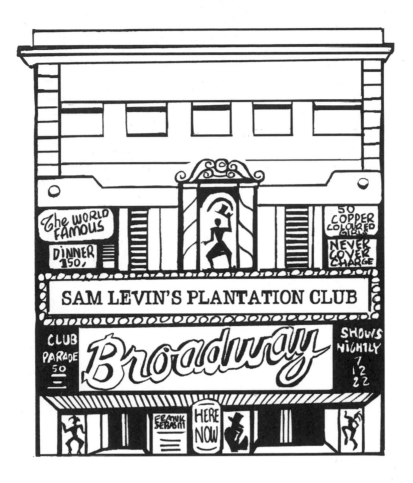

1925: Broadway, New York, USA

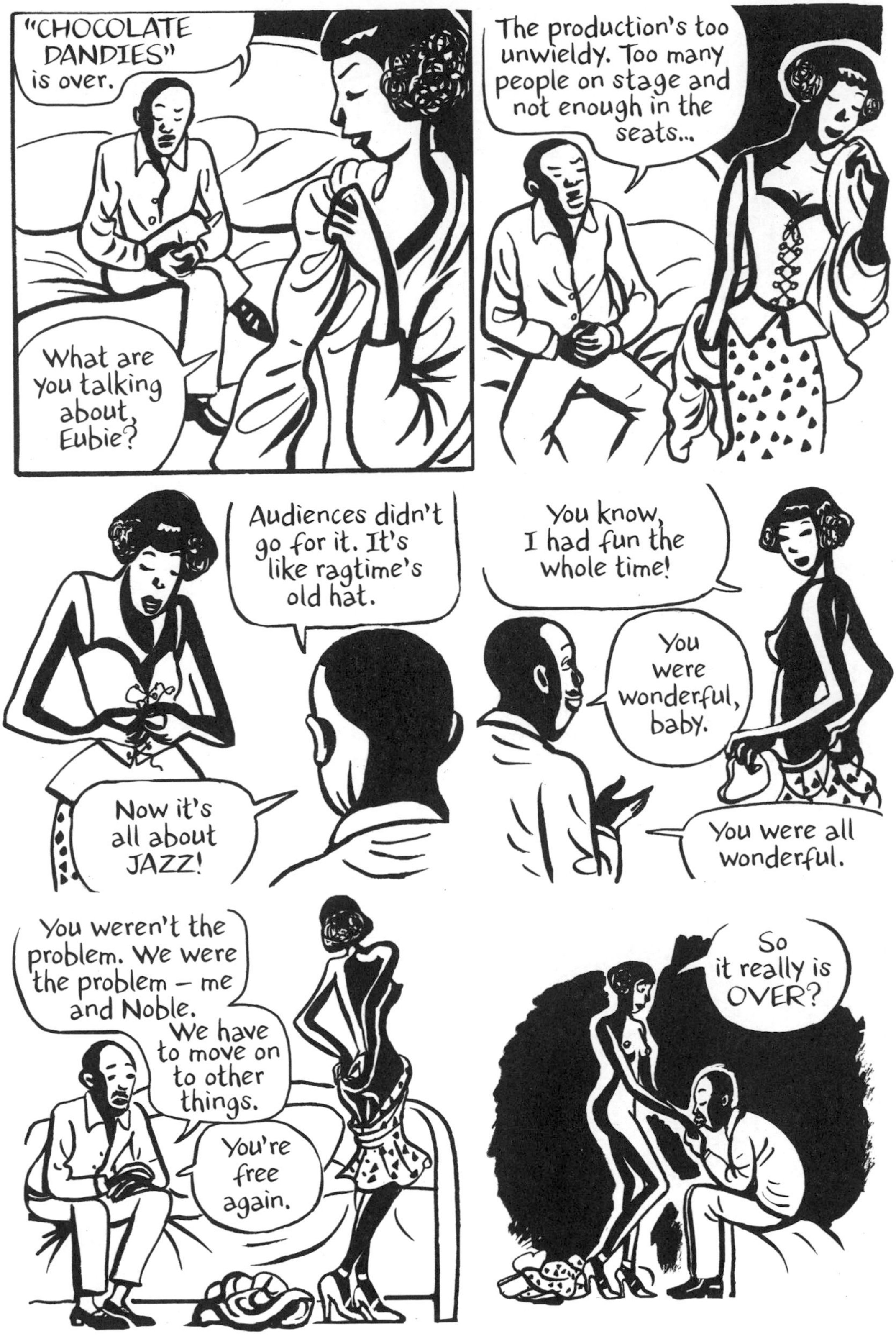
"CHOCOLATE DANDIES" is over.
What are you talking about, Eubie?
The production's too unwieldy. Too many people on stage and not enough in the seats...
Audiences didn't go for it. It's like ragtime's old hat.
Now it's all about JAZZ!
You know, I had fun the whole time!
You were wonderful, baby.
You were all wonderful.
You weren't the problem. We were the problem – me and Noble.
We have to move on to other things.
You're free again.
So it really is OVER?

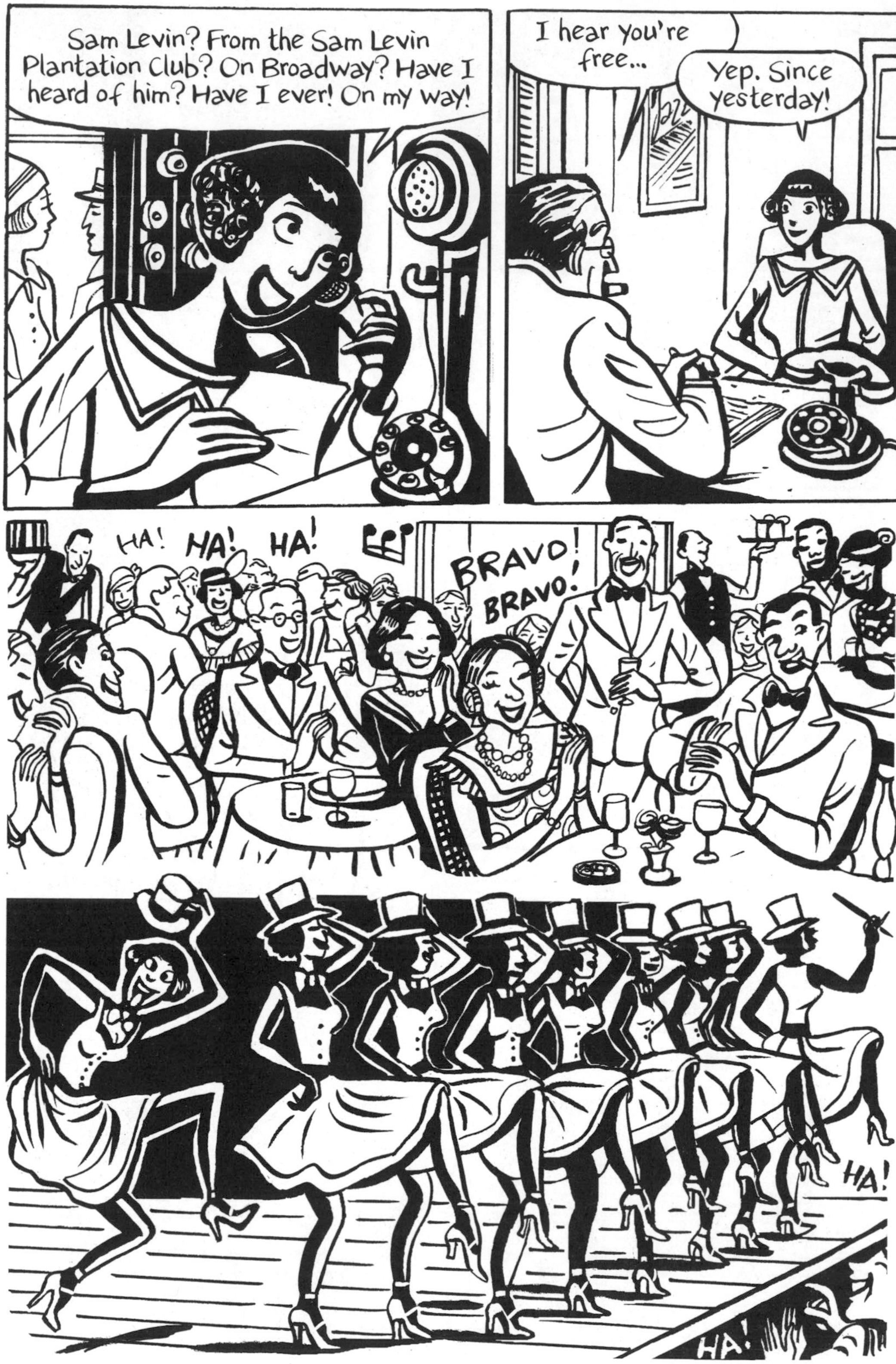
Sam Levin? From the Sam Levin Plantation Club? On Broadway? Have I heard of him? Have I ever! On my way!
I hear you're free...
Yep. Since yesterday!
HA! HA! HA!
BRAVO! BRAVO!
HA!
HA

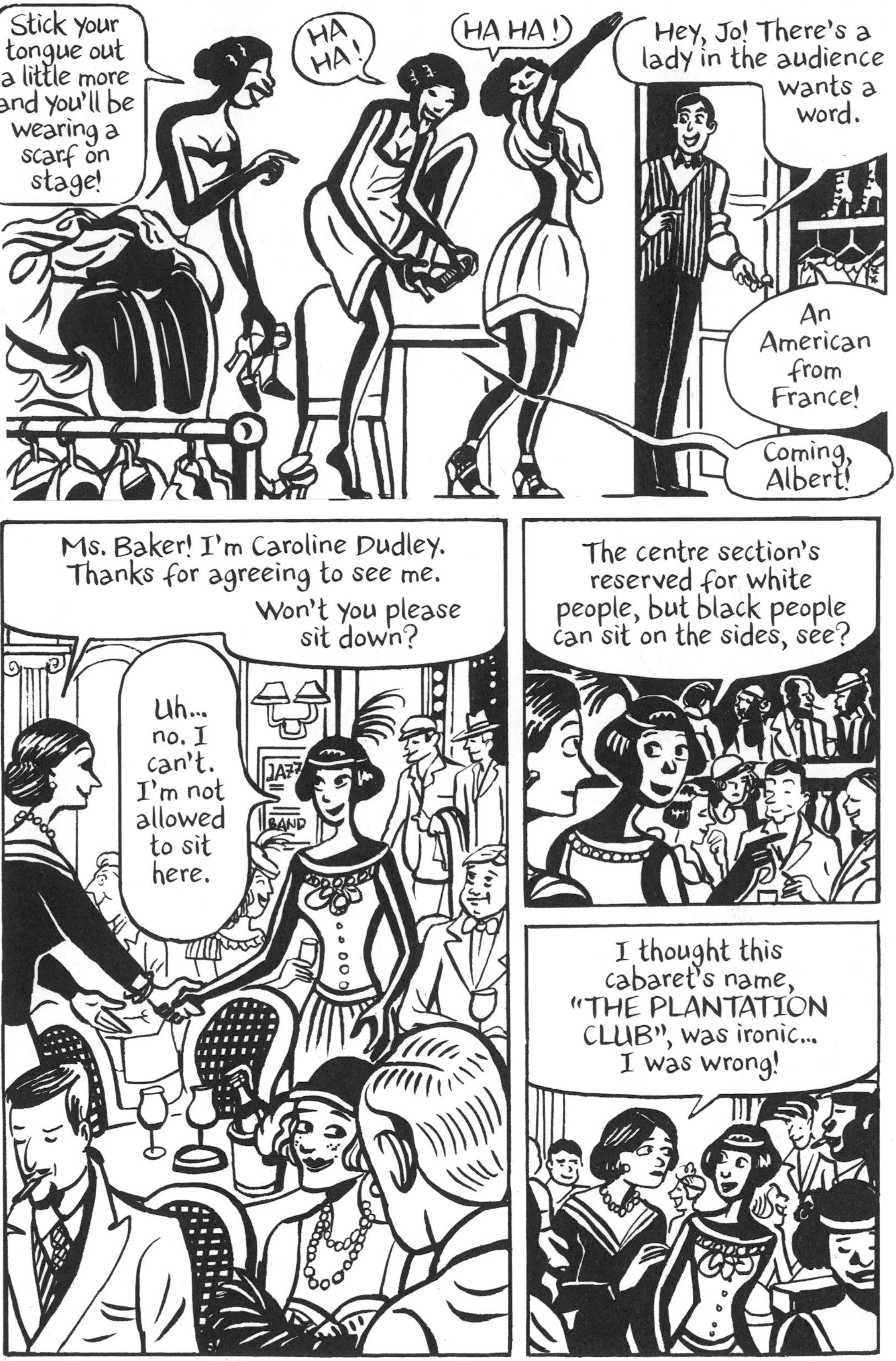
Stick your tongue out a little more and you'll be wearing a scarf on stage!
HA HA!
HA HA!
Hey, Jo! There's a lady in the audience wants a word.
An American from France!
Coming, Albert!
Ms. Baker! I'm Caroline Dudley. Thanks for agreeing to see me.
Won't you please sit down?
Uh... no. I can't. I'm not allowed to sit here.
JAZZ
BAND
The centre section's reserved for white people, but black people can sit on the sides, see?
I thought this cabaret's name, "THE PLANTATION CLUB", was ironic... I was wrong!

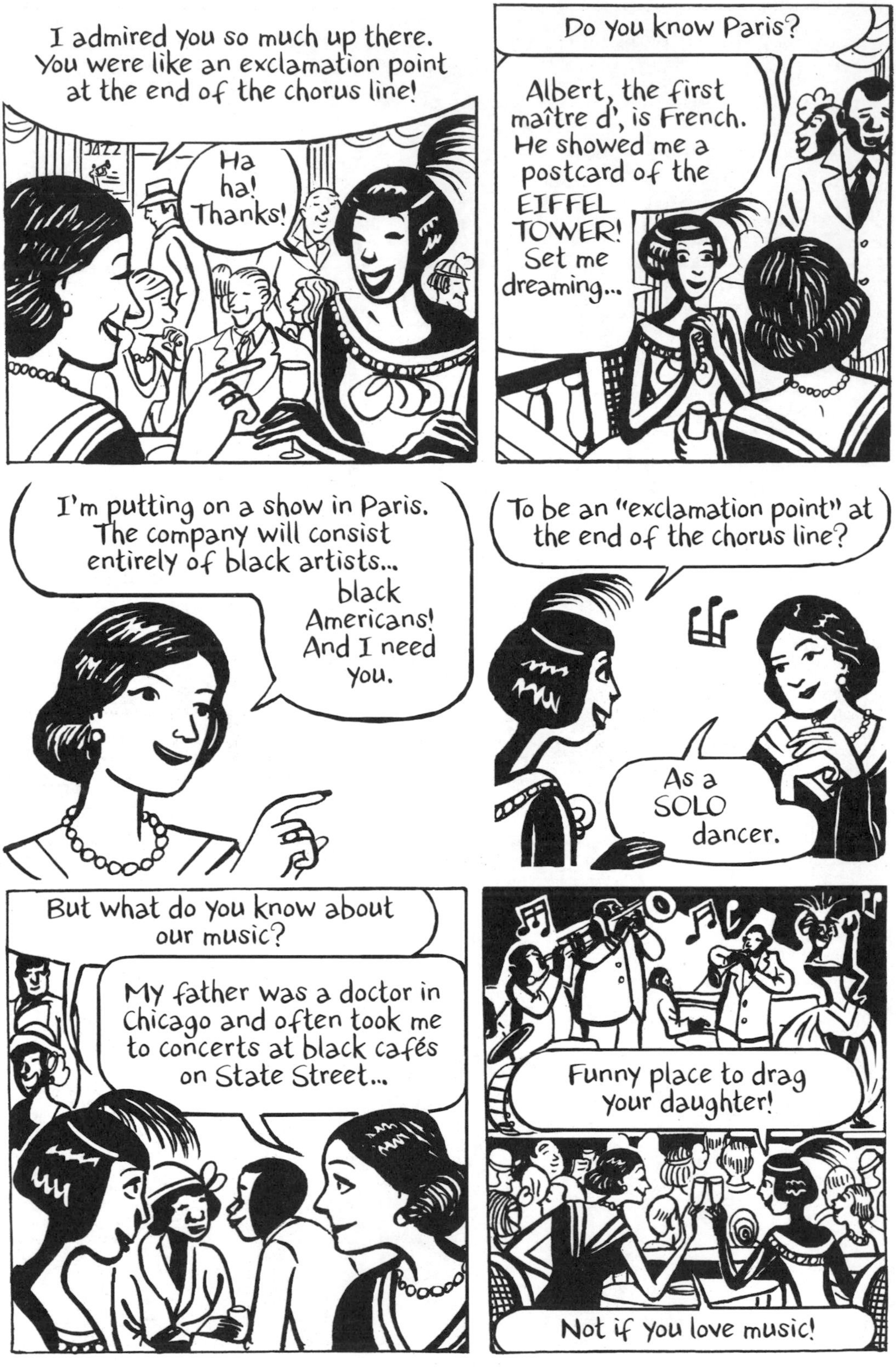
I admired you so much up there. You were like an exclamation point at the end of the chorus line!
JAZZ
Ha ha! Thanks!
Do you know Paris?
Albert, the first maître d', is French. He showed me a postcard of the EIFFEL TOWER! Set me dreaming...
I'm putting on a show in Paris. The company will consist entirely of black artists...
black Americans! And I need you.
To be an "exclamation point" at the end of the chorus line?
As a SOLO dancer.
But what do you know about our music?
My father was a doctor in Chicago and often took me to concerts at black cafés on State Street...
Funny place to drag your daughter!
Not if you love music!

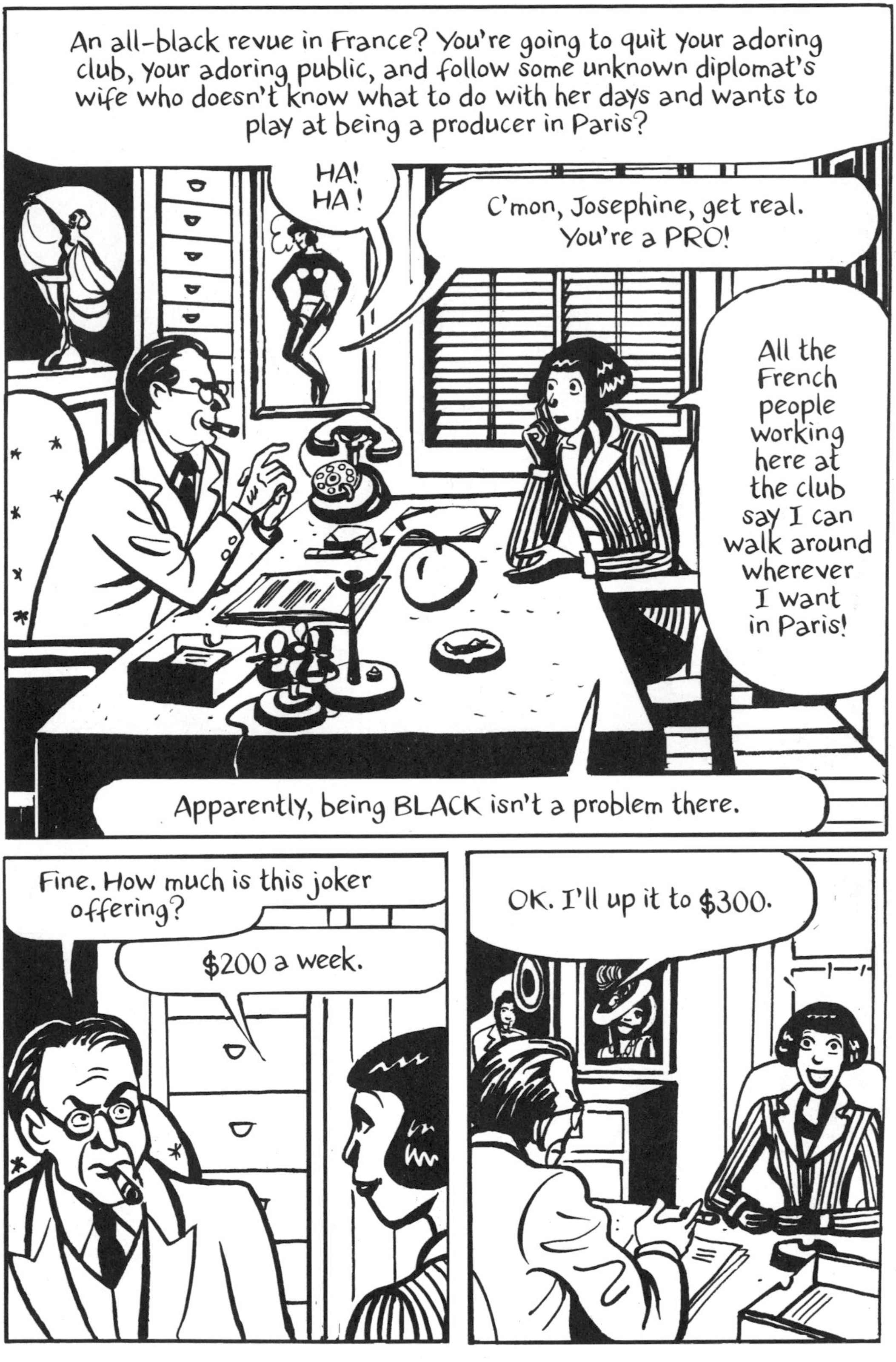

An all-black revue in France? You're going to quit your adoring club, your adoring public, and follow some unknown diplomat's wife who doesn't know what to do with her days and wants to play at being a producer in Paris?
HA! HA!
C'mon, Josephine, get real. You're a PRO!
All the French people working here at the club say I can walk around wherever I want in Paris!
Apparently, being BLACK isn't a problem there.
Fine. How much is this joker offering?
$200 a week.
OK. I'll up it to $300.

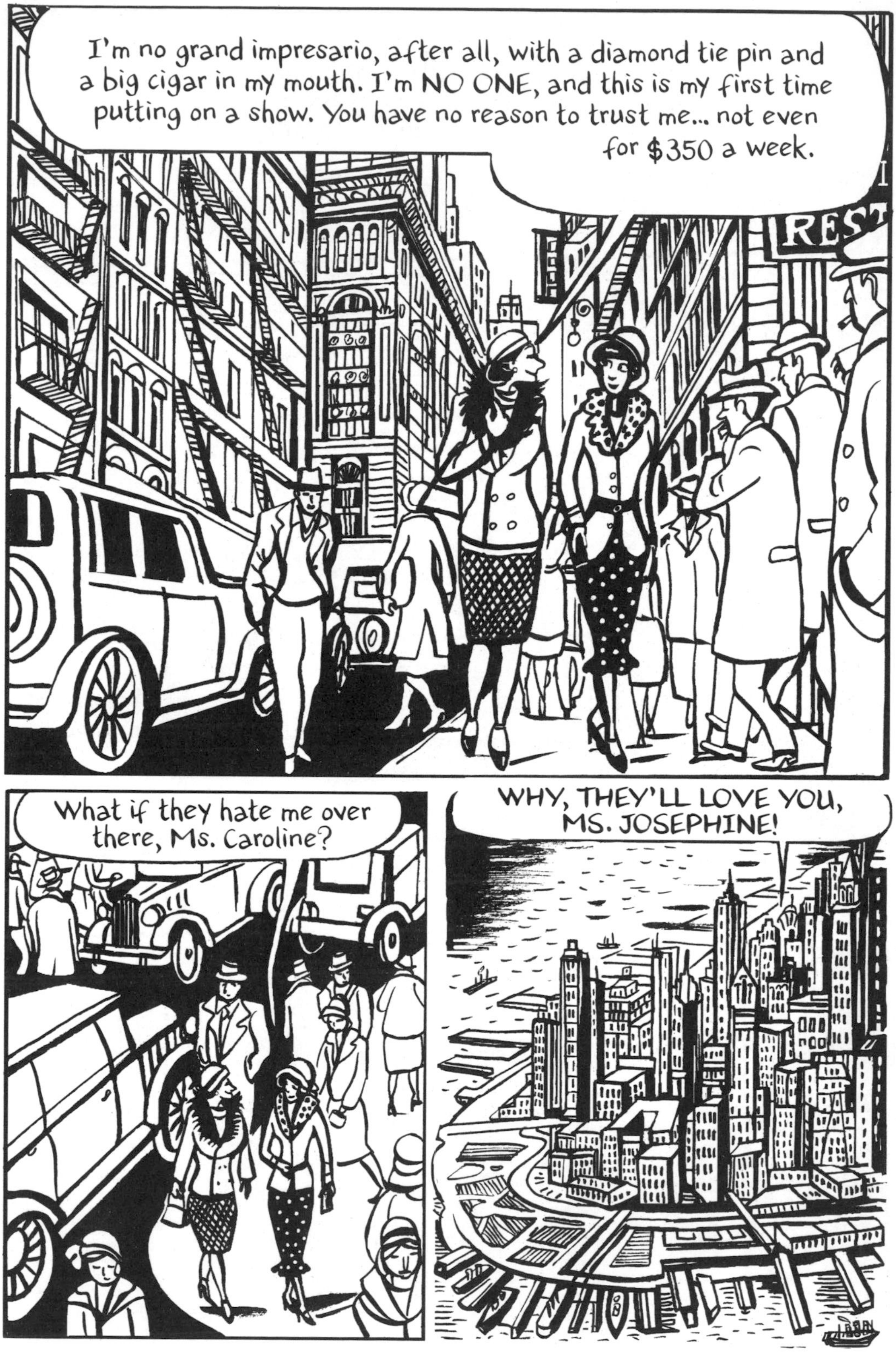
I'm no grand impresario, after all, with a diamond tie pin and a big cigar in my mouth. I'm NO ONE, and this is my first time putting on a show. You have no reason to trust me... not even for $350 a week.
What if they hate me over there, Ms. Caroline?
WHY, THEY'LL LOVE YOU, MS. JOSEPHINE!

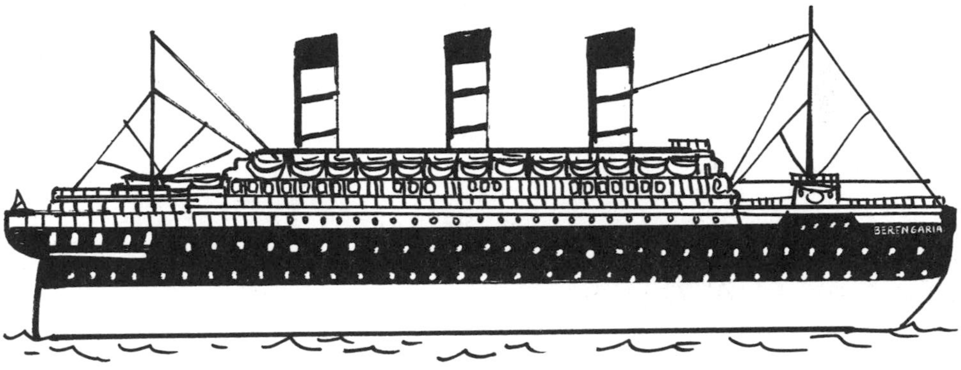
BERENGARIA

1925: The *Berengaria*, Atlantic Ocean

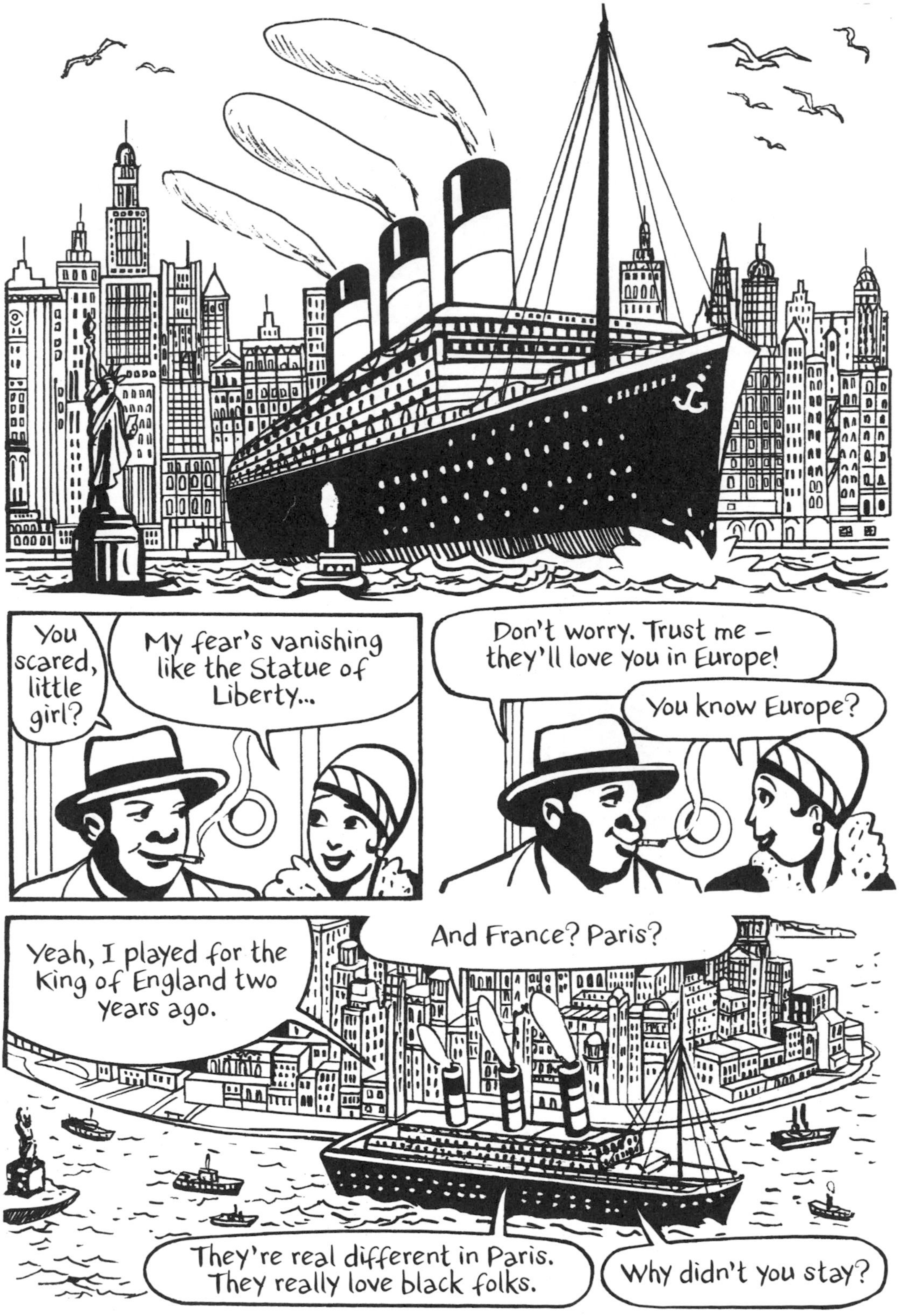
You scared, little girl?
My fear's vanishing like the Statue of Liberty...
Don't worry. Trust me – they'll love you in Europe!
You know Europe?
Yeah, I played for the King of England two years ago.
And France? Paris?
They're real different in Paris. They really love black folks.
Why didn't you stay?

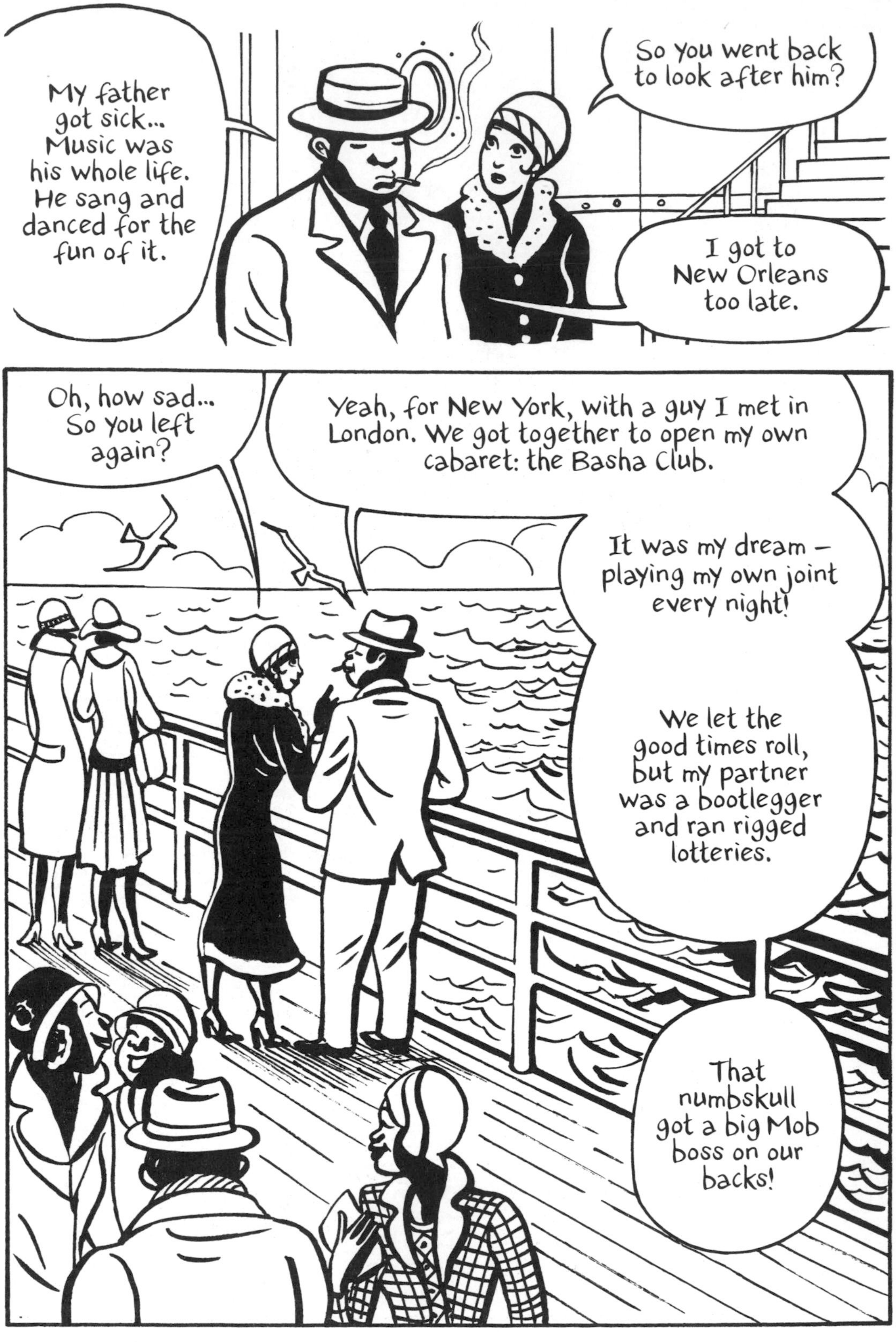
My father got sick... Music was his whole life. He sang and danced for the fun of it.
So you went back to look after him?
I got to New Orleans too late.
Oh, how sad... So you left again?
Yeah, for New York, with a guy I met in London. We got together to open my own cabaret: the Basha Club.
It was my dream – playing my own joint every night!
We let the good times roll, but my partner was a bootlegger and ran rigged lotteries.
That numbskull got a big Mob boss on our backs!

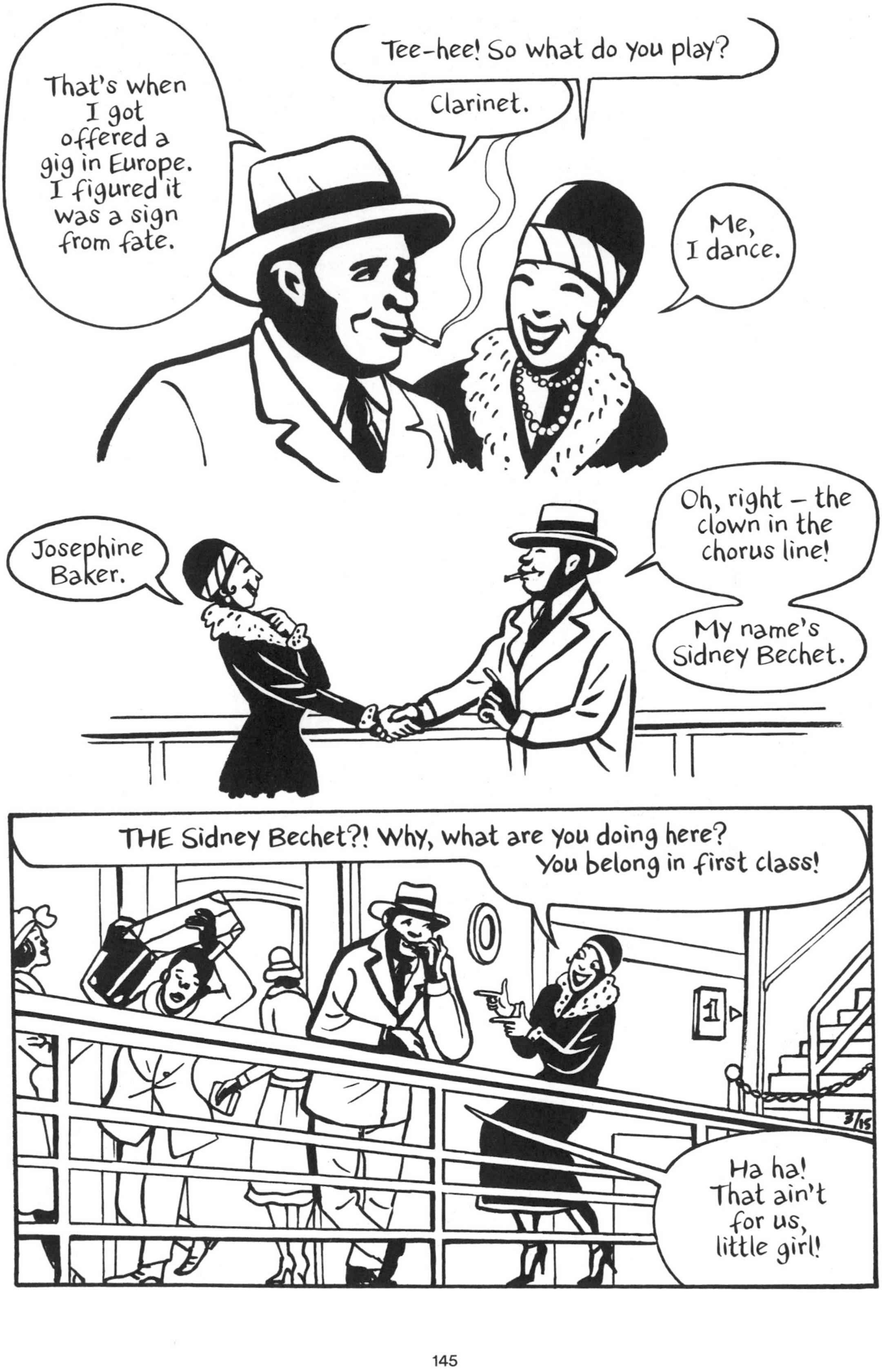

That's when I got offered a gig in Europe. I figured it was a sign from fate.
Tee-hee! So what do you play?
Clarinet.
Me, I dance.
Josephine Baker.
Oh, right – the clown in the chorus line!
My name's Sidney Bechet.
THE Sidney Bechet?! Why, what are you doing here? You belong in first class!
Ha ha! That ain't for us, little girl!

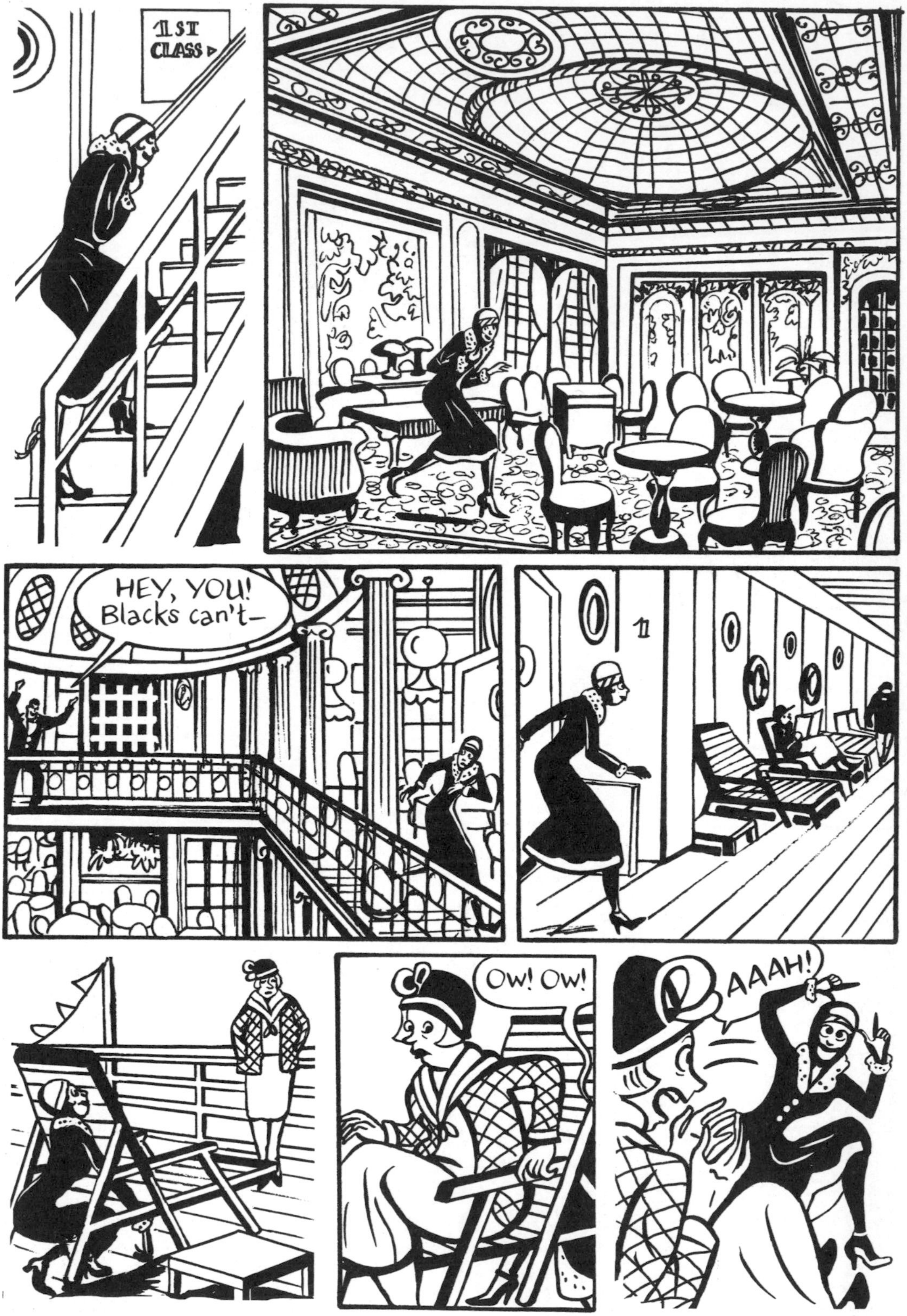

1ST CLASS ▹
HEY, YOU! Blacks can't—
OW! OW!
AAAH!

I understand, steward. Her intrusion into first class was unacceptable!
Ms. Paxton almost died of a heart attack!
You should lock that piccaninny up in her cell – I mean, cabin – till we reach Cherbourg!
Show me who did it and I'll make sure no such incident ever happens again, Ms. Paxton.
How am I supposed to point her out...?
They all look the same!
Well, either I punish all of them or none of them!
Josephine!
It was a joke, Ms. Caroline!

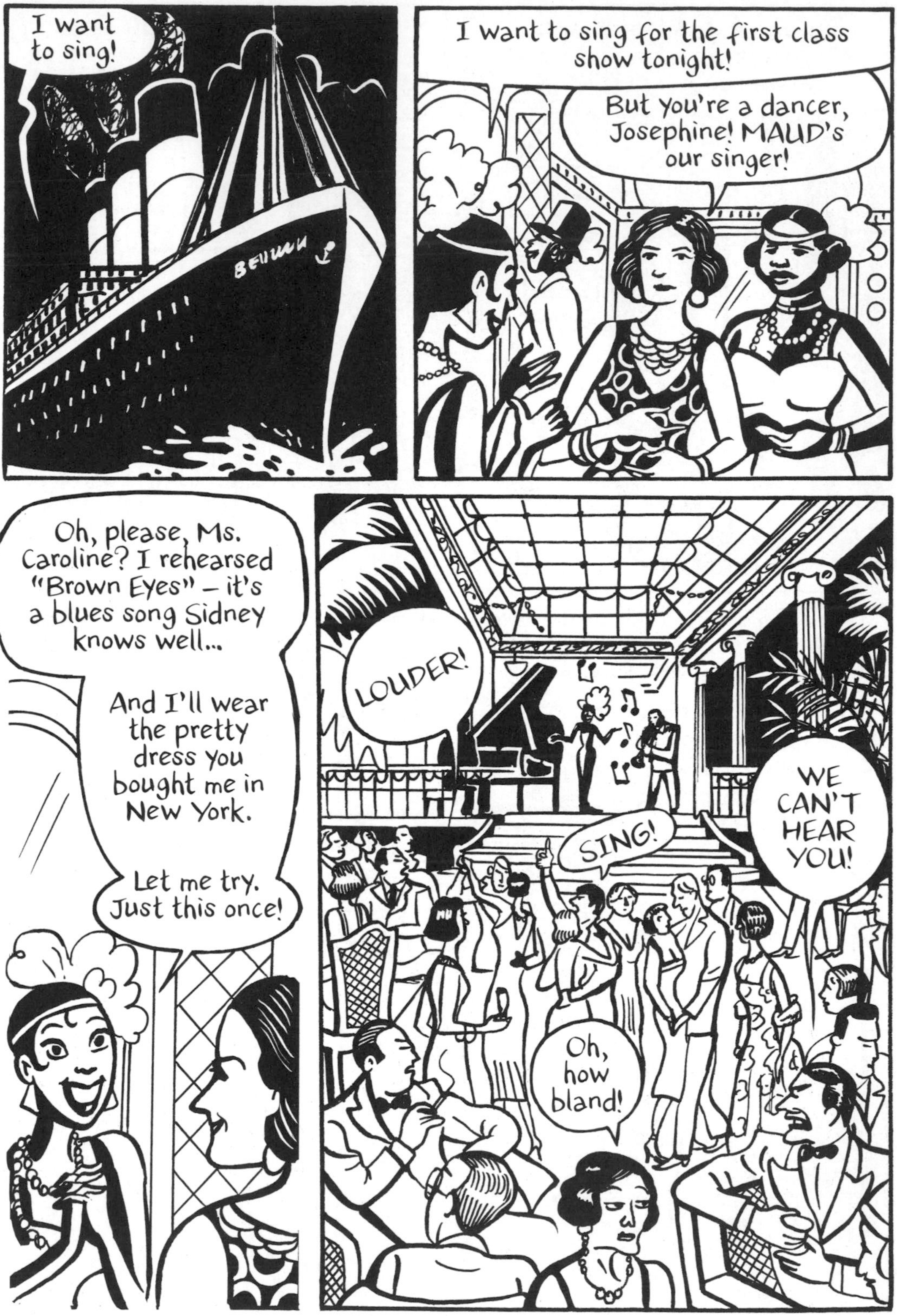
I want to sing!
BEIIWIN
I want to sing for the first class show tonight!
But you're a dancer, Josephine! MAUD's our singer!
Oh, please, Ms. Caroline? I rehearsed "Brown Eyes" – it's a blues song Sidney knows well...
And I'll wear the pretty dress you bought me in New York.
Let me try. Just this once!
LOUDER!
SING!
WE CAN'T HEAR YOU!
Oh, how bland!

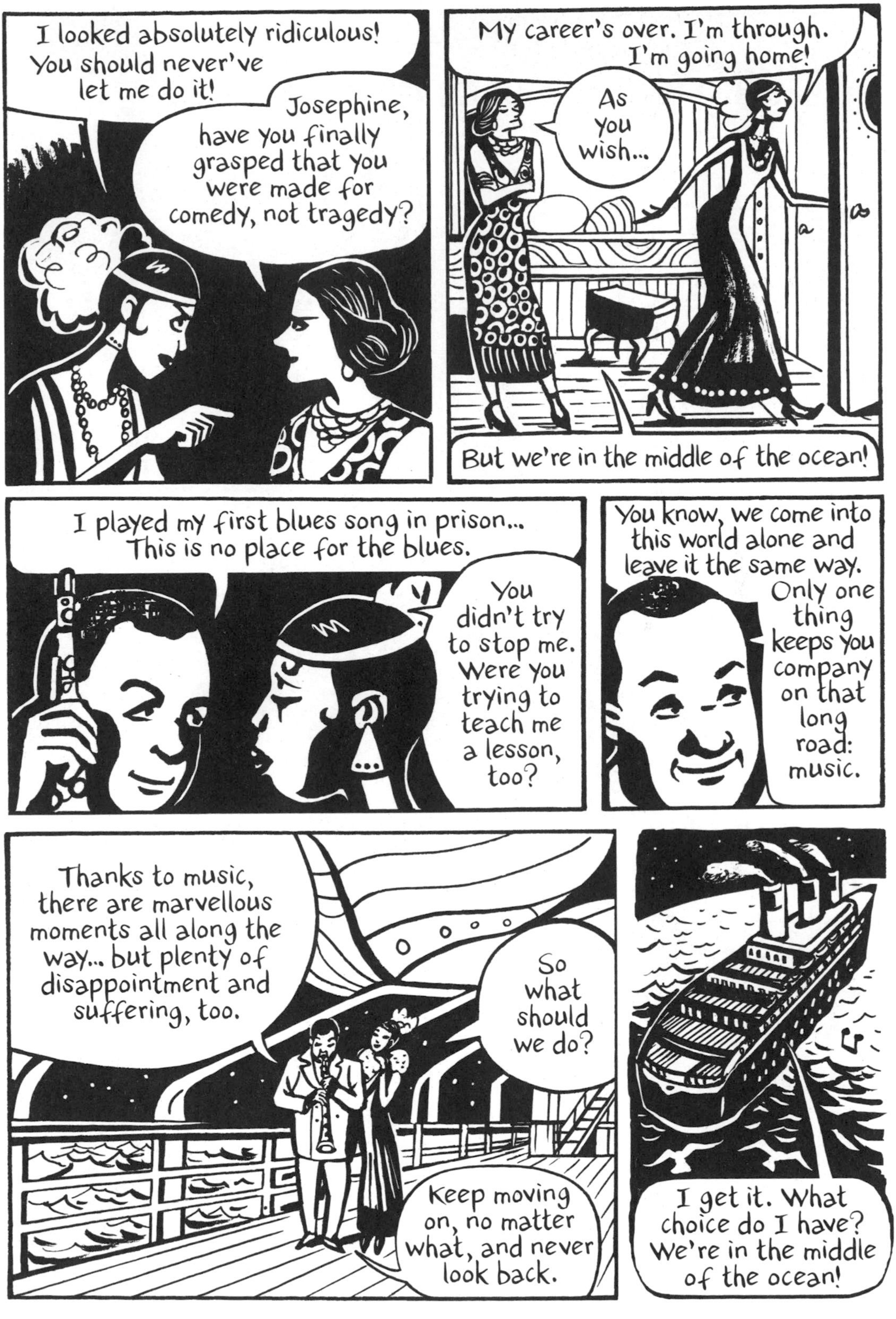

I looked absolutely ridiculous! You should never've let me do it!
Josephine, have you finally grasped that you were made for comedy, not tragedy?
My career's over. I'm through. I'm going home!
As you wish...
But we're in the middle of the ocean!
I played my first blues song in prison... This is no place for the blues.
You didn't try to stop me. Were you trying to teach me a lesson, too?
You know, we come into this world alone and leave it the same way.
Only one thing keeps you company on that long road: music.
Thanks to music, there are marvellous moments all along the way... but plenty of disappointment and suffering, too.
So what should we do?
Keep moving on, no matter what, and never look back.
I get it. What choice do I have? We're in the middle of the ocean!

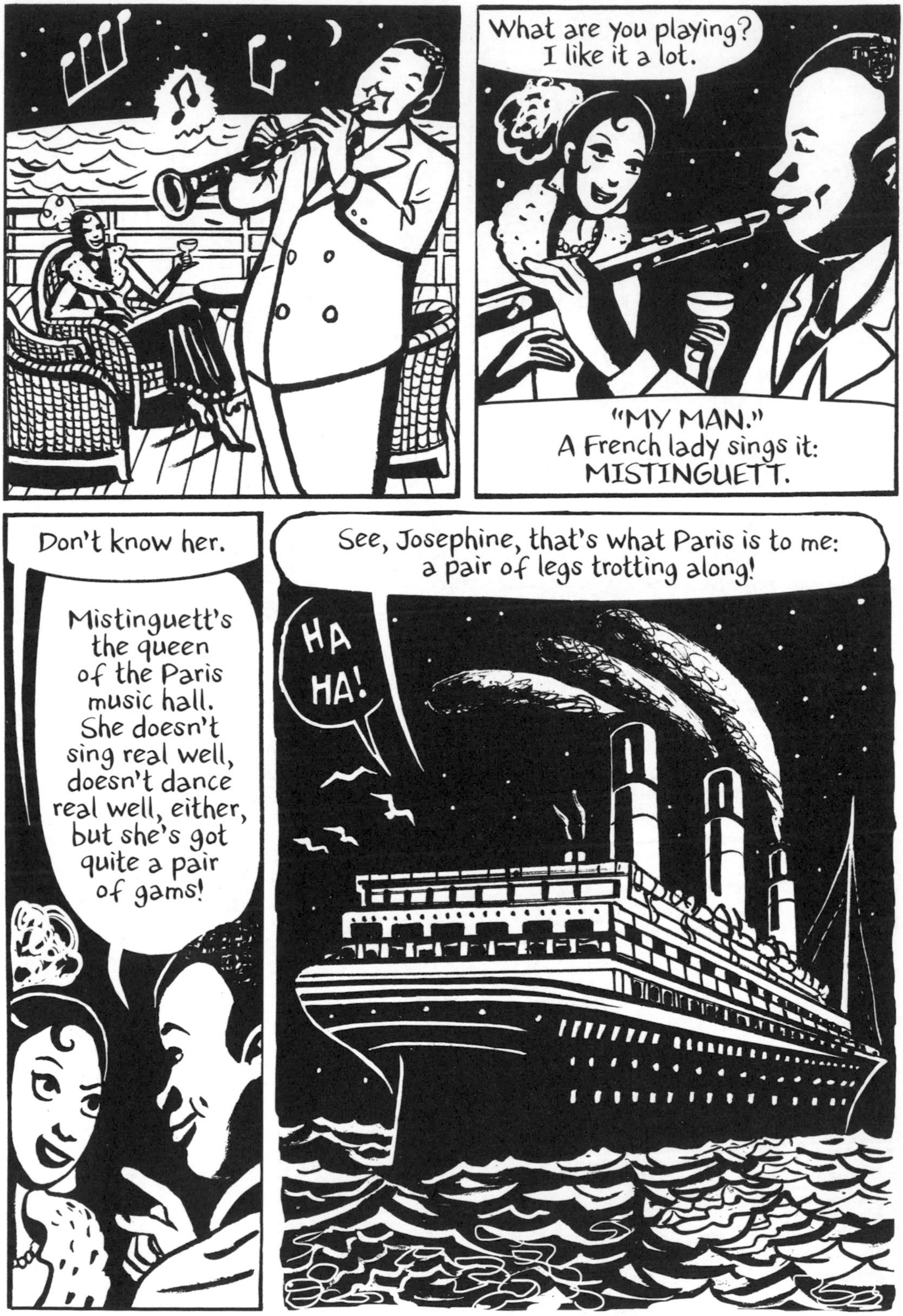
What are you playing? I like it a lot.
"MY MAN." A French lady sings it: MISTINGUETT.
Don't know her.
Mistinguett's the queen of the Paris music hall. She doesn't sing real well, doesn't dance real well, either, but she's got quite a pair of gams!
See, Josephine, that's what Paris is to me: a pair of legs trotting along!
HA HA!

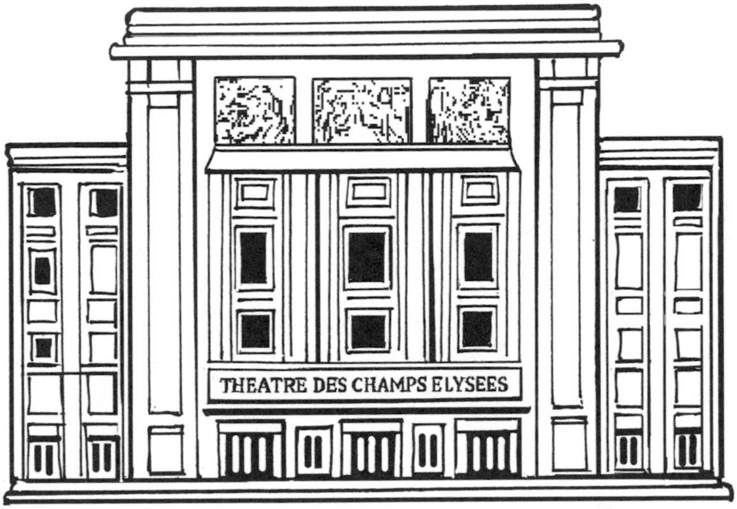
THEATRE DES CHAMPS ELYSEES

1925: Théâtre des Champs-Élysées,
Avenue Montaigne, Paris, France

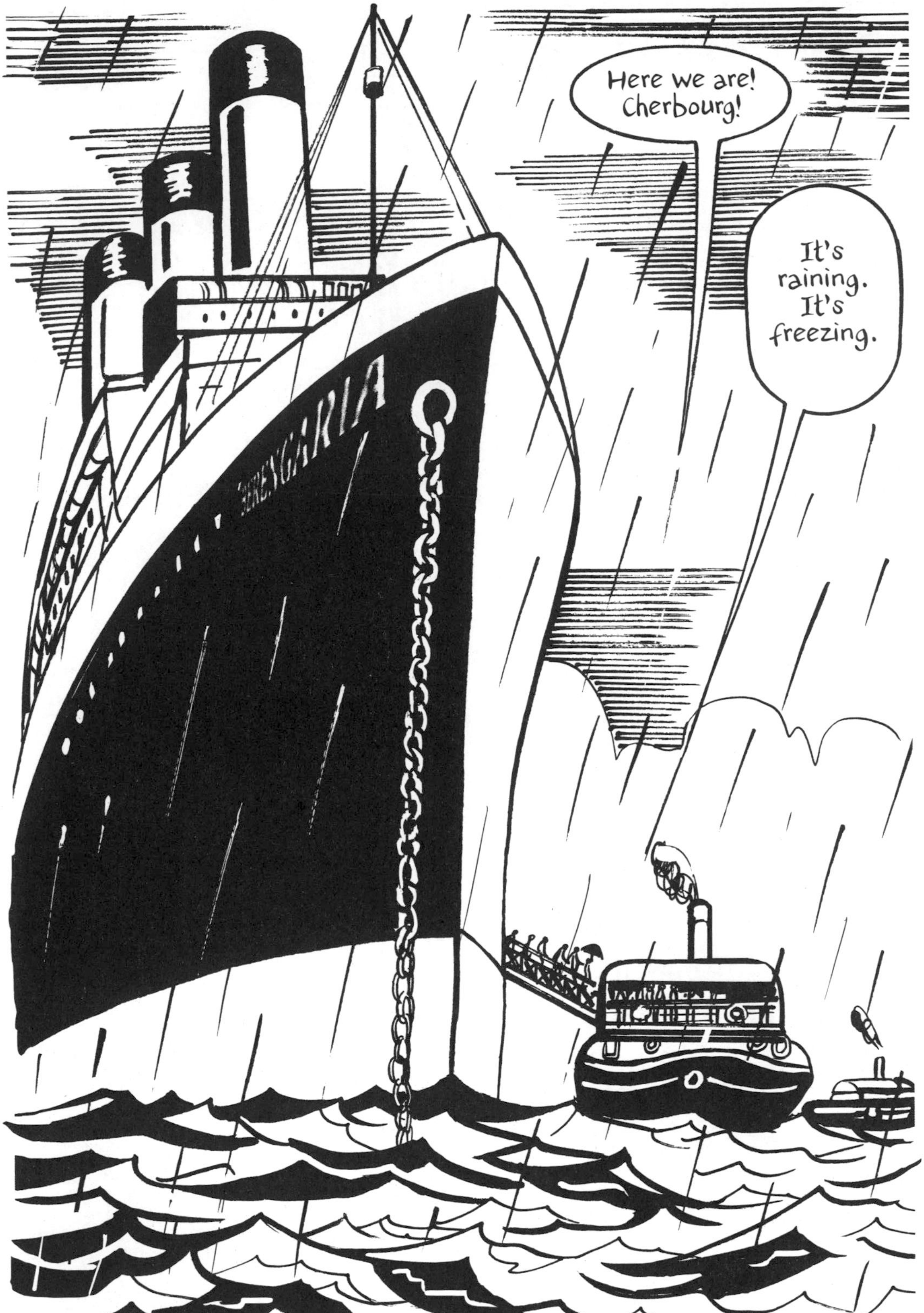
BERENGARIA
Here we are! Cherbourg!
It's raining. It's freezing.

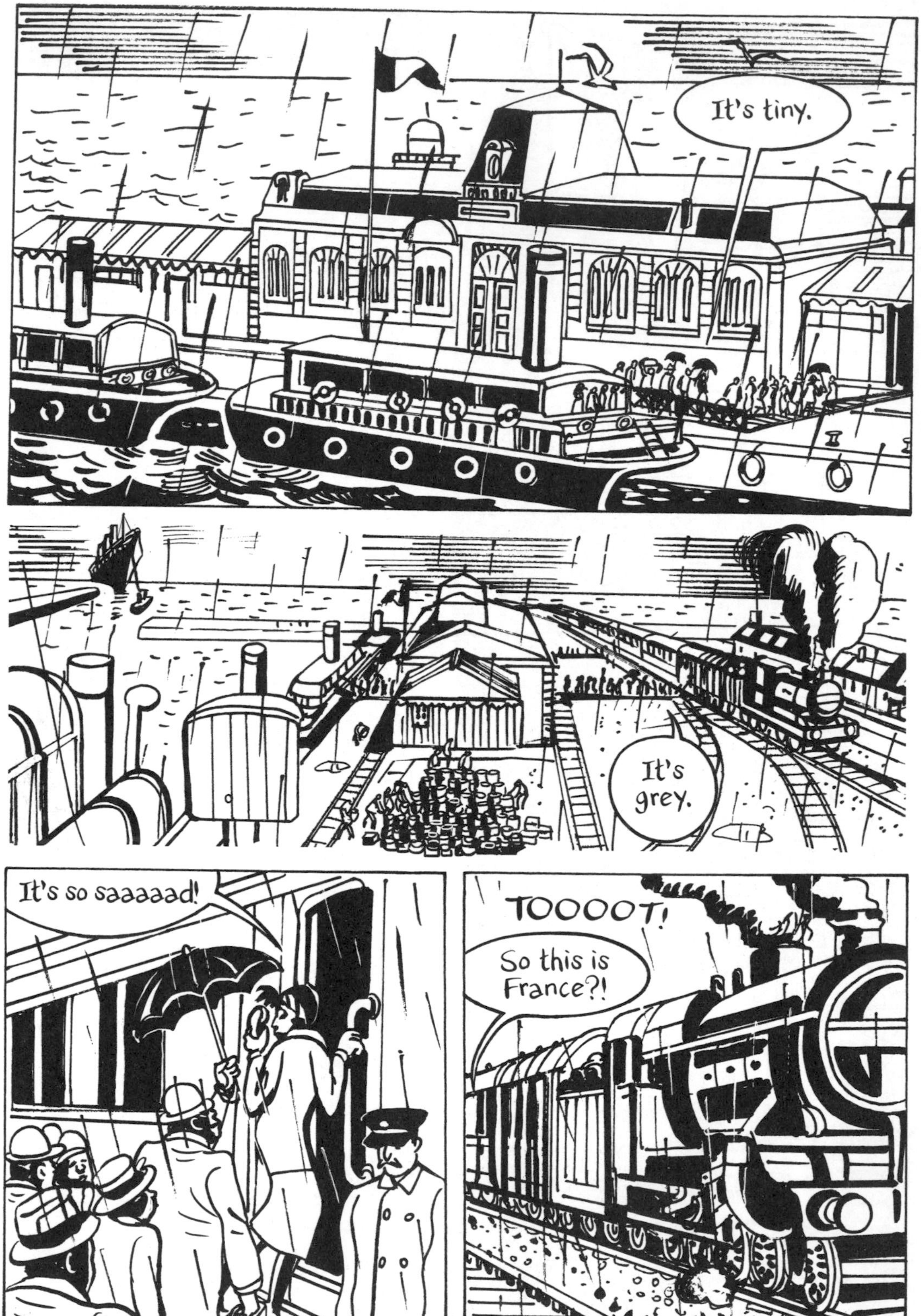
It's tiny.
It's grey.
It's so saaaaad!
TOOOOT!
So this is France?!

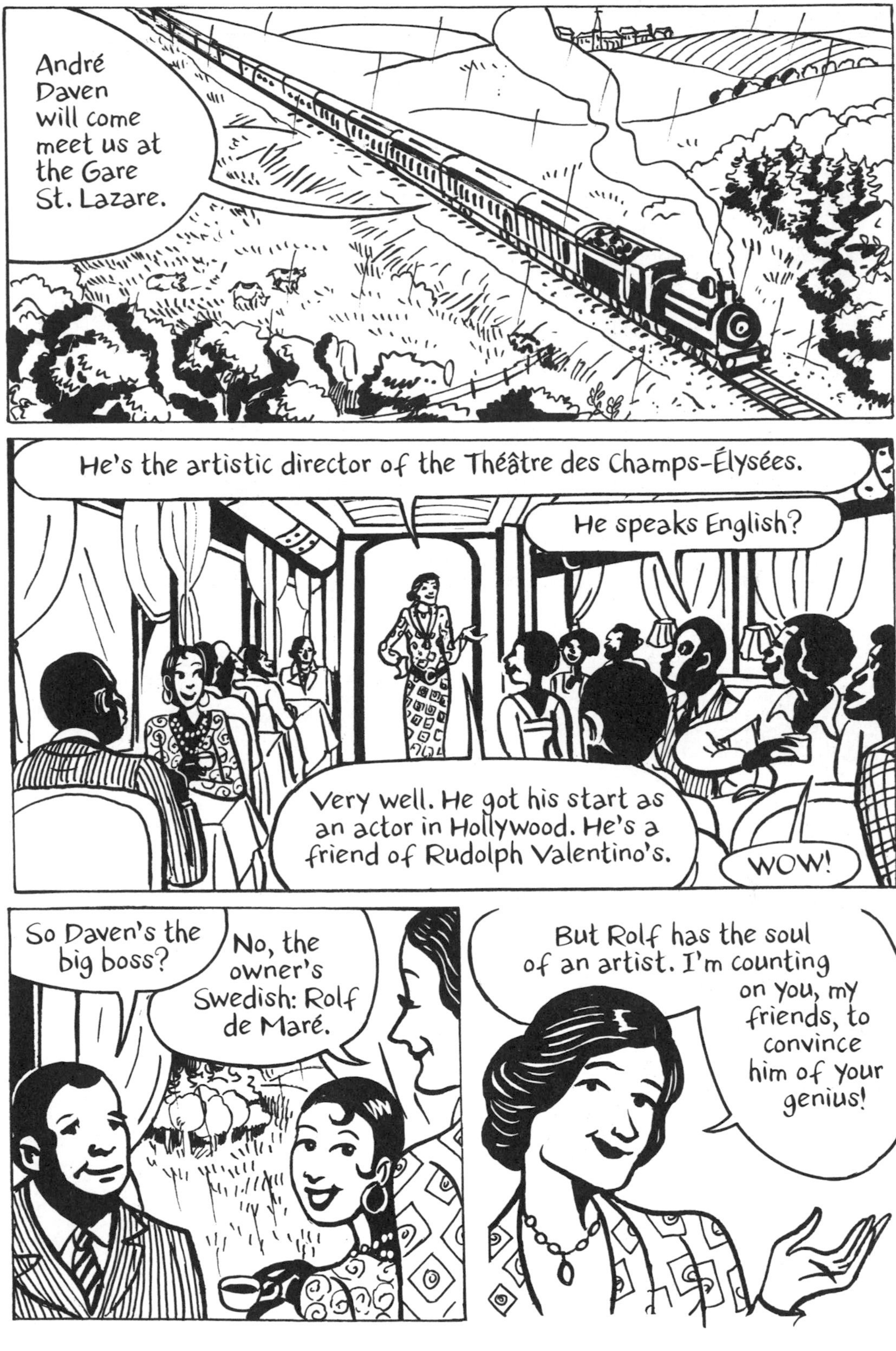
André Daven will come meet us at the Gare St. Lazare.
He's the artistic director of the Théâtre des Champs-Élysées.
He speaks English?
Very well. He got his start as an actor in Hollywood. He's a friend of Rudolph Valentino's.
WOW!
So Daven's the big boss?
No, the owner's Swedish: Rolf de Maré.
But Rolf has the soul of an artist. I'm counting on you, my friends, to convince him of your genius!

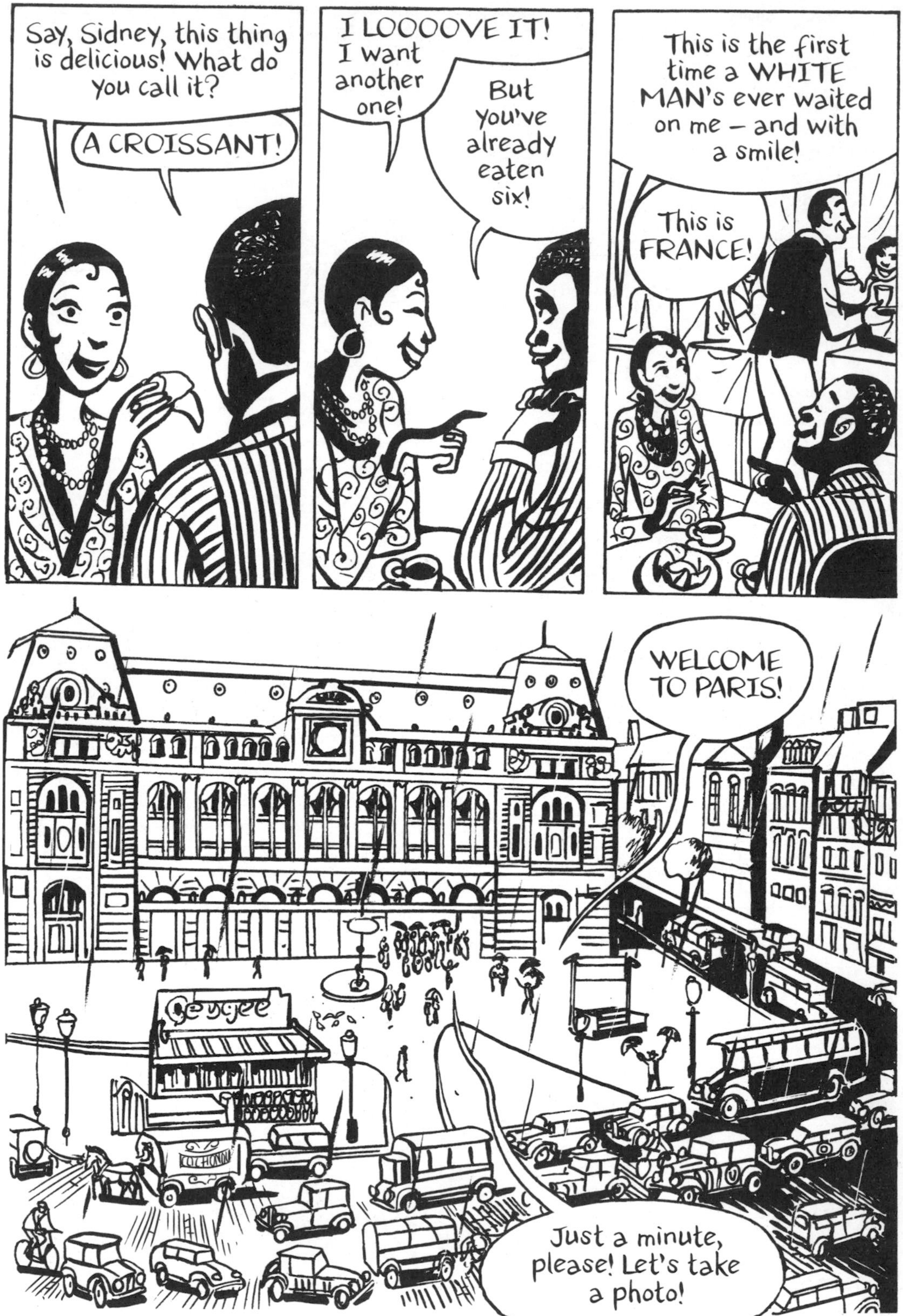
Say, Sidney, this thing is delicious! What do you call it?
A CROISSANT!
I LOOOOVE IT! I want another one!
But you've already eaten six!
This is the first time a WHITE MAN's ever waited on me – and with a smile!
This is FRANCE!
WELCOME TO PARIS!
Just a minute, please! Let's take a photo!

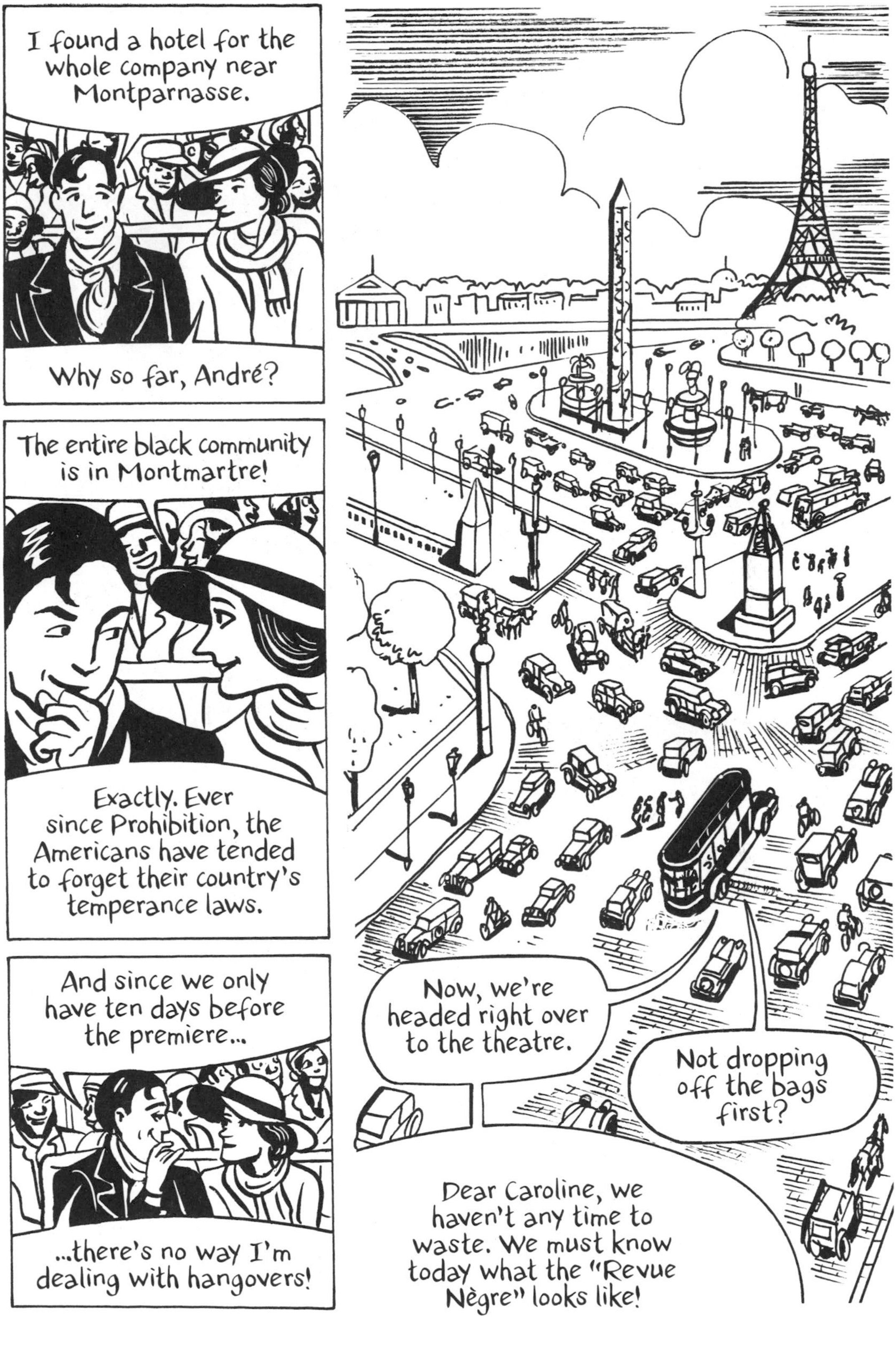
I found a hotel for the whole company near Montparnasse.
Why so far, André?
The entire black community is in Montmartre!
Exactly. Ever since Prohibition, the Americans have tended to forget their country's temperance laws.
And since we only have ten days before the premiere...
...there's no way I'm dealing with hangovers!
Now, we're headed right over to the theatre.
Not dropping off the bags first?
Dear Caroline, we haven't any time to waste. We must know today what the "Revue Nègre" looks like!

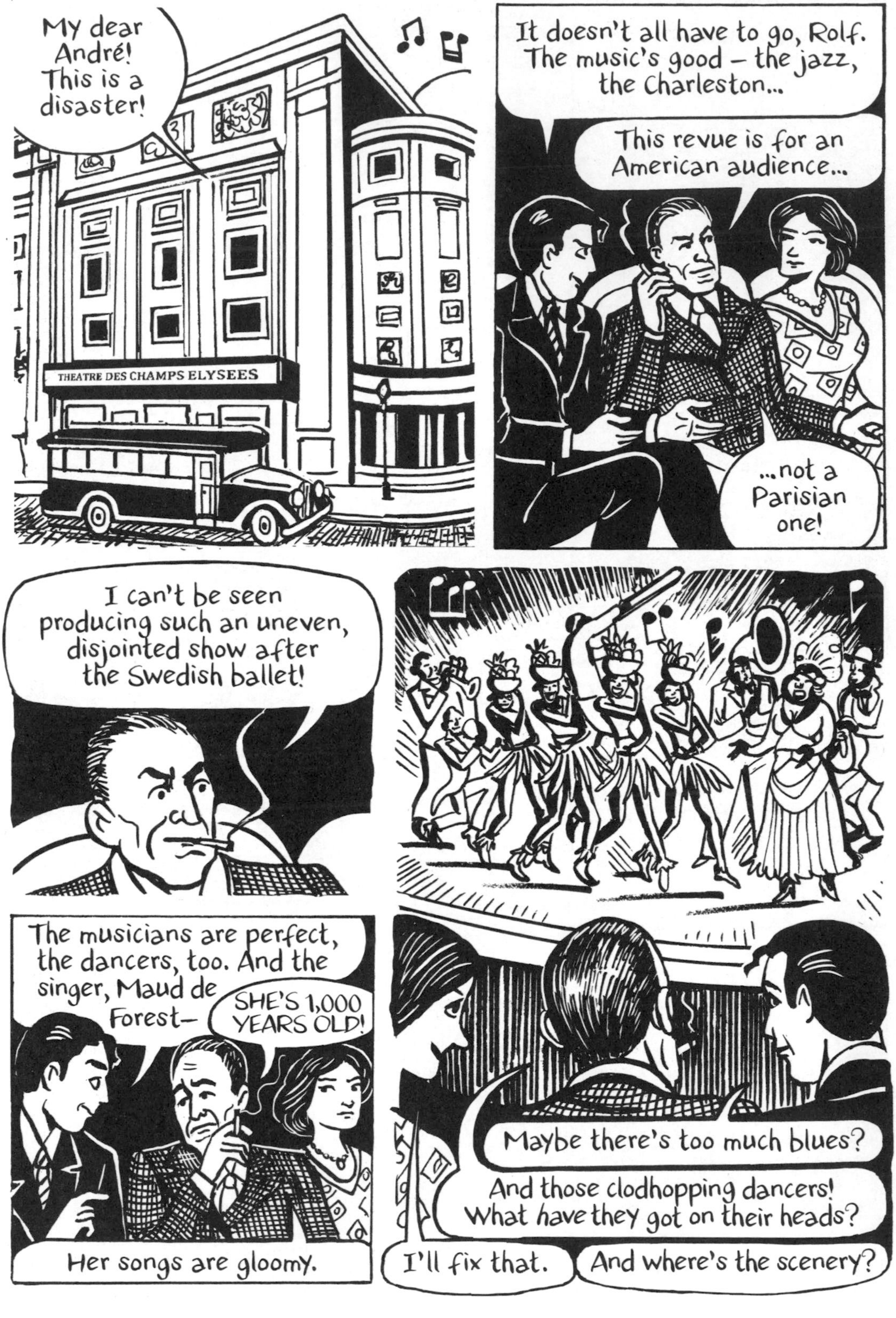
My dear André! This is a disaster!
THEATRE DES CHAMPS ELYSEES
It doesn't all have to go, Rolf. The music's good – the jazz, the Charleston...
This revue is for an American audience...
...not a Parisian one!
I can't be seen producing such an uneven, disjointed show after the Swedish ballet!
The musicians are perfect, the dancers, too. And the singer, Maud de Forest–
SHE'S 1,000 YEARS OLD!
Her songs are gloomy.
Maybe there's too much blues?
And those clodhopping dancers! What *have* they got on their heads?
I'll fix that.
And where's the scenery?

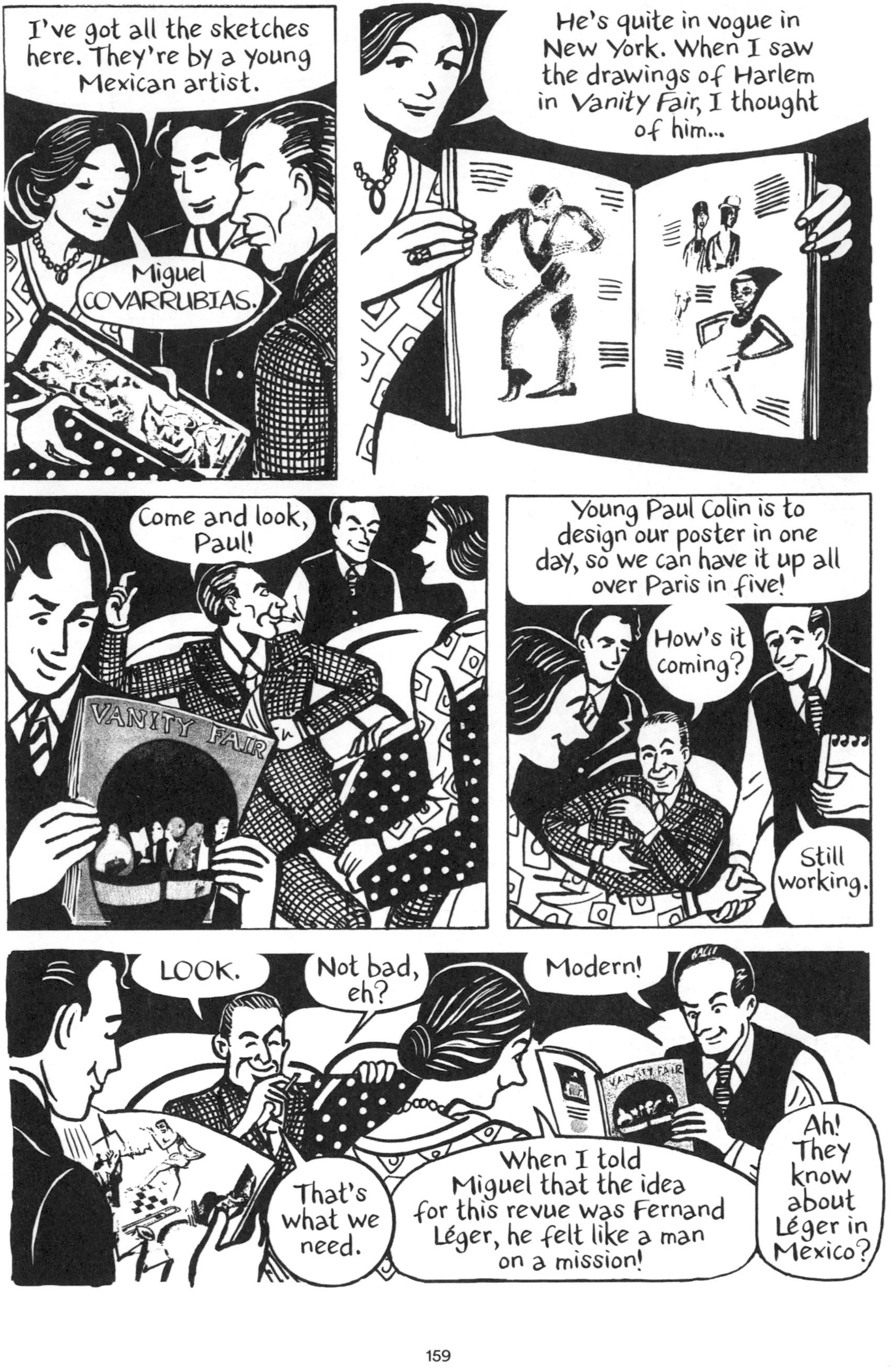
I've got all the sketches here. They're by a young Mexican artist.
Miguel COVARRUBIAS.
He's quite in vogue in New York. When I saw the drawings of Harlem in *Vanity Fair*, I thought of him...
Come and look, Paul!
VANITY FAIR
Young Paul Colin is to design our poster in one day, so we can have it up all over Paris in five!
How's it coming?
Still working.
LOOK.
Not bad, eh?
Modern!
VANITY FAIR
That's what we need.
When I told Miguel that the idea for this revue was Fernand Léger, he felt like a man on a mission!
Ah! They know about Léger in Mexico?

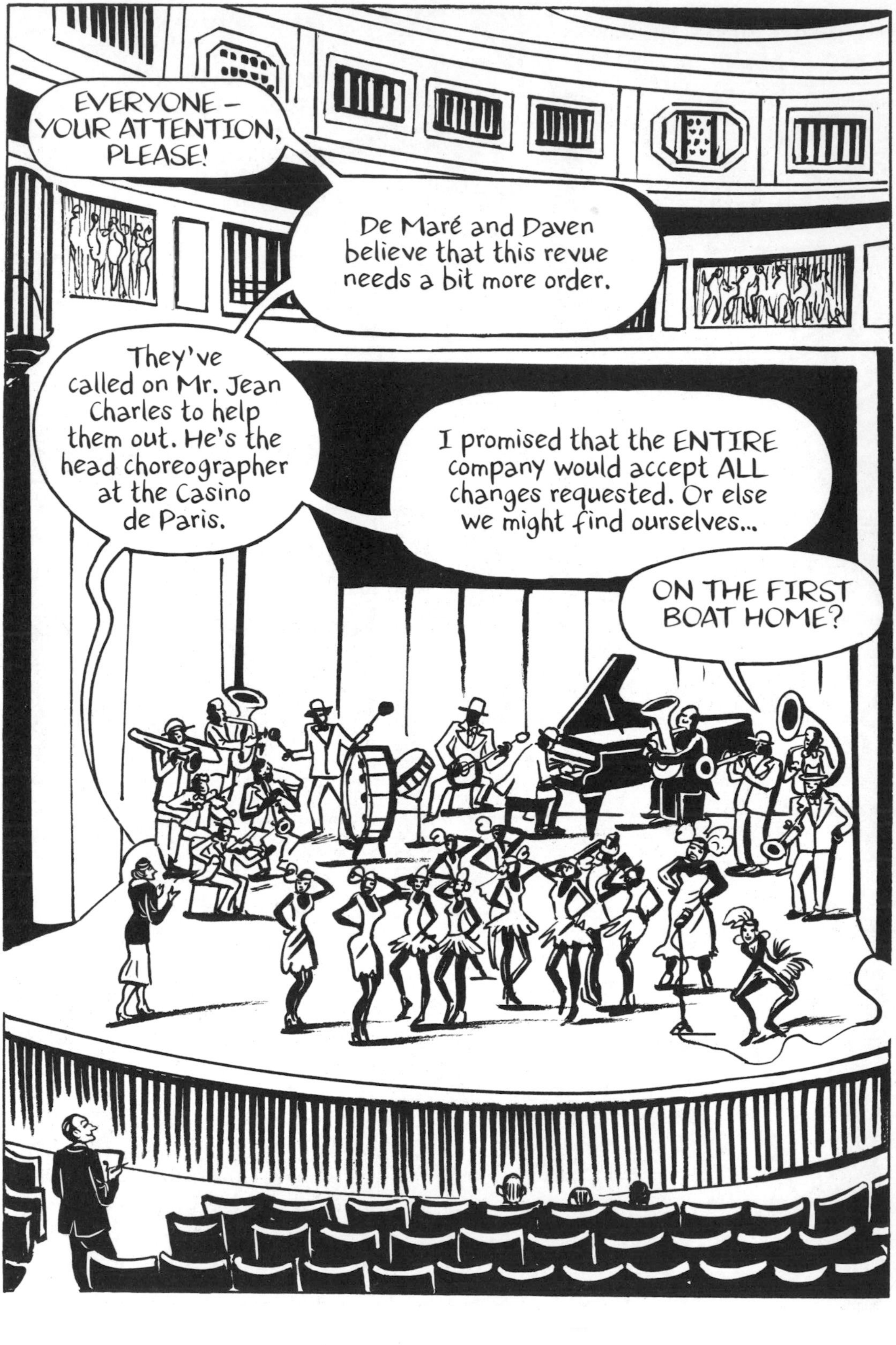
EVERYONE – YOUR ATTENTION, PLEASE!
De Maré and Daven believe that this revue needs a bit more order.
They've called on Mr. Jean Charles to help them out. He's the head choreographer at the Casino de Paris.
I promised that the ENTIRE company would accept ALL changes requested. Or else we might find ourselves...
ON THE FIRST BOAT HOME?

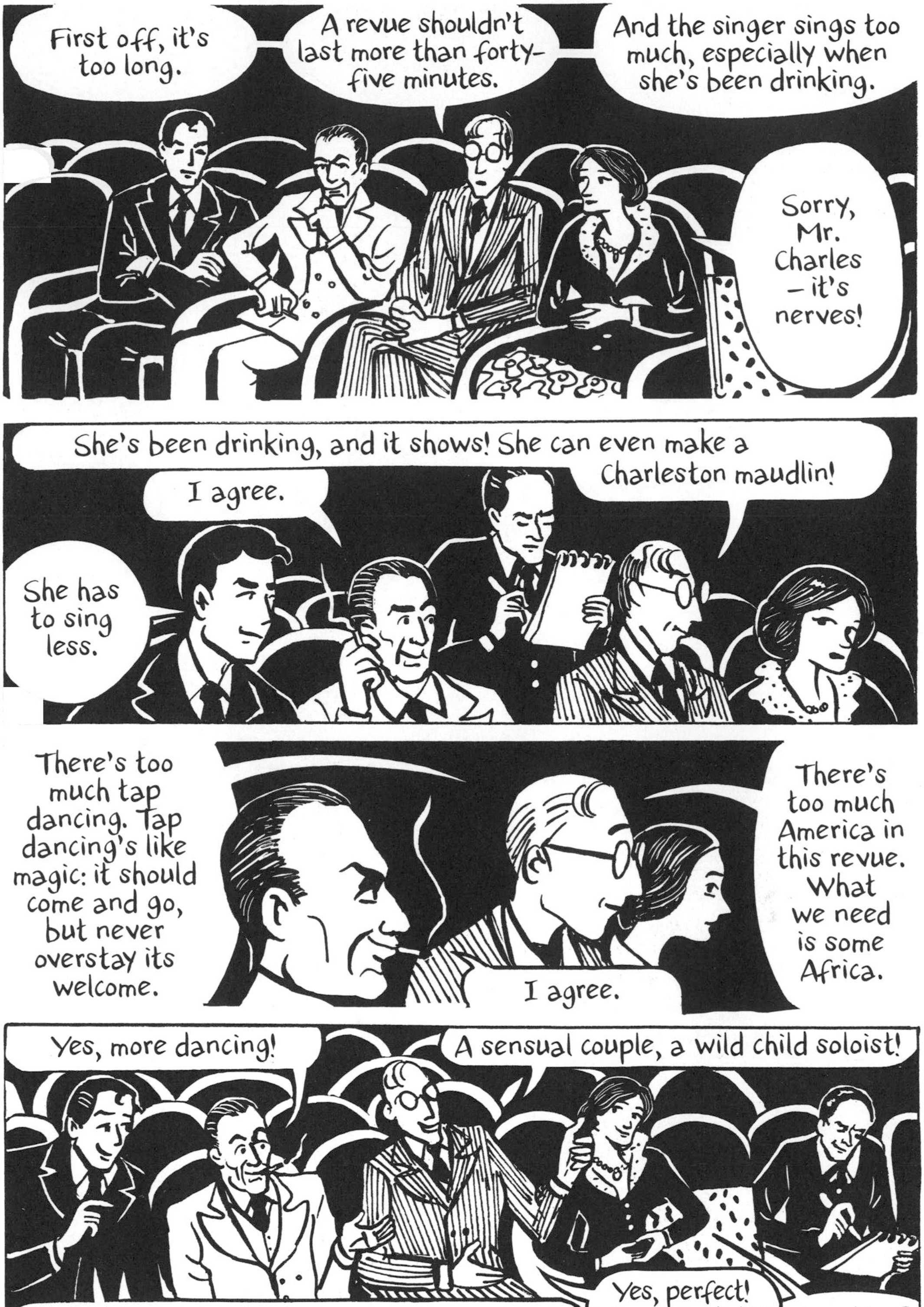
First off, it's too long.
A revue shouldn't last more than forty-five minutes.
And the singer sings too much, especially when she's been drinking.
Sorry, Mr. Charles – it's nerves!
She's been drinking, and it shows! She can even make a Charleston maudlin!
I agree.
She has to sing less.
There's too much tap dancing. Tap dancing's like magic: it should come and go, but never overstay its welcome.
I agree.
There's too much America in this revue. What we need is some Africa.
Yes, more dancing!
A sensual couple, a wild child soloist!
Like that funny-looking, cross-eyed gal over there?
Yes, perfect! Very animalistic!
Josephine?

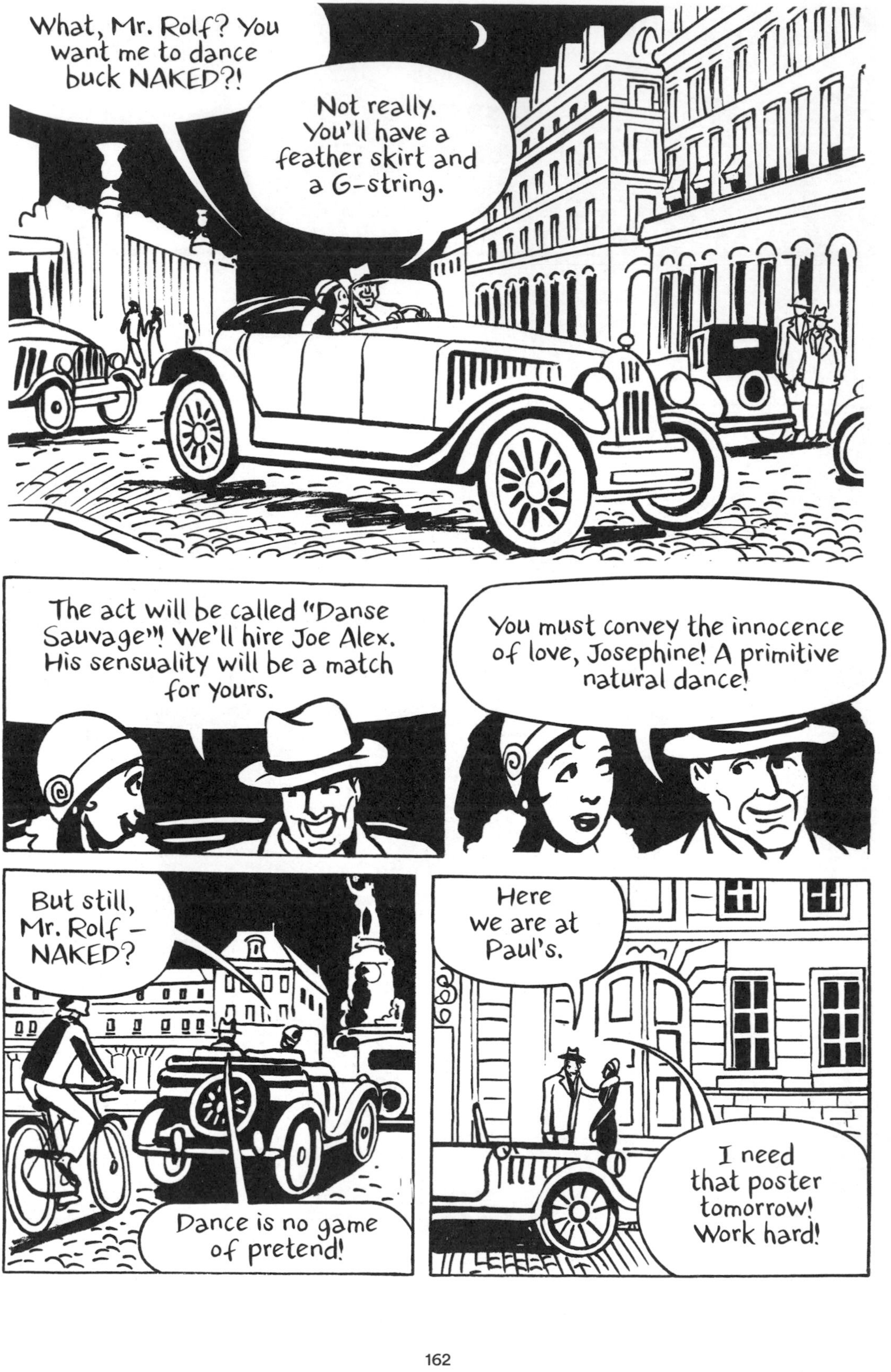
What, Mr. Rolf? You want me to dance buck NAKED?!
Not really. You'll have a feather skirt and a G-string.
The act will be called "Danse Sauvage"! We'll hire Joe Alex. His sensuality will be a match for yours.
You must convey the innocence of love, Josephine! A primitive natural dance!
But still, Mr. Rolf – NAKED?
Dance is no game of pretend!
Here we are at Paul's.
I need that poster tomorrow! Work hard!

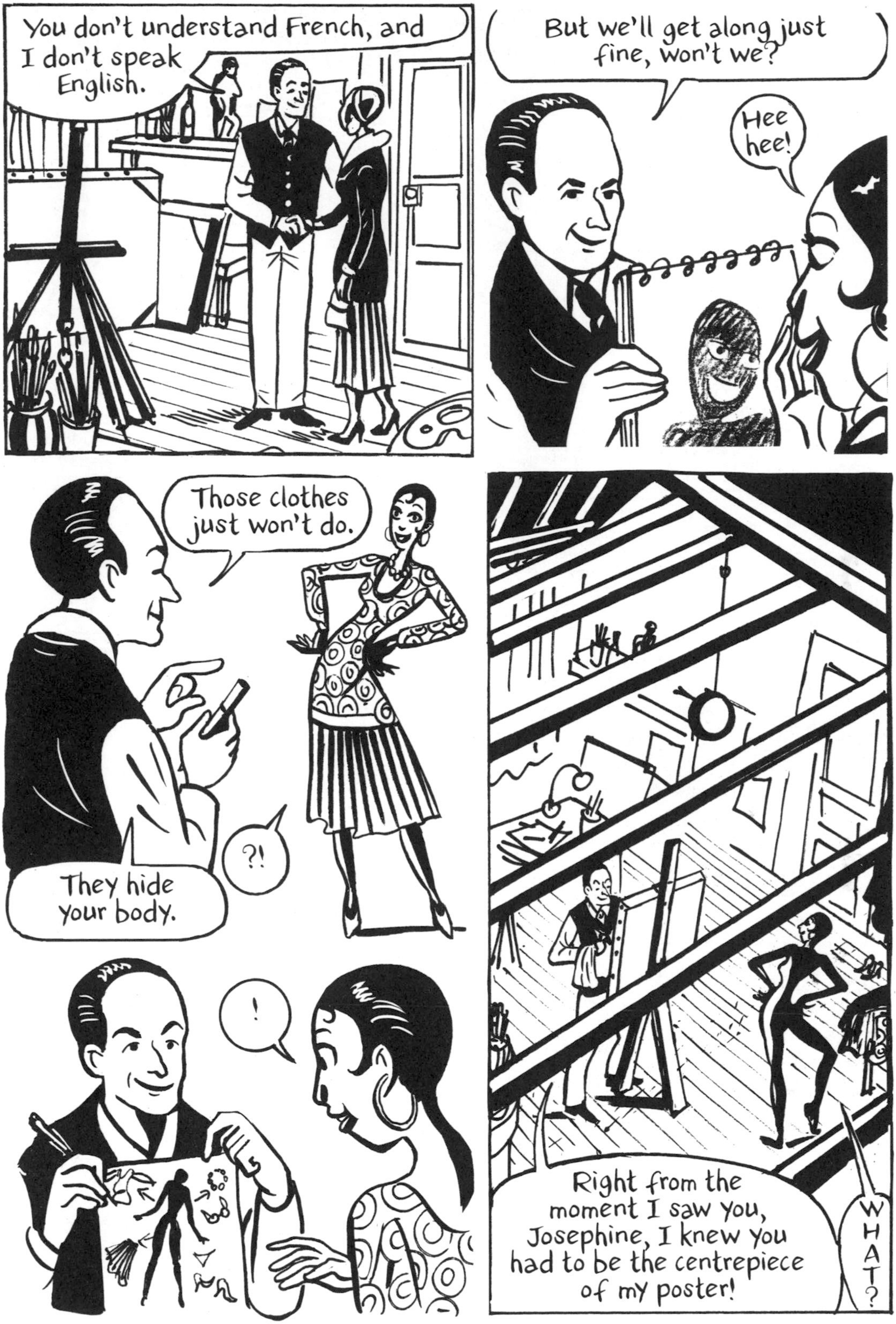
You don't understand French, and I don't speak English.
But we'll get along just fine, won't we?
Hee hee!
Those clothes just won't do.
They hide your body.
?!
!
Right from the moment I saw you, Josephine, I knew you had to be the centrepiece of my poster!
WHAT?

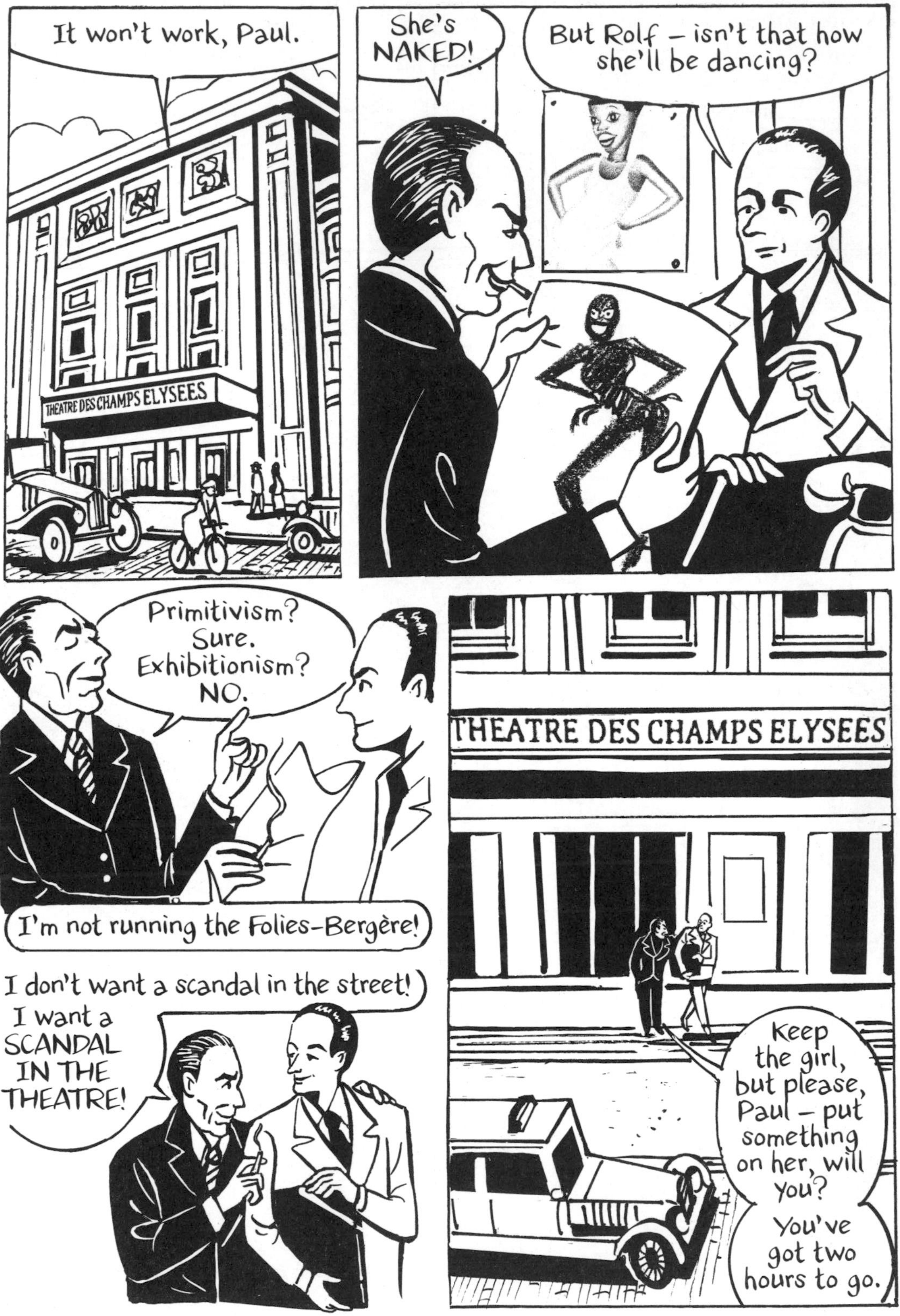
It won't work, Paul.
THEATRE DES CHAMPS ELYSEES
She's NAKED!
But Rolf – isn't that how she'll be dancing?
Primitivism? Sure. Exhibitionism? NO.
I'm not running the Folies-Bergère!
I don't want a scandal in the street!
I want a SCANDAL IN THE THEATRE!
THEATRE DES CHAMPS ELYSEES
Keep the girl, but please, Paul – put something on her, will you?
You've got two hours to go.

Waiter! TWO more croissants!
Oh, PAUL!
REVUE NÈGRE
AU
Music-hall
REVUE NEGRE
Music-hall
THEATRE DES CHAMPS ELYSEES

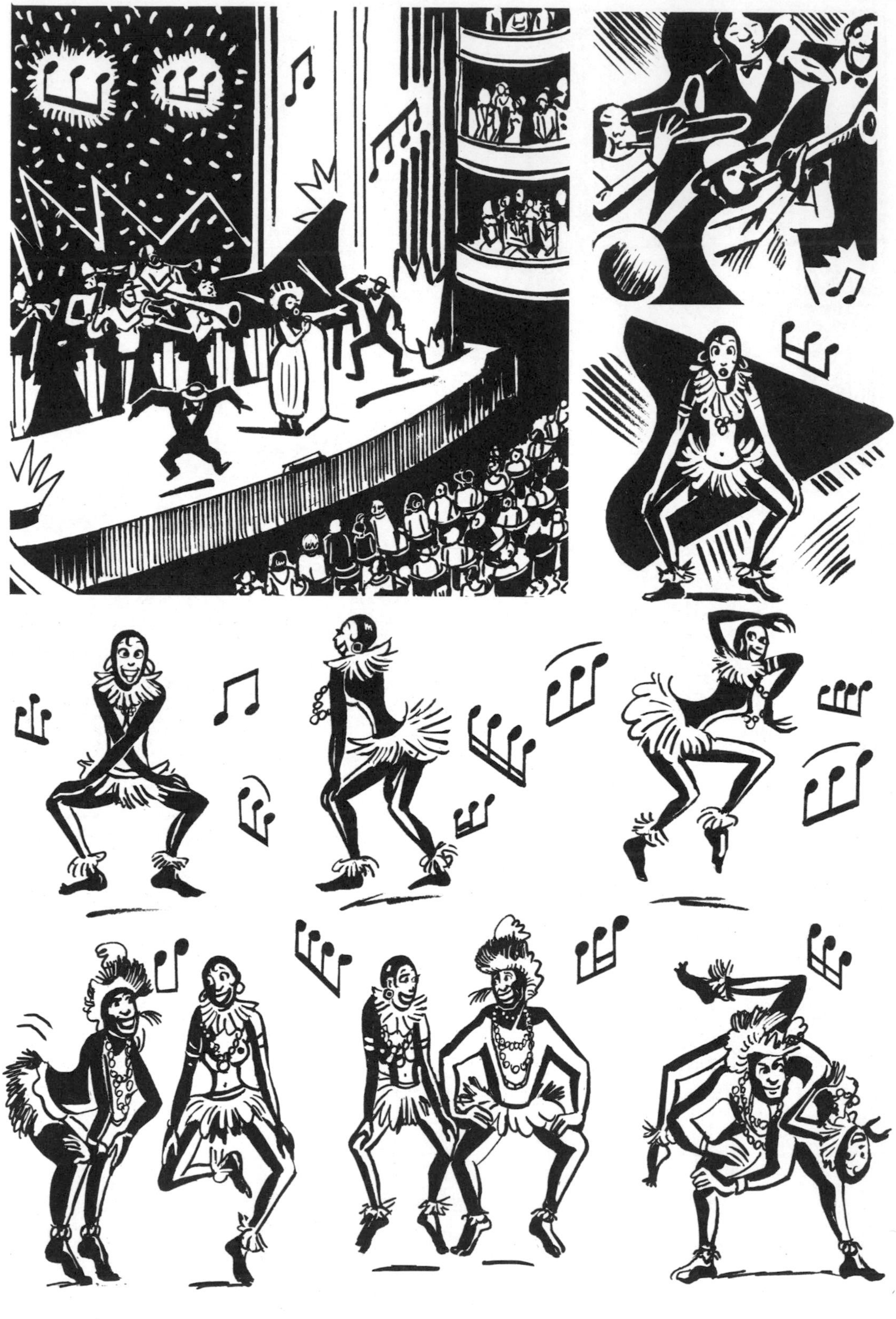

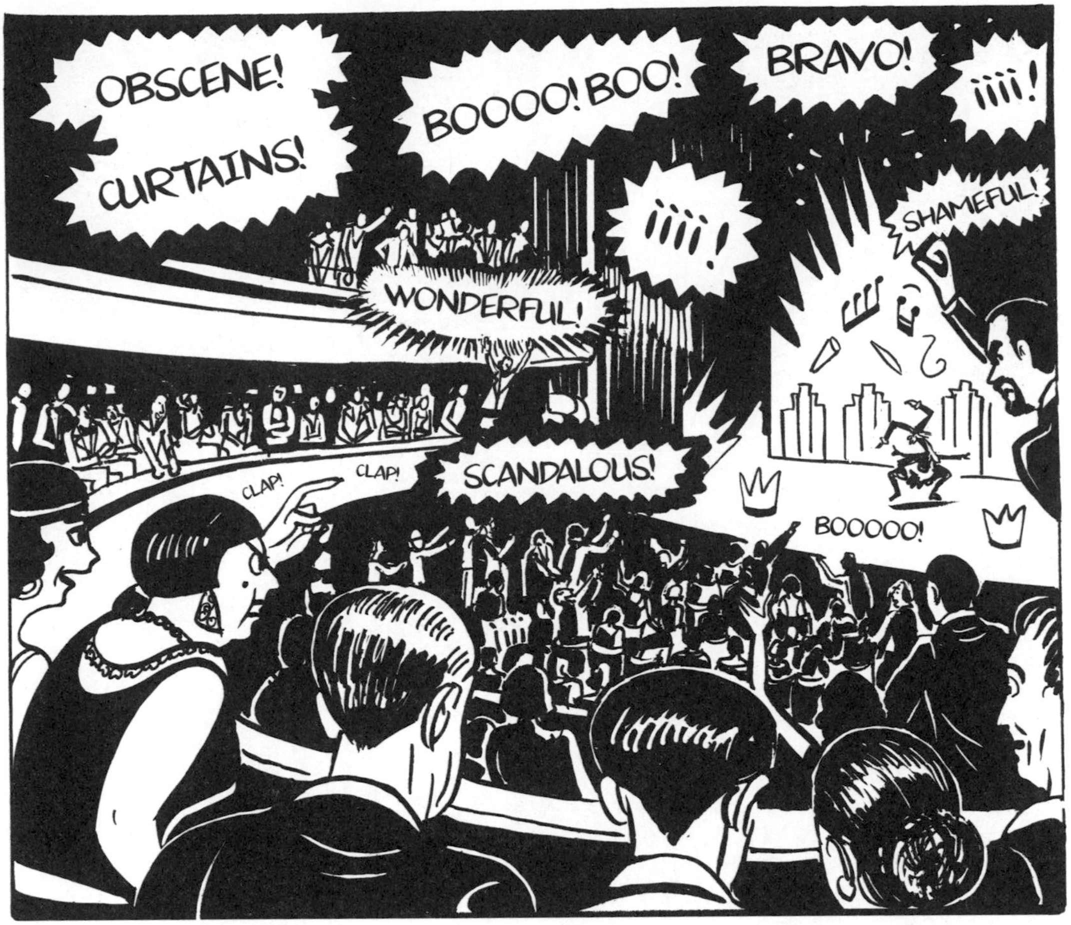

OBSCENE!
CURTAINS!
BOOOO! BOO!
BRAVO!
¡¡¡¡!
¡¡¡¡!
SHAMEFUL!
WONDERFUL!
SCANDALOUS!
CLAP!
CLAP!
BOOOOO!

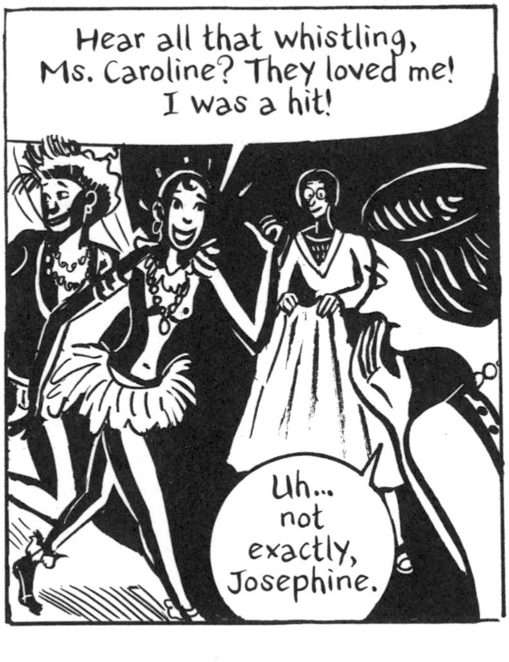

Hear all that whistling, Ms. Caroline? They loved me! I was a hit!
Uh... not exactly, Josephine.

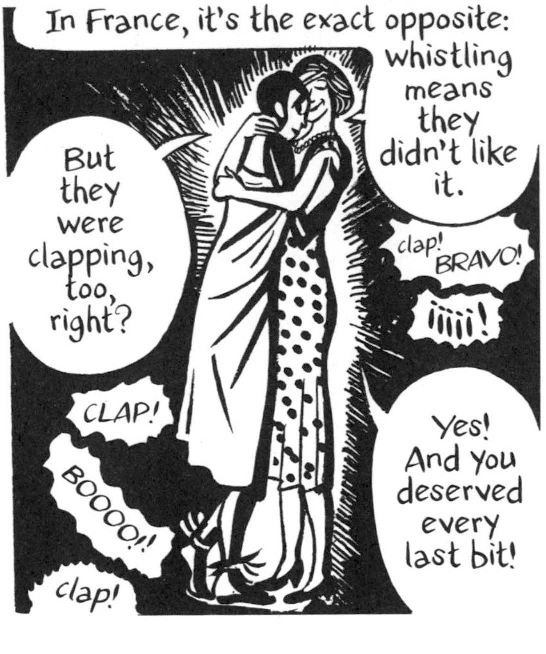

In France, it's the exact opposite: whistling means they didn't like it.
But they were clapping, too, right?
clap!
BRAVO!
¡¡¡¡!
CLAP!
BOOOO!!
clap!
Yes! And you deserved every last bit!

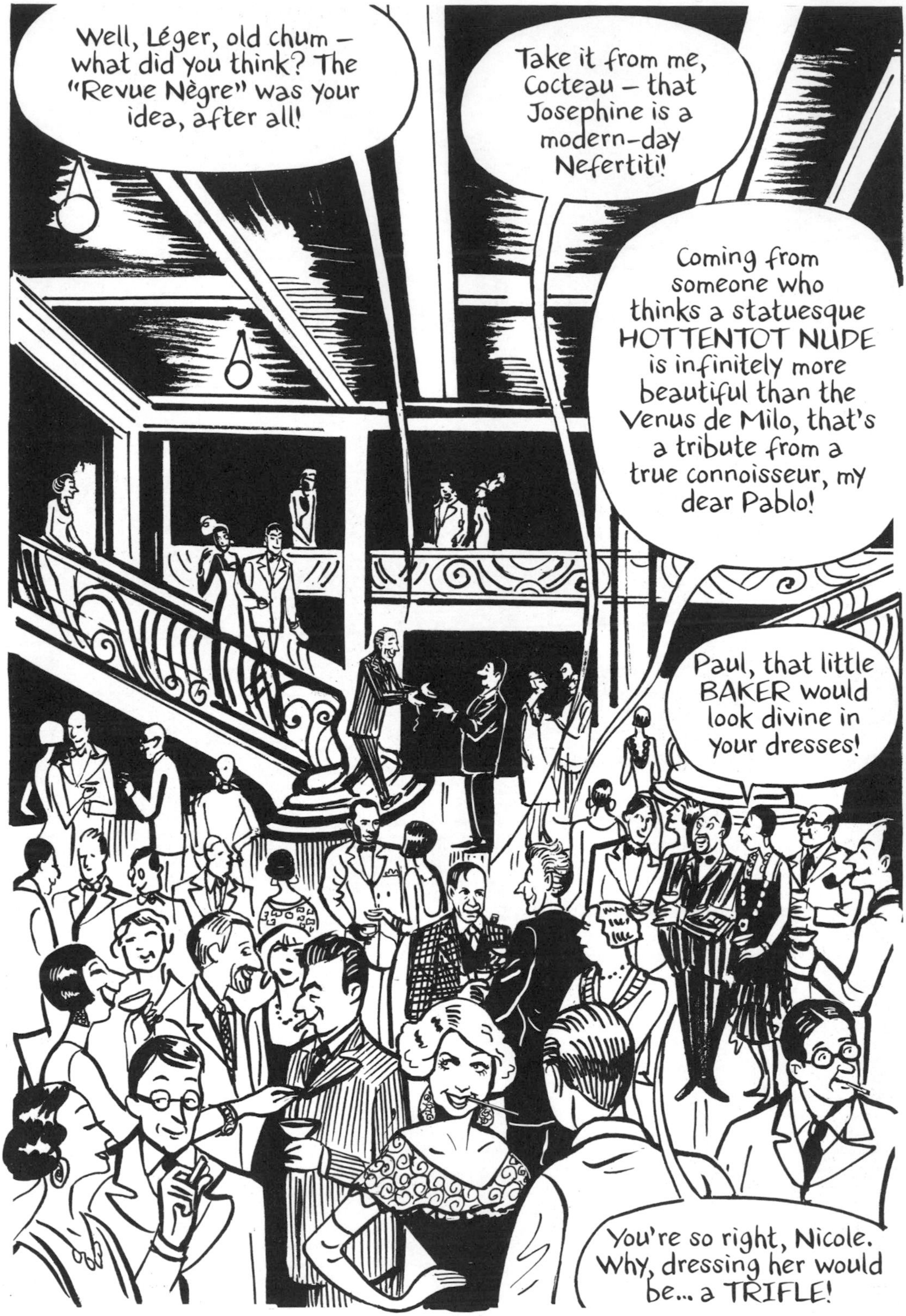
Well, Léger, old chum – what did you think? The "Revue Nègre" was your idea, after all!
Take it from me, Cocteau – that Josephine is a modern-day Nefertiti!
Coming from someone who thinks a statuesque HOTTENTOT NUDE is infinitely more beautiful than the Venus de Milo, that's a tribute from a true connoisseur, my dear Pablo!
Paul, that little BAKER would look divine in your dresses!
You're so right, Nicole. Why, dressing her would be... a TRIFLE!

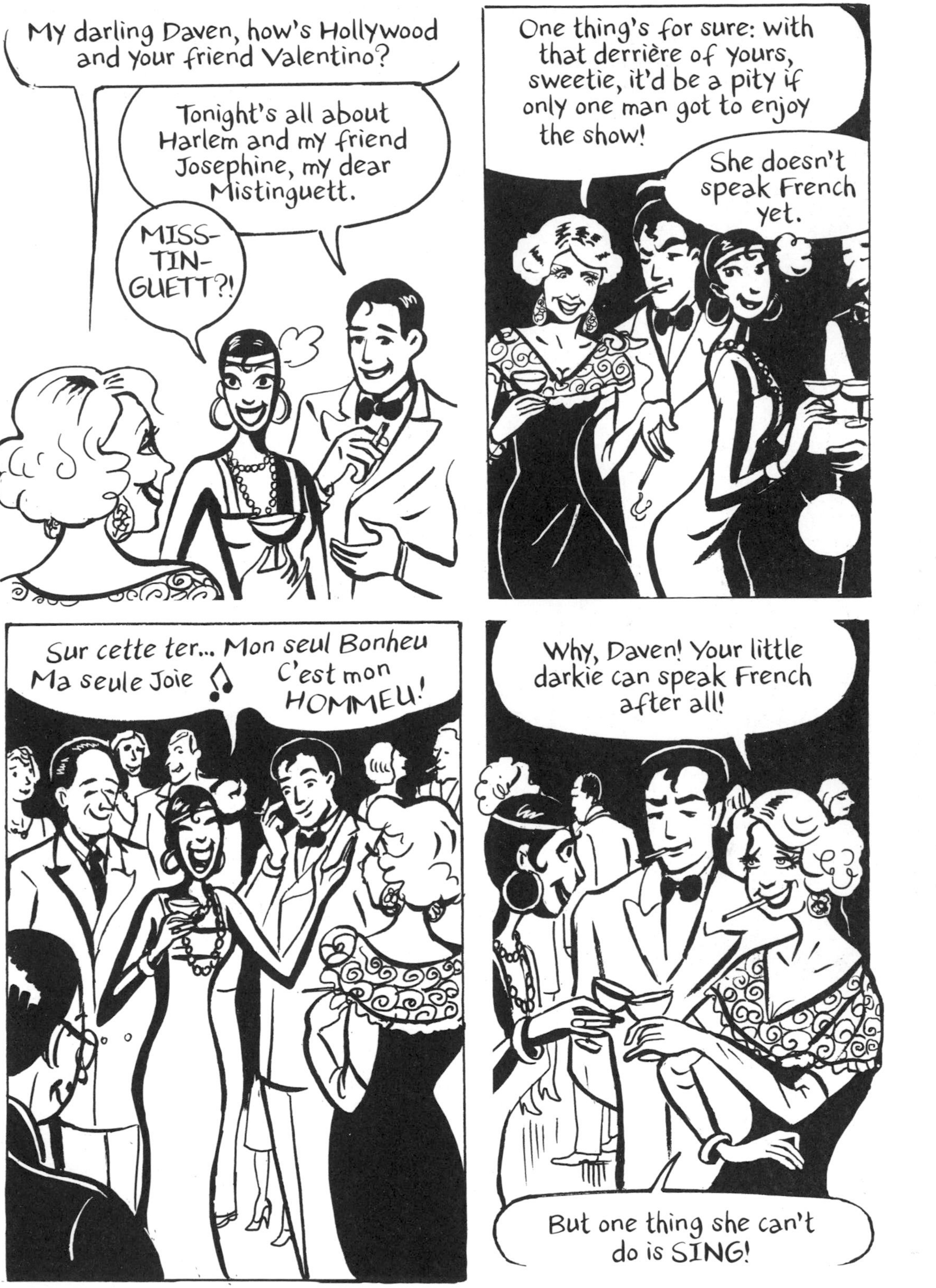
My darling Daven, how's Hollywood and your friend Valentino?
Tonight's all about Harlem and my friend Josephine, my dear Mistinguett.
MISS-TIN-GUETT?!
One thing's for sure: with that derrière of yours, sweetie, it'd be a pity if only one man got to enjoy the show!
She doesn't speak French yet.
Sur cette ter... Mon seul Bonheu Ma seule Joie C'est mon HOMMEU!
Why, Daven! Your little darkie can speak French after all!
But one thing she can't do is SING!

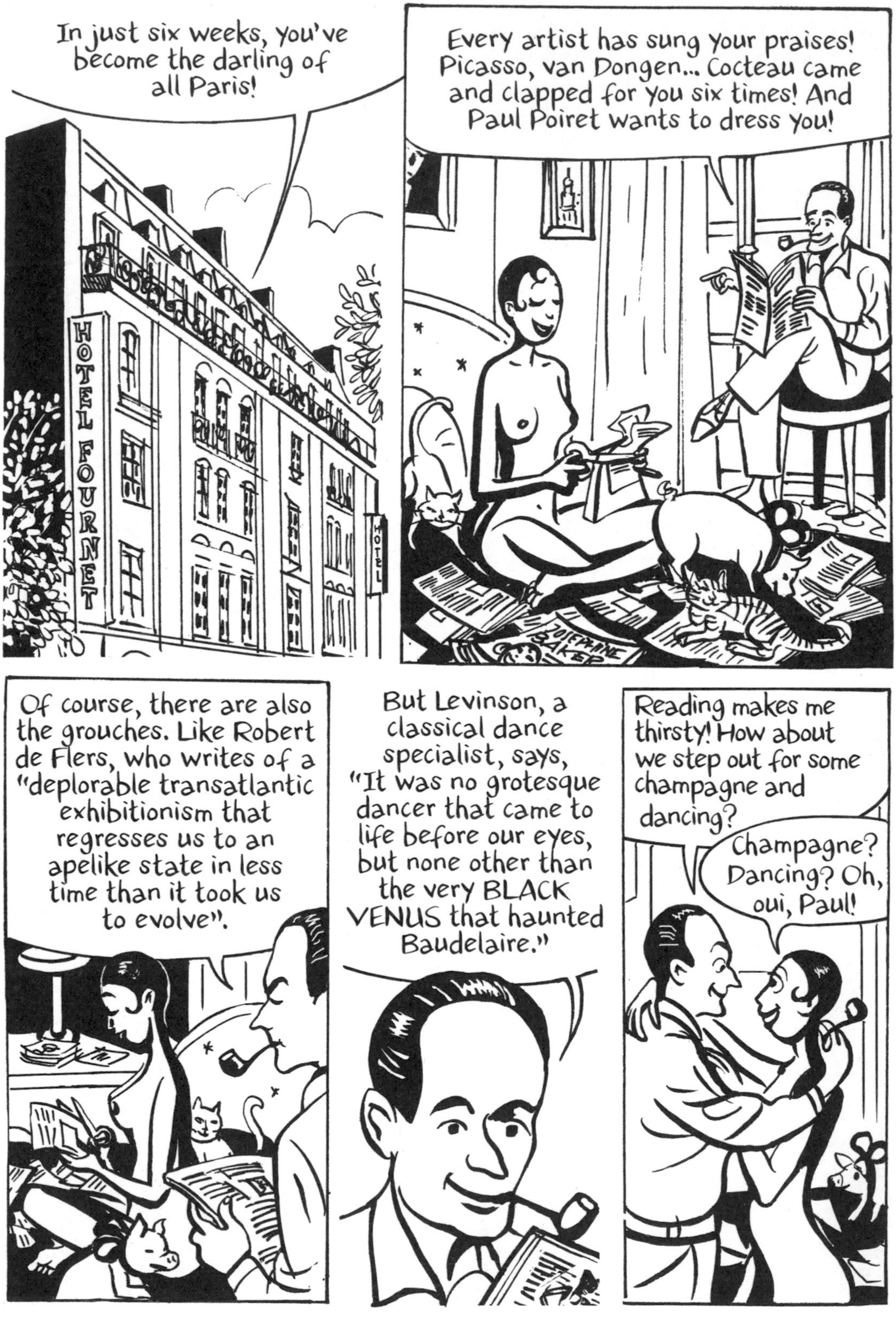

In just six weeks, you've become the darling of all Paris!
Every artist has sung your praises! Picasso, van Dongen... Cocteau came and clapped for you six times! And Paul Poiret wants to dress you!
HOTEL FOURNET
HOTEL
JOSEPHINE BAKER
Of course, there are also the grouches. Like Robert de Flers, who writes of a "deplorable transatlantic exhibitionism that regresses us to an apelike state in less time than it took us to evolve".
But Levinson, a classical dance specialist, says, "It was no grotesque dancer that came to life before our eyes, but none other than the very BLACK VENUS that haunted Baudelaire."
Reading makes me thirsty! How about we step out for some champagne and dancing?
Champagne? Dancing? Oh, oui, Paul!

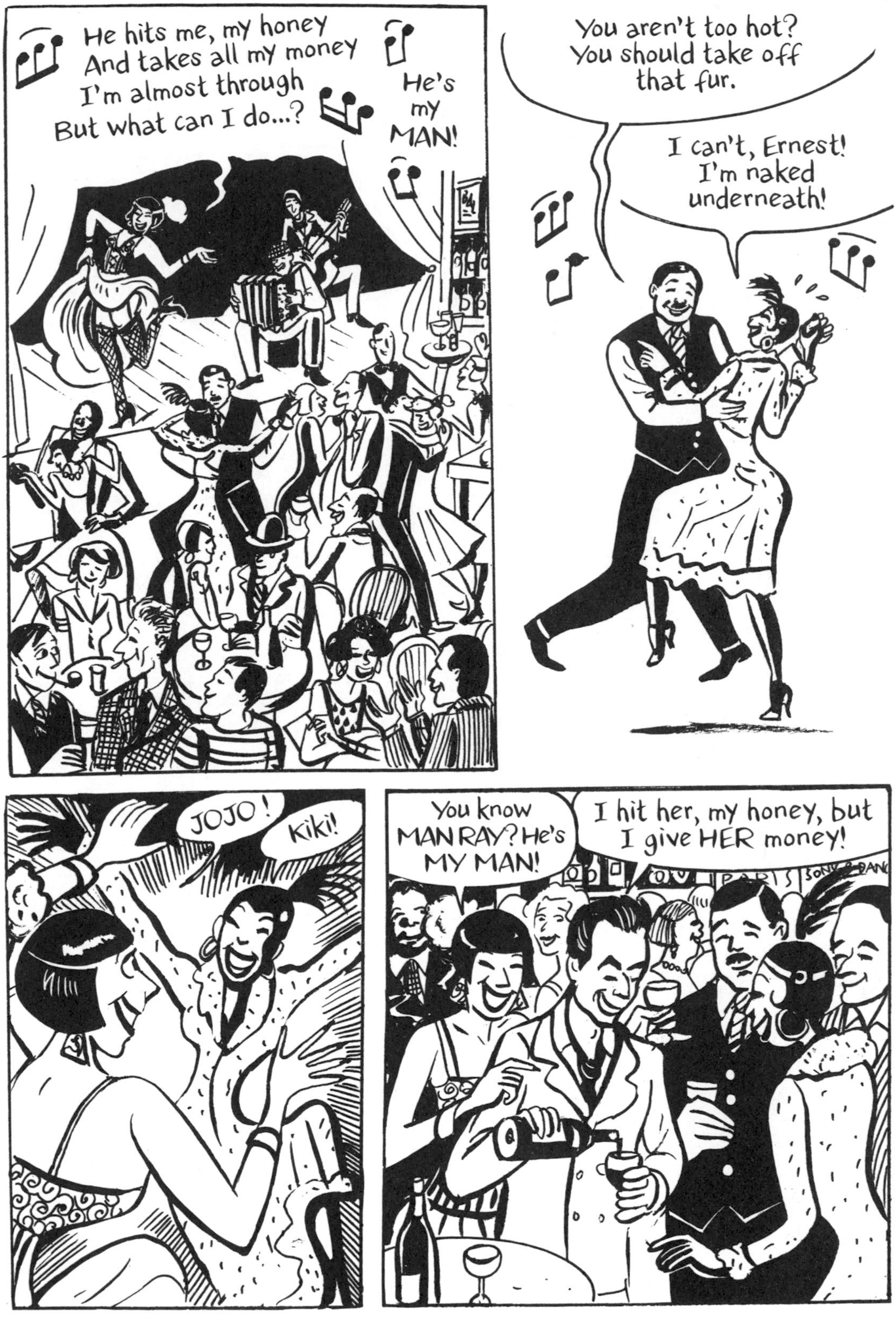
He hits me, my honey
And takes all my money
I'm almost through
But what can I do...?
He's my MAN!
You aren't too hot? You should take off that fur.
I can't, Ernest! I'm naked underneath!
JOJO!
Kiki!
You know MAN RAY? He's MY MAN!
I hit her, my honey, but I give HER money!
PARIS

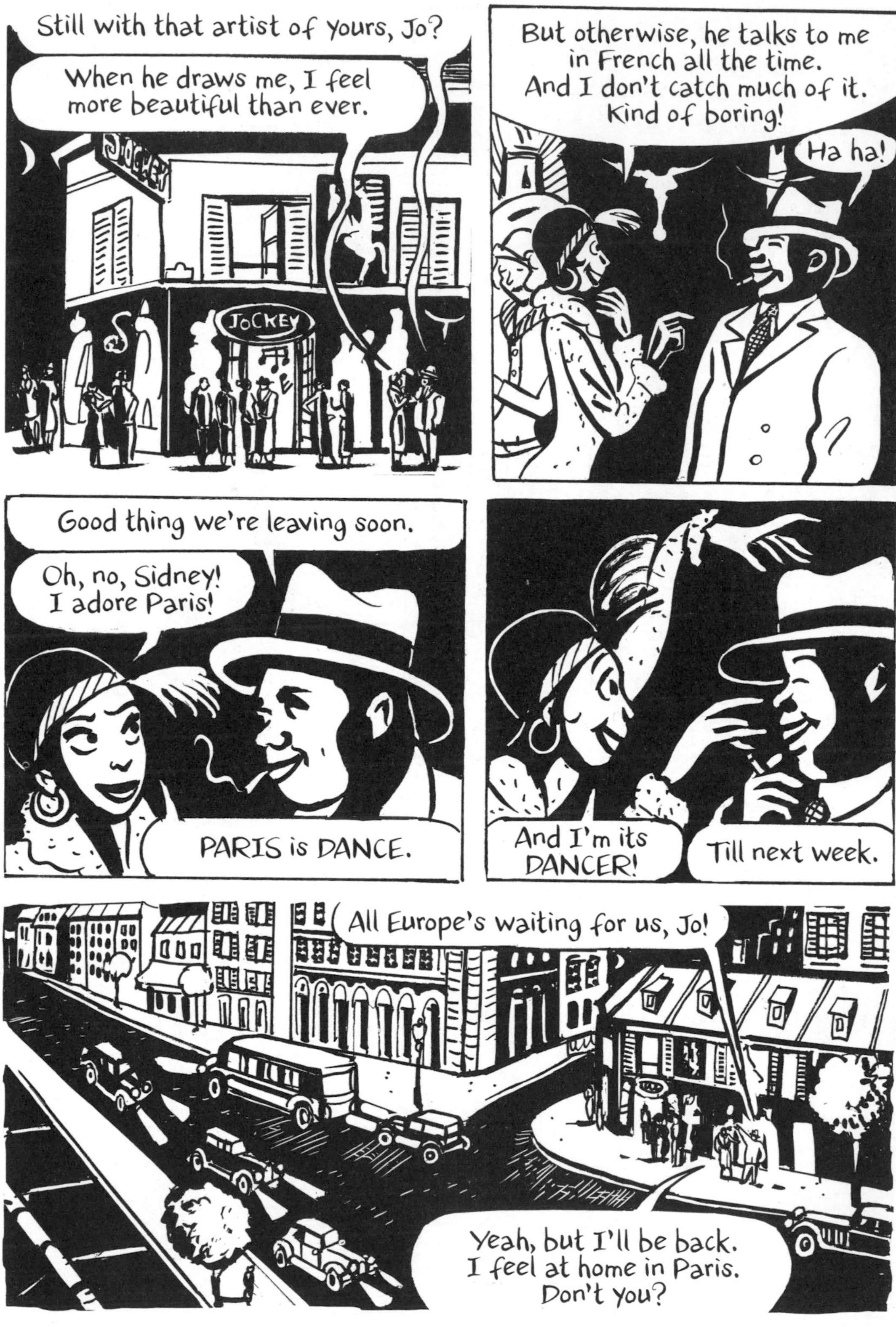
Still with that artist of yours, Jo?
When he draws me, I feel more beautiful than ever.
JOCKEY
JOCKEY
But otherwise, he talks to me in French all the time. And I don't catch much of it. Kind of boring!
Ha ha!
Good thing we're leaving soon.
Oh, no, Sidney! I adore Paris!
PARIS is DANCE.
And I'm its DANCER!
Till next week.
All Europe's waiting for us, Jo!
Yeah, but I'll be back. I feel at home in Paris. Don't you?

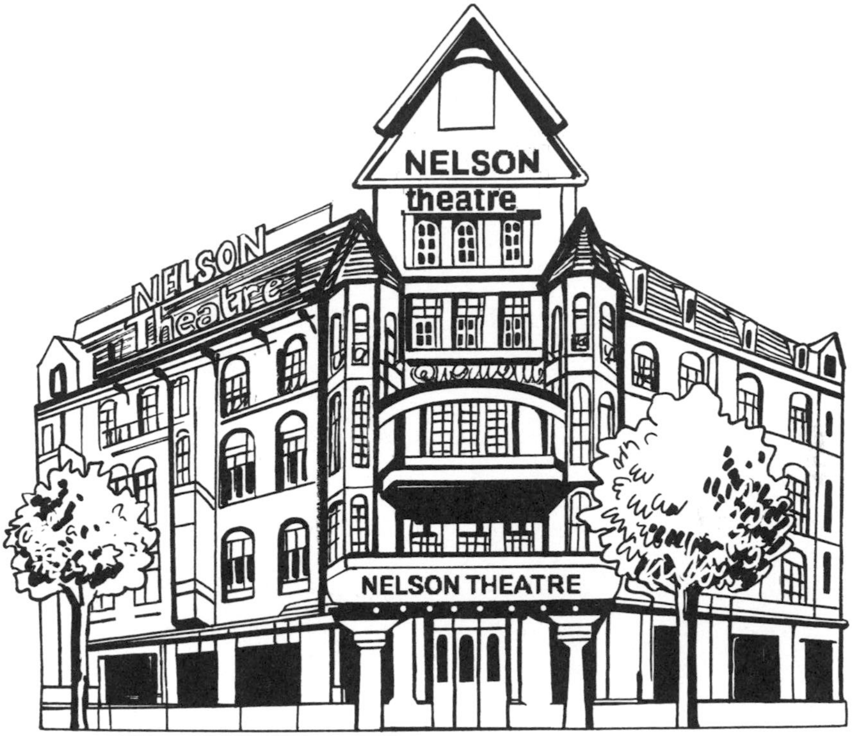
NELSON
theatre
NELSON
Theatre
NELSON THEATRE

1926: Nelson Theatre, Berlin, Germany

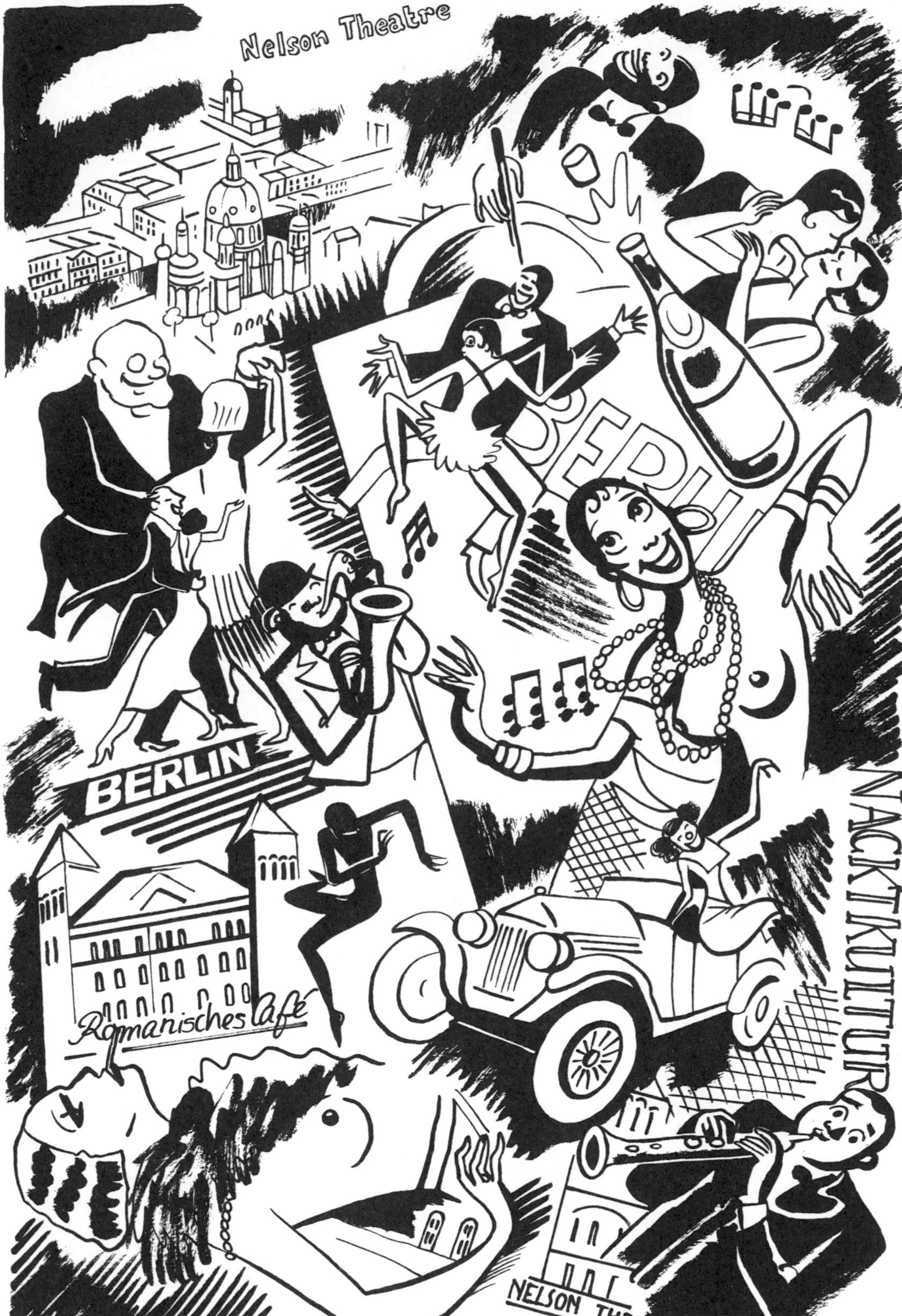
Nelson Theatre
BERLIN
BERLIN
Romanisches Café
NACKTKULTUR
NELSON THEA

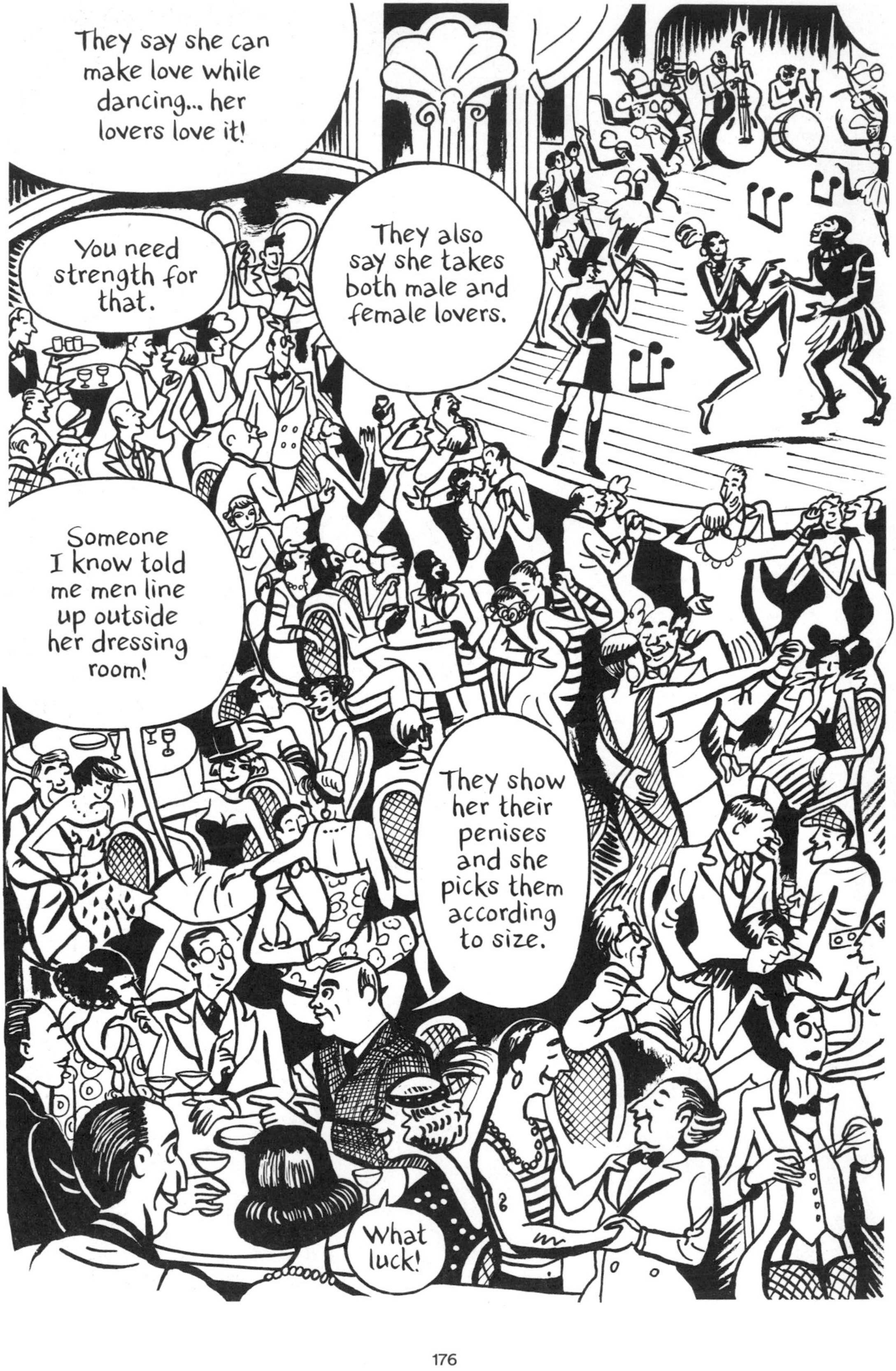
They say she can make love while dancing... her lovers love it!
You need strength for that.
They also say she takes both male and female lovers.
Someone I know told me men line up outside her dressing room!
They show her their penises and she picks them according to size.
What luck!

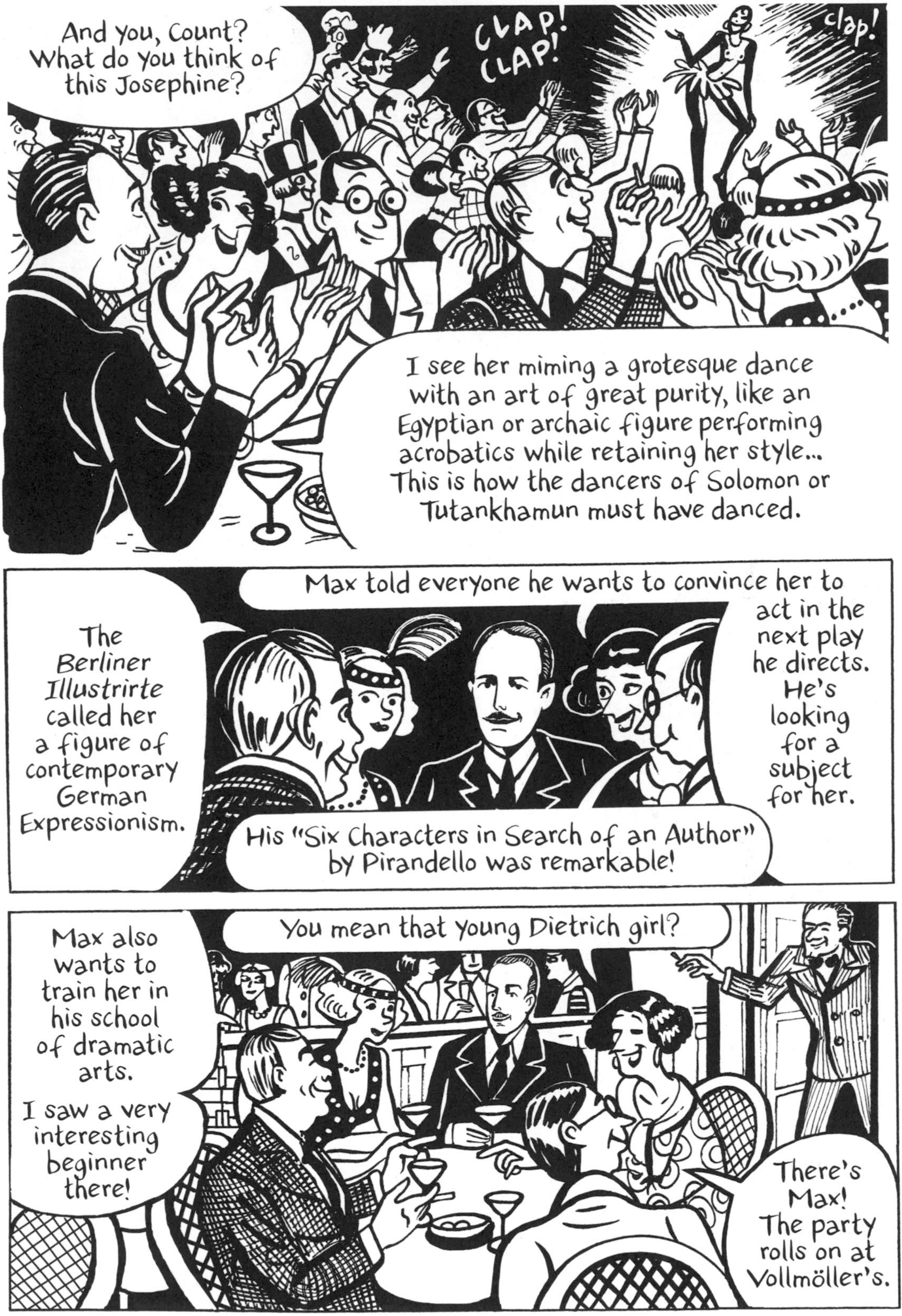
And you, Count? What do you think of this Josephine?
CLAP! CLAP!
clap!
I see her miming a grotesque dance with an art of great purity, like an Egyptian or archaic figure performing acrobatics while retaining her style... This is how the dancers of Solomon or Tutankhamun must have danced.
The *Berliner Illustrirte* called her a figure of contemporary German Expressionism.
Max told everyone he wants to convince her to act in the next play he directs. He's looking for a subject for her.
His "Six Characters in Search of an Author" by Pirandello was remarkable!
Max also wants to train her in his school of dramatic arts.
You mean that young Dietrich girl?
I saw a very interesting beginner there!
There's Max! The party rolls on at Vollmöller's.

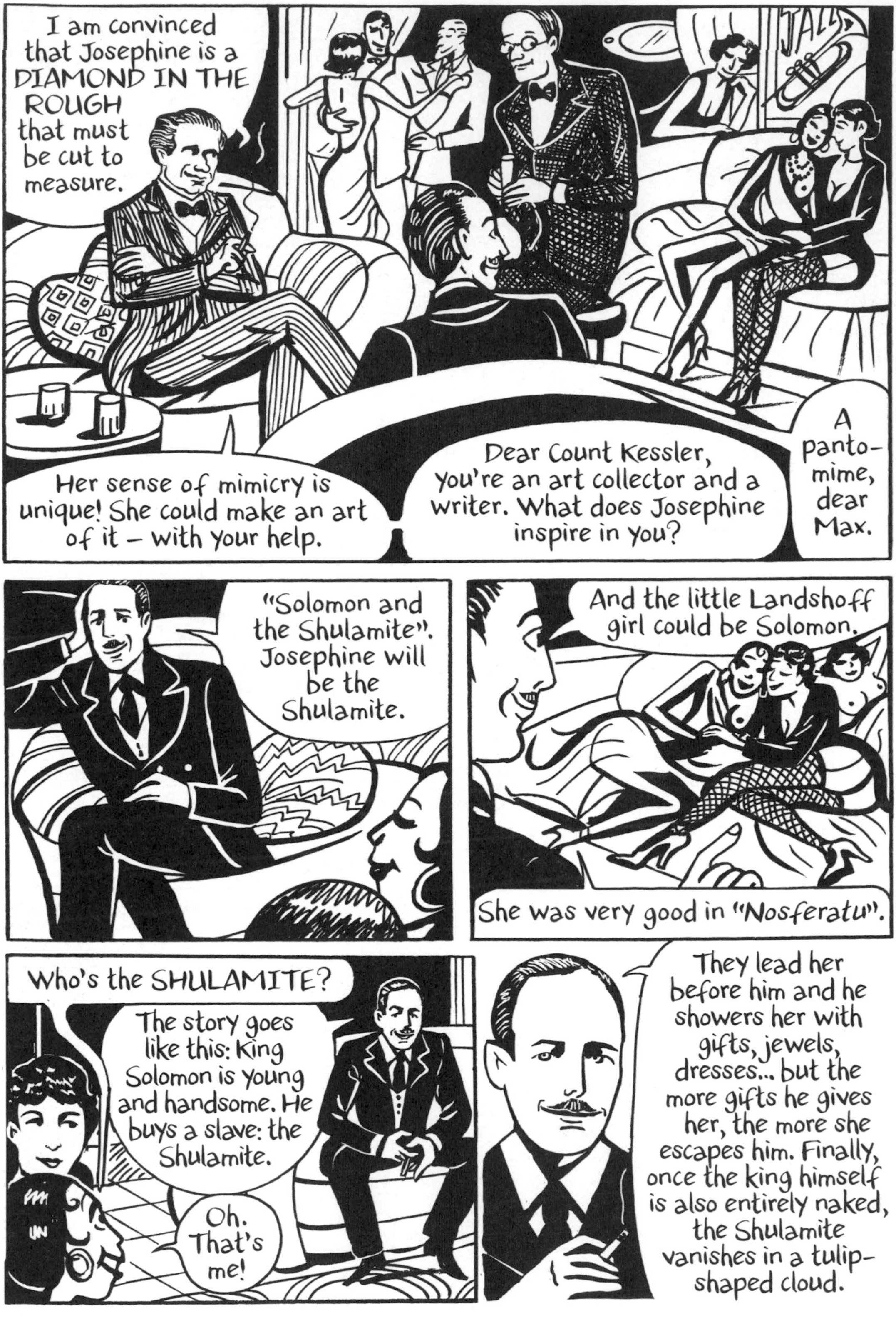

I am convinced that Josephine is a DIAMOND IN THE ROUGH that must be cut to measure.
JAZZ
Her sense of mimicry is unique! She could make an art of it – with your help.
Dear Count Kessler, You're an art collector and a writer. What does Josephine inspire in you?
A panto-mime, dear Max.
"Solomon and the Shulamite". Josephine will be the Shulamite.
And the little Landshoff girl could be Solomon.
She was very good in "Nosferatu".
Who's the SHULAMITE?
The story goes like this: King Solomon is young and handsome. He buys a slave: the Shulamite.
Oh. That's me!
They lead her before him and he showers her with gifts, jewels, dresses... but the more gifts he gives her, the more she escapes him. Finally, once the king himself is also entirely naked, the Shulamite vanishes in a tulip-shaped cloud.

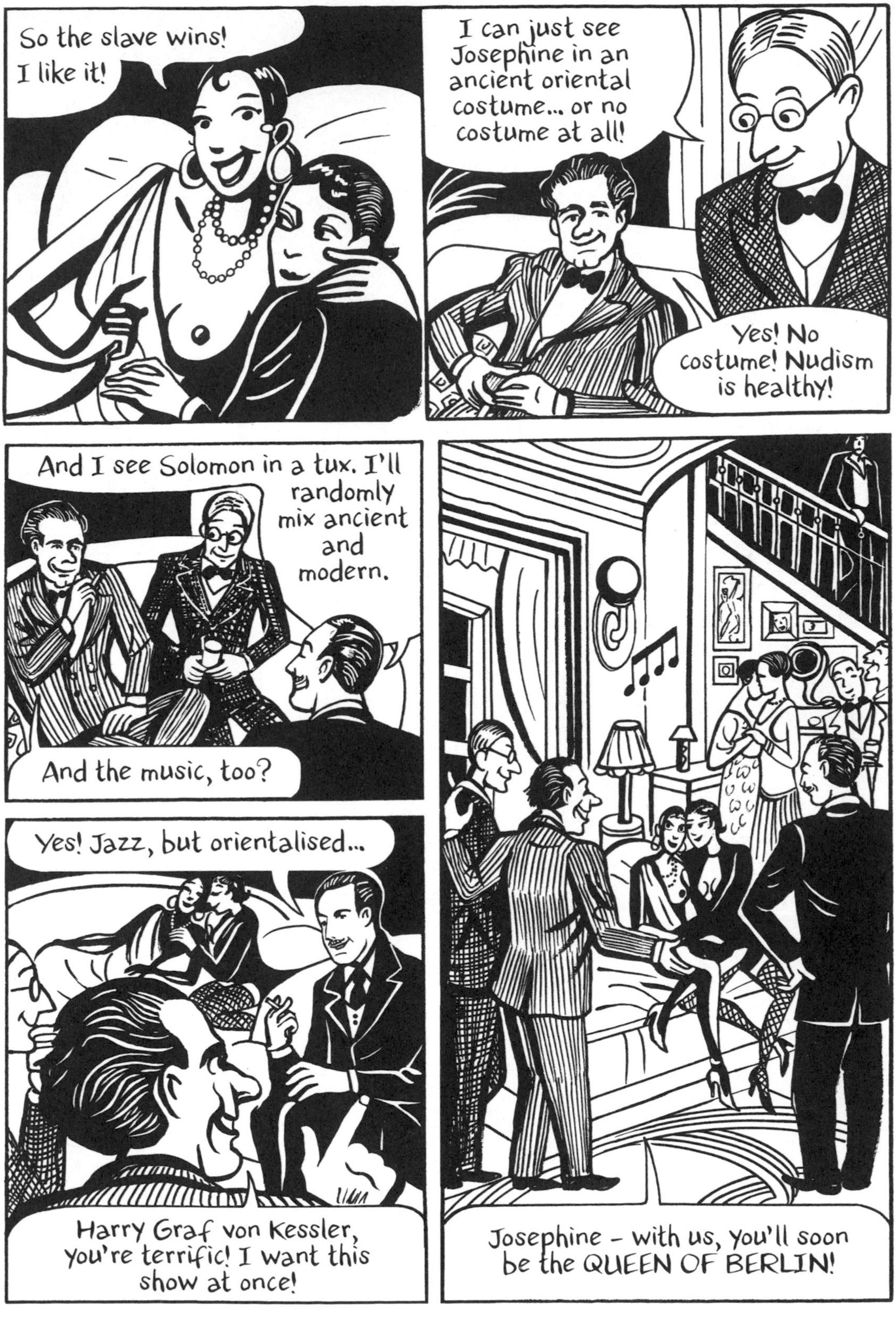
So the slave wins! I like it!
I can just see Josephine in an ancient oriental costume... or no costume at all!
Yes! No costume! Nudism is healthy!
And I see Solomon in a tux. I'll randomly mix ancient and modern.
And the music, too?
Yes! Jazz, but orientalised...
Harry Graf von Kessler, you're terrific! I want this show at once!
Josephine – with us, you'll soon be the QUEEN OF BERLIN!

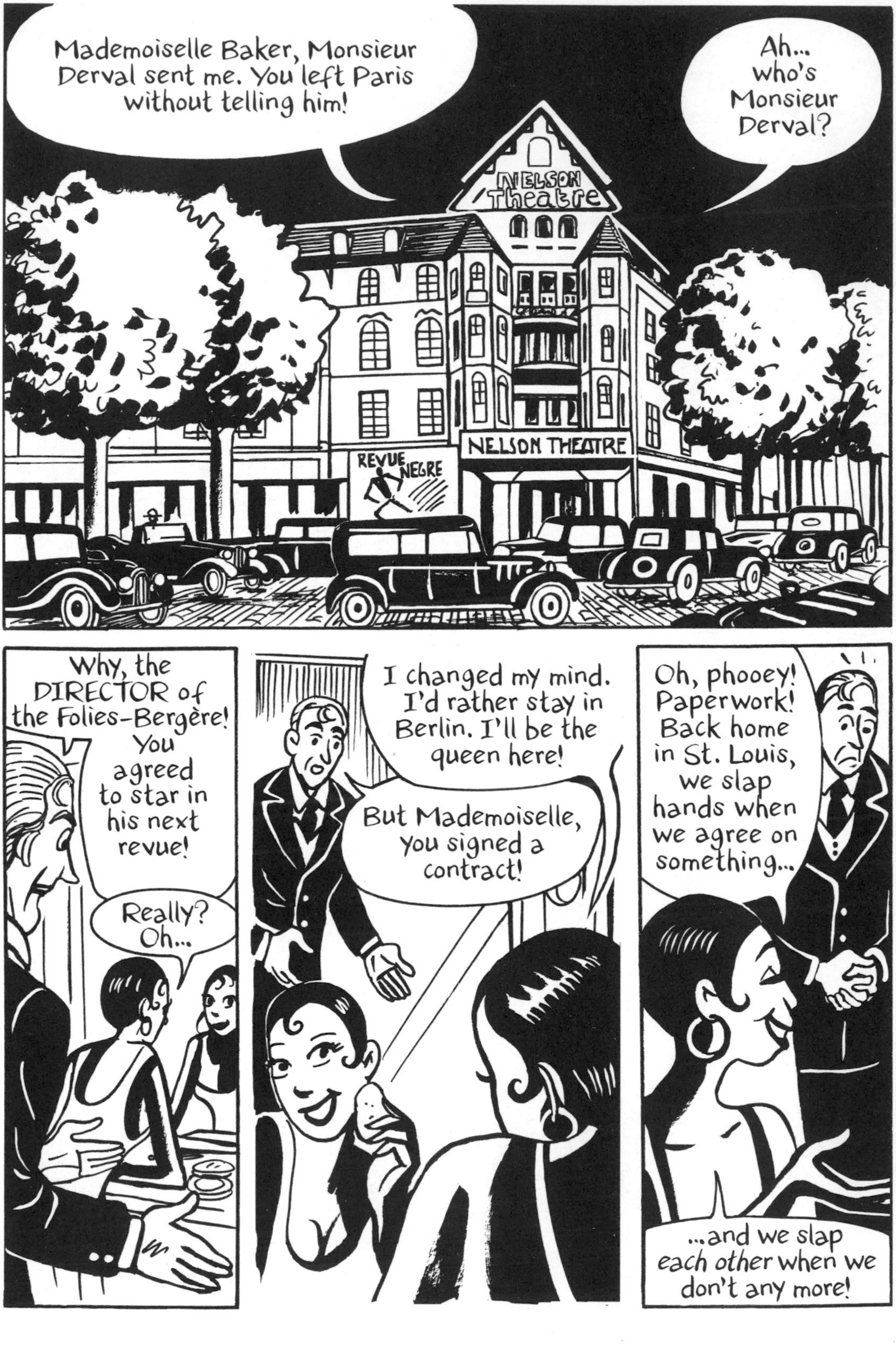

Mademoiselle Baker, Monsieur Derval sent me. You left Paris without telling him!
Ah... who's Monsieur Derval?
NIELSON Theatre
NELSON THEATRE
REVUE NEGRE
Why, the DIRECTOR of the Folies-Bergère! You agreed to star in his next revue!
Really? Oh...
I changed my mind. I'd rather stay in Berlin. I'll be the queen here!
But Mademoiselle, you signed a contract!
Oh, phooey! Paperwork! Back home in St. Louis, we slap hands when we agree on something...
...and we slap each other when we don't any more!

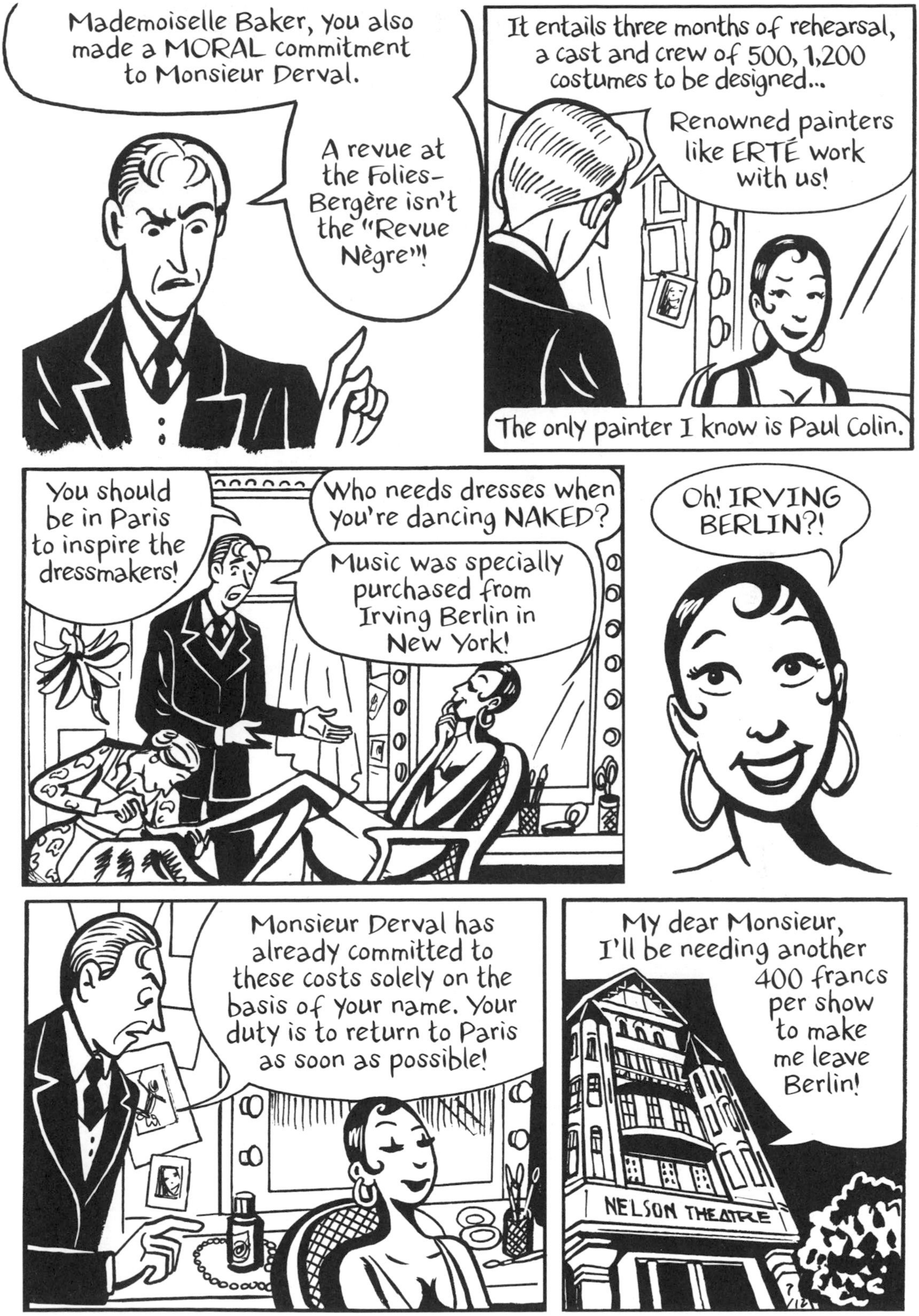
Mademoiselle Baker, you also made a MORAL commitment to Monsieur Derval.
A revue at the Folies-Bergère isn't the "Revue Nègre"!
It entails three months of rehearsal, a cast and crew of 500, 1,200 costumes to be designed...
Renowned painters like ERTÉ work with us!
The only painter I know is Paul Colin.
You should be in Paris to inspire the dressmakers!
Who needs dresses when you're dancing NAKED?
Music was specially purchased from Irving Berlin in New York!
Oh! IRVING BERLIN?!
Monsieur Derval has already committed to these costs solely on the basis of your name. Your duty is to return to Paris as soon as possible!
My dear Monsieur, I'll be needing another 400 francs per show to make me leave Berlin!
NELSON THEATRE

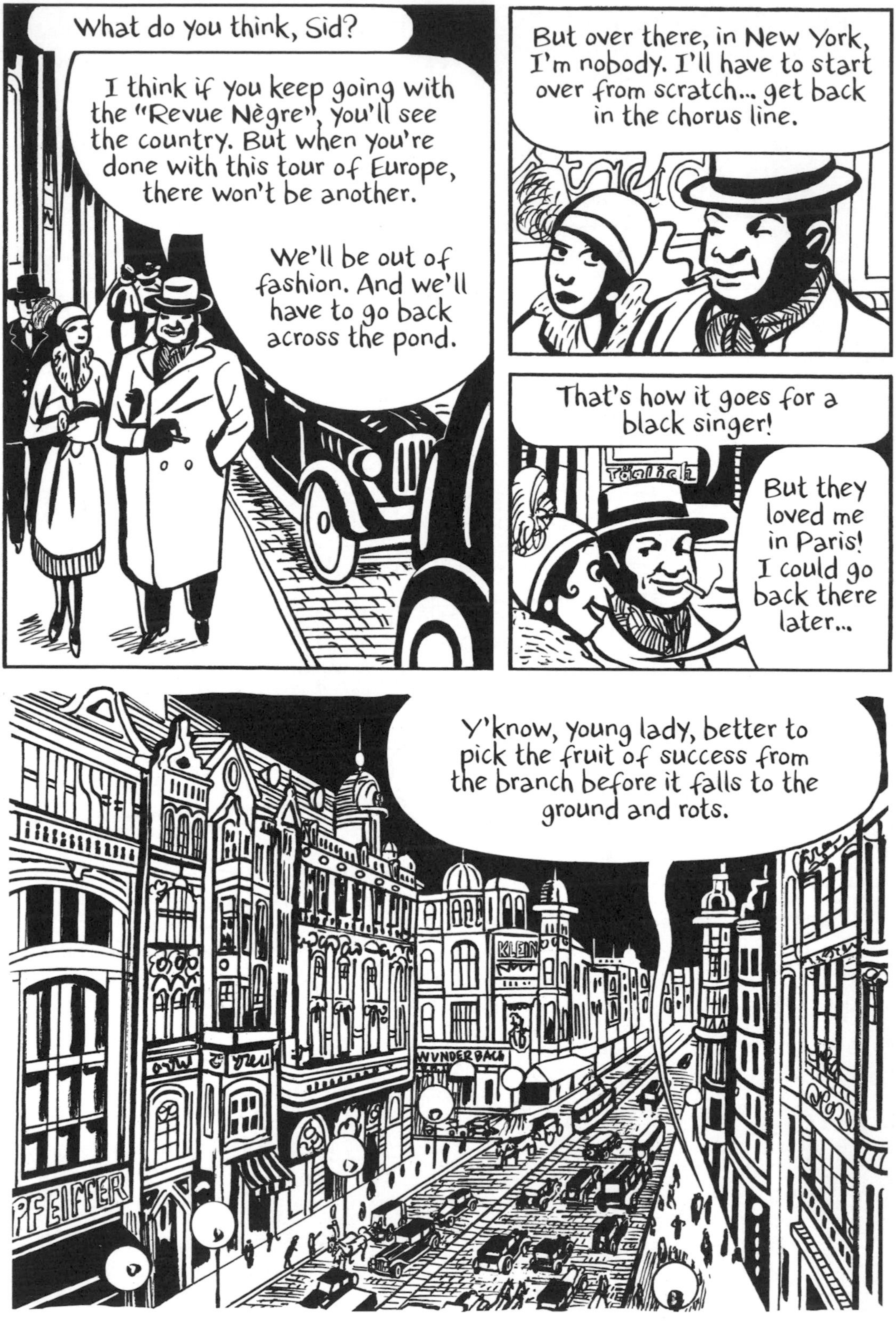
What do you think, Sid?
I think if you keep going with the "Revue Nègre", you'll see the country. But when you're done with this tour of Europe, there won't be another.
We'll be out of fashion. And we'll have to go back across the pond.
But over there, in New York, I'm nobody. I'll have to start over from scratch... get back in the chorus line.
That's how it goes for a black singer!
Täglich
But they loved me in Paris! I could go back there later...
Y'know, young lady, better to pick the fruit of success from the branch before it falls to the ground and rots.
KLEIN
WUNDERBACH
PFEIFFER

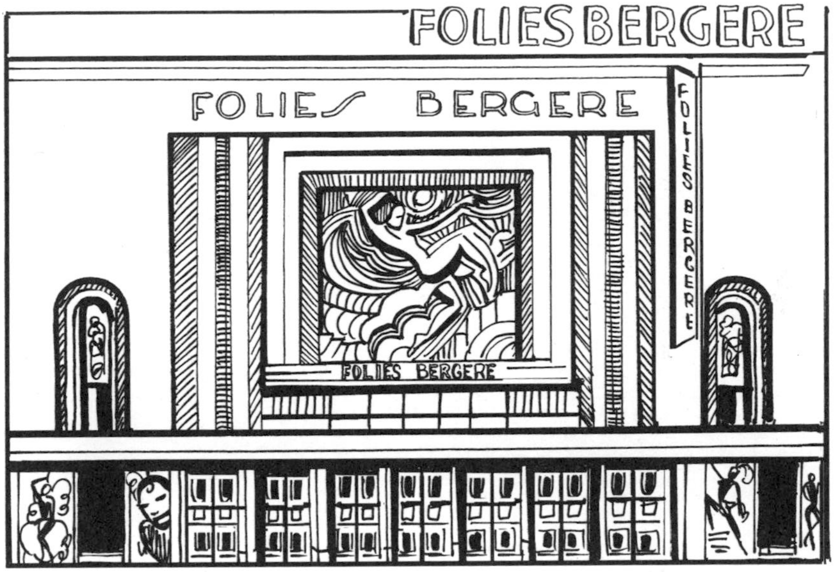
FOLIES BERGERE
FOLIES BERGERE
FOLIES BERGERE
FOLIES BERGERE

1926: Folies-Bergère, Rue Richer, Paris, France

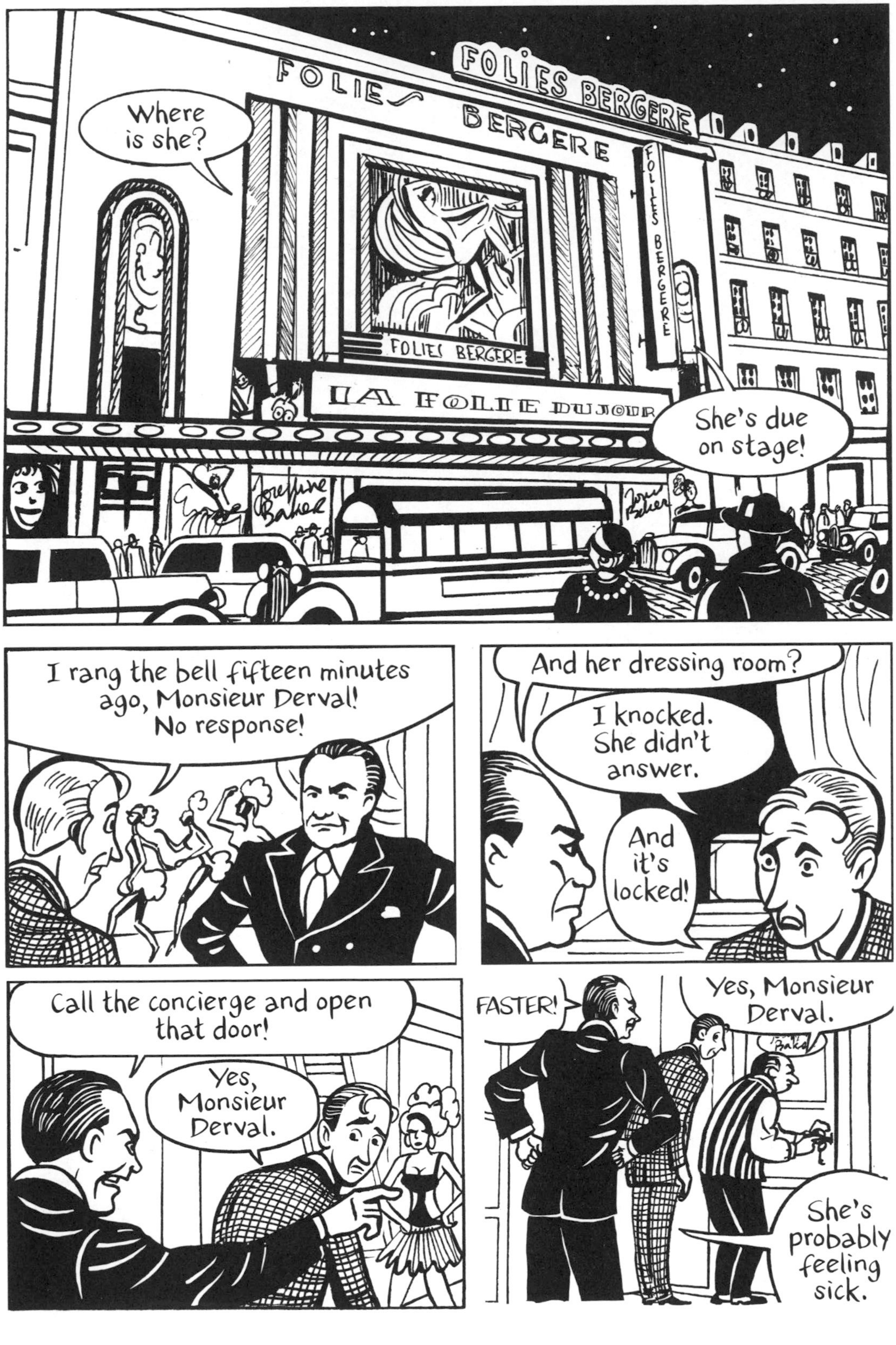
FOLIES BERGERE
FOLIES BERGERE
Where is she?
FOLIES BERGERE
FOLIES BERGERE
LA FOLIE DU JOUR
She's due on stage!
I rang the bell fifteen minutes ago, Monsieur Derval! No response!
And her dressing room?
I knocked. She didn't answer.
And it's locked!
Call the concierge and open that door!
Yes, Monsieur Derval.
FASTER!
Yes, Monsieur Derval.
She's probably feeling sick.

Josephine! What are you doing?!

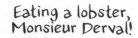

Eating a lobster, Monsieur Derval!

But you're not even in your costume, my girl! And they're waiting for you!

Don't fret, my costume doesn't take long to slip on!

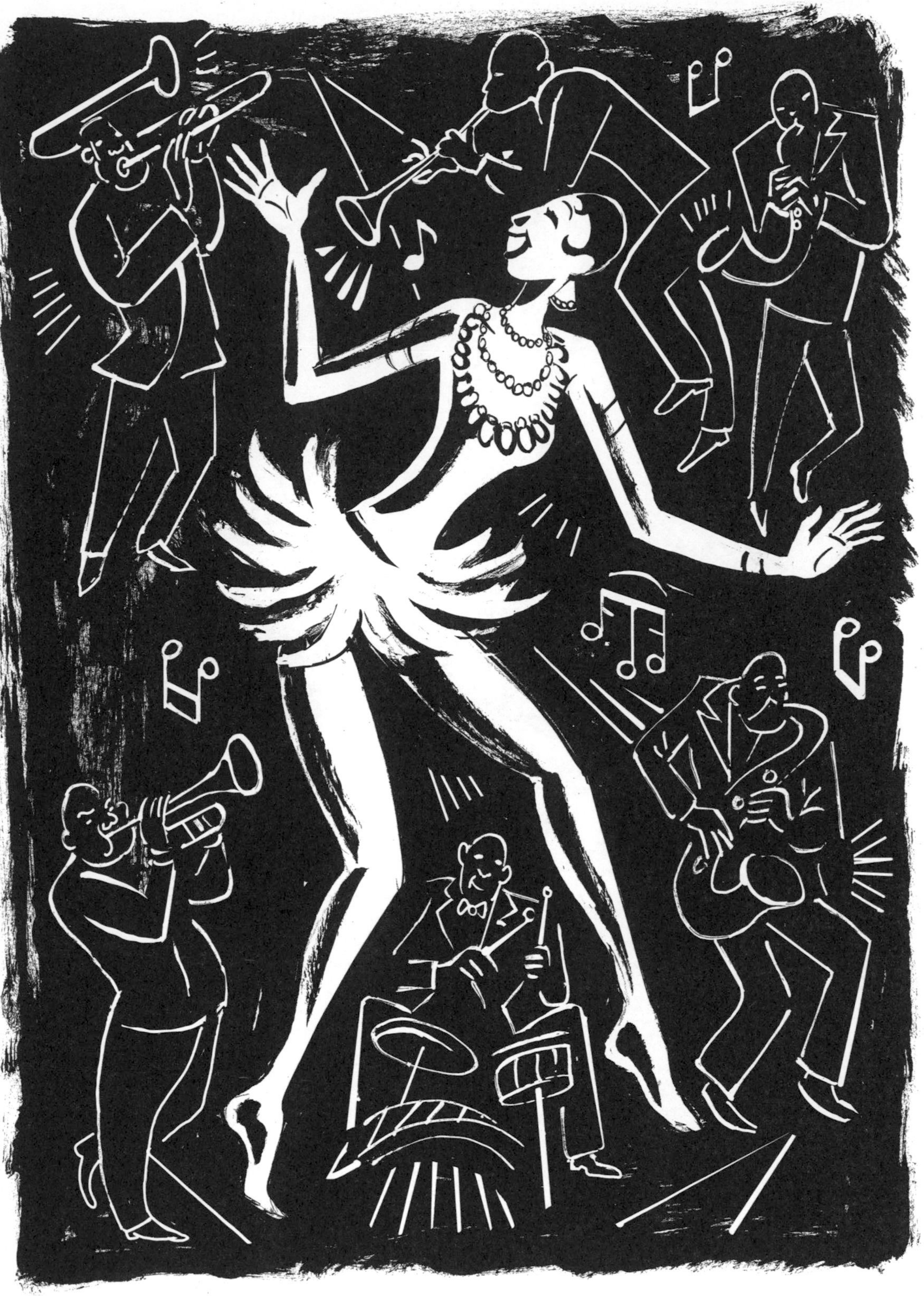

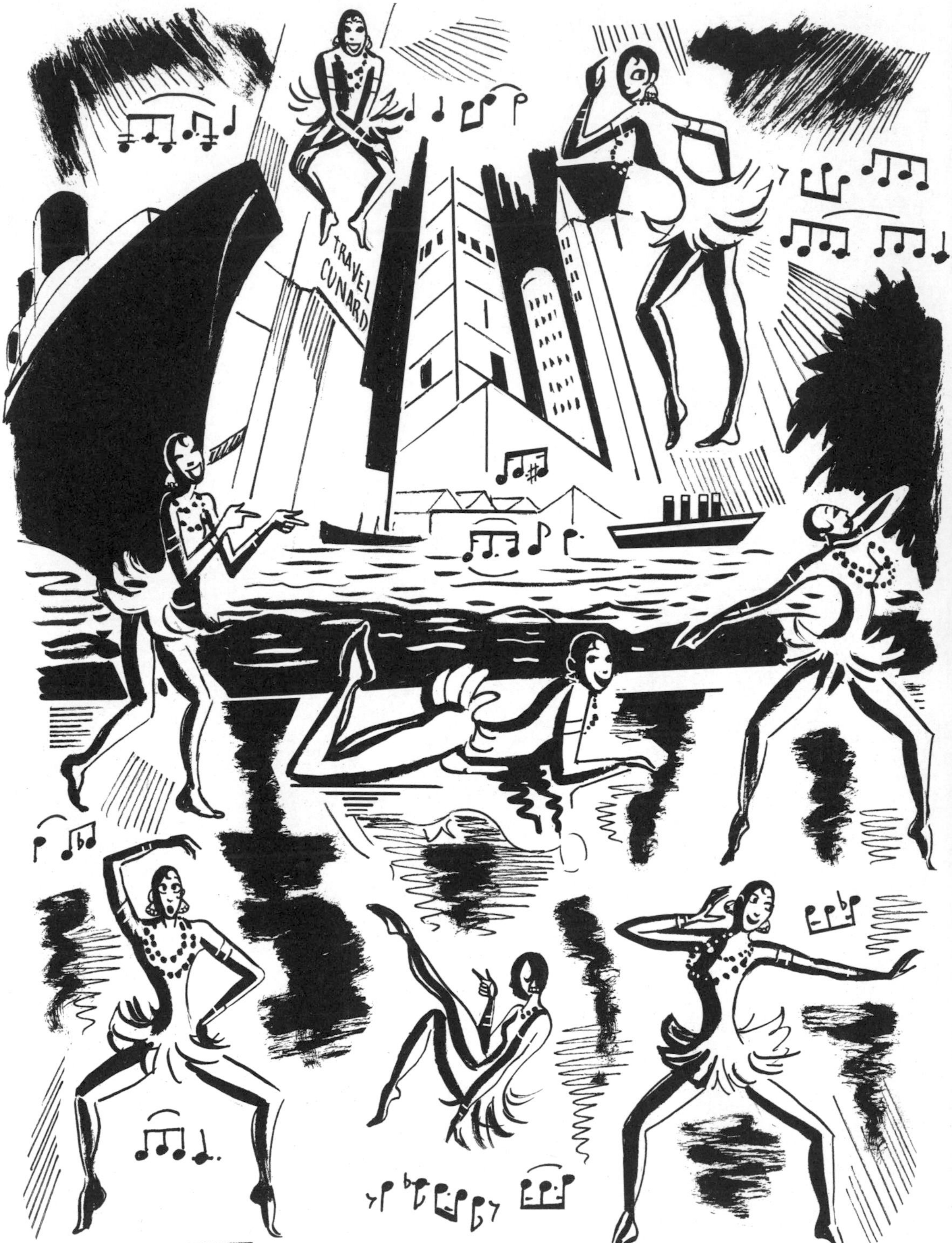
TRAVEL
CUNARD

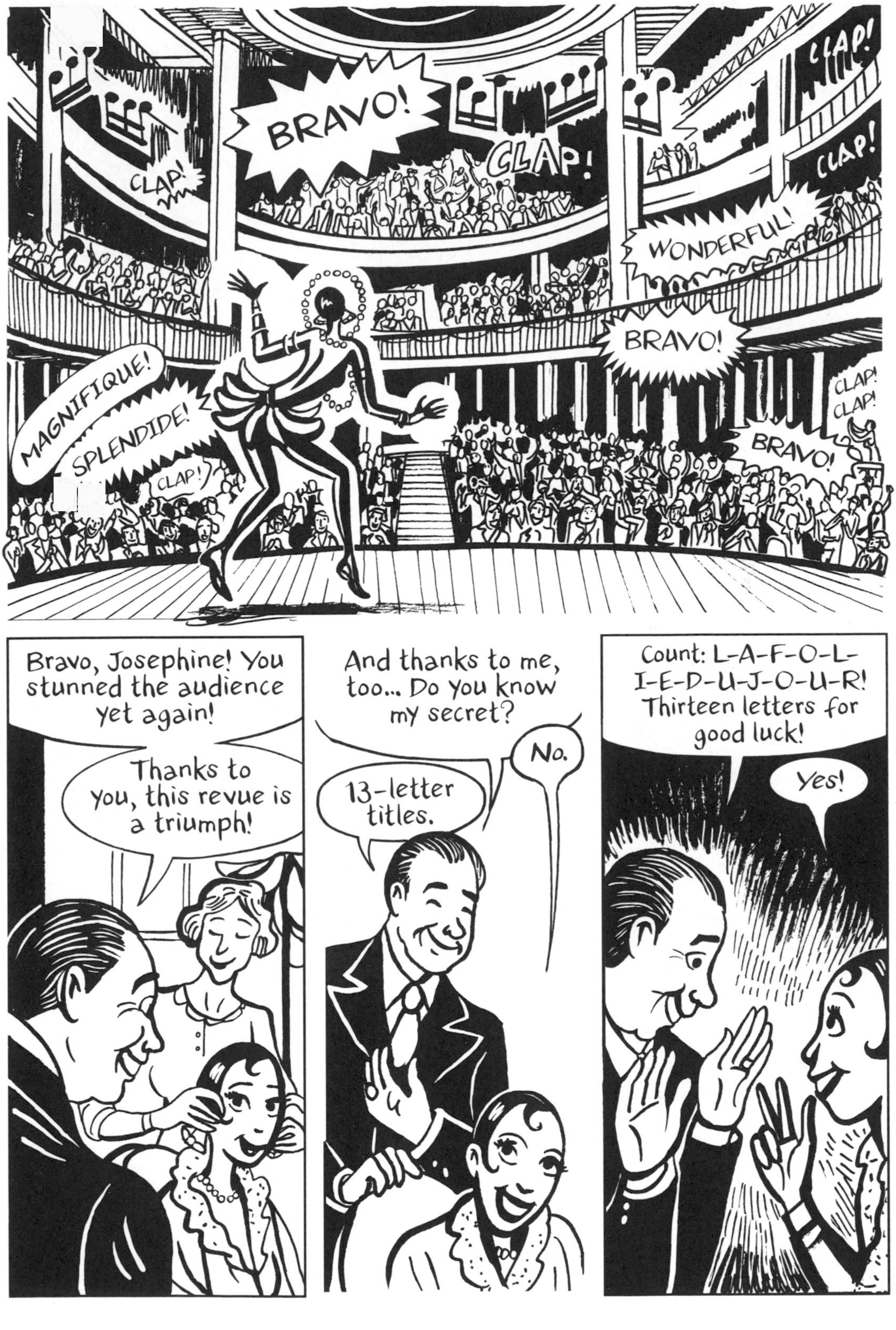
BRAVO!
CLAP!
CLAP!
CLAP!
CLAP!
WONDERFUL!
BRAVO!
MAGNIFIQUE!
SPLENDIDE!
CLAP!
CLAP! CLAP!
BRAVO!
Bravo, Josephine! You stunned the audience yet again!
Thanks to you, this revue is a triumph!
And thanks to me, too... Do you know my secret?
No.
13-letter titles.
Count: L-A-F-O-L-I-E-D-U-J-O-U-R! Thirteen letters for good luck!
Yes!

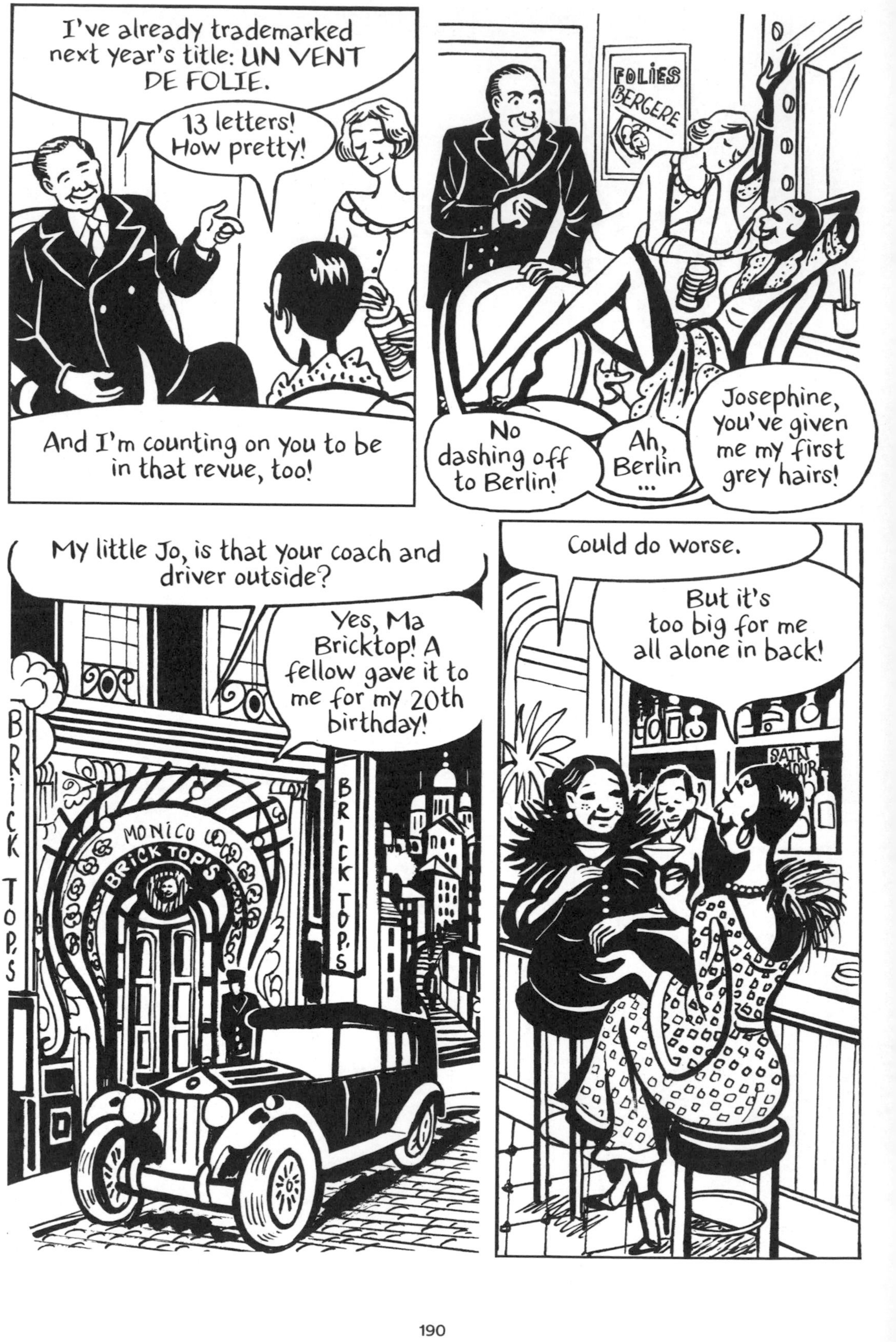
I've already trademarked next year's title: UN VENT DE FOLIE.
13 letters! How pretty!
And I'm counting on you to be in that revue, too!
FOLIES BERGERE
No dashing off to Berlin!
Ah, Berlin ...
Josephine, you've given me my first grey hairs!
My little Jo, is that your coach and driver outside?
Yes, Ma Bricktop! A fellow gave it to me for my 20th birthday!
BRICK TOPS
MONICO
BRICK TOP'S
BRICK TOPS
Could do worse.
But it's too big for me all alone in back!

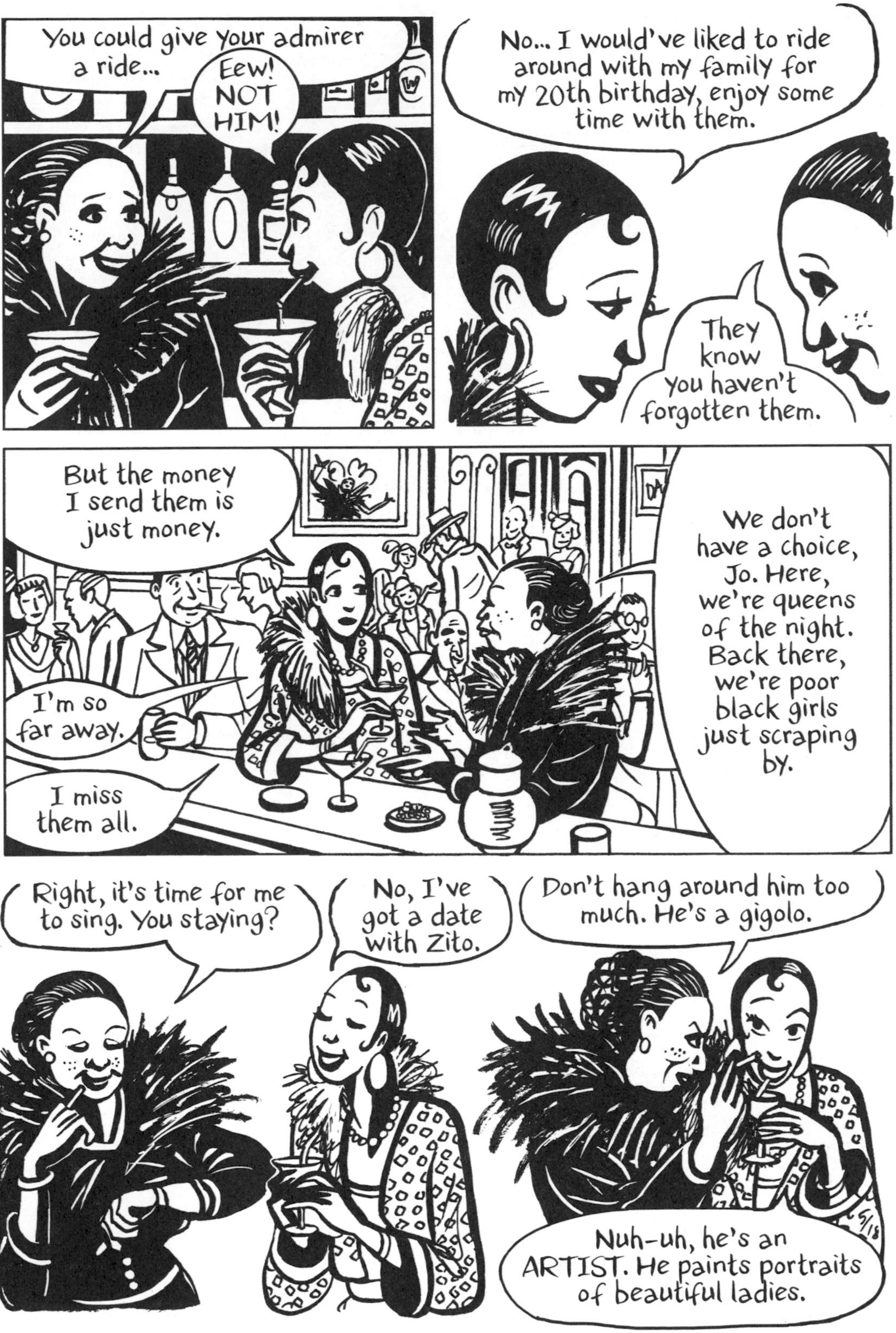

You could give your admirer a ride...
Eew! NOT HIM!
No... I would've liked to ride around with my family for my 20th birthday, enjoy some time with them.
They know you haven't forgotten them.
But the money I send them is just money.
I'm so far away.
I miss them all.
We don't have a choice, Jo. Here, we're queens of the night. Back there, we're poor black girls just scraping by.
Right, it's time for me to sing. You staying?
No, I've got a date with Zito.
Don't hang around him too much. He's a gigolo.
Nuh-uh, he's an ARTIST. He paints portraits of beautiful ladies.

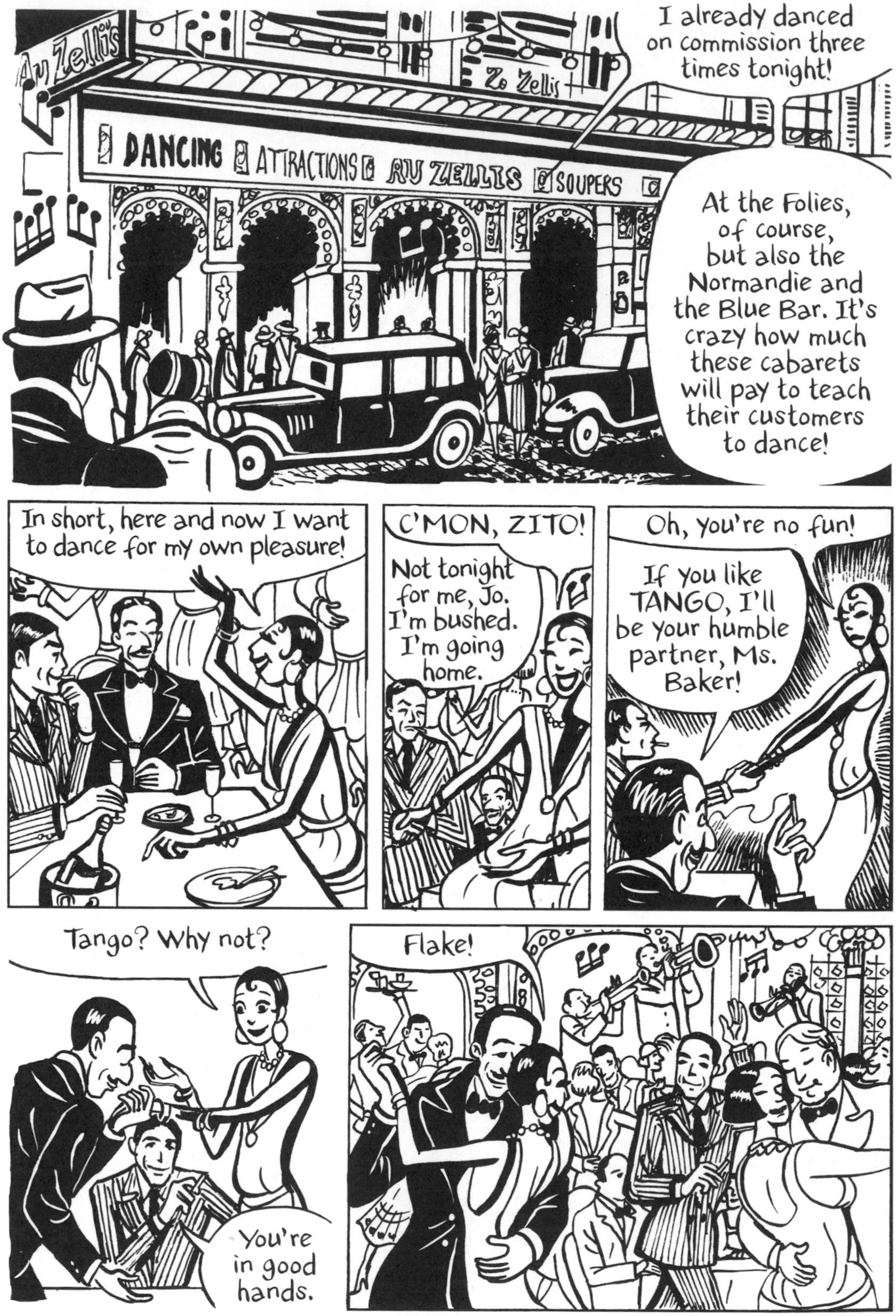
AU ZELLIS
ZO ZELLIS
DANCING
ATTRACTIONS
AU ZELLIS
SOUPERS
I already danced on commission three times tonight!
At the Folies, of course, but also the Normandie and the Blue Bar. It's crazy how much these cabarets will pay to teach their customers to dance!
In short, here and now I want to dance for my own pleasure!
C'MON, ZITO!
Not tonight for me, Jo. I'm bushed. I'm going home.
Oh, you're no fun!
If you like TANGO, I'll be your humble partner, Ms. Baker!
Tango? Why not?
You're in good hands.
Flake!

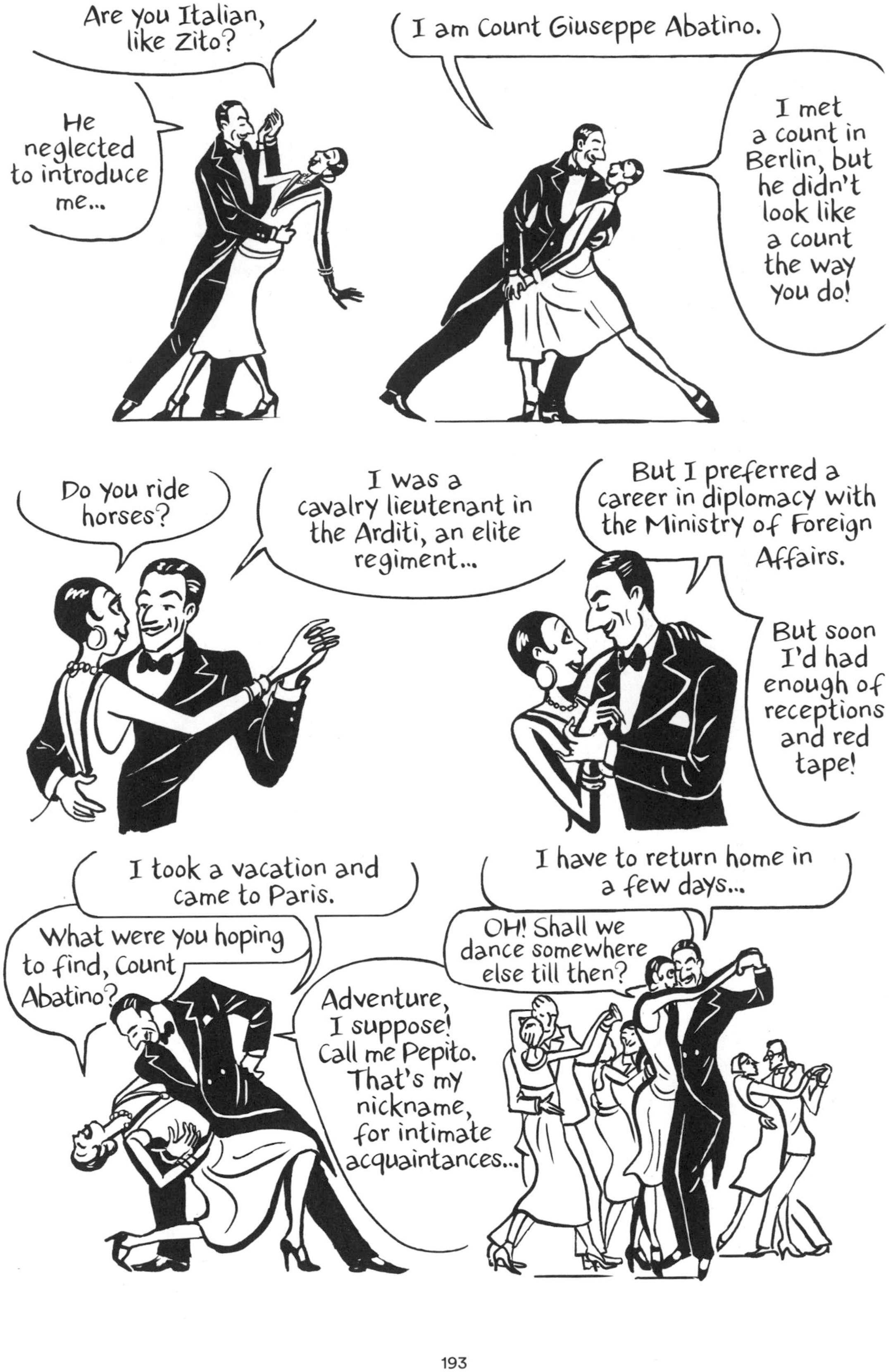
Are you Italian, like Zito?
He neglected to introduce me...
I am Count Giuseppe Abatino.
I met a count in Berlin, but he didn't look like a count the way you do!
Do you ride horses?
I was a cavalry lieutenant in the Arditi, an elite regiment...
But I preferred a career in diplomacy with the Ministry of Foreign Affairs.
But soon I'd had enough of receptions and red tape!
I took a vacation and came to Paris.
What were you hoping to find, Count Abatino?
Adventure, I suppose! Call me Pepito. That's my nickname, for intimate acquaintances...
I have to return home in a few days...
OH! Shall we dance somewhere else till then?

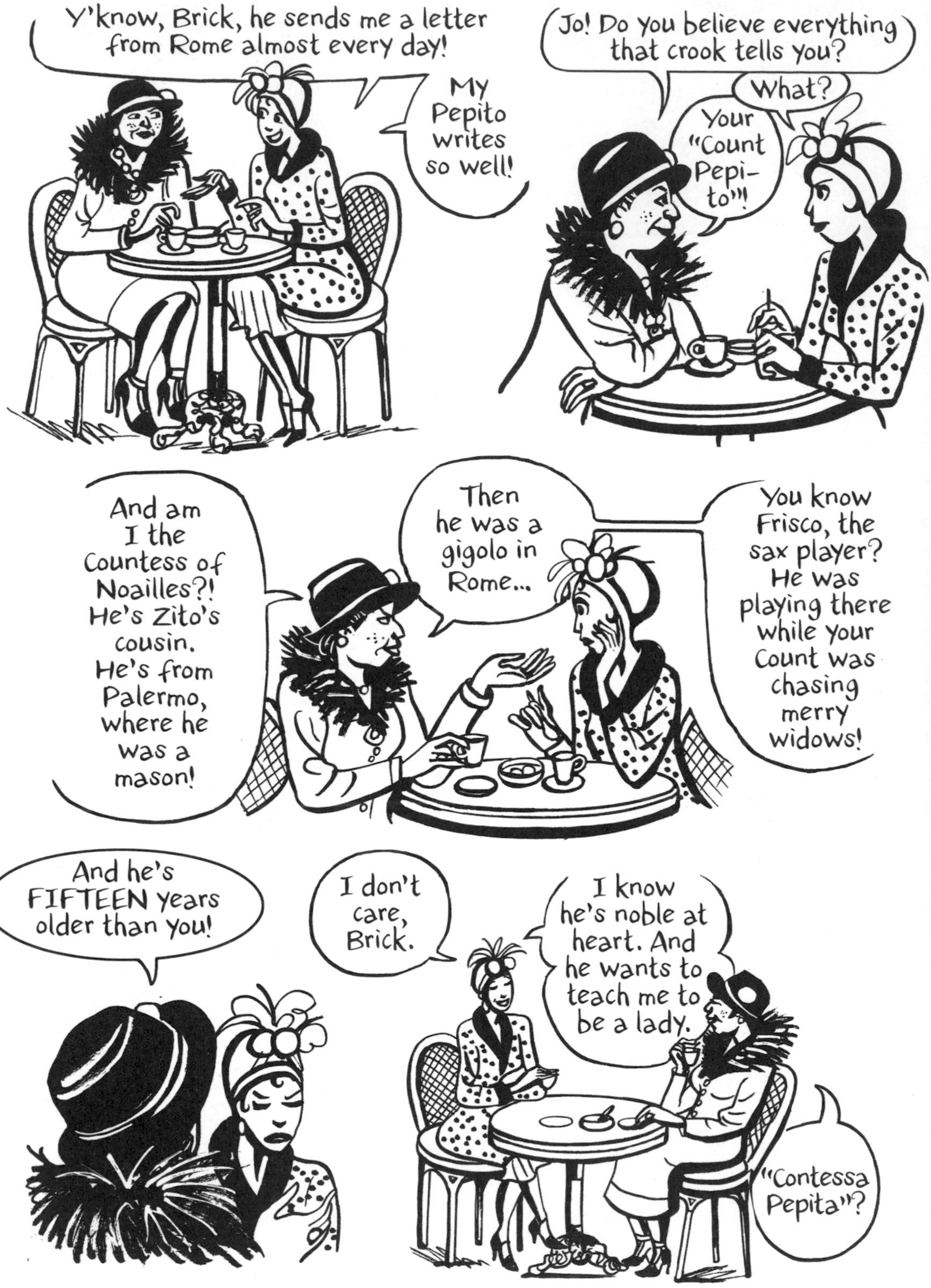
Y'know, Brick, he sends me a letter from Rome almost every day!
My Pepito writes so well!
Jo! Do you believe everything that crook tells you?
What?
Your "Count Pepi-to"!
And am I the Countess of Noailles?! He's Zito's cousin. He's from Palermo, where he was a mason!
Then he was a gigolo in Rome...
You know Frisco, the sax player? He was playing there while your Count was chasing merry widows!
And he's FIFTEEN years older than you!
I don't care, Brick.
I know he's noble at heart. And he wants to teach me to be a lady.
"Contessa Pepita"?

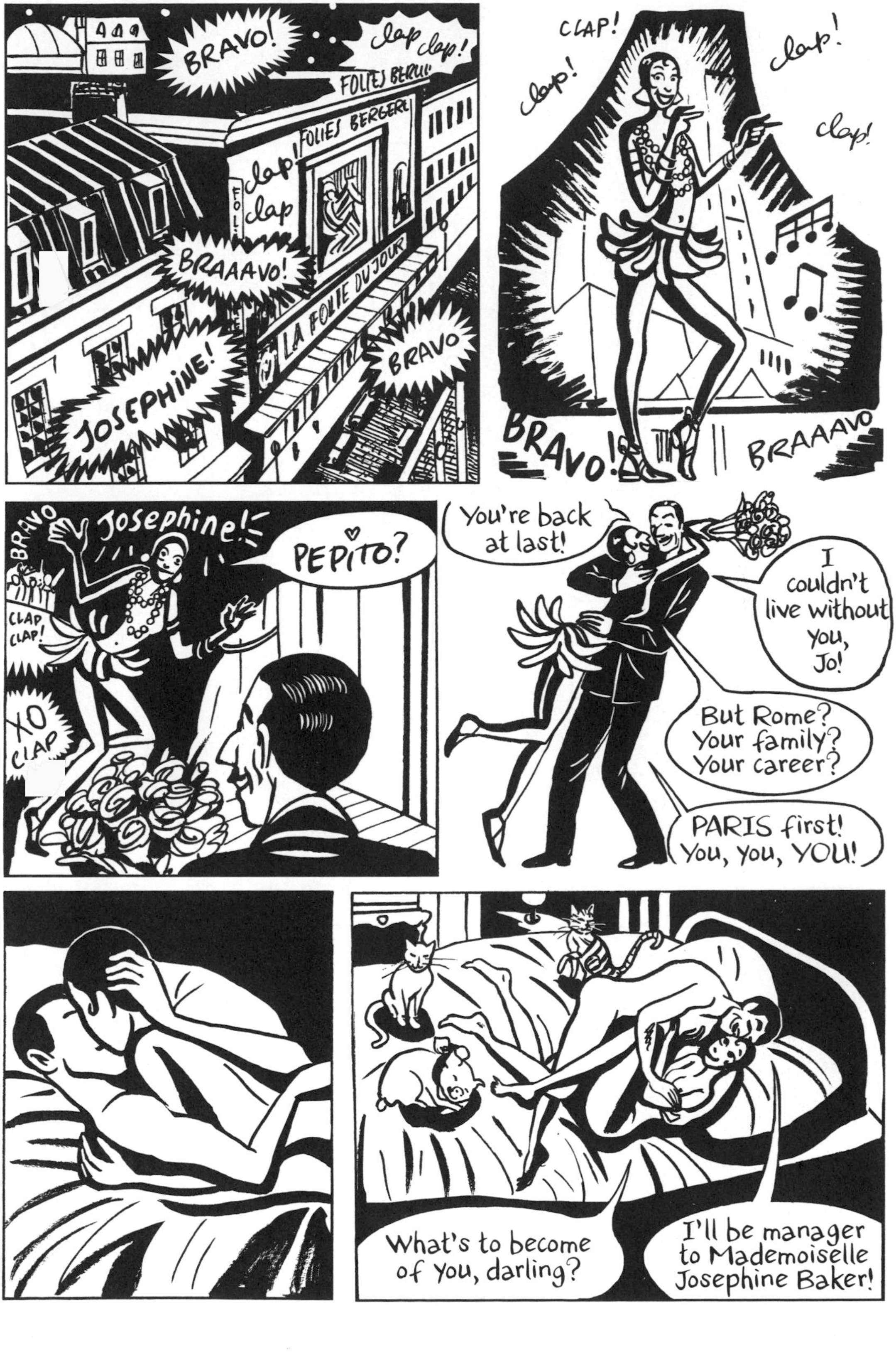
BRAVO!
clap clap!
FOLIES BERGÈRE
clap clap
BRAAAVO!
LA FOLIE DU JOUR
JOSEPHINE!
BRAVO
CLAP!
clap!
clap!
clap!
BRAVO!
BRAAAVO
BRAVO
Josephine!
CLAP, CLAP!
XO CLAP
PEPITO?
You're back at last!
I couldn't live without you, Jo!
But Rome? Your family? Your career?
PARIS first! You, you, YOU!
What's to become of you, darling?
I'll be manager to Mademoiselle Josephine Baker!

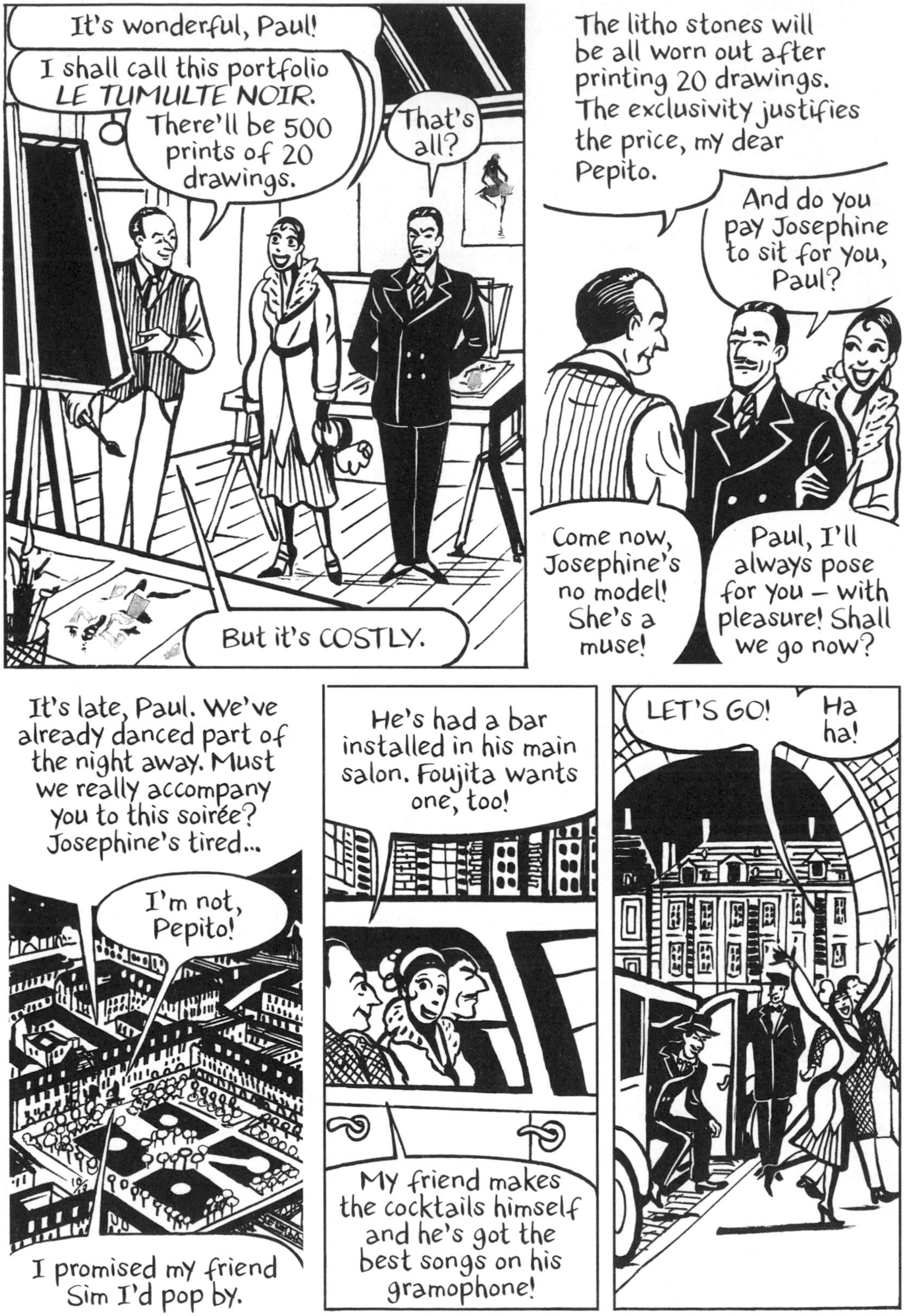
It's wonderful, Paul!
I shall call this portfolio LE TUMULTE NOIR. There'll be 500 prints of 20 drawings.
That's all?
But it's COSTLY.
The litho stones will be all worn out after printing 20 drawings. The exclusivity justifies the price, my dear Pepito.
And do you pay Josephine to sit for you, Paul?
Come now, Josephine's no model! She's a muse!
Paul, I'll always pose for you – with pleasure! Shall we go now?
It's late, Paul. We've already danced part of the night away. Must we really accompany you to this soirée? Josephine's tired...
I'm not, Pepito!
I promised my friend Sim I'd pop by.
He's had a bar installed in his main salon. Foujita wants one, too!
My friend makes the cocktails himself and he's got the best songs on his gramophone!
LET'S GO!
Ha ha!

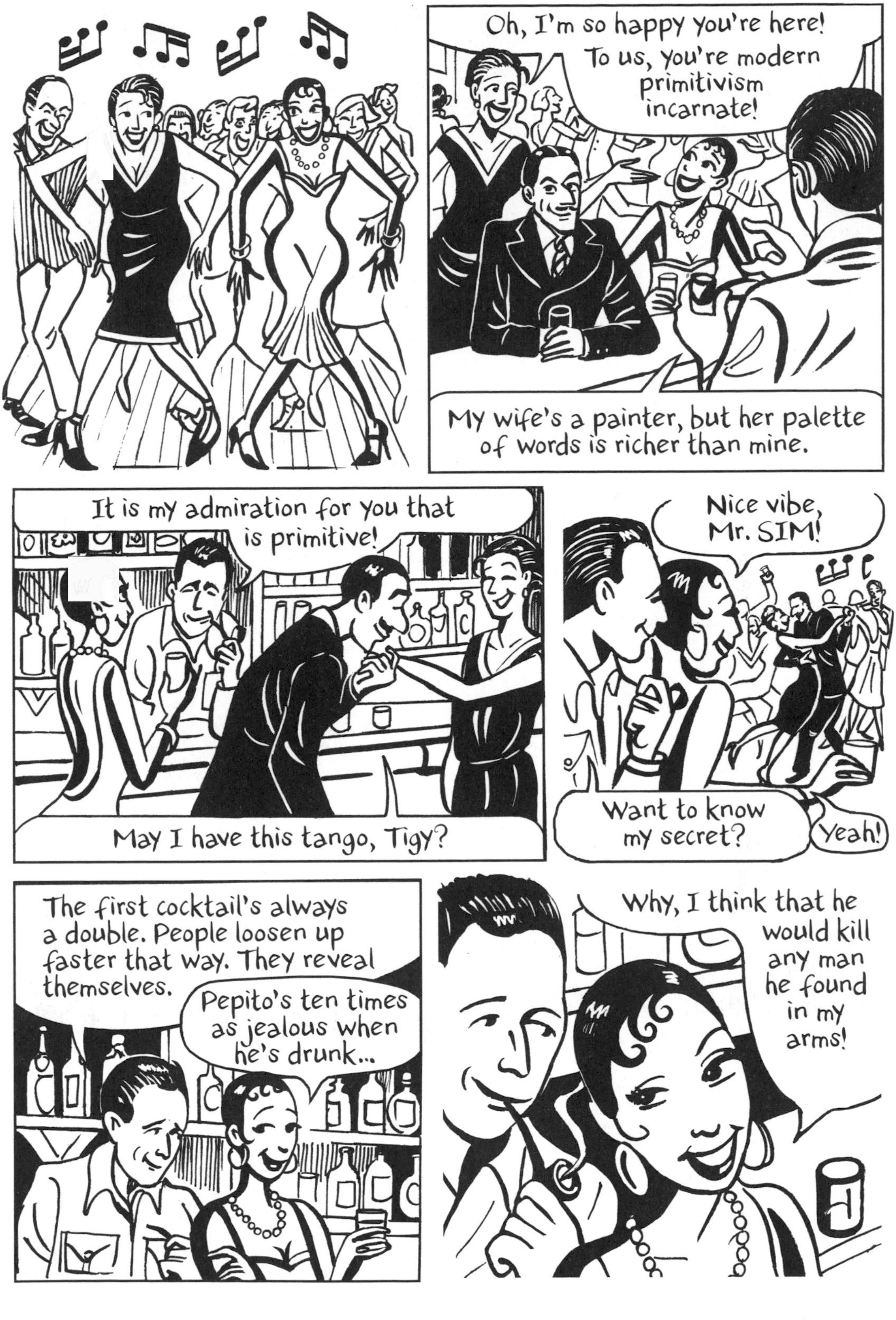
Oh, I'm so happy you're here!
To us, you're modern primitivism incarnate!
My wife's a painter, but her palette of words is richer than mine.
It is my admiration for you that is primitive!
May I have this tango, Tigy?
Nice vibe, Mr. SIM!
Want to know my secret?
Yeah!
The first cocktail's always a double. People loosen up faster that way. They reveal themselves.
Pepito's ten times as jealous when he's drunk...
Why, I think that he would kill any man he found in my arms!

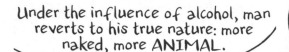

Under the influence of alcohol, man reverts to his true nature: more naked, more ANIMAL.

I like watching men in their natural state. And women, too!

I know. You were watching me while I danced...

You were watching me, too, while you danced.

What do you want, Georges Sim?

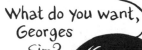

When?

Right now.

Where?

In the stairwell.

To dance on your merry derrière, beautiful Josephine.

RISKY.

It'll have to be a quickie.

OK.

You've got ten minutes to pleasure me.

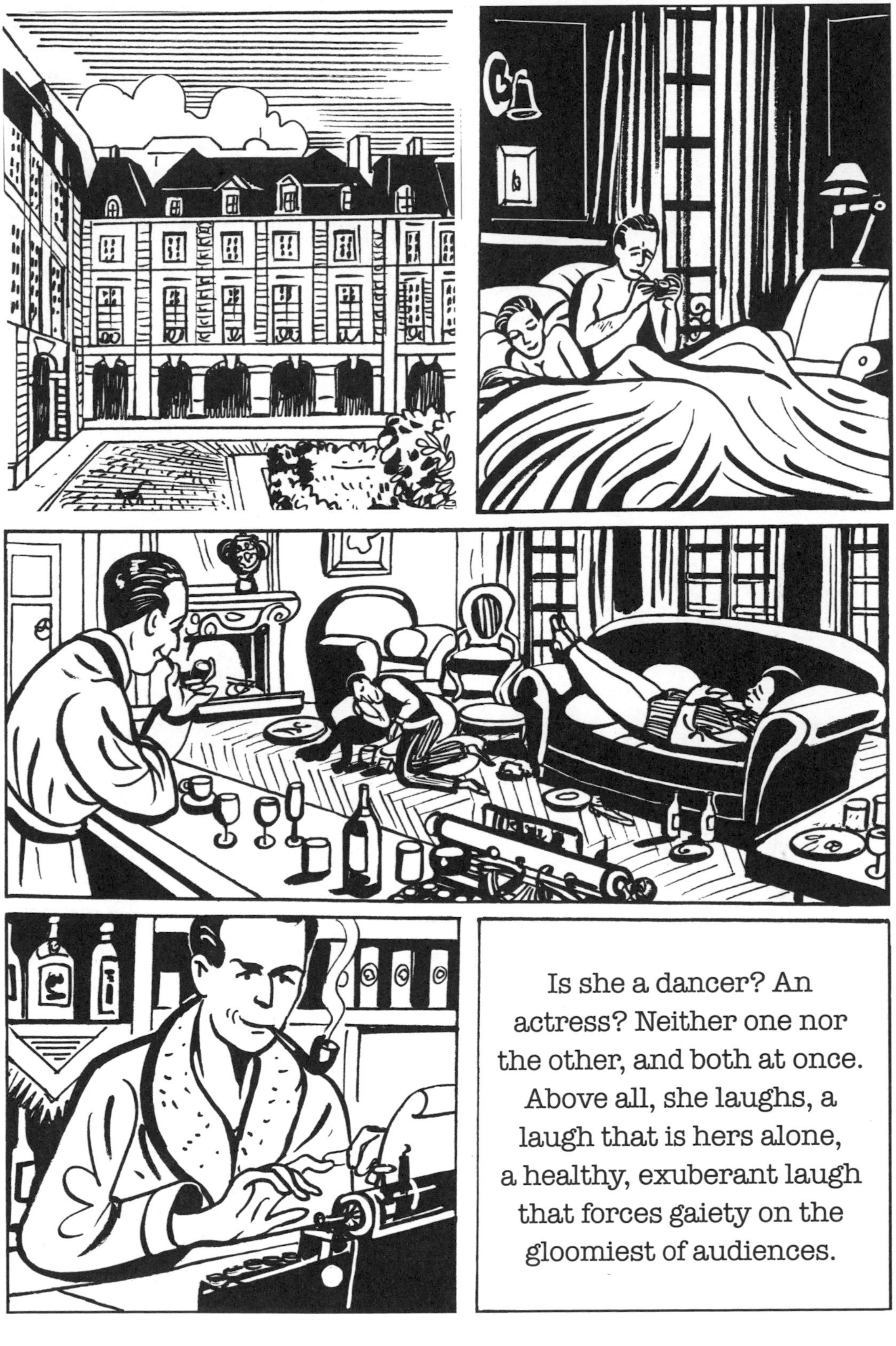
Is she a dancer? An actress? Neither one nor the other, and both at once. Above all, she laughs, a laugh that is hers alone, a healthy, exuberant laugh that forces gaiety on the gloomiest of audiences.

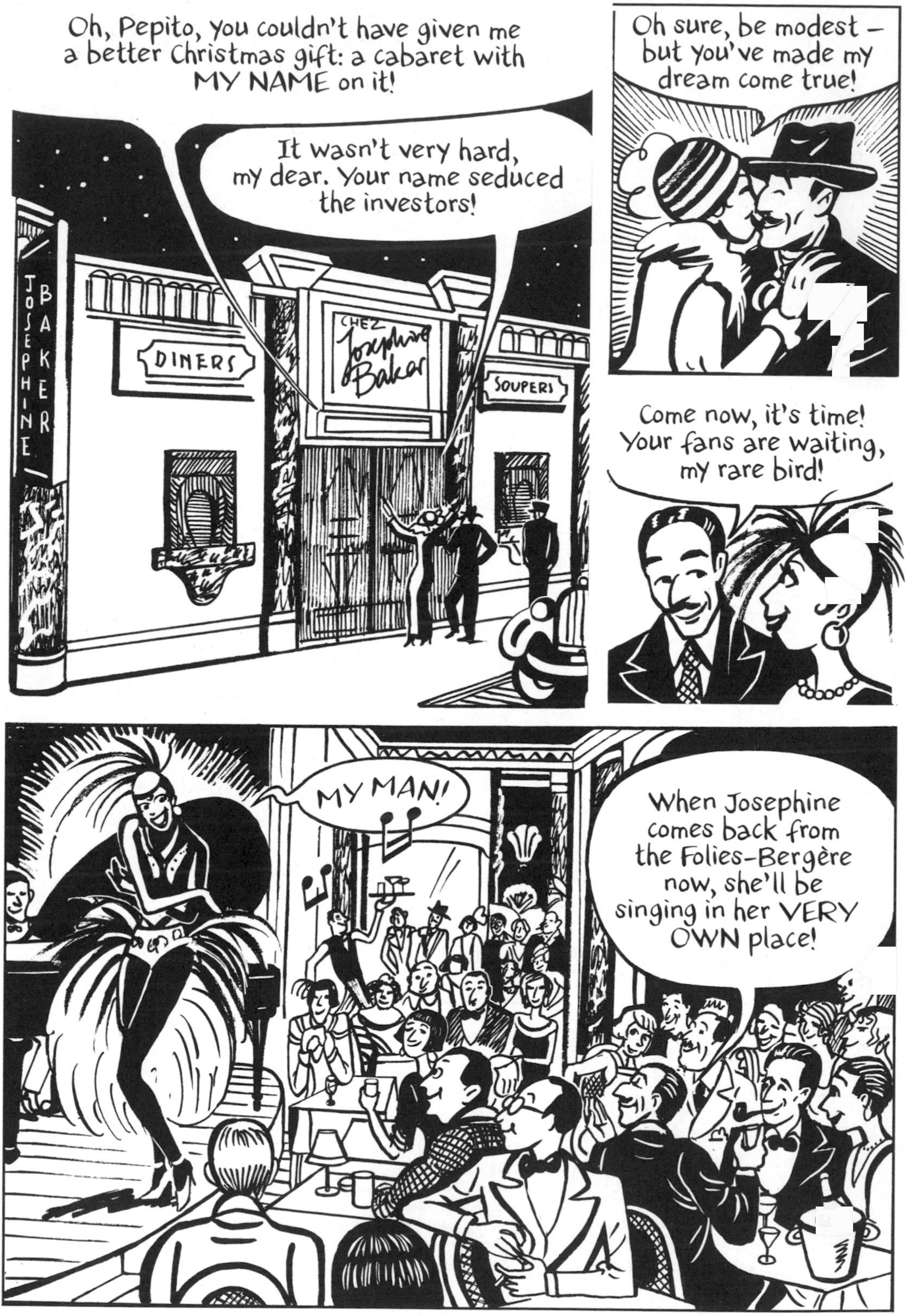

Oh, Pepito, you couldn't have given me a better Christmas gift: a cabaret with MY NAME on it!
It wasn't very hard, my dear. Your name seduced the investors!
JOSEPHINE BAKER
DINERS
CHEZ Josephine Baker
SOUPERS
Oh sure, be modest – but you've made my dream come true!
Come now, it's time! Your fans are waiting, my rare bird!
MY MAN!
When Josephine comes back from the Folies-Bergère now, she'll be singing in her VERY OWN place!

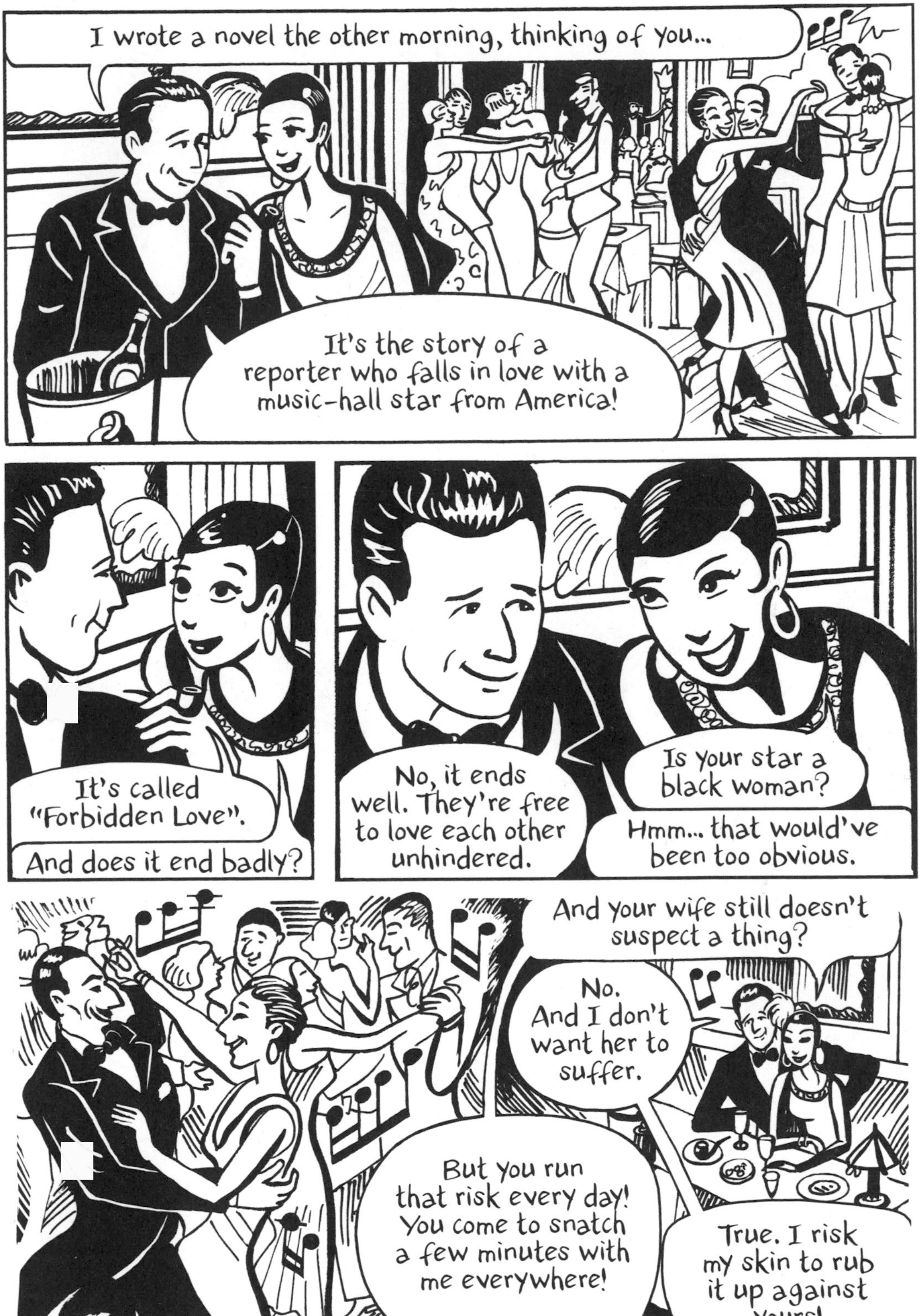
I wrote a novel the other morning, thinking of you...
It's the story of a reporter who falls in love with a music-hall star from America!
It's called "Forbidden Love".
And does it end badly?
No, it ends well. They're free to love each other unhindered.
Is your star a black woman?
Hmm... that would've been too obvious.
And your wife still doesn't suspect a thing?
No. And I don't want her to suffer.
But you run that risk every day! You come to snatch a few minutes with me everywhere!
True. I risk my skin to rub it up against yours!

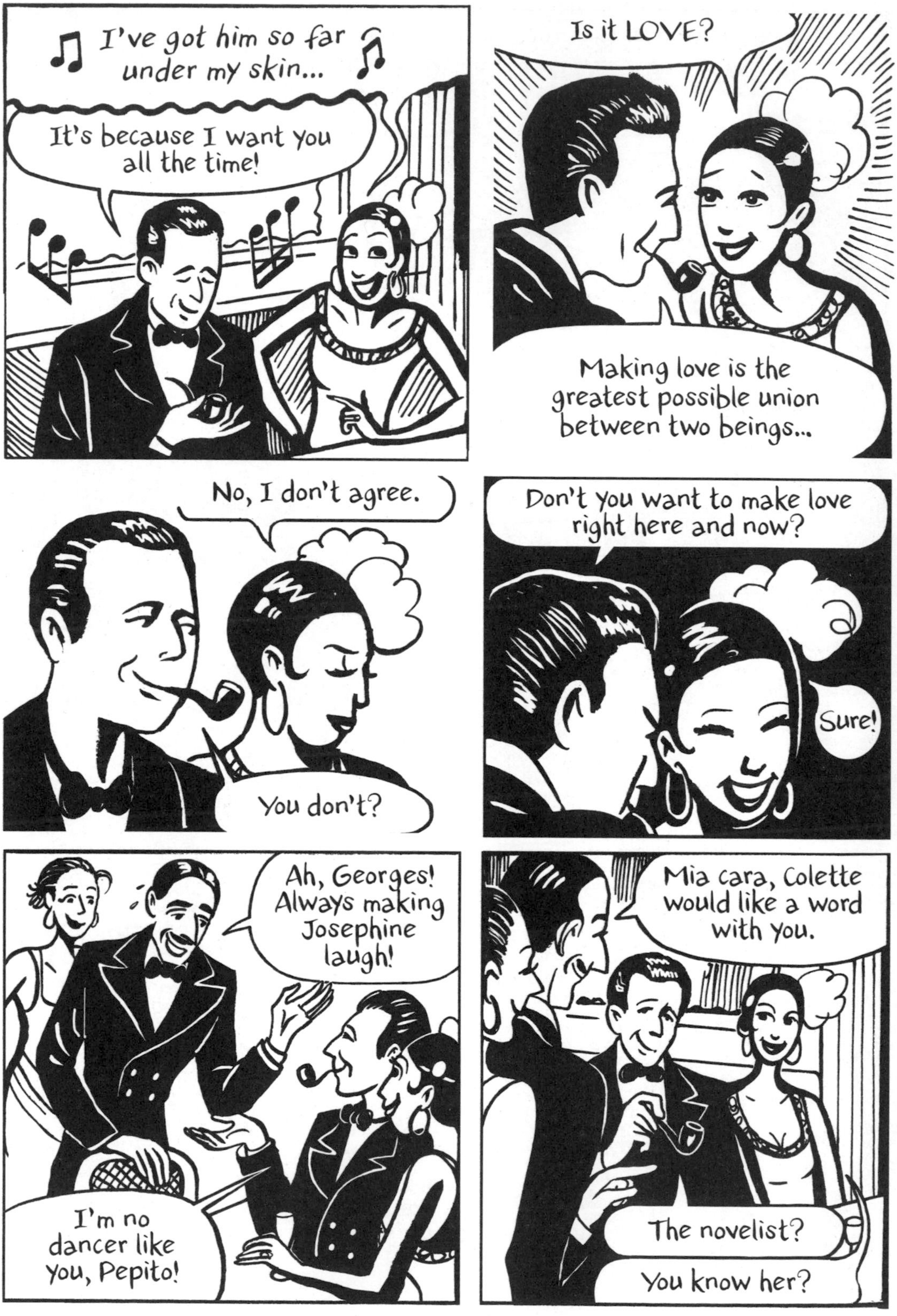
I've got him so far under my skin...
It's because I want you all the time!
Is it LOVE?
Making love is the greatest possible union between two beings...
No, I don't agree.
You don't?
Don't you want to make love right here and now?
Sure!
Ah, Georges! Always making Josephine laugh!
I'm no dancer like you, Pepito!
Mia cara, Colette would like a word with you.
The novelist?
You know her?

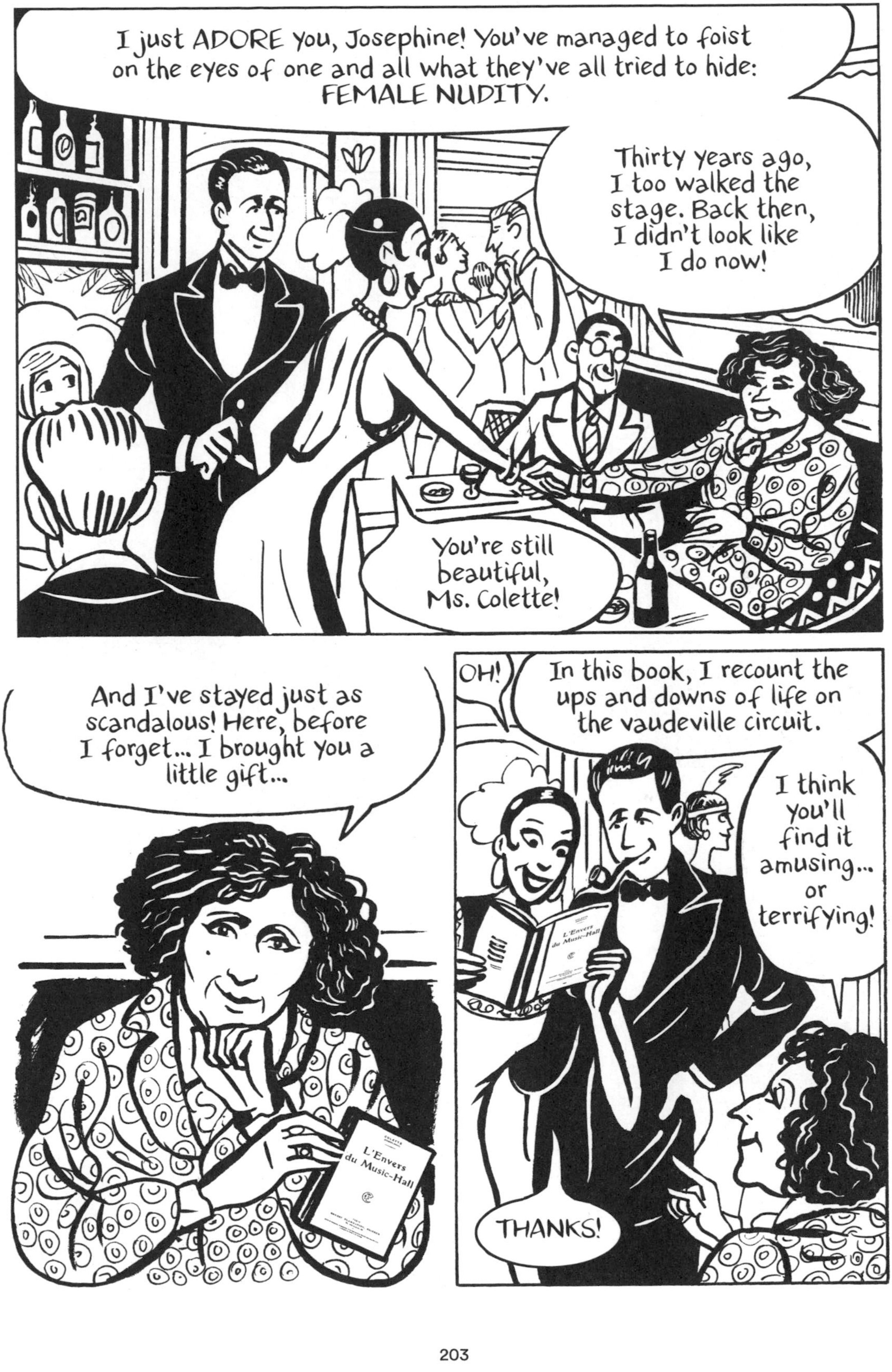
I just ADORE you, Josephine! You've managed to foist on the eyes of one and all what they've all tried to hide: FEMALE NUDITY.
Thirty years ago, I too walked the stage. Back then, I didn't look like I do now!
You're still beautiful, Ms. Colette!
And I've stayed just as scandalous! Here, before I forget... I brought you a little gift...
L'Envers du Music-Hall
OH!
In this book, I recount the ups and downs of life on the vaudeville circuit.
I think you'll find it amusing... or terrifying!
L'Envers du Music-Hall
THANKS!

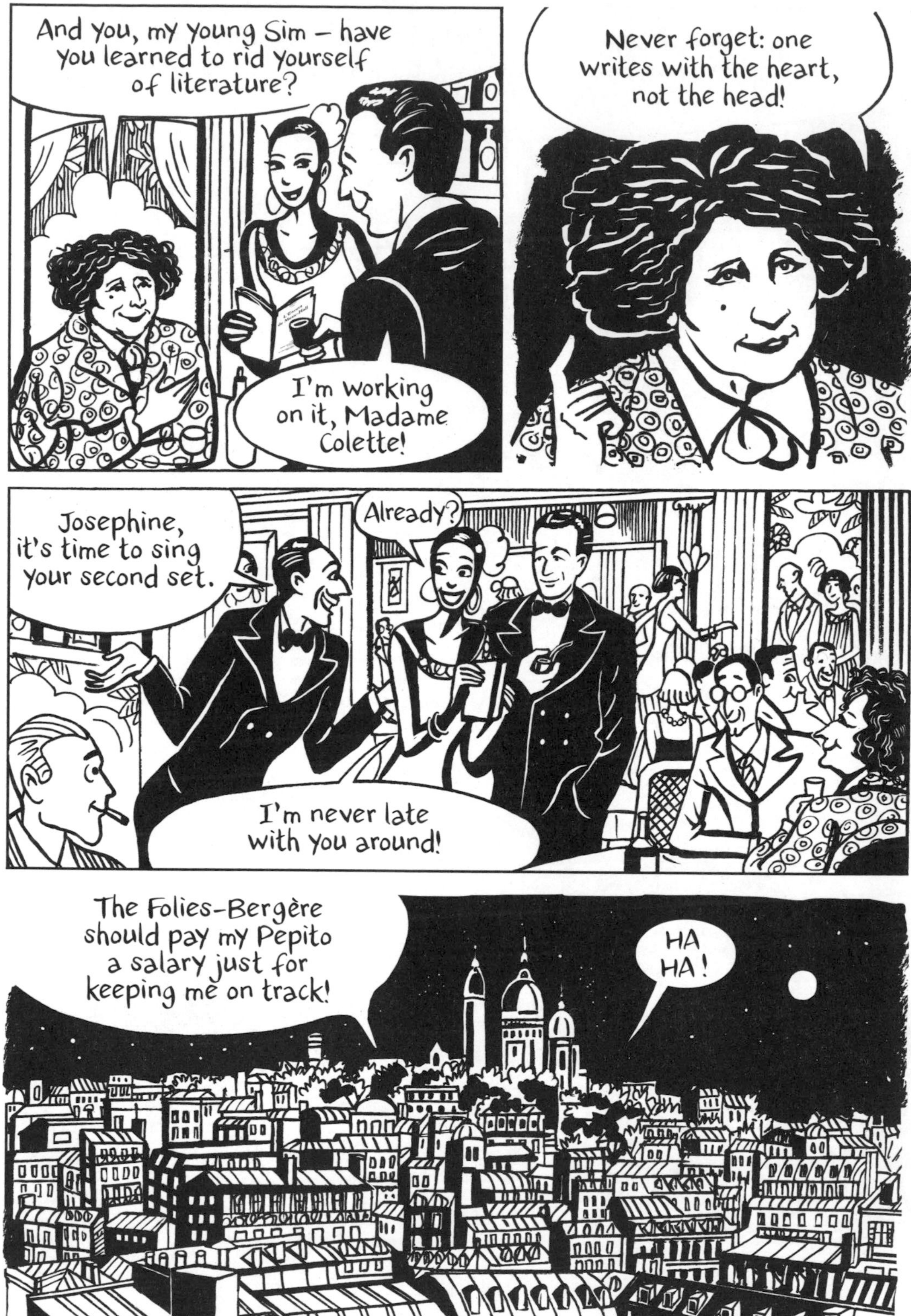
And you, my young Sim – have you learned to rid yourself of literature?
I'm working on it, Madame Colette!
Never forget: one writes with the heart, not the head!
Josephine, it's time to sing your second set.
Already?
I'm never late with you around!
The Folies-Bergère should pay my Pepito a salary just for keeping me on track!
HA HA!

1927: Rue Mallet-Stevens, Paris, France

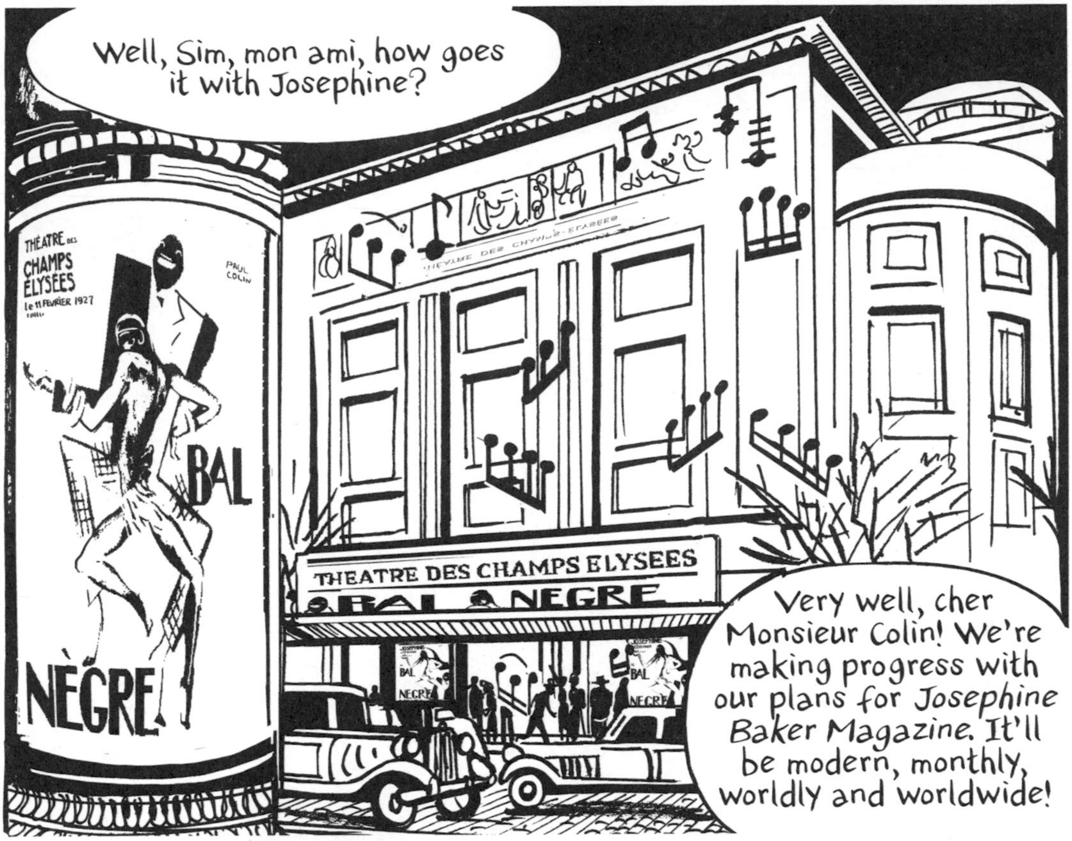
Well, Sim, mon ami, how goes it with Josephine?
THÉATRE DES CHAMPS ELYSÉES le 11 FEVRIER 1927
PAUL COLIN
BAL
NÈGRE
THEATRE DES CHAMPS ELYSEES
BAL NEGRE
Very well, cher Monsieur Colin! We're making progress with our plans for Josephine Baker Magazine. It'll be modern, monthly, worldly and worldwide!

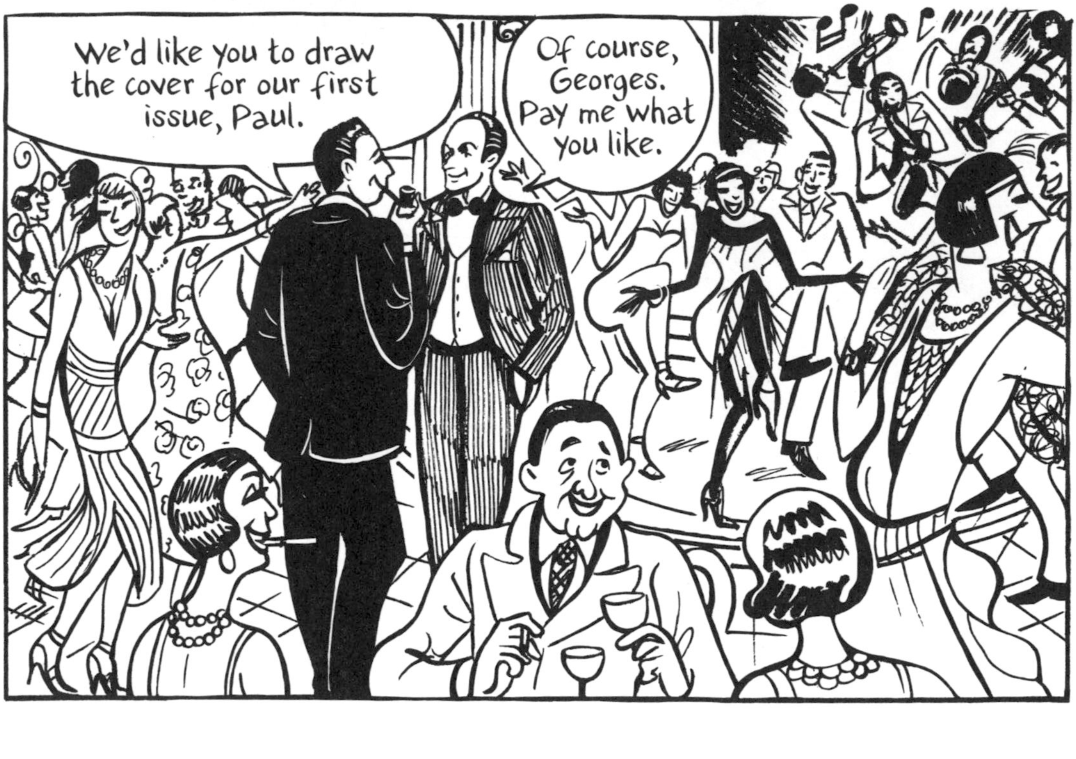
We'd like you to draw the cover for our first issue, Paul.
Of course, Georges. Pay me what you like.

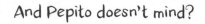

And Pepito doesn't mind?

I've put together part of the backing already...

But he wants his cut, of course!

I told him it's free publicity for Jo, but he says my backers are getting rich at his expense!

Sounds just like him!

I'm not worried. He'll end up seeing things my way.

Hey there, fellas! Plotting away?

For your HAPPINESS, darling! Paul wants to contribute to our magazine.

TERRIFIC!

I'M HOT!

Me, too!

Wanna dance, mon petit Sim?

Only on your derrière!

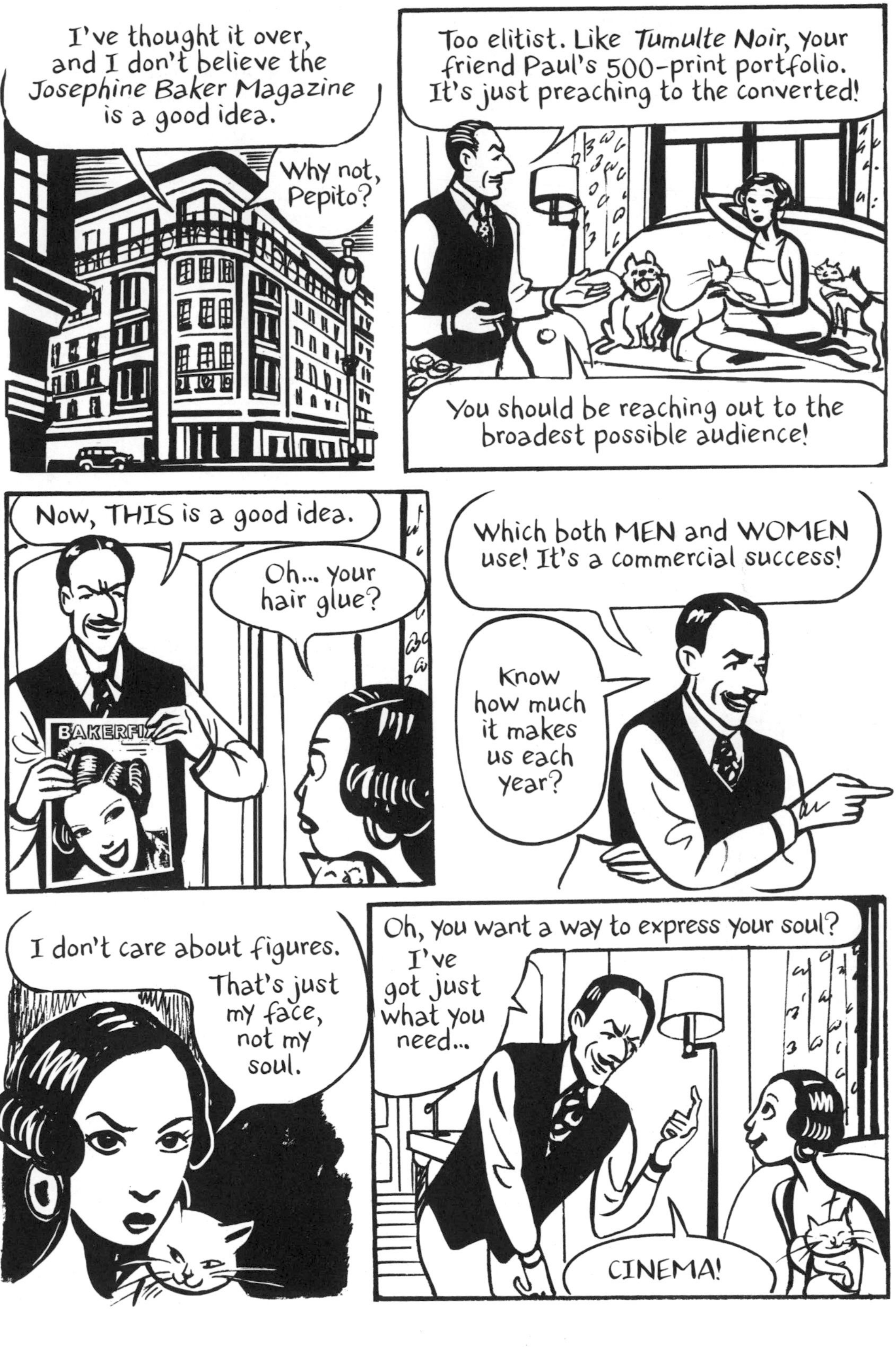

I've thought it over, and I don't believe the *Josephine Baker Magazine* is a good idea.
Why not, Pepito?
Too elitist. Like *Tumulte Noir*, your friend Paul's 500-print portfolio. It's just preaching to the converted!
You should be reaching out to the broadest possible audience!
Now, THIS is a good idea.
Oh... your hair glue?
BAKERFIX
Which both MEN and WOMEN use! It's a commercial success!
Know how much it makes us each year?
I don't care about figures.
That's just my face, not my soul.
Oh, you want a way to express your soul?
I've got just what you need...
CINEMA!

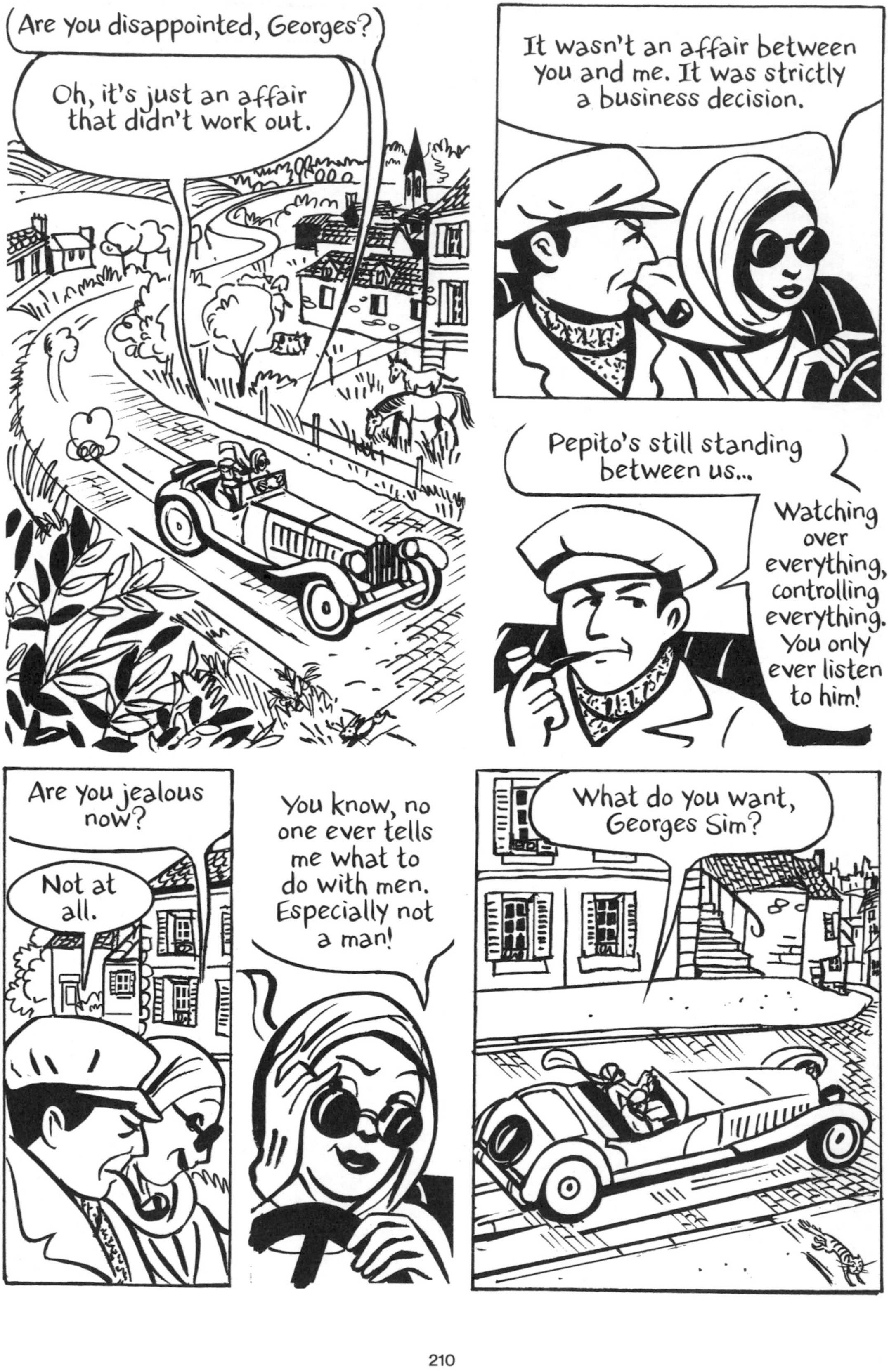
Are you disappointed, Georges?
Oh, it's just an affair that didn't work out.
It wasn't an affair between you and me. It was strictly a business decision.
Pepito's still standing between us...
Watching over everything, controlling everything. You only ever listen to him!
Are you jealous now?
Not at all.
You know, no one ever tells me what to do with men. Especially not a man!
What do you want, Georges Sim?

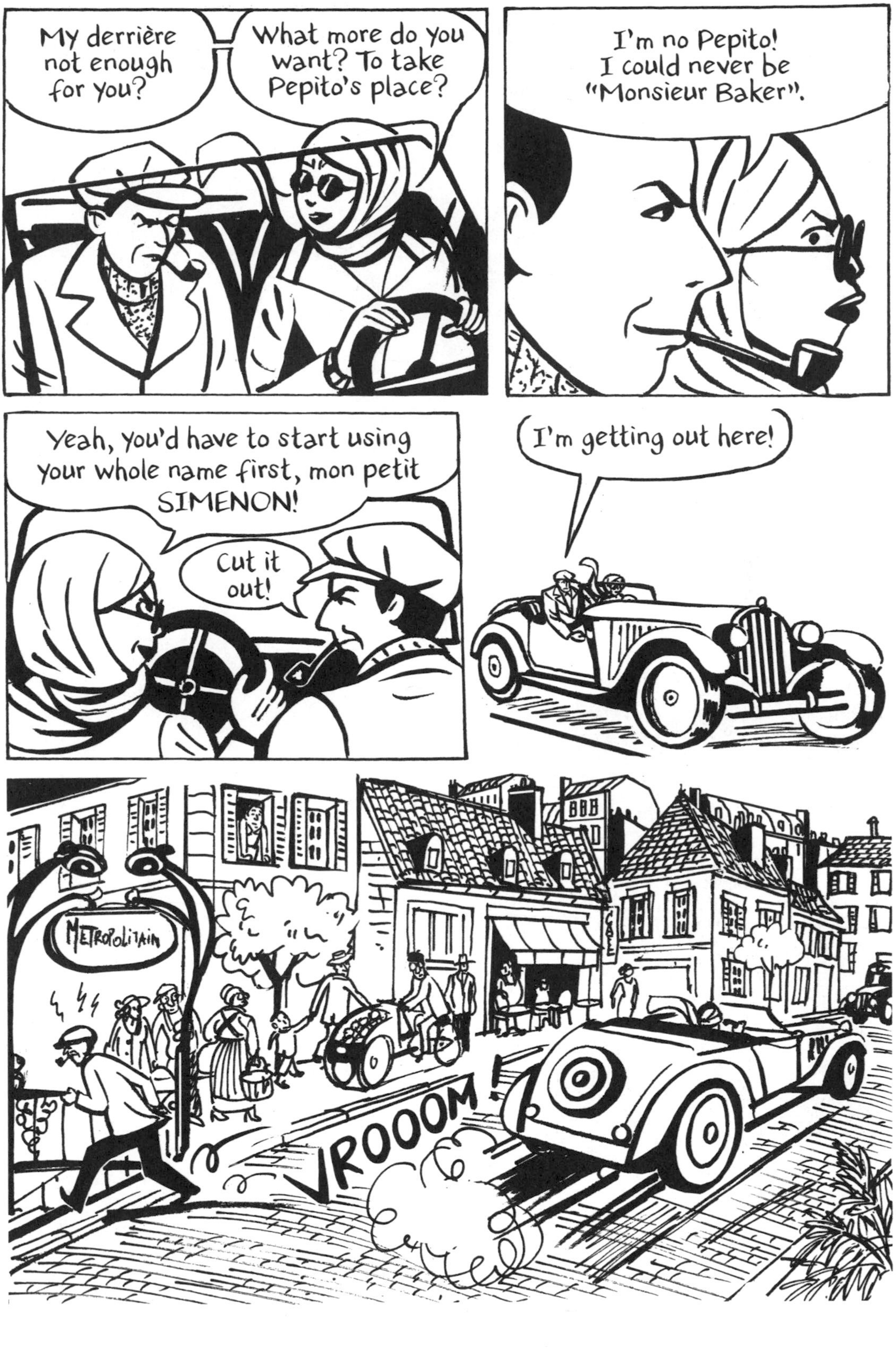
My derrière not enough for you?
What more do you want? To take Pepito's place?
I'm no Pepito! I could never be "Monsieur Baker".
Yeah, you'd have to start using your whole name first, mon petit SIMENON!
Cut it out!
I'm getting out here!
METROPOLITAIN
CAFÉ
VROOOM!

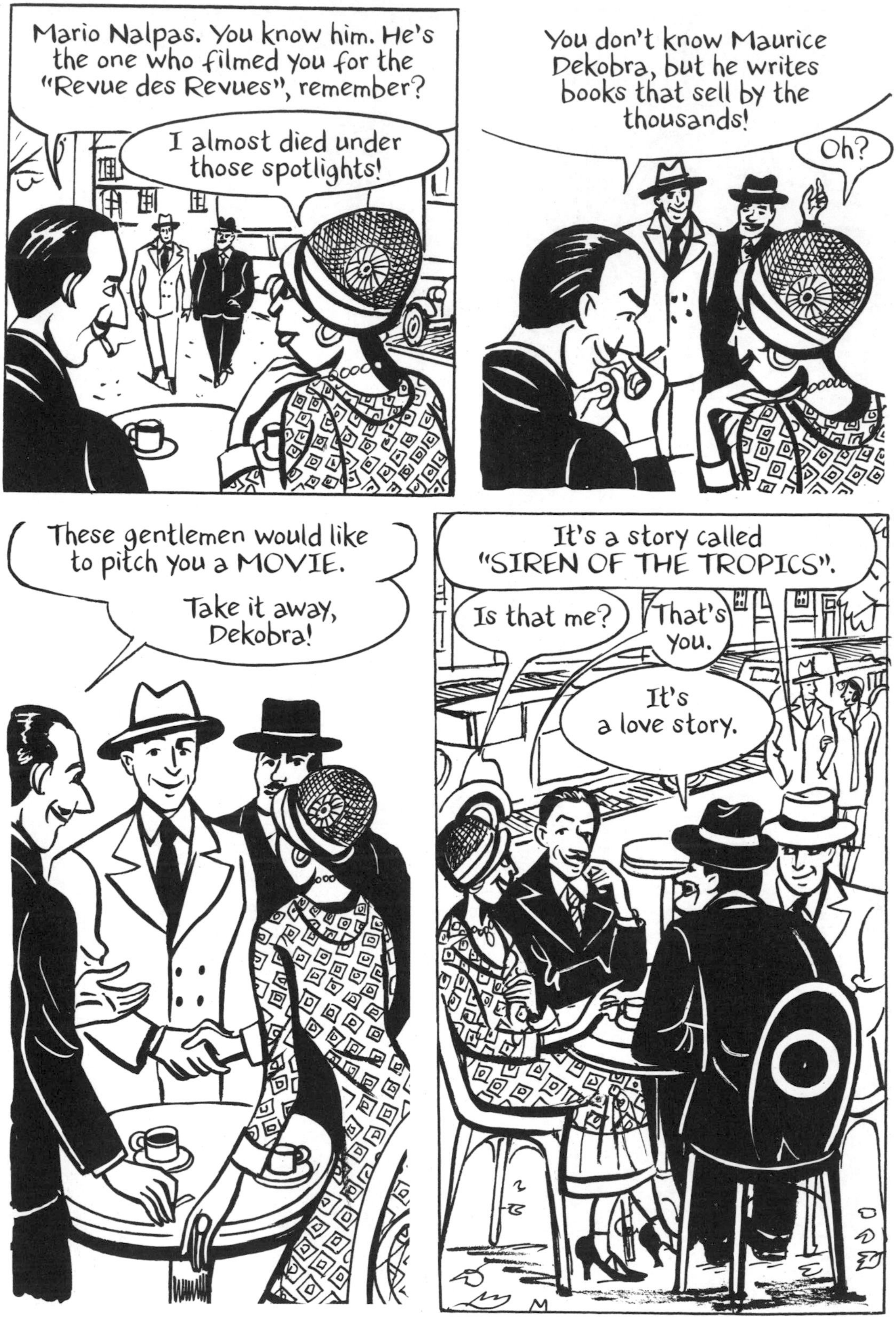

Mario Nalpas. You know him. He's the one who filmed you for the "Revue des Revues", remember?
I almost died under those spotlights!
You don't know Maurice Dekobra, but he writes books that sell by the thousands!
Oh?
These gentlemen would like to pitch you a MOVIE.
Take it away, Dekobra!
It's a story called "SIREN OF THE TROPICS".
Is that me?
That's you.
It's a love story.

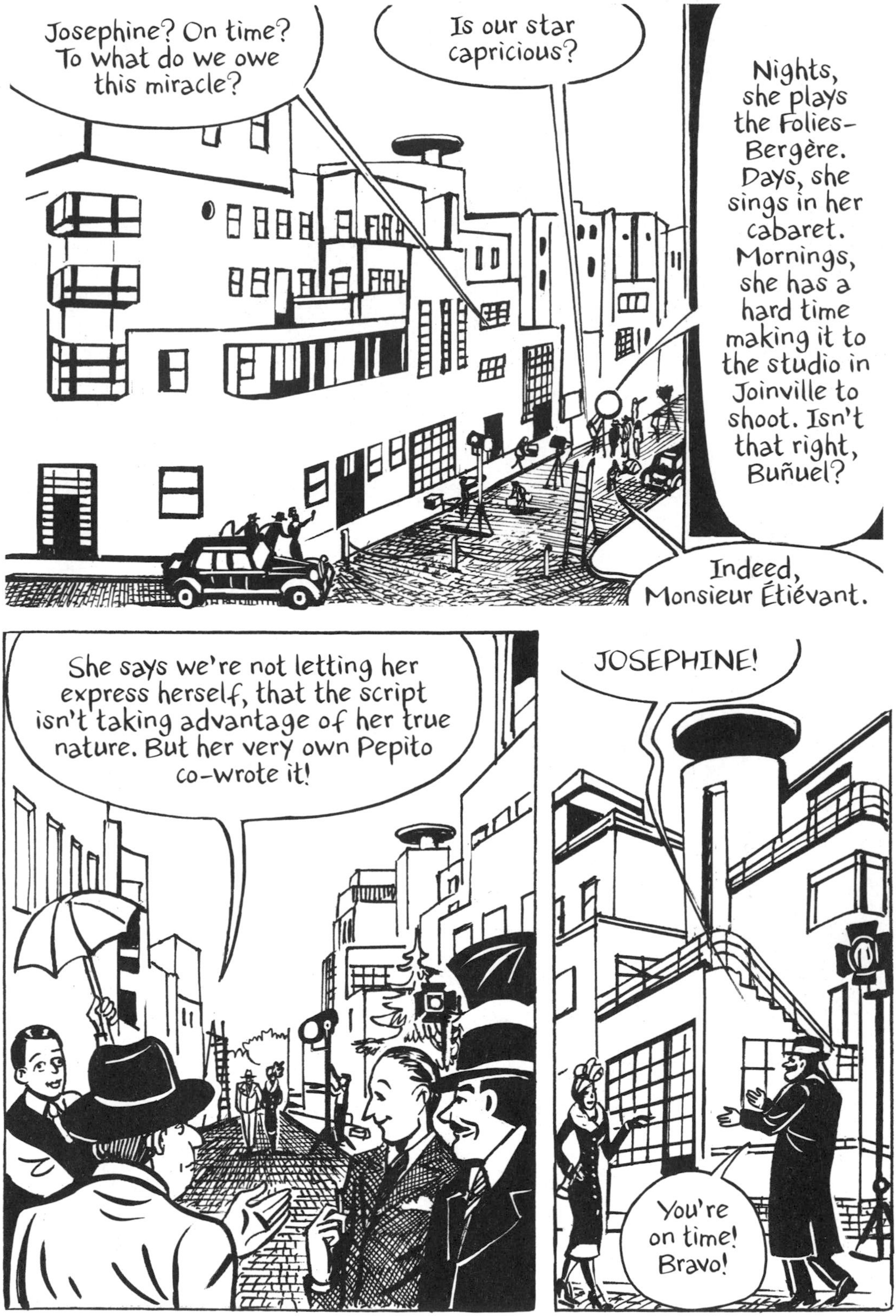
Josephine? On time? To what do we owe this miracle?
Is our star capricious?
Nights, she plays the Folies-Bergère. Days, she sings in her cabaret. Mornings, she has a hard time making it to the studio in Joinville to shoot. Isn't that right, Buñuel?
Indeed, Monsieur Étiévant.
She says we're not letting her express herself, that the script isn't taking advantage of her true nature. But her very own Pepito co-wrote it!
JOSEPHINE!
You're on time! Bravo!

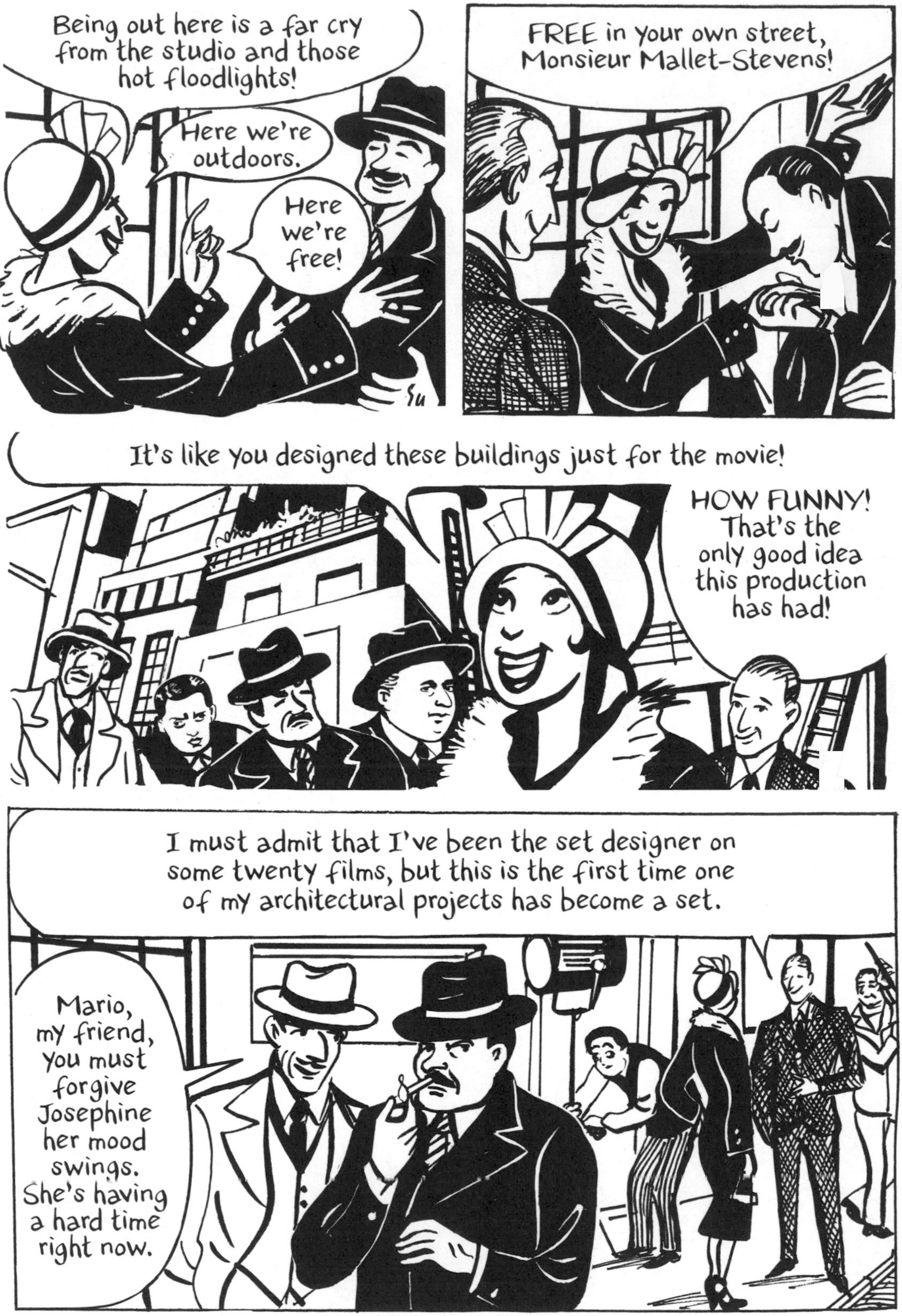
Being out here is a far cry from the studio and those hot floodlights!
Here we're outdoors.
Here we're free!
FREE in your own street, Monsieur Mallet-Stevens!
It's like you designed these buildings just for the movie!
HOW FUNNY! That's the only good idea this production has had!
I must admit that I've been the set designer on some twenty films, but this is the first time one of my architectural projects has become a set.
Mario, my friend, you must forgive Josephine her mood swings. She's having a hard time right now.

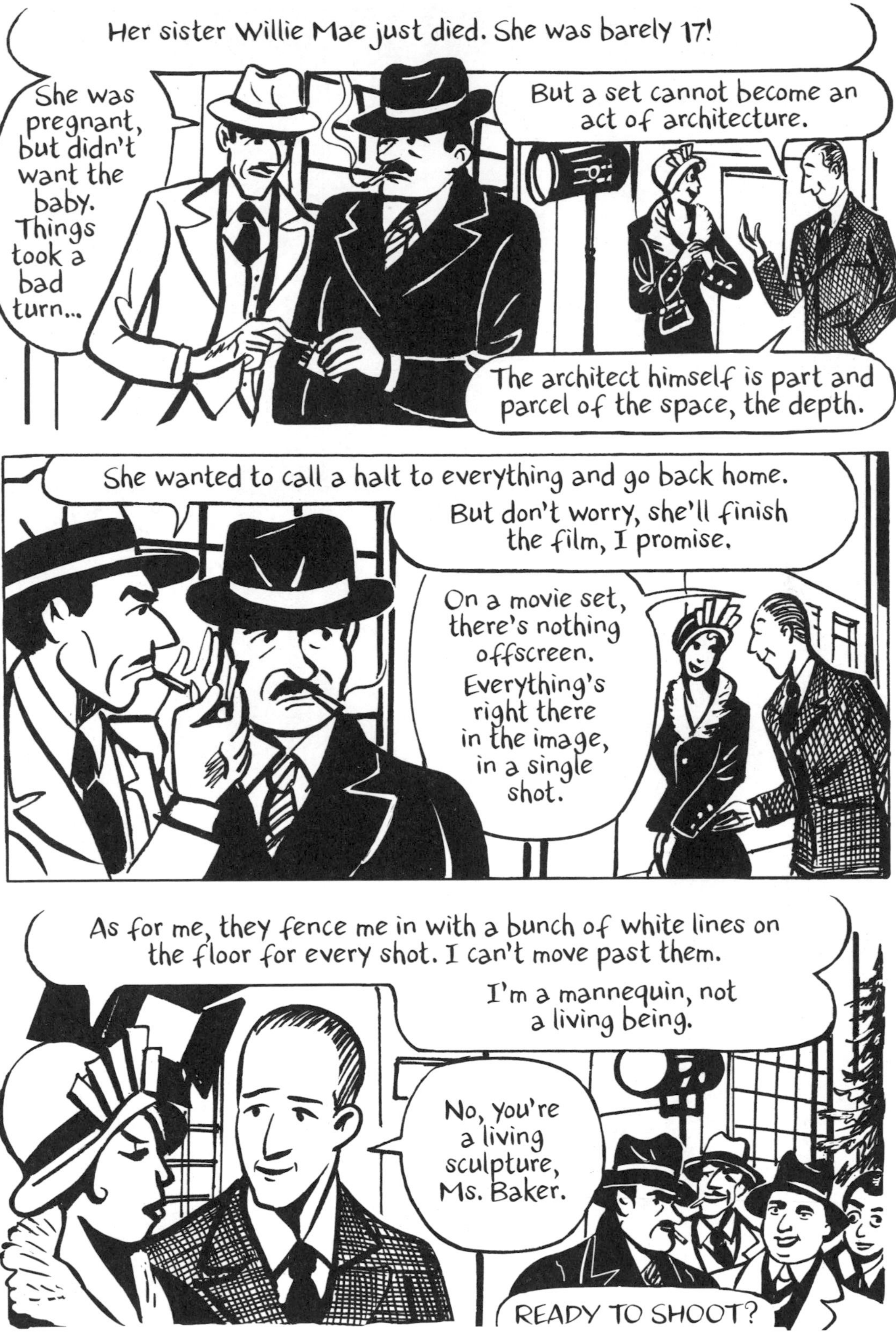
Her sister Willie Mae just died. She was barely 17!
She was pregnant, but didn't want the baby. Things took a bad turn...
But a set cannot become an act of architecture.
The architect himself is part and parcel of the space, the depth.
She wanted to call a halt to everything and go back home.
But don't worry, she'll finish the film, I promise.
On a movie set, there's nothing offscreen. Everything's right there in the image, in a single shot.
As for me, they fence me in with a bunch of white lines on the floor for every shot. I can't move past them.
I'm a mannequin, not a living being.
No, you're a living sculpture, Ms. Baker.
READY TO SHOOT?

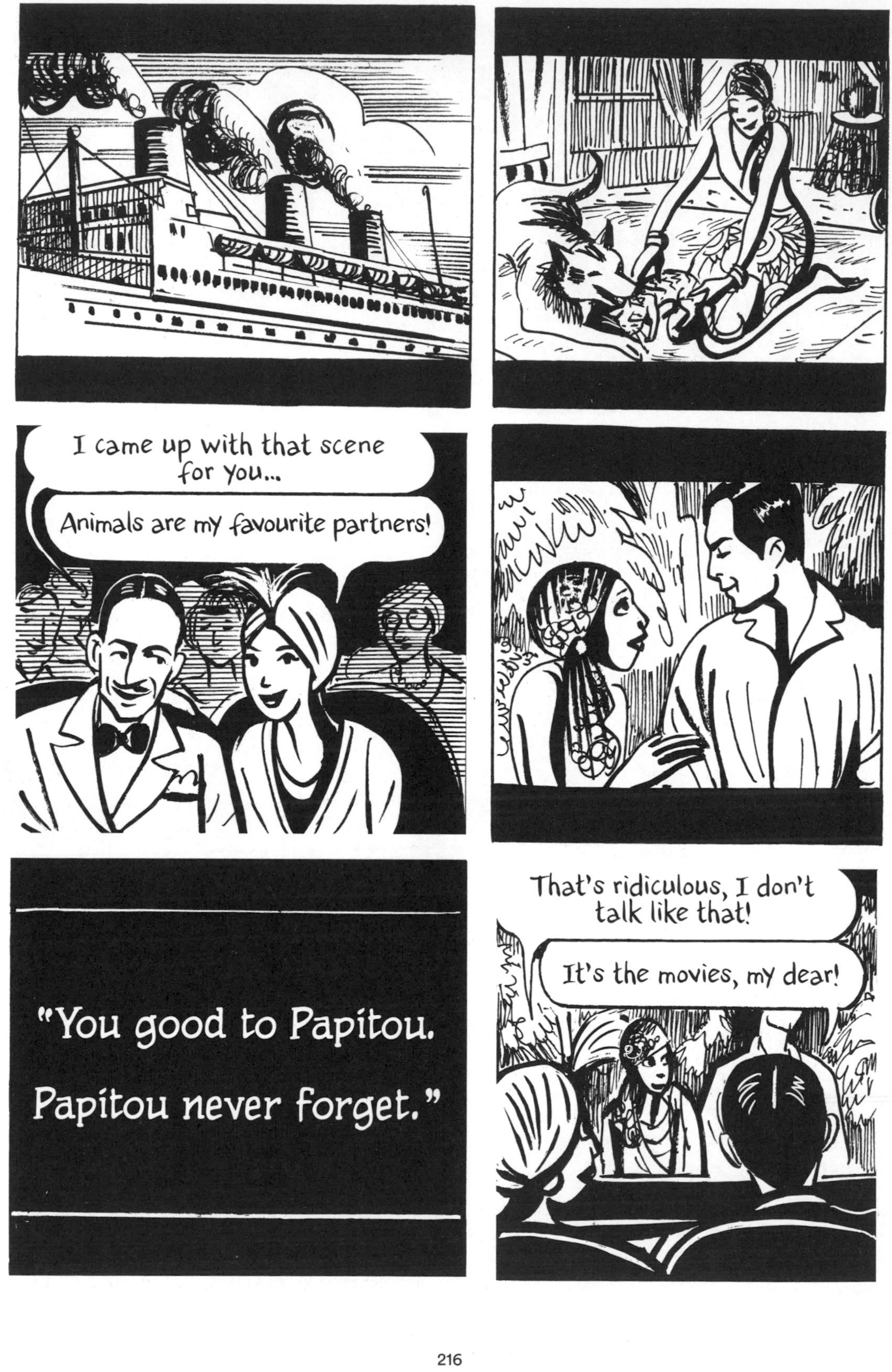
I came up with that scene for you...
Animals are my favourite partners!
"You good to Papitou. Papitou never forget."
That's ridiculous, I don't talk like that!
It's the movies, my dear!

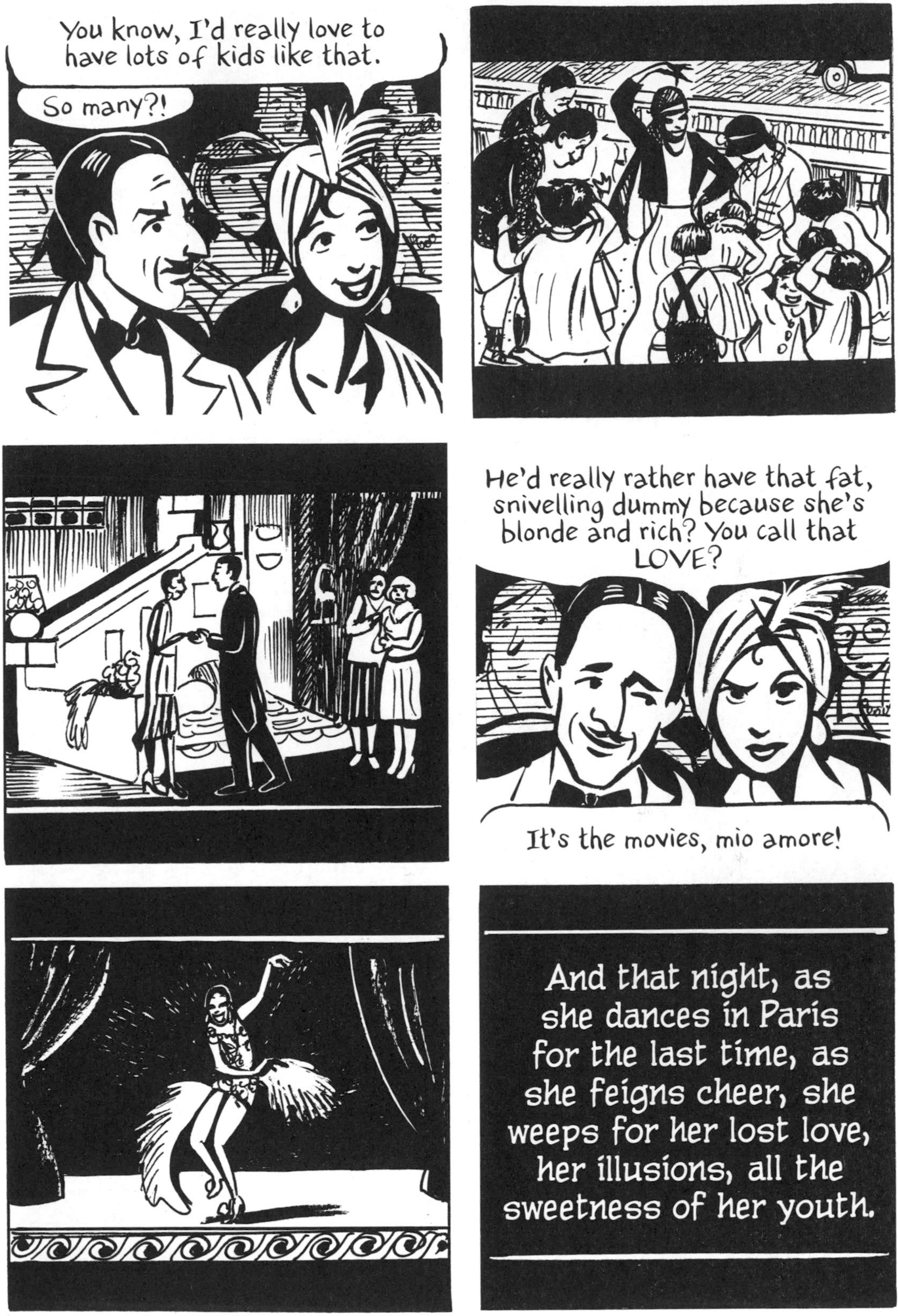
You know, I'd really love to have lots of kids like that.
So many?!
He'd really rather have that fat, snivelling dummy because she's blonde and rich? You call that LOVE?
It's the movies, mio amore!
And that night, as she dances in Paris for the last time, as she feigns cheer, she weeps for her lost love, her illusions, all the sweetness of her youth.

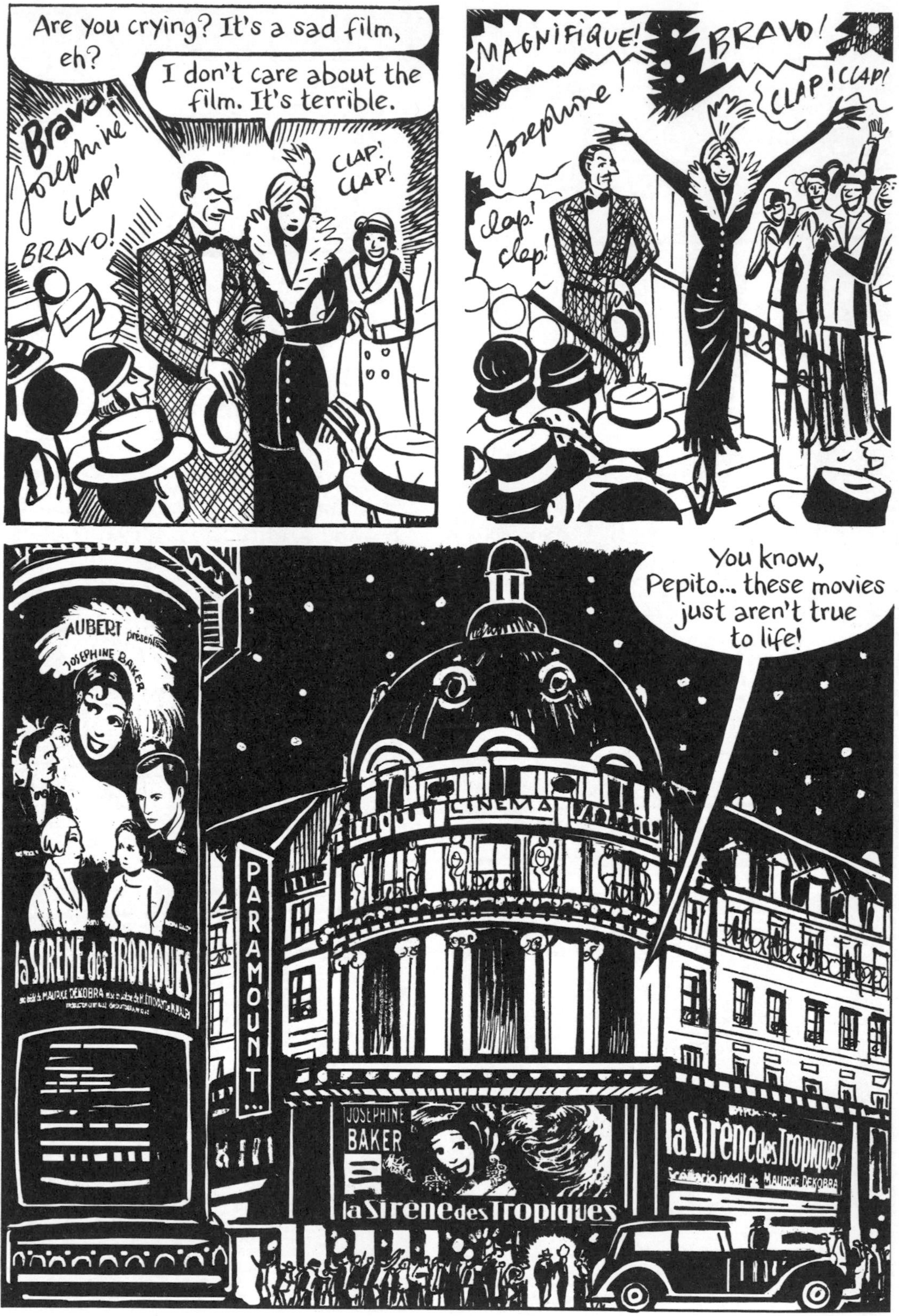
Are you crying? It's a sad film, eh?
I don't care about the film. It's terrible.
Bravo! Josephine!
CLAP!
BRAVO!
CLAP! CLAP!
MAGNIFIQUE!
BRAVO!
Josephine!
CLAP! CLAP!
clap! clap!
AUBERT présente
JOSEPHINE BAKER
la SIRENE des TROPIQUES
CINEMA
PARAMOUNT
JOSEPHINE BAKER
la Sirène des Tropiques
la Sirène des Tropiques
scénario inédit ★ MAURICE DEKOBRA
You know, Pepito... these movies just aren't true to life!

1929: SS *Lutetia*, South Atlantic

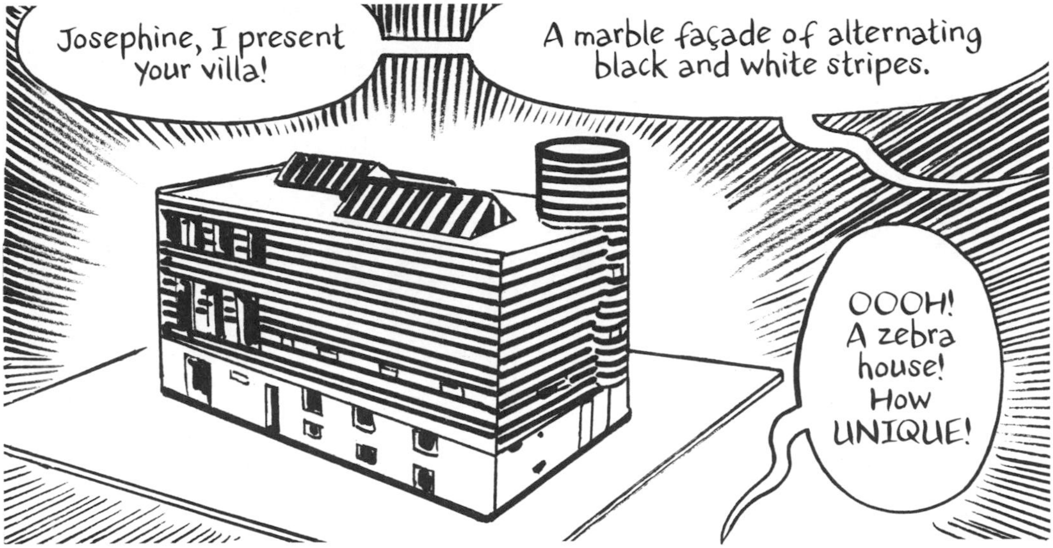
Josephine, I present your villa!
A marble façade of alternating black and white stripes.
OOOH! A zebra house! How UNIQUE!

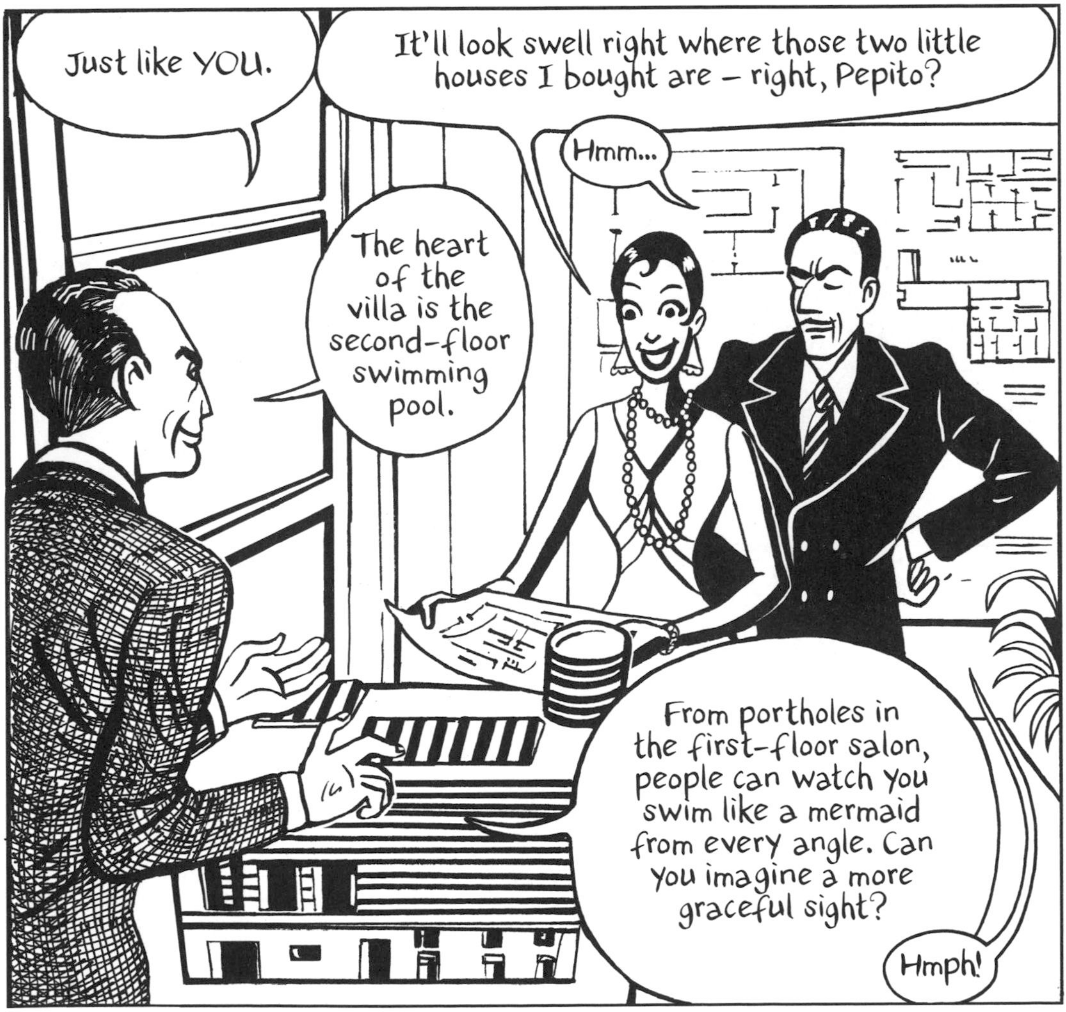
Just like YOU.
It'll look swell right where those two little houses I bought are – right, Pepito?
Hmm...
The heart of the villa is the second-floor swimming pool.
From portholes in the first-floor salon, people can watch you swim like a mermaid from every angle. Can you imagine a more graceful sight?
Hmph!

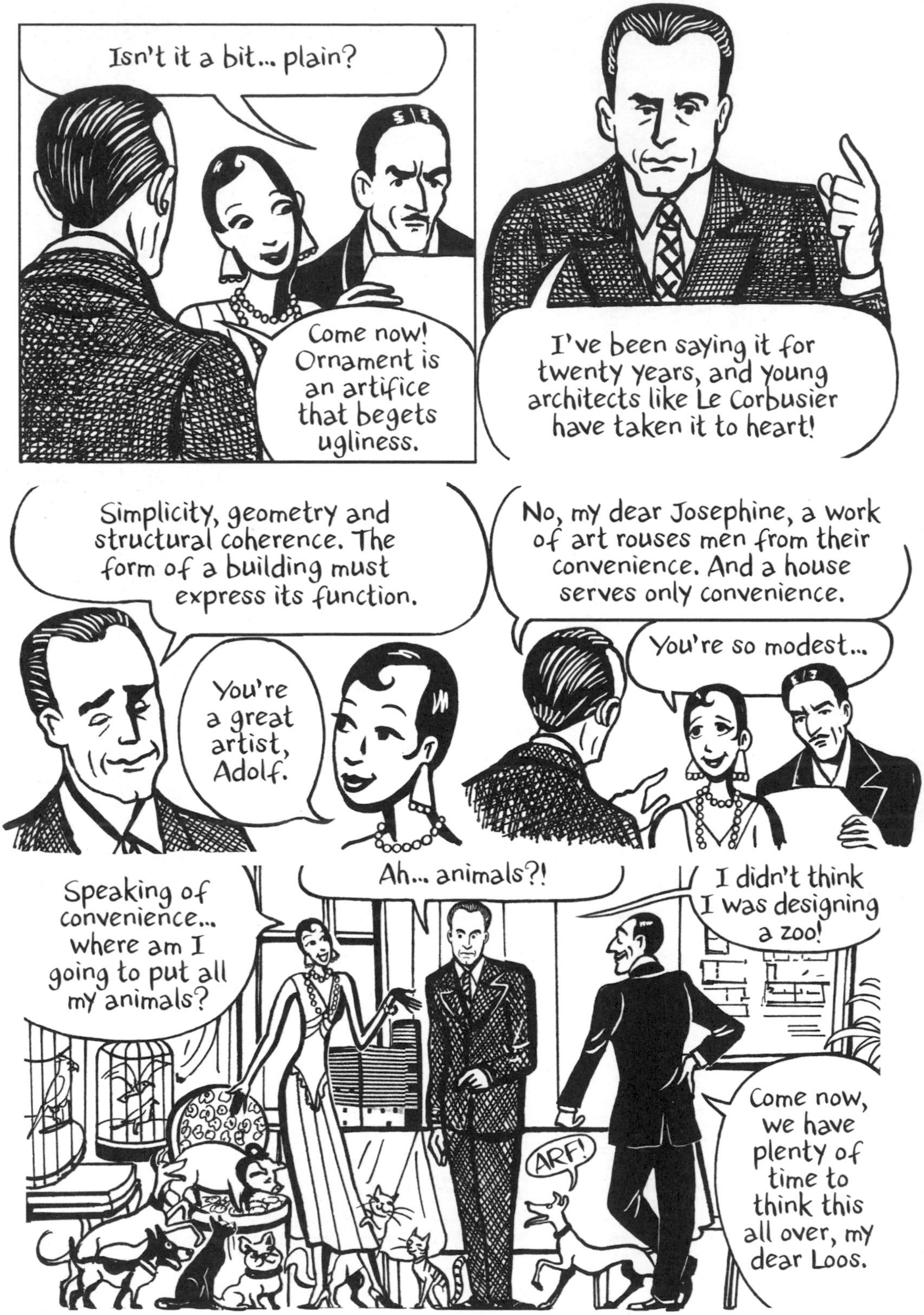
Isn't it a bit... plain?
Come now! Ornament is an artifice that begets ugliness.
I've been saying it for twenty years, and young architects like Le Corbusier have taken it to heart!
Simplicity, geometry and structural coherence. The form of a building must express its function.
You're a great artist, Adolf.
No, my dear Josephine, a work of art rouses men from their convenience. And a house serves only convenience.
You're so modest...
Speaking of convenience... where am I going to put all my animals?
Ah... animals?!
I didn't think I was designing a zoo!
ARF!
Come now, we have plenty of time to think this all over, my dear Loos.

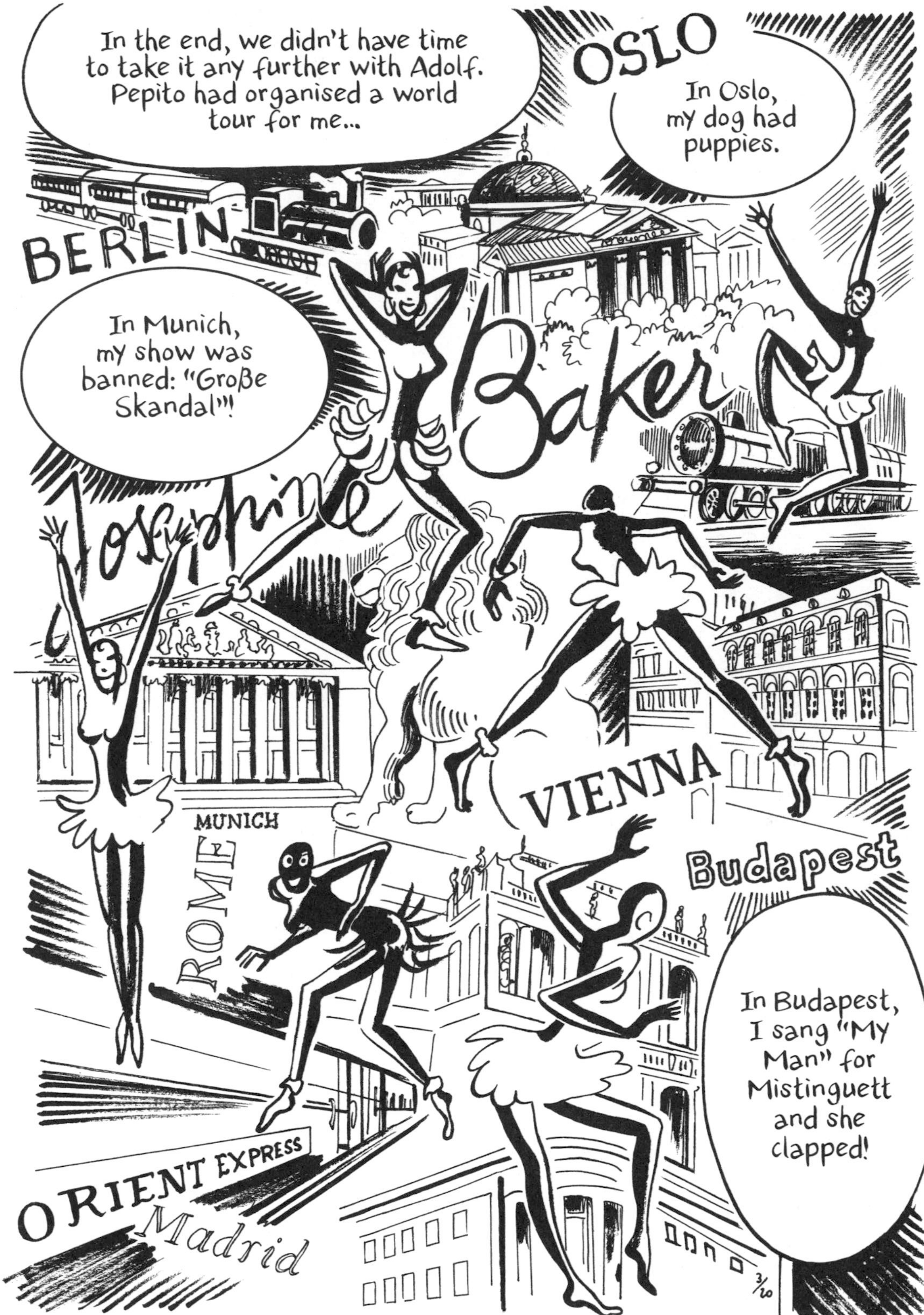

In the end, we didn't have time to take it any further with Adolf. Pepito had organised a world tour for me...
OSLO
In Oslo, my dog had puppies.
BERLIN
In Munich, my show was banned: "Große Skandal"!
Baker
Josephine
VIENNA
MUNICH
ROME
Budapest
In Budapest, I sang "My Man" for Mistinguett and she clapped!
ORIENT EXPRESS
Madrid

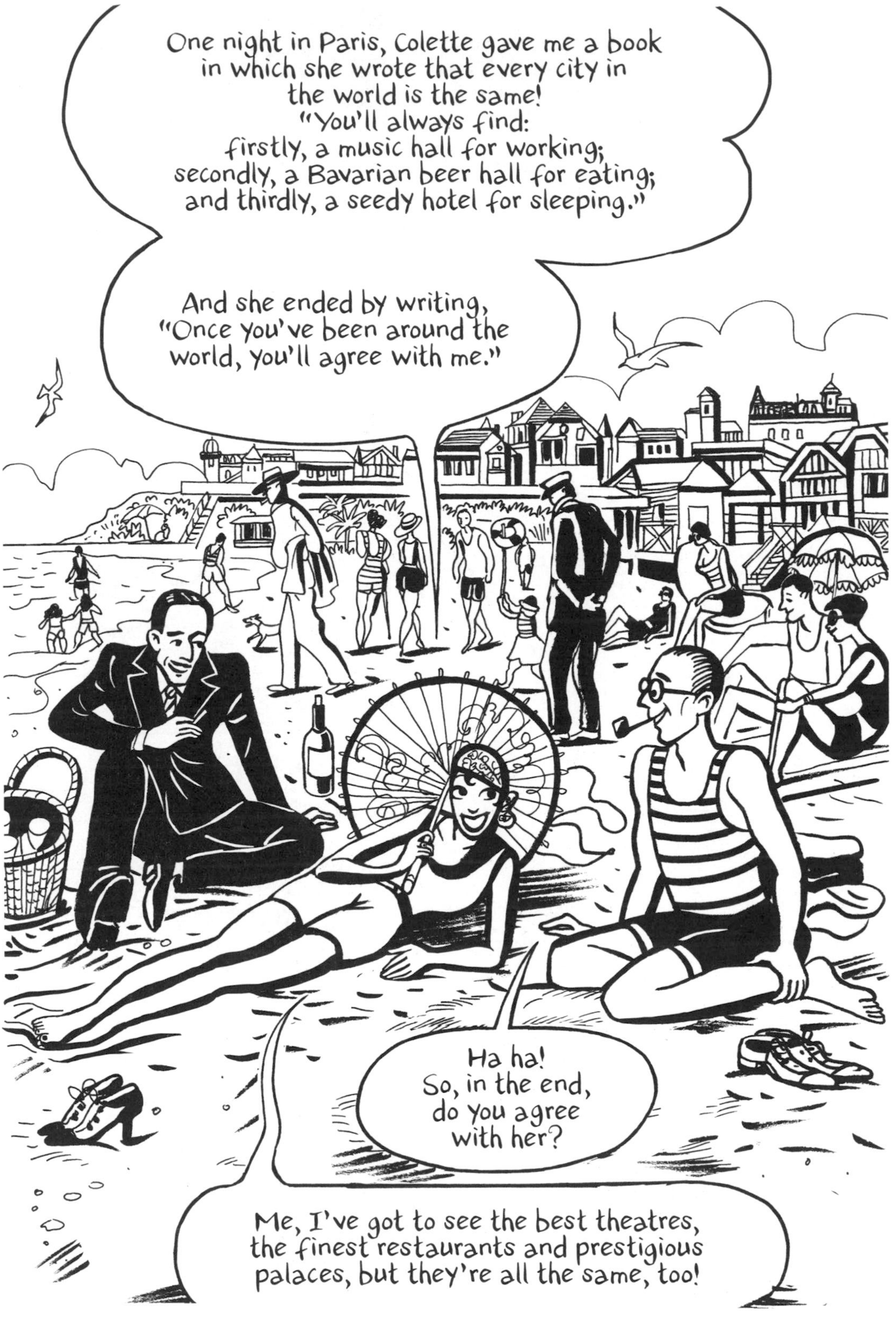
One night in Paris, Colette gave me a book in which she wrote that every city in the world is the same! "You'll always find: firstly, a music hall for working; secondly, a Bavarian beer hall for eating; and thirdly, a seedy hotel for sleeping."
And she ended by writing, "Once you've been around the world, you'll agree with me."
Ha ha! So, in the end, do you agree with her?
Me, I've got to see the best theatres, the finest restaurants and prestigious palaces, but they're all the same, too!

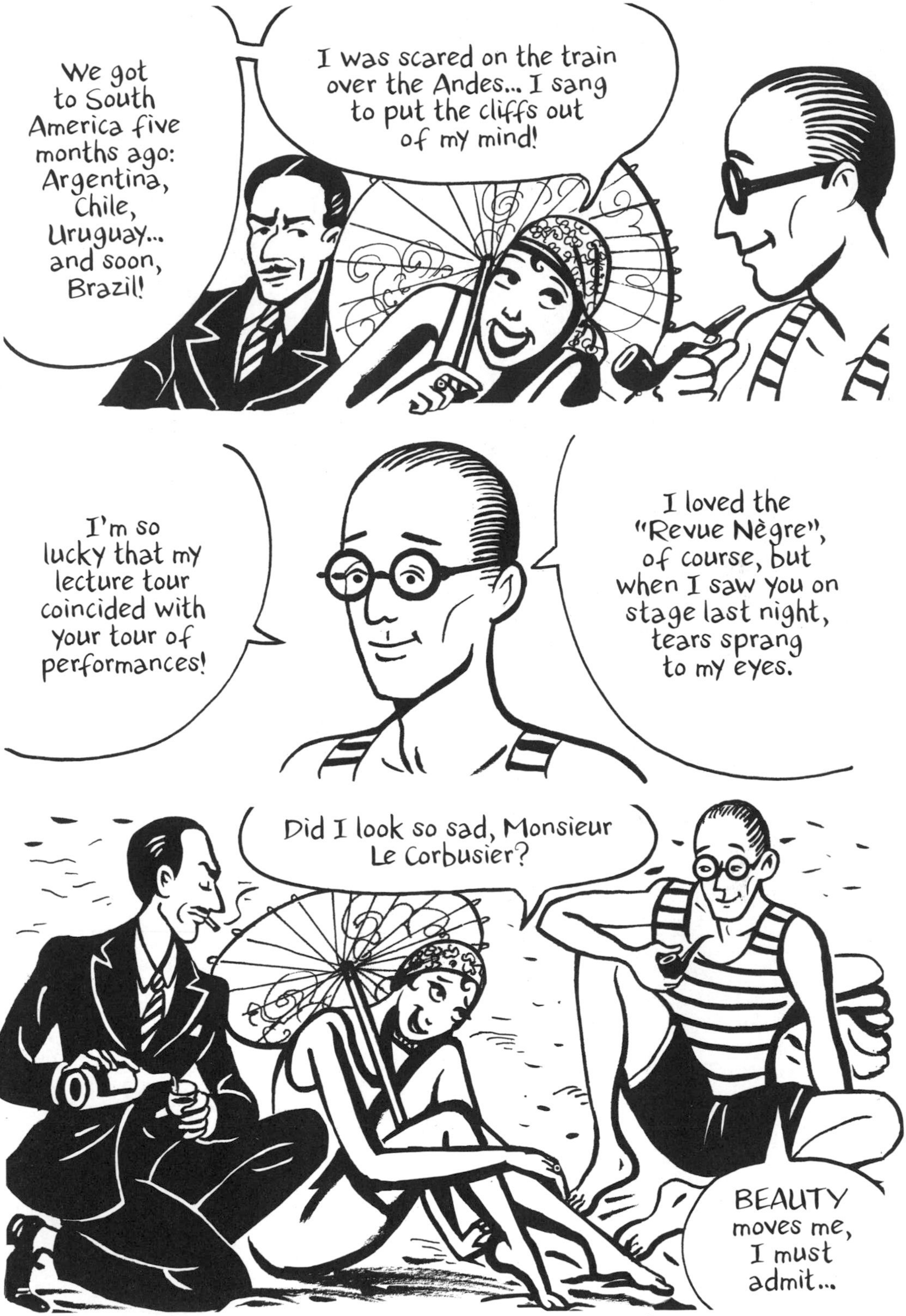
We got to South America five months ago: Argentina, Chile, Uruguay... and soon, Brazil!
I was scared on the train over the Andes... I sang to put the cliffs out of my mind!
I'm so lucky that my lecture tour coincided with your tour of performances!
I loved the "Revue Nègre", of course, but when I saw you on stage last night, tears sprang to my eyes.
Did I look so sad, Monsieur Le Corbusier?
BEAUTY moves me, I must admit...

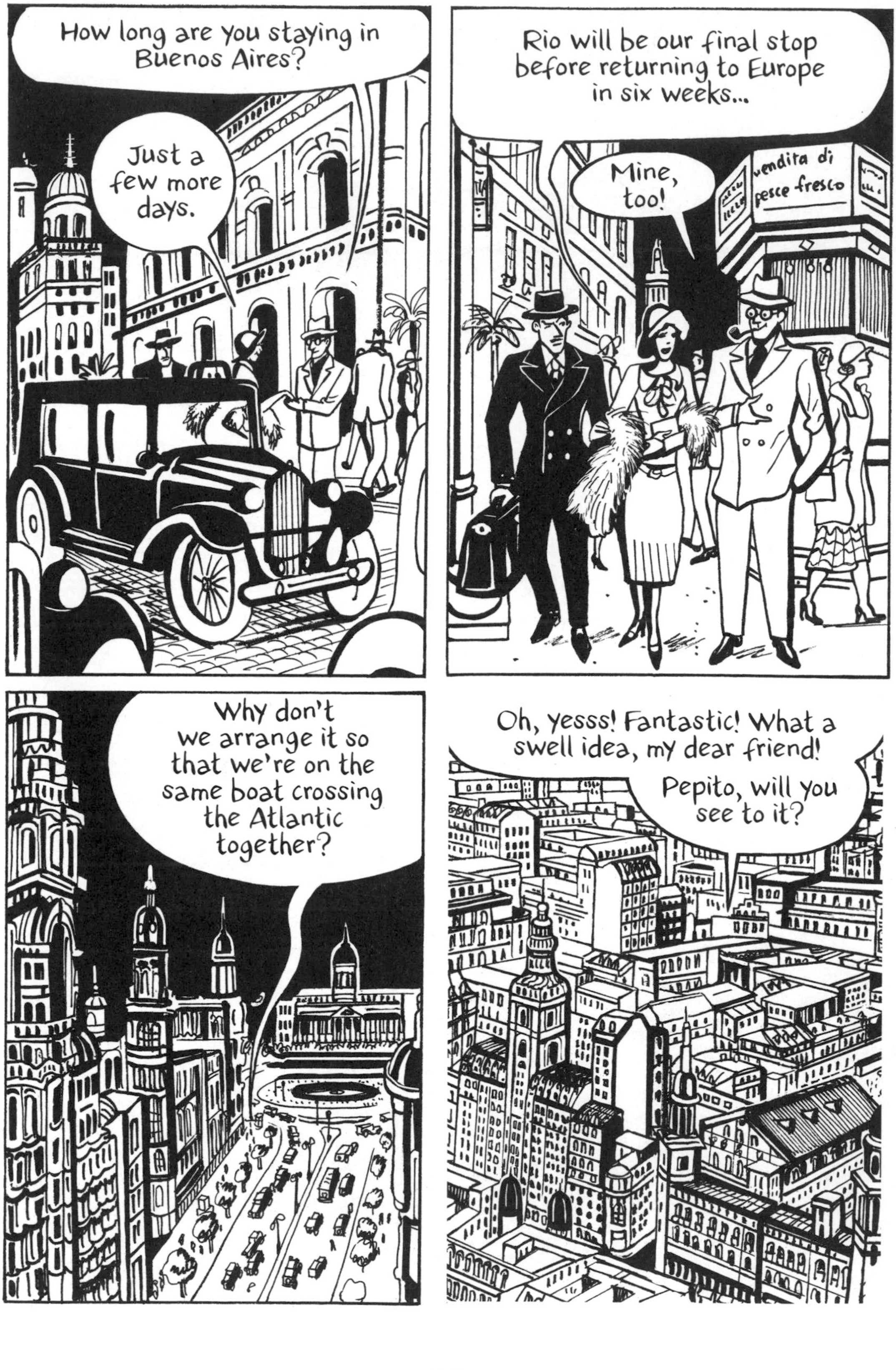
How long are you staying in Buenos Aires?
Just a few more days.
Rio will be our final stop before returning to Europe in six weeks...
Mine, too!
vendita di pesce fresco
Why don't we arrange it so that we're on the same boat crossing the Atlantic together?
Oh, yesss! Fantastic! What a swell idea, my dear friend!
Pepito, will you see to it?

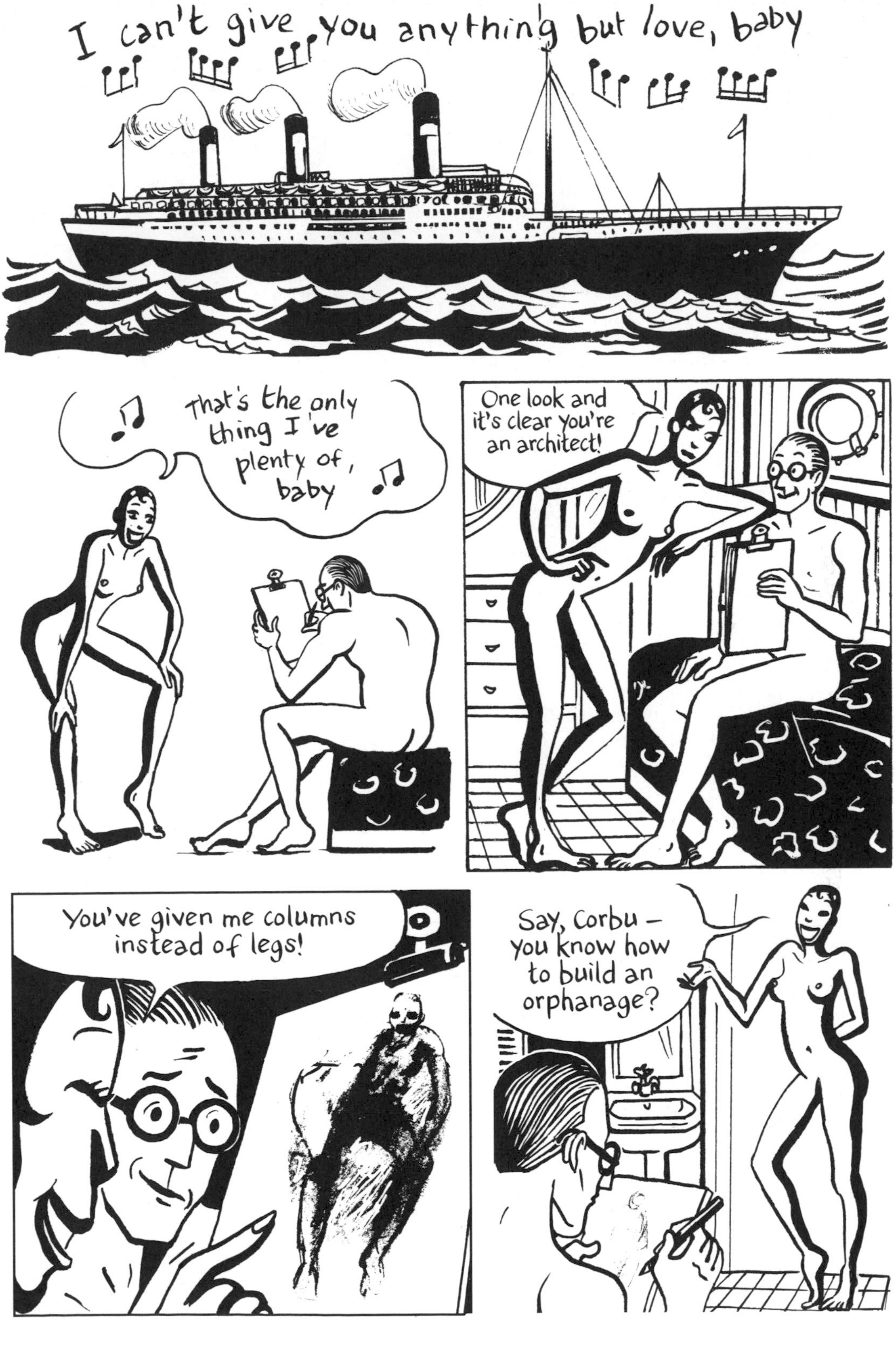
I can't give you anything but love, baby
That's the only thing I've plenty of, baby
One look and it's clear you're an architect!
You've given me columns instead of legs!
Say, Corbu – you know how to build an orphanage?

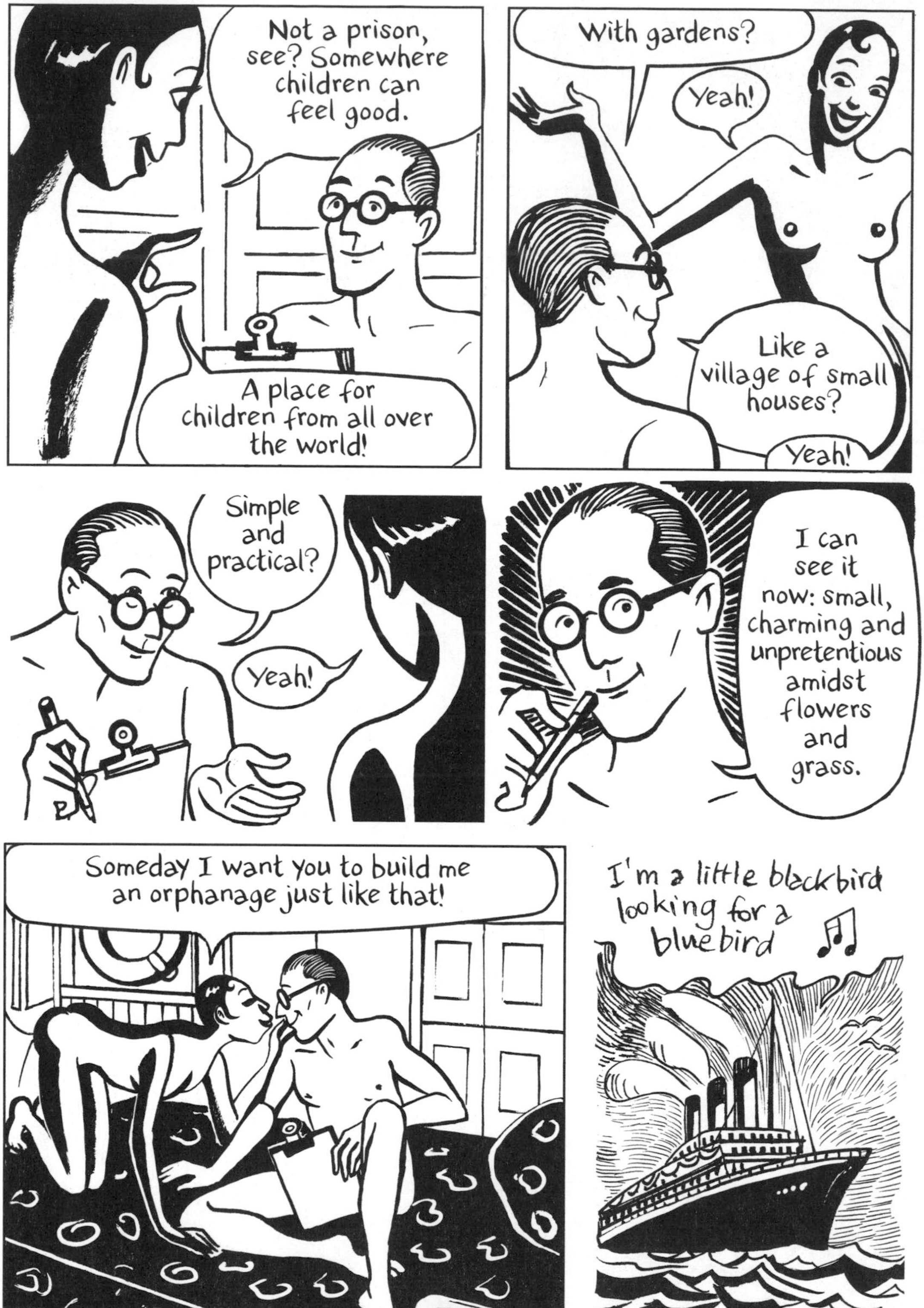
Not a prison, see? Somewhere children can feel good.
A place for children from all over the world!
With gardens?
Yeah!
Like a village of small houses?
Yeah!
Simple and practical?
Yeah!
I can see it now: small, charming and unpretentious amidst flowers and grass.
Someday I want you to build me an orphanage just like that!
I'm a little blackbird looking for a bluebird

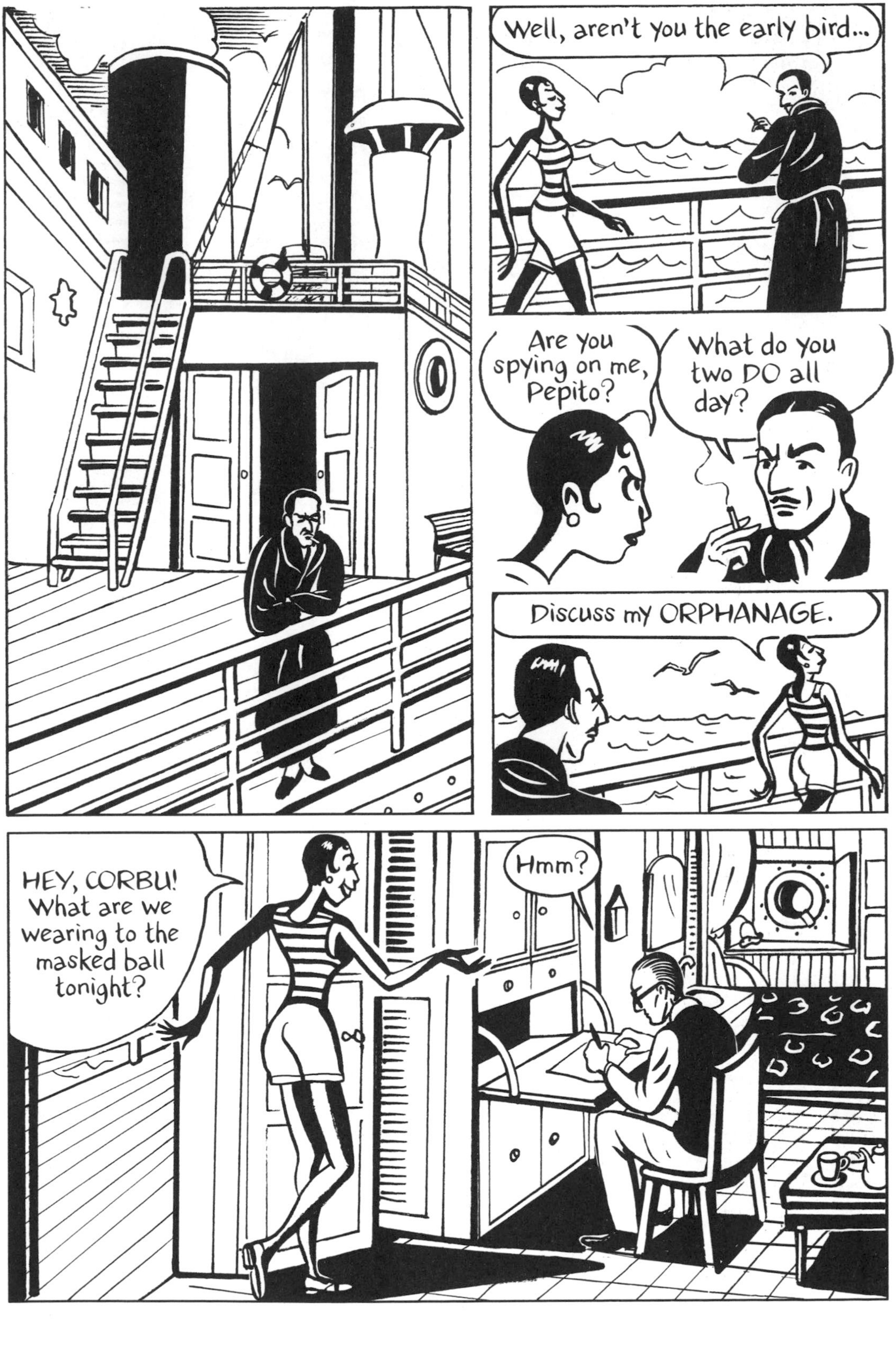
Well, aren't you the early bird...
Are you spying on me, Pepito?
What do you two DO all day?
Discuss my ORPHANAGE.
HEY, CORBU! What are we wearing to the masked ball tonight?
Hmm?

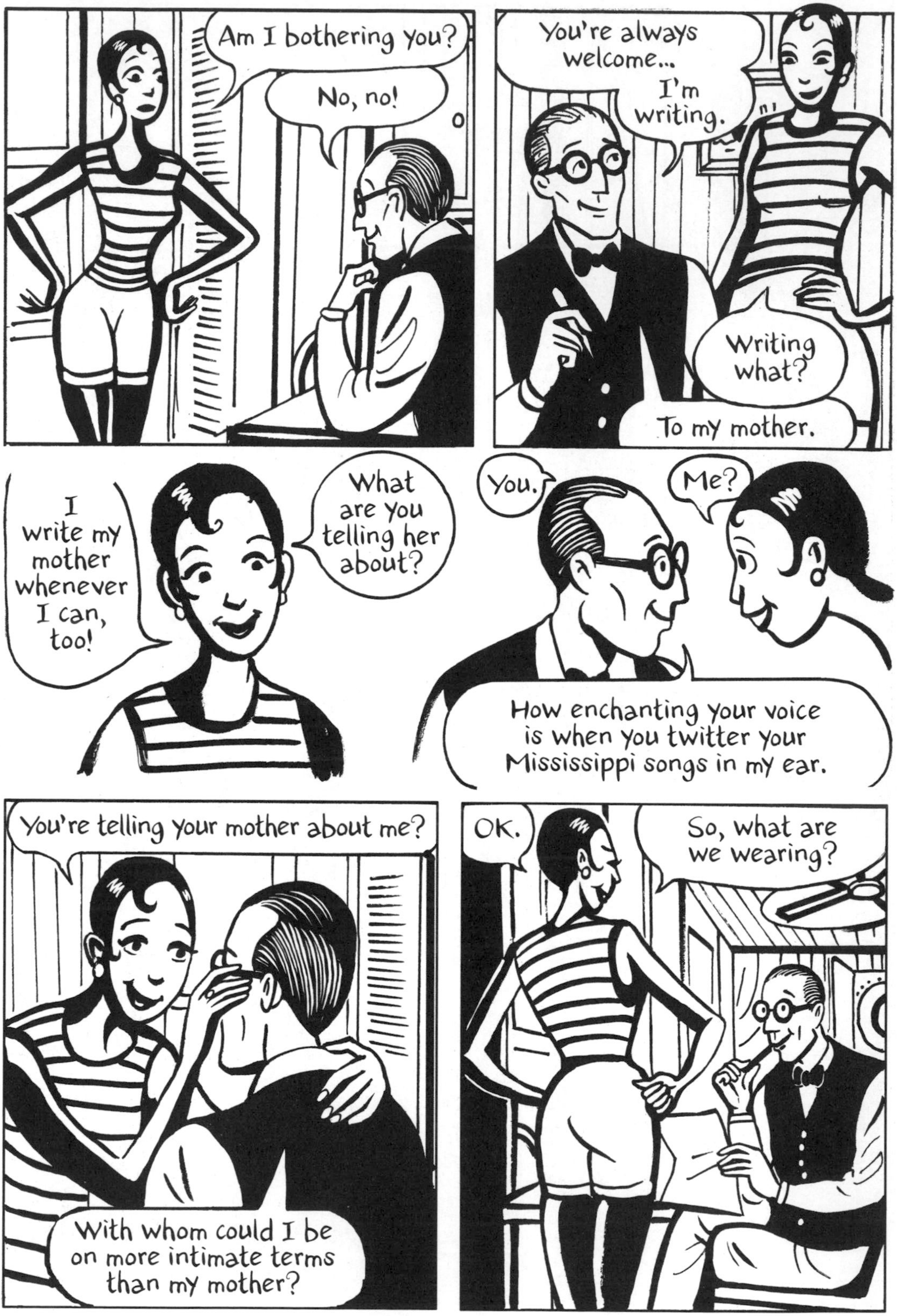
Am I bothering you?
No, no!
You're always welcome...
I'm writing.
Writing what?
To my mother.
I write my mother whenever I can, too!
What are you telling her about?
You.
Me?
How enchanting your voice is when you twitter your Mississippi songs in my ear.
You're telling your mother about me?
With whom could I be on more intimate terms than my mother?
OK.
So, what are we wearing?

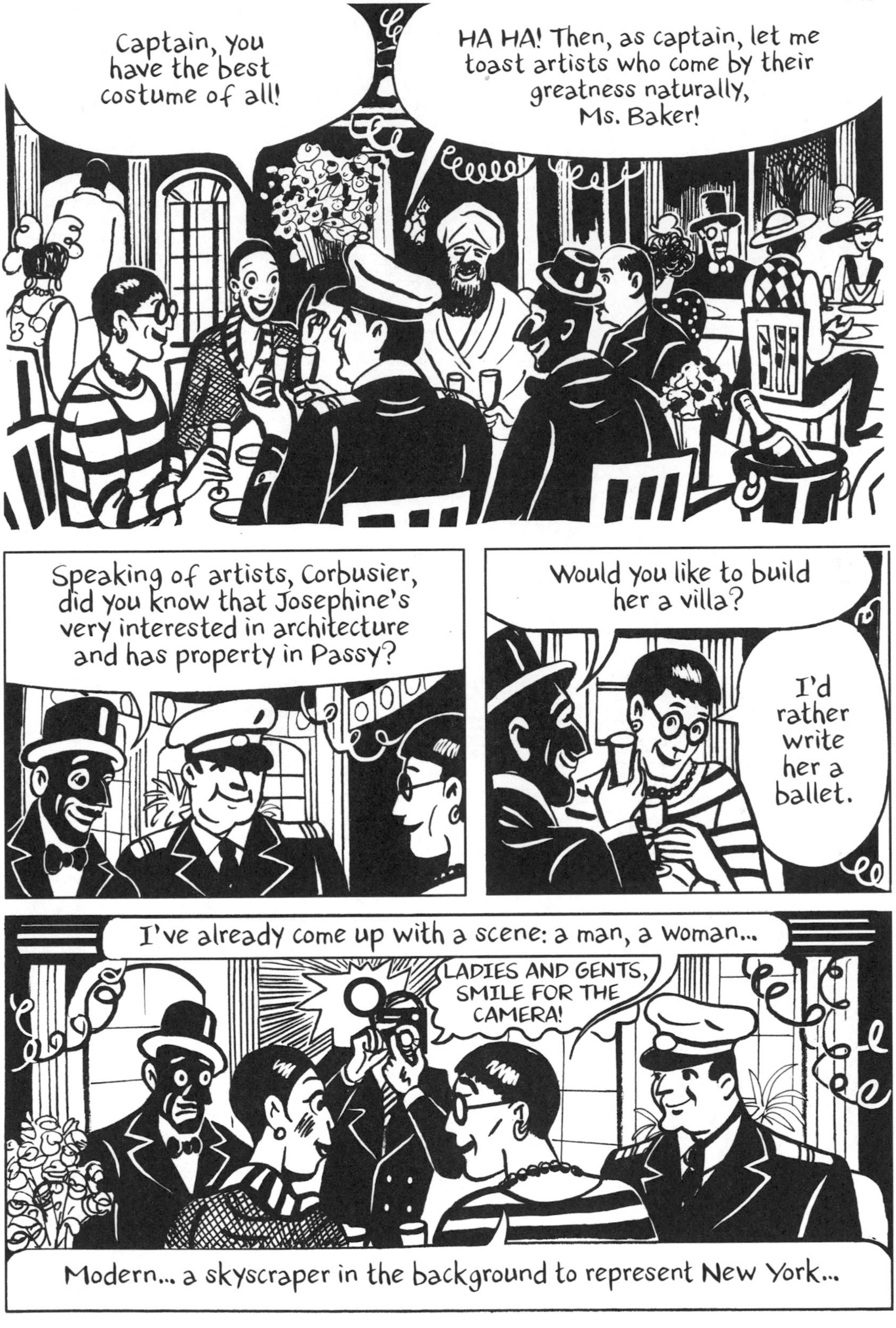

Captain, you have the best costume of all!
HA HA! Then, as captain, let me toast artists who come by their greatness naturally, Ms. Baker!
Speaking of artists, Corbusier, did you know that Josephine's very interested in architecture and has property in Passy?
Would you like to build her a villa?
I'd rather write her a ballet.
I've already come up with a scene: a man, a woman...
LADIES AND GENTS, SMILE FOR THE CAMERA!
Modern... a skyscraper in the background to represent New York...

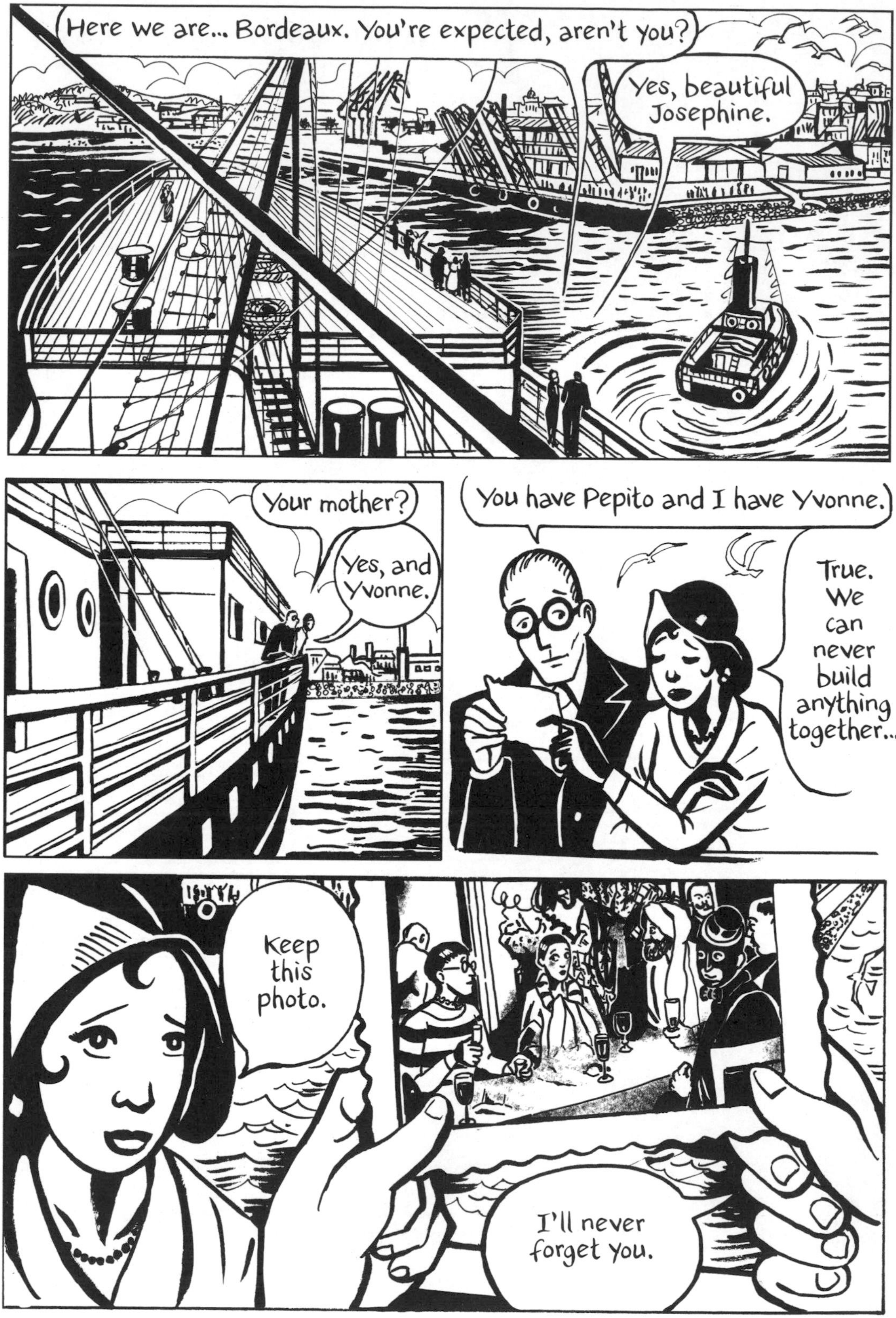
Here we are... Bordeaux. You're expected, aren't you?
Yes, beautiful Josephine.
Your mother?
Yes, and Yvonne.
You have Pepito and I have Yvonne.
True. We can never build anything together...
Keep this photo.
I'll never forget you.

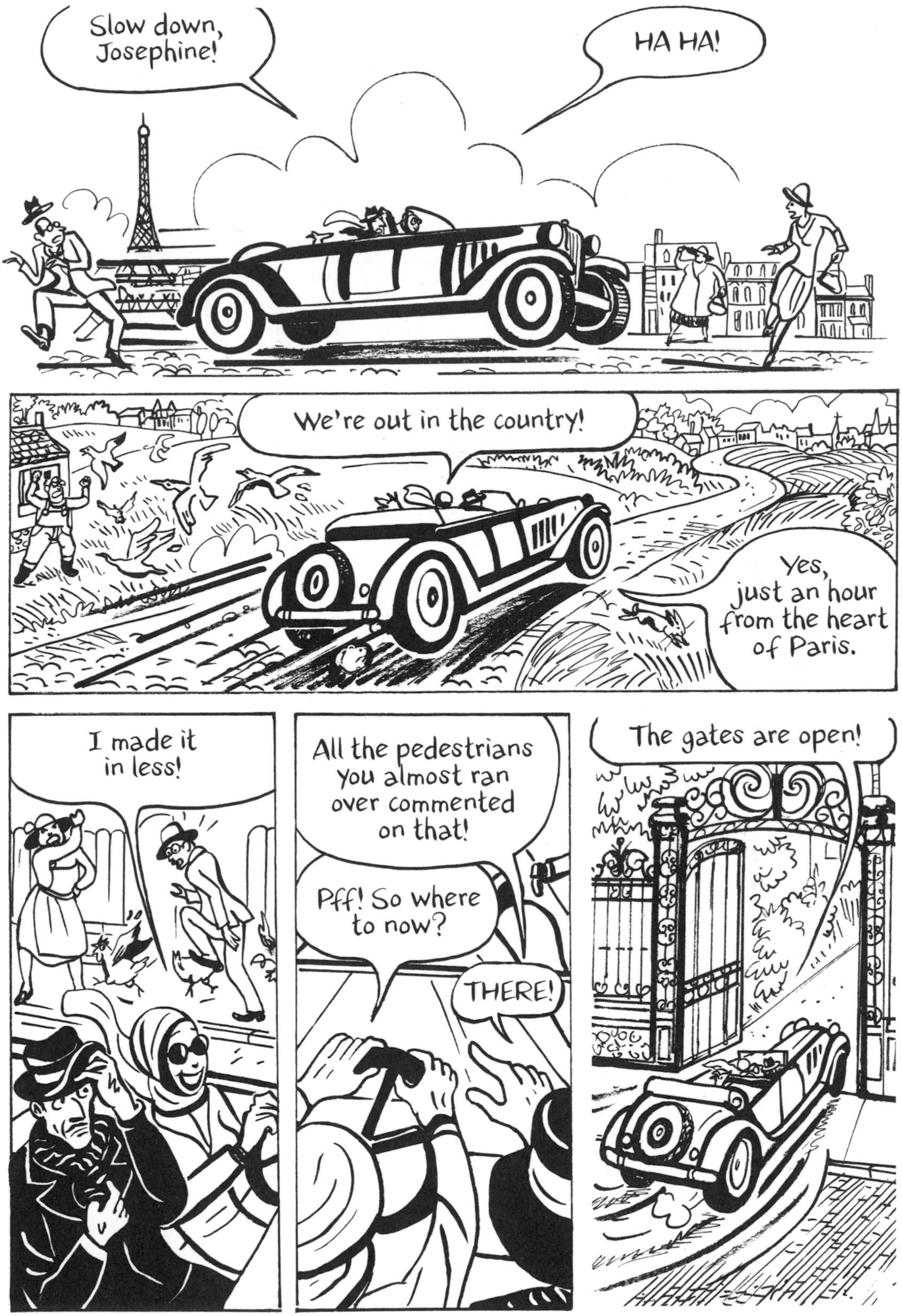
Slow down, Josephine!
HA HA!
We're out in the country!
Yes, just an hour from the heart of Paris.
I made it in less!
All the pedestrians you almost ran over commented on that!
Pff! So where to now?
THERE!
The gates are open!

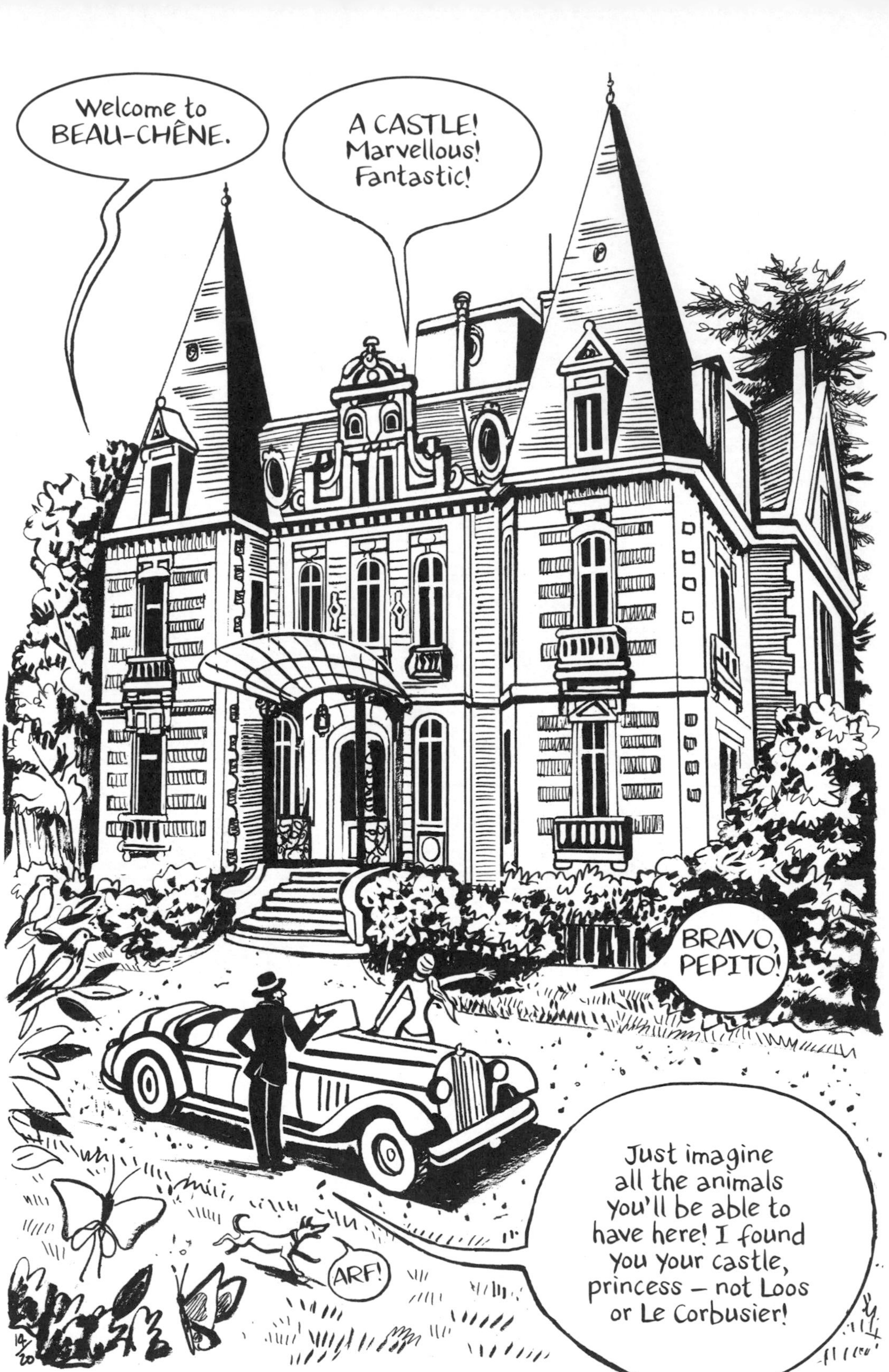
Welcome to BEAU-CHÊNE.
A CASTLE! Marvellous! Fantastic!
BRAVO, PEPITO!
ARF!
Just imagine all the animals you'll be able to have here! I found you your castle, princess – not Loos or Le Corbusier!
14/20

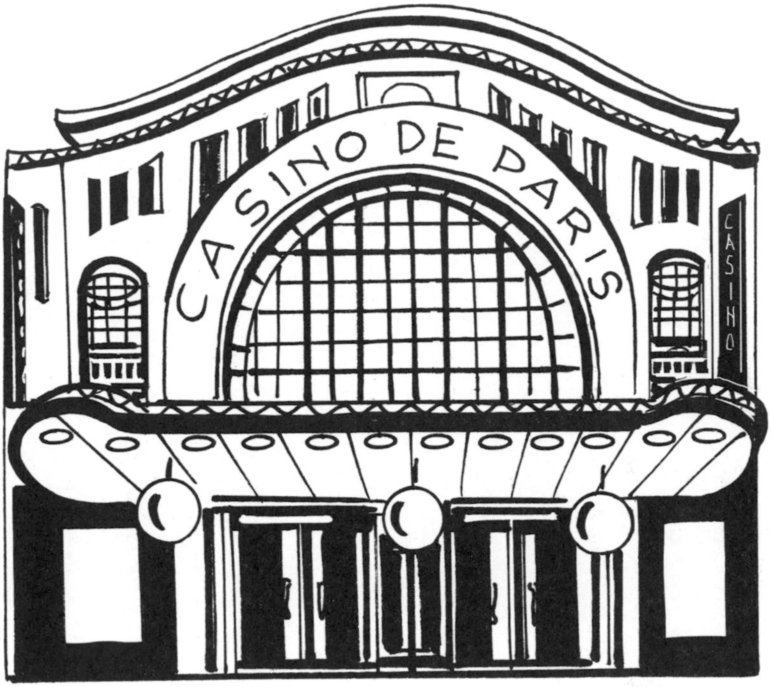
CASINO DE PARIS
CASINO

1930: Casino de Paris, Rue de Clichy, Paris, France

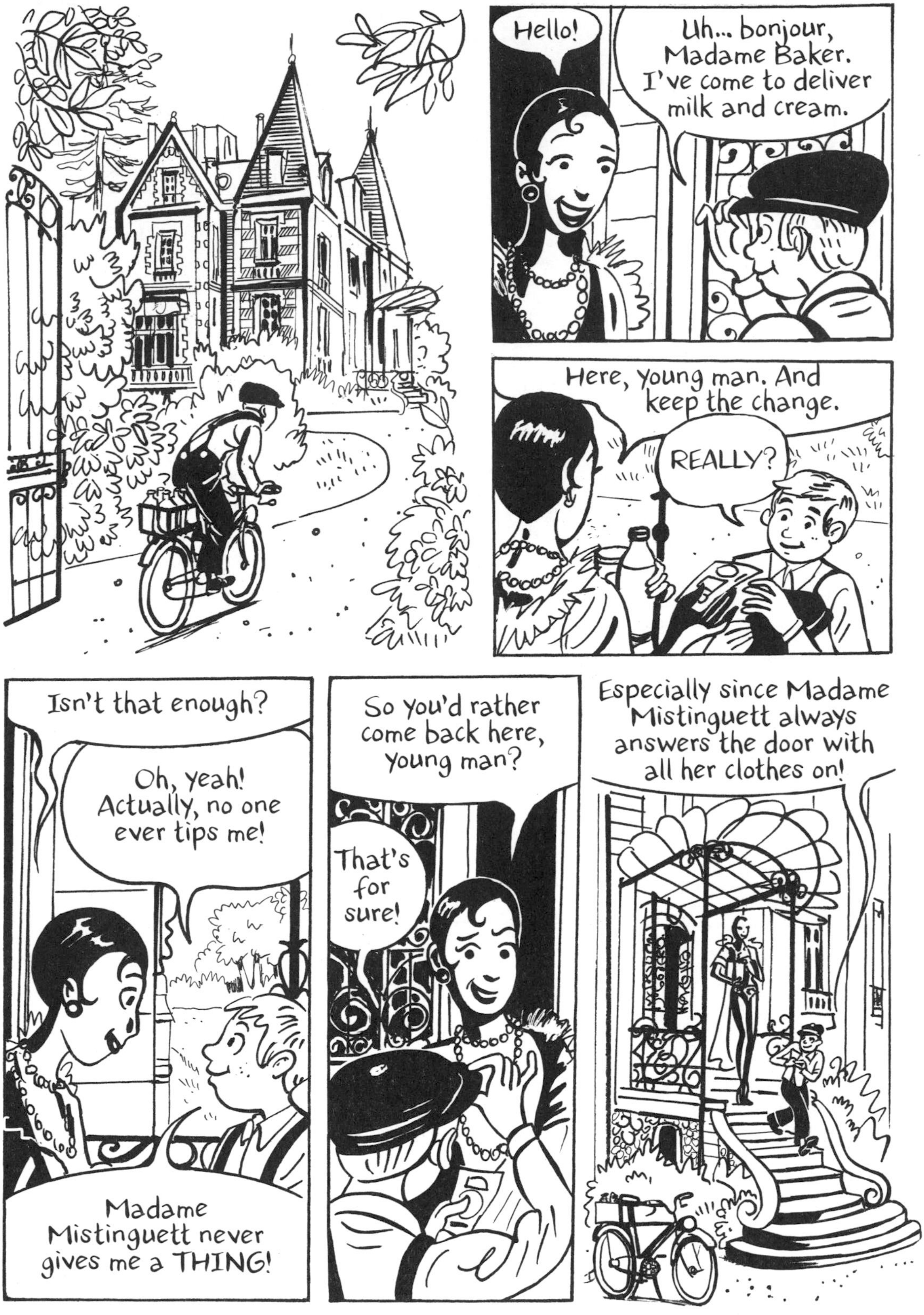
Hello!
Uh... bonjour, Madame Baker. I've come to deliver milk and cream.
Here, young man. And keep the change.
REALLY?
Isn't that enough?
Oh, yeah! Actually, no one ever tips me!
Madame Mistinguett never gives me a THING!
So you'd rather come back here, young man?
That's for sure!
Especially since Madame Mistinguett always answers the door with all her clothes on!

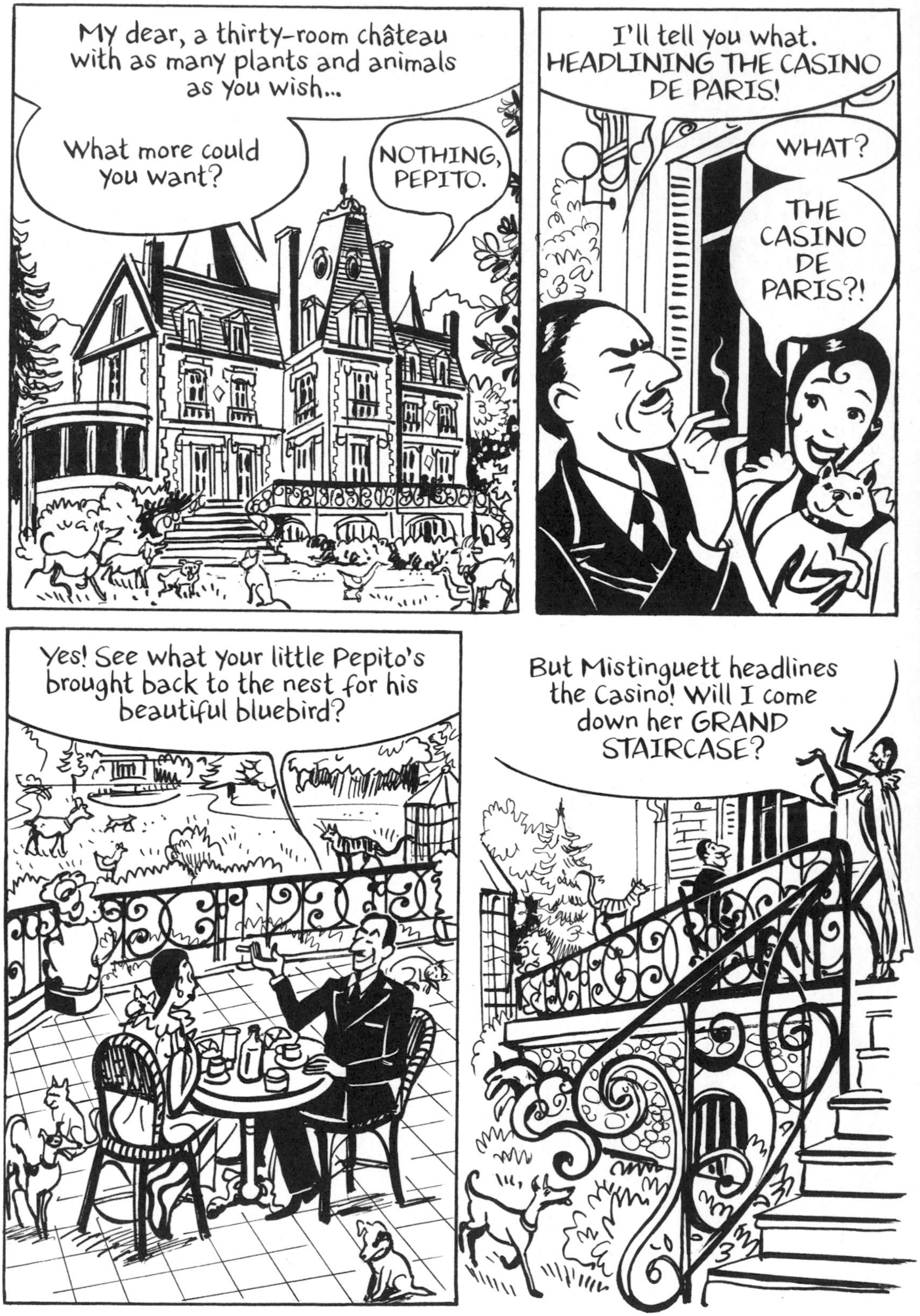
My dear, a thirty-room château with as many plants and animals as you wish...
What more could you want?
NOTHING, PEPITO.
I'll tell you what. HEADLINING THE CASINO DE PARIS!
WHAT?
THE CASINO DE PARIS?!
Yes! See what your little Pepito's brought back to the nest for his beautiful bluebird?
But Mistinguett headlines the Casino! Will I come down her GRAND STAIRCASE?

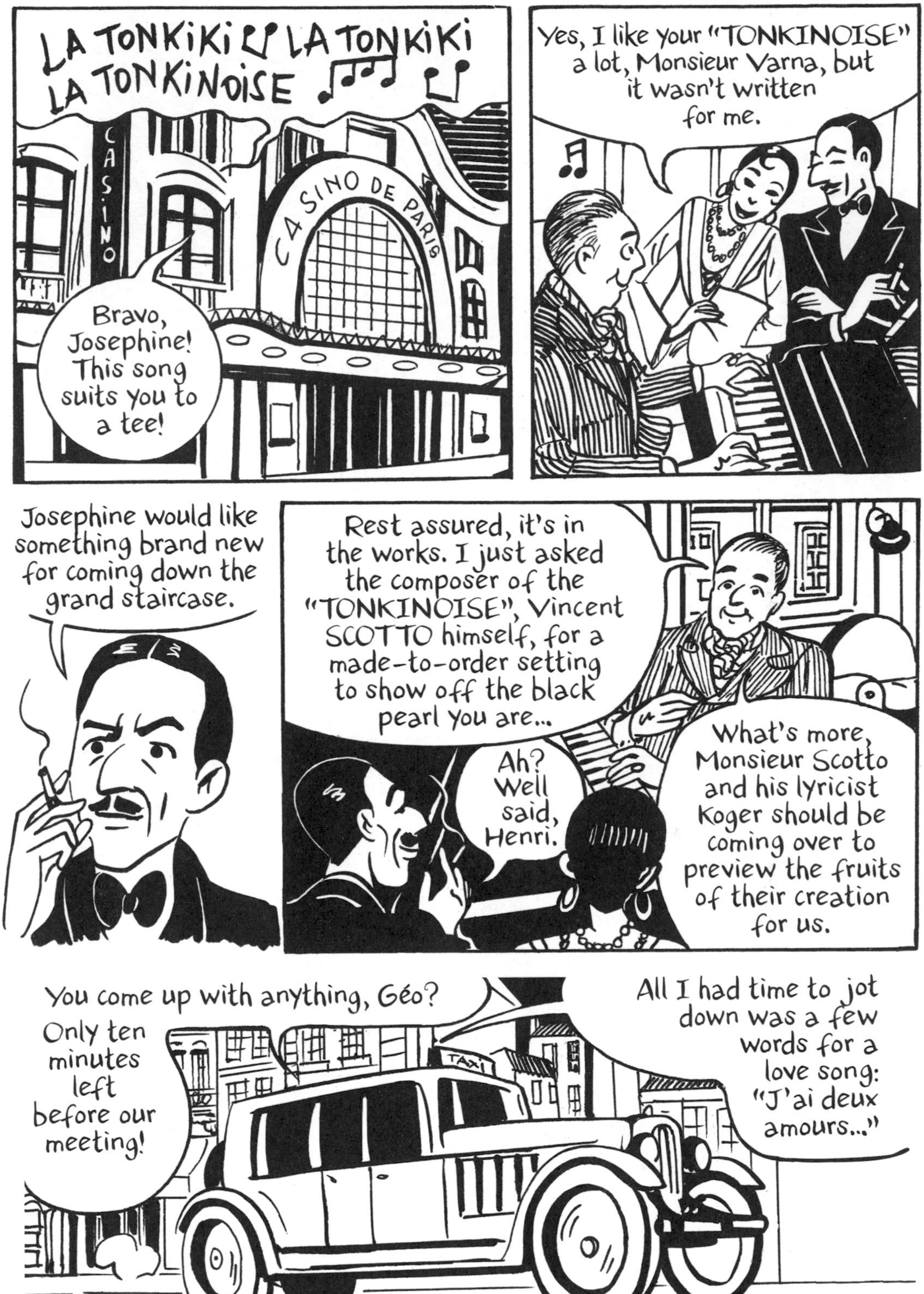

LA TONKIKI LA TONKIKI LA TONKINOISE
CASINO
CASINO DE PARIS
Bravo, Josephine! This song suits you to a tee!
Yes, I like your "TONKINOISE" a lot, Monsieur Varna, but it wasn't written for me.
Josephine would like something brand new for coming down the grand staircase.
Rest assured, it's in the works. I just asked the composer of the "TONKINOISE", Vincent SCOTTO himself, for a made-to-order setting to show off the black pearl you are...
Ah? Well said, Henri.
What's more, Monsieur Scotto and his lyricist Koger should be coming over to preview the fruits of their creation for us.
You come up with anything, Géo?
Only ten minutes left before our meeting!
TAXI
All I had time to jot down was a few words for a love song: "J'ai deux amours..."

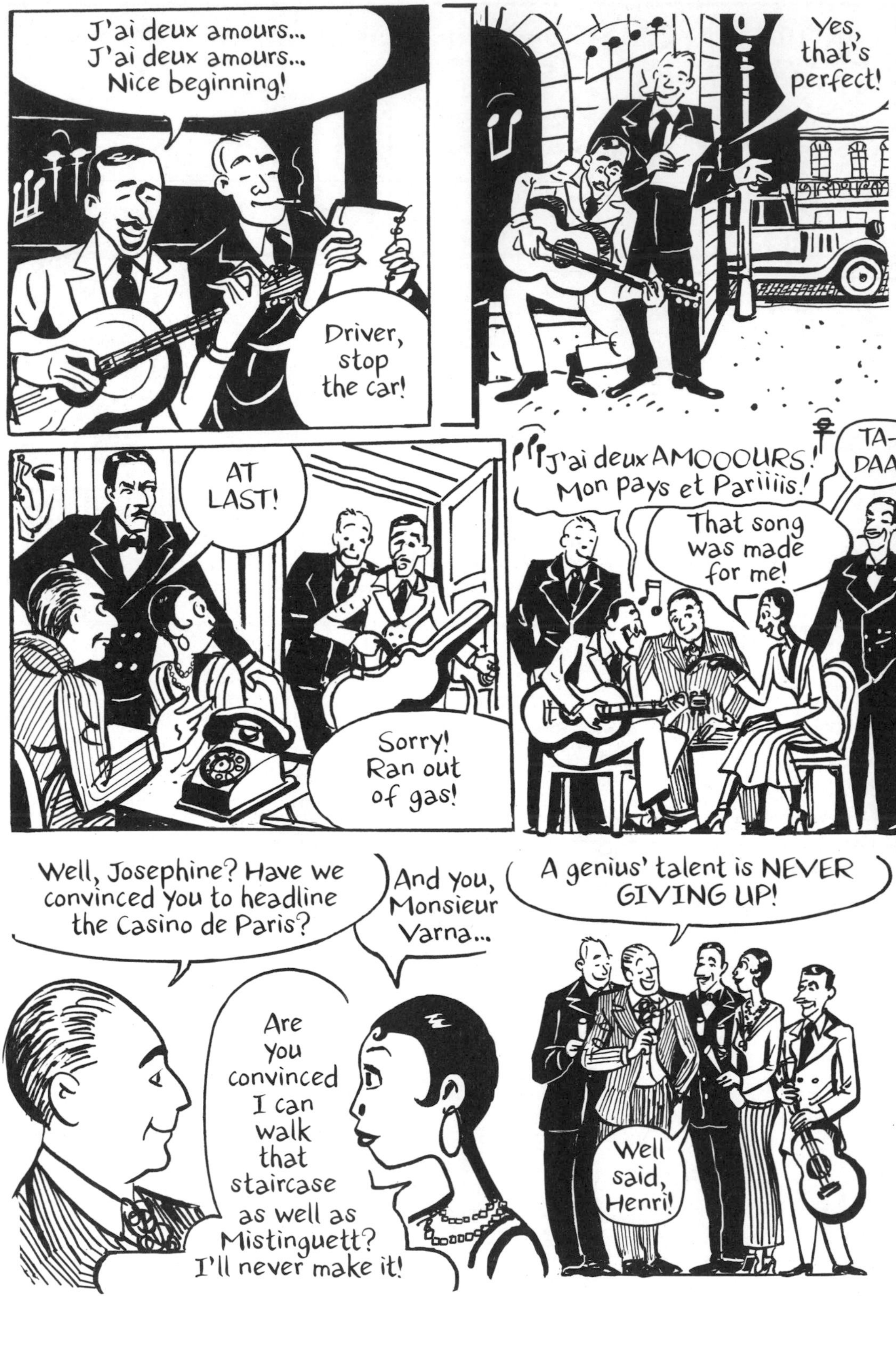

J'ai deux amours...
J'ai deux amours...
Nice beginning!
Driver, stop the car!
Yes, that's perfect!
AT LAST!
Sorry! Ran out of gas!
J'ai deux AMOOOURS! Mon pays et Pariiiis!
TA-DAA!
That song was made for me!
Well, Josephine? Have we convinced you to headline the Casino de Paris?
And you, Monsieur Varna...
Are you convinced I can walk that staircase as well as Mistinguett? I'll never make it!
A genius' talent is NEVER GIVING UP!
Well said, Henri!

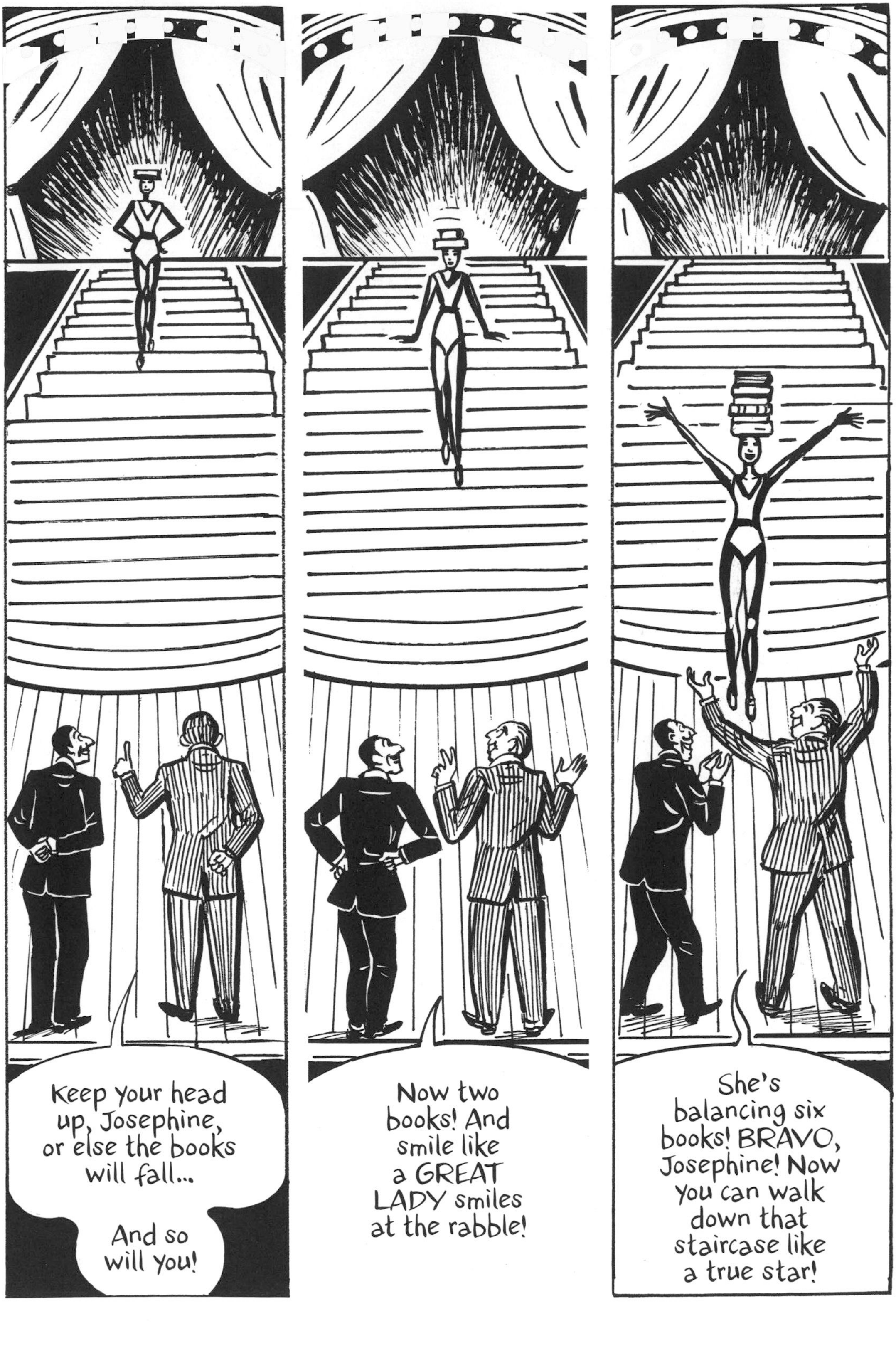

Keep your head up, Josephine, or else the books will fall...
And so will you!
Now two books! And smile like a GREAT LADY smiles at the rabble!
She's balancing six books! BRAVO, Josephine! Now you can walk down that staircase like a true star!

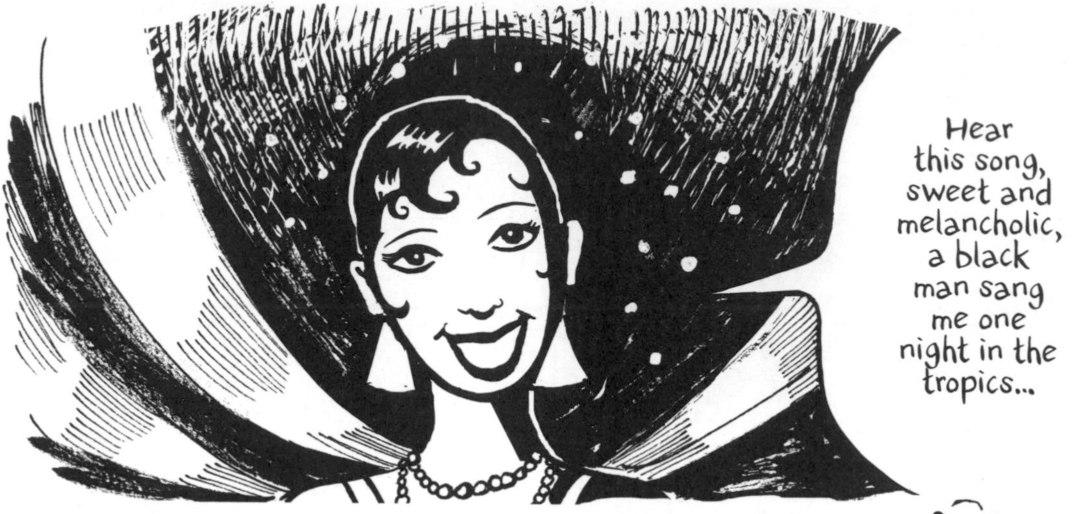
Hear this song, sweet and melancholic, a black man sang me one night in the tropics...

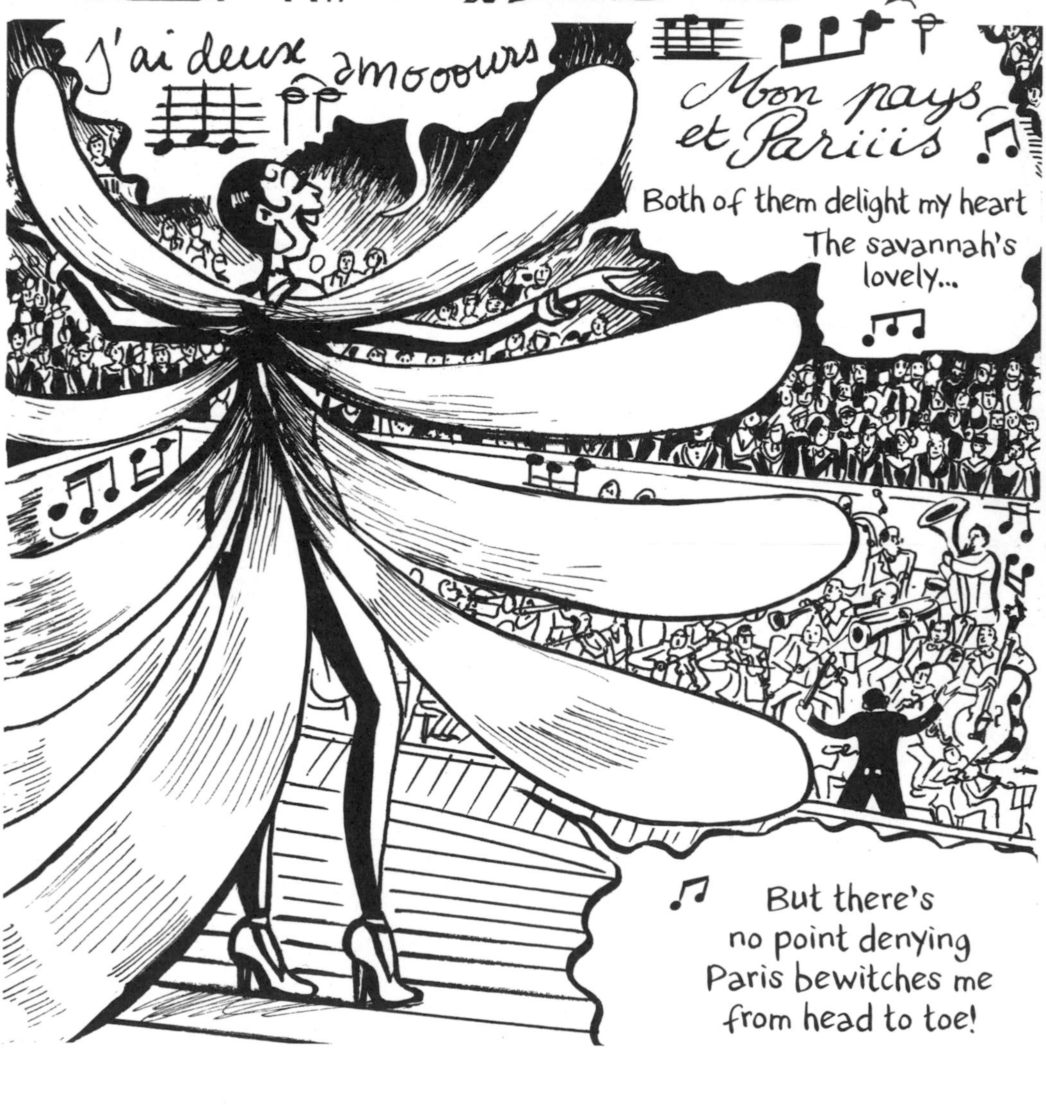
J'ai deux amooours
Mon pays et Pariiis
Both of them delight my heart
The savannah's lovely...
But there's no point denying Paris bewitches me from head to toe!

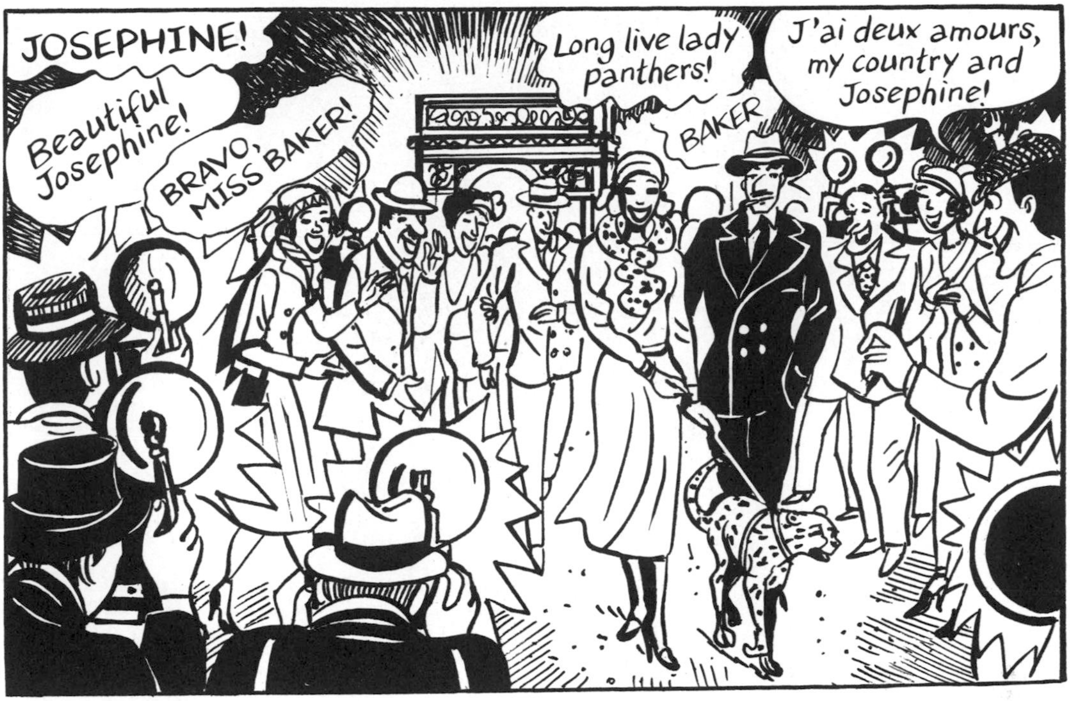
JOSEPHINE!
Beautiful Josephine!
BRAVO, MISS BAKER!
Long live lady panthers!
BAKER
J'ai deux amours, my country and Josephine!

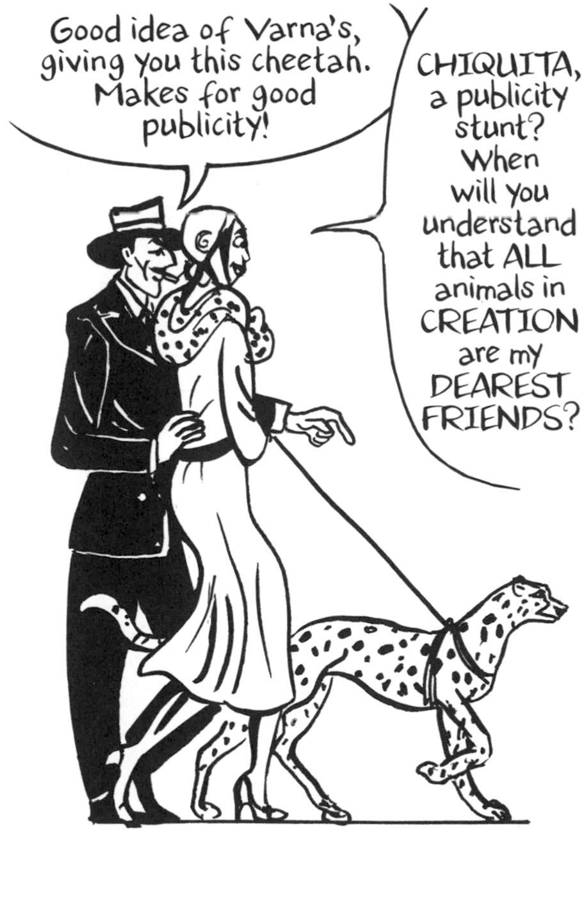
Good idea of Varna's, giving you this cheetah. Makes for good publicity!
CHIQUITA, a publicity stunt? When will you understand that ALL animals in CREATION are my DEAREST FRIENDS?

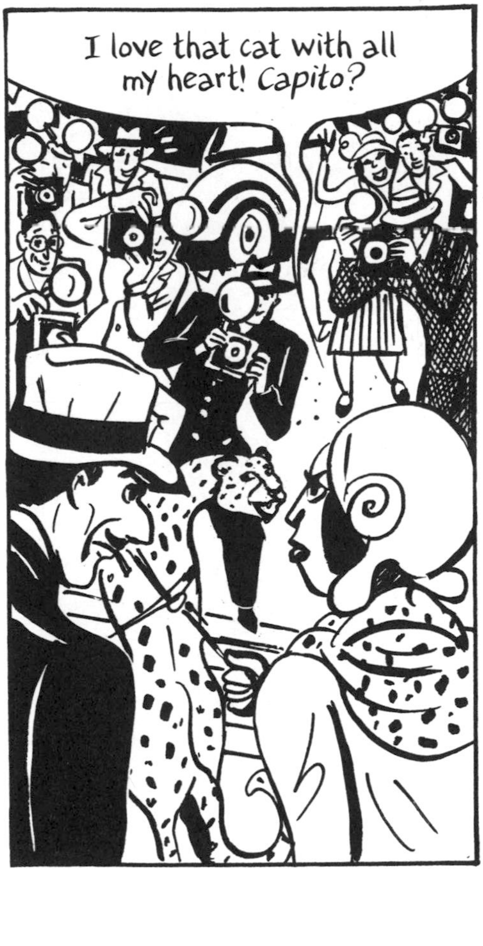
I love that cat with all my heart! Capito?

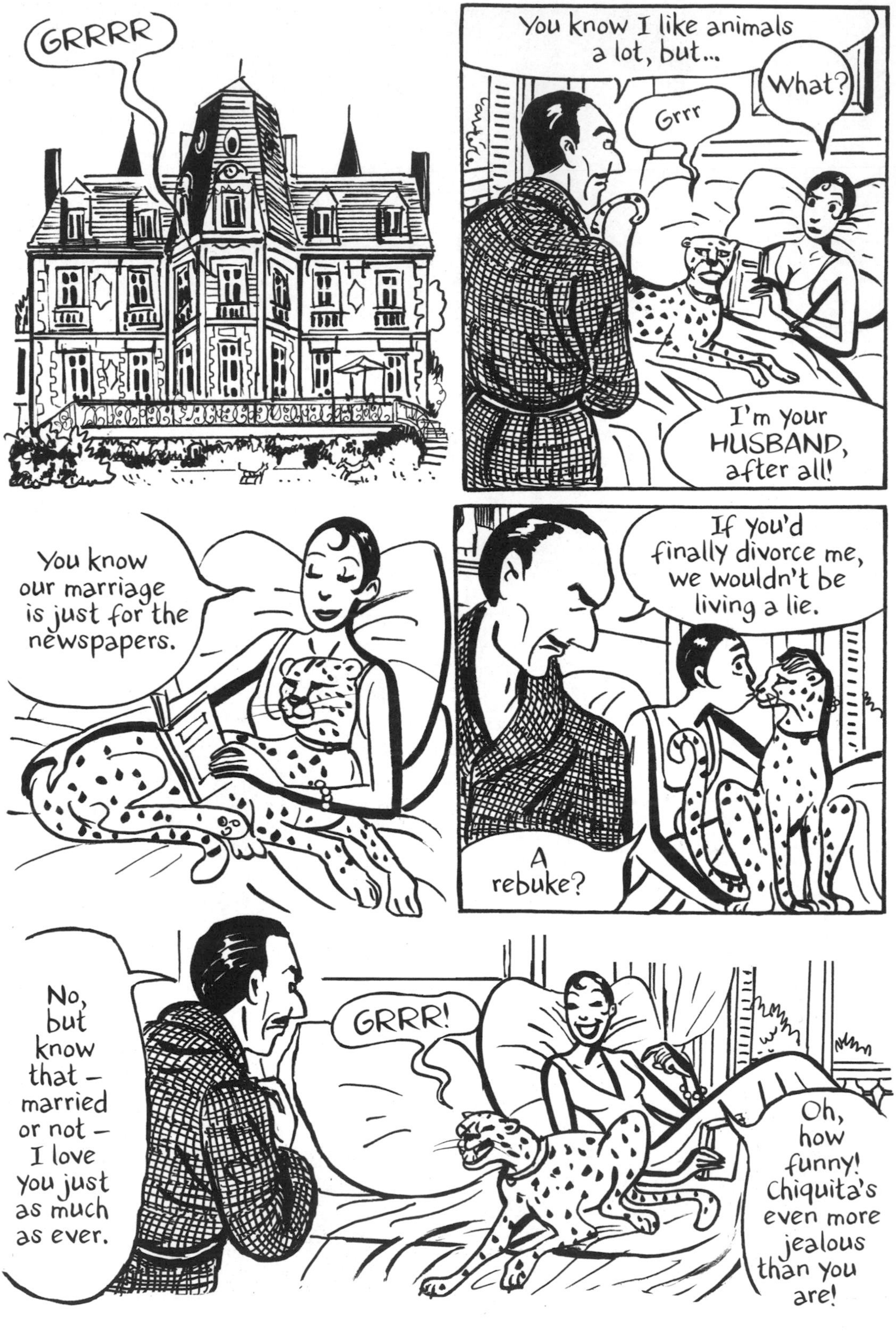
GRRRR
You know I like animals a lot, but...
Grrr
What?
I'm your HUSBAND, after all!
You know our marriage is just for the newspapers.
If you'd finally divorce me, we wouldn't be living a lie.
A rebuke?
No, but know that – married or not – I love you just as much as ever.
GRRR!
Oh, how funny! Chiquita's even more jealous than you are!

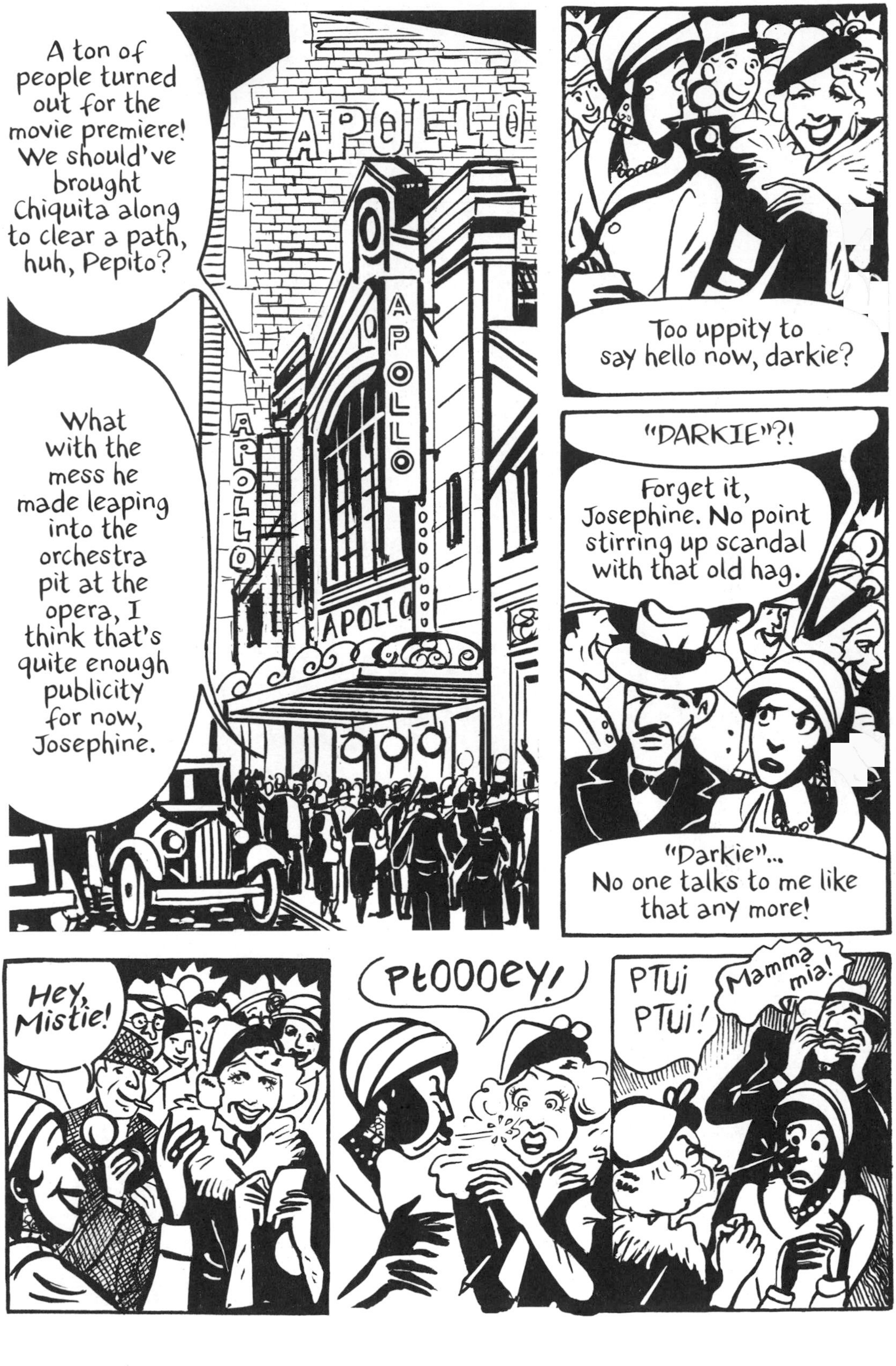

A ton of people turned out for the movie premiere! We should've brought Chiquita along to clear a path, huh, Pepito?
What with the mess he made leaping into the orchestra pit at the opera, I think that's quite enough publicity for now, Josephine.
APOLLO
APOLLO
APOLLO
APOLLO
Too uppity to say hello now, darkie?
"DARKIE"?!
Forget it, Josephine. No point stirring up scandal with that old hag.
"Darkie"... No one talks to me like that any more!
Hey, Mistie!
PtOOOey!
PTUi PTUi!
Mamma mia!

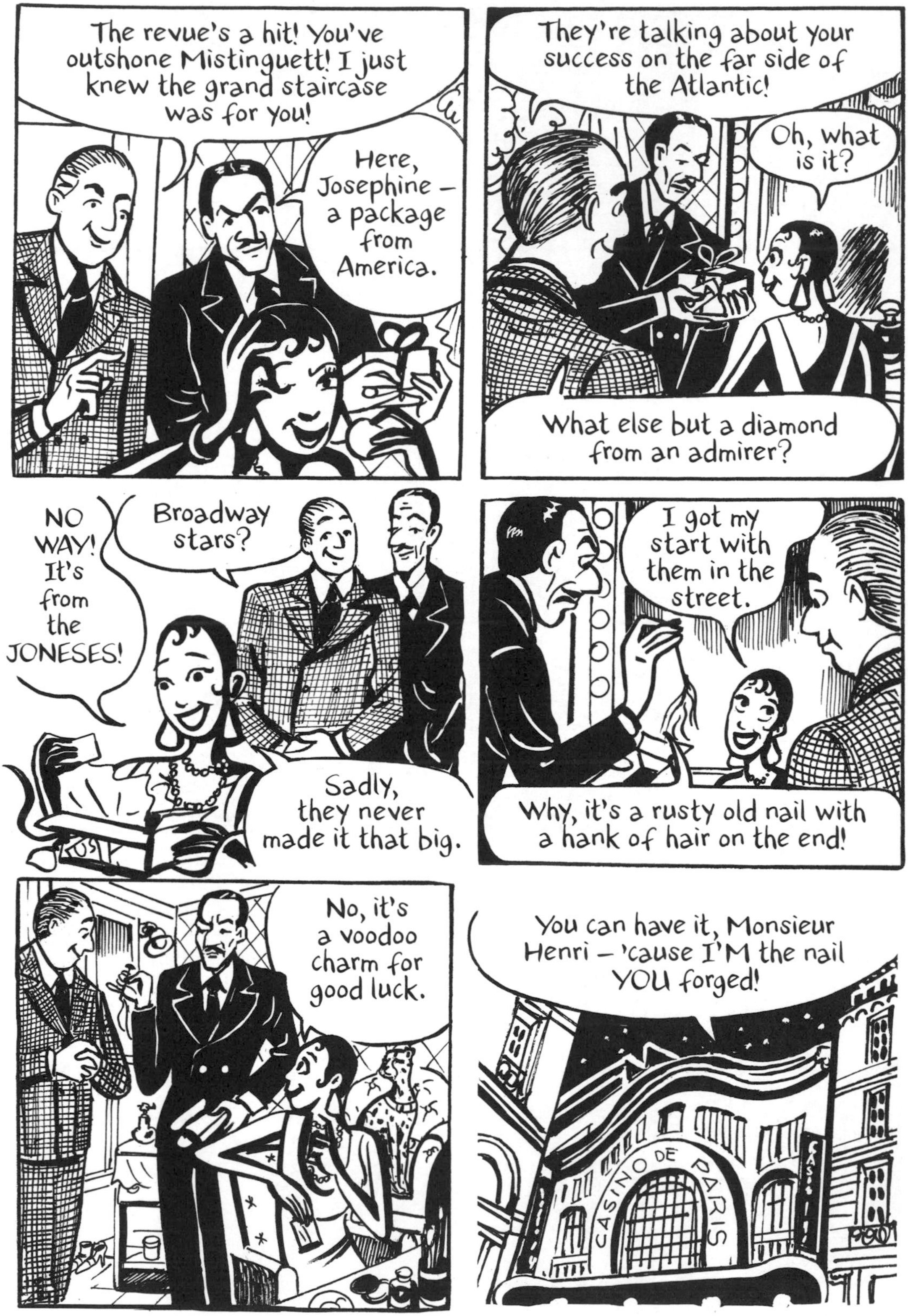
The revue's a hit! You've outshone Mistinguett! I just knew the grand staircase was for you!
Here, Josephine – a package from America.
They're talking about your success on the far side of the Atlantic!
Oh, what is it?
What else but a diamond from an admirer?
Broadway stars?
NO WAY! It's from the JONESES!
Sadly, they never made it that big.
I got my start with them in the street.
Why, it's a rusty old nail with a hank of hair on the end!
No, it's a voodoo charm for good luck.
You can have it, Monsieur Henri – 'cause I'M the nail YOU forged!
CASINO DE PARIS

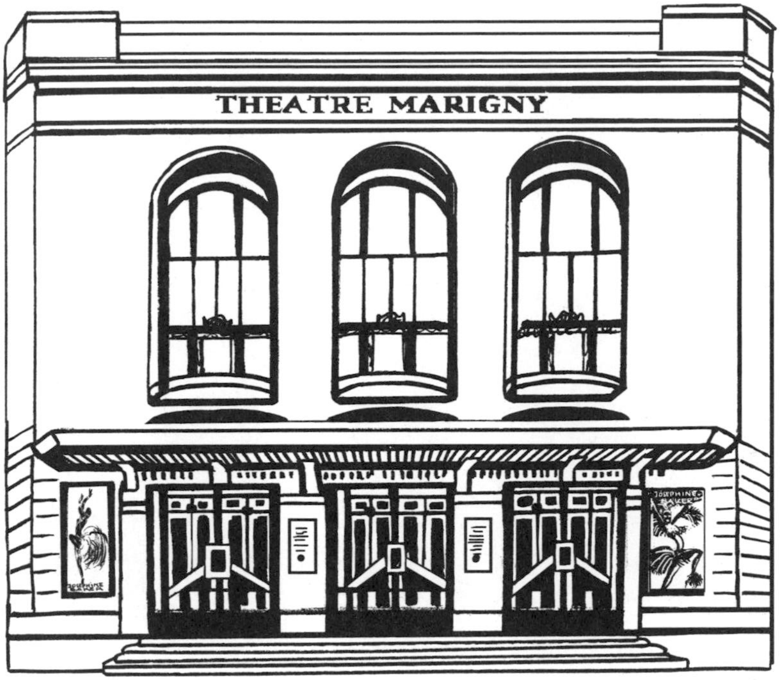
THEATRE MARIGNY
JOSEPHINE BAKER

1934: Théâtre Marigny, Paris, France

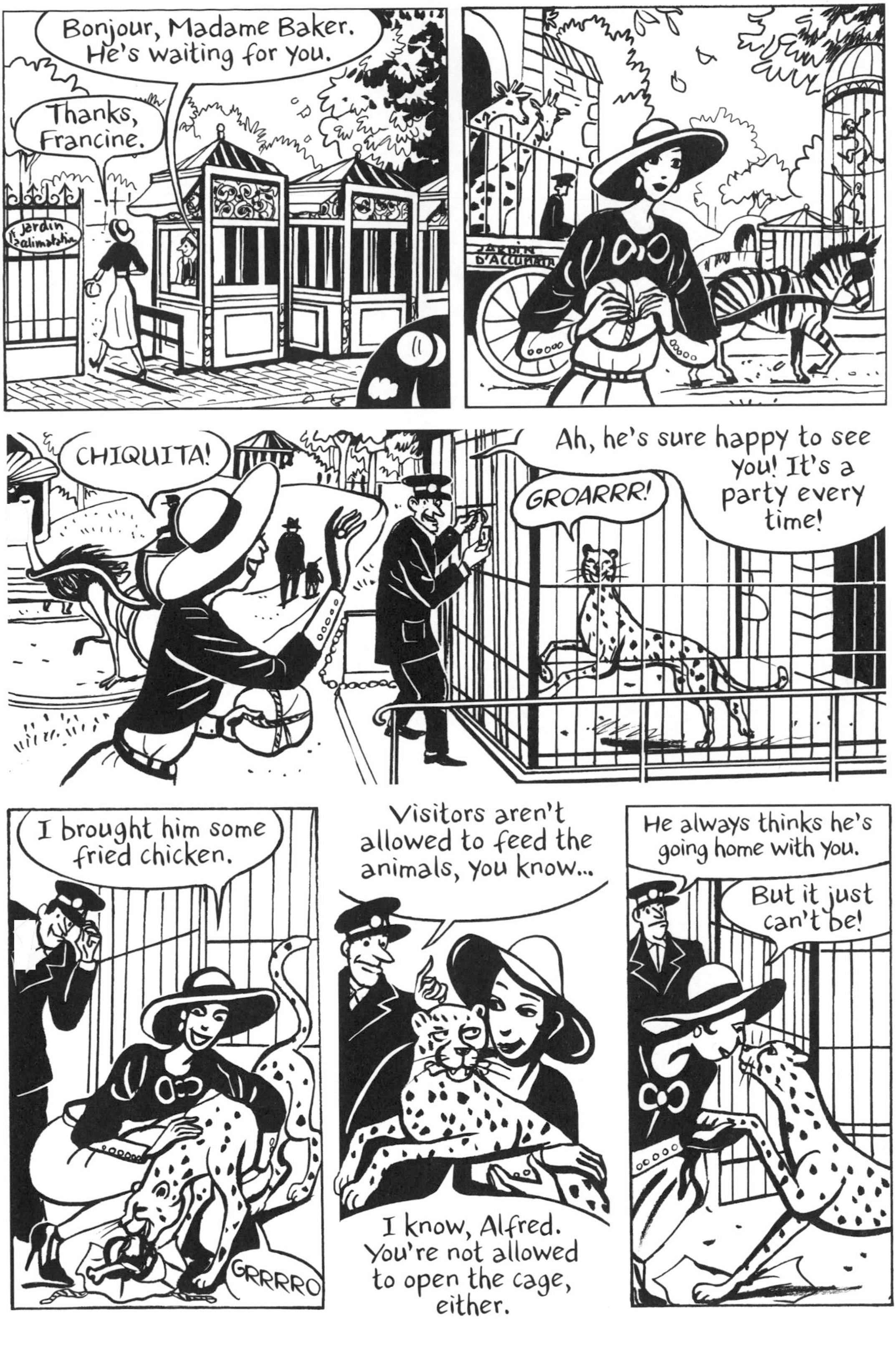

Bonjour, Madame Baker. He's waiting for you.
Thanks, Francine.
Jardin d'alimatation
JARDIN D'ACCLIMATA
CHIQUITA!
GROARRR!
Ah, he's sure happy to see you! It's a party every time!
I brought him some fried chicken.
GRRRRO
Visitors aren't allowed to feed the animals, you know...
I know, Alfred. You're not allowed to open the cage, either.
He always thinks he's going home with you.
But it just can't be!

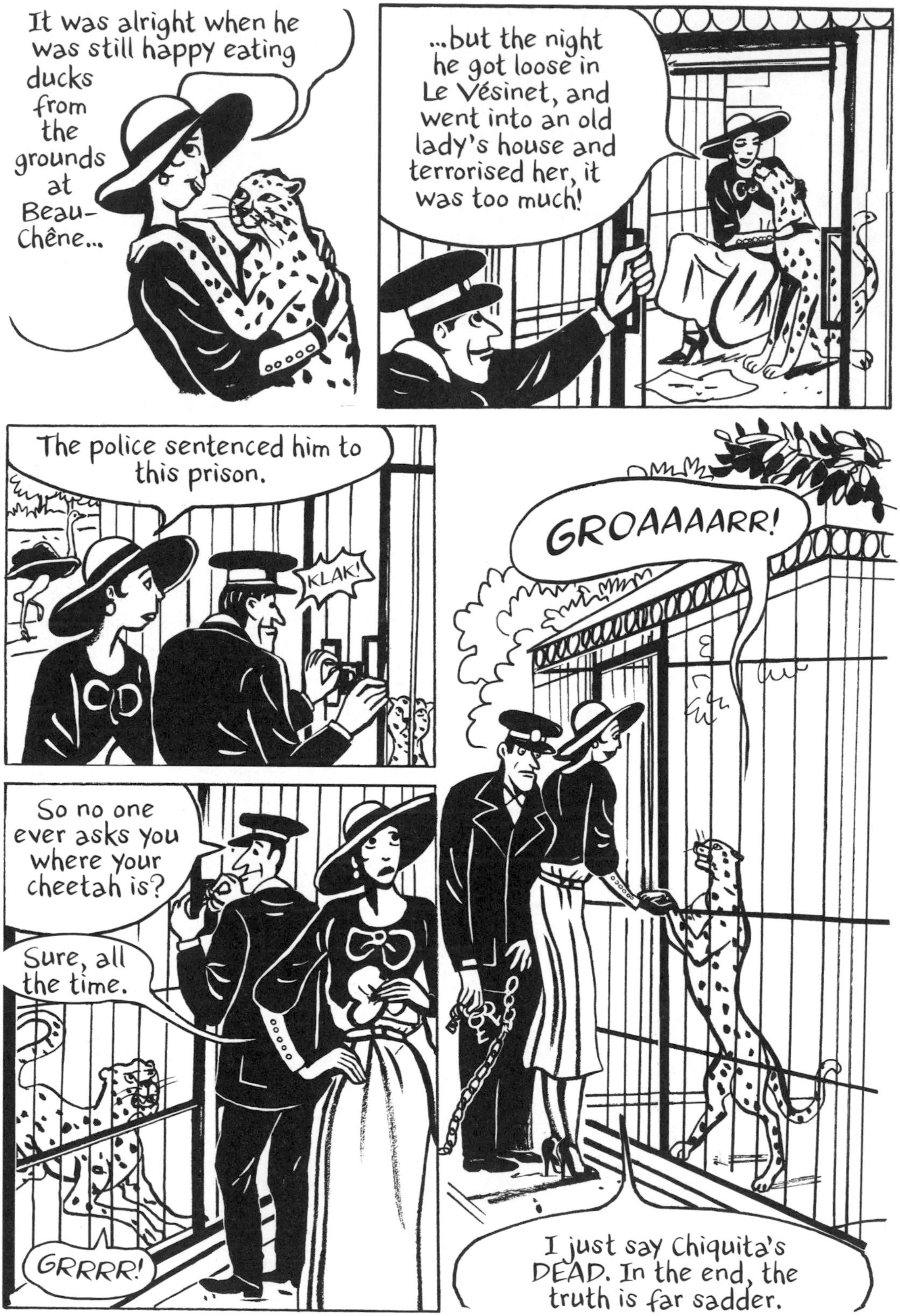
It was alright when he was still happy eating ducks from the grounds at Beau-Chêne...
...but the night he got loose in Le Vésinet, and went into an old lady's house and terrorised her, it was too much!
The police sentenced him to this prison.
KLAK!
GROAAAARR!
So no one ever asks you where your cheetah is?
Sure, all the time.
GRRRR!
I just say Chiquita's DEAD. In the end, the truth is far sadder.

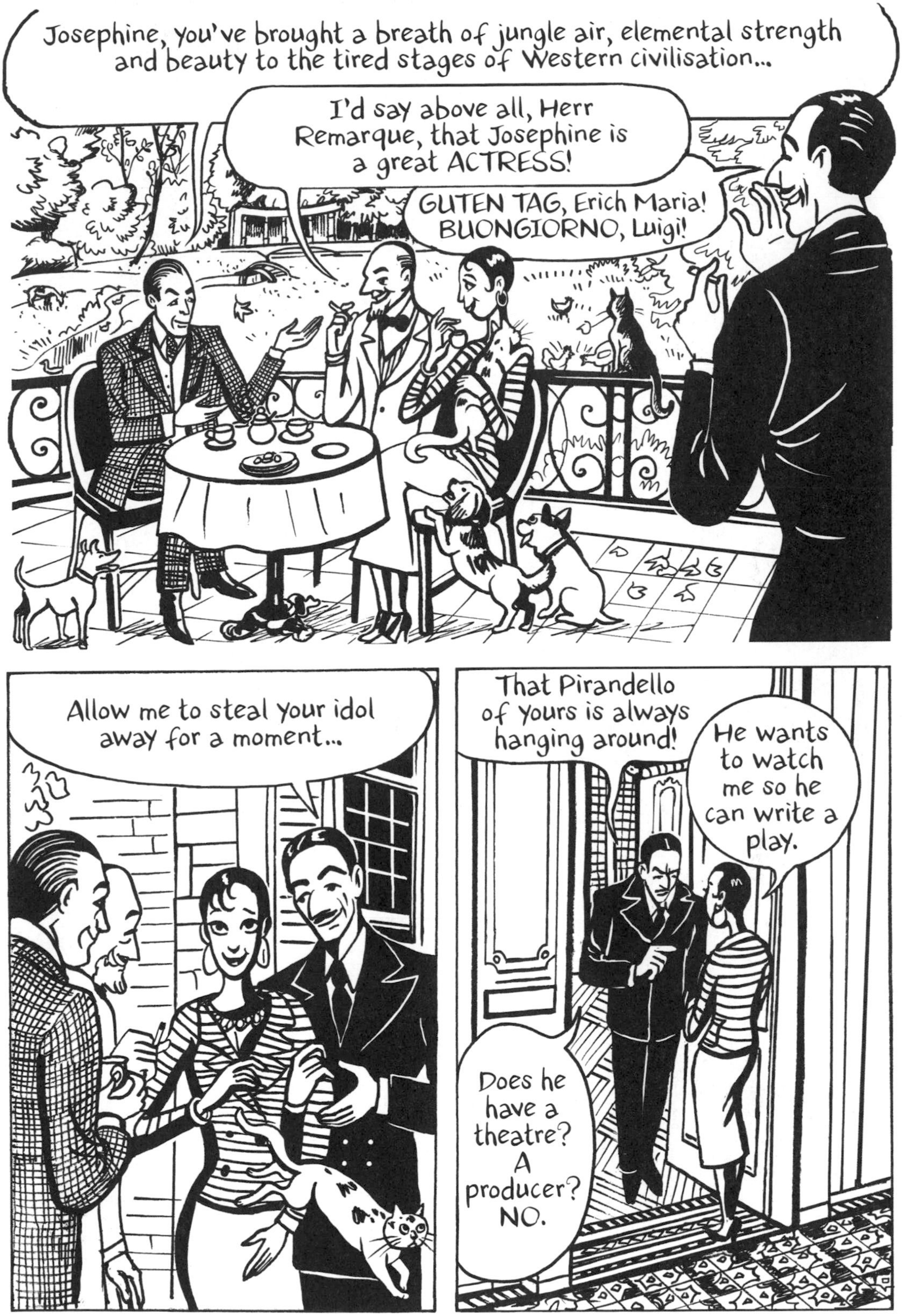

Josephine, you've brought a breath of jungle air, elemental strength and beauty to the tired stages of Western civilisation...
I'd say above all, Herr Remarque, that Josephine is a great ACTRESS!
GUTEN TAG, Erich Maria! BUONGIORNO, Luigi!
Allow me to steal your idol away for a moment...
That Pirandello of yours is always hanging around!
He wants to watch me so he can write a play.
Does he have a theatre? A producer? NO.

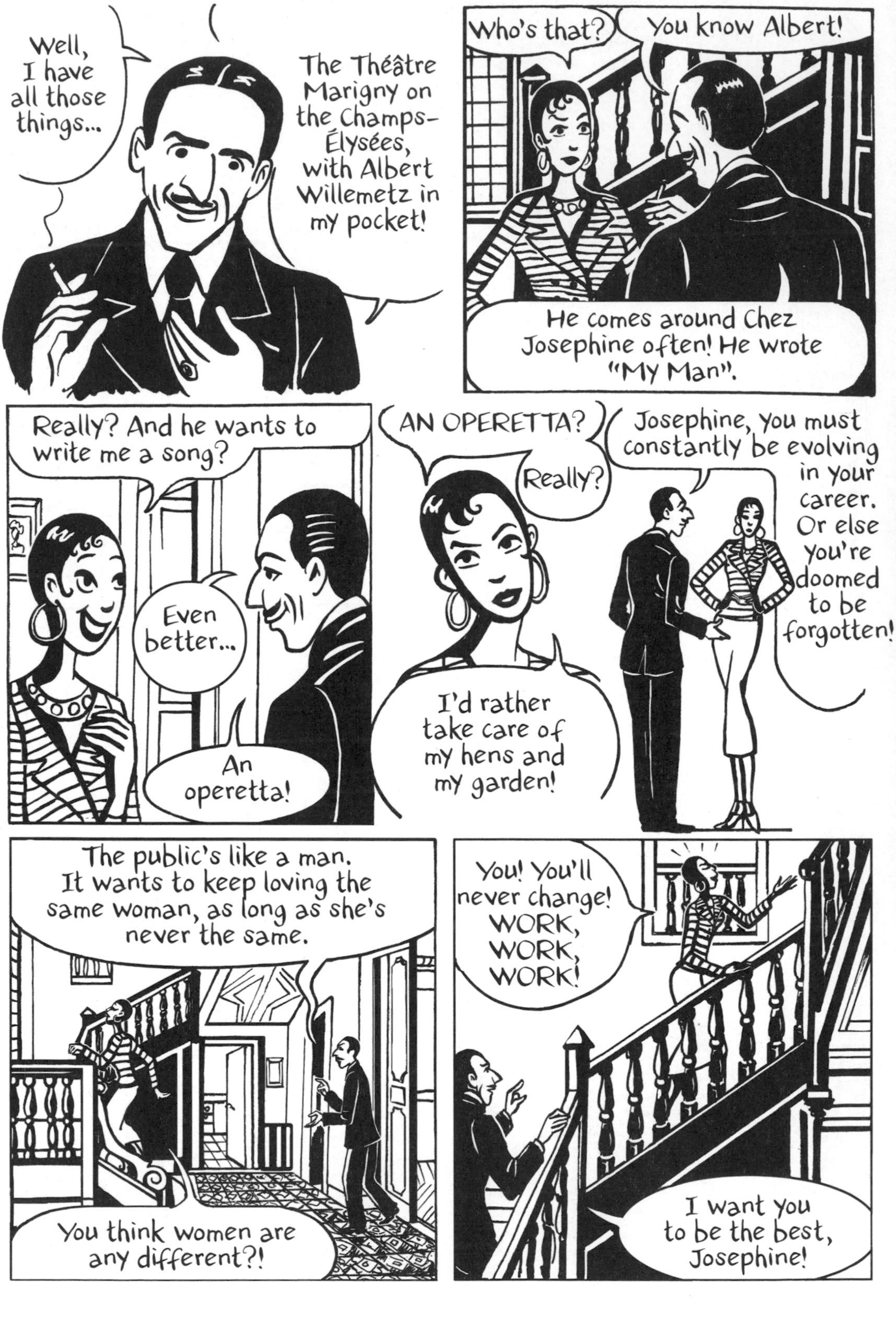

Well, I have all those things...
The Théâtre Marigny on the Champs-Élysées, with Albert Willemetz in my pocket!
Who's that?
You know Albert!
He comes around Chez Josephine often! He wrote "My Man".
Really? And he wants to write me a song?
Even better...
An operetta!
AN OPERETTA?
Really?
I'd rather take care of my hens and my garden!
Josephine, you must constantly be evolving in your career. Or else you're doomed to be forgotten!
The public's like a man. It wants to keep loving the same woman, as long as she's never the same.
You think women are any different?!
You! You'll never change! WORK, WORK, WORK!
I want you to be the best, Josephine!

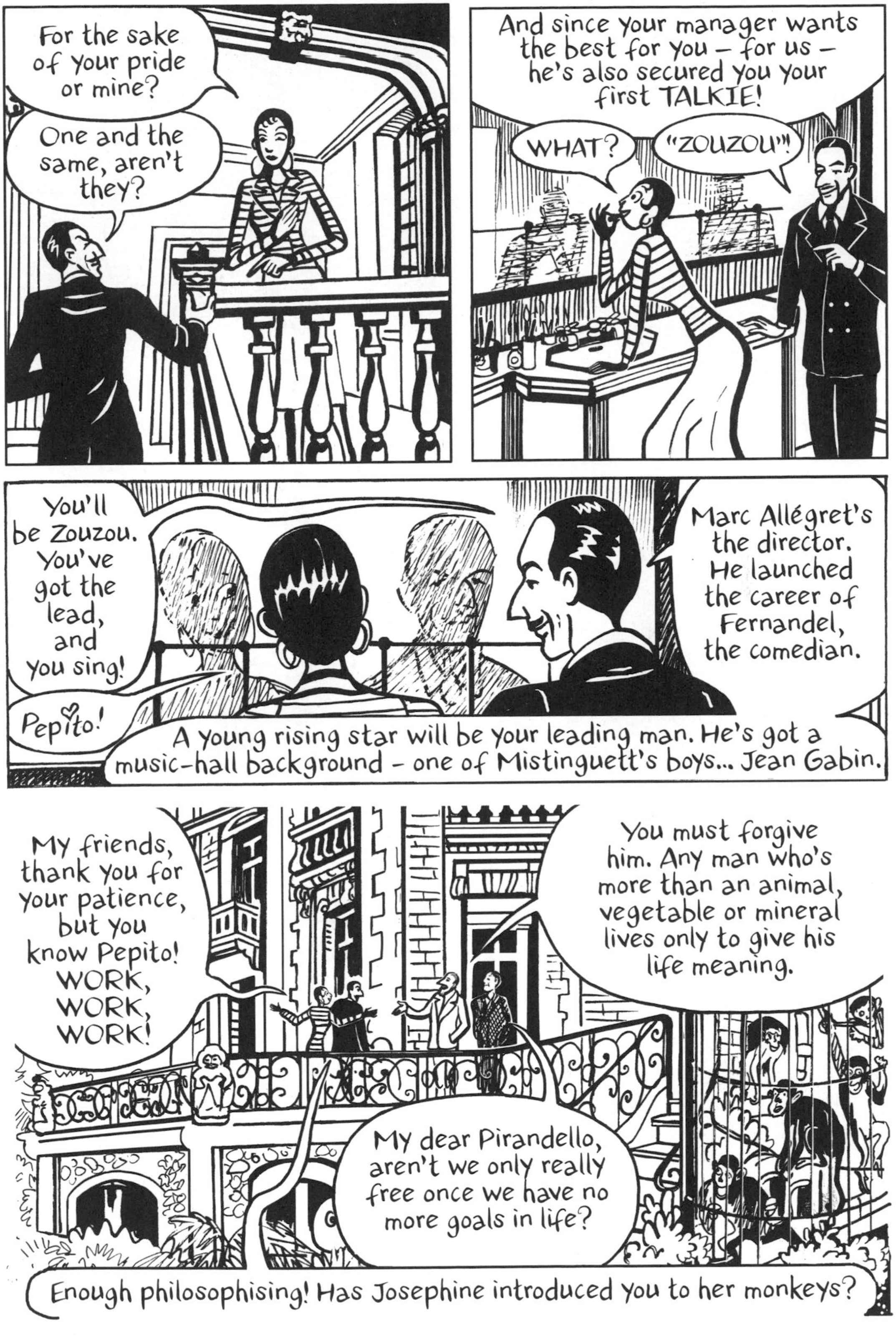

For the sake of your pride or mine?
One and the same, aren't they?
And since your manager wants the best for you – for us – he's also secured you your first TALKIE!
WHAT?
"ZOUZOU"!
You'll be Zouzou. You've got the lead, and you sing!
Marc Allégret's the director. He launched the career of Fernandel, the comedian.
Pepito!
A young rising star will be your leading man. He's got a music-hall background – one of Mistinguett's boys... Jean Gabin.
My friends, thank you for your patience, but you know Pepito! WORK, WORK, WORK!
You must forgive him. Any man who's more than an animal, vegetable or mineral lives only to give his life meaning.
My dear Pirandello, aren't we only really free once we have no more goals in life?
Enough philosophising! Has Josephine introduced you to her monkeys?

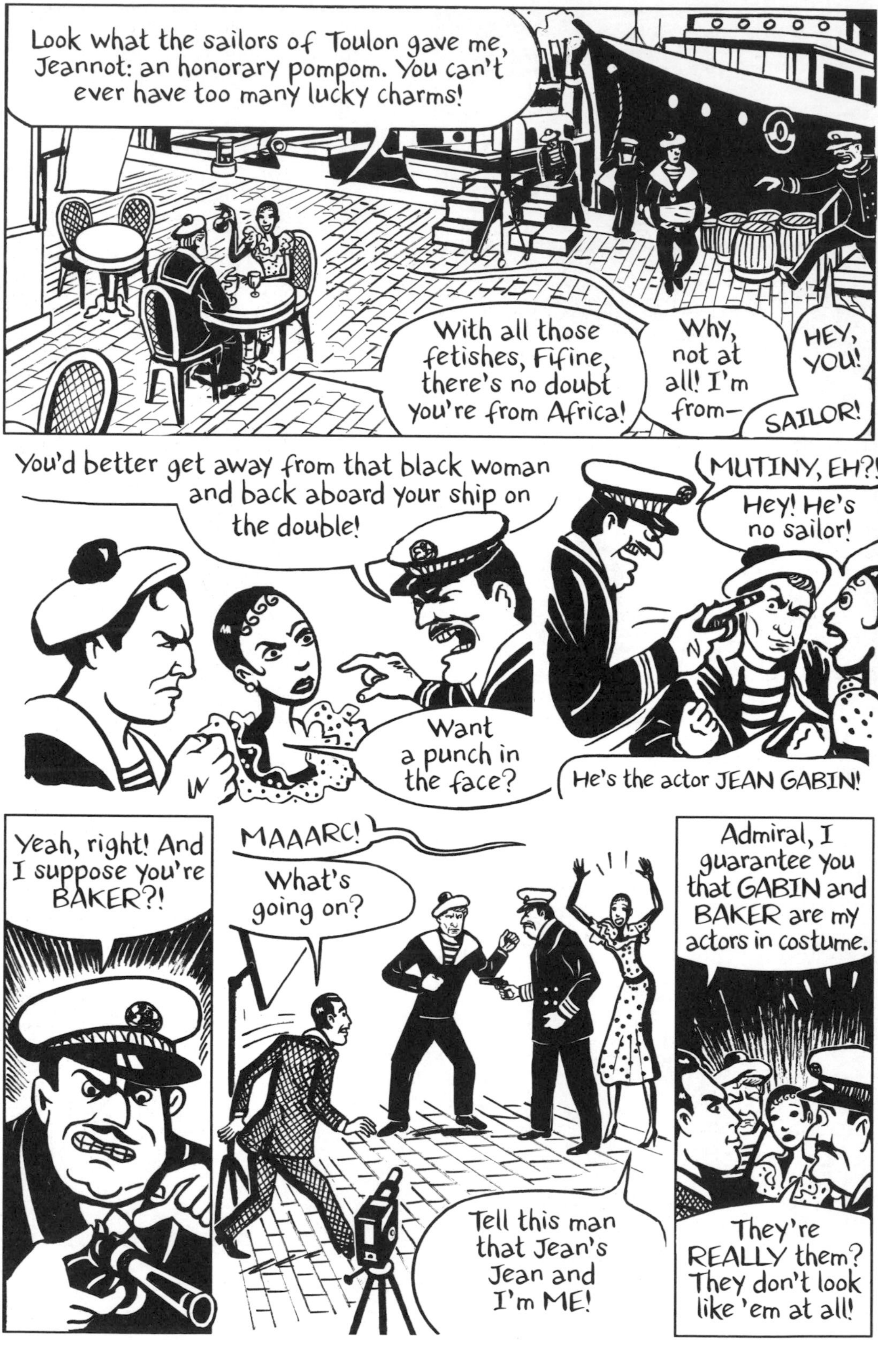
Look what the sailors of Toulon gave me, Jeannot: an honorary pompom. You can't ever have too many lucky charms!
With all those fetishes, Fifine, there's no doubt you're from Africa!
Why, not at all! I'm from—
HEY, YOU!
SAILOR!
You'd better get away from that black woman and back aboard your ship on the double!
Want a punch in the face?
MUTINY, EH?!
Hey! He's no sailor!
He's the actor JEAN GABIN!
Yeah, right! And I suppose you're BAKER?!
MAAARC!
What's going on?
Tell this man that Jean's Jean and I'm ME!
Admiral, I guarantee you that GABIN and BAKER are my actors in costume.
They're REALLY them? They don't look like 'em at all!

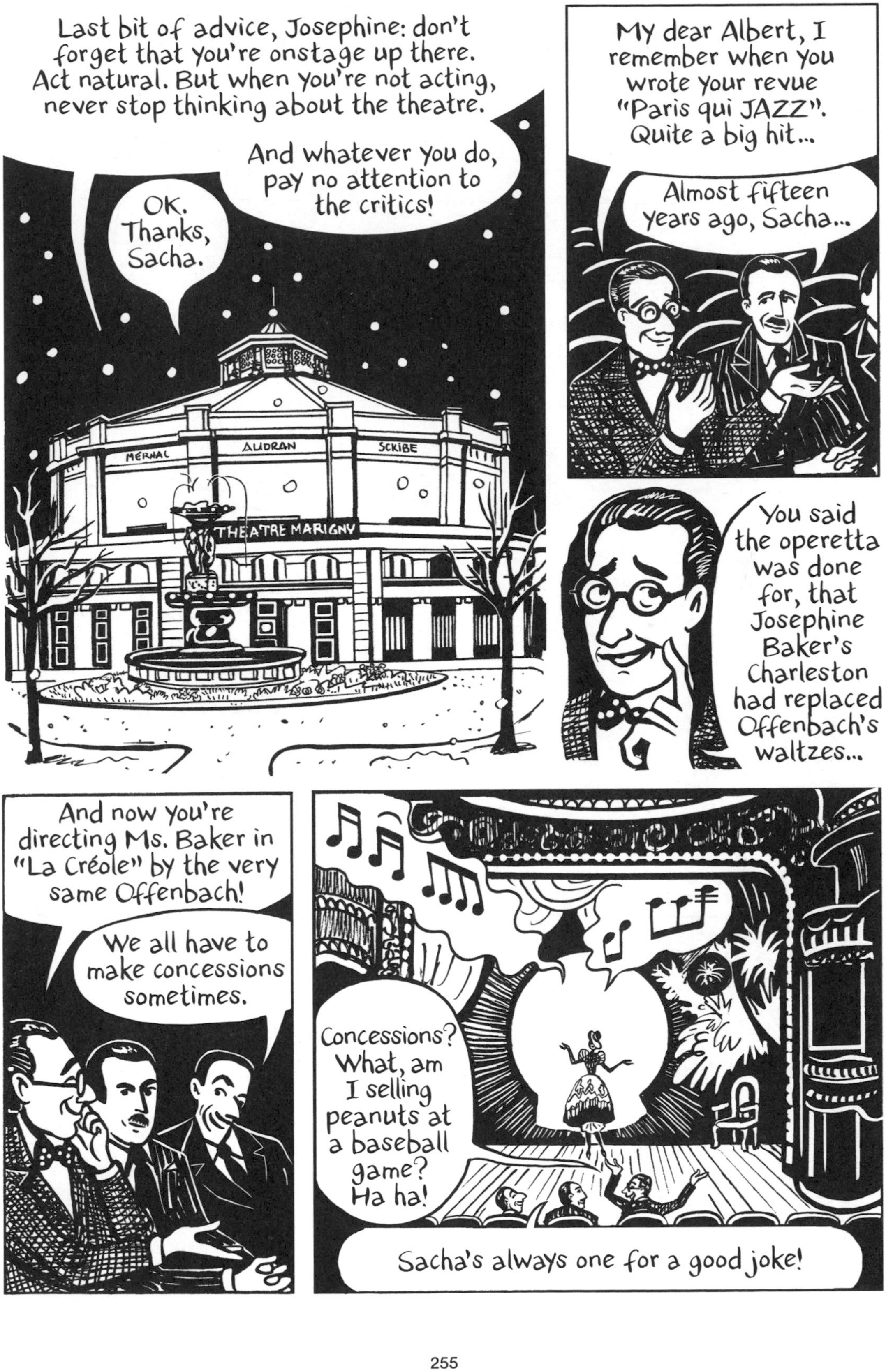
Last bit of advice, Josephine: don't forget that you're onstage up there. Act natural. But when you're not acting, never stop thinking about the theatre.
And whatever you do, pay no attention to the critics!
OK. Thanks, Sacha.
MERNAL
AUDRAN
SCRIBE
THEATRE MARIGNY
My dear Albert, I remember when you wrote your revue "Paris qui JAZZ". Quite a big hit...
Almost fifteen years ago, Sacha...
You said the operetta was done for, that Josephine Baker's Charleston had replaced Offenbach's waltzes...
And now you're directing Ms. Baker in "La Créole" by the very same Offenbach!
We all have to make concessions sometimes.
Concessions? What, am I selling peanuts at a baseball game? Ha ha!
Sacha's always one for a good joke!

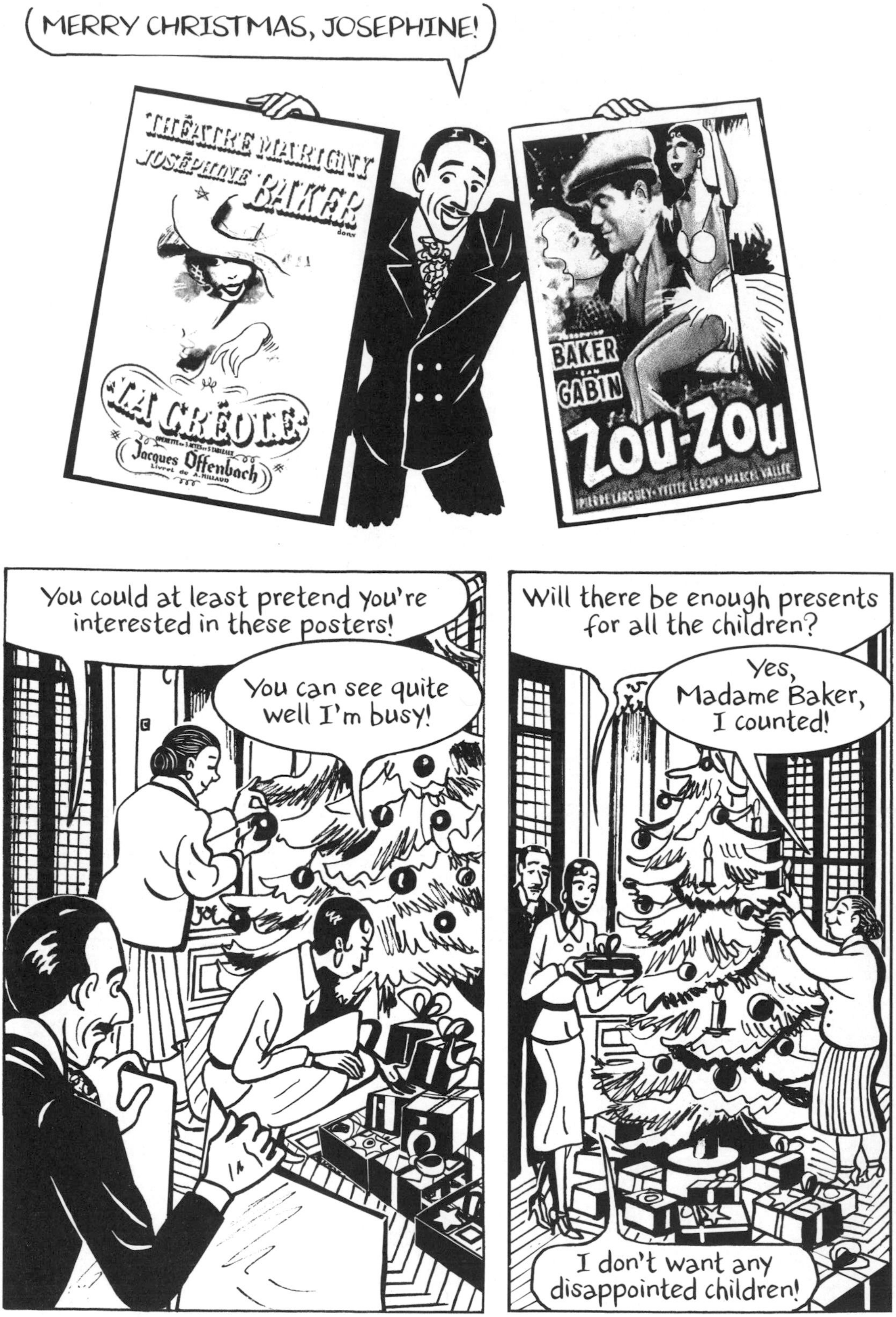
MERRY CHRISTMAS, JOSEPHINE!
THÉÂTRE MARIGNY
JOSÉPHINE BAKER
LA CRÉOLE
Jacques Offenbach
BAKER
GABIN
ZOU-ZOU
You could at least pretend you're interested in these posters!
You can see quite well I'm busy!
Will there be enough presents for all the children?
Yes, Madame Baker, I counted!
I don't want any disappointed children!

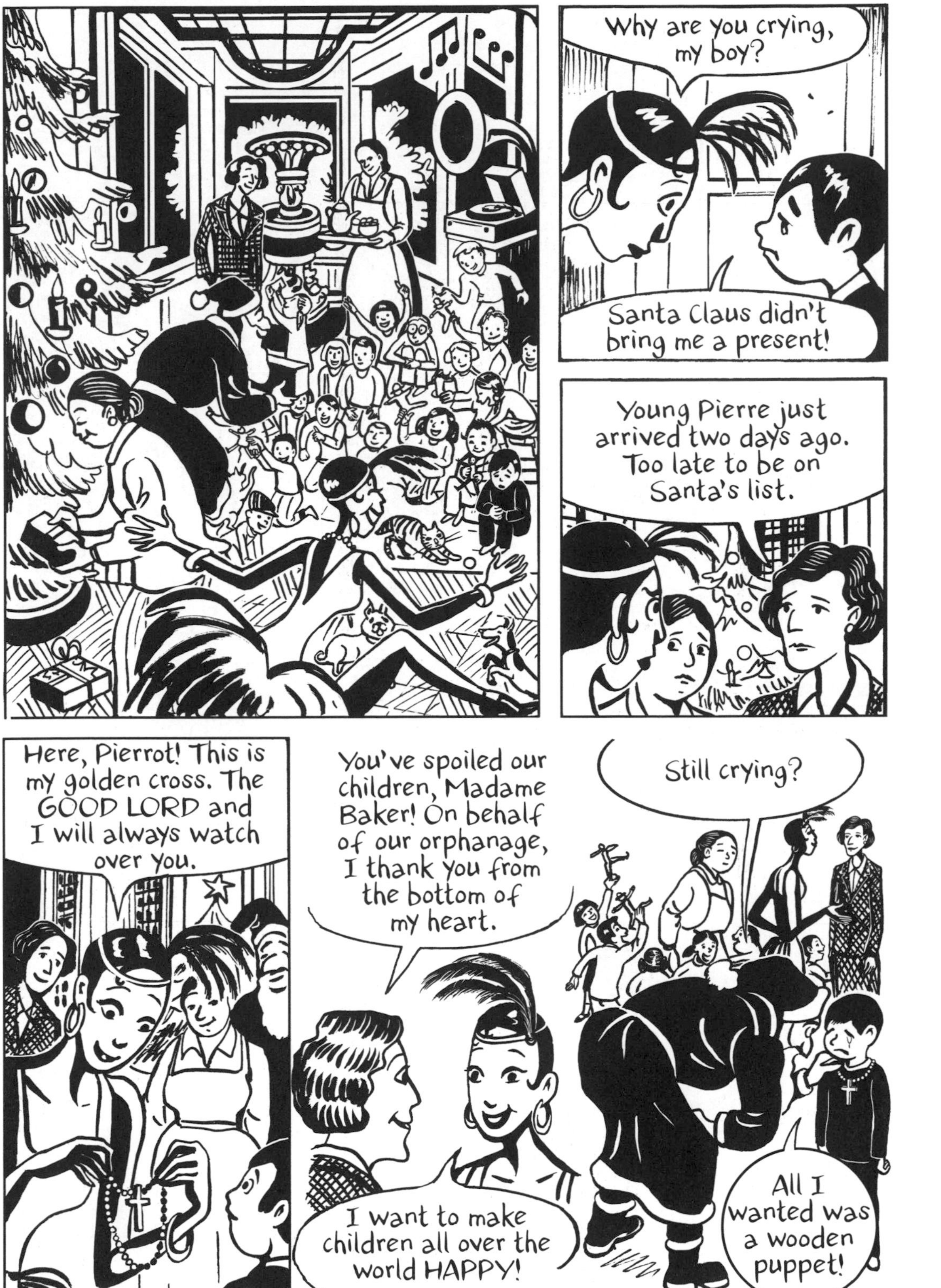
Why are you crying, my boy?
Santa Claus didn't bring me a present!
Young Pierre just arrived two days ago. Too late to be on Santa's list.
Here, Pierrot! This is my golden cross. The GOOD LORD and I will always watch over you.
You've spoiled our children, Madame Baker! On behalf of our orphanage, I thank you from the bottom of my heart.
I want to make children all over the world HAPPY!
Still crying?
All I wanted was a wooden puppet!

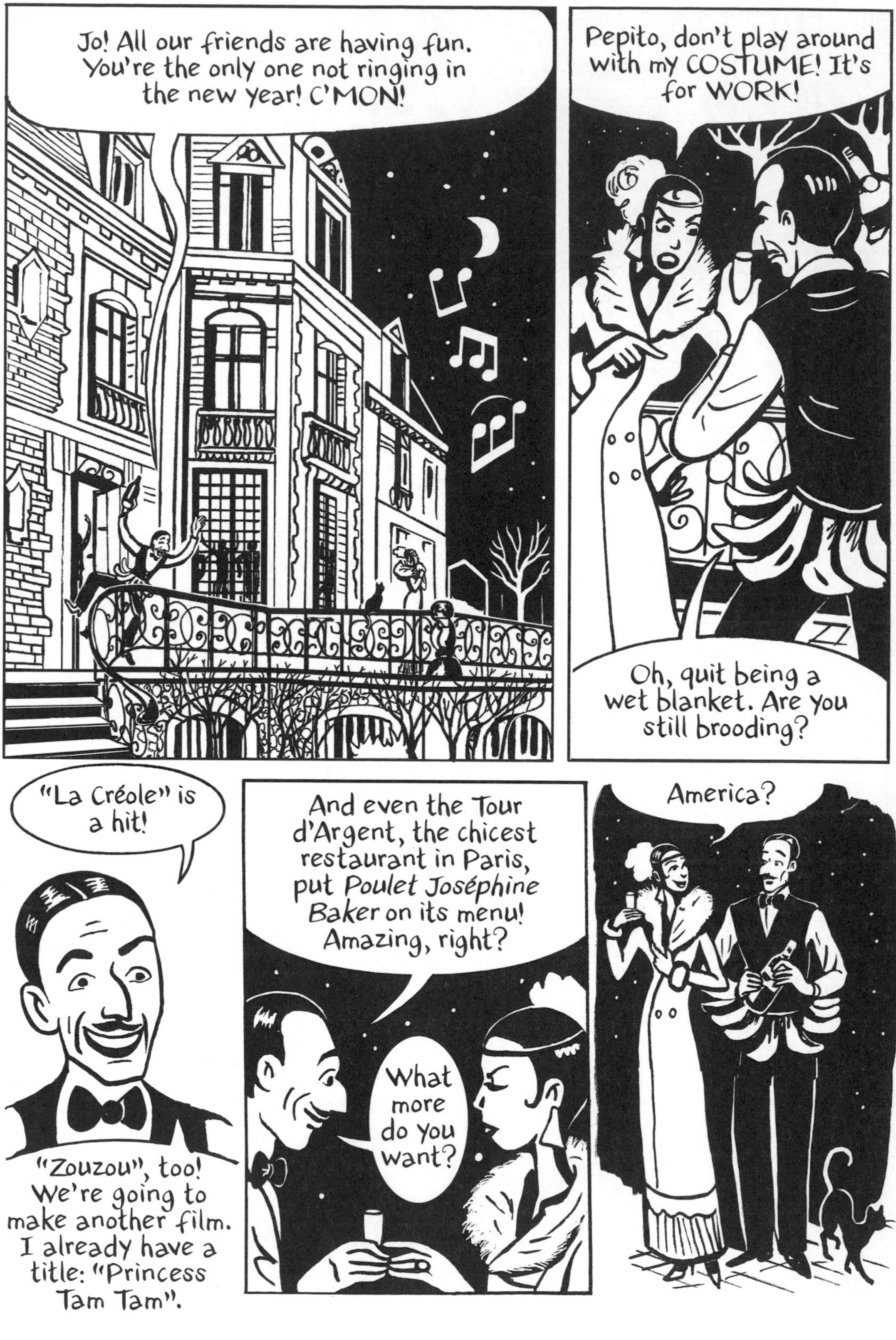
Jo! All our friends are having fun. You're the only one not ringing in the new year! C'MON!
Pepito, don't play around with my COSTUME! It's for WORK!
Oh, quit being a wet blanket. Are you still brooding?
"La Créole" is a hit!
"Zouzou", too! We're going to make another film. I already have a title: "Princess Tam Tam".
And even the Tour d'Argent, the chicest restaurant in Paris, put *Poulet Joséphine Baker* on its menu! Amazing, right?
What more do you want?
America?

1935: Central West End, St. Louis, Missouri, USA

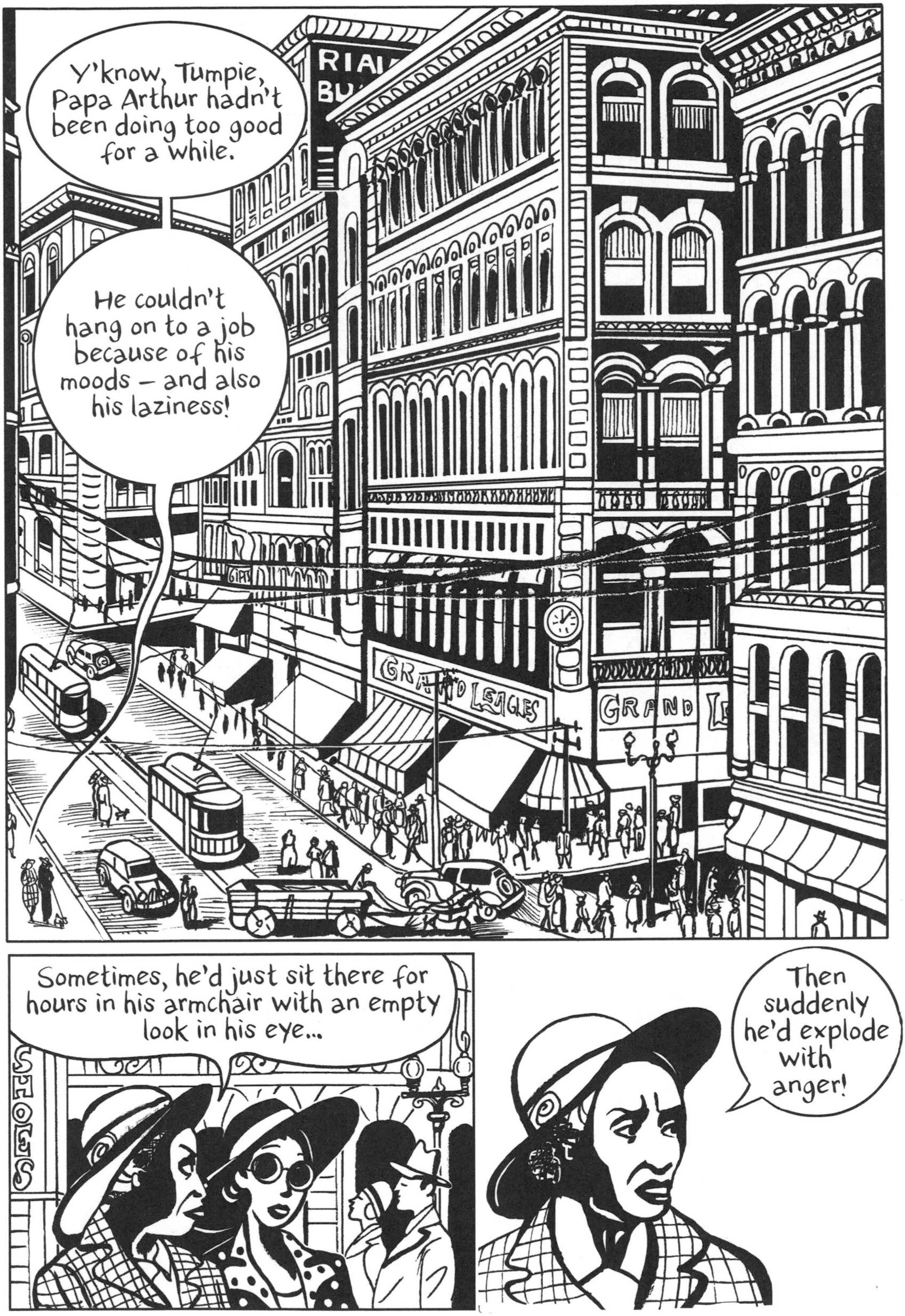
Y'know, Tumpie, Papa Arthur hadn't been doing too good for a while.
He couldn't hang on to a job because of his moods – and also his laziness!
RIAL
BU
GIFTS
GRAND LEAGLES
GRAND
Sometimes, he'd just sit there for hours in his armchair with an empty look in his eye...
SHOES
Then suddenly he'd explode with anger!

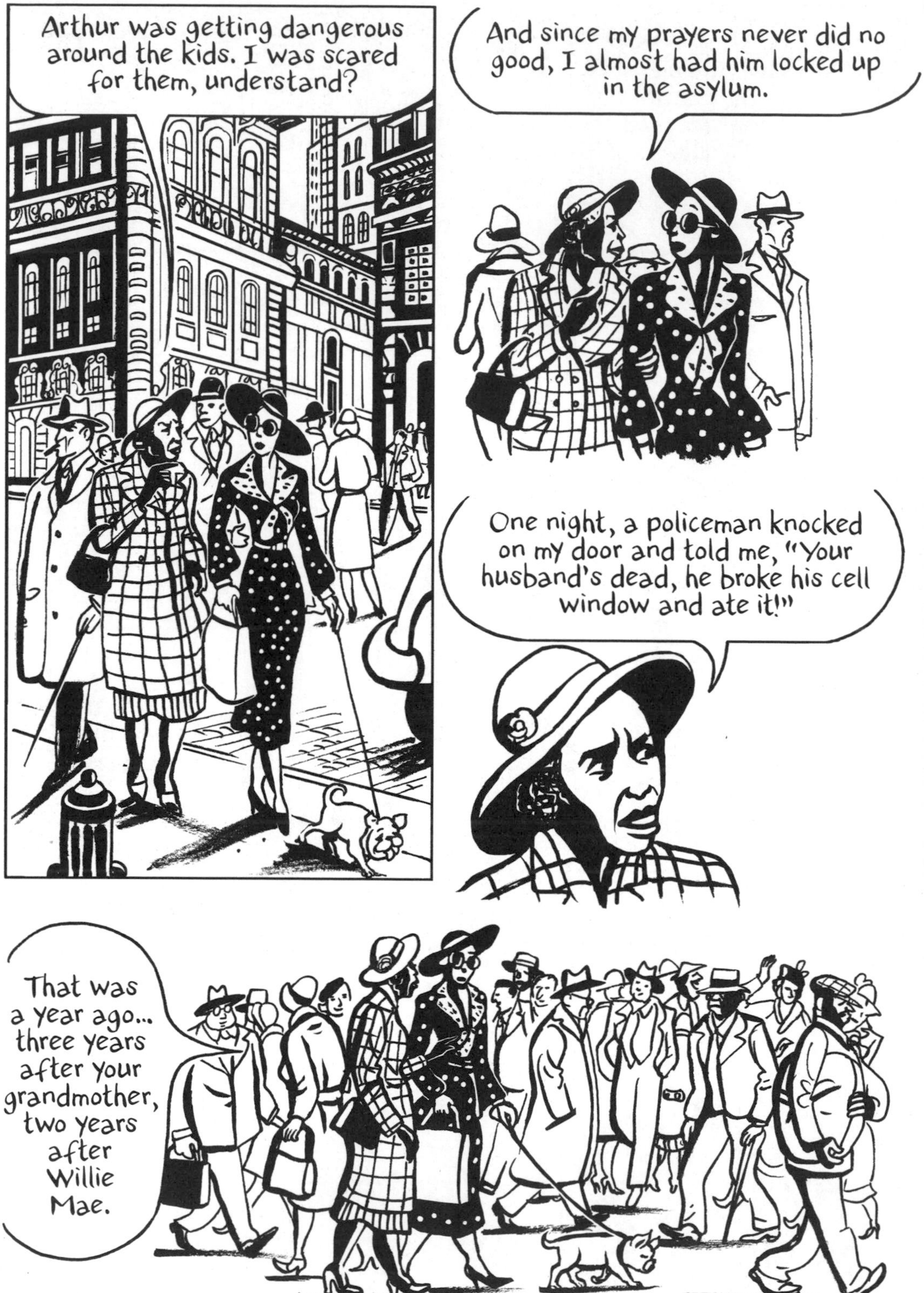

Arthur was getting dangerous around the kids. I was scared for them, understand?
And since my prayers never did no good, I almost had him locked up in the asylum.
One night, a policeman knocked on my door and told me, "Your husband's dead, he broke his cell window and ate it!"
That was a year ago... three years after your grandmother, two years after Willie Mae.

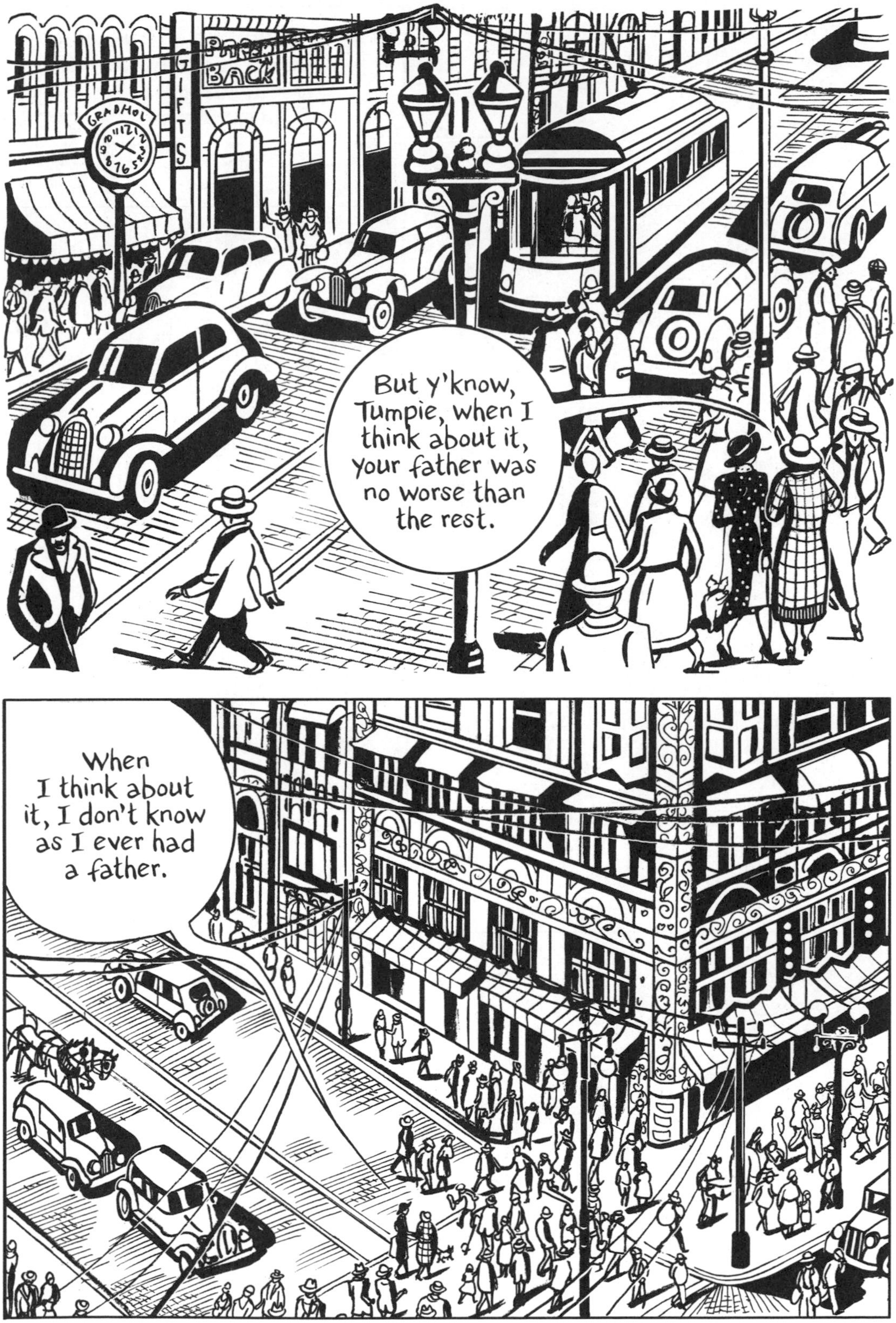
But y'know, Tumpie, when I think about it, your father was no worse than the rest.
When I think about it, I don't know as I ever had a father.

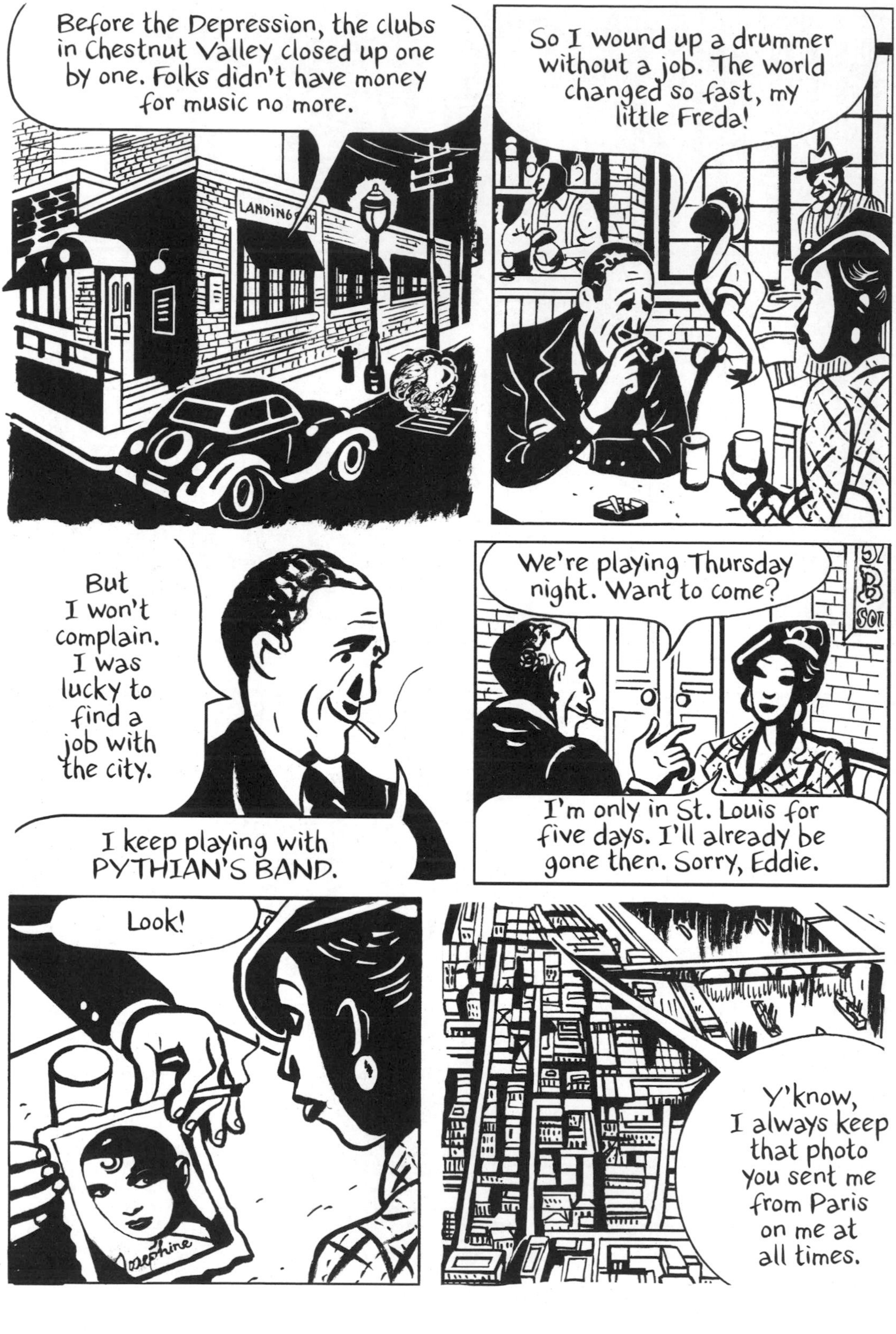
Before the Depression, the clubs in Chestnut Valley closed up one by one. Folks didn't have money for music no more.
LANDING
So I wound up a drummer without a job. The world changed so fast, my little Freda!
But I won't complain. I was lucky to find a job with the city.
I keep playing with PYTHIAN'S BAND.
We're playing Thursday night. Want to come?
I'm only in St. Louis for five days. I'll already be gone then. Sorry, Eddie.
Look!
Josephine
Y'know, I always keep that photo you sent me from Paris on me at all times.

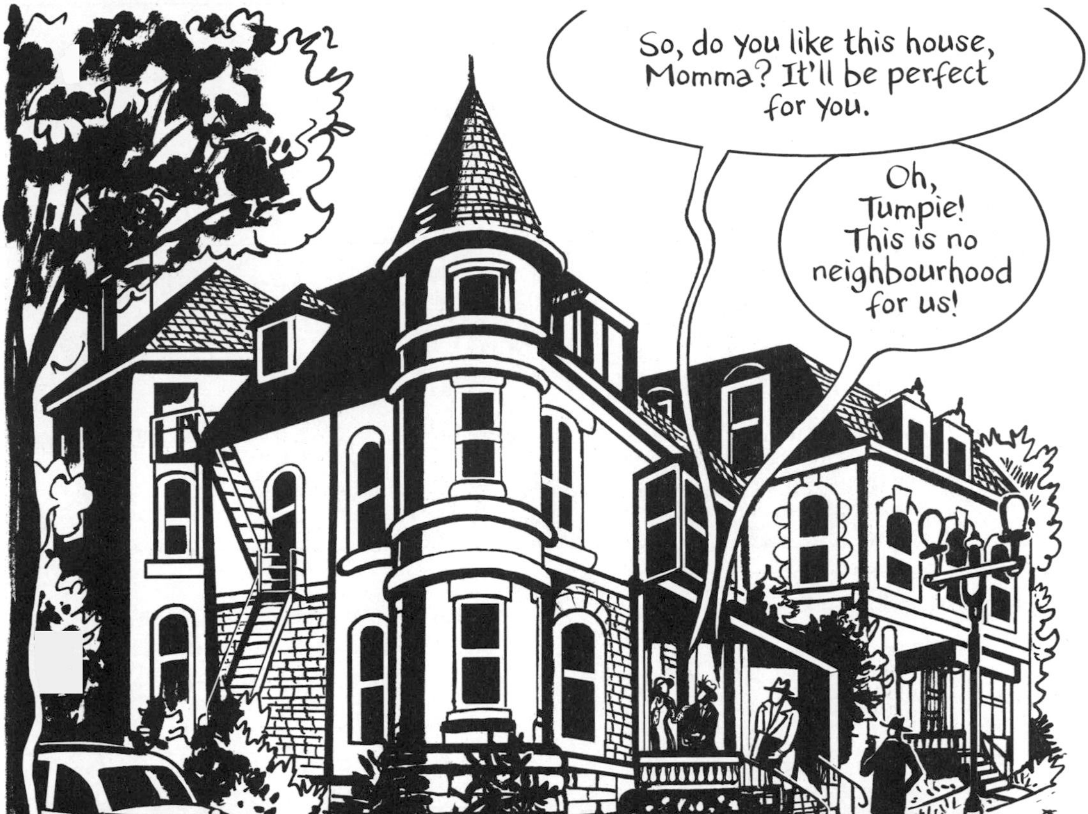
So, do you like this house, Momma? It'll be perfect for you.
Oh, Tumpie! This is no neighbourhood for us!

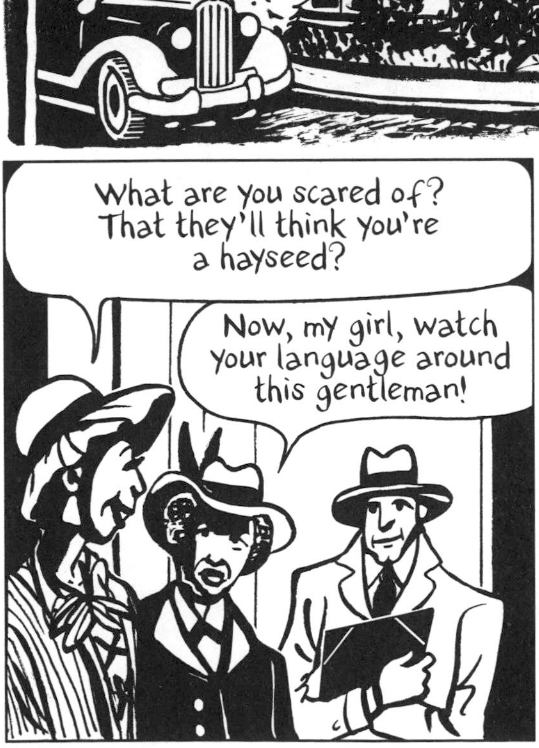
What are you scared of? That they'll think you're a hayseed?
Now, my girl, watch your language around this gentleman!

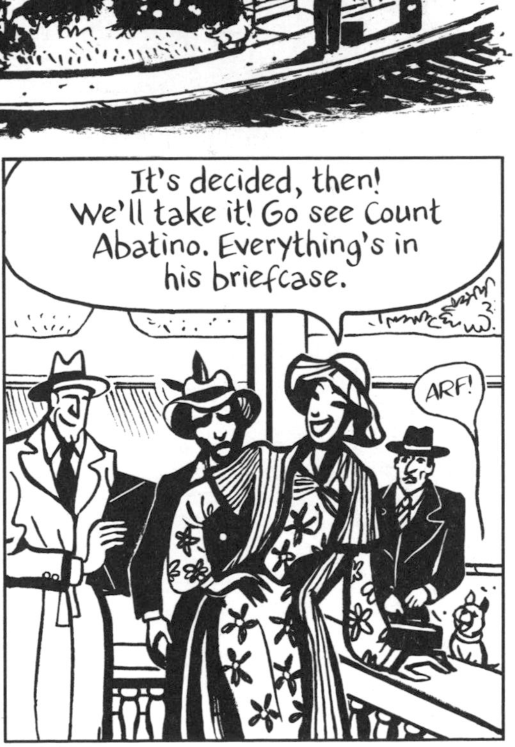
It's decided, then! We'll take it! Go see Count Abatino. Everything's in his briefcase.
ARF!

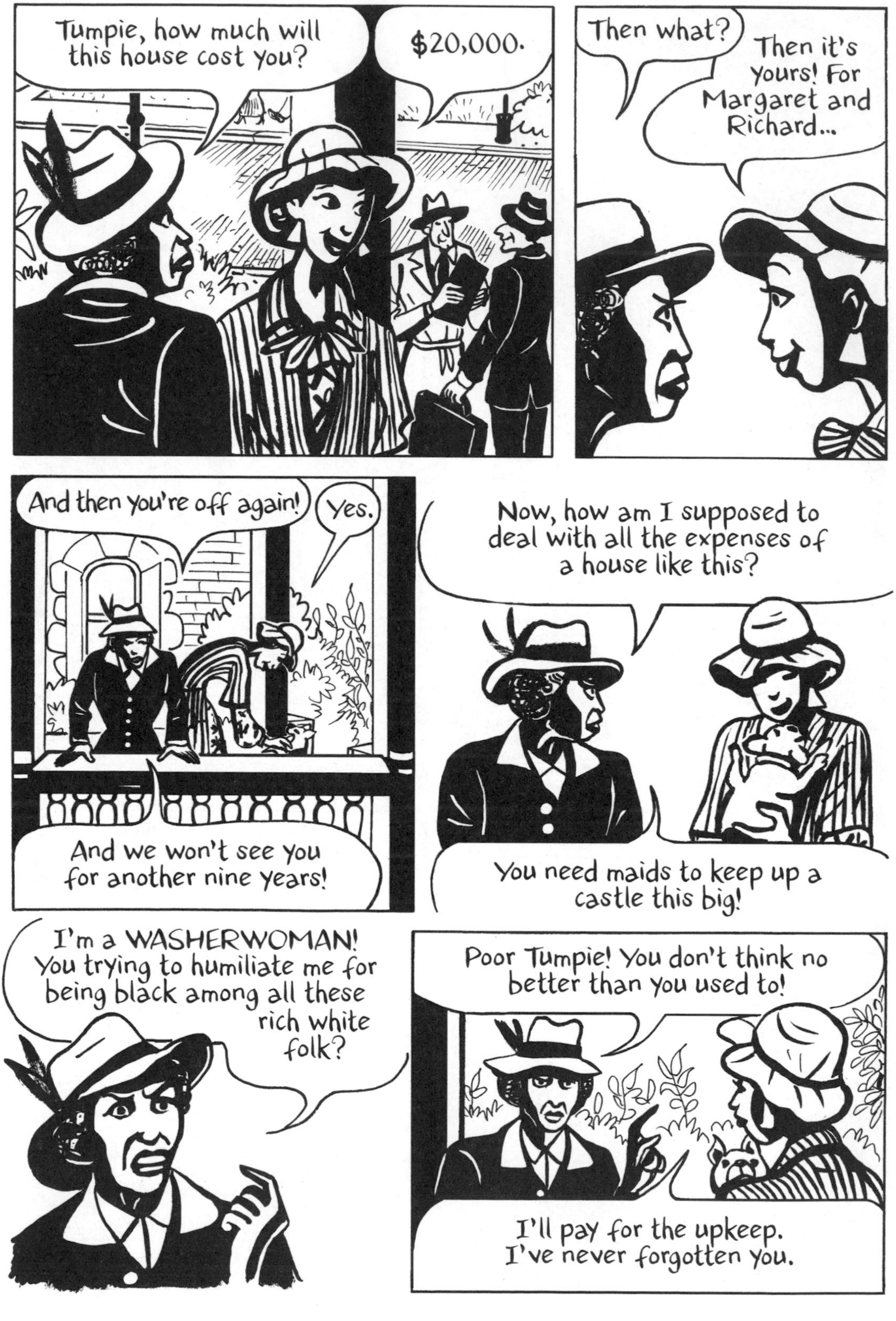
Tumpie, how much will this house cost you?
$20,000.
Then what?
Then it's yours! For Margaret and Richard...
And then you're off again!
Yes.
And we won't see you for another nine years!
Now, how am I supposed to deal with all the expenses of a house like this?
You need maids to keep up a castle this big!
I'm a WASHERWOMAN! You trying to humiliate me for being black among all these rich white folk?
Poor Tumpie! You don't think no better than you used to!
I'll pay for the upkeep. I've never forgotten you.

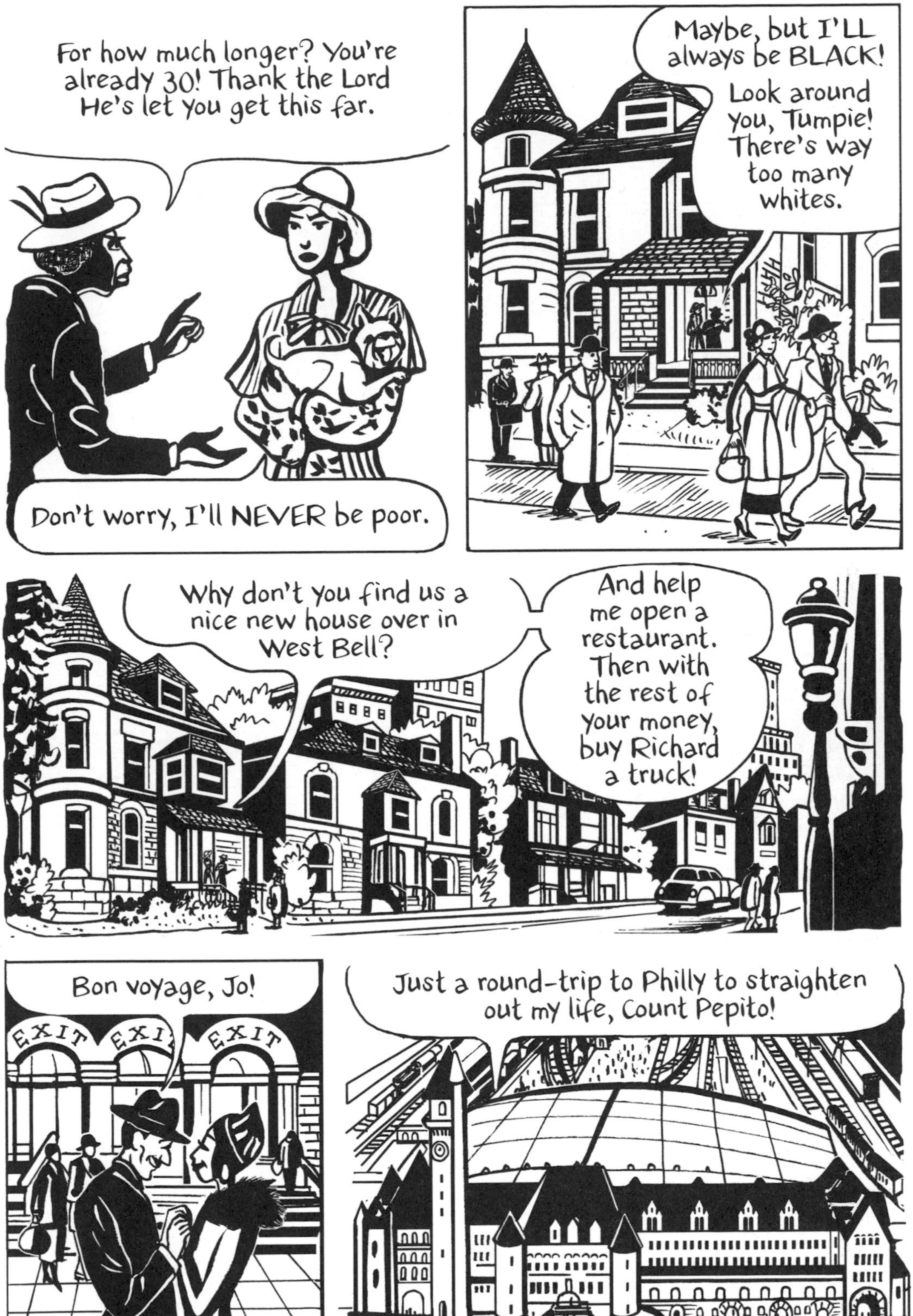
For how much longer? You're already 30! Thank the Lord He's let you get this far.
Don't worry, I'll NEVER be poor.
Maybe, but I'LL always be BLACK!
Look around you, Tumpie! There's way too many whites.
Why don't you find us a nice new house over in West Bell?
And help me open a restaurant. Then with the rest of your money, buy Richard a truck!
Bon voyage, Jo!
EXIT
EXIT
EXIT
Just a round-trip to Philly to straighten out my life, Count Pepito!

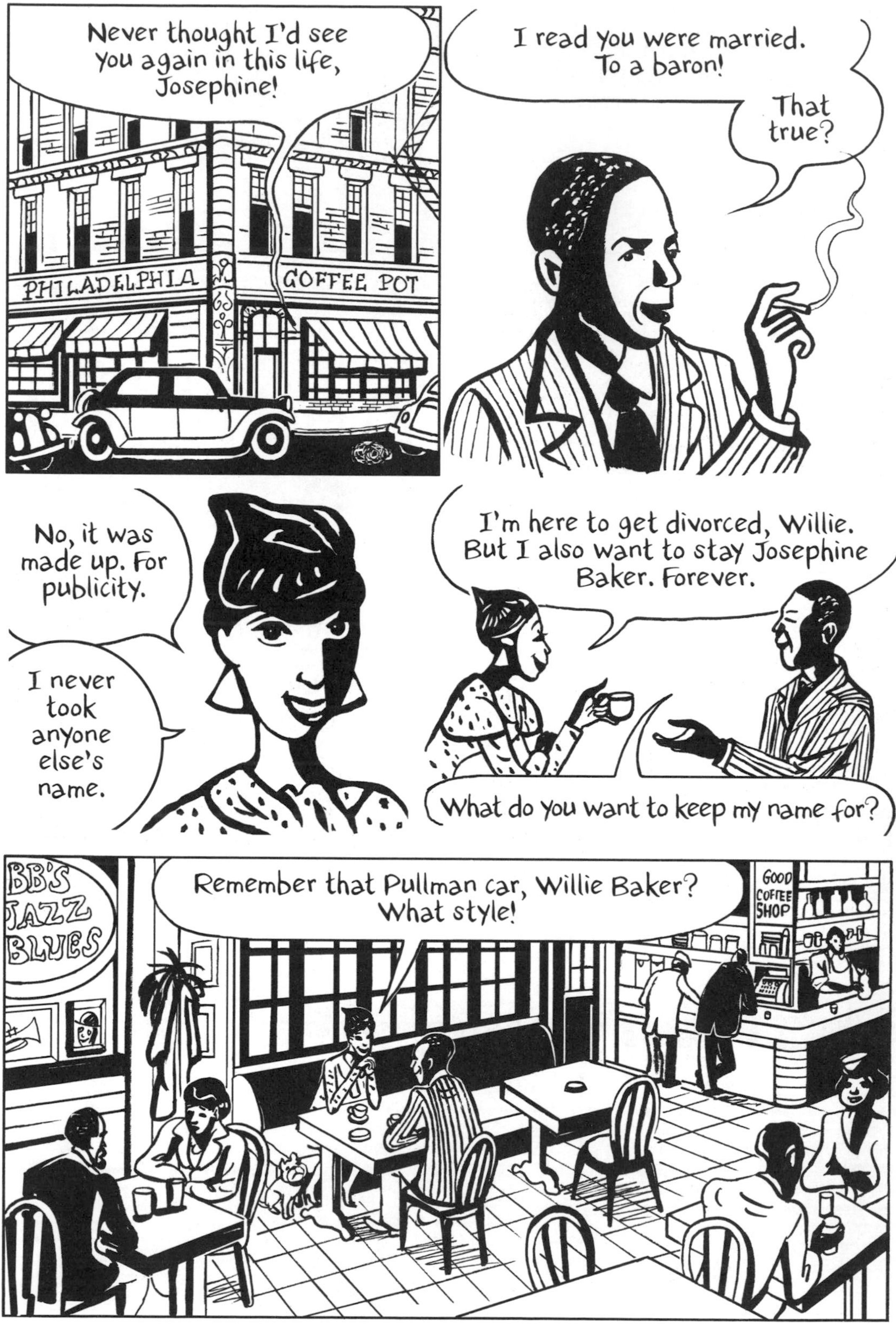
Never thought I'd see you again in this life, Josephine!
PHILADELPHIA
COFFEE POT
I read you were married. To a baron!
That true?
No, it was made up. For publicity.
I never took anyone else's name.
I'm here to get divorced, Willie. But I also want to stay Josephine Baker. Forever.
What do you want to keep my name for?
BB'S JAZZ BLUES
GOOD COFFEE SHOP
Remember that Pullman car, Willie Baker? What style!

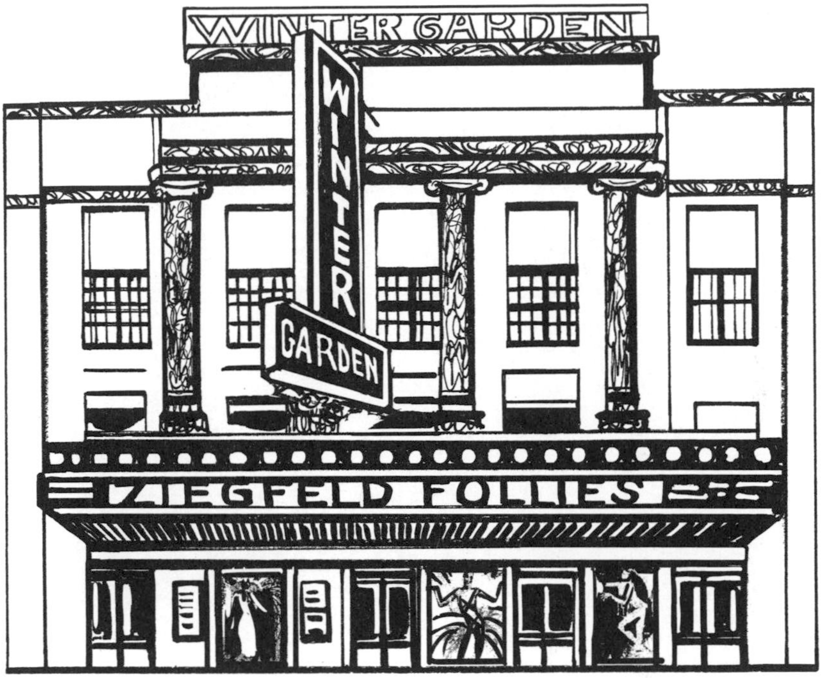
WINTER GARDEN
WINTER
GARDEN
ZIEGFELD FOLLIES

1936: Winter Garden Theatre, Broadway, New York, USA

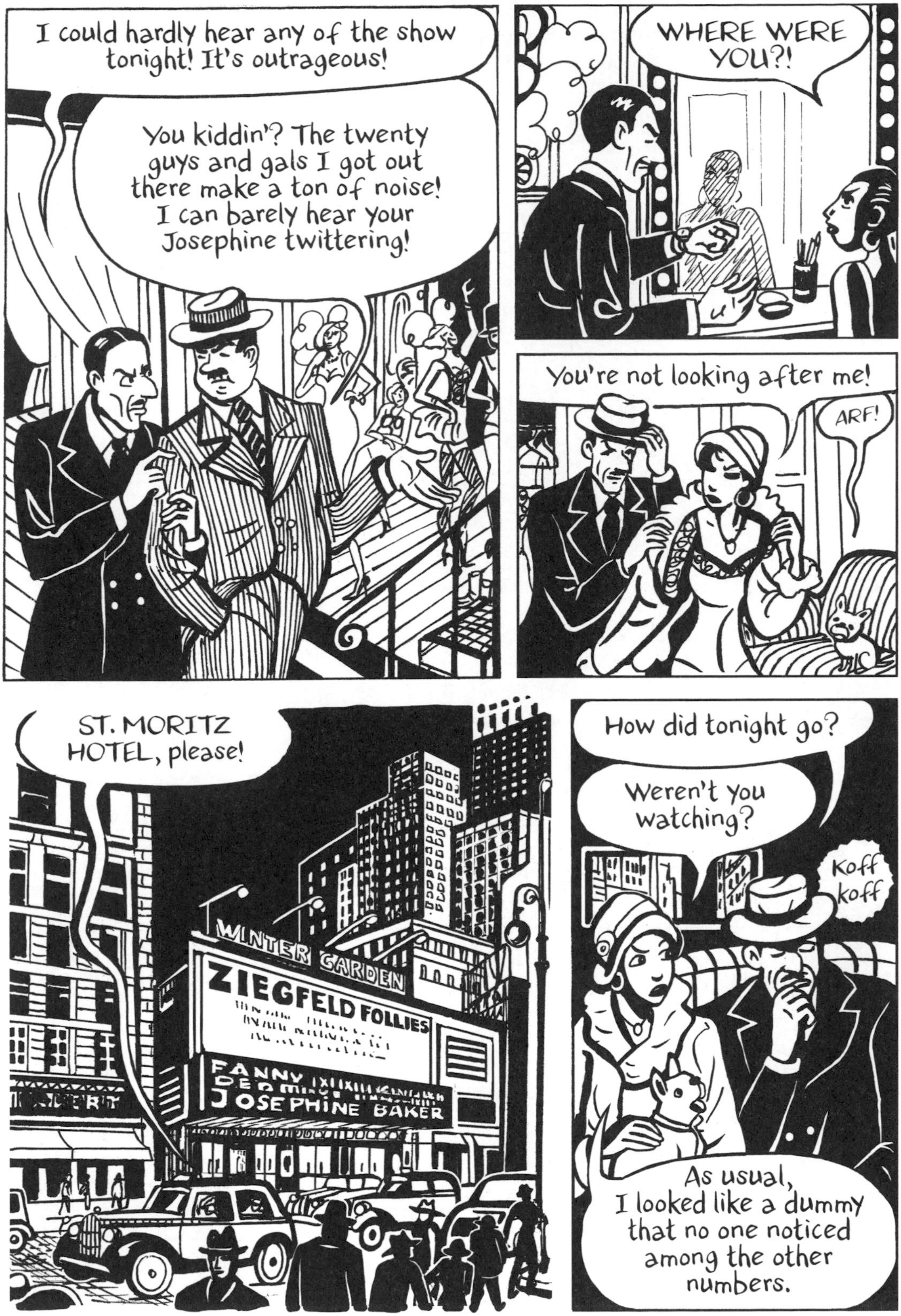
I could hardly hear any of the show tonight! It's outrageous!
You kiddin'? The twenty guys and gals I got out there make a ton of noise! I can barely hear your Josephine twittering!
WHERE WERE YOU?!
You're not looking after me!
ARF!
ST. MORITZ HOTEL, please!
WINTER GARDEN
ZIEGFELD FOLLIES
FANNY
JOSEPHINE BAKER
How did tonight go?
Weren't you watching?
Koff koff
As usual, I looked like a dummy that no one noticed among the other numbers.

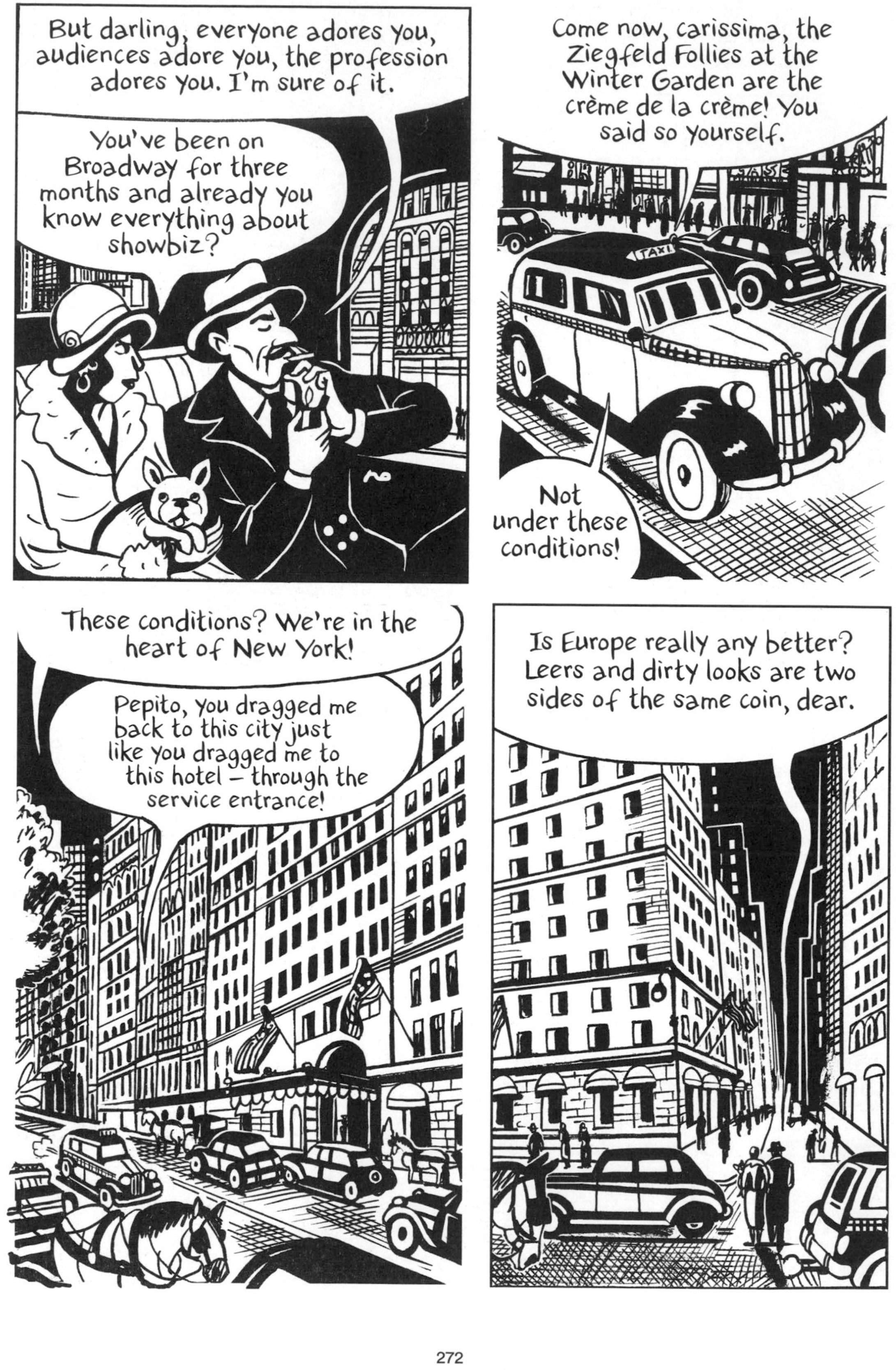

But darling, everyone adores you, audiences adore you, the profession adores you. I'm sure of it.
You've been on Broadway for three months and already you know everything about showbiz?
Come now, carissima, the Ziegfeld Follies at the Winter Garden are the crème de la crème! You said so yourself.
TAXI
Not under these conditions!
These conditions? We're in the heart of New York!
Pepito, you dragged me back to this city just like you dragged me to this hotel – through the service entrance!
Is Europe really any better? Leers and dirty looks are two sides of the same coin, dear.

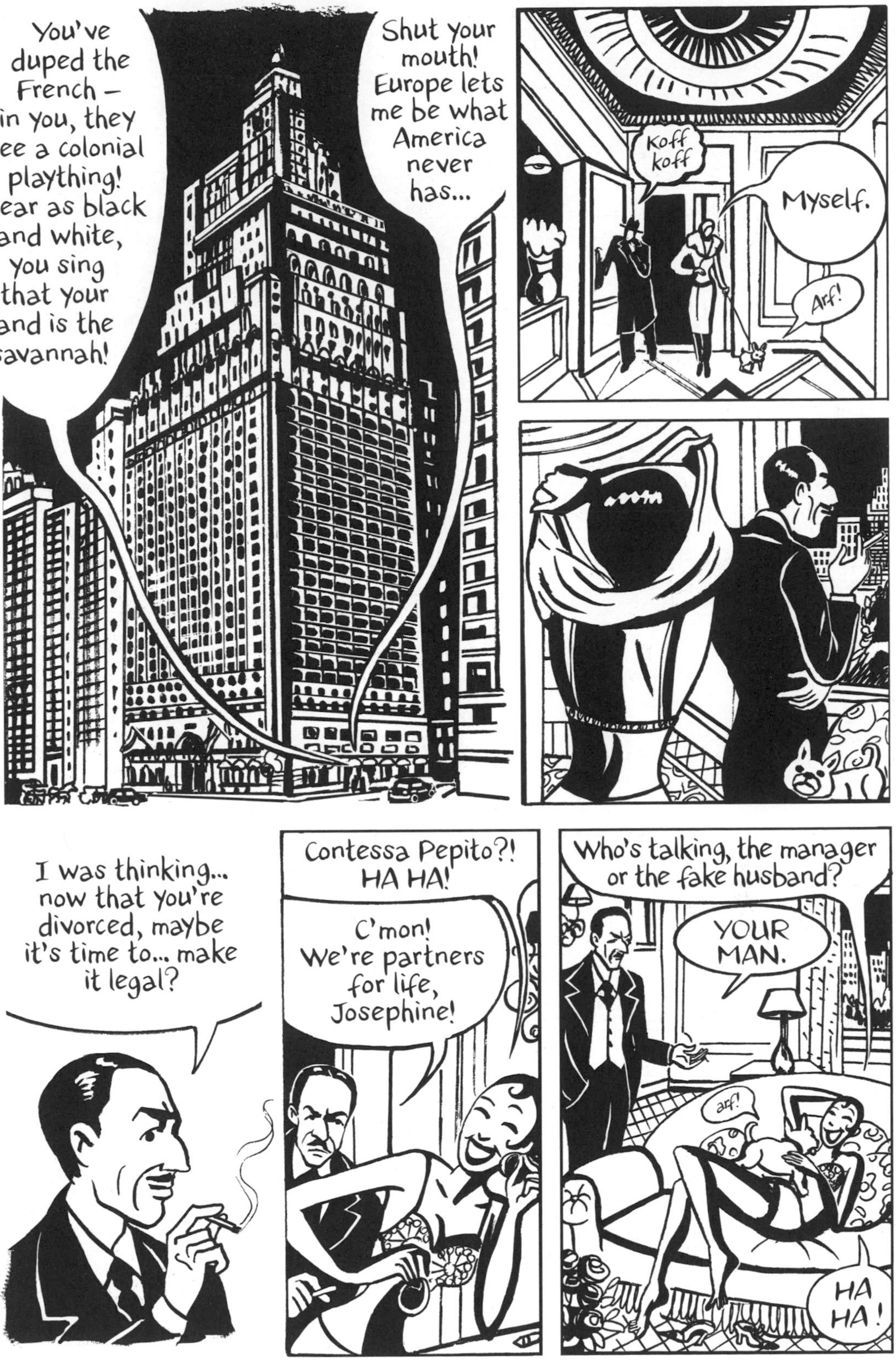
You've duped the French – in you, they see a colonial plaything! Clear as black and white, you sing that your land is the savannah!
Shut your mouth! Europe lets me be what America never has...
Koff koff
Myself.
Arf!
I was thinking... now that you're divorced, maybe it's time to... make it legal?
Contessa Pepito?! HA HA!
C'mon! We're partners for life, Josephine!
Who's talking, the manager or the fake husband?
YOUR MAN.
arf!
HA HA!

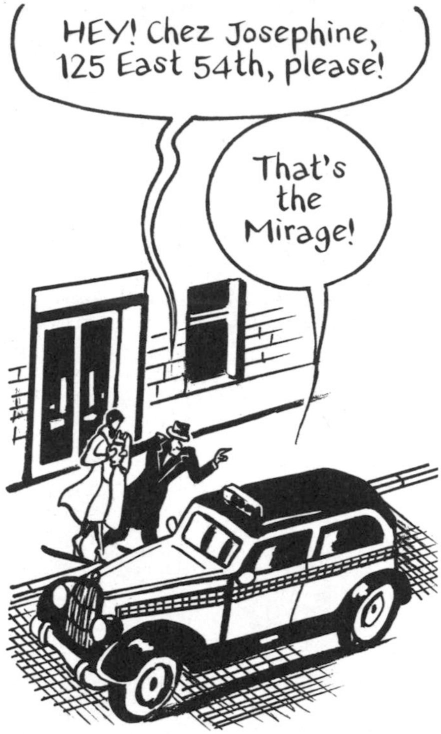
HEY! Chez Josephine, 125 East 54th, please!
That's the Mirage!

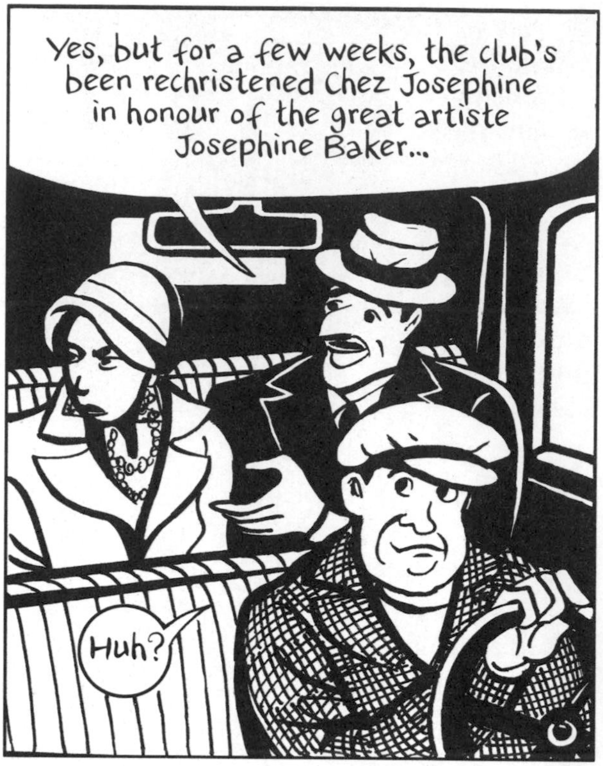
Yes, but for a few weeks, the club's been rechristened Chez Josephine in honour of the great artiste Josephine Baker...
Huh?

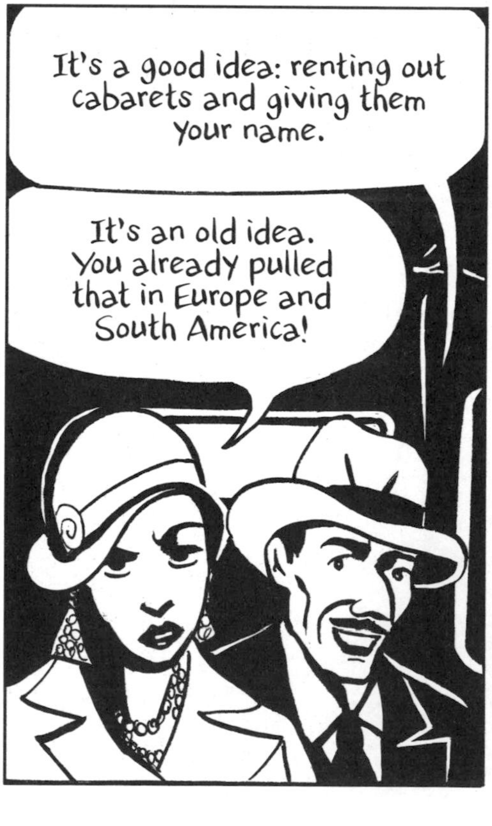
It's a good idea: renting out cabarets and giving them your name.
It's an old idea. You already pulled that in Europe and South America!

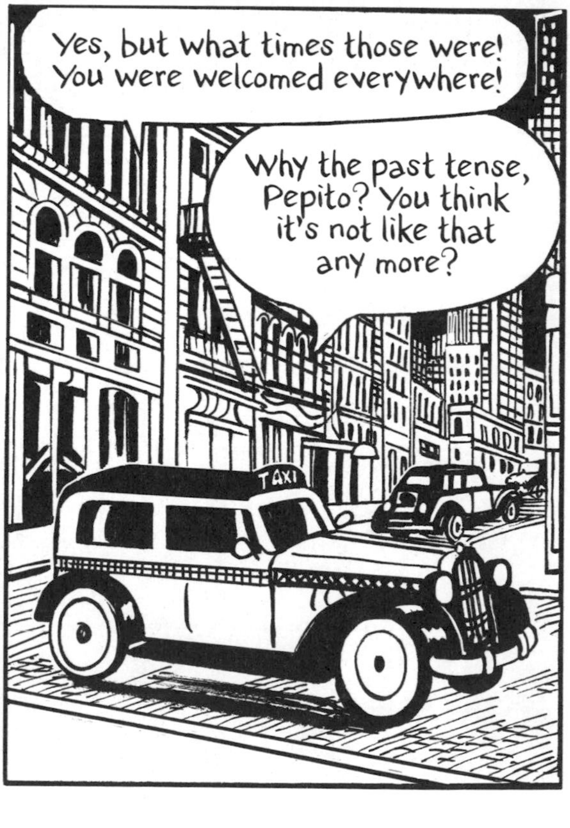
Yes, but what times those were! You were welcomed everywhere!
Why the past tense, Pepito? You think it's not like that any more?
TAXI

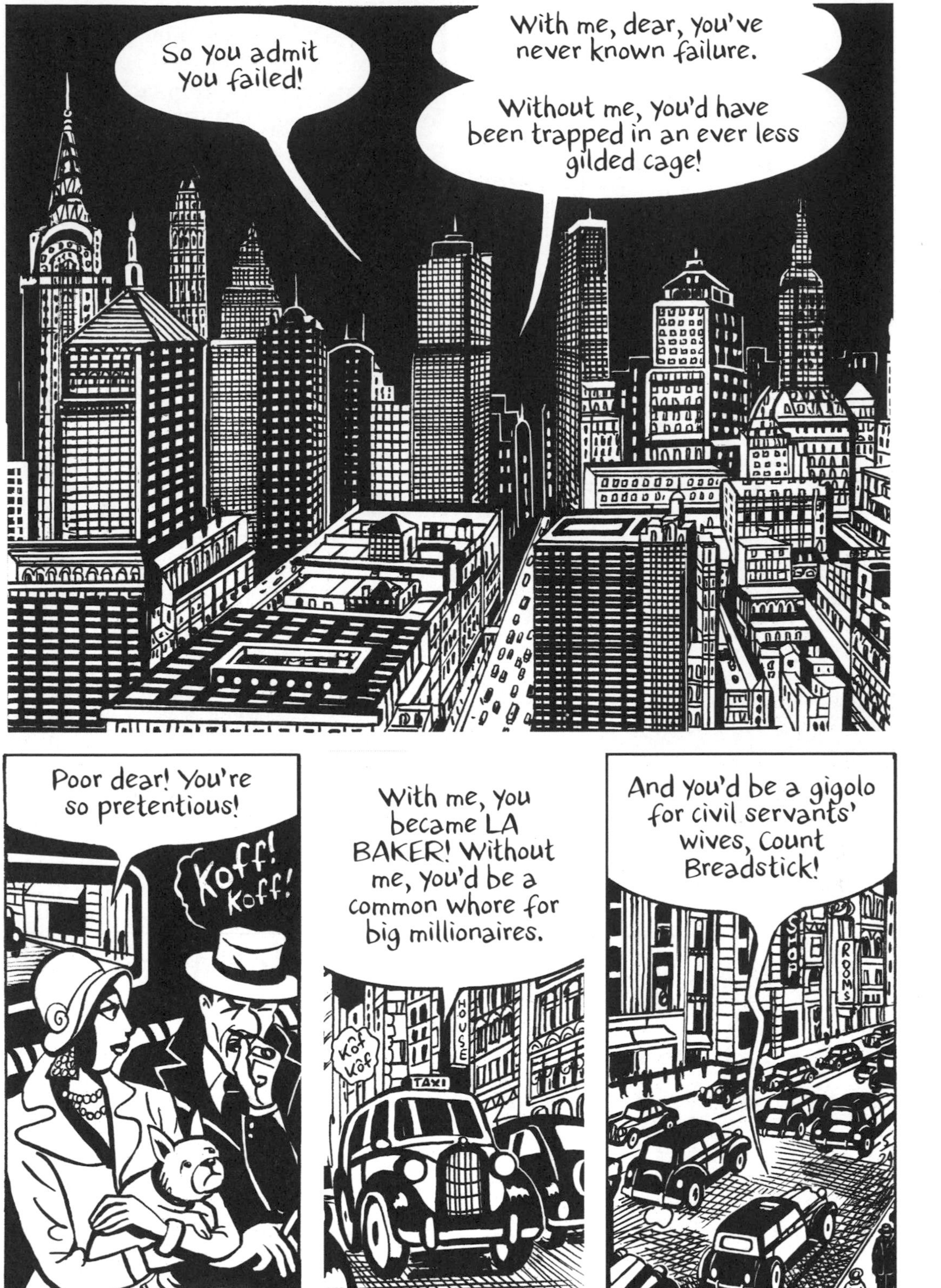
So you admit you failed!
With me, dear, you've never known failure.
Without me, you'd have been trapped in an ever less gilded cage!
Poor dear! You're so pretentious!
Koff! Koff!
With me, you became LA BAKER! Without me, you'd be a common whore for big millionaires.
Kôf Kôf
HOUSE
TAXI
And you'd be a gigolo for civil servants' wives, Count Breadstick!
SHOP
ROOMS

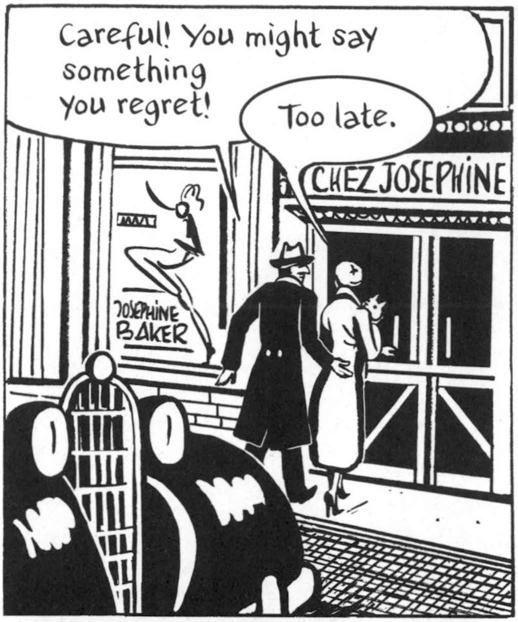
Careful! You might say something you regret!
Too late.
CHEZ JOSEPHINE
JOSEPHINE BAKER

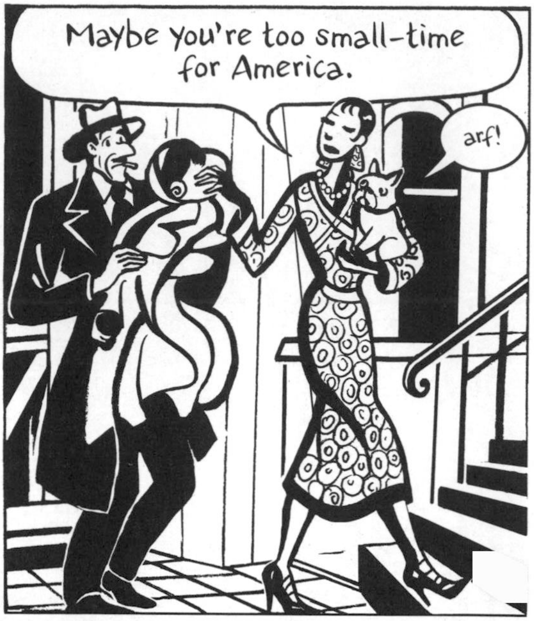
Maybe you're too small-time for America.
arf!

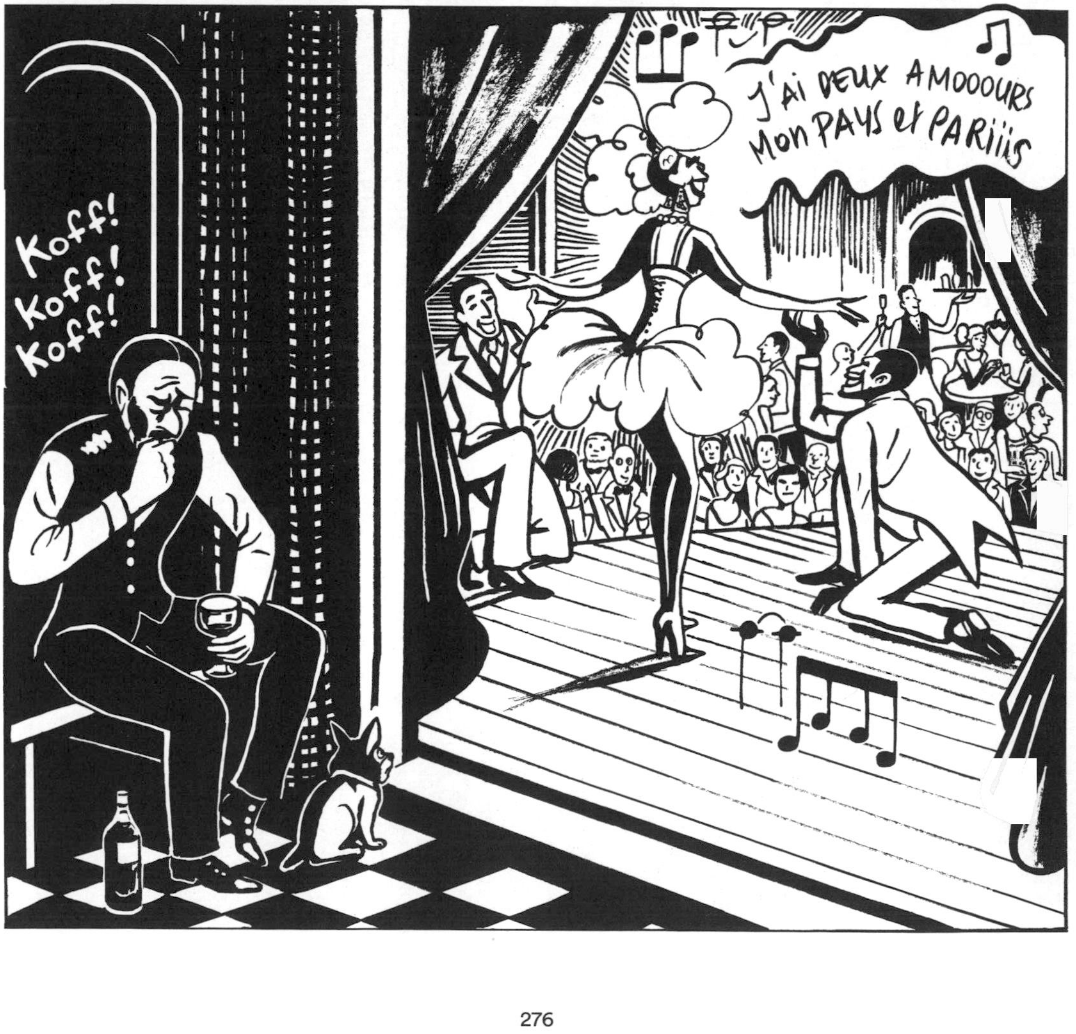
J'AI DEUX AMOOOURS
Mon PAYS et PARiiis
Koff! Koff! Koff!

1936: Beau-Chêne, Le Vésinet, France

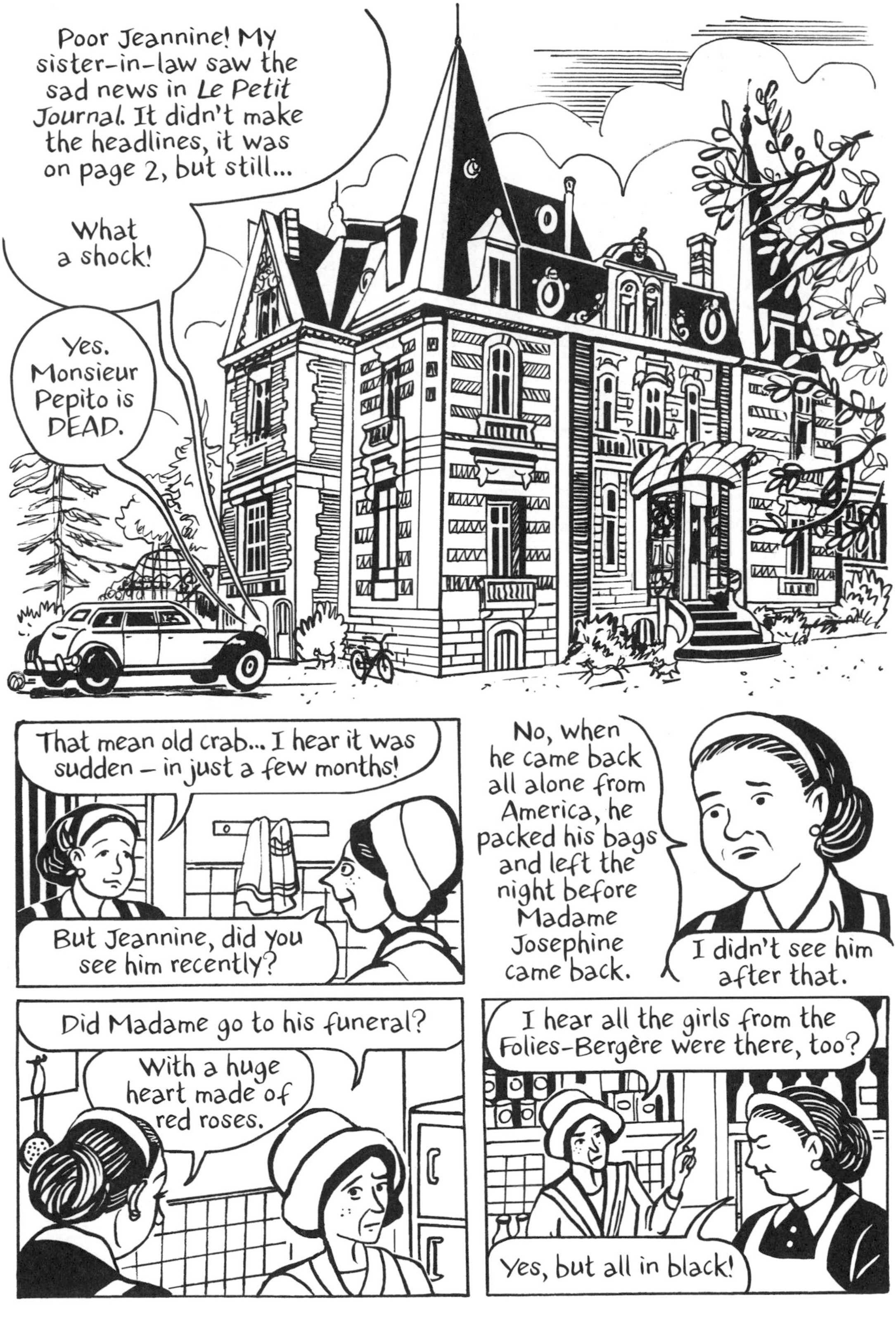
Poor Jeannine! My sister-in-law saw the sad news in Le Petit Journal. It didn't make the headlines, it was on page 2, but still...
What a shock!
Yes. Monsieur Pepito is DEAD.
That mean old crab... I hear it was sudden – in just a few months!
But Jeannine, did you see him recently?
No, when he came back all alone from America, he packed his bags and left the night before Madame Josephine came back.
I didn't see him after that.
Did Madame go to his funeral?
With a huge heart made of red roses.
I hear all the girls from the Folies-Bergère were there, too?
Yes, but all in black!

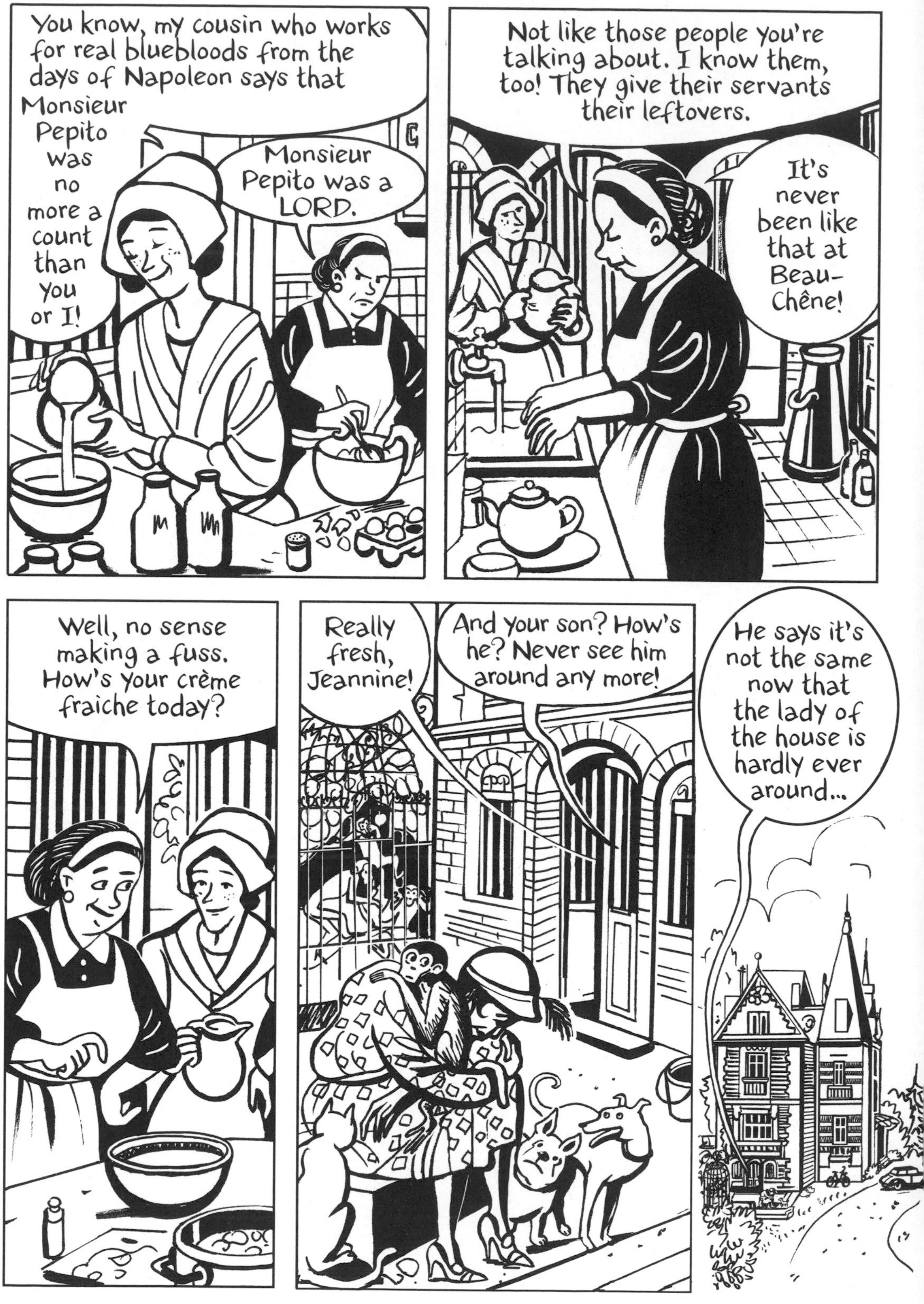
You know, my cousin who works for real bluebloods from the days of Napoleon says that Monsieur Pepito was no more a count than you or I!
Monsieur Pepito was a LORD.
Not like those people you're talking about. I know them, too! They give their servants their leftovers.
It's never been like that at Beau-Chêne!
Well, no sense making a fuss. How's your crème fraiche today?
Really fresh, Jeannine!
And your son? How's he? Never see him around any more!
He says it's not the same now that the lady of the house is hardly ever around...

1937: Pavillon Dauphine, Bois de Boulogne, Paris, France

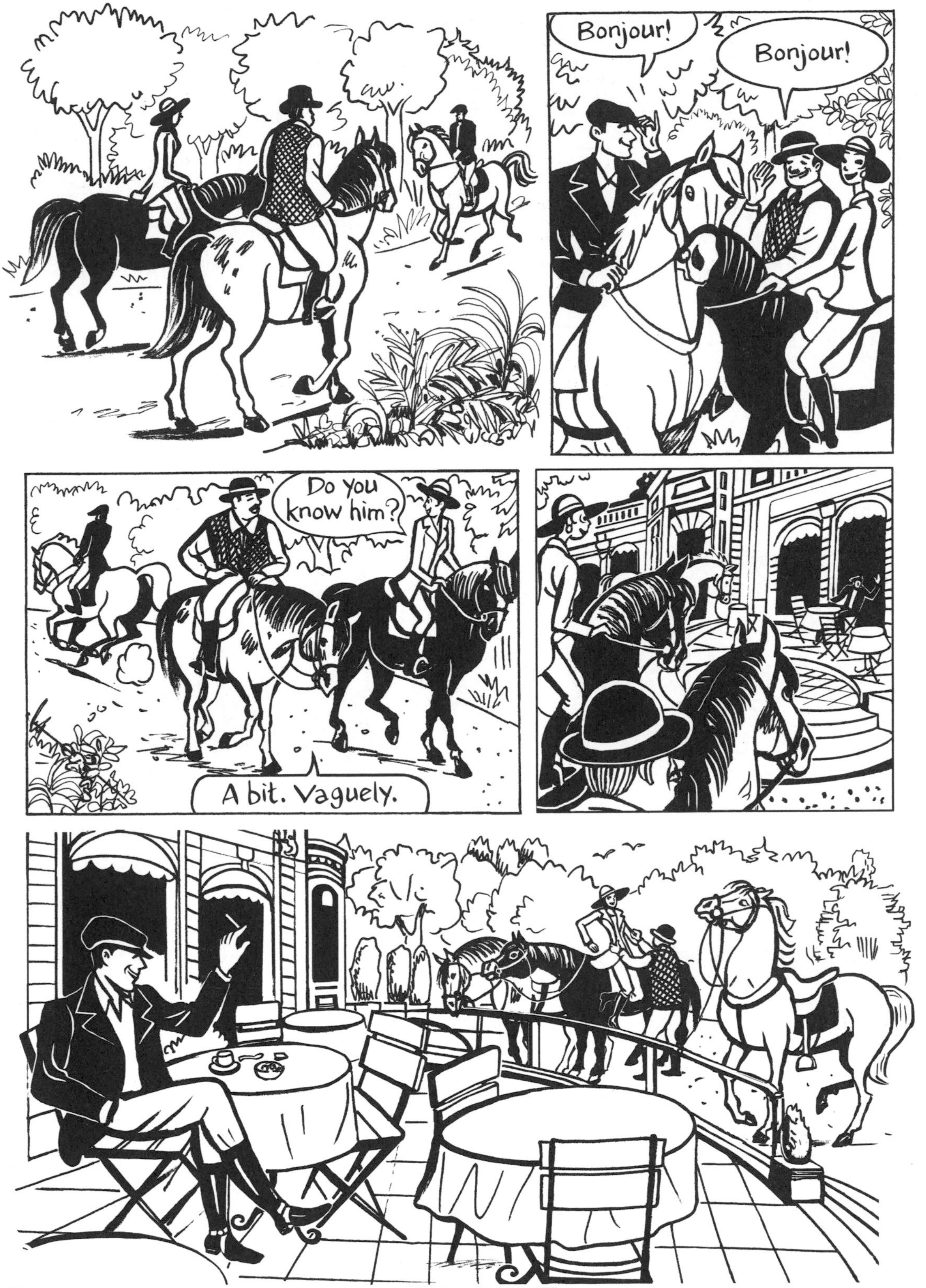
Bonjour!
Bonjour!
Do you know him?
A bit. Vaguely.

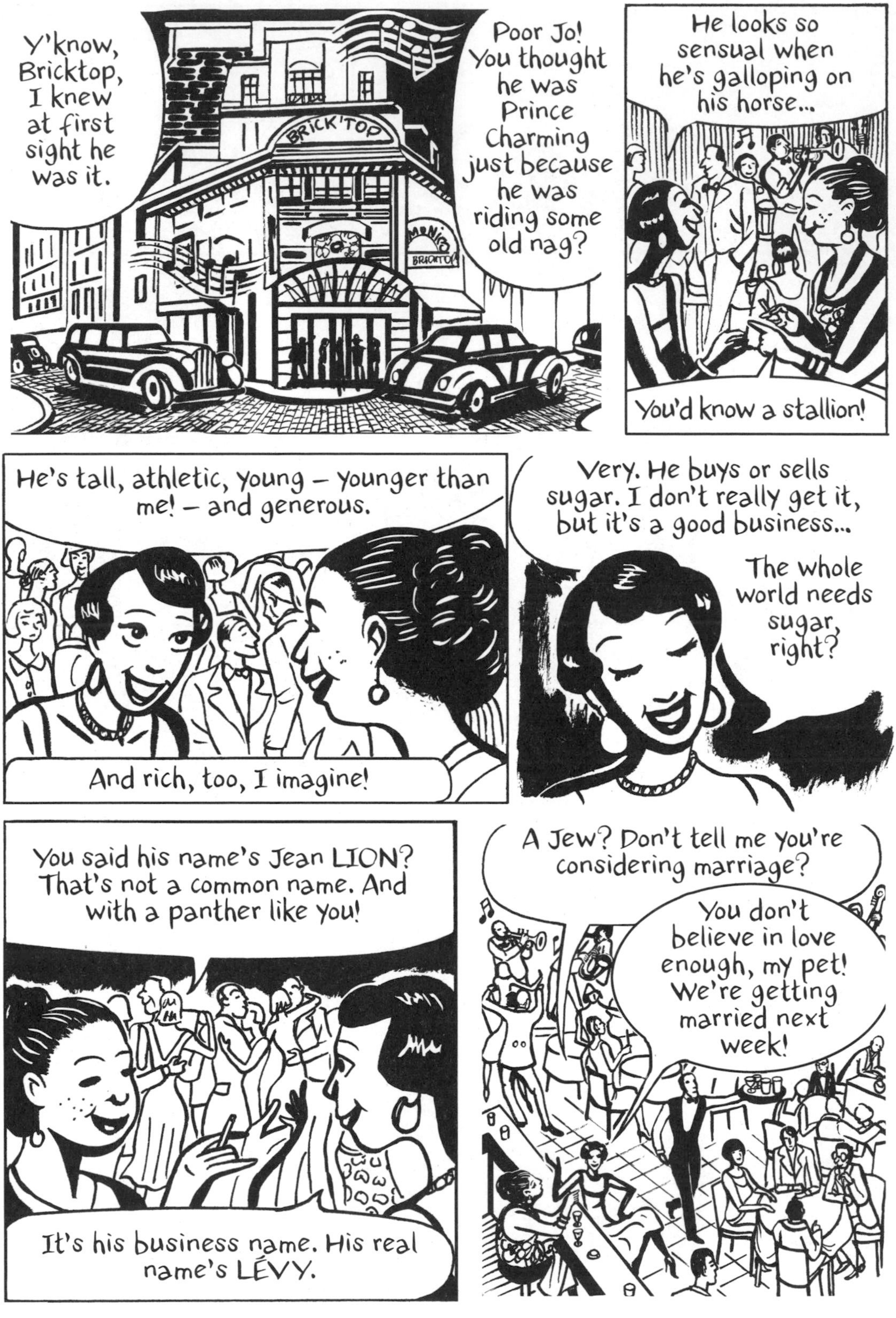
Y'know, Bricktop, I knew at first sight he was it.
BRICK'TOP
Poor Jo! You thought he was Prince Charming just because he was riding some old nag?
He looks so sensual when he's galloping on his horse...
You'd know a stallion!
He's tall, athletic, young – younger than me! – and generous.
And rich, too, I imagine!
Very. He buys or sells sugar. I don't really get it, but it's a good business...
The whole world needs sugar, right?
You said his name's Jean LION? That's not a common name. And with a panther like you!
It's his business name. His real name's LÉVY.
A Jew? Don't tell me you're considering marriage?
You don't believe in love enough, my pet! We're getting married next week!

1938: Château des Mirandes, Périgord, France

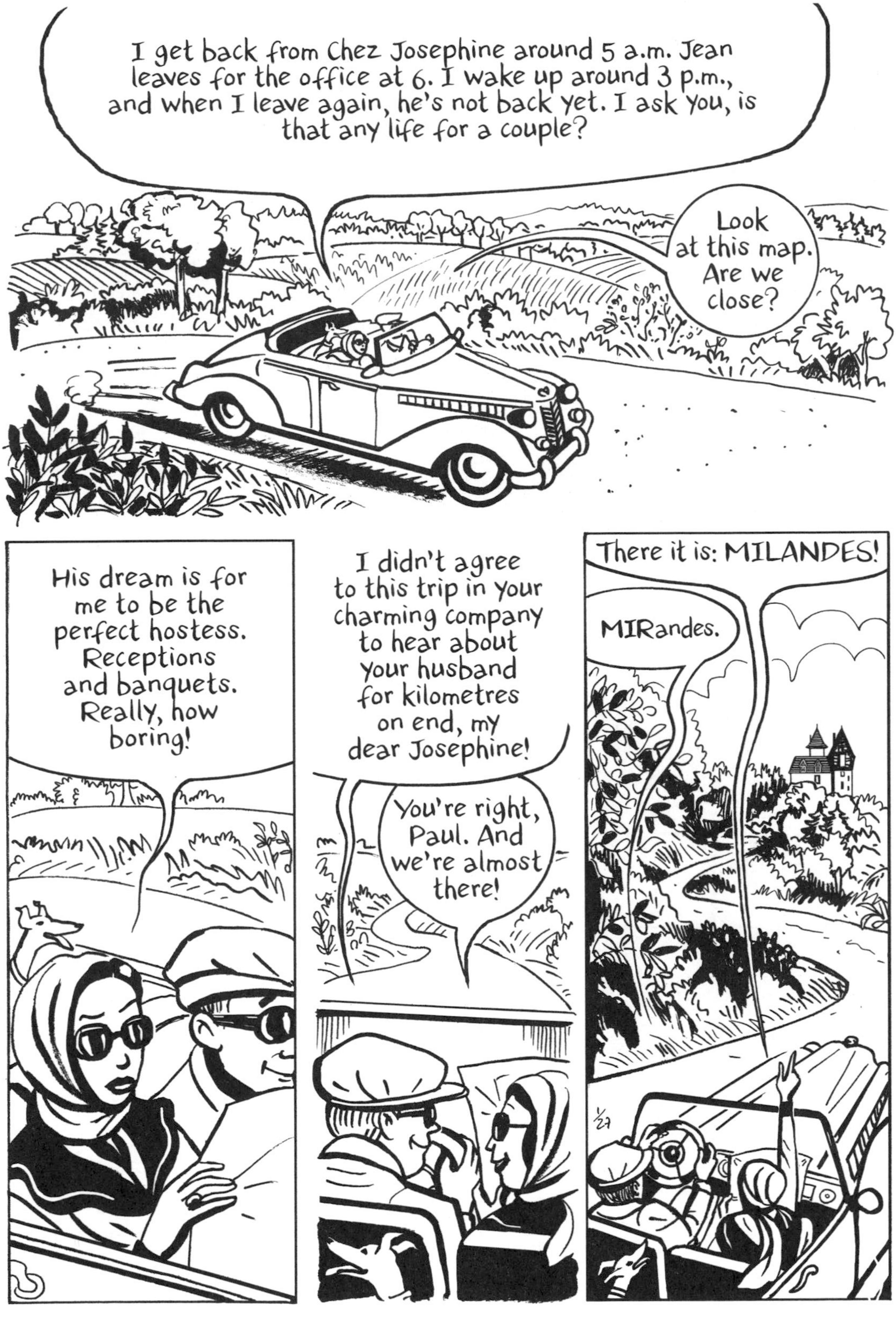
I get back from Chez Josephine around 5 a.m. Jean leaves for the office at 6. I wake up around 3 p.m., and when I leave again, he's not back yet. I ask you, is that any life for a couple?
Look at this map. Are we close?
His dream is for me to be the perfect hostess. Receptions and banquets. Really, how boring!
I didn't agree to this trip in your charming company to hear about your husband for kilometres on end, my dear Josephine!
You're right, Paul. And we're almost there!
There it is: MILANDES!
MIRandes.

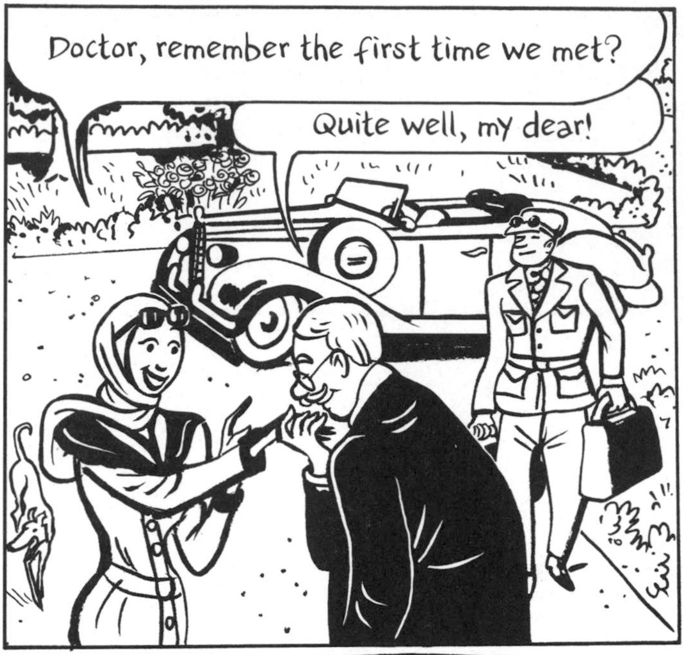
Doctor, remember the first time we met?
Quite well, my dear!

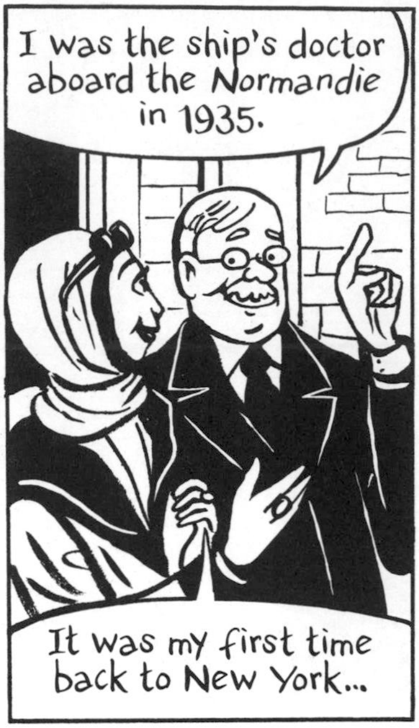
I was the ship's doctor aboard the Normandie in 1935.
It was my first time back to New York...

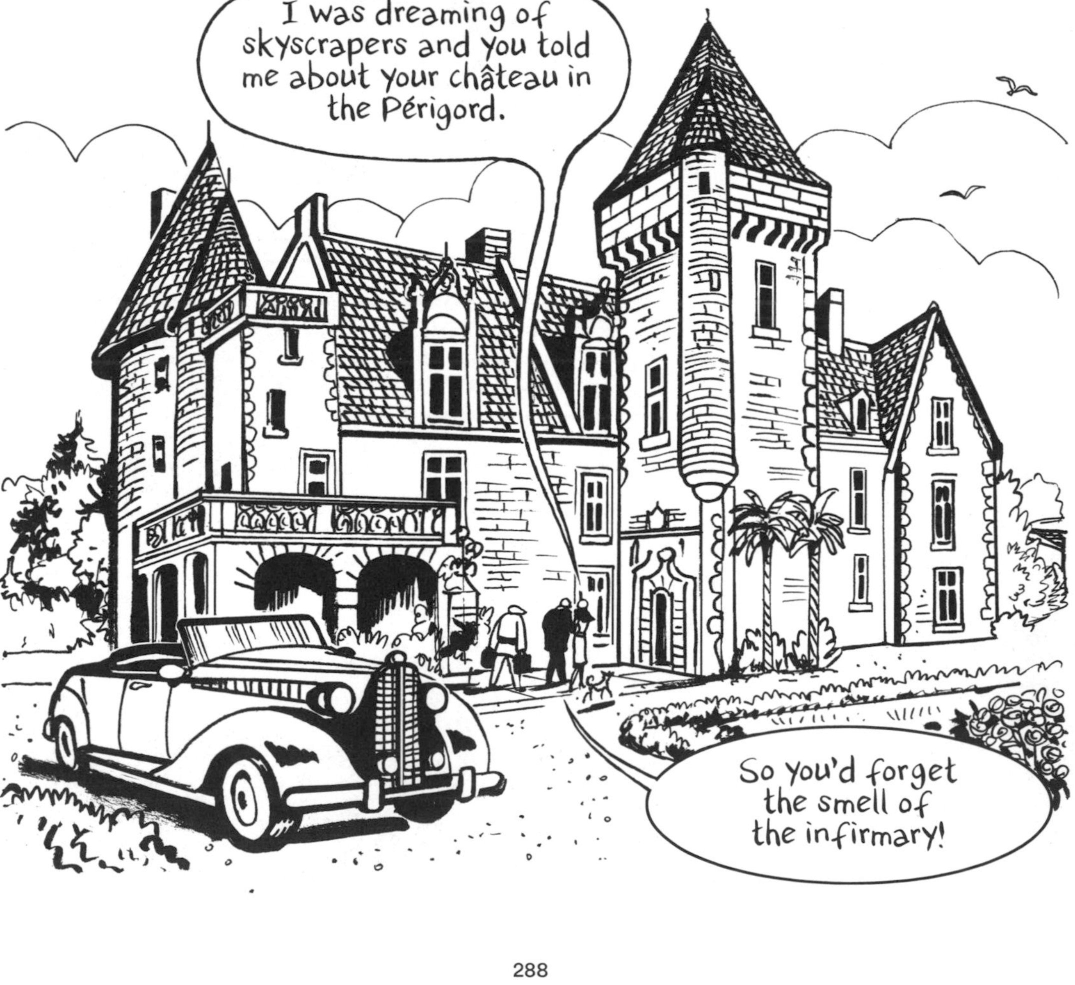
I was dreaming of skyscrapers and you told me about your château in the Périgord.
So you'd forget the smell of the infirmary!

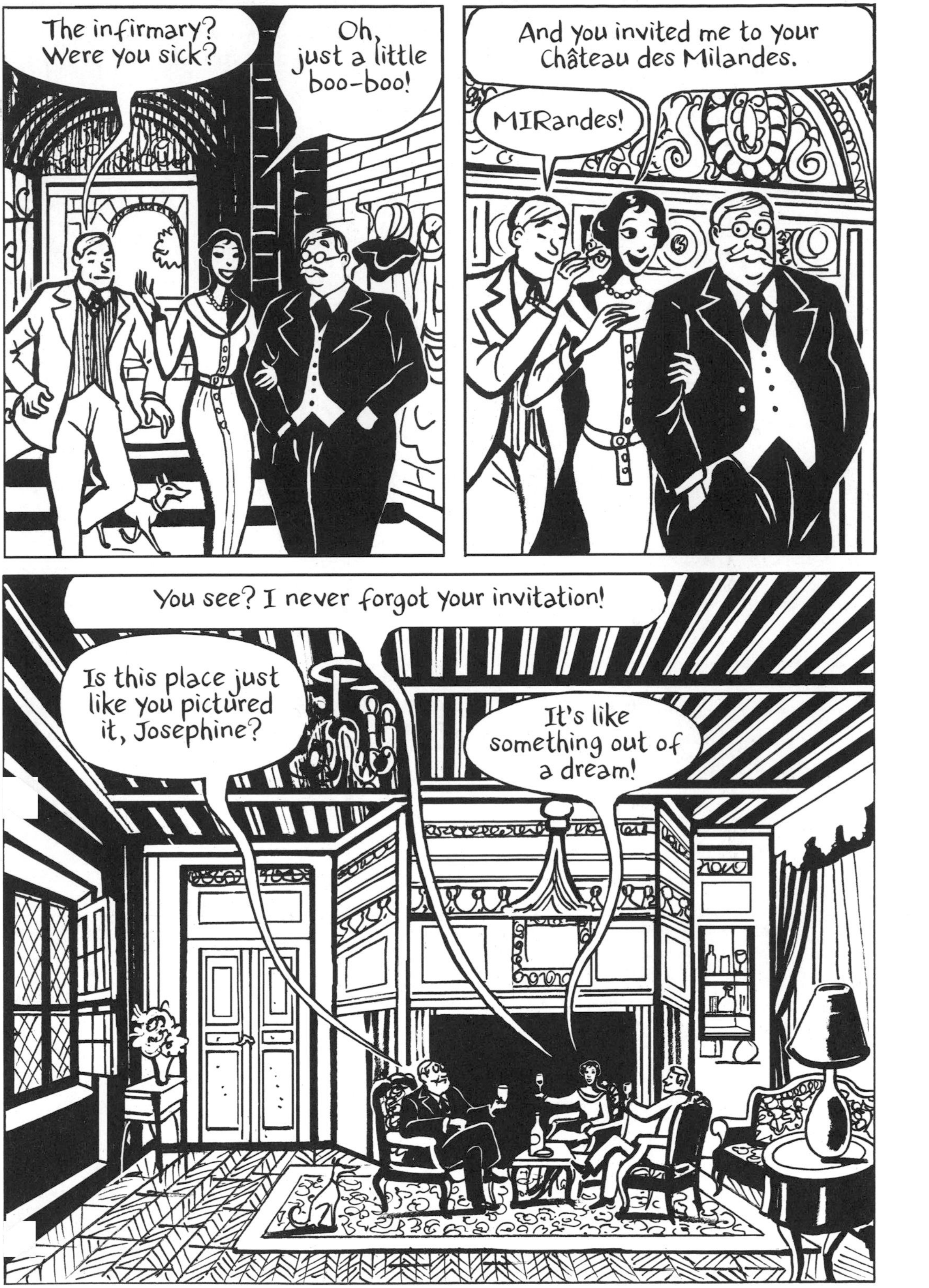
The infirmary? Were you sick?
Oh, just a little boo-boo!
And you invited me to your Château des Milandes.
MIRandes!
You see? I never forgot your invitation!
Is this place just like you pictured it, Josephine?
It's like something out of a dream!

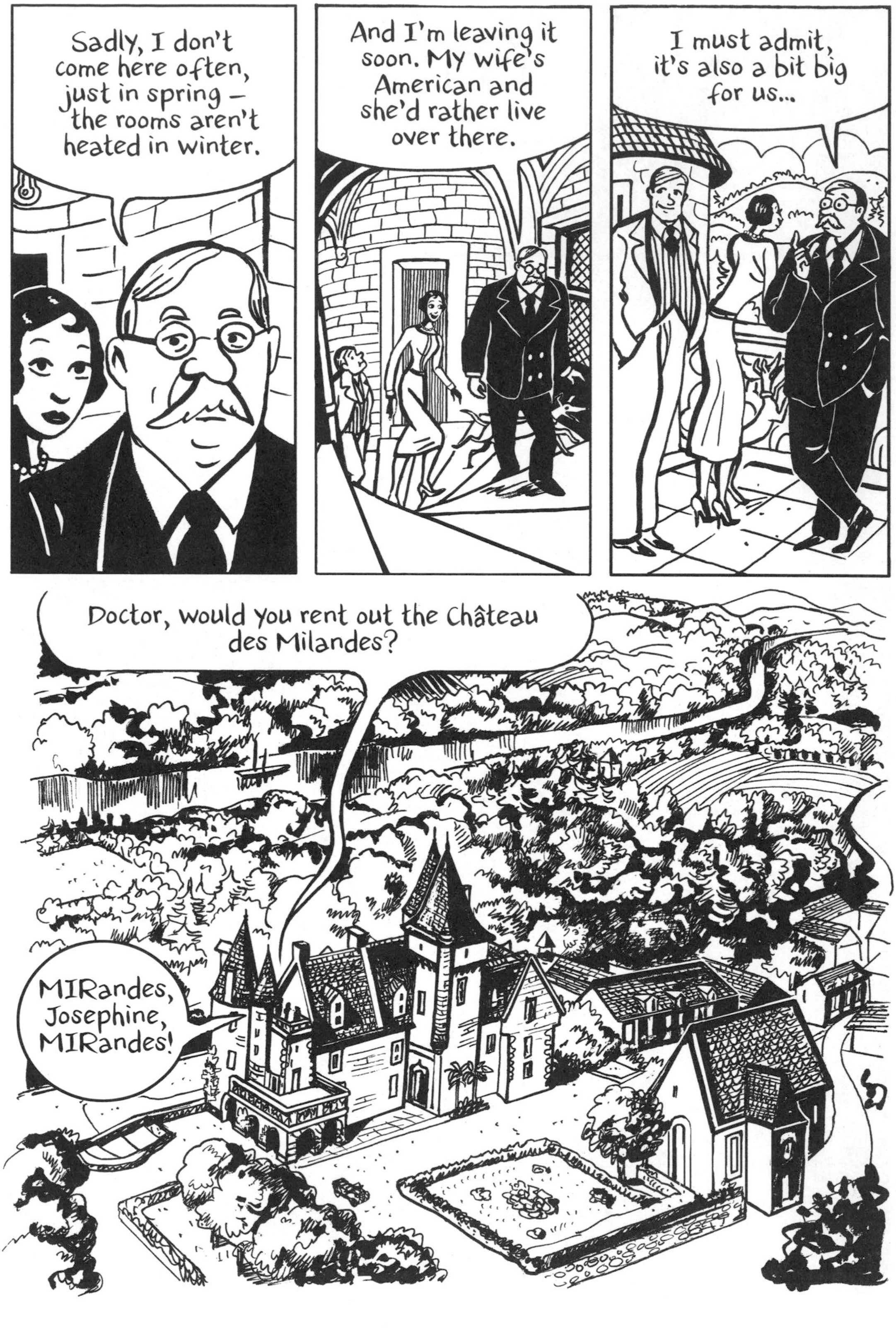
Sadly, I don't come here often, just in spring – the rooms aren't heated in winter.
And I'm leaving it soon. My wife's American and she'd rather live over there.
I must admit, it's also a bit big for us...
Doctor, would you rent out the Château des Milandes?
MIRandes, Josephine, MIRandes!

1939: Montmartre, Paris, France

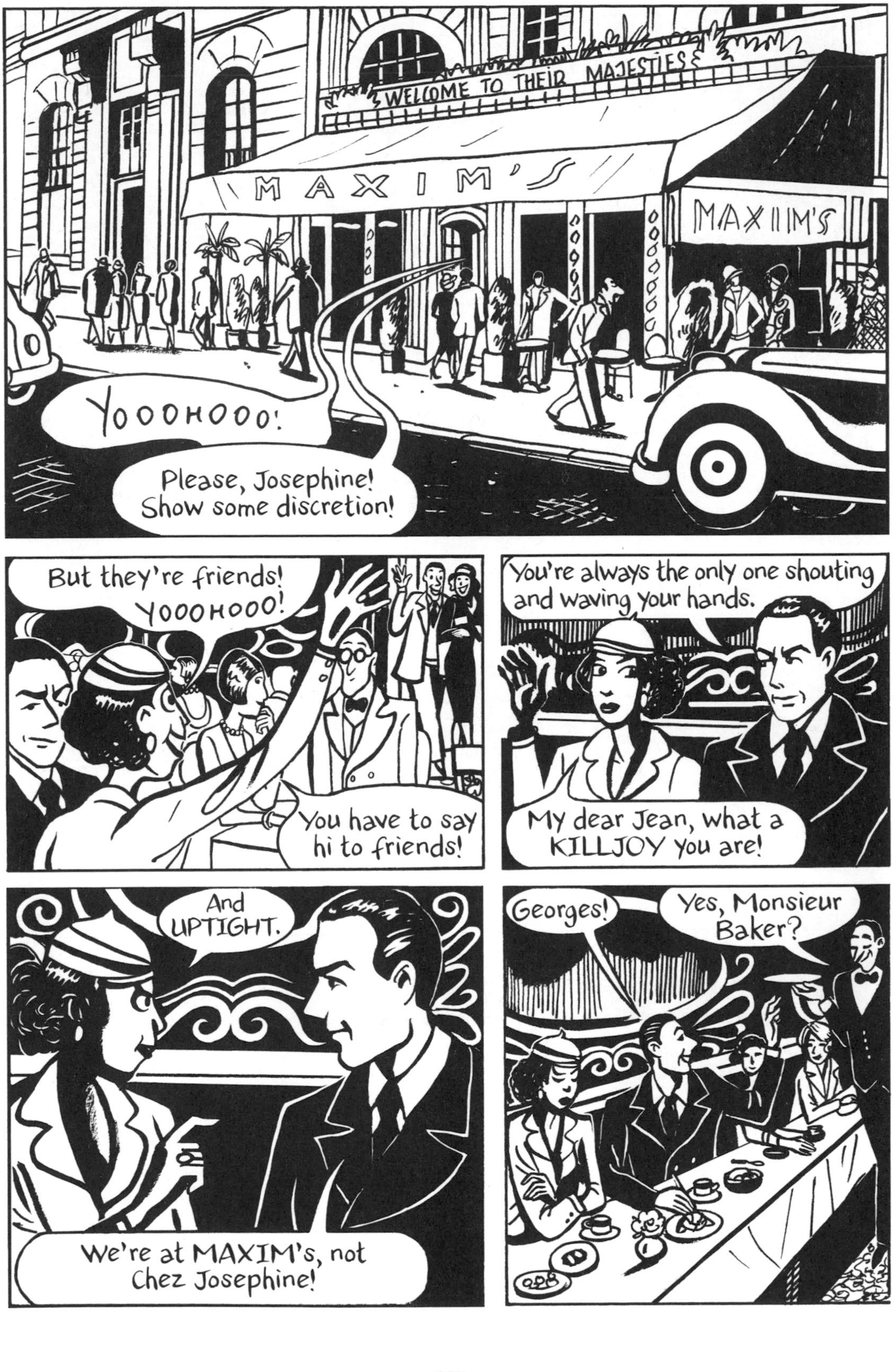
WELCOME TO THEIR MAJESTIES
MAXIM'S
MAXIM'S
YOOOHOOO!
Please, Josephine! Show some discretion!
But they're friends! YOOOHOOO!
You have to say hi to friends!
You're always the only one shouting and waving your hands.
My dear Jean, what a KILLJOY you are!
And UPTIGHT.
We're at MAXIM's, not Chez Josephine!
Georges!
Yes, Monsieur Baker?

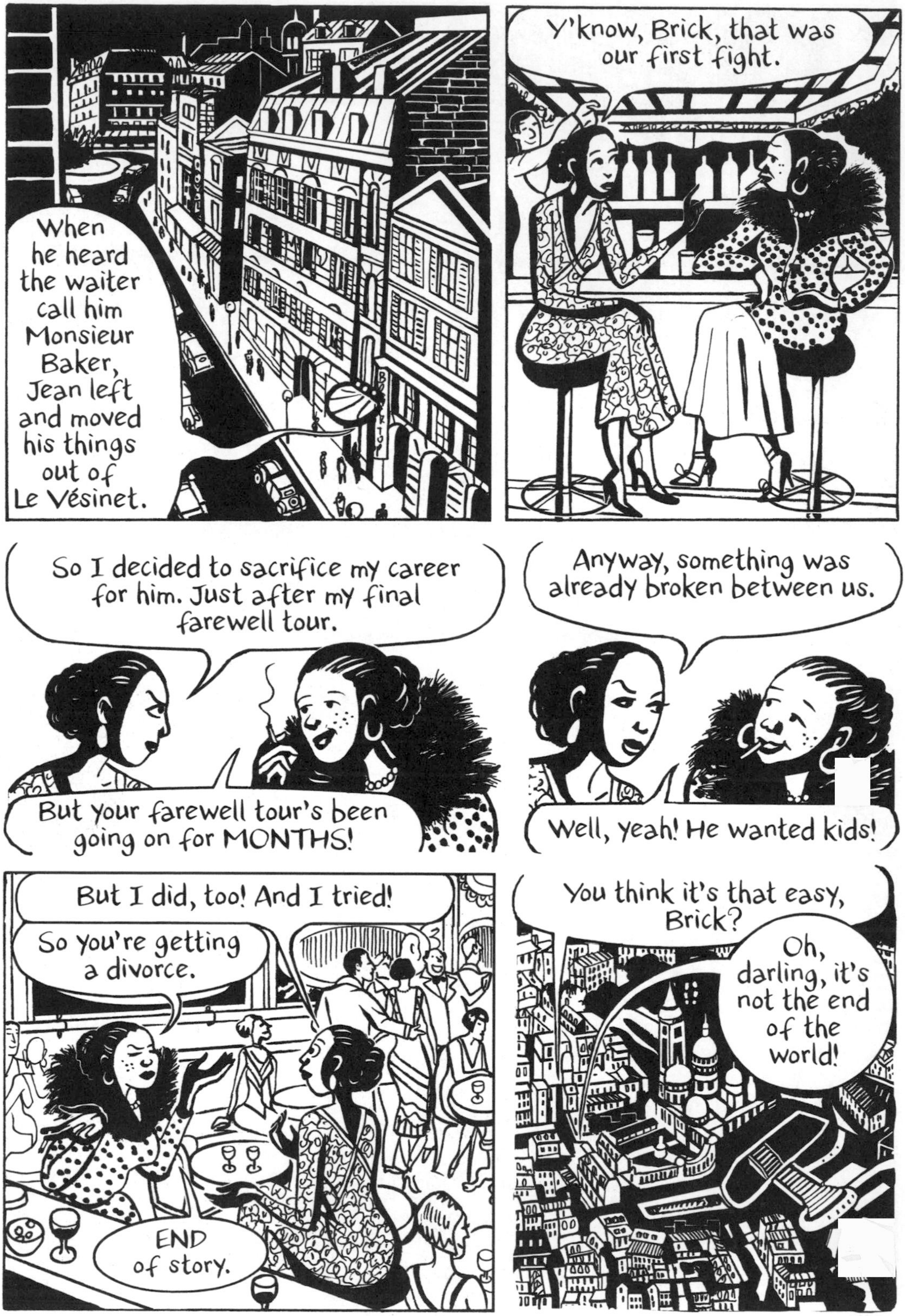
When he heard the waiter call him Monsieur Baker, Jean left and moved his things out of Le Vésinet.
Y'know, Brick, that was our first fight.
So I decided to sacrifice my career for him. Just after my final farewell tour.
But your farewell tour's been going on for MONTHS!
Anyway, something was already broken between us.
Well, yeah! He wanted kids!
But I did, too! And I tried!
So you're getting a divorce.
END of story.
You think it's that easy, Brick?
Oh, darling, it's not the end of the world!

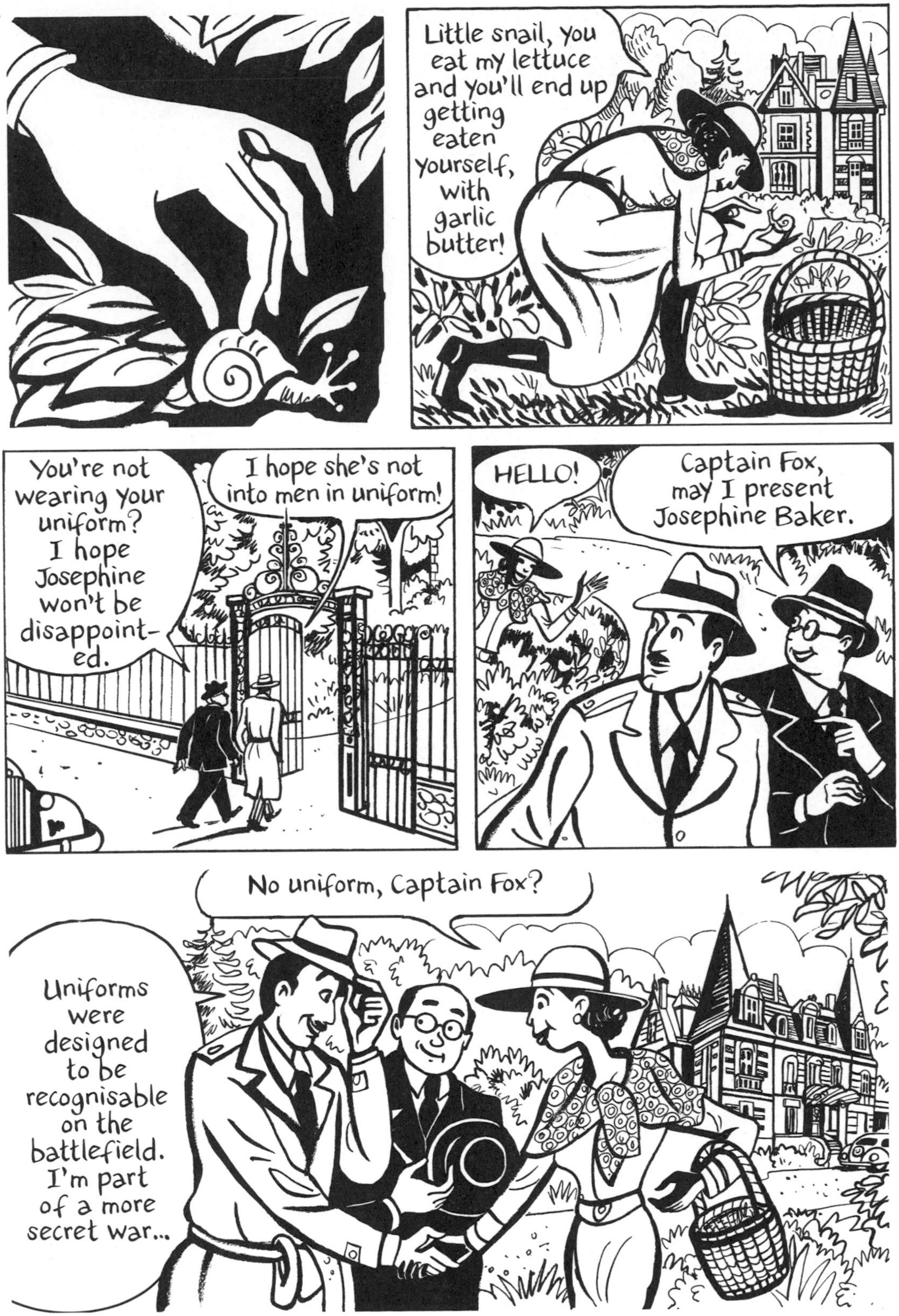
Little snail, you eat my lettuce and you'll end up getting eaten yourself, with garlic butter!
You're not wearing your uniform? I hope Josephine won't be disappoint-ed.
I hope she's not into men in uniform!
HELLO!
Captain Fox, may I present Josephine Baker.
No uniform, Captain Fox?
Uniforms were designed to be recognisable on the battlefield. I'm part of a more secret war...

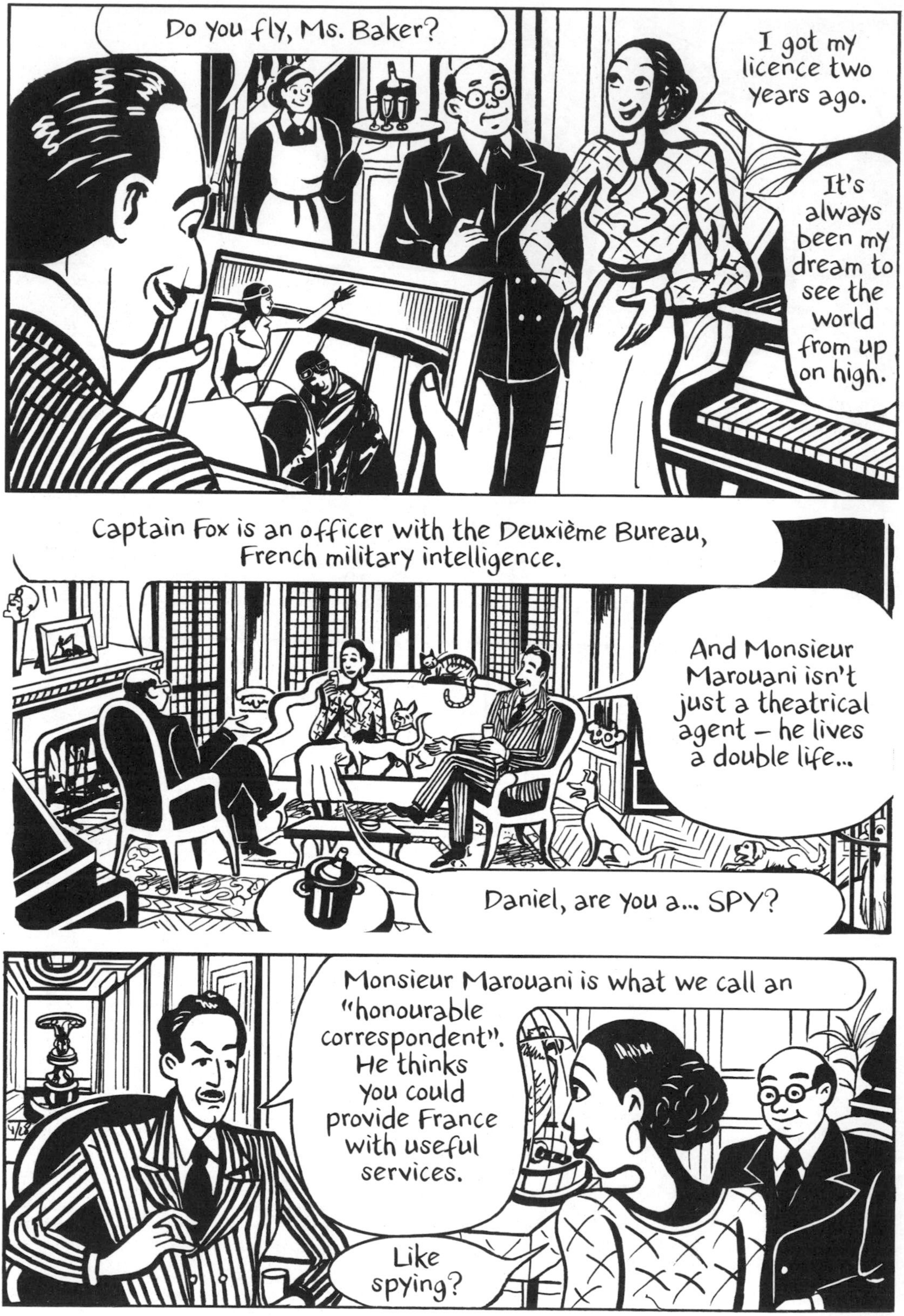
Do you fly, Ms. Baker?
I got my licence two years ago.
It's always been my dream to see the world from up on high.
Captain Fox is an officer with the Deuxième Bureau, French military intelligence.
And Monsieur Marouani isn't just a theatrical agent – he lives a double life...
Daniel, are you a... SPY?
Monsieur Marouani is what we call an "honourable correspondent". He thinks you could provide France with useful services.
Like spying?

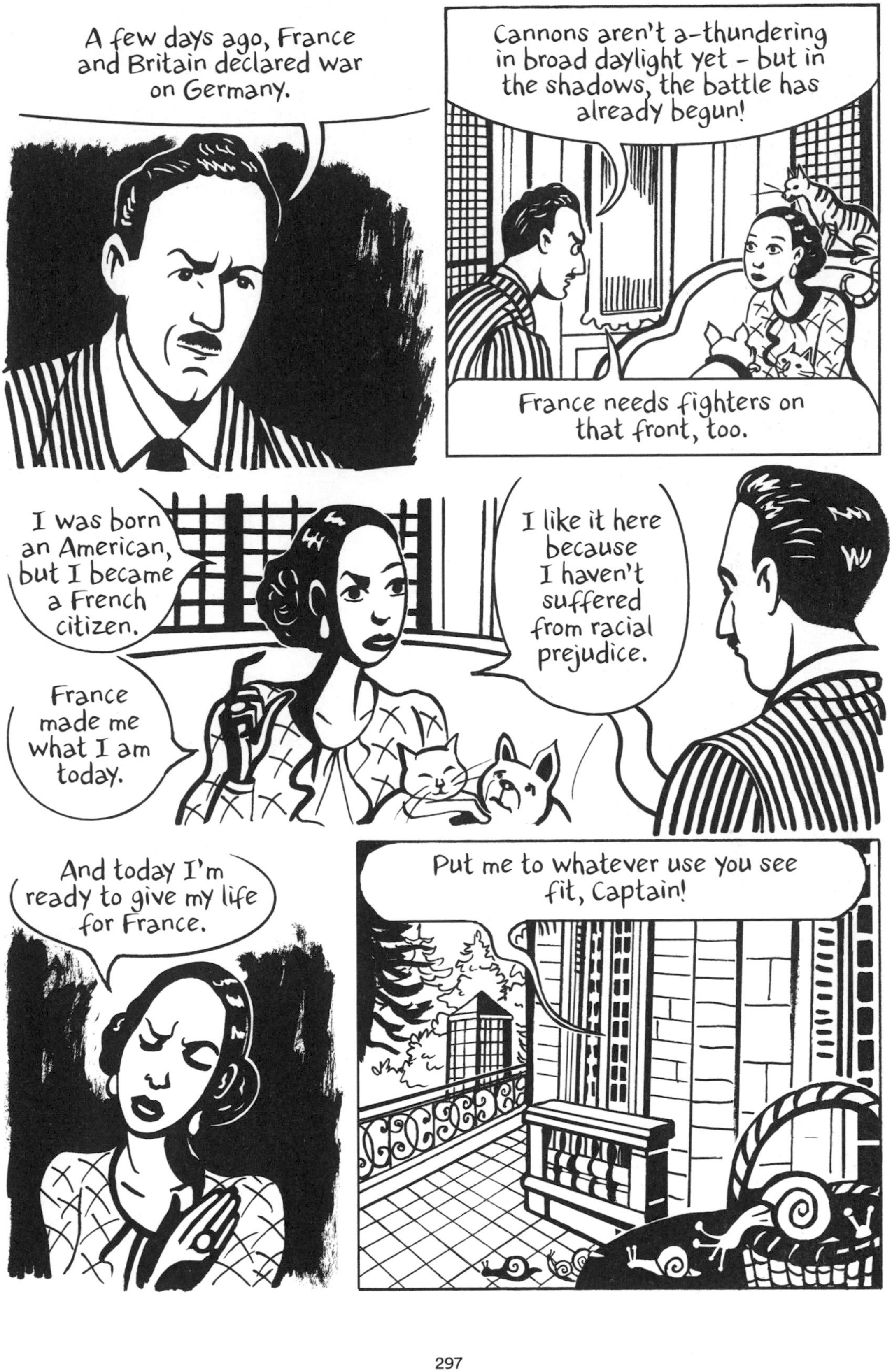
A few days ago, France and Britain declared war on Germany.
Cannons aren't a-thundering in broad daylight yet - but in the shadows, the battle has already begun!
France needs fighters on that front, too.
I was born an American, but I became a French citizen.
France made me what I am today.
I like it here because I haven't suffered from racial prejudice.
And today I'm ready to give my life for France.
Put me to whatever use you see fit, Captain!

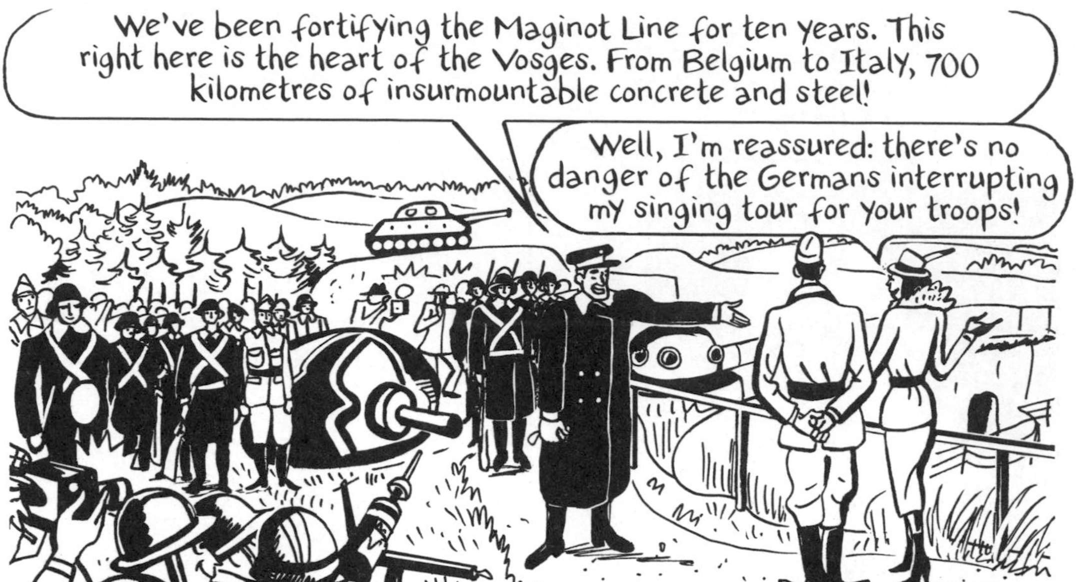
We've been fortifying the Maginot Line for ten years. This right here is the heart of the Vosges. From Belgium to Italy, 700 kilometres of insurmountable concrete and steel!
Well, I'm reassured: there's no danger of the Germans interrupting my singing tour for your troops!

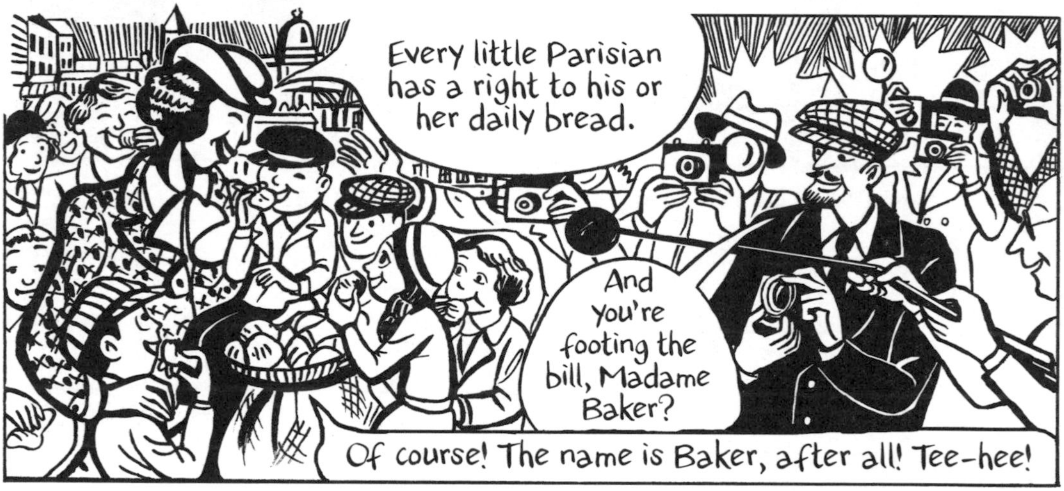
Every little Parisian has a right to his or her daily bread.
And you're footing the bill, Madame Baker?
Of course! The name is Baker, after all! Tee-hee!

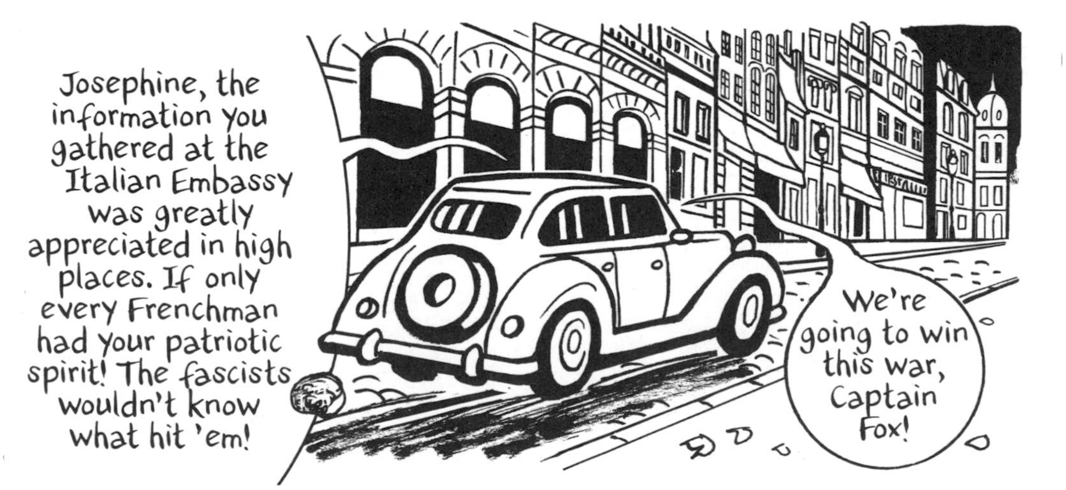
Josephine, the information you gathered at the Italian Embassy was greatly appreciated in high places. If only every Frenchman had your patriotic spirit! The fascists wouldn't know what hit 'em!
We're going to win this war, Captain Fox!

1940 : Château des Milandes, Périgord, France

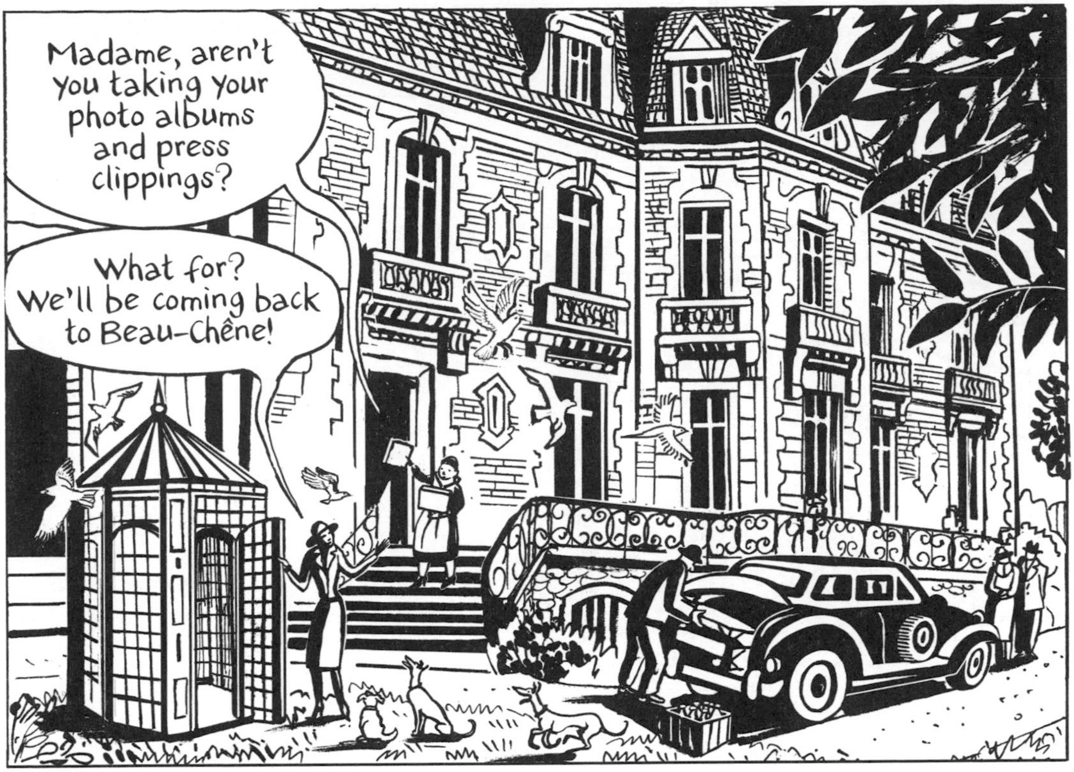
Madame, aren't you taking your photo albums and press clippings?
What for? We'll be coming back to Beau-Chêne!

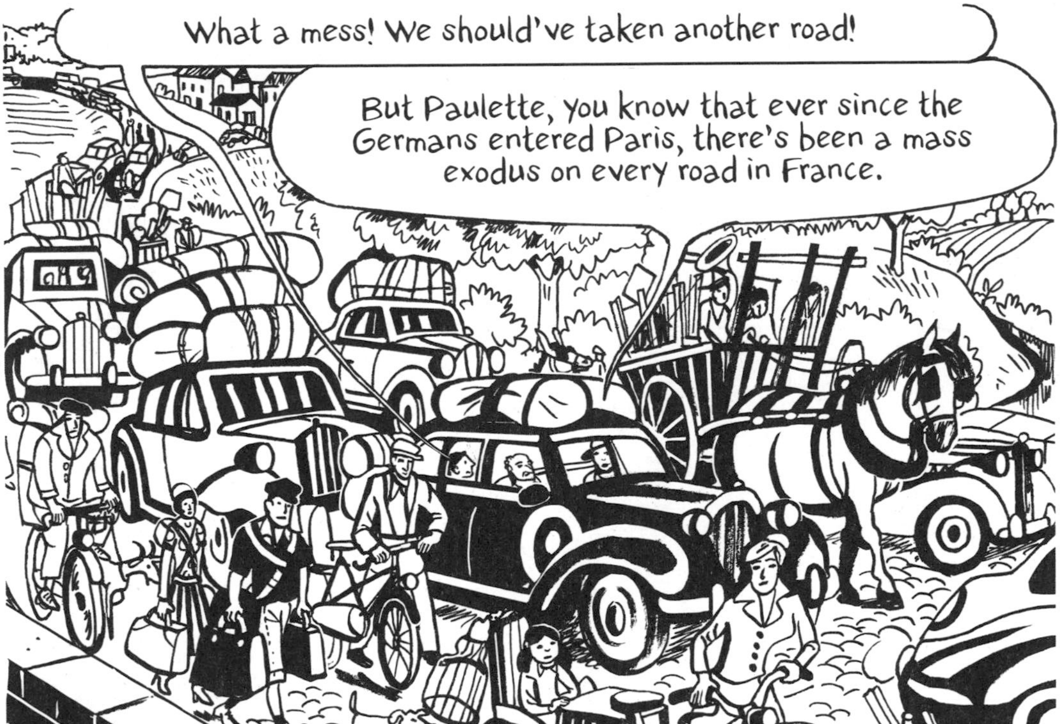
What a mess! We should've taken another road!
But Paulette, you know that ever since the Germans entered Paris, there's been a mass exodus on every road in France.

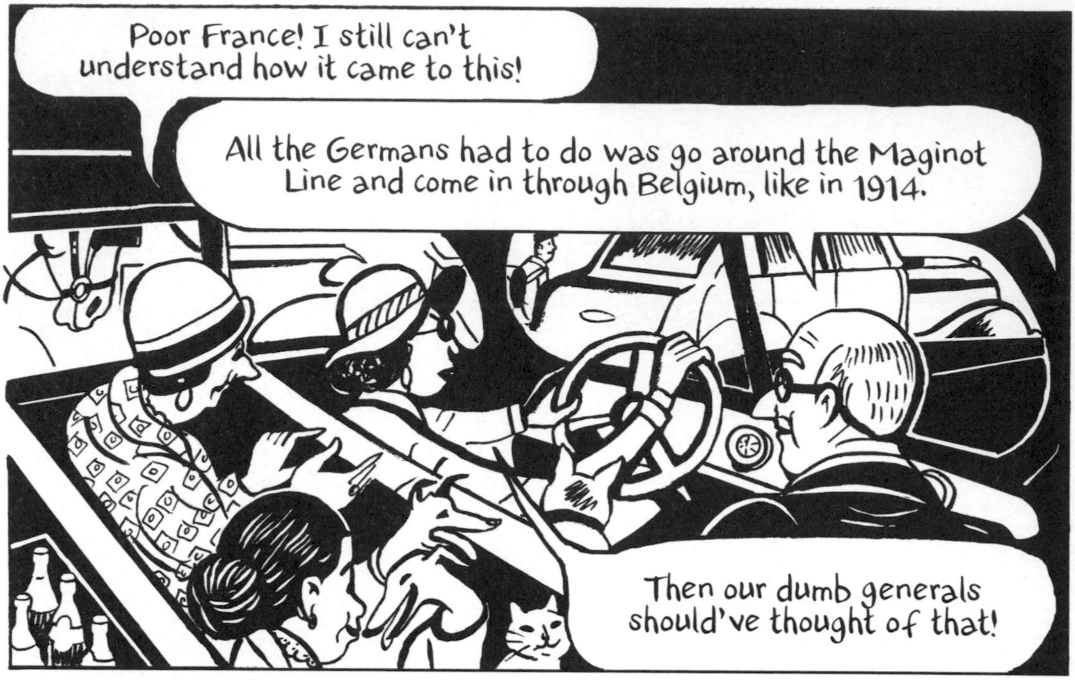
Poor France! I still can't understand how it came to this!
All the Germans had to do was go around the Maginot Line and come in through Belgium, like in 1914.
Then our dumb generals should've thought of that!

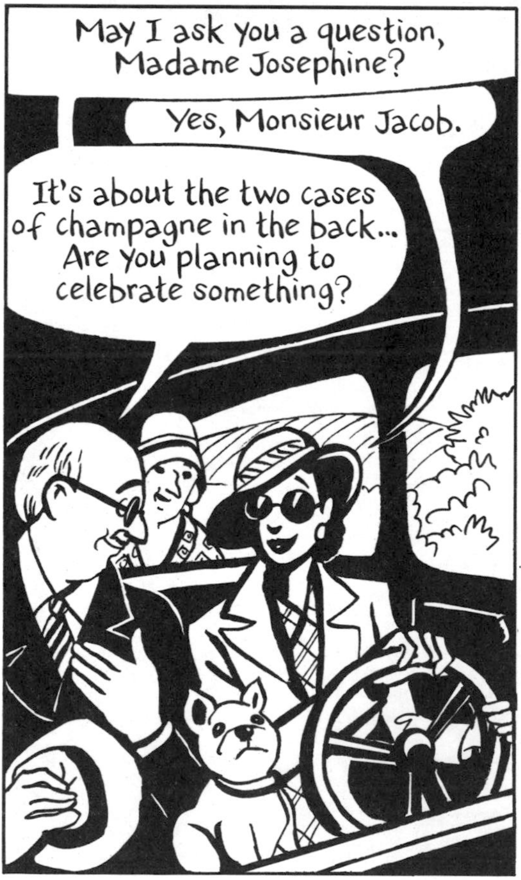
May I ask you a question, Madame Josephine?
Yes, Monsieur Jacob.
It's about the two cases of champagne in the back... Are you planning to celebrate something?

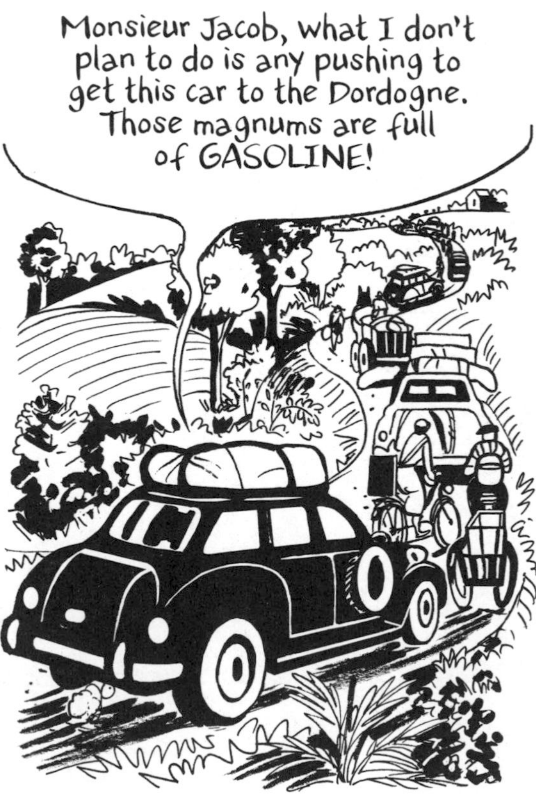
Monsieur Jacob, what I don't plan to do is any pushing to get this car to the Dordogne. Those magnums are full of GASOLINE!

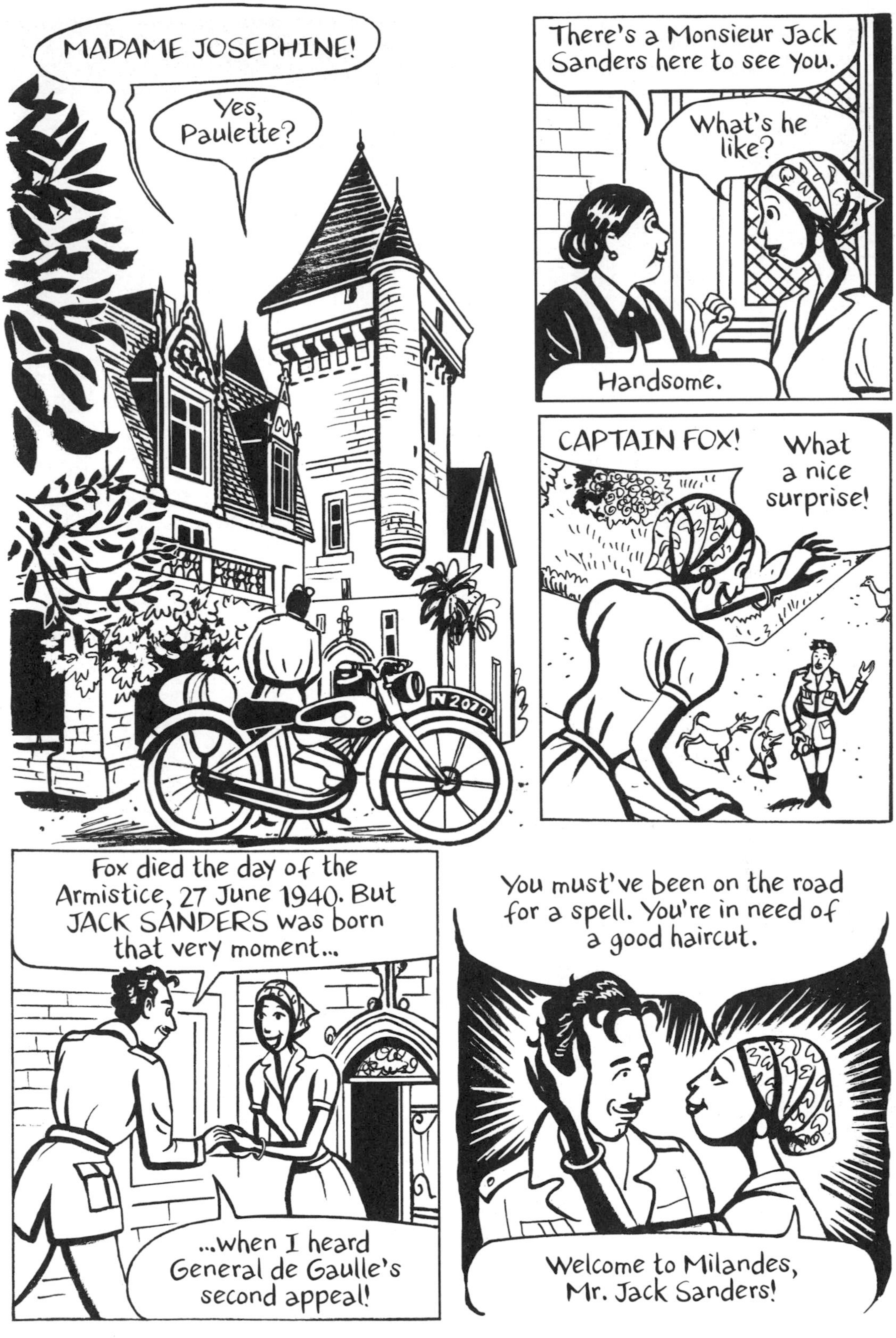
MADAME JOSEPHINE!
Yes, Paulette?
There's a Monsieur Jack Sanders here to see you.
What's he like?
Handsome.
CAPTAIN FOX!
What a nice surprise!
N 2070
Fox died the day of the Armistice, 27 June 1940. But JACK SANDERS was born that very moment...
...when I heard General de Gaulle's second appeal!
You must've been on the road for a spell. You're in need of a good haircut.
Welcome to Milandes, Mr. Jack Sanders!

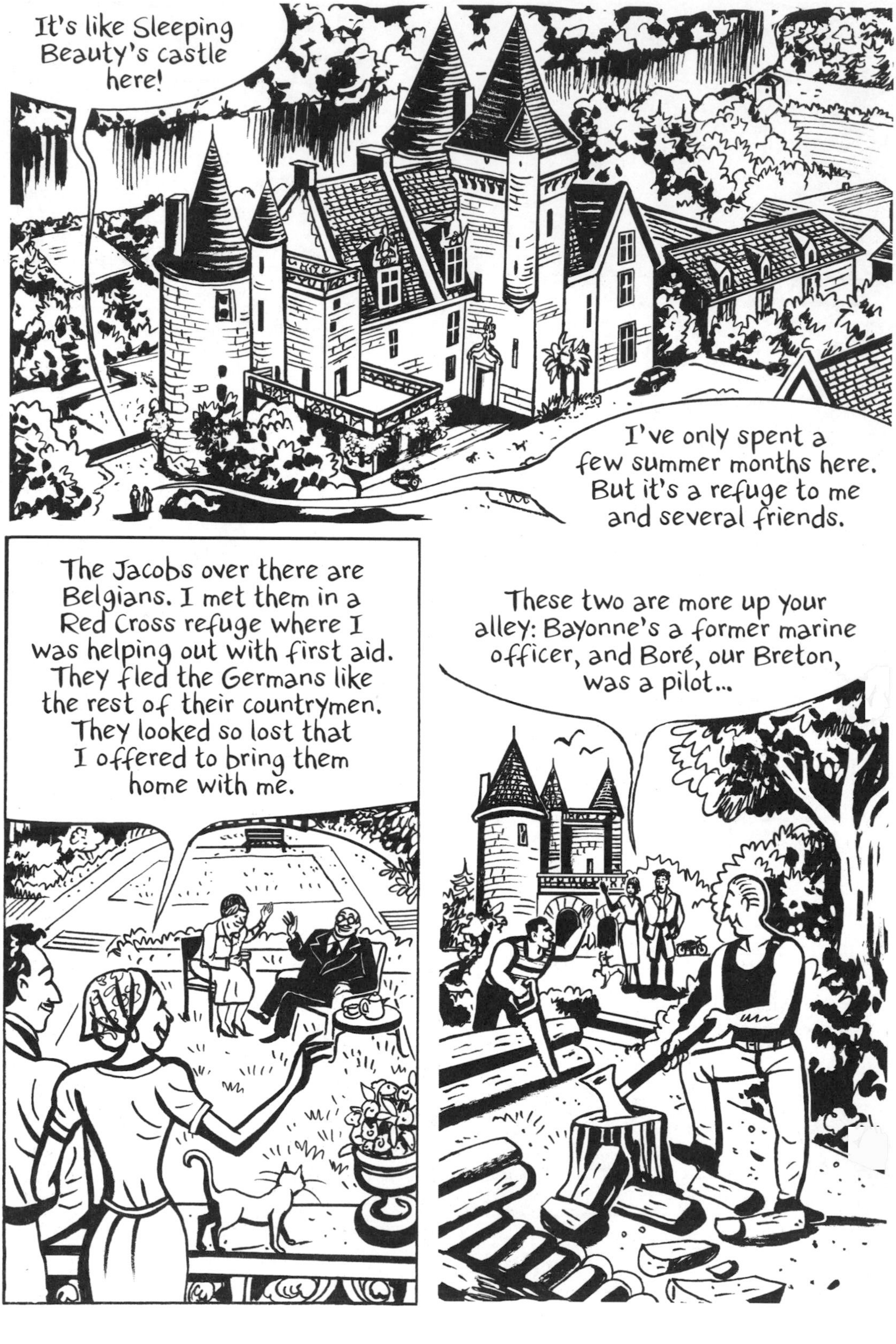
It's like Sleeping Beauty's castle here!
I've only spent a few summer months here. But it's a refuge to me and several friends.
The Jacobs over there are Belgians. I met them in a Red Cross refuge where I was helping out with first aid. They fled the Germans like the rest of their countrymen. They looked so lost that I offered to bring them home with me.
These two are more up your alley: Bayonne's a former marine officer, and Boré, our Breton, was a pilot...

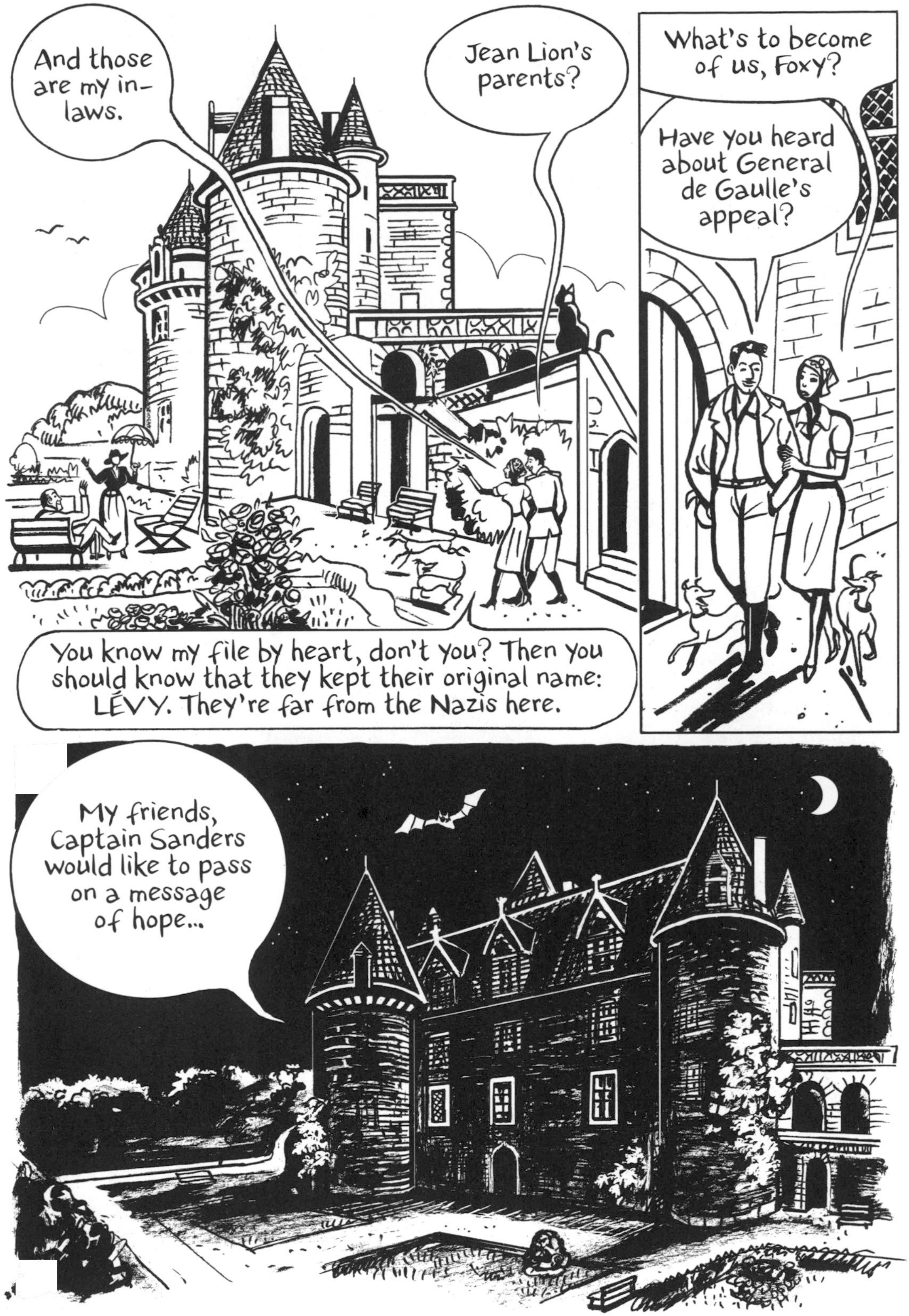
And those are my in-laws.
Jean Lion's parents?
You know my file by heart, don't you? Then you should know that they kept their original name: LÉVY. They're far from the Nazis here.
What's to become of us, Foxy?
Have you heard about General de Gaulle's appeal?
My friends, Captain Sanders would like to pass on a message of hope...

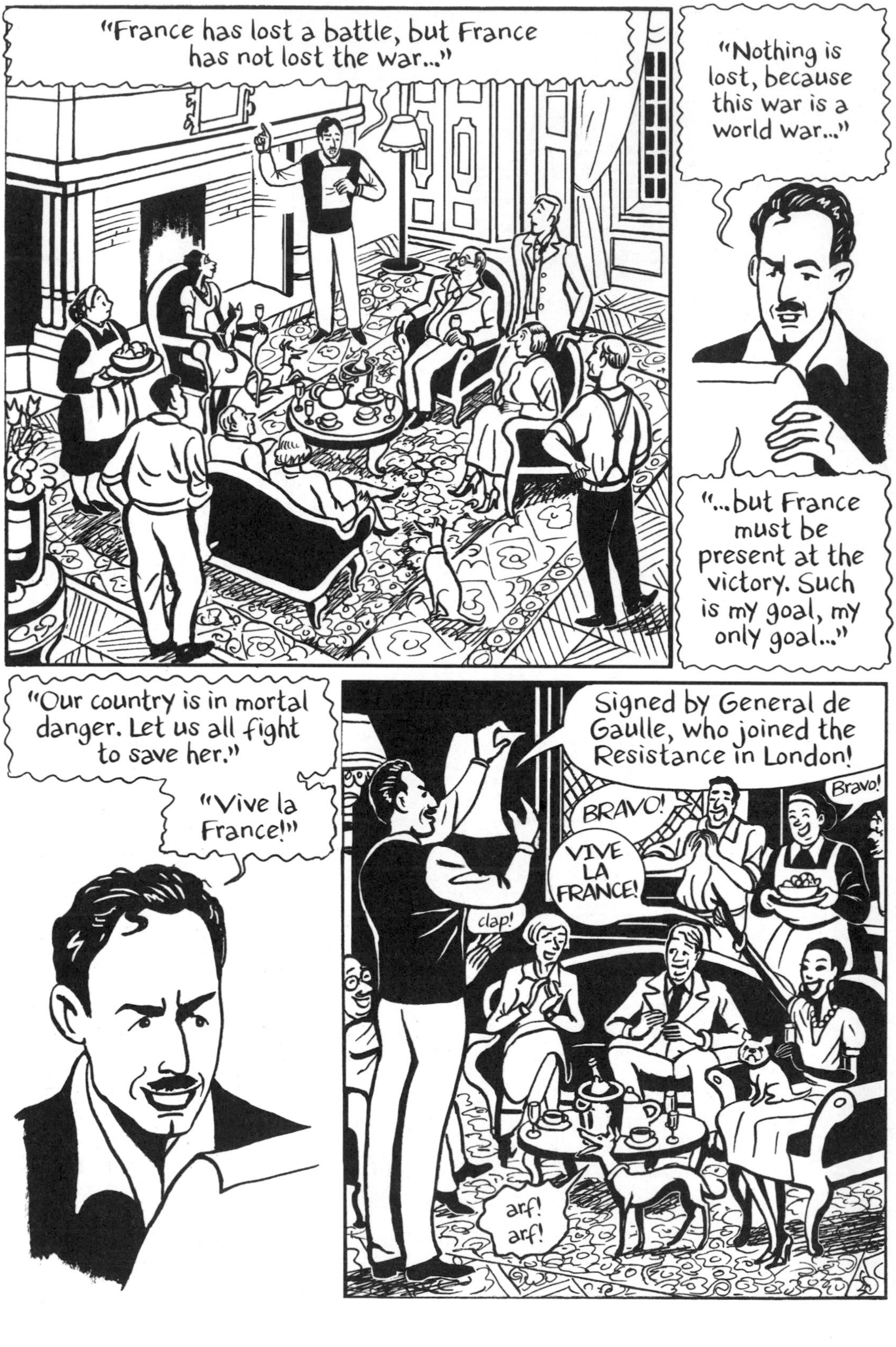
"France has lost a battle, but France has not lost the war..."
"Nothing is lost, because this war is a world war..."
"...but France must be present at the victory. Such is my goal, my only goal..."
"Our country is in mortal danger. Let us all fight to save her."
"Vive la France!"
Signed by General de Gaulle, who joined the Resistance in London!
BRAVO!
Bravo!
VIVE LA FRANCE!
clap!
arf! arf!

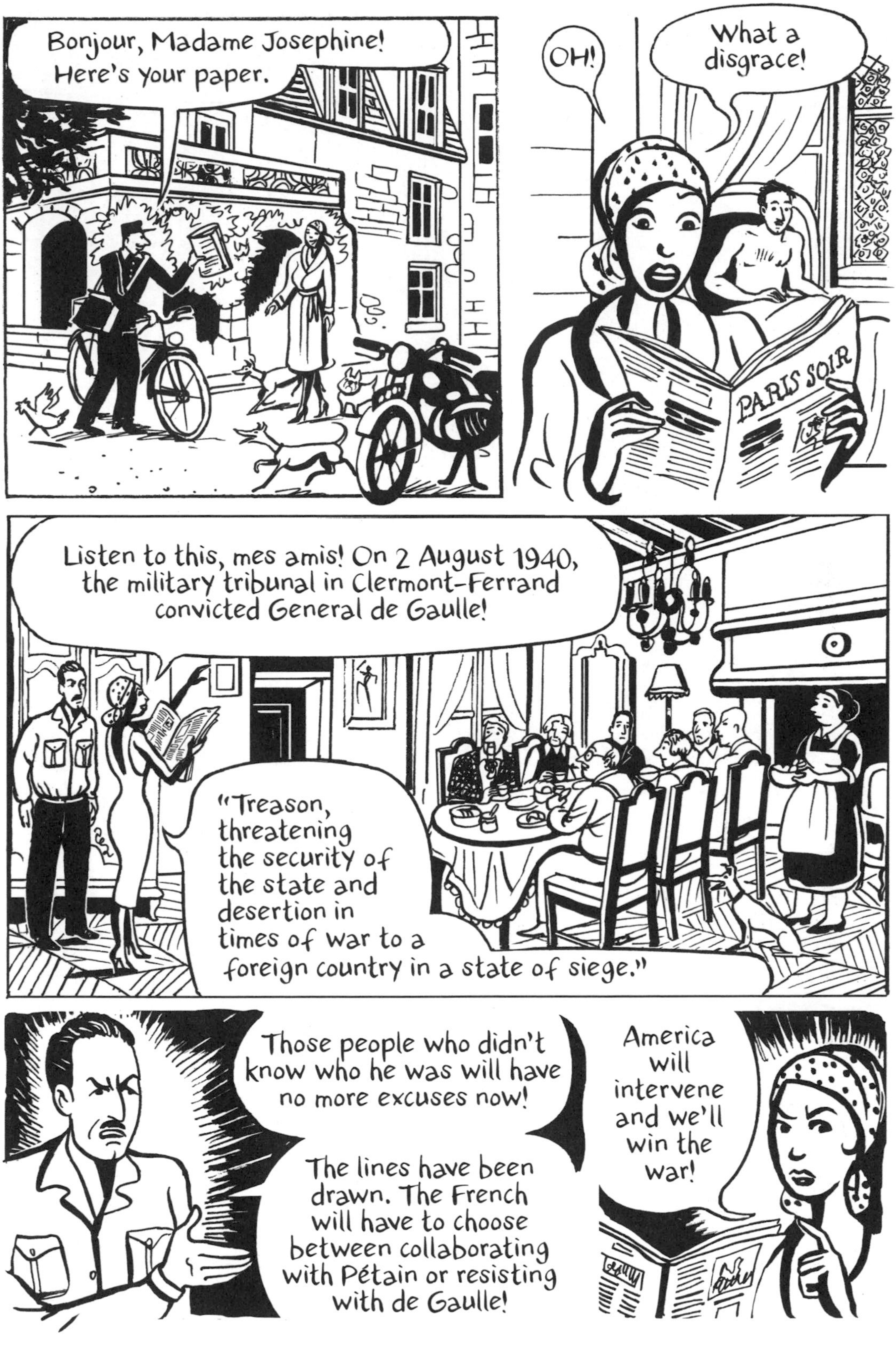
Bonjour, Madame Josephine! Here's your paper.
OH!
What a disgrace!
PARIS SOIR
Listen to this, mes amis! On 2 August 1940, the military tribunal in Clermont-Ferrand convicted General de Gaulle!
"Treason, threatening the security of the state and desertion in times of war to a foreign country in a state of siege."
Those people who didn't know who he was will have no more excuses now!
The lines have been drawn. The French will have to choose between collaborating with Pétain or resisting with de Gaulle!
America will intervene and we'll win the war!

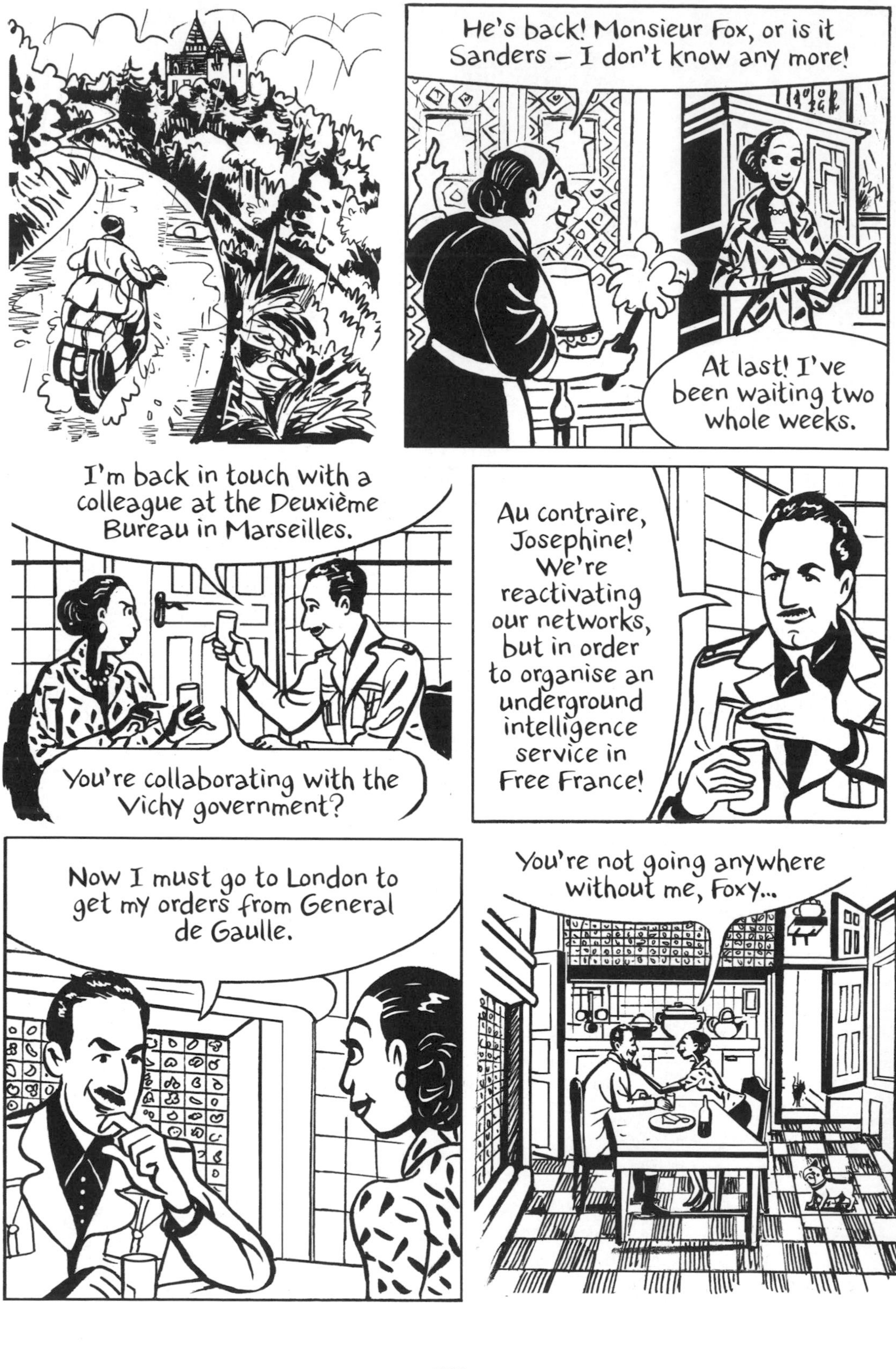
He's back! Monsieur Fox, or is it Sanders – I don't know any more!
At last! I've been waiting two whole weeks.
I'm back in touch with a colleague at the Deuxième Bureau in Marseilles.
You're collaborating with the Vichy government?
Au contraire, Josephine! We're reactivating our networks, but in order to organise an underground intelligence service in Free France!
Now I must go to London to get my orders from General de Gaulle.
You're not going anywhere without me, Foxy...

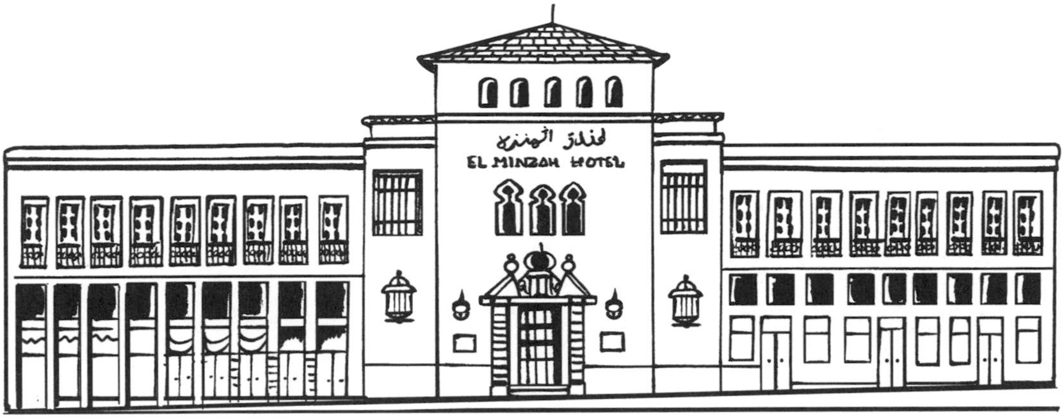
EL MINZAH HOTEL

1941: El Minzah Hotel, Tangier, Morocco

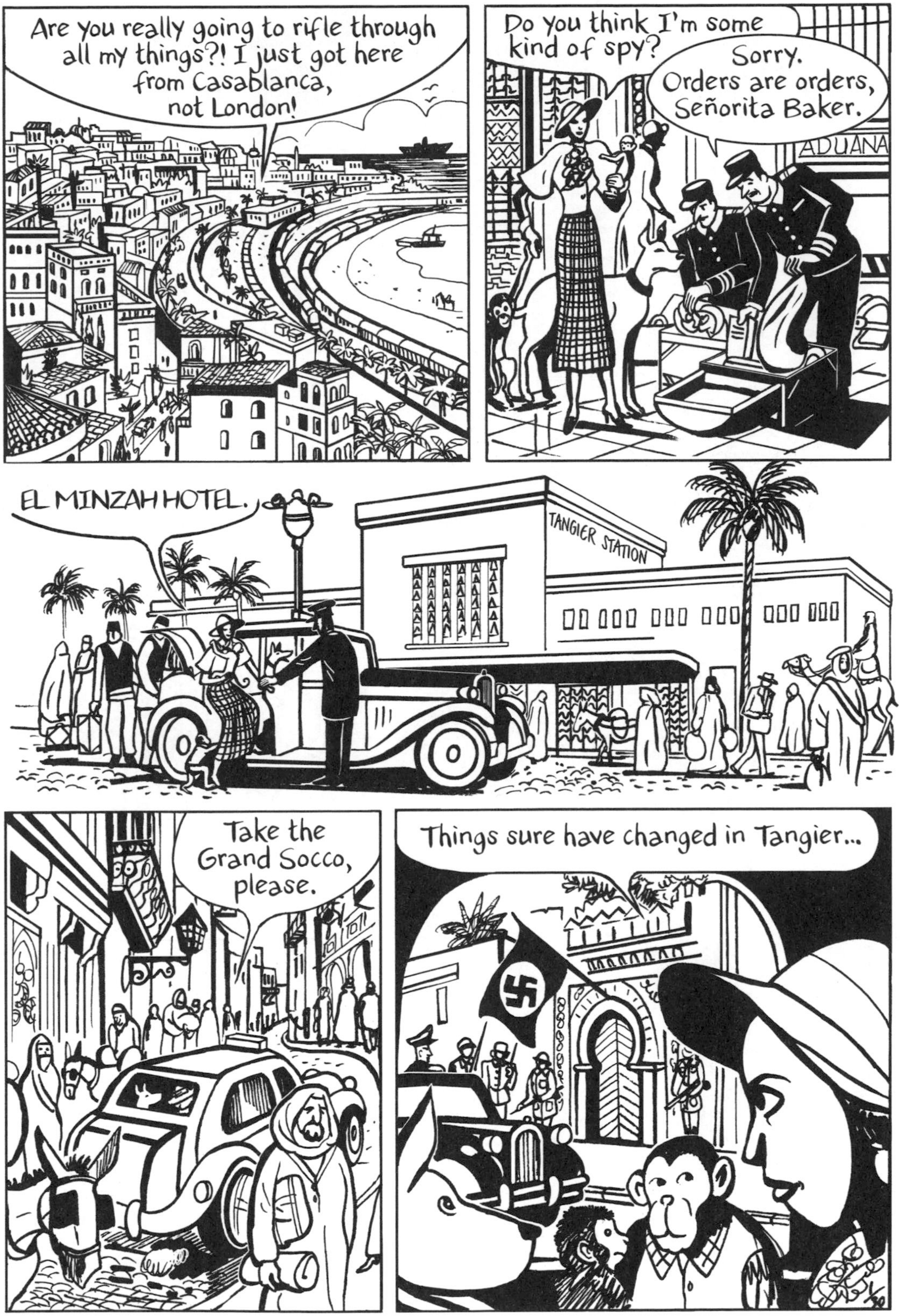
Are you really going to rifle through all my things?! I just got here from Casablanca, not London!
Do you think I'm some kind of spy?
Sorry. Orders are orders, Señorita Baker.
ADUANA
EL MINZAH HOTEL.
TANGIER STATION
Take the Grand Socco, please.
Things sure have changed in Tangier...

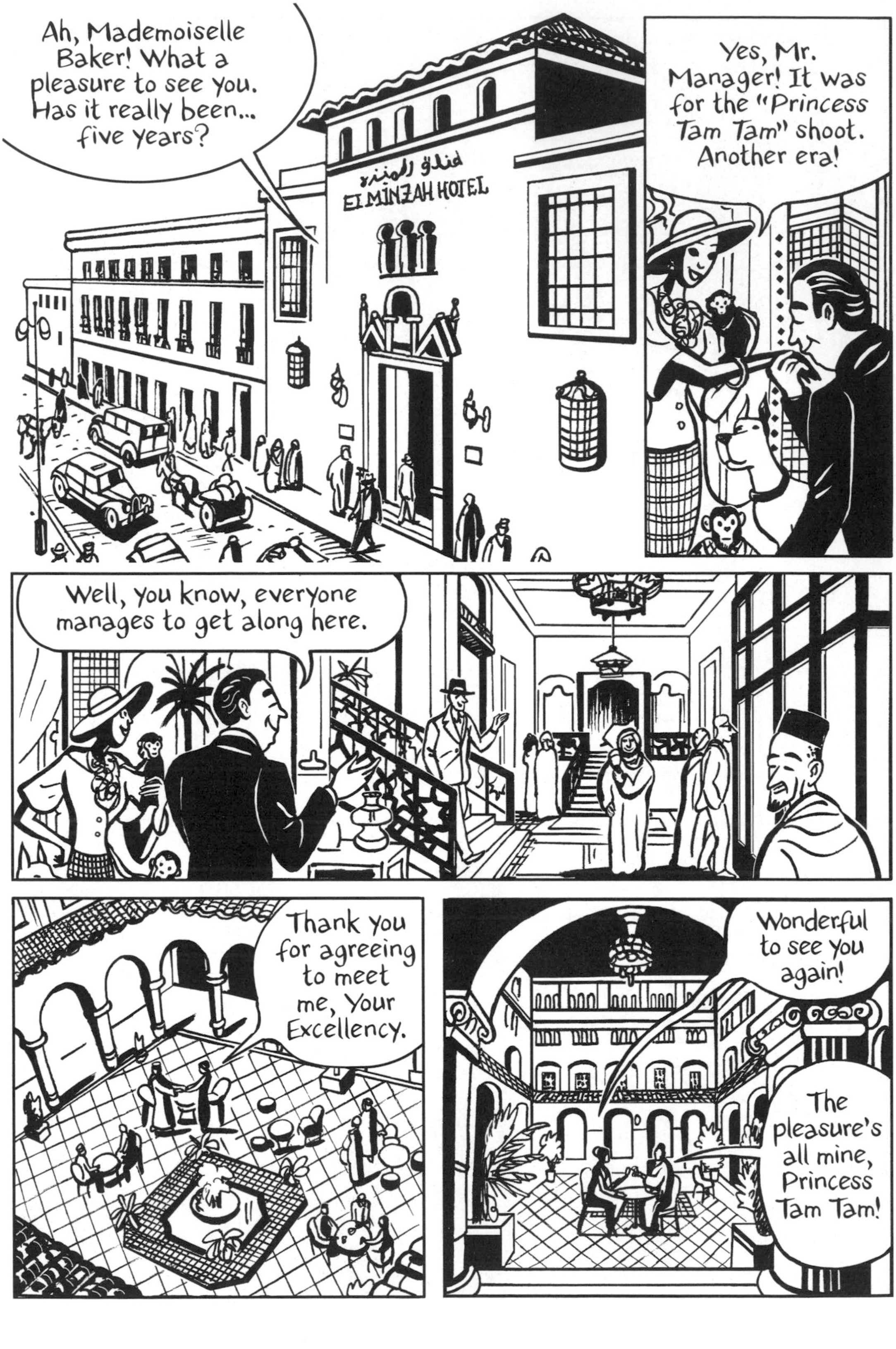
Ah, Mademoiselle Baker! What a pleasure to see you. Has it really been... five years?
EL MINZAH HOTEL
Yes, Mr. Manager! It was for the "Princess Tam Tam" shoot. Another era!
Well, you know, everyone manages to get along here.
Thank you for agreeing to meet me, Your Excellency.
Wonderful to see you again!
The pleasure's all mine, Princess Tam Tam!

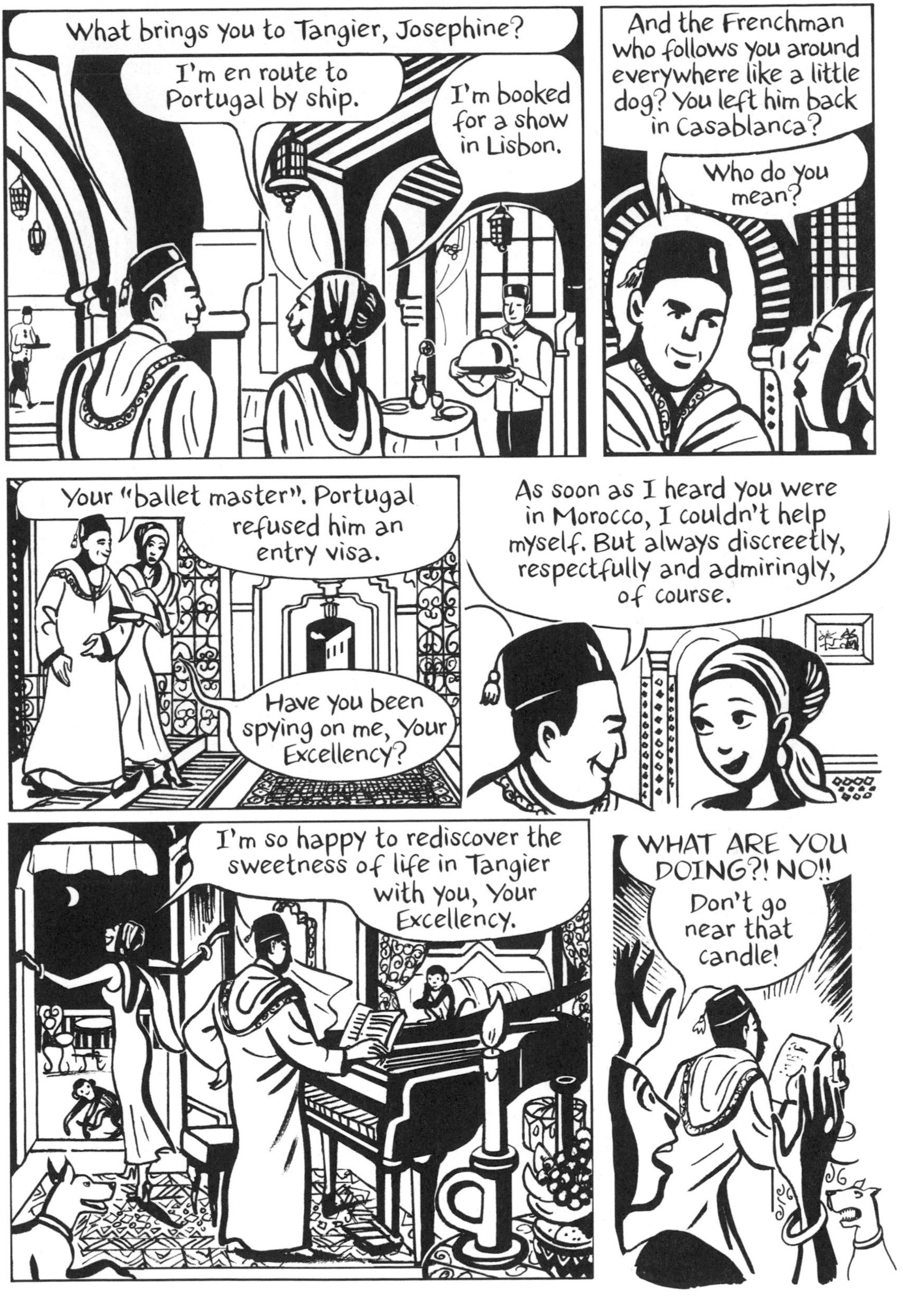
What brings you to Tangier, Josephine?
I'm en route to Portugal by ship.
I'm booked for a show in Lisbon.
And the Frenchman who follows you around everywhere like a little dog? You left him back in Casablanca?
Who do you mean?
Your "ballet master". Portugal refused him an entry visa.
Have you been spying on me, Your Excellency?
As soon as I heard you were in Morocco, I couldn't help myself. But always discreetly, respectfully and admiringly, of course.
I'm so happy to rediscover the sweetness of life in Tangier with you, Your Excellency.
WHAT ARE YOU DOING?! NO!!
Don't go near that candle!

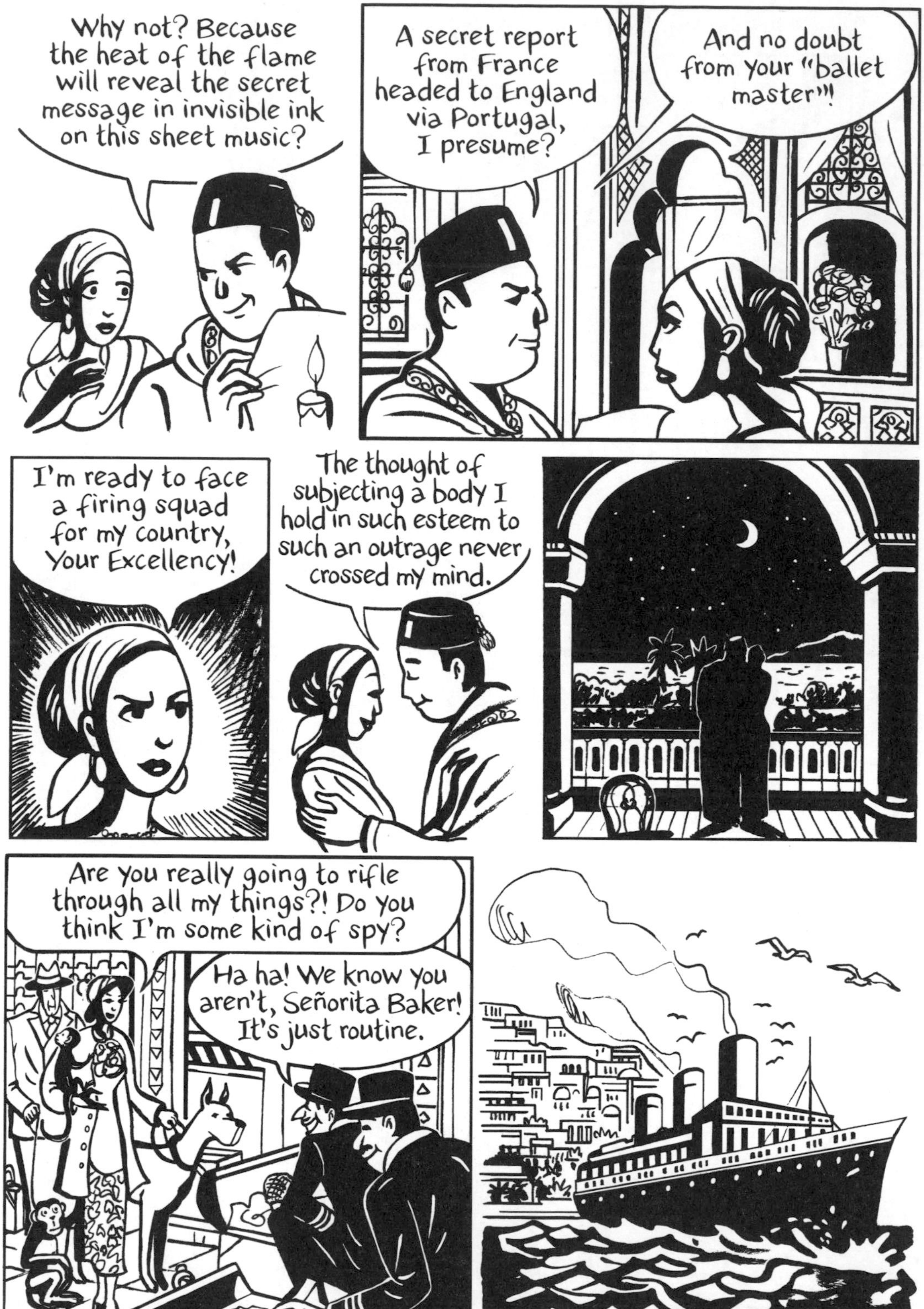
Why not? Because the heat of the flame will reveal the secret message in invisible ink on this sheet music?
A secret report from France headed to England via Portugal, I presume?
And no doubt from your "ballet master"!
I'm ready to face a firing squad for my country, Your Excellency!
The thought of subjecting a body I hold in such esteem to such an outrage never crossed my mind.
Are you really going to rifle through all my things?! Do you think I'm some kind of spy?
Ha ha! We know you aren't, Señorita Baker! It's just routine.

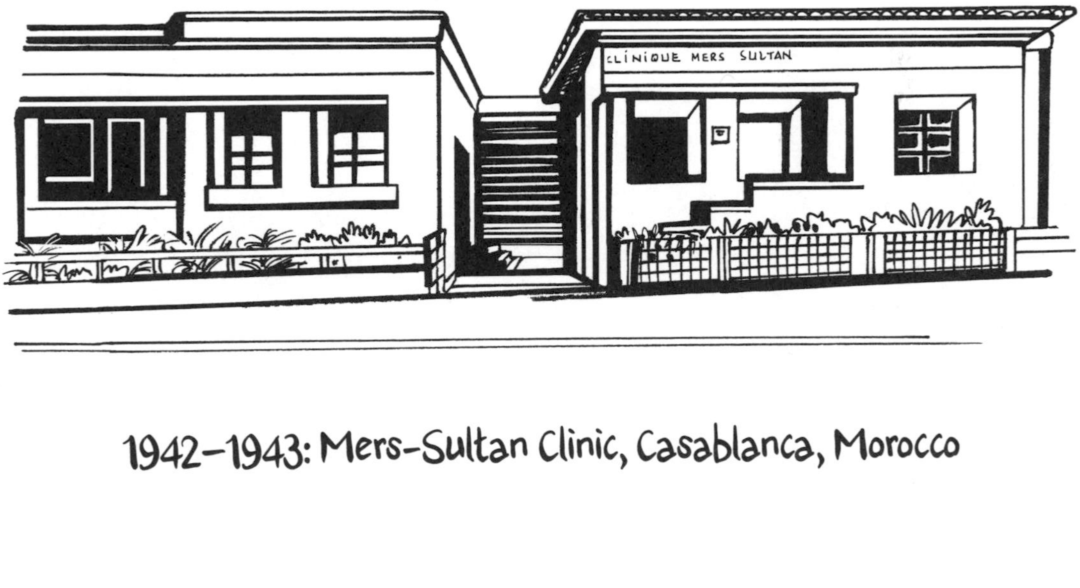
CLINIQUE MERS SULTAN

1942–1943: Mers-Sultan Clinic, Casablanca, Morocco

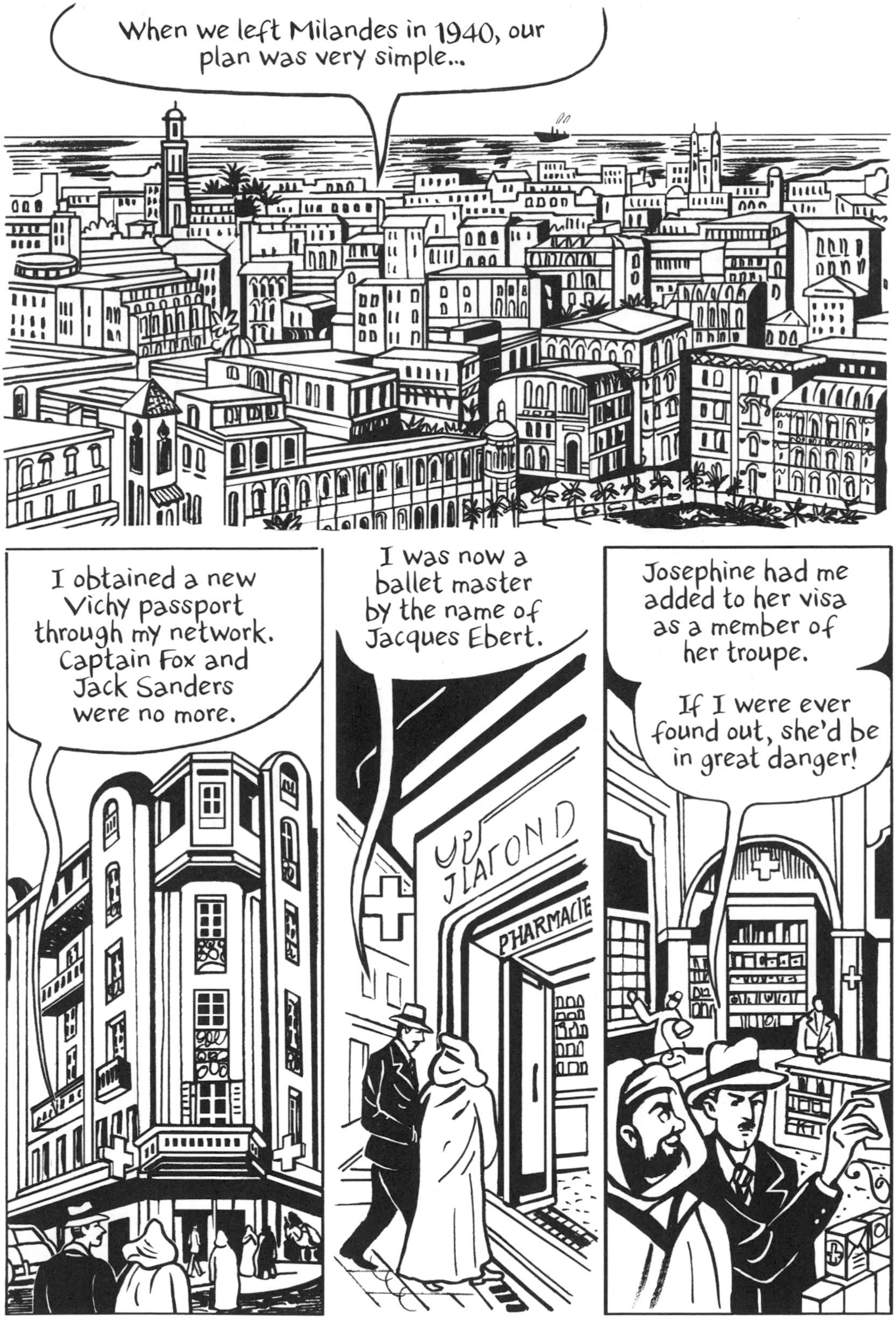
When we left Milandes in 1940, our plan was very simple...
I obtained a new Vichy passport through my network. Captain Fox and Jack Sanders were no more.
I was now a ballet master by the name of Jacques Ebert.
PHARMACIE
Josephine had me added to her visa as a member of her troupe.
If I were ever found out, she'd be in great danger!

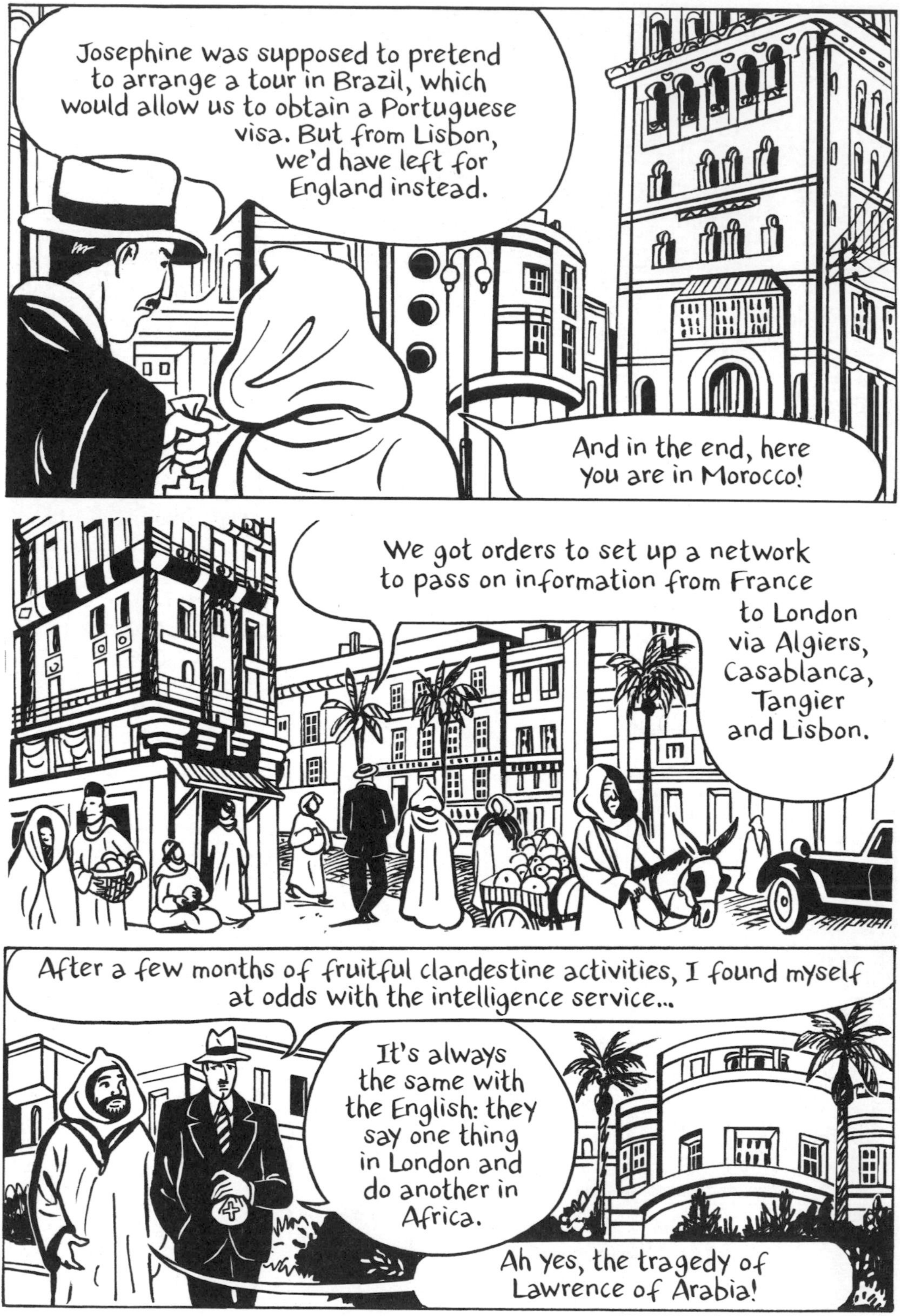
Josephine was supposed to pretend to arrange a tour in Brazil, which would allow us to obtain a Portuguese visa. But from Lisbon, we'd have left for England instead.
And in the end, here you are in Morocco!
We got orders to set up a network to pass on information from France to London via Algiers, Casablanca, Tangier and Lisbon.
After a few months of fruitful clandestine activities, I found myself at odds with the intelligence service...
It's always the same with the English: they say one thing in London and do another in Africa.
Ah yes, the tragedy of Lawrence of Arabia!

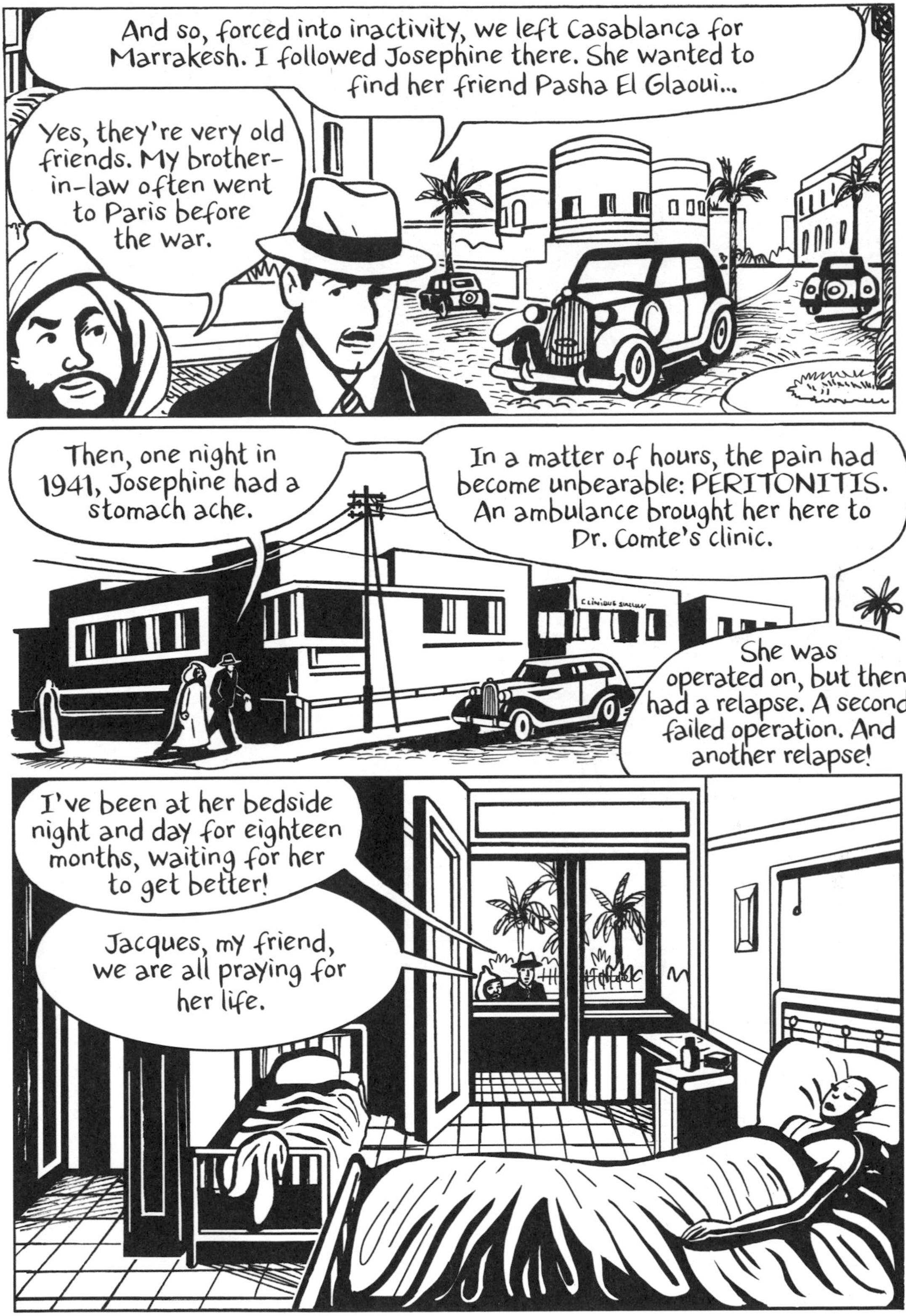
And so, forced into inactivity, we left Casablanca for Marrakesh. I followed Josephine there. She wanted to find her friend Pasha El Glaoui...
Yes, they're very old friends. My brother-in-law often went to Paris before the war.
Then, one night in 1941, Josephine had a stomach ache.
In a matter of hours, the pain had become unbearable: PERITONITIS. An ambulance brought her here to Dr. Comte's clinic.
She was operated on, but then had a relapse. A second, failed operation. And another relapse!
I've been at her bedside night and day for eighteen months, waiting for her to get better!
Jacques, my friend, we are all praying for her life.

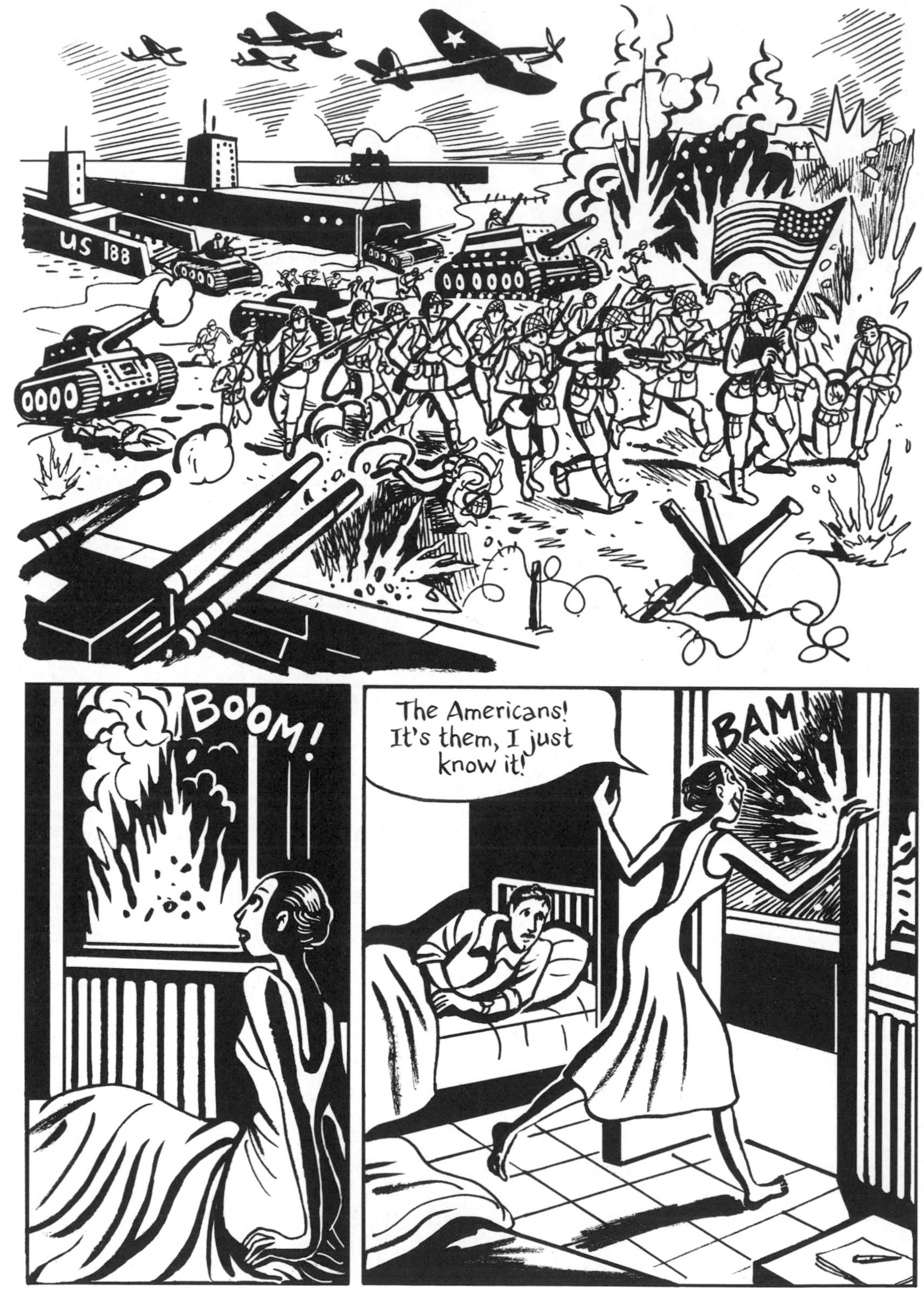
US 188
BOOM!
The Americans! It's them, I just know it!
BAM!

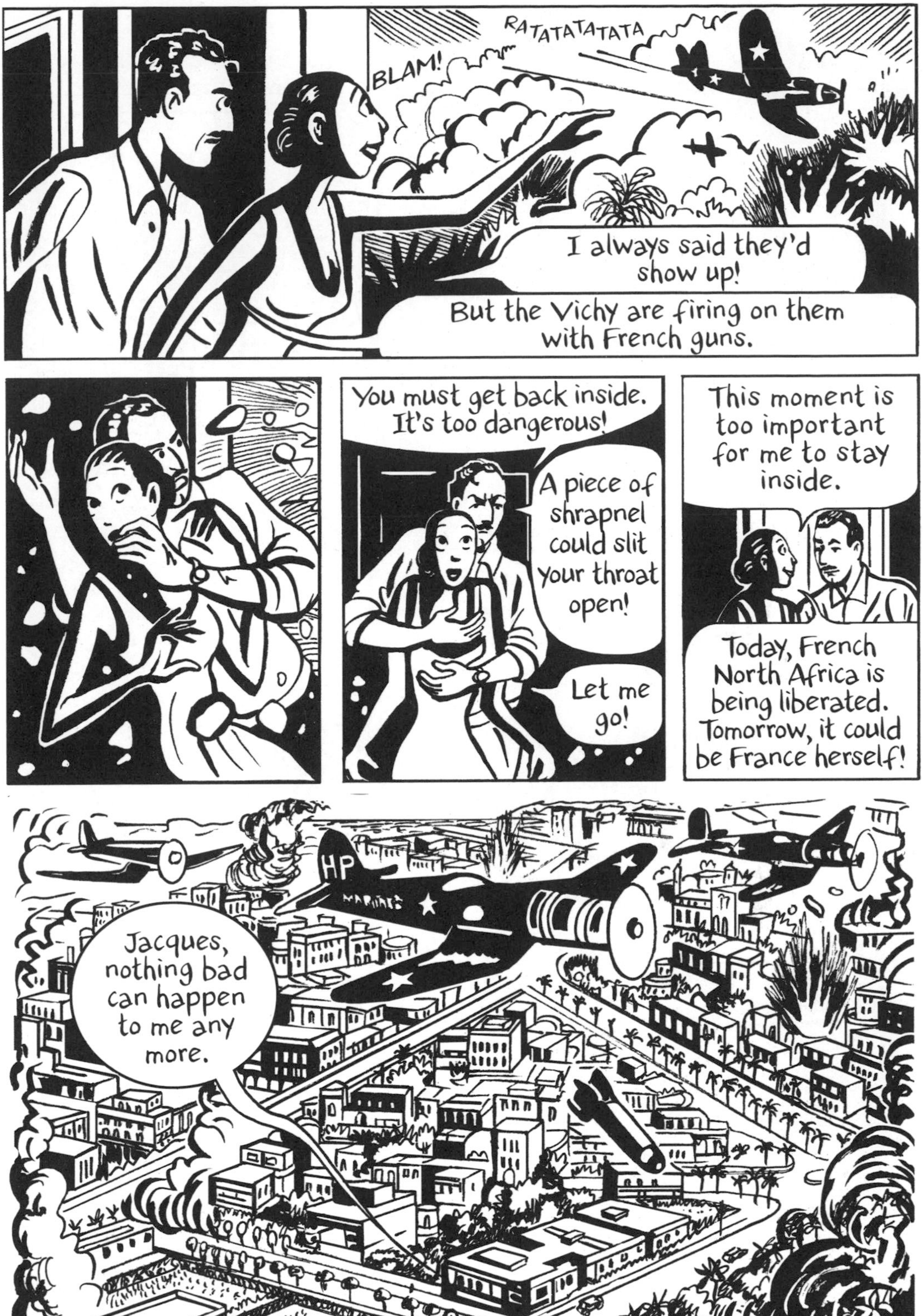
RATATATATATA
BLAM!
I always said they'd show up!
But the Vichy are firing on them with French guns.
You must get back inside. It's too dangerous!
A piece of shrapnel could slit your throat open!
Let me go!
This moment is too important for me to stay inside.
Today, French North Africa is being liberated. Tomorrow, it could be France herself!
HP
Jacques, nothing bad can happen to me any more.

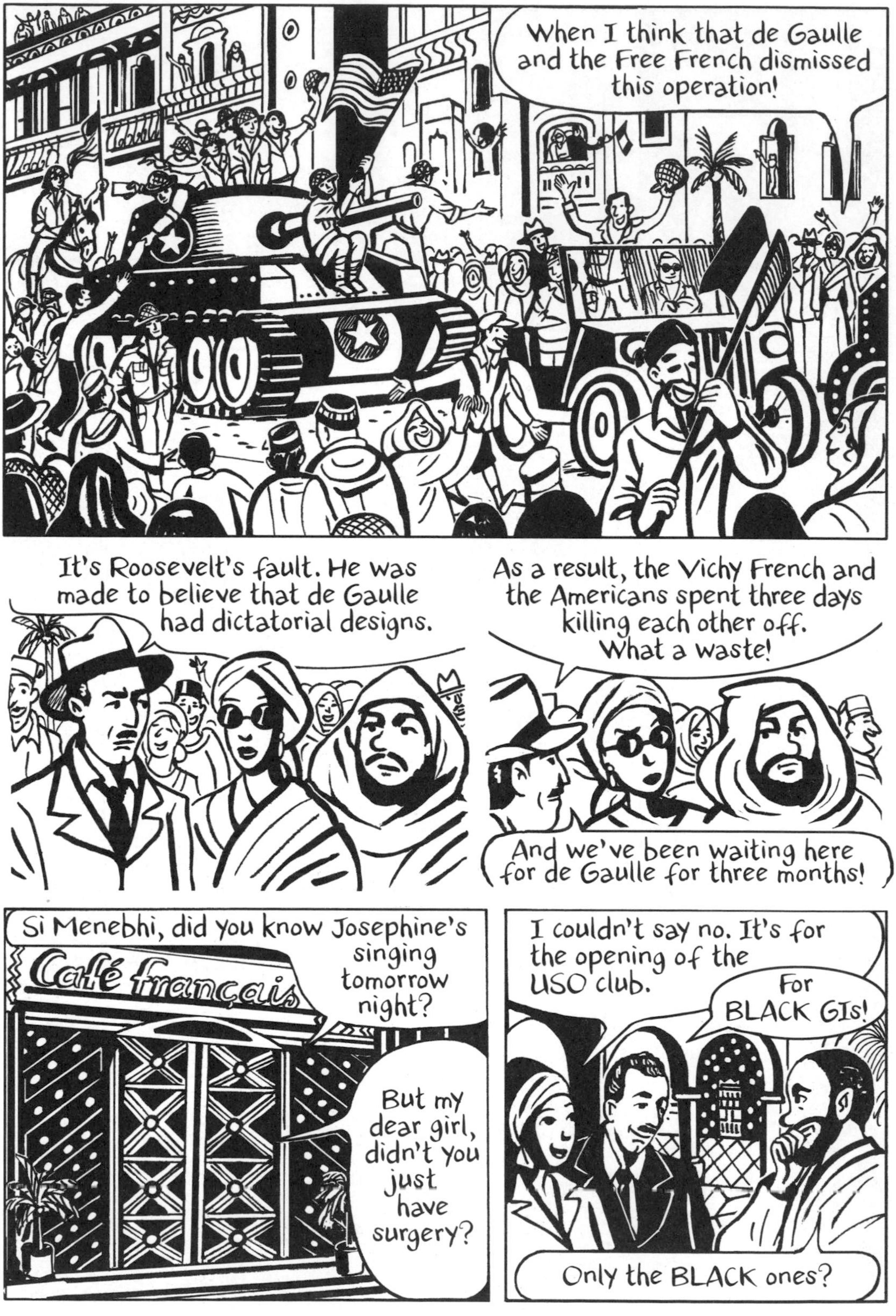
When I think that de Gaulle and the Free French dismissed this operation!
It's Roosevelt's fault. He was made to believe that de Gaulle had dictatorial designs.
As a result, the Vichy French and the Americans spent three days killing each other off. What a waste!
And we've been waiting here for de Gaulle for three months!
Si Menebhi, did you know Josephine's singing tomorrow night?
Café français
But my dear girl, didn't you just have surgery?
I couldn't say no. It's for the opening of the USO club.
For BLACK GIs!
Only the BLACK ones?

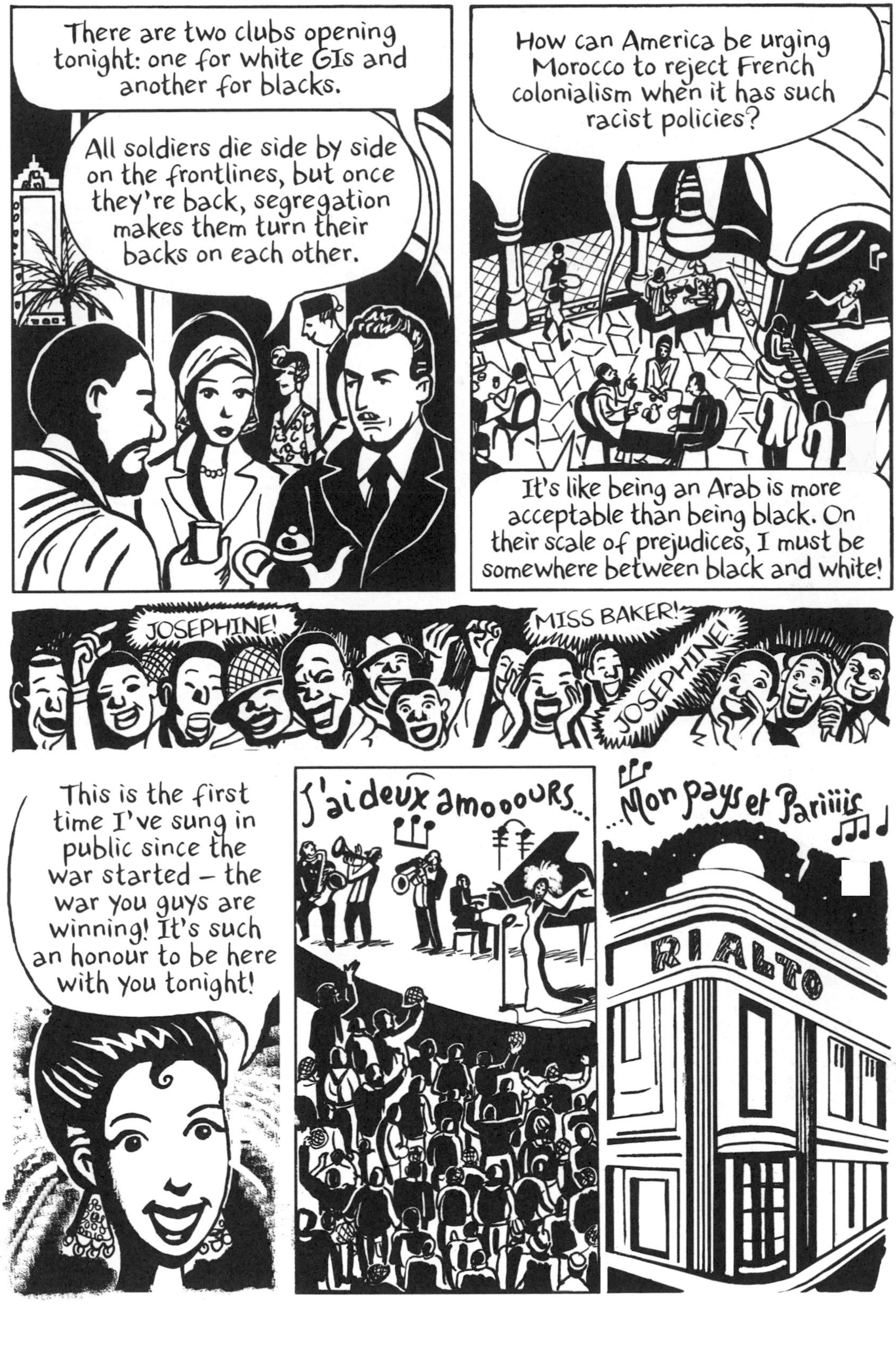

There are two clubs opening tonight: one for white GIs and another for blacks.
All soldiers die side by side on the frontlines, but once they're back, segregation makes them turn their backs on each other.
How can America be urging Morocco to reject French colonialism when it has such racist policies?
It's like being an Arab is more acceptable than being black. On their scale of prejudices, I must be somewhere between black and white!
JOSEPHINE!
MISS BAKER!
JOSEPHINE!
This is the first time I've sung in public since the war started – the war you guys are winning! It's such an honour to be here with you tonight!
J'ai deux amooouRS...
...Mon pays et Pariiiis
RIALTO

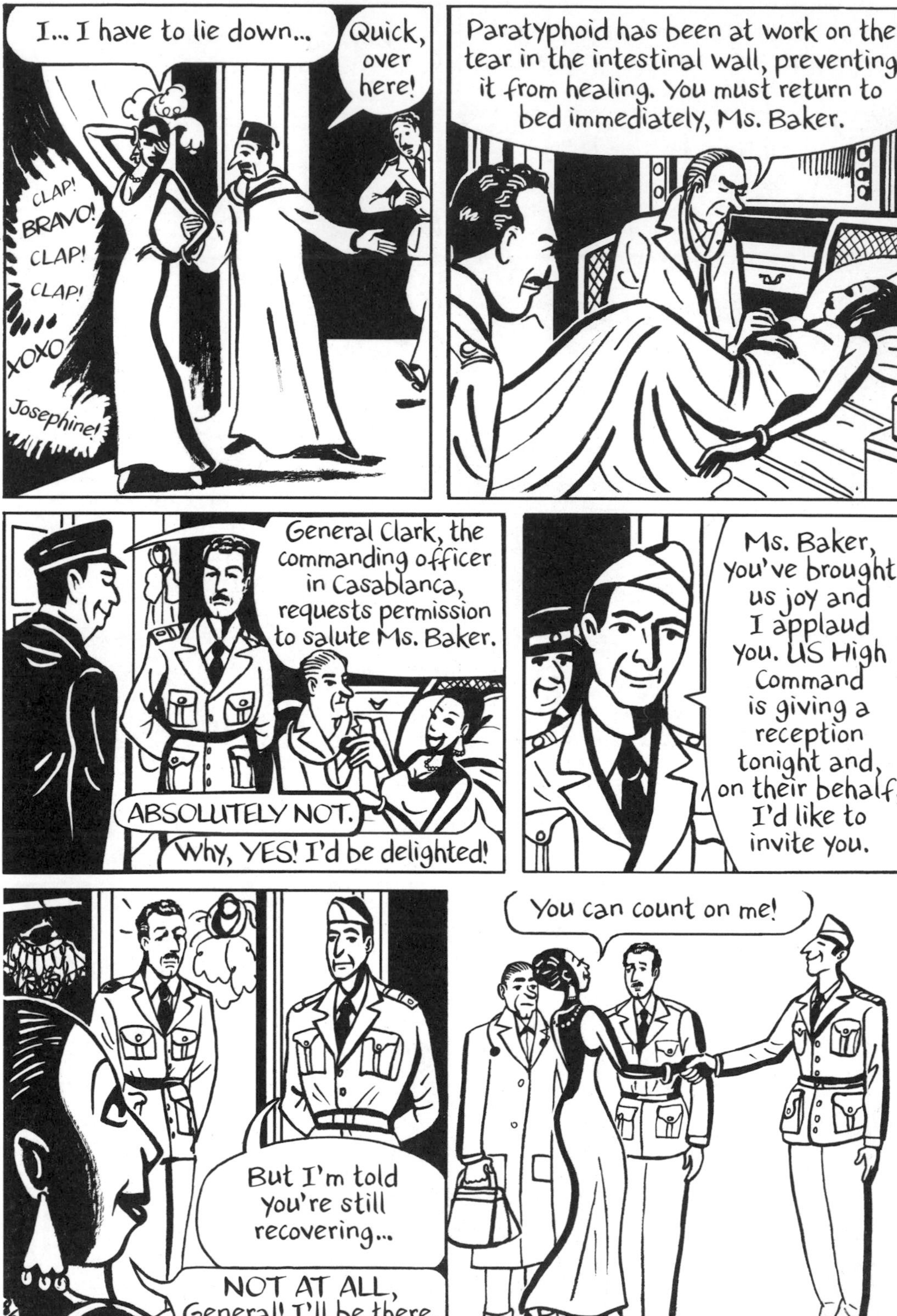
I... I have to lie down...
Quick, over here!
CLAP! BRAVO! CLAP! CLAP!
XOXO
Josephine!
Paratyphoid has been at work on the tear in the intestinal wall, preventing it from healing. You must return to bed immediately, Ms. Baker.
General Clark, the commanding officer in Casablanca, requests permission to salute Ms. Baker.
ABSOLUTELY NOT.
Why, YES! I'd be delighted!
Ms. Baker, you've brought us joy and I applaud you. US High Command is giving a reception tonight and, on their behalf, I'd like to invite you.
But I'm told you're still recovering...
NOT AT ALL, General! I'll be there.
You can count on me!

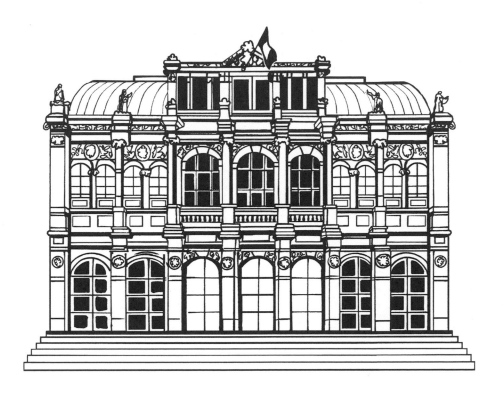

1943: Algiers Opera House, Algeria

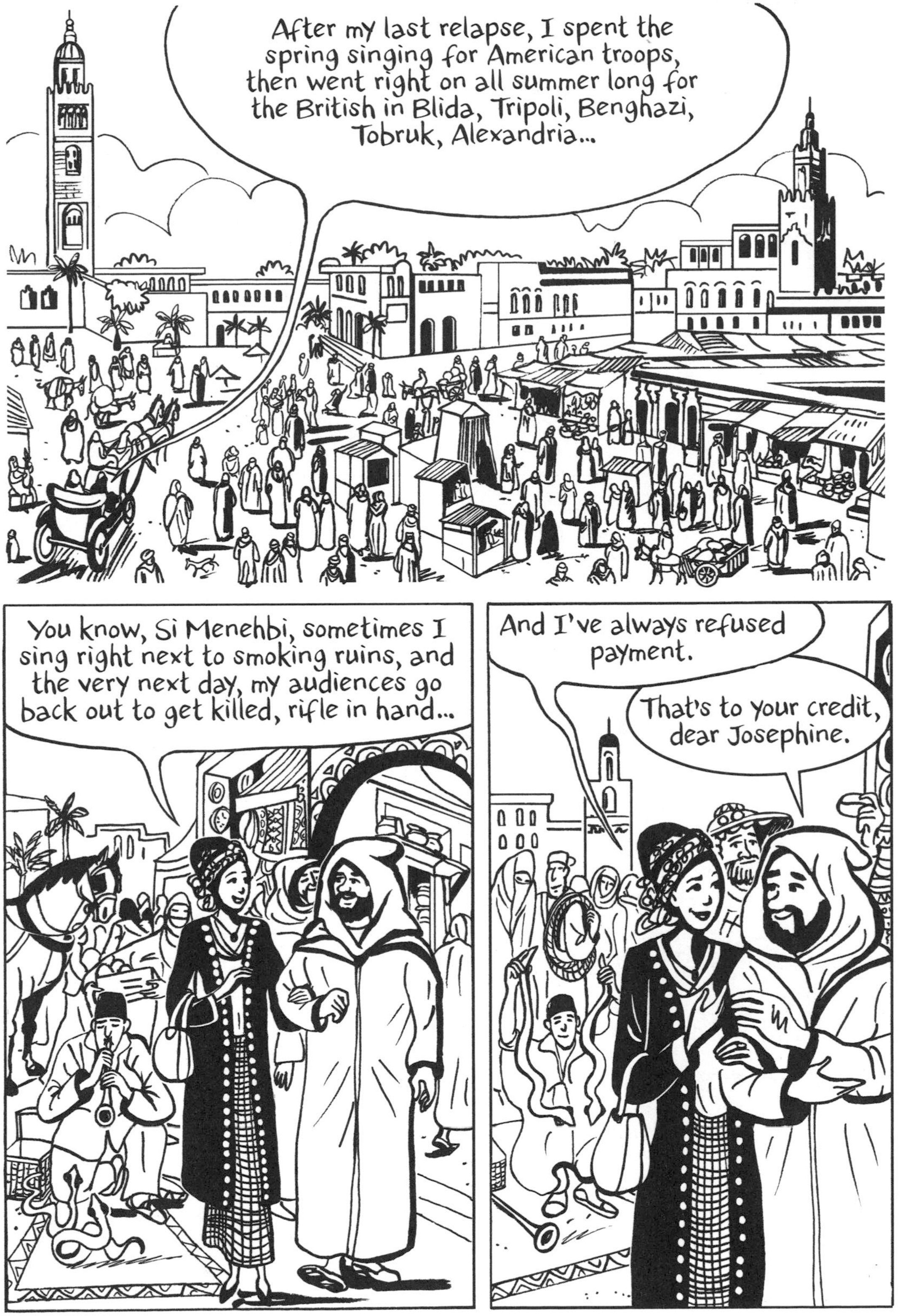
After my last relapse, I spent the spring singing for American troops, then went right on all summer long for the British in Blida, Tripoli, Benghazi, Tobruk, Alexandria...
You know, Si Menehbi, sometimes I sing right next to smoking ruins, and the very next day, my audiences go back out to get killed, rifle in hand...
And I've always refused payment.
That's to your credit, dear Josephine.

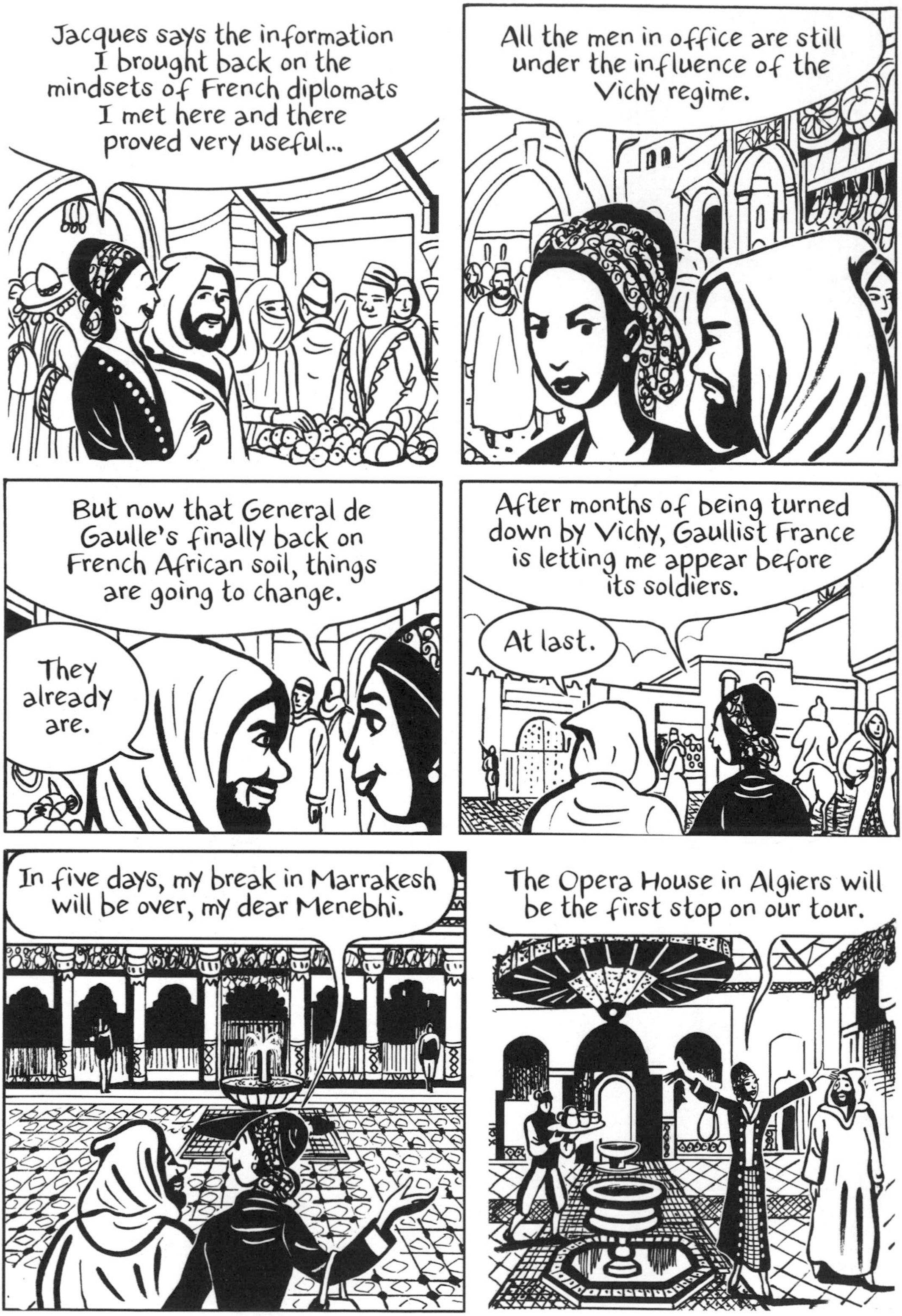
Jacques says the information I brought back on the mindsets of French diplomats I met here and there proved very useful...
All the men in office are still under the influence of the Vichy regime.
But now that General de Gaulle's finally back on French African soil, things are going to change.
They already are.
After months of being turned down by Vichy, Gaullist France is letting me appear before its soldiers.
At last.
In five days, my break in Marrakesh will be over, my dear Menebhi.
The Opera House in Algiers will be the first stop on our tour.

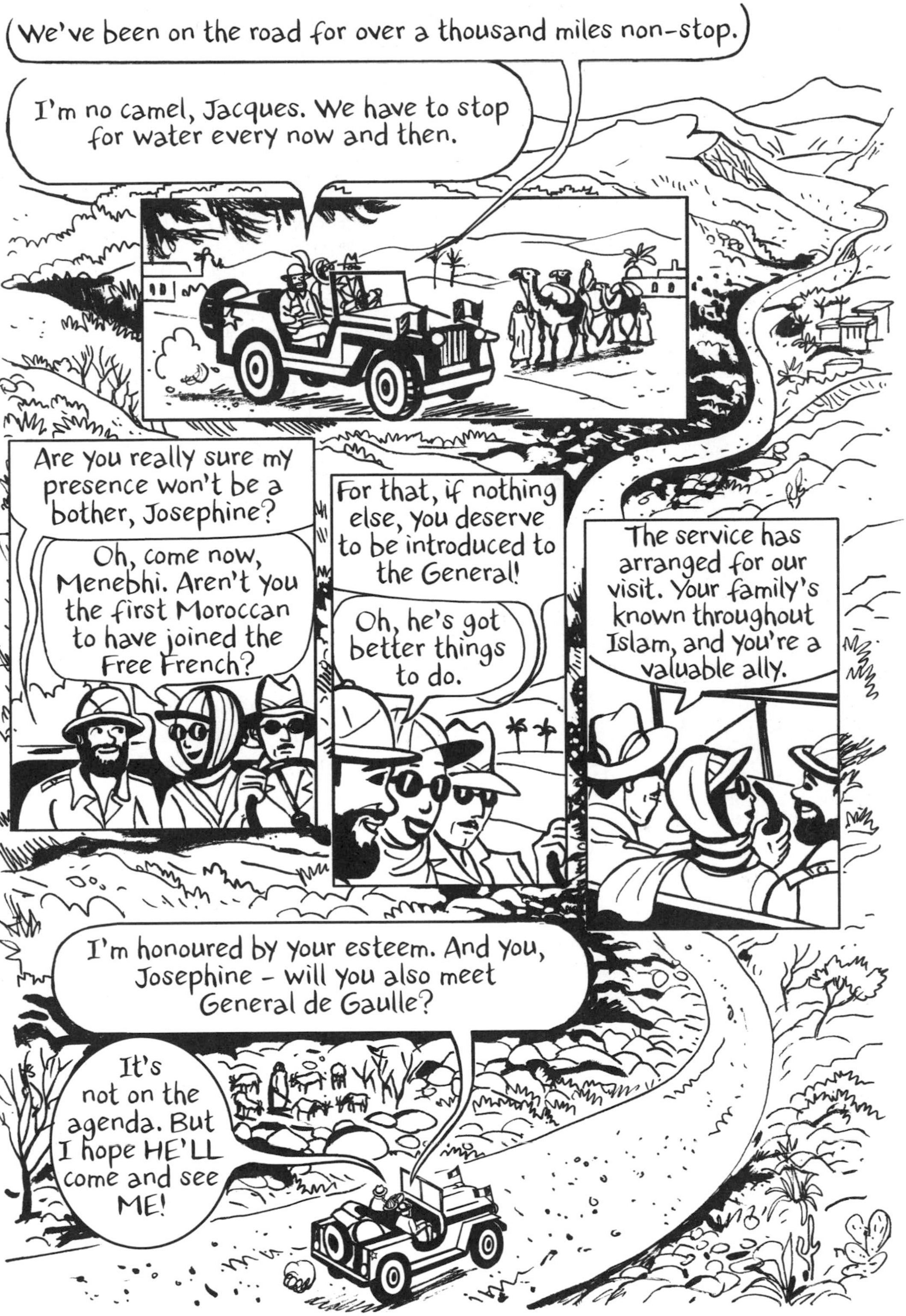
We've been on the road for over a thousand miles non-stop.
I'm no camel, Jacques. We have to stop for water every now and then.
Are you really sure my presence won't be a bother, Josephine?
Oh, come now, Menebhi. Aren't you the first Moroccan to have joined the Free French?
For that, if nothing else, you deserve to be introduced to the General!
Oh, he's got better things to do.
The service has arranged for our visit. Your family's known throughout Islam, and you're a valuable ally.
I'm honoured by your esteem. And you, Josephine - will you also meet General de Gaulle?
It's not on the agenda. But I hope HE'LL come and see ME!

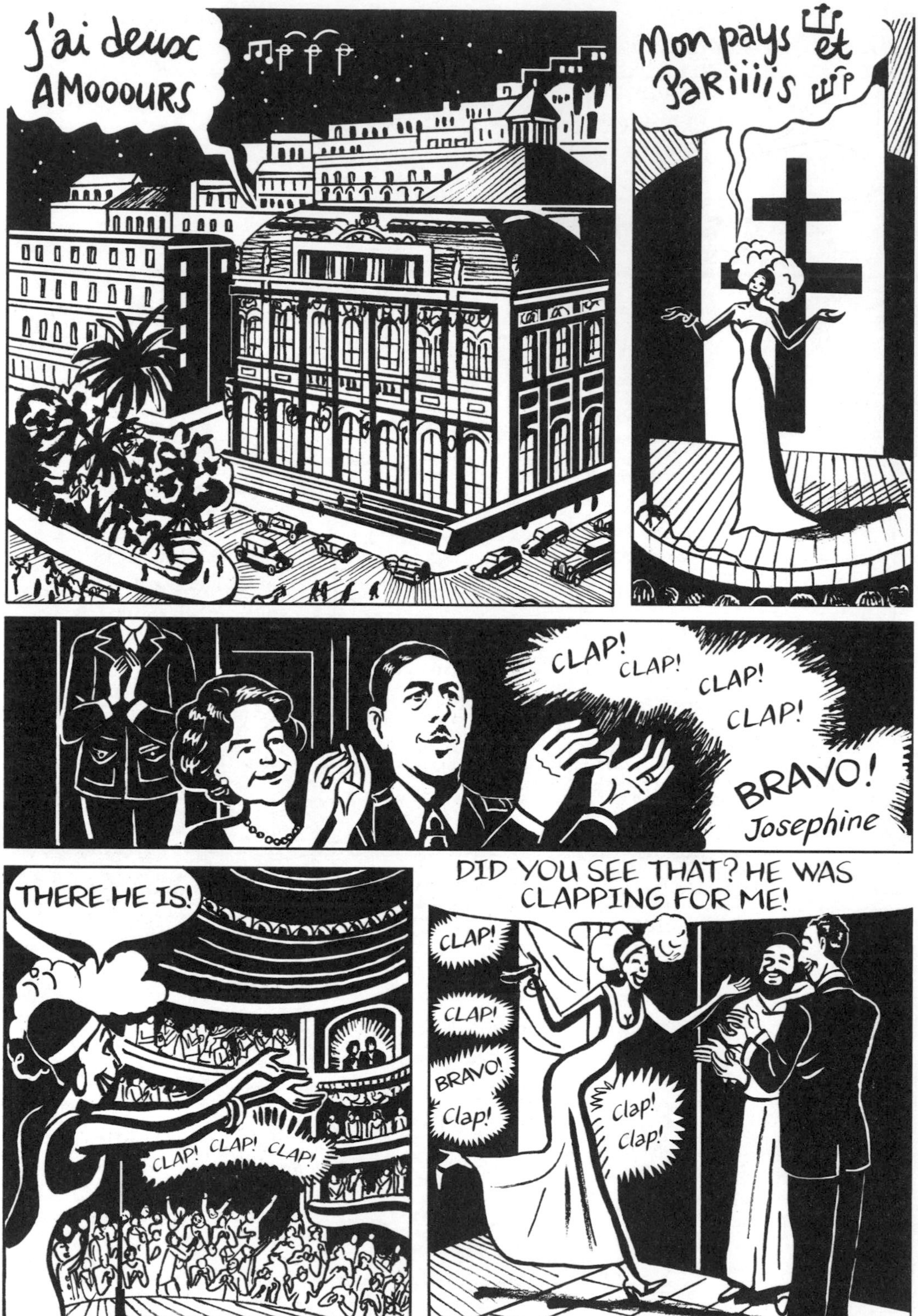
J'ai deux AMooours
Mon pays et Pariiiis
CLAP! CLAP! CLAP! CLAP!
BRAVO! Josephine
THERE HE IS!
CLAP! CLAP! CLAP!
DID YOU SEE THAT? HE WAS CLAPPING FOR ME!
CLAP!
CLAP!
BRAVO! Clap!
Clap! Clap!

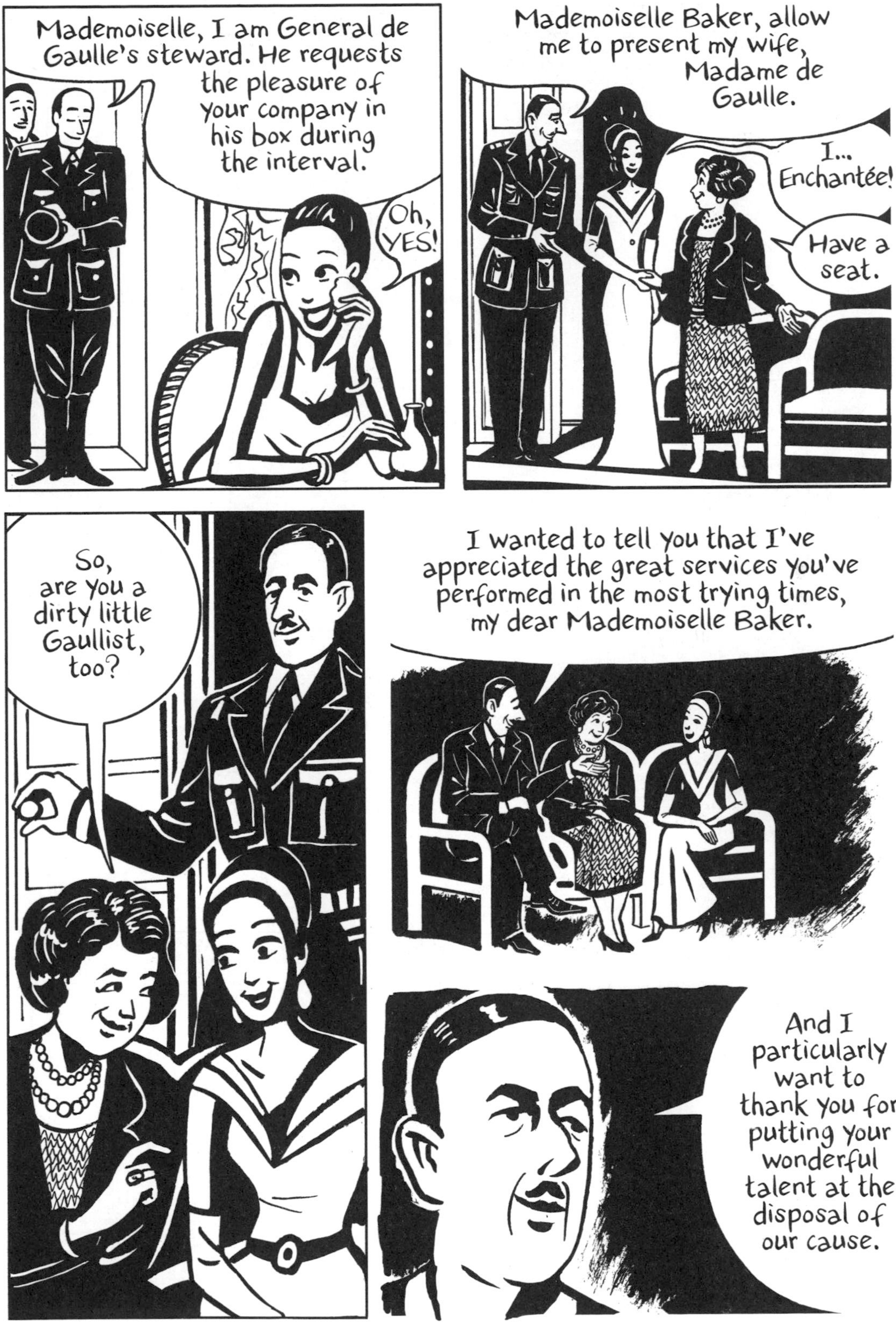
Mademoiselle, I am General de Gaulle's steward. He requests the pleasure of your company in his box during the interval.
Oh, YES!
Mademoiselle Baker, allow me to present my wife, Madame de Gaulle.
I... Enchantée!
Have a seat.
So, are you a dirty little Gaullist, too?
I wanted to tell you that I've appreciated the great services you've performed in the most trying times, my dear Mademoiselle Baker.
And I particularly want to thank you for putting your wonderful talent at the disposal of our cause.

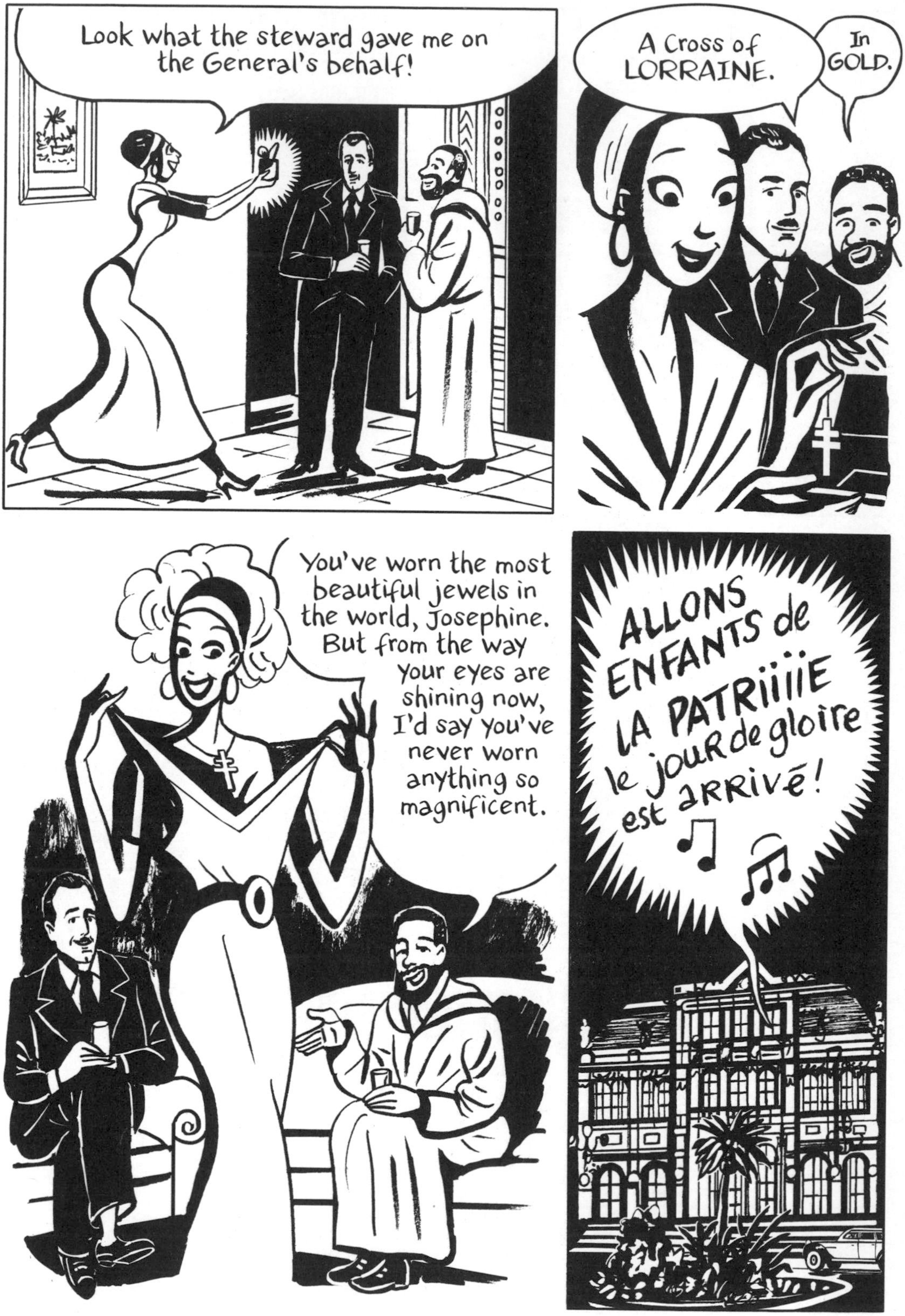
Look what the steward gave me on the General's behalf!
A Cross of LORRAINE.
In GOLD.
You've worn the most beautiful jewels in the world, Josephine. But from the way your eyes are shining now, I'd say you've never worn anything so magnificent.
ALLONS ENFANTS de LA PATRIiiiE le jour de gloire est arrivé!

1944: Arc de Triomphe, Paris, France

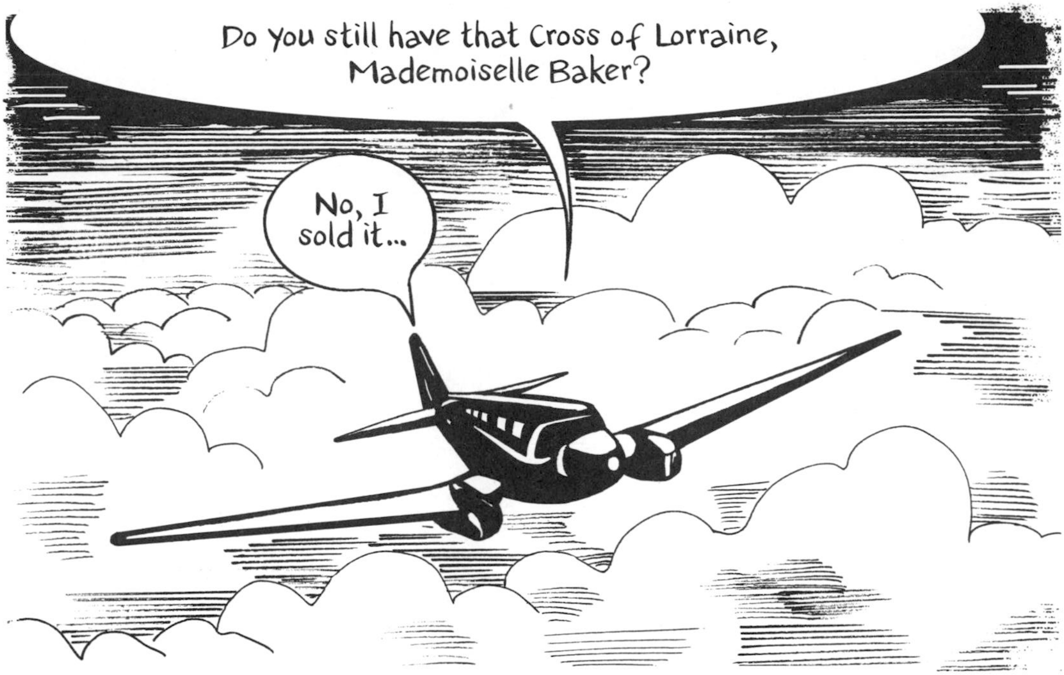
Do you still have that Cross of Lorraine, Mademoiselle Baker?
No, I sold it...

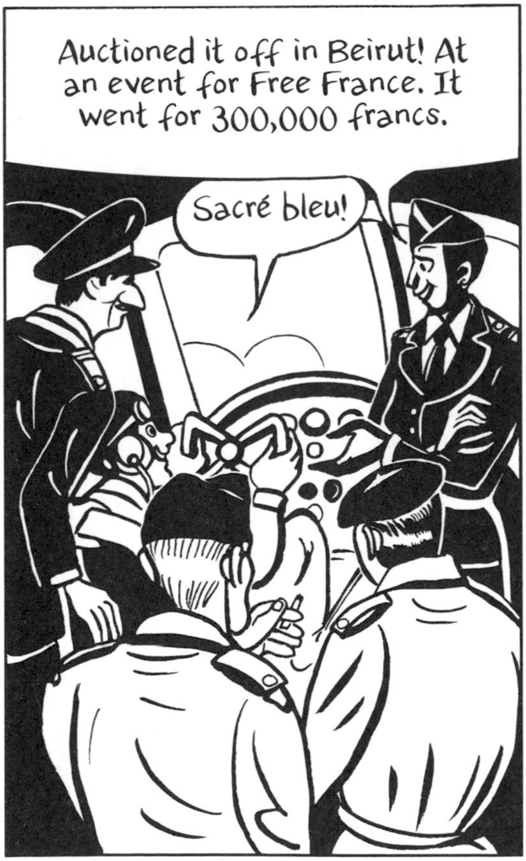
Auctioned it off in Beirut! At an event for Free France. It went for 300,000 francs.
Sacré bleu!

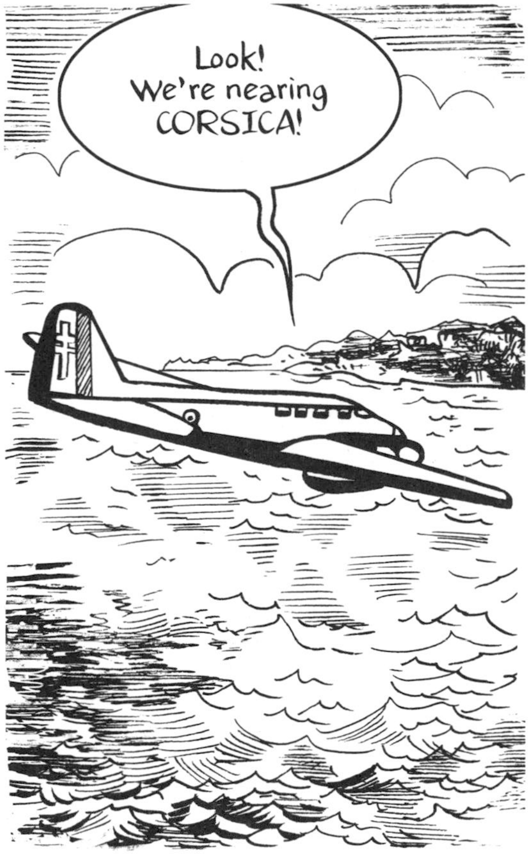
Look! We're nearing CORSICA!

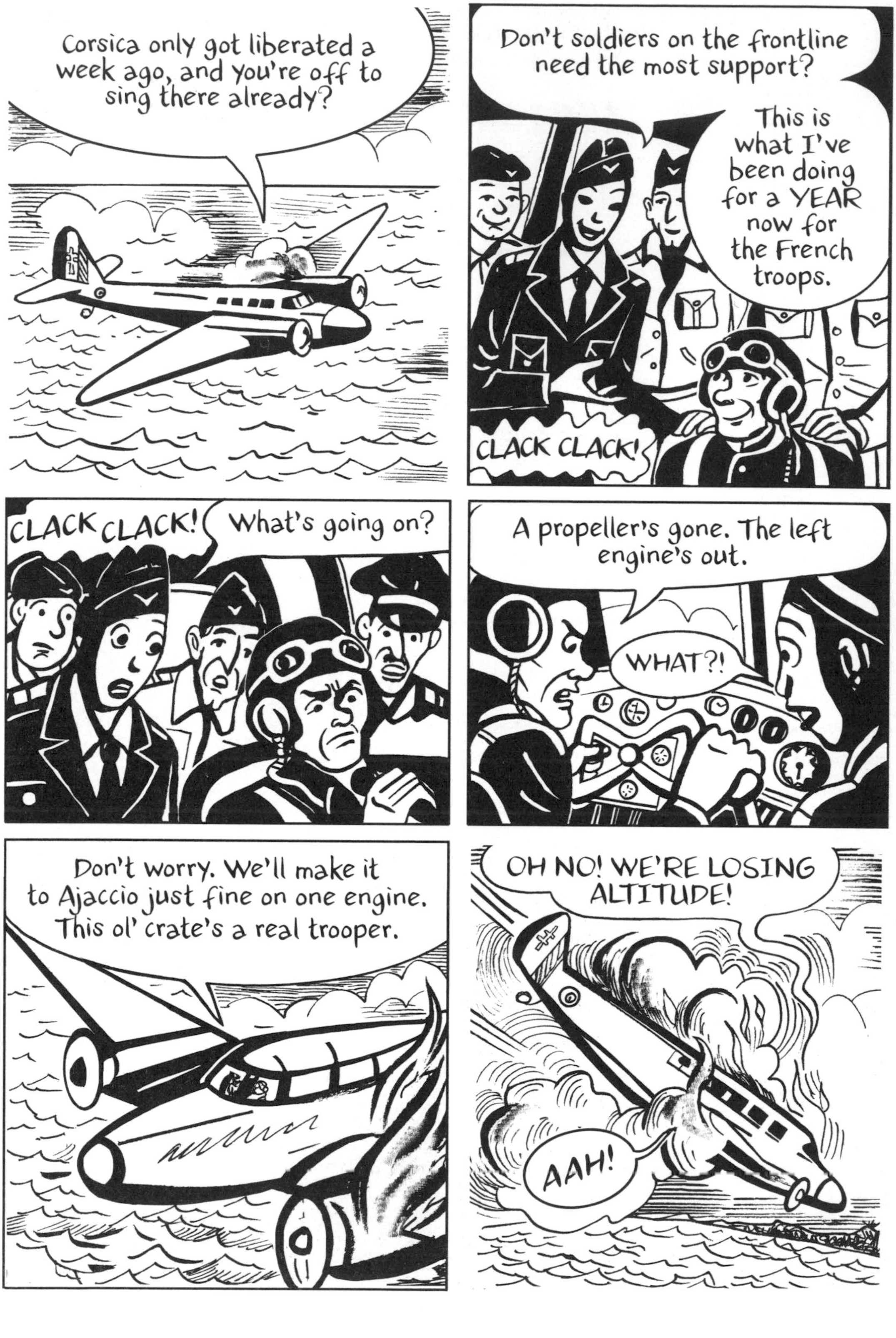
Corsica only got liberated a week ago, and you're off to sing there already?
Don't soldiers on the frontline need the most support?
This is what I've been doing for a YEAR now for the French troops.
CLACK CLACK!
CLACK CLACK!
What's going on?
A propeller's gone. The left engine's out.
WHAT?!
Don't worry. We'll make it to Ajaccio just fine on one engine. This ol' crate's a real trooper.
OH NO! WE'RE LOSING ALTITUDE!
AAH!

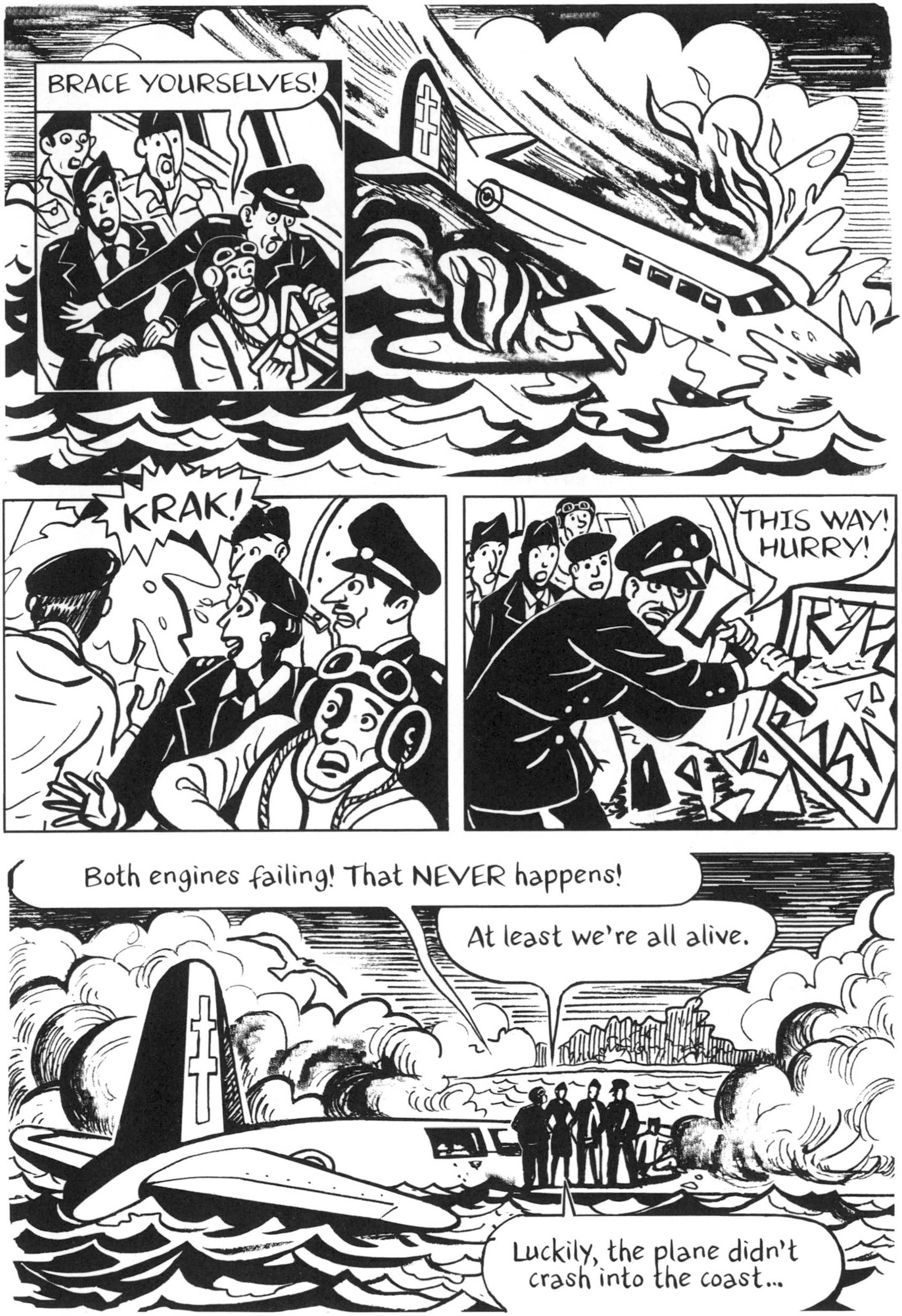
BRACE YOURSELVES!
KRAK!
THIS WAY! HURRY!
Both engines failing! That NEVER happens!
At least we're all alive.
Luckily, the plane didn't crash into the coast...

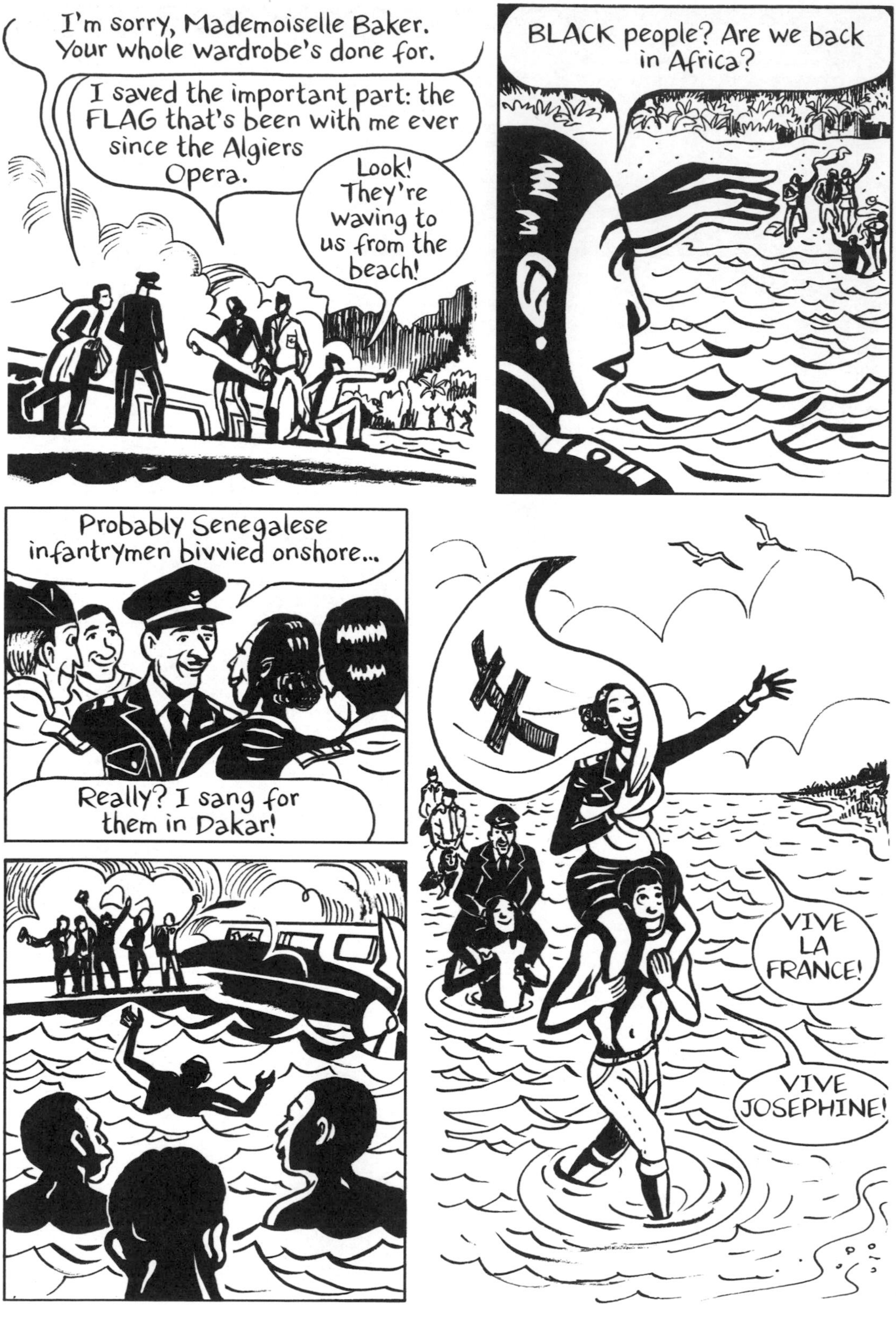
I'm sorry, Mademoiselle Baker. Your whole wardrobe's done for.
I saved the important part: the FLAG that's been with me ever since the Algiers Opera.
Look! They're waving to us from the beach!
BLACK people? Are we back in Africa?
Probably Senegalese infantrymen bivvied onshore...
Really? I sang for them in Dakar!
VIVE LA FRANCE!
VIVE JOSEPHINE!

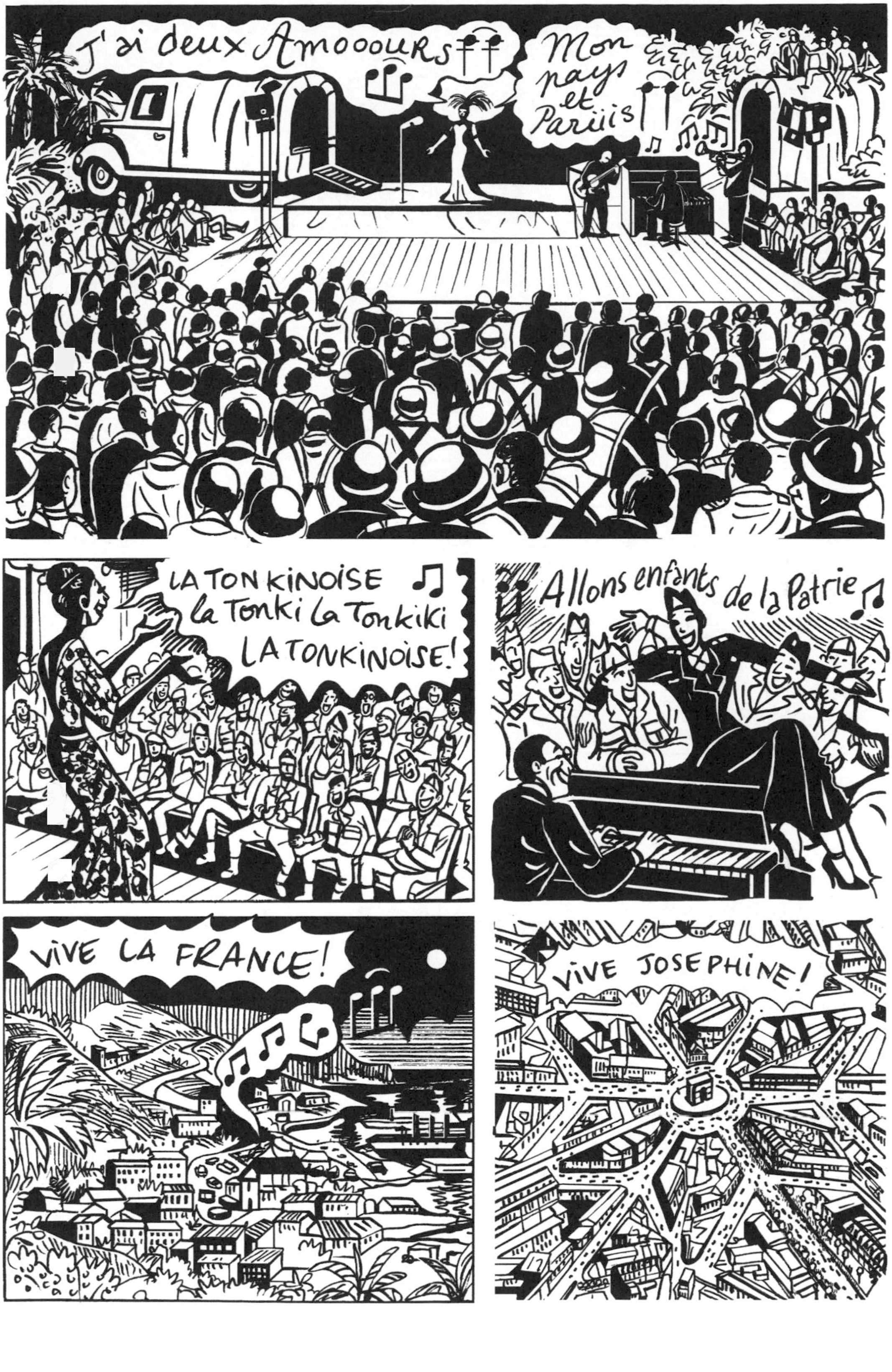
J'ai deux Amooours
Mon pays et Pariiis
LA TONKINOISE
la Tonki la Tonkiki
LA TONKINOISE!
Allons enfants de la Patrie
VIVE LA FRANCE!
VIVE JOSEPHINE!

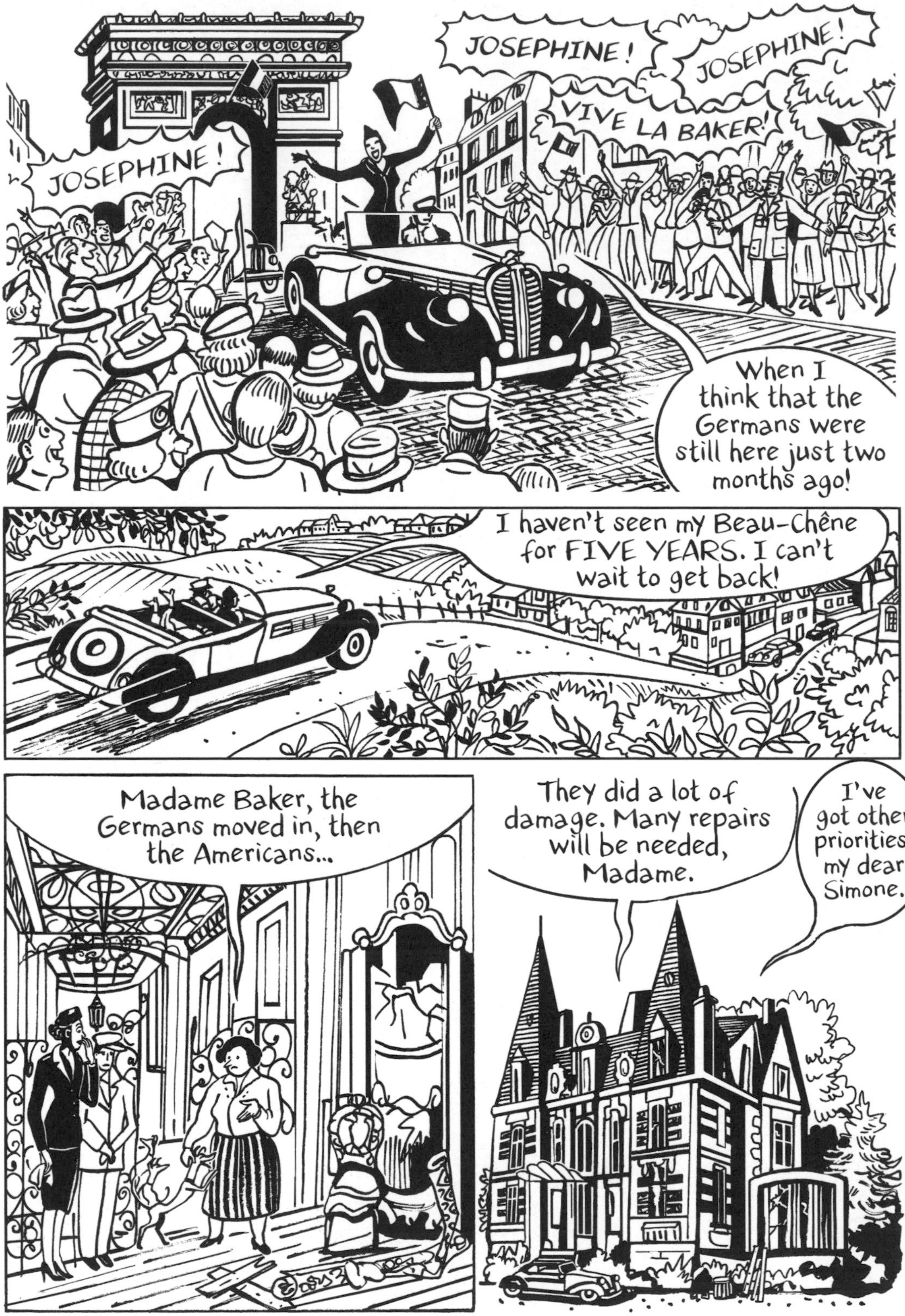
JOSEPHINE!
JOSEPHINE!
JOSEPHINE!
VIVE LA BAKER!
When I think that the Germans were still here just two months ago!
I haven't seen my Beau-Chêne for FIVE YEARS. I can't wait to get back!
Madame Baker, the Germans moved in, then the Americans...
They did a lot of damage. Many repairs will be needed, Madame.
I've got other priorities, my dear Simone.

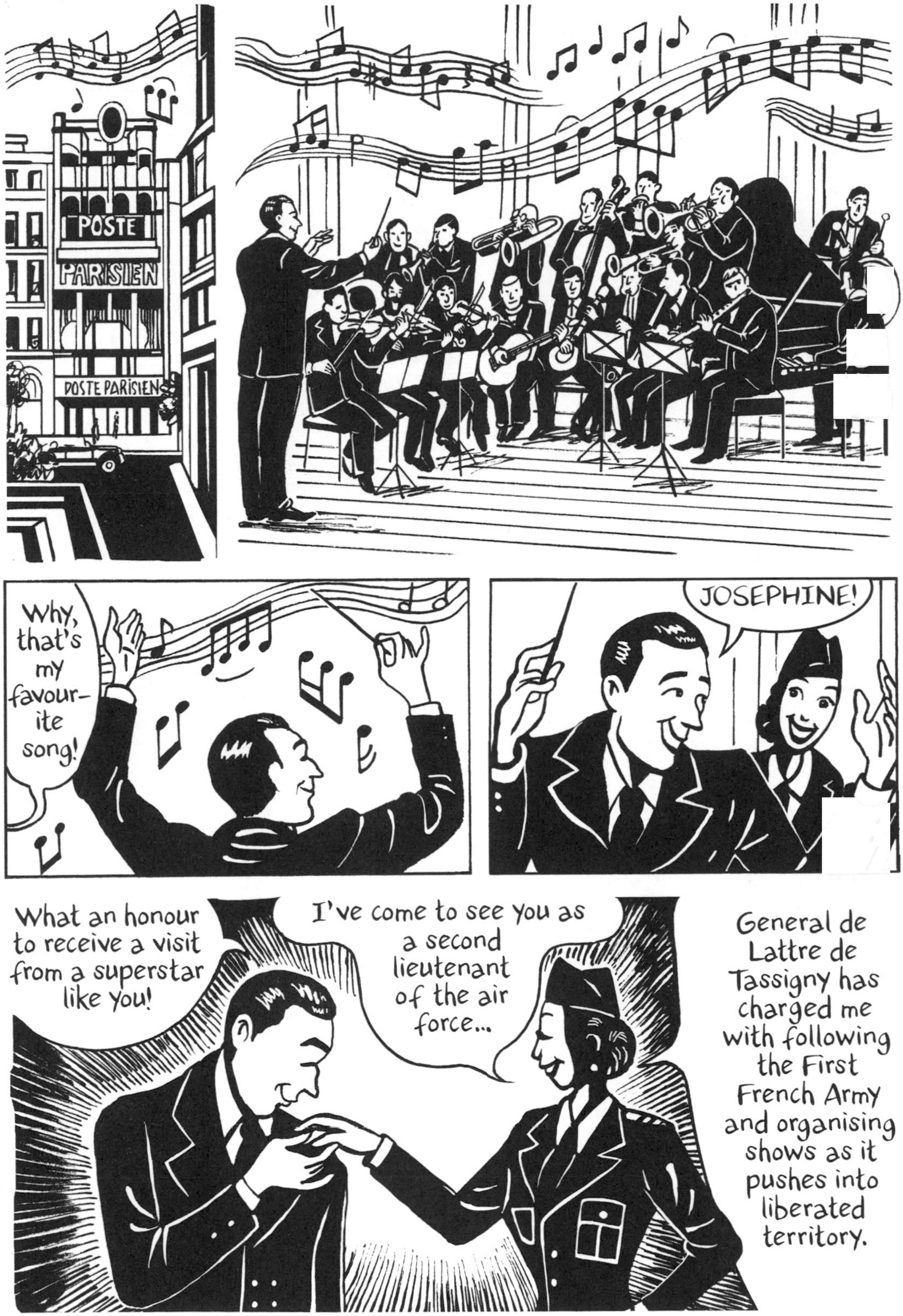
POSTE
PARISIEN
POSTE PARISIEN
Why, that's my favourite song!
JOSEPHINE!
What an honour to receive a visit from a superstar like you!
I've come to see you as a second lieutenant of the air force...
General de Lattre de Tassigny has charged me with following the First French Army and organising shows as it pushes into liberated territory.

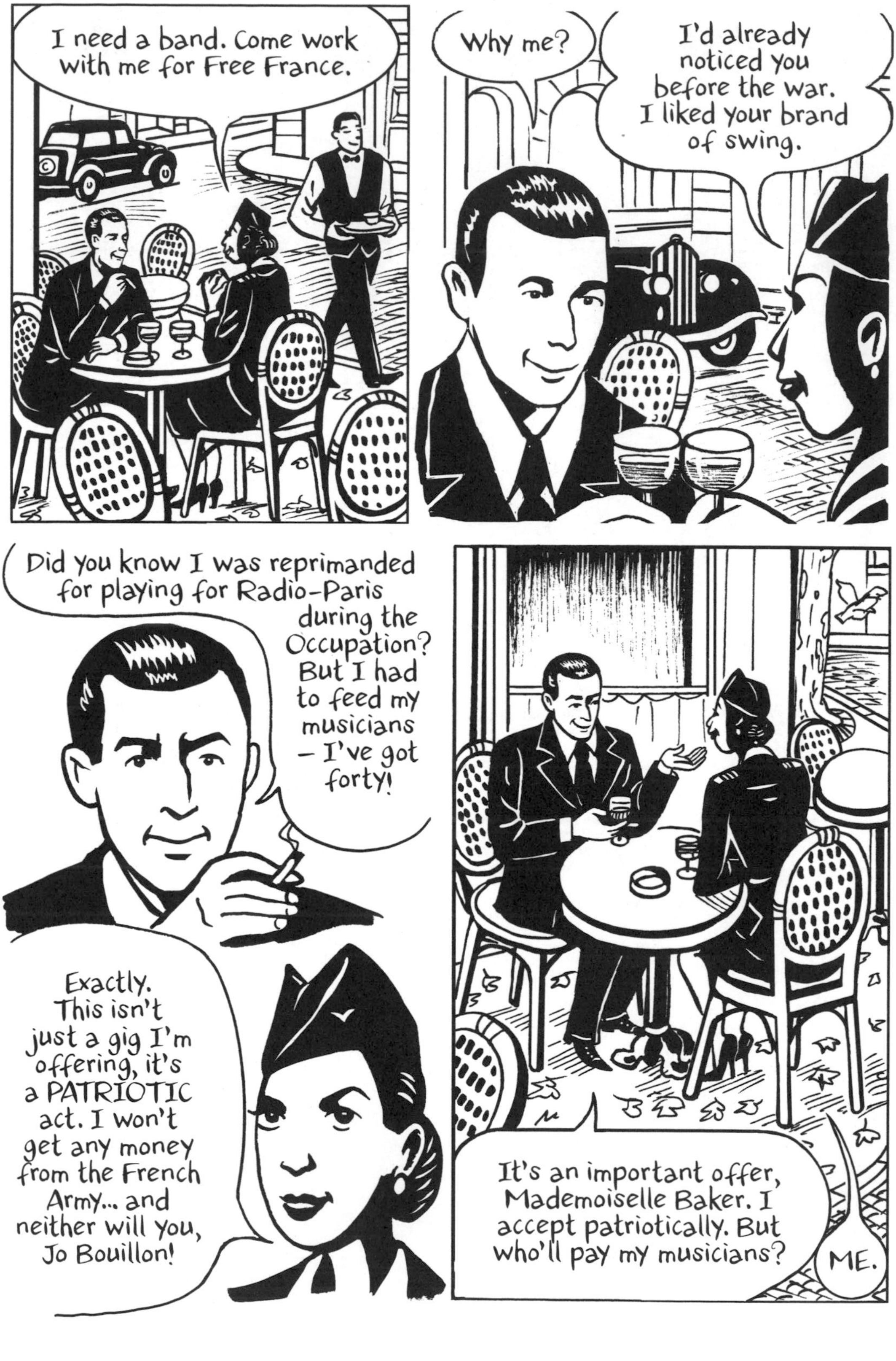

I need a band. Come work with me for Free France.
Why me?
I'd already noticed you before the war. I liked your brand of swing.
Did you know I was reprimanded for playing for Radio-Paris during the Occupation? But I had to feed my musicians – I've got forty!
Exactly. This isn't just a gig I'm offering, it's a PATRIOTIC act. I won't get any money from the French Army... and neither will you, Jo Bouillon!
It's an important offer, Mademoiselle Baker. I accept patriotically. But who'll pay my musicians?
ME.

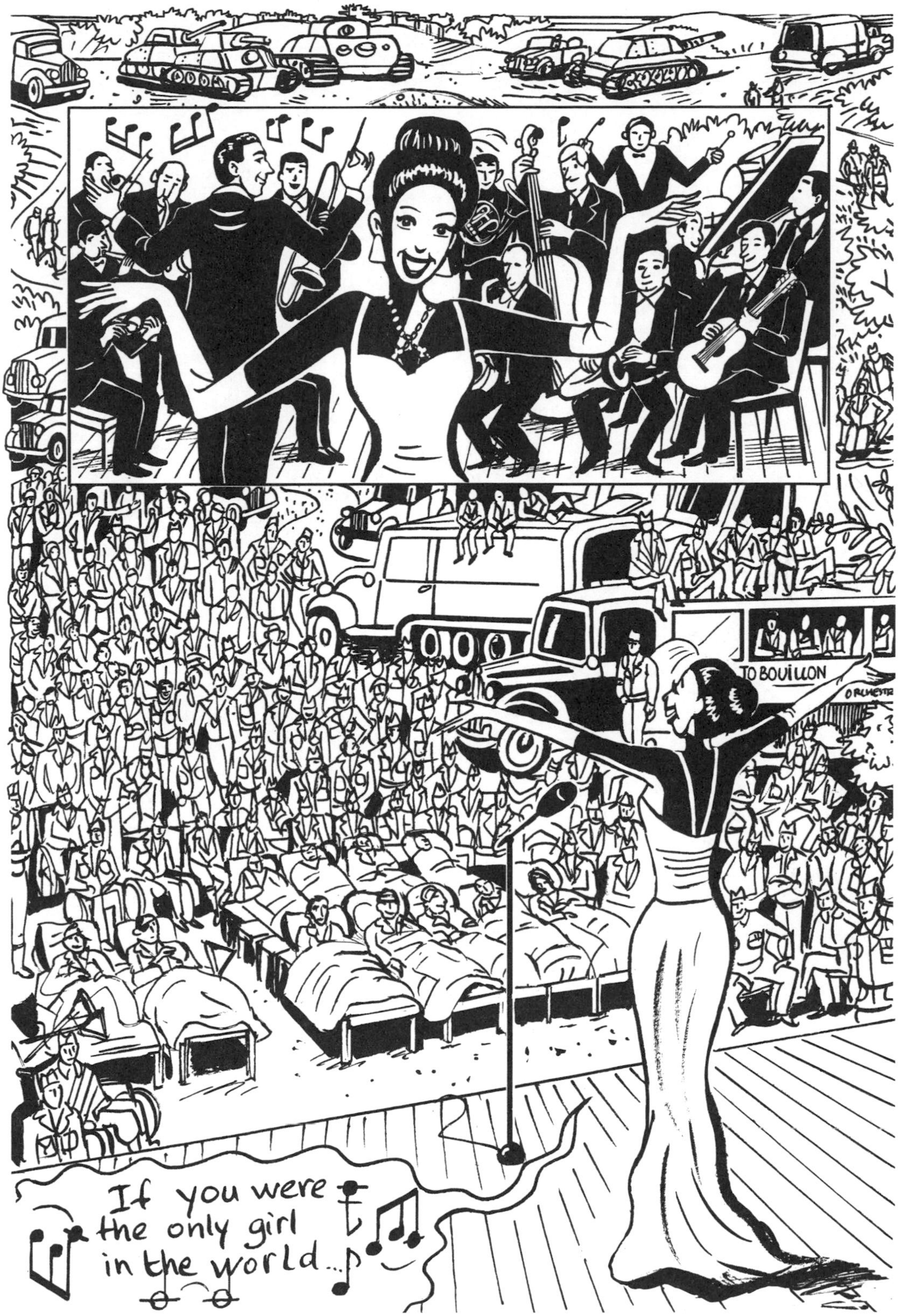
TO BOUILLON
If you were the only girl in the world...

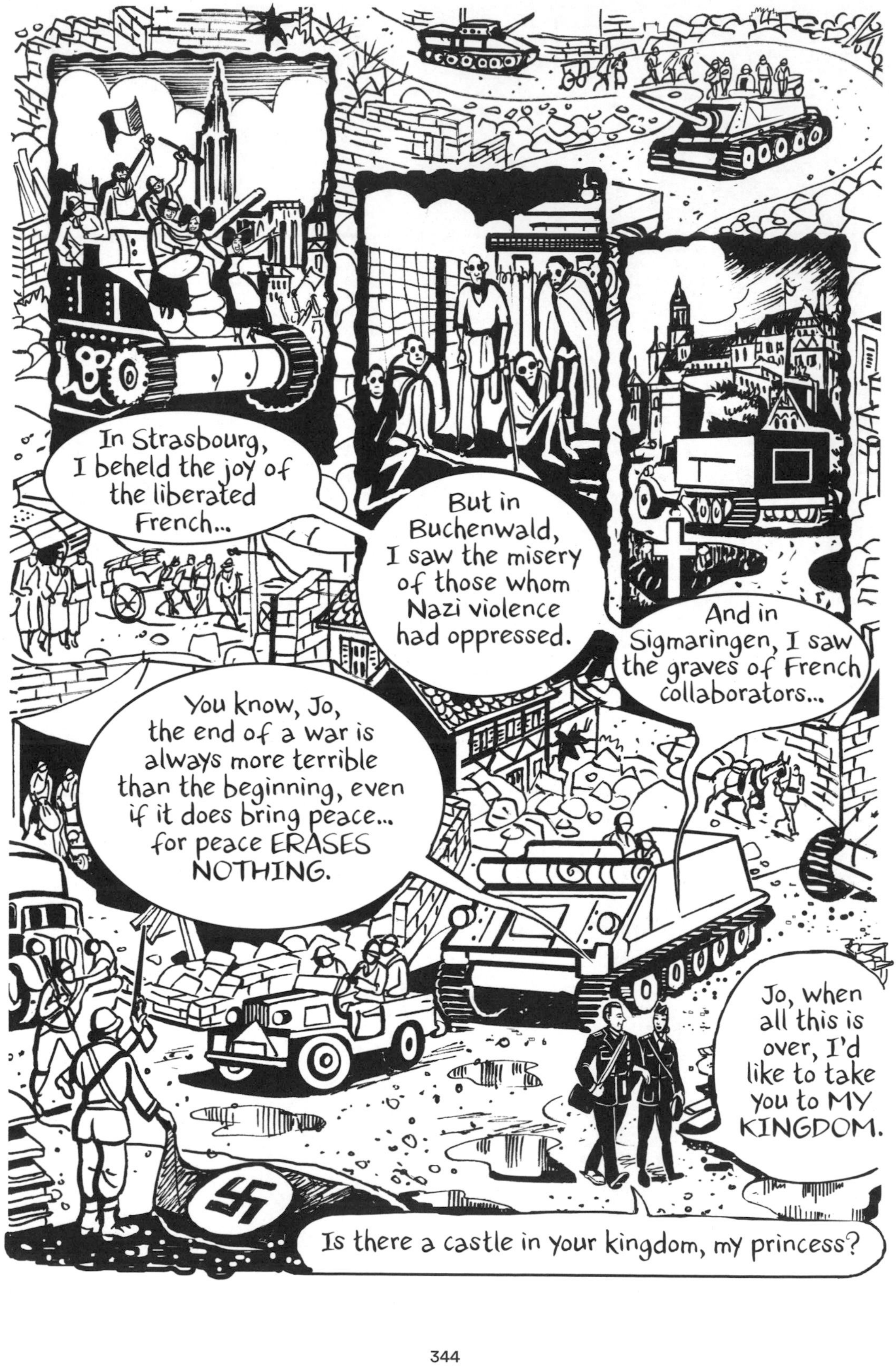
In Strasbourg, I beheld the joy of the liberated French...
But in Buchenwald, I saw the misery of those whom Nazi violence had oppressed.
And in Sigmaringen, I saw the graves of French collaborators...
You know, Jo, the end of a war is always more terrible than the beginning, even if it does bring peace... for peace ERASES NOTHING.
Jo, when all this is over, I'd like to take you to MY KINGDOM.
Is there a castle in your kingdom, my princess?

1947: Milandes Chapel, Périgord, France

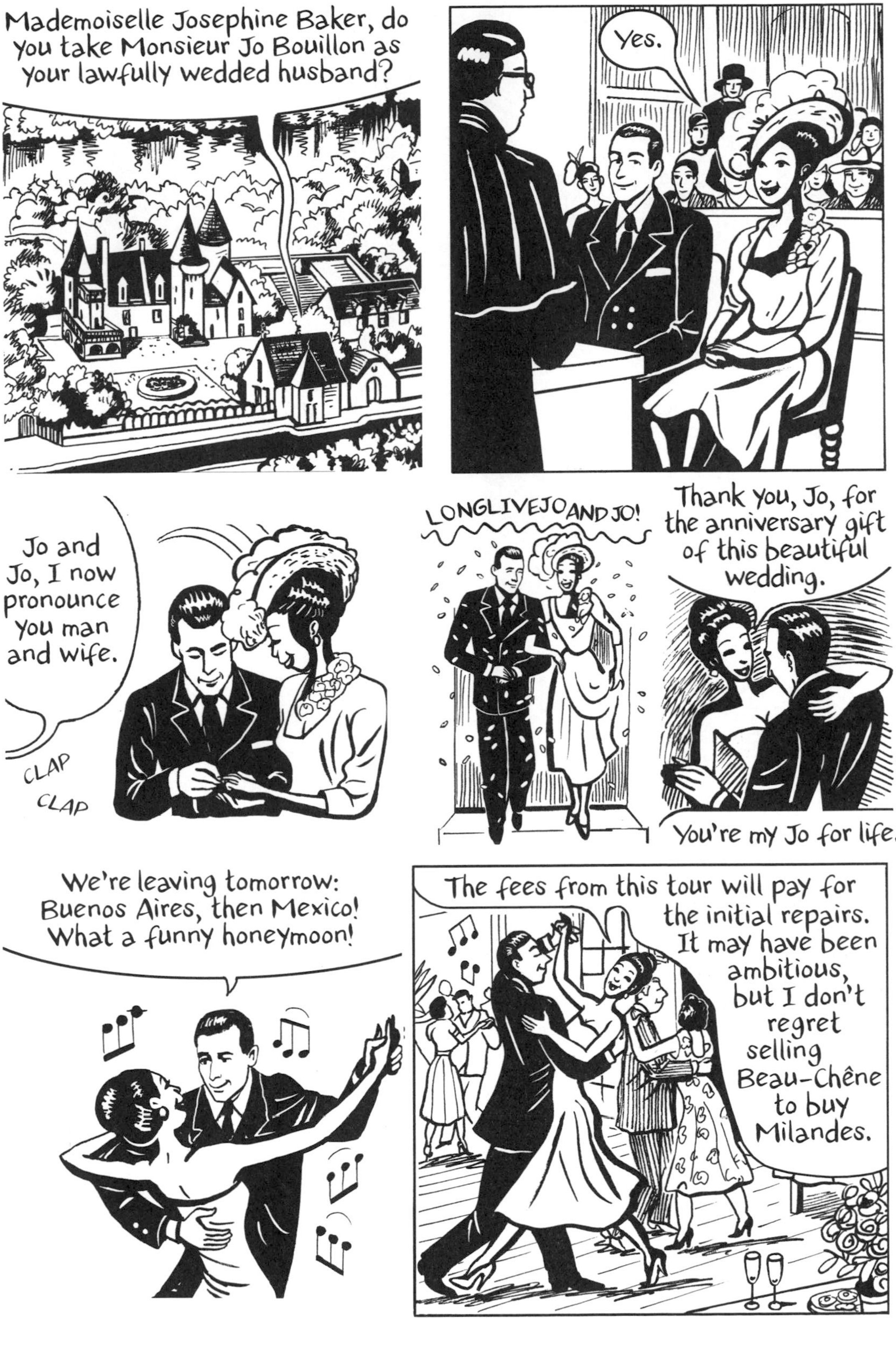
Mademoiselle Josephine Baker, do you take Monsieur Jo Bouillon as your lawfully wedded husband?
Yes.
Jo and Jo, I now pronounce you man and wife.
CLAP
CLAP
LONGLIVEJOANDJO!
Thank you, Jo, for the anniversary gift of this beautiful wedding.
You're my Jo for life.
We're leaving tomorrow: Buenos Aires, then Mexico! What a funny honeymoon!
The fees from this tour will pay for the initial repairs. It may have been ambitious, but I don't regret selling Beau-Chêne to buy Milandes.

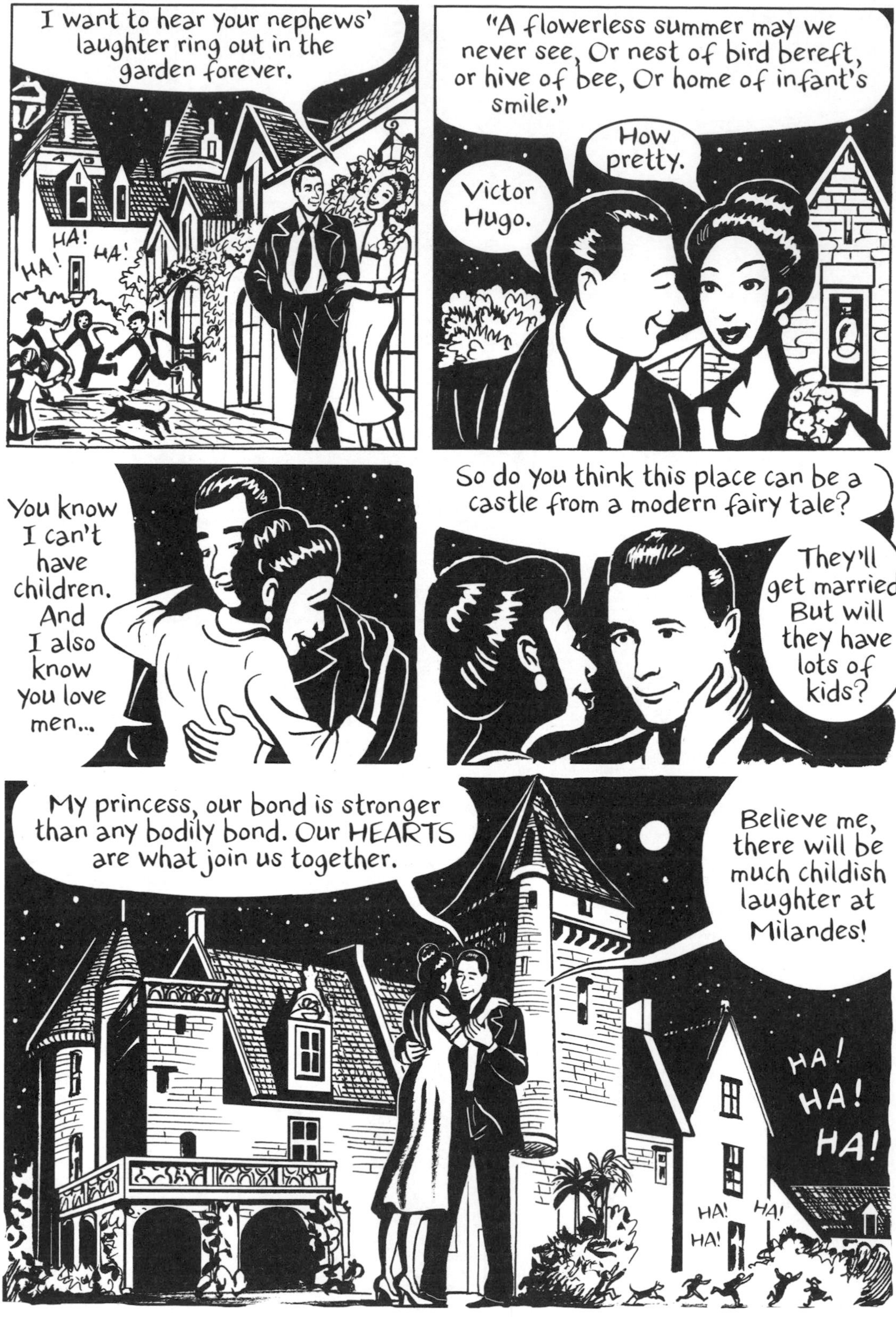
I want to hear your nephews' laughter ring out in the garden forever.
HA! HA! HA!
"A flowerless summer may we never see, Or nest of bird bereft, or hive of bee, Or home of infant's smile."
Victor Hugo.
How pretty.
You know I can't have children. And I also know you love men...
So do you think this place can be a castle from a modern fairy tale?
They'll get married. But will they have lots of kids?
My princess, our bond is stronger than any bodily bond. Our HEARTS are what join us together.
Believe me, there will be much childish laughter at Milandes!
HA! HA! HA!
HA! HA! HA!

1949: Milandes Farm, Périgord, France

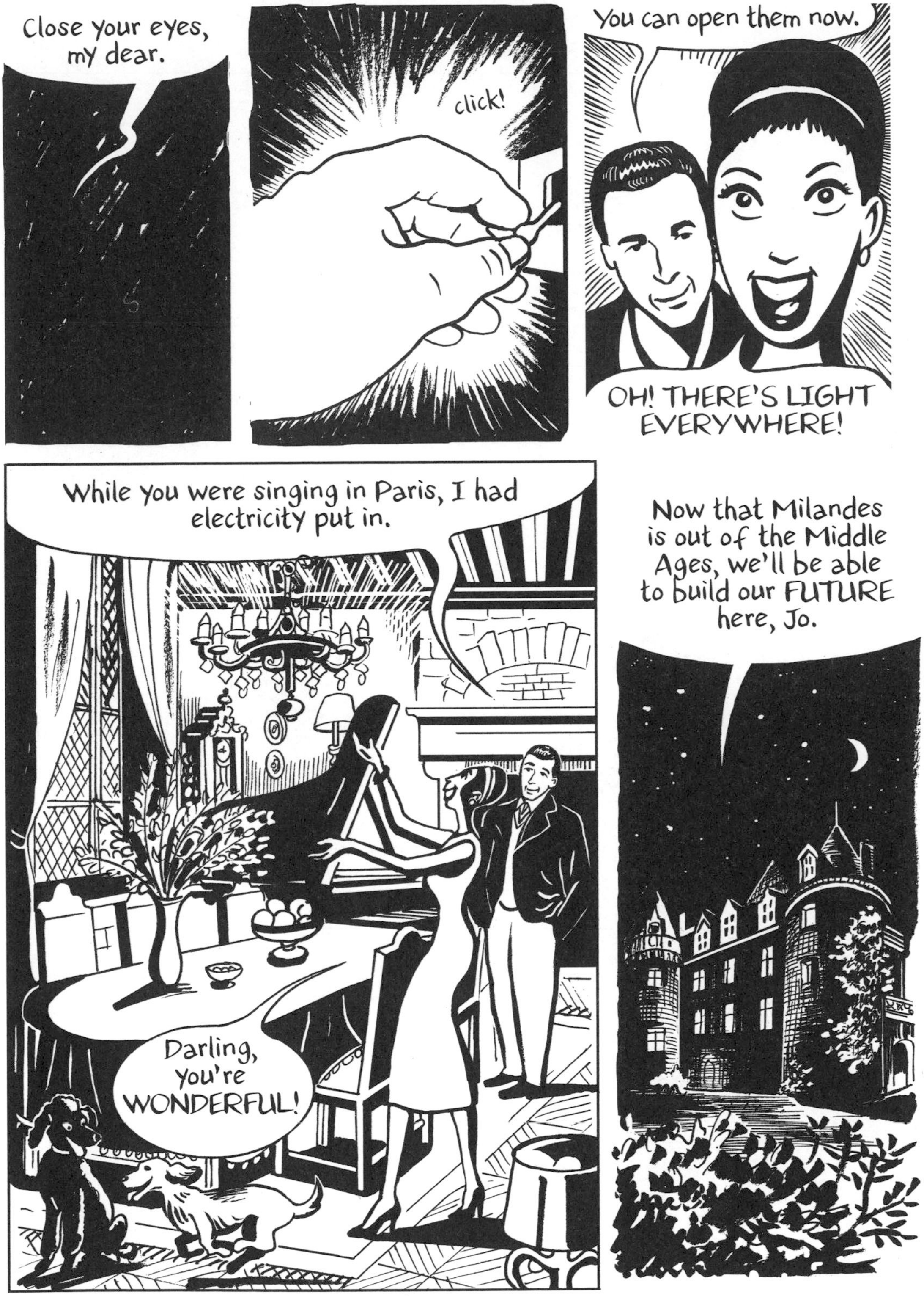
Close your eyes, my dear.
click!
You can open them now.
OH! THERE'S LIGHT EVERYWHERE!
While you were singing in Paris, I had electricity put in.
Darling, you're WONDERFUL!
Now that Milandes is out of the Middle Ages, we'll be able to build our FUTURE here, Jo.

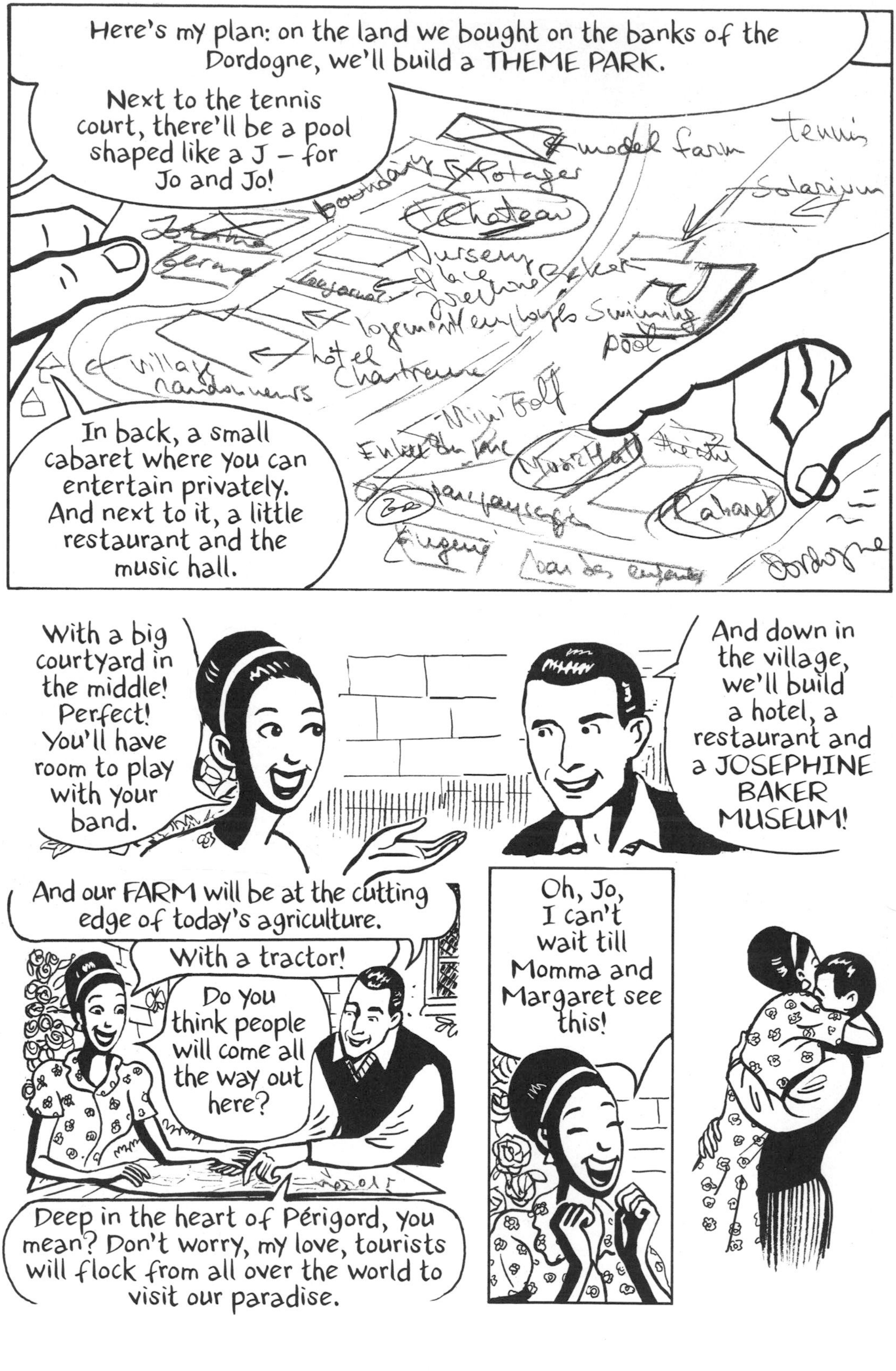

Here's my plan: on the land we bought on the banks of the Dordogne, we'll build a THEME PARK.
Next to the tennis court, there'll be a pool shaped like a J – for Jo and Jo!
model farm
Tennis
boundary
Potager
Chateau
Swimming pool
Dordogne
In back, a small cabaret where you can entertain privately. And next to it, a little restaurant and the music hall.
With a big courtyard in the middle! Perfect! You'll have room to play with your band.
And down in the village, we'll build a hotel, a restaurant and a JOSEPHINE BAKER MUSEUM!
And our FARM will be at the cutting edge of today's agriculture.
With a tractor!
Do you think people will come all the way out here?
Deep in the heart of Périgord, you mean? Don't worry, my love, tourists will flock from all over the world to visit our paradise.
Oh, Jo, I can't wait till Momma and Margaret see this!

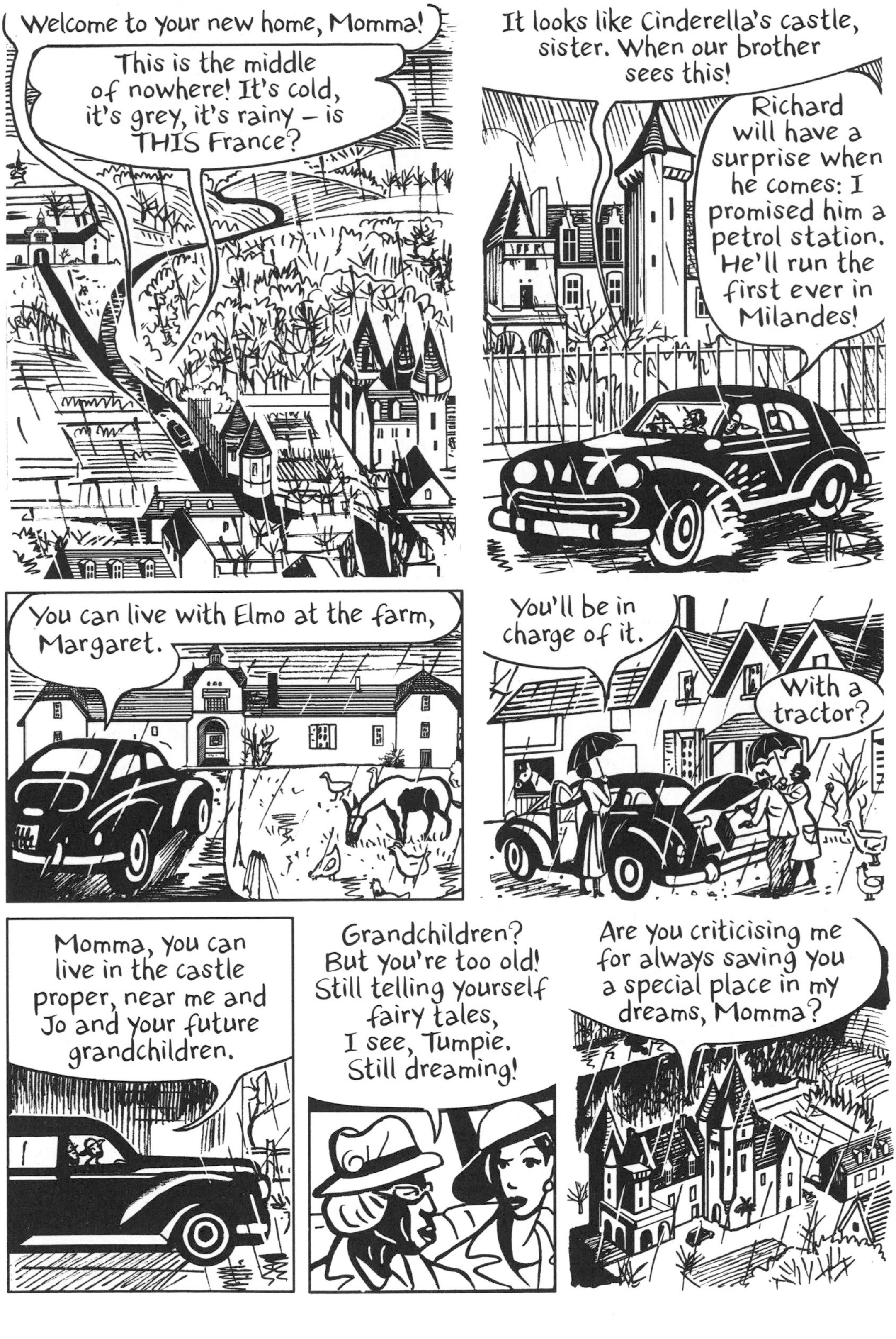
Welcome to your new home, Momma!
This is the middle of nowhere! It's cold, it's grey, it's rainy – is THIS France?
It looks like Cinderella's castle, sister. When our brother sees this!
Richard will have a surprise when he comes: I promised him a petrol station. He'll run the first ever in Milandes!
You can live with Elmo at the farm, Margaret.
You'll be in charge of it.
With a tractor?
Momma, you can live in the castle proper, near me and Jo and your future grandchildren.
Grandchildren? But you're too old! Still telling yourself fairy tales, I see, Tumpie. Still dreaming!
Are you criticising me for always saving you a special place in my dreams, Momma?

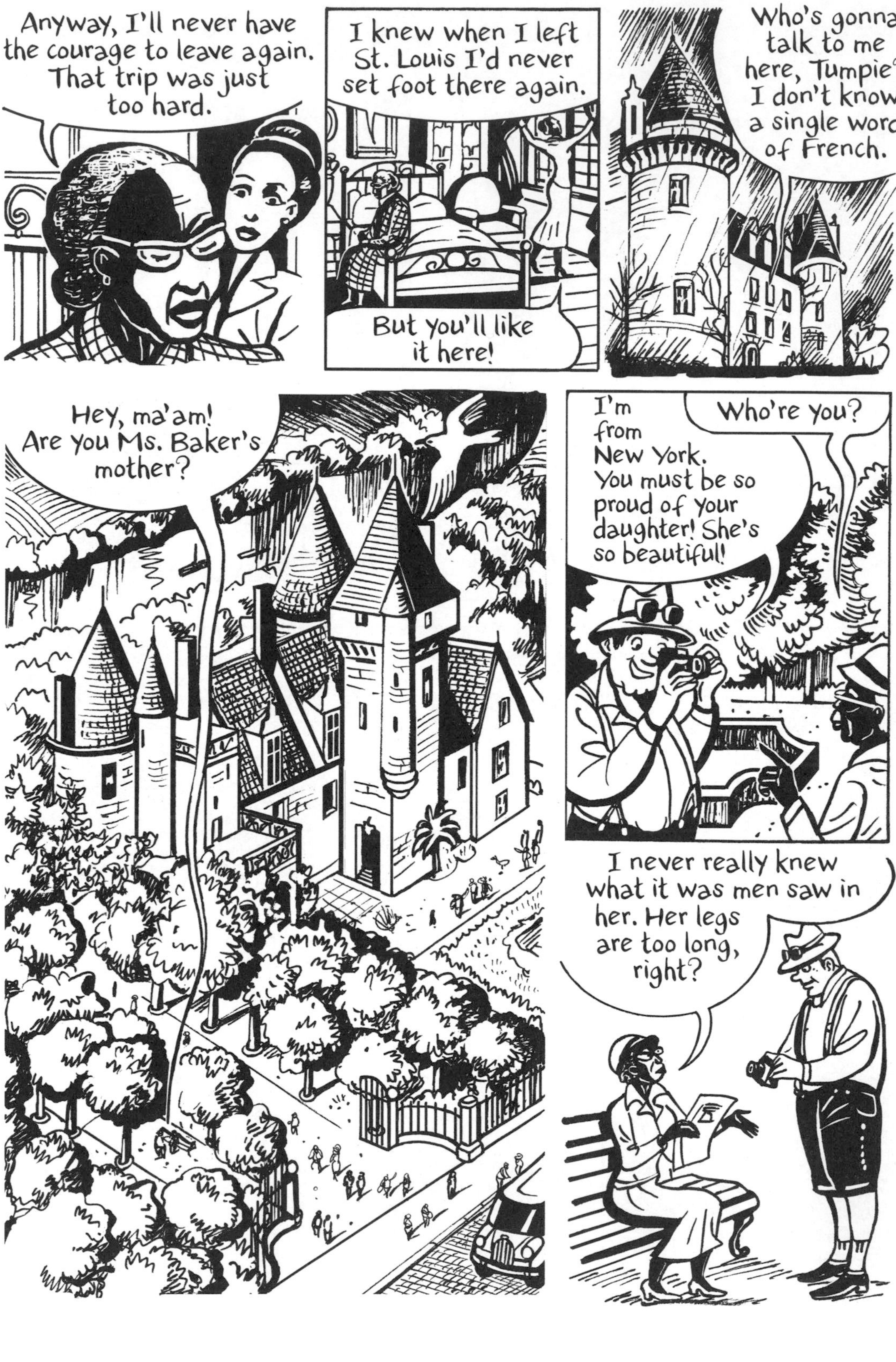
Anyway, I'll never have the courage to leave again. That trip was just too hard.
I knew when I left St. Louis I'd never set foot there again.
But you'll like it here!
Who's gonna talk to me here, Tumpie? I don't know a single word of French.
Hey, ma'am! Are you Ms. Baker's mother?
Who're you?
I'm from New York. You must be so proud of your daughter! She's so beautiful!
I never really knew what it was men saw in her. Her legs are too long, right?

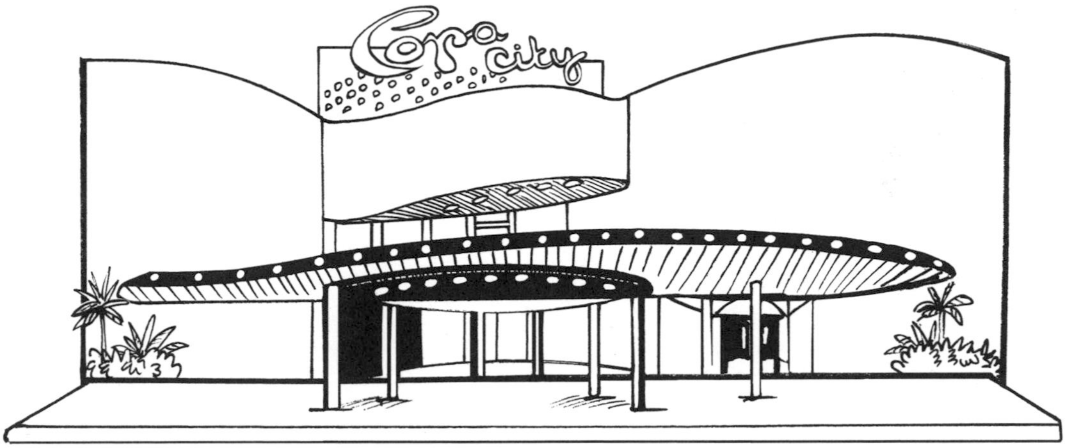
Copa city

1951: Copa City Club, Miami, Florida, USA

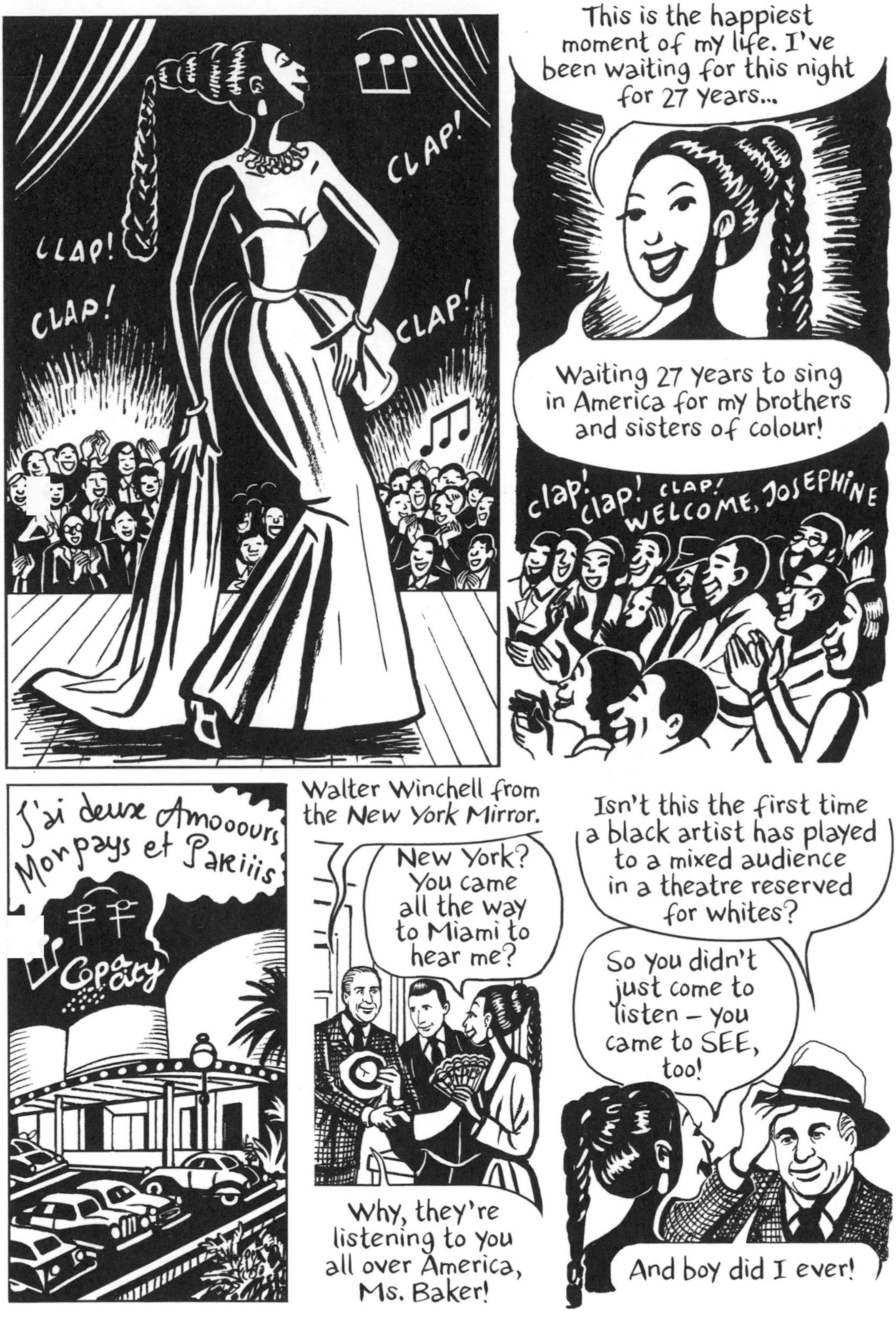
CLAP!
CLAP!
CLAP!
CLAP!
This is the happiest moment of my life. I've been waiting for this night for 27 years...
Waiting 27 years to sing in America for my brothers and sisters of colour!
clap! clap! CLAP! WELCOME, JOSEPHINE
J'ai deux Amooours
Mon pays et Pariiis
Copa city
Walter Winchell from the New York Mirror.
New York? You came all the way to Miami to hear me?
Why, they're listening to you all over America, Ms. Baker!
Isn't this the first time a black artist has played to a mixed audience in a theatre reserved for whites?
So you didn't just come to listen – you came to SEE, too!
And boy did I ever!

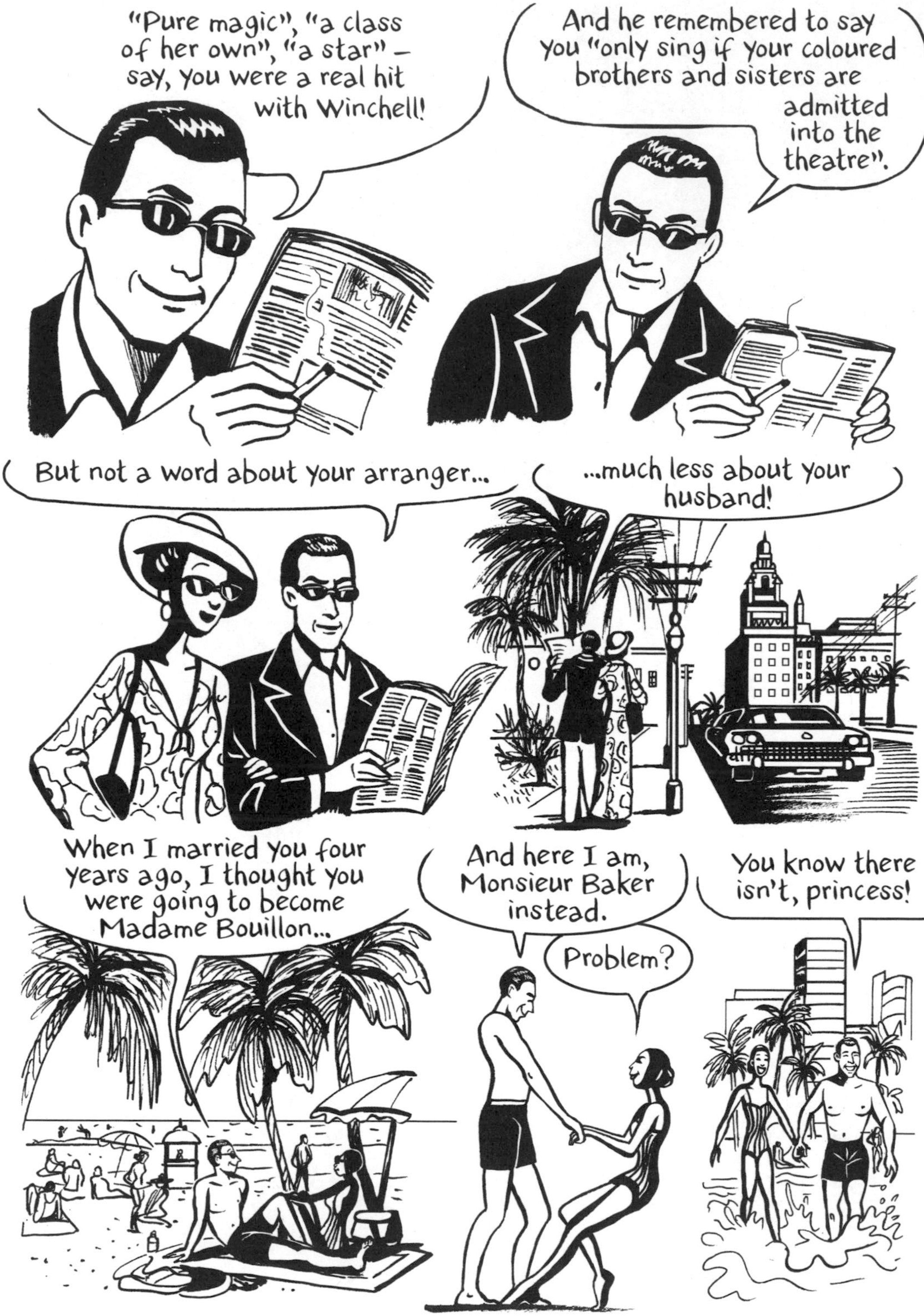
"Pure magic", "a class of her own", "a star" – say, you were a real hit with Winchell!
And he remembered to say you "only sing if your coloured brothers and sisters are admitted into the theatre".
But not a word about your arranger...
...much less about your husband!
When I married you four years ago, I thought you were going to become Madame Bouillon...
And here I am, Monsieur Baker instead.
Problem?
You know there isn't, princess!

STORK CLUB
STORK CLUB
STORK CLUB
STORK CLUB

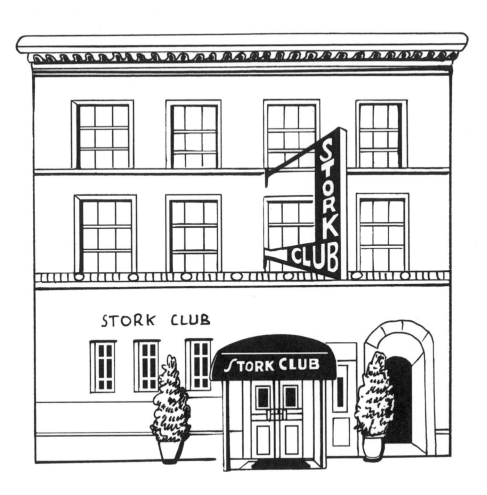

1951: Stork Club, New York, USA

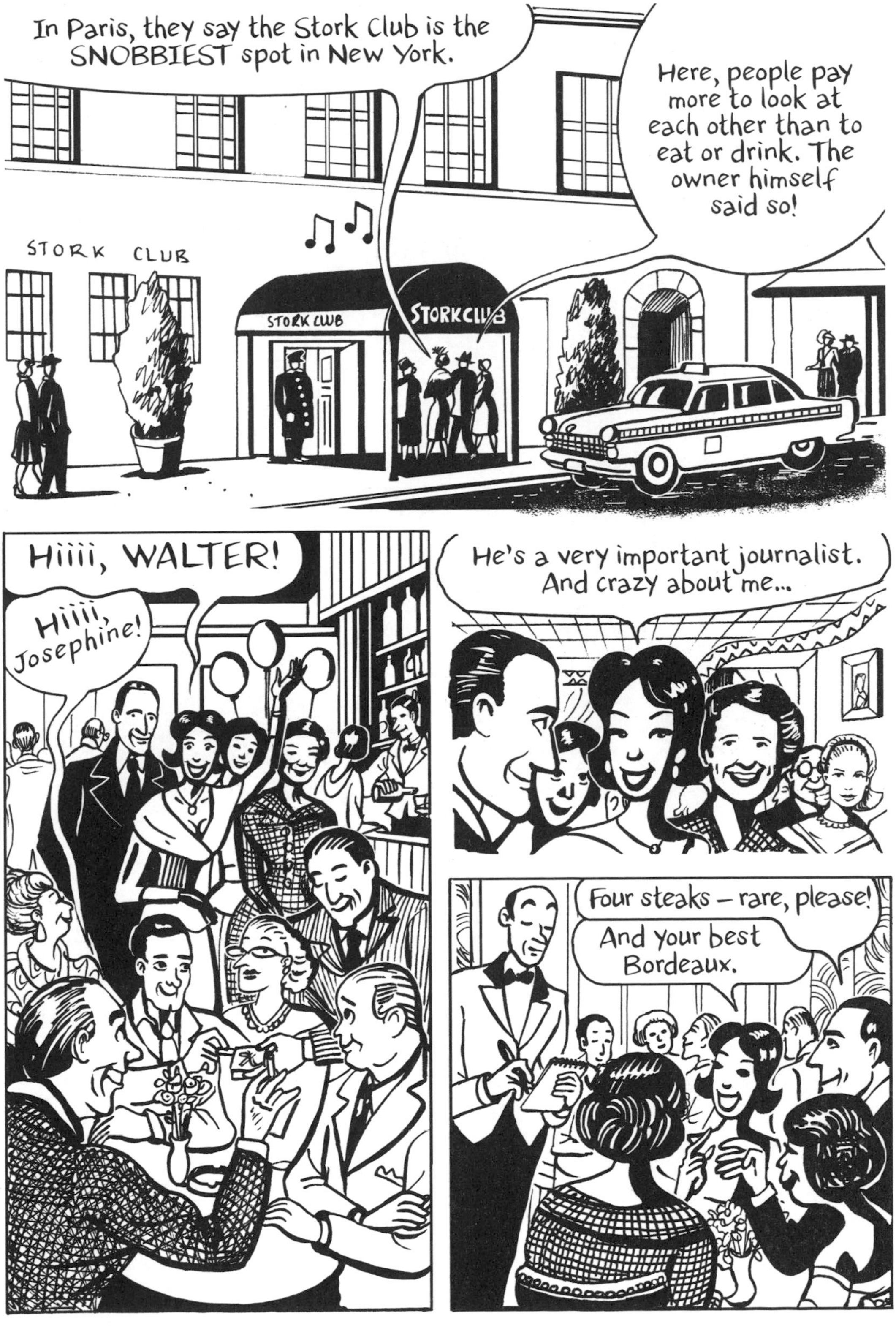
In Paris, they say the Stork Club is the SNOBBIEST spot in New York.
Here, people pay more to look at each other than to eat or drink. The owner himself said so!
STORK CLUB
STORK CLUB
STORKCLUB
Hiiii, WALTER!
Hiiii, Josephine!
He's a very important journalist. And crazy about me...
Four steaks – rare, please!
And your best Bordeaux.

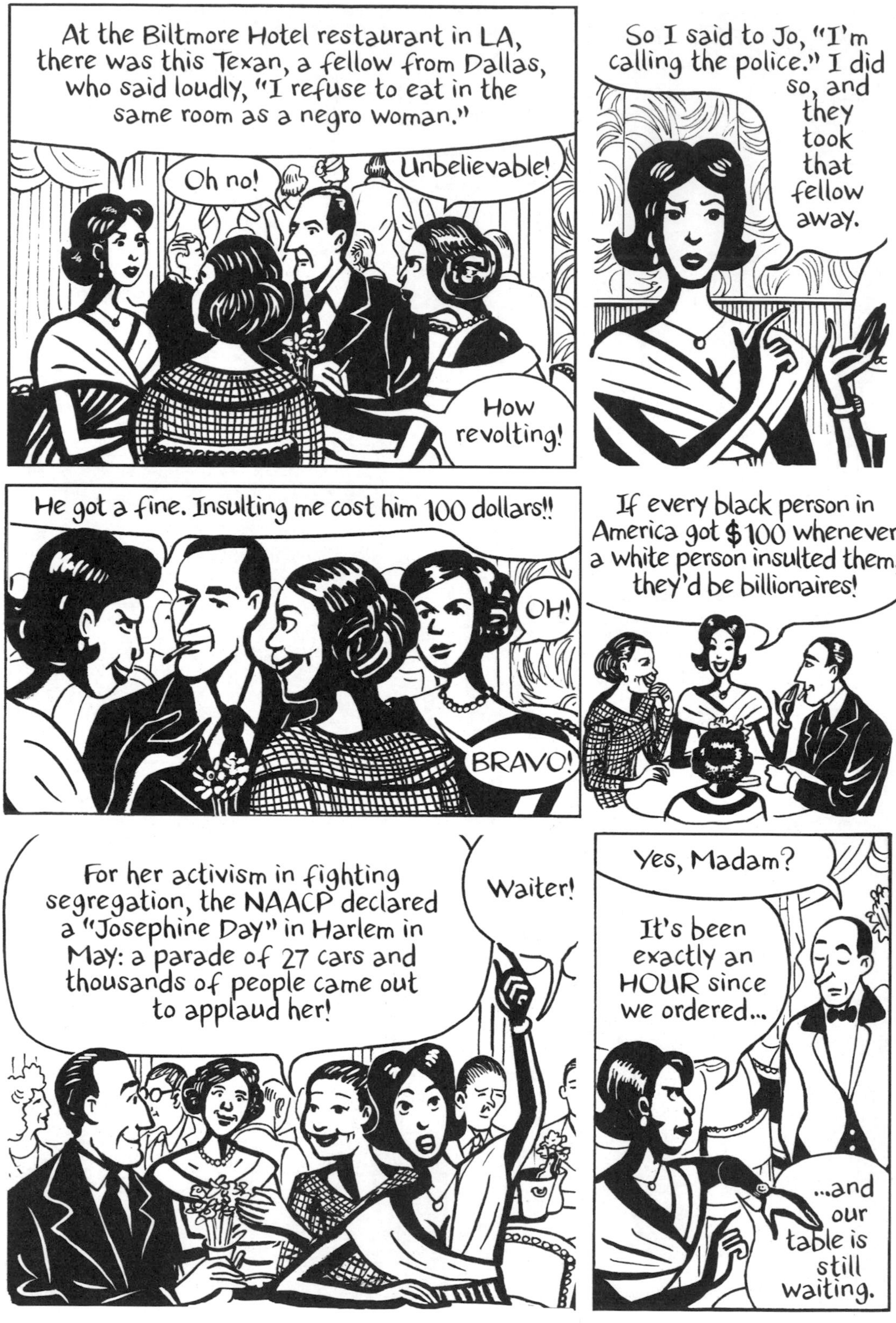
At the Biltmore Hotel restaurant in LA, there was this Texan, a fellow from Dallas, who said loudly, "I refuse to eat in the same room as a negro woman."
Oh no!
Unbelievable!
How revolting!
So I said to Jo, "I'm calling the police." I did so, and they took that fellow away.
He got a fine. Insulting me cost him 100 dollars!!
OH!
BRAVO!
If every black person in America got $100 whenever a white person insulted them, they'd be billionaires!
For her activism in fighting segregation, the NAACP declared a "Josephine Day" in Harlem in May: a parade of 27 cars and thousands of people came out to applaud her!
Waiter!
Yes, Madam?
It's been exactly an HOUR since we ordered...
...and our table is still waiting.

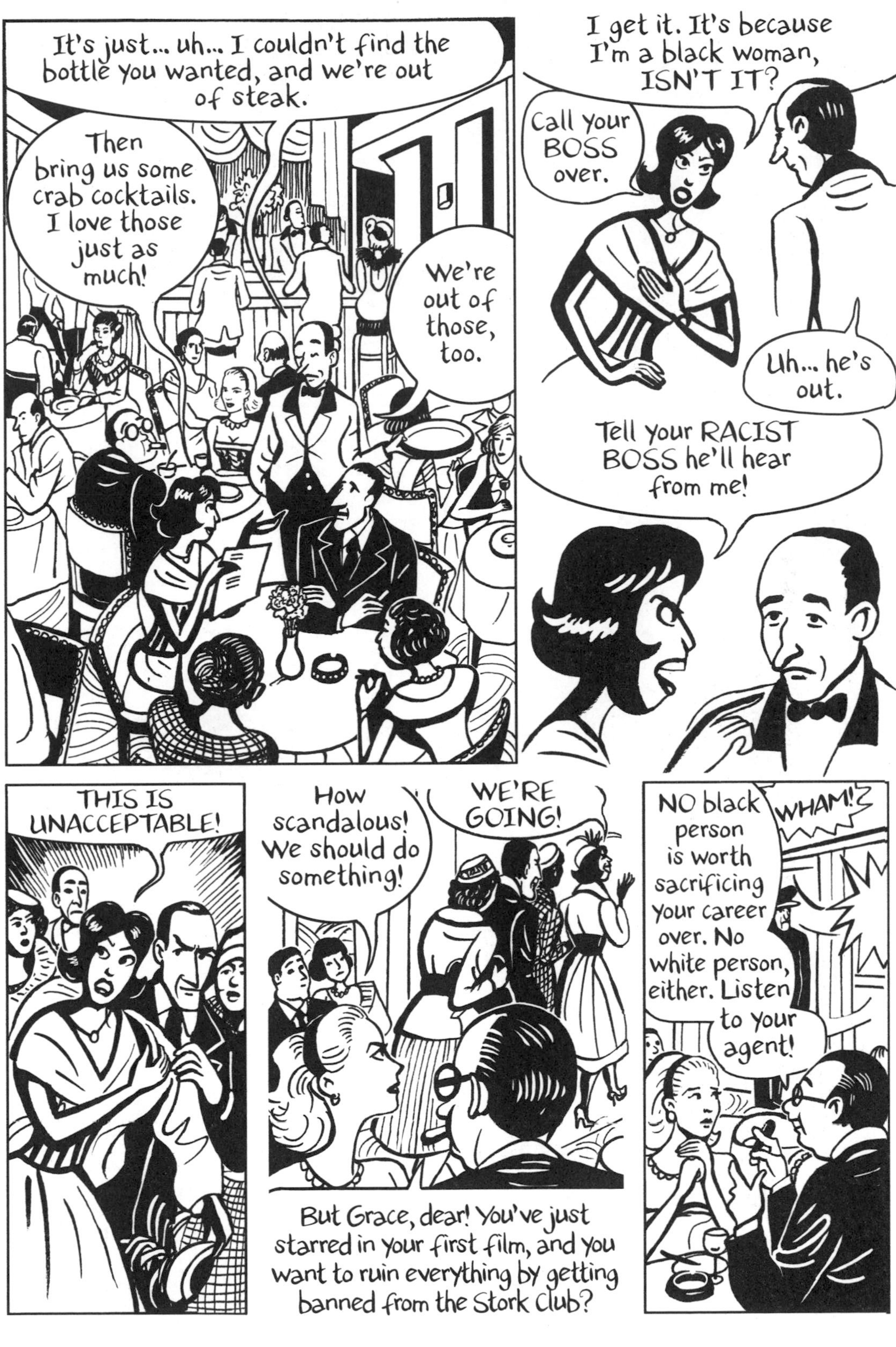
It's just... uh... I couldn't find the bottle you wanted, and we're out of steak.
Then bring us some crab cocktails. I love those just as much!
We're out of those, too.
I get it. It's because I'm a black woman, ISN'T IT?
Call your BOSS over.
Uh... he's out.
Tell your RACIST BOSS he'll hear from me!
THIS IS UNACCEPTABLE!
How scandalous! We should do something!
WE'RE GOING!
But Grace, dear! You've just starred in your first film, and you want to ruin everything by getting banned from the Stork Club?
NO black person is worth sacrificing your career over. No white person, either. Listen to your agent!
WHAM!

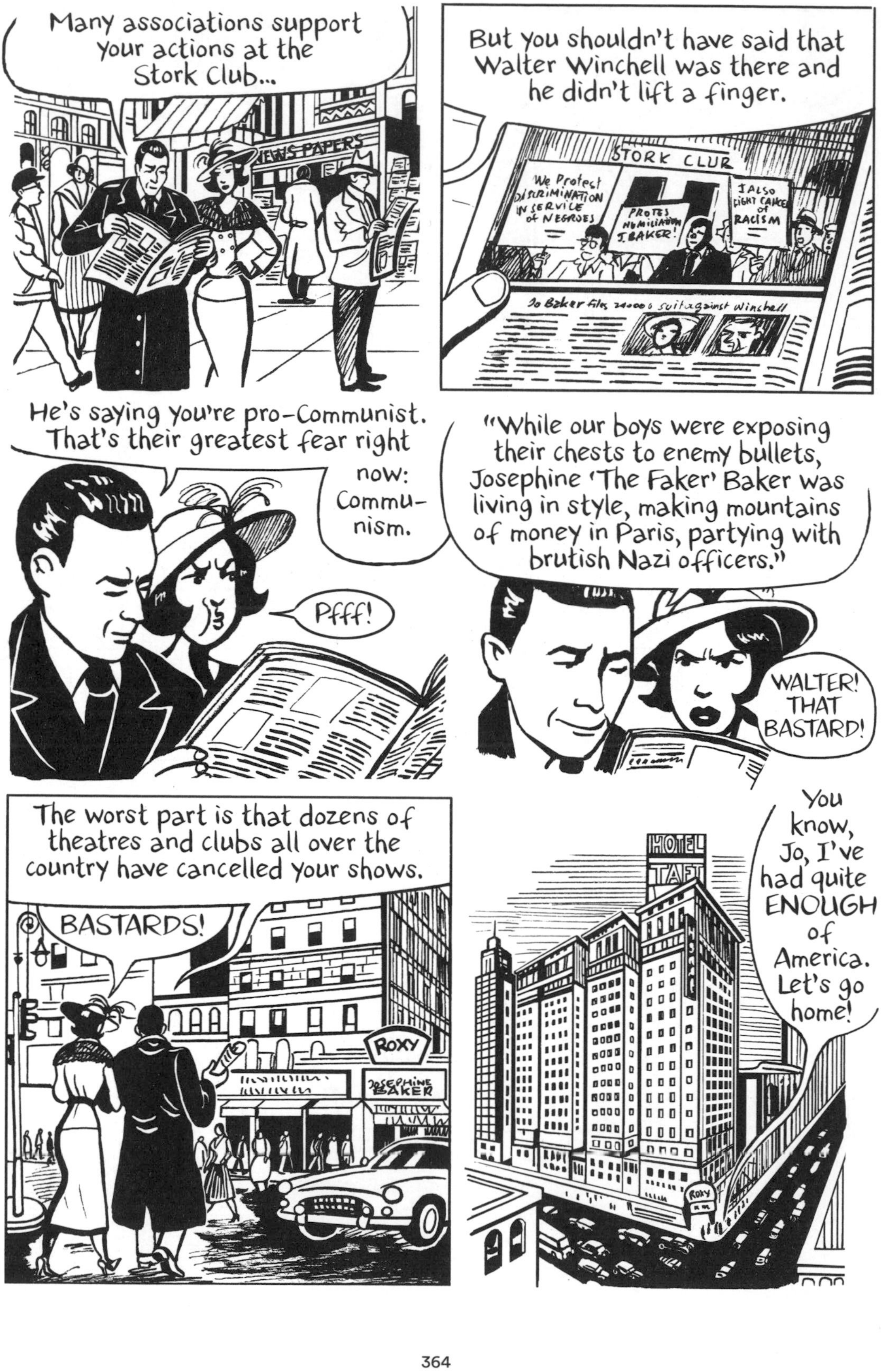
Many associations support your actions at the Stork Club...
NEWS PAPERS
But you shouldn't have said that Walter Winchell was there and he didn't lift a finger.
STORK CLUB
We Protest DISCRIMINATION IN SERVICE of NEGROES
I ALSO FIGHT CANCER of RACISM
He's saying you're pro-Communist. That's their greatest fear right now: Communism.
Pfff!
"While our boys were exposing their chests to enemy bullets, Josephine 'The Faker' Baker was living in style, making mountains of money in Paris, partying with brutish Nazi officers."
WALTER! THAT BASTARD!
The worst part is that dozens of theatres and clubs all over the country have cancelled your shows.
BASTARDS!
ROXY
JOSEPHINE BAKER
HOTEL TAFT
You know, Jo, I've had quite ENOUGH of America. Let's go home!

1954: Imperial Hotel, Tokyo, Japan

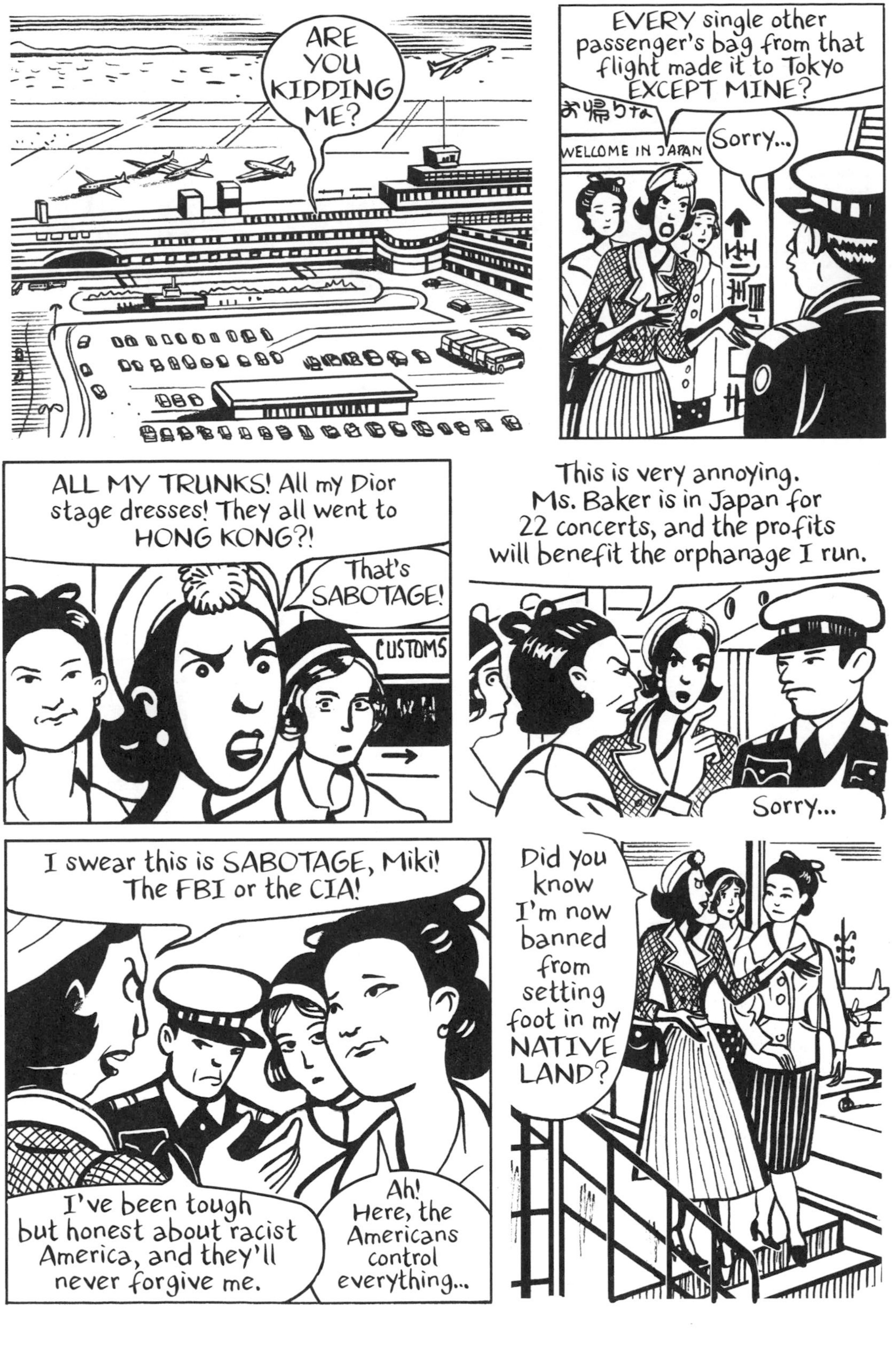
ARE YOU KIDDING ME?
EVERY single other passenger's bag from that flight made it to Tokyo EXCEPT MINE?
WELCOME IN JAPAN
Sorry...
ALL MY TRUNKS! All my Dior stage dresses! They all went to HONG KONG?!
That's SABOTAGE!
CUSTOMS
This is very annoying. Ms. Baker is in Japan for 22 concerts, and the profits will benefit the orphanage I run.
Sorry...
I swear this is SABOTAGE, Miki! The FBI or the CIA!
I've been tough but honest about racist America, and they'll never forgive me.
Ah! Here, the Americans control everything...
Did you know I'm now banned from setting foot in my NATIVE LAND?

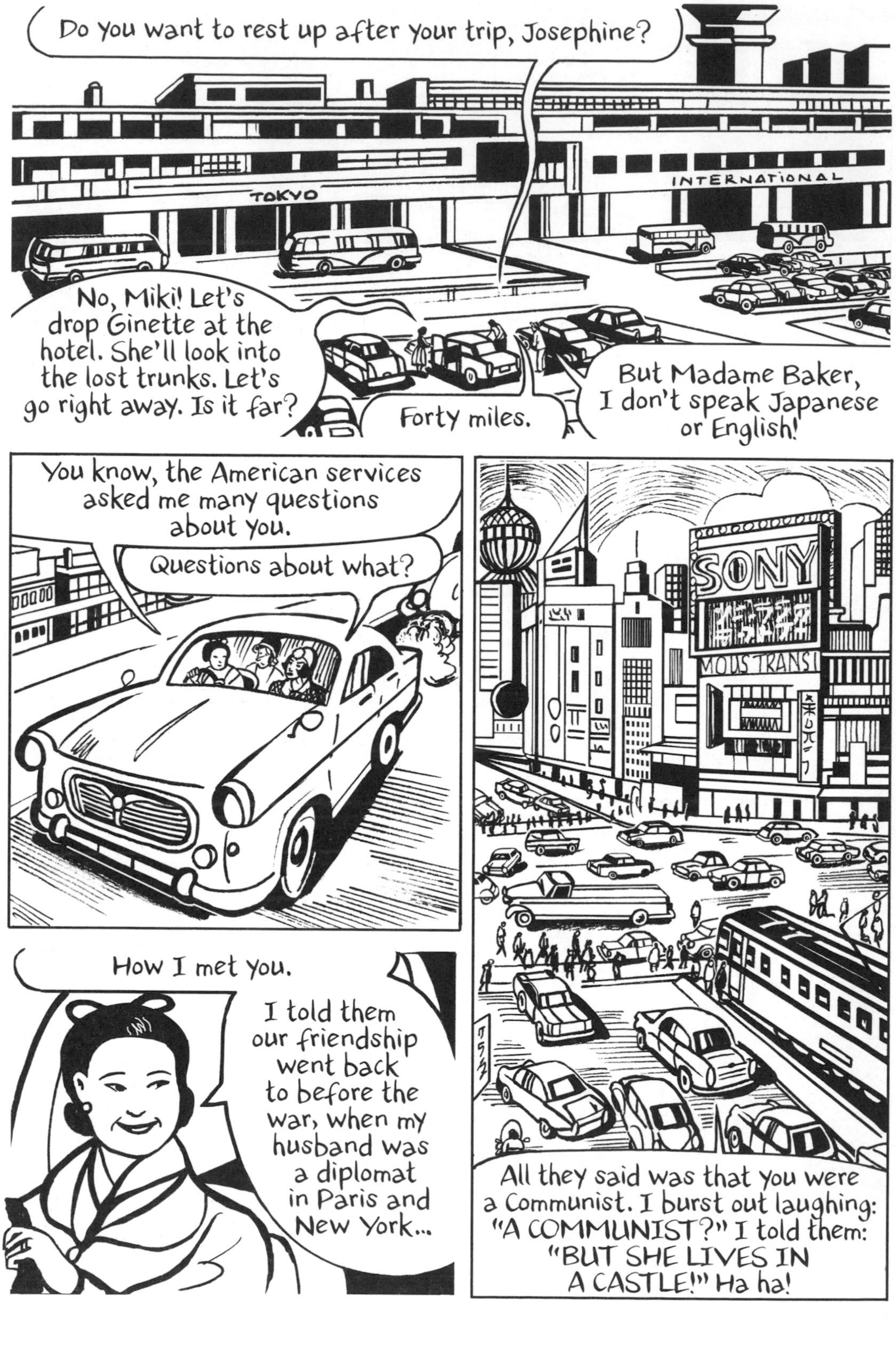
Do you want to rest up after your trip, Josephine?
TOKYO
INTERNATIONAL
No, Miki! Let's drop Ginette at the hotel. She'll look into the lost trunks. Let's go right away. Is it far?
Forty miles.
But Madame Baker, I don't speak Japanese or English!
You know, the American services asked me many questions about you.
Questions about what?
How I met you.
I told them our friendship went back to before the war, when my husband was a diplomat in Paris and New York...
SONY
All they said was that you were a Communist. I burst out laughing: "A COMMUNIST?" I told them: "BUT SHE LIVES IN A CASTLE!" Ha ha!

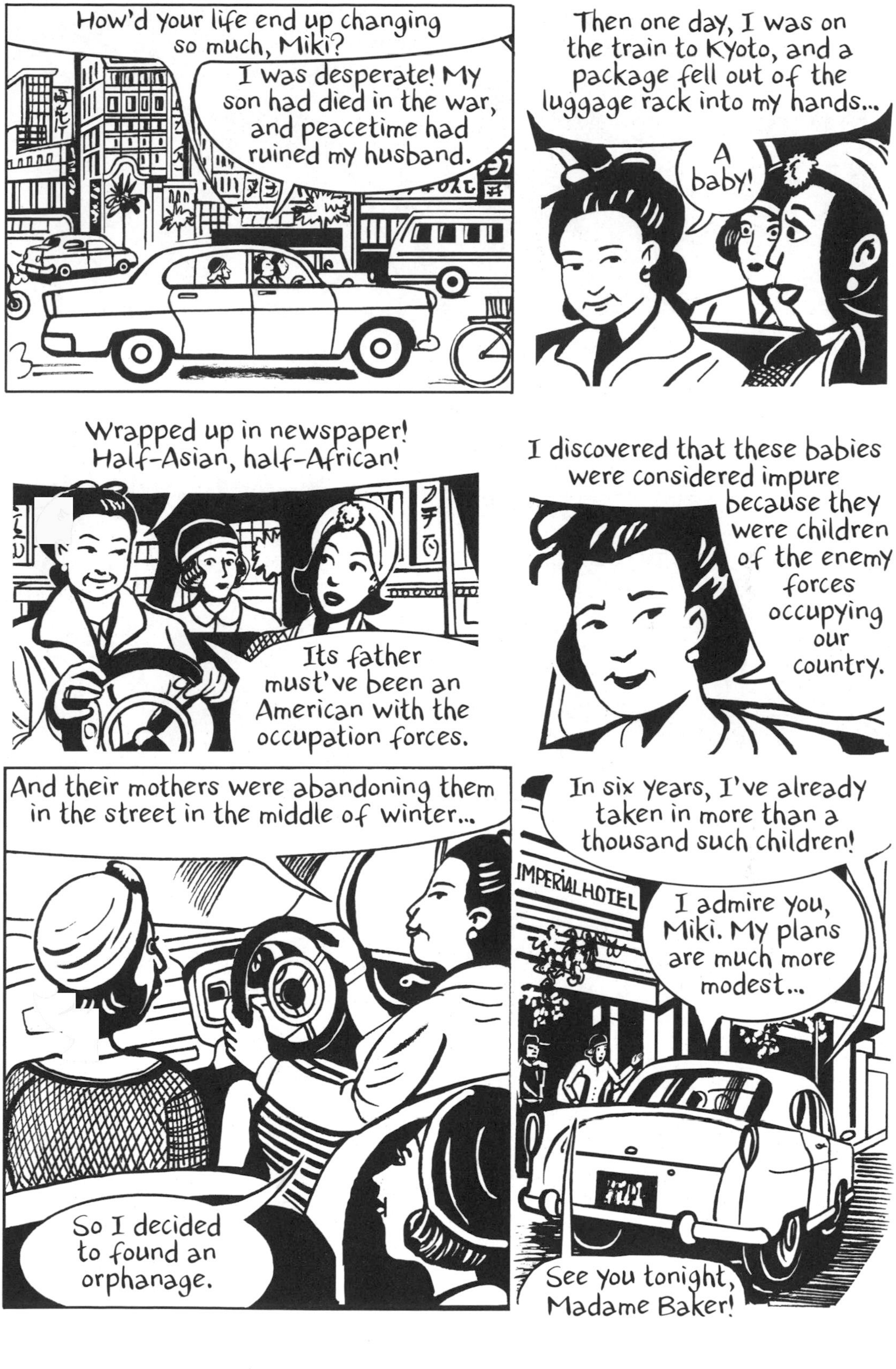
How'd your life end up changing so much, Miki?
I was desperate! My son had died in the war, and peacetime had ruined my husband.
Then one day, I was on the train to Kyoto, and a package fell out of the luggage rack into my hands...
A baby!
Wrapped up in newspaper! Half-Asian, half-African!
Its father must've been an American with the occupation forces.
I discovered that these babies were considered impure because they were children of the enemy forces occupying our country.
And their mothers were abandoning them in the street in the middle of winter...
So I decided to found an orphanage.
In six years, I've already taken in more than a thousand such children!
IMPERIAL HOTEL
I admire you, Miki. My plans are much more modest...
See you tonight, Madame Baker!

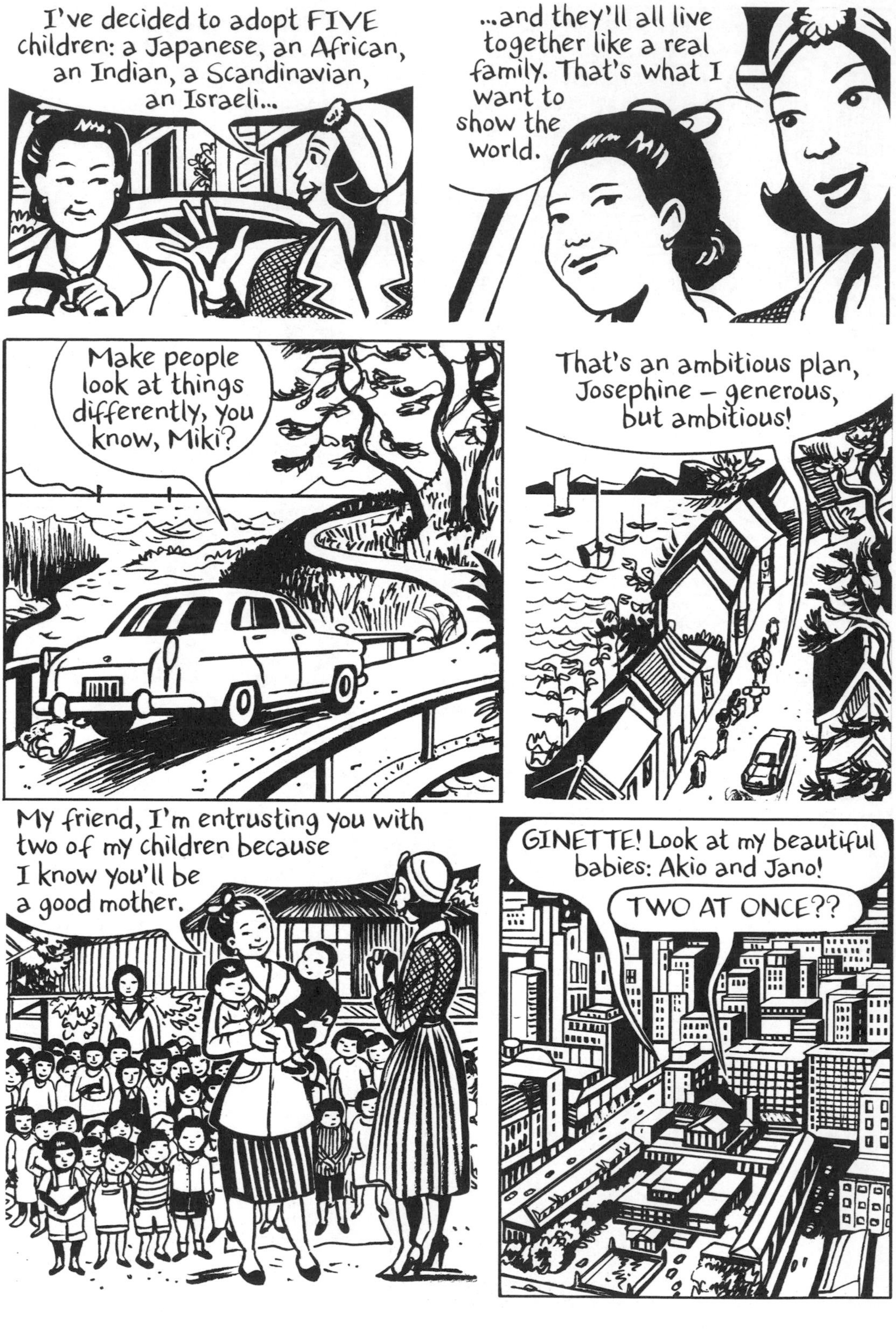
I've decided to adopt FIVE children: a Japanese, an African, an Indian, a Scandinavian, an Israeli...
...and they'll all live together like a real family. That's what I want to show the world.
Make people look at things differently, you know, Miki?
That's an ambitious plan, Josephine – generous, but ambitious!
My friend, I'm entrusting you with two of my children because I know you'll be a good mother.
GINETTE! Look at my beautiful babies: Akio and Jano!
TWO AT ONCE??

I'm so happy!

Um... how do you prepare a bottle?

WAAAAH!

Any news of my wardrobe, Ginette?

Still nothing, Madame.

The first concert's tonight! How infuriating!

Goo

Say, Miki, did we ever swap dresses before?

LA TONKINOISE LA TONKIKI! LA TONKIKI LA TONKINOISE

LA TONKIKI LA TONKINOISE

BRAVO! clap! clap! Josephine!

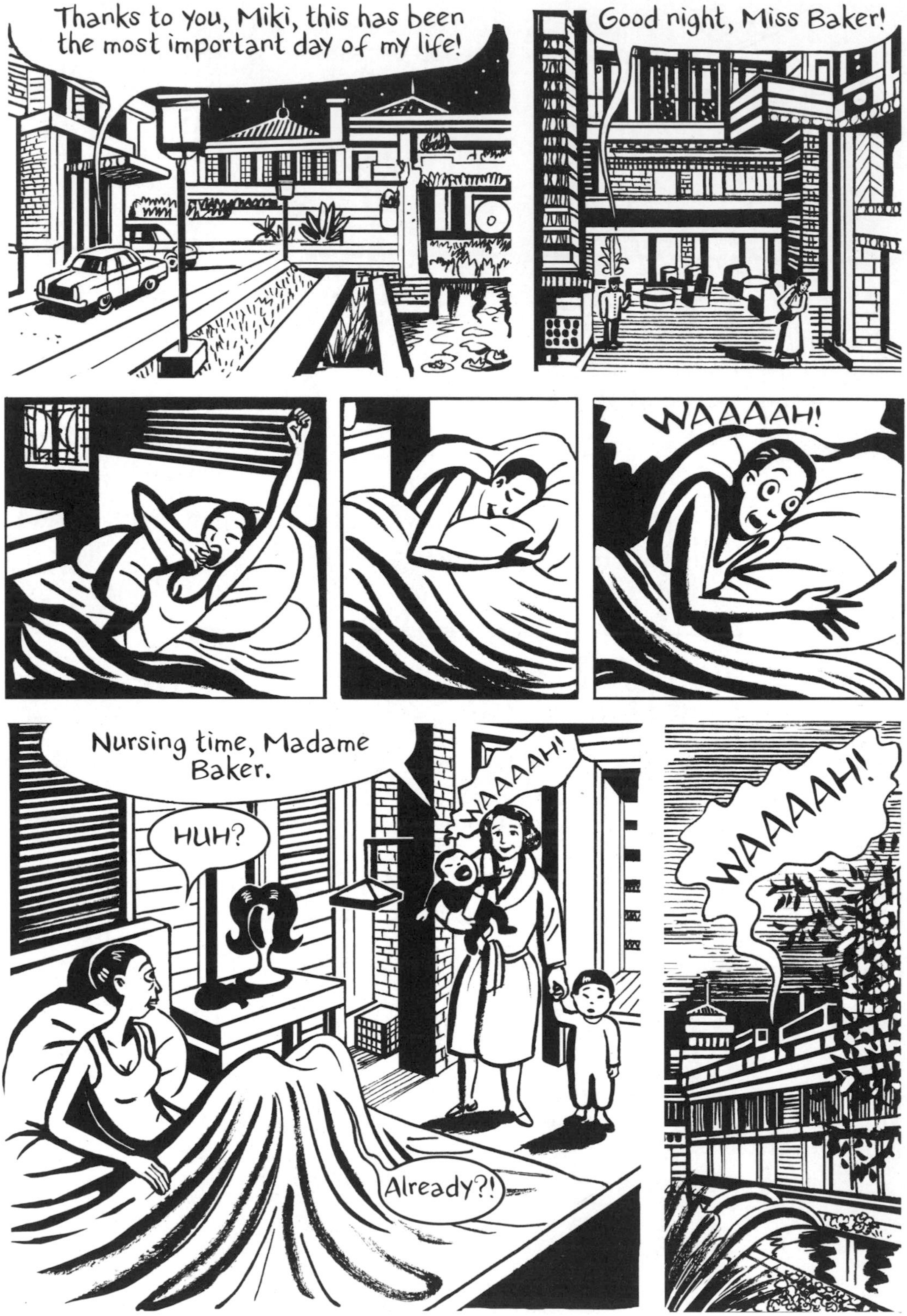
Thanks to you, Miki, this has been the most important day of my life!
Good night, Miss Baker!
WAAAAH!
Nursing time, Madame Baker.
HUH?
WAAAAAH!
Already?!
WAAAAAH!

1957: Milandes, Périgord, France

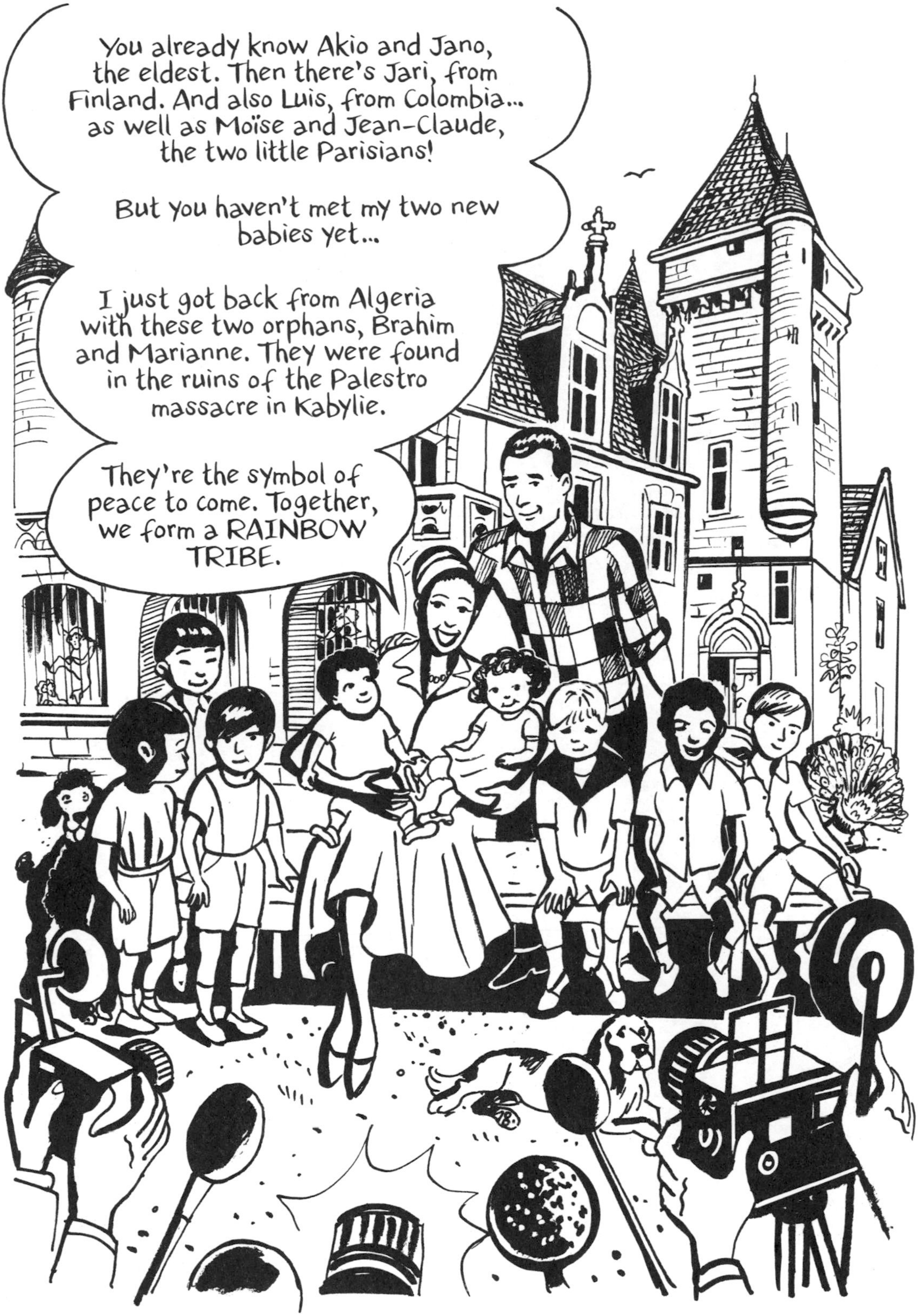
You already know Akio and Jano, the eldest. Then there's Jari, from Finland. And also Luis, from Colombia... as well as Moïse and Jean-Claude, the two little Parisians!
But you haven't met my two new babies yet...
I just got back from Algeria with these two orphans, Brahim and Marianne. They were found in the ruins of the Palestro massacre in Kabylie.
They're the symbol of peace to come. Together, we form a RAINBOW TRIBE.

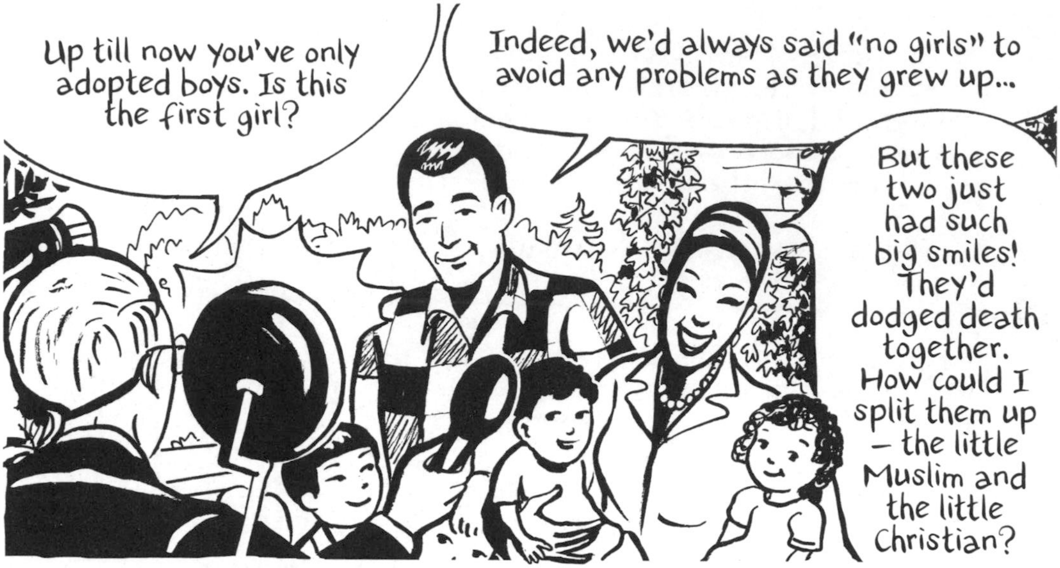
Up till now you've only adopted boys. Is this the first girl?
Indeed, we'd always said "no girls" to avoid any problems as they grew up...
But these two just had such big smiles! They'd dodged death together. How could I split them up – the little Muslim and the little Christian?

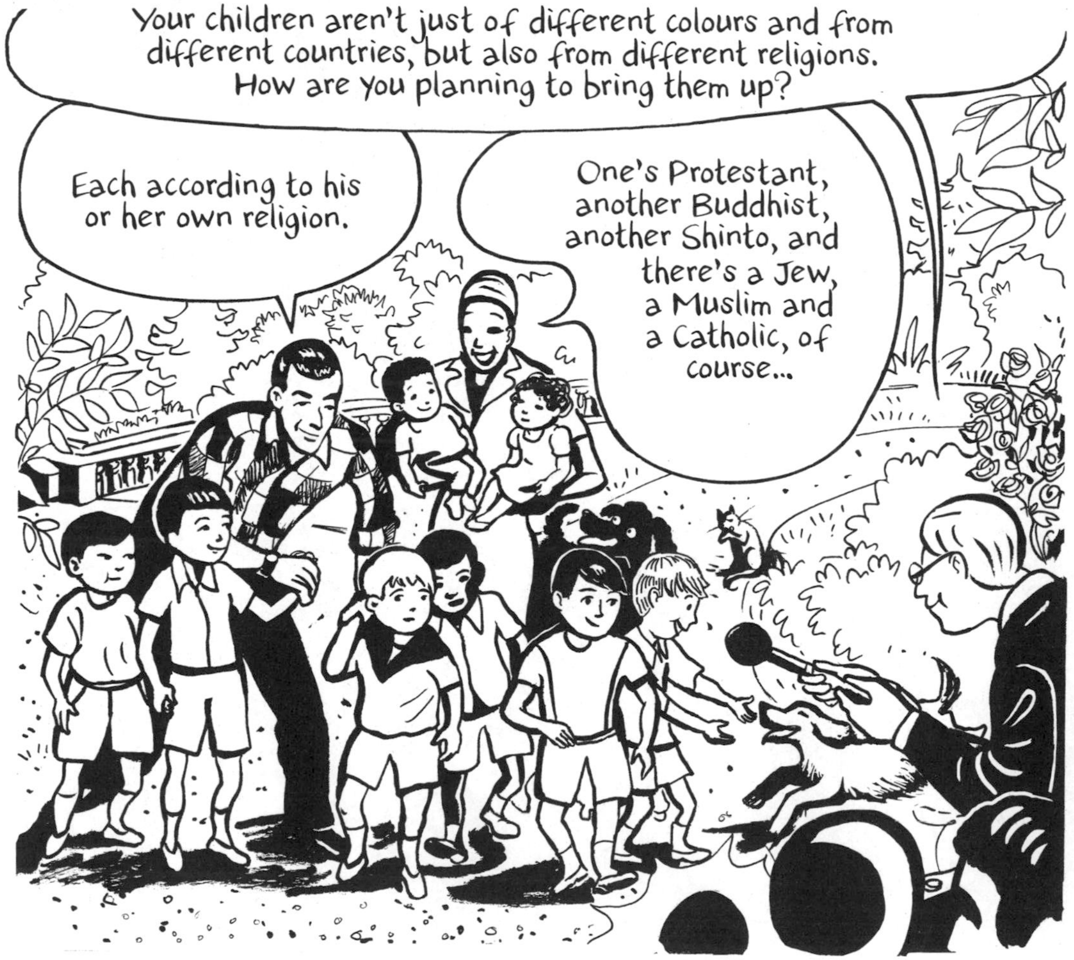
Your children aren't just of different colours and from different countries, but also from different religions. How are you planning to bring them up?
Each according to his or her own religion.
One's Protestant, another Buddhist, another Shinto, and there's a Jew, a Muslim and a Catholic, of course...

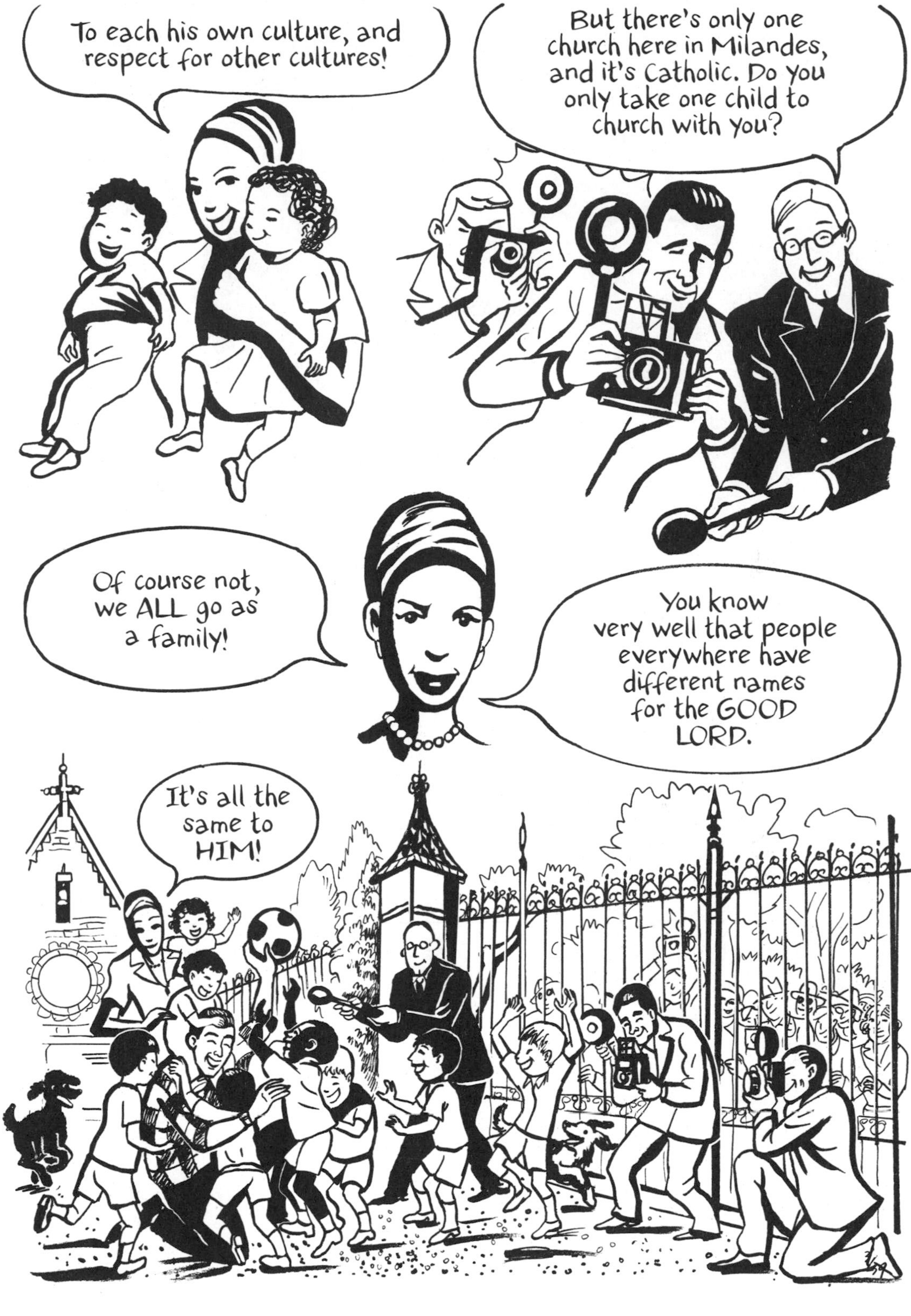
To each his own culture, and respect for other cultures!
But there's only one church here in Milandes, and it's Catholic. Do you only take one child to church with you?
Of course not, we ALL go as a family!
You know very well that people everywhere have different names for the GOOD LORD.
It's all the same to HIM!

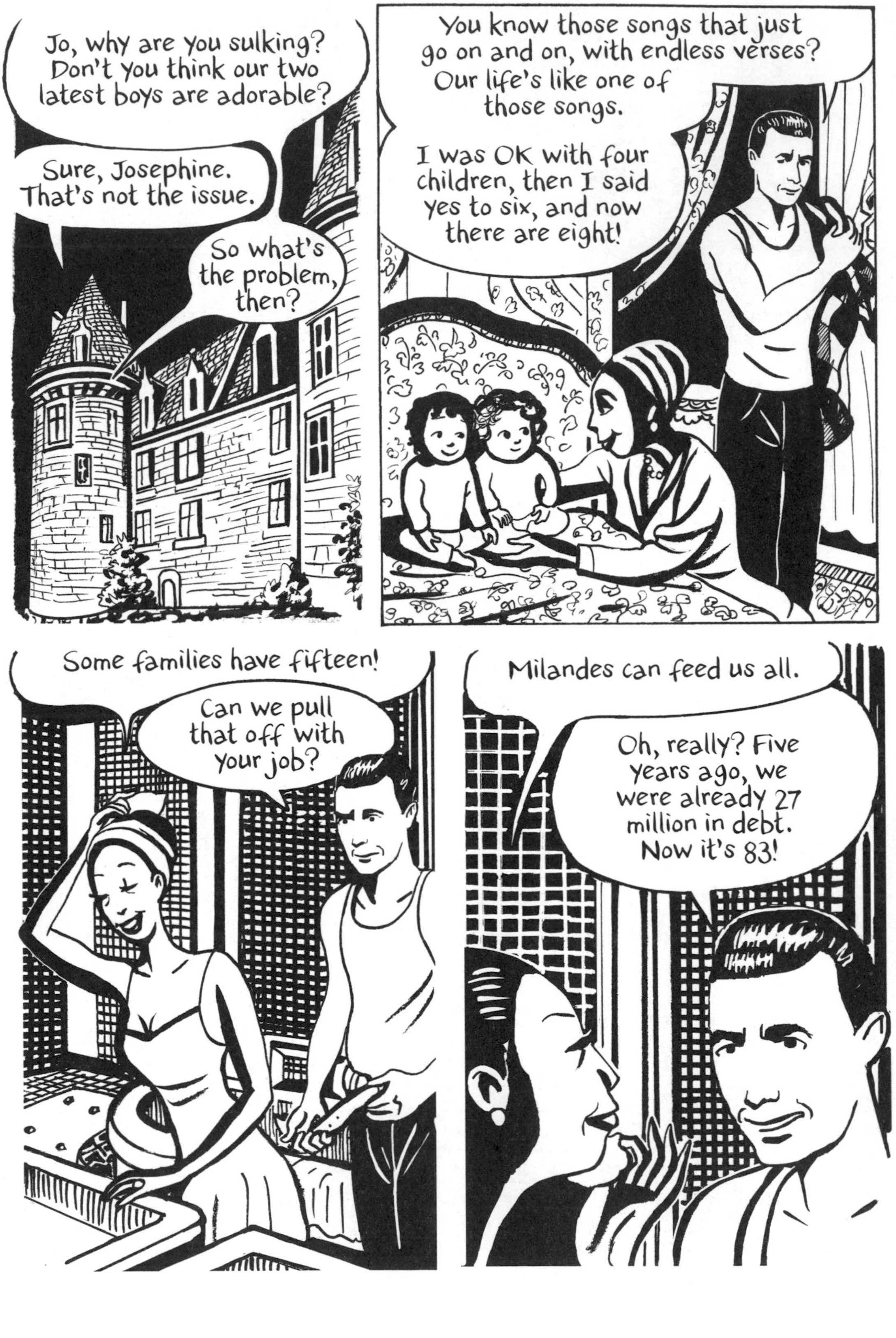
Jo, why are you sulking? Don't you think our two latest boys are adorable?
Sure, Josephine. That's not the issue.
So what's the problem, then?
You know those songs that just go on and on, with endless verses? Our life's like one of those songs.
I was OK with four children, then I said yes to six, and now there are eight!
Some families have fifteen!
Can we pull that off with your job?
Milandes can feed us all.
Oh, really? Five years ago, we were already 27 million in debt. Now it's 83!

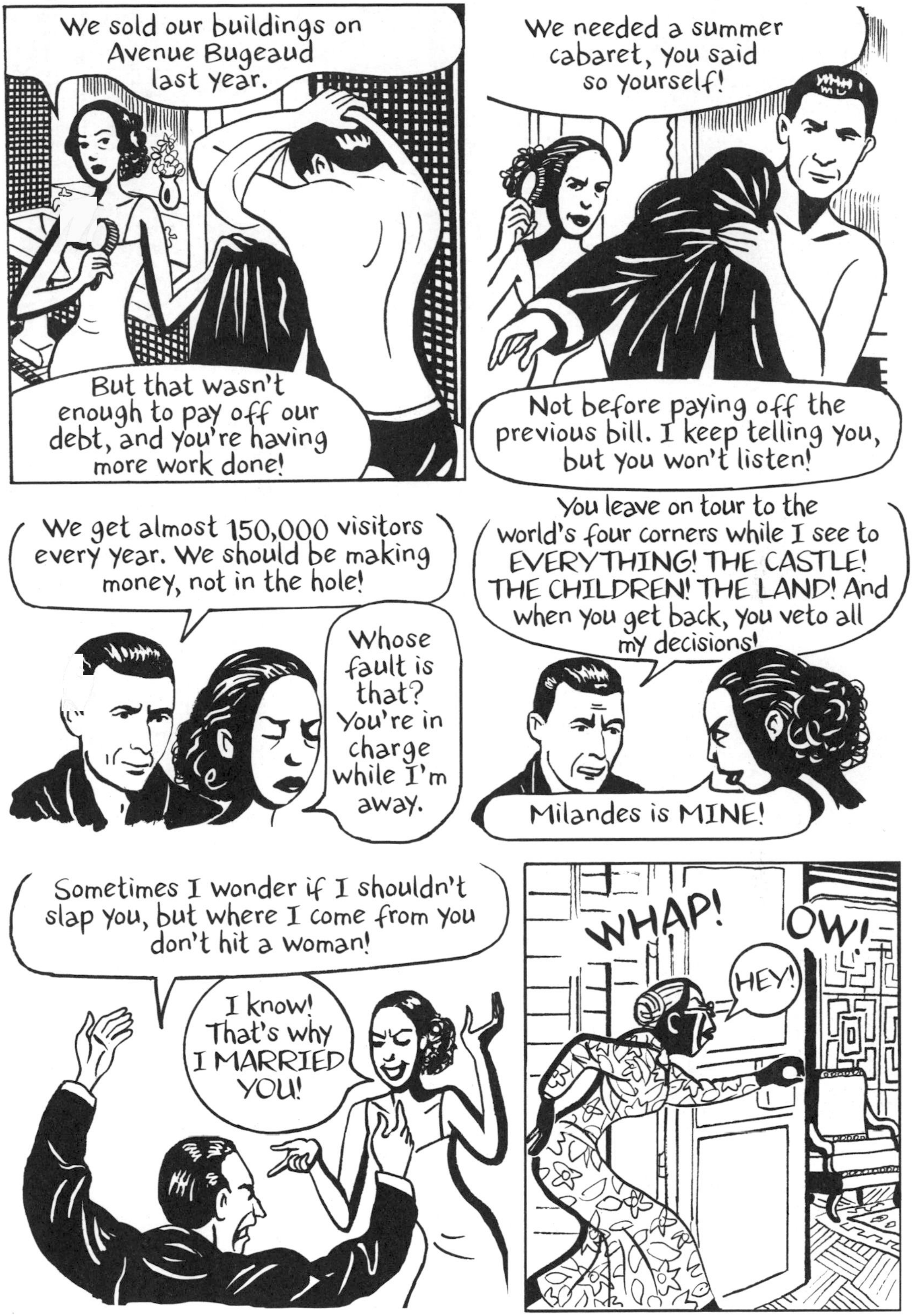
We sold our buildings on Avenue Bugeaud last year.
But that wasn't enough to pay off our debt, and you're having more work done!
We needed a summer cabaret, you said so yourself!
Not before paying off the previous bill. I keep telling you, but you won't listen!
We get almost 150,000 visitors every year. We should be making money, not in the hole!
Whose fault is that? You're in charge while I'm away.
You leave on tour to the world's four corners while I see to EVERYTHING! THE CASTLE! THE CHILDREN! THE LAND! And when you get back, you veto all my decisions!
Milandes is MINE!
Sometimes I wonder if I shouldn't slap you, but where I come from you don't hit a woman!
I know! That's why I MARRIED YOU!
WHAP!
OW!
HEY!

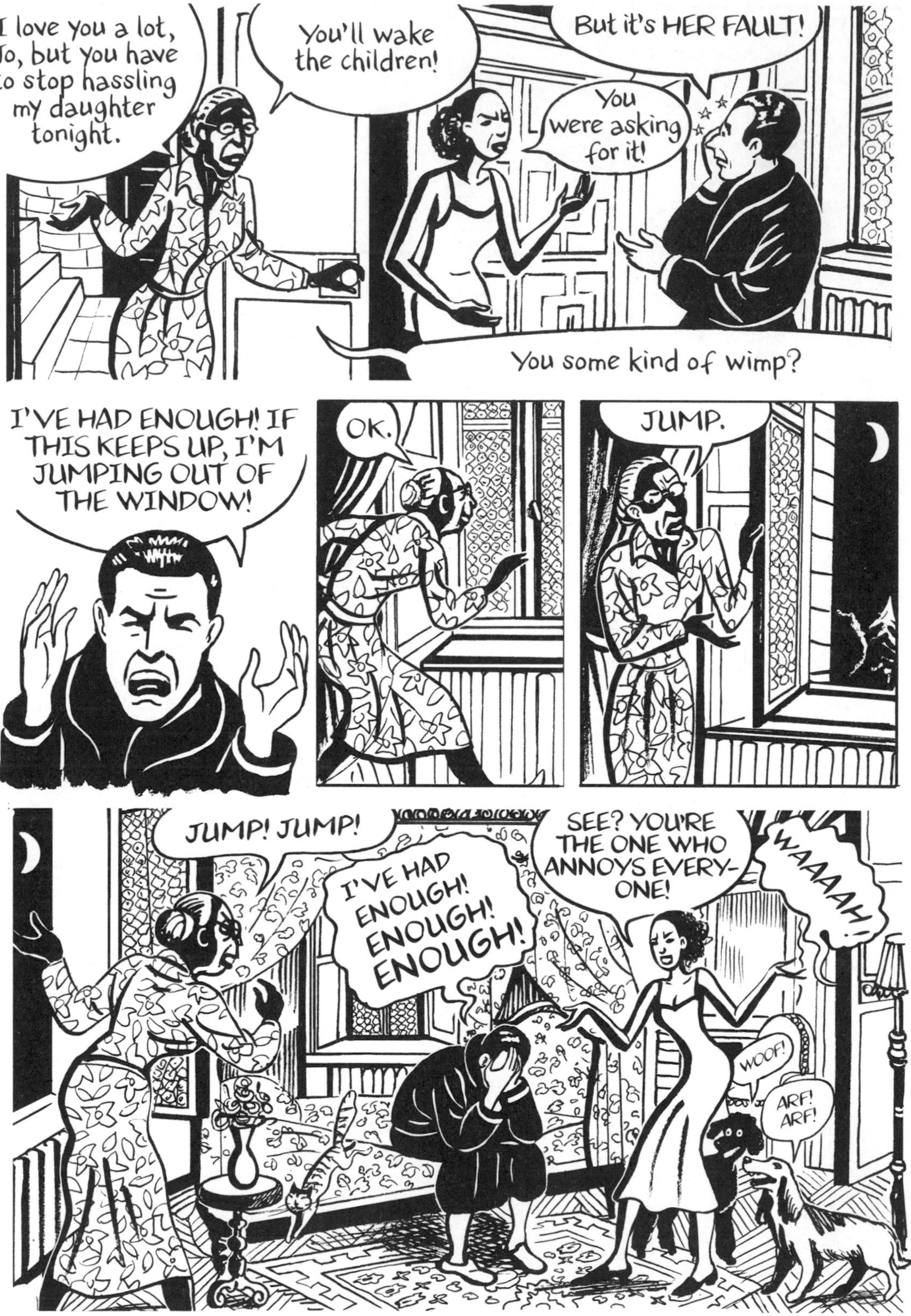
I love you a lot, Jo, but you have to stop hassling my daughter tonight.
You'll wake the children!
But it's HER FAULT!
You were asking for it!
You some kind of wimp?
I'VE HAD ENOUGH! IF THIS KEEPS UP, I'M JUMPING OUT OF THE WINDOW!
OK.
JUMP.
JUMP! JUMP!
I'VE HAD ENOUGH! ENOUGH! ENOUGH!
SEE? YOU'RE THE ONE WHO ANNOYS EVERY-ONE!
WAAAAH!
WOOF!
ARF! ARF!

1959: Pera Palace Hotel, Istanbul, Turkey

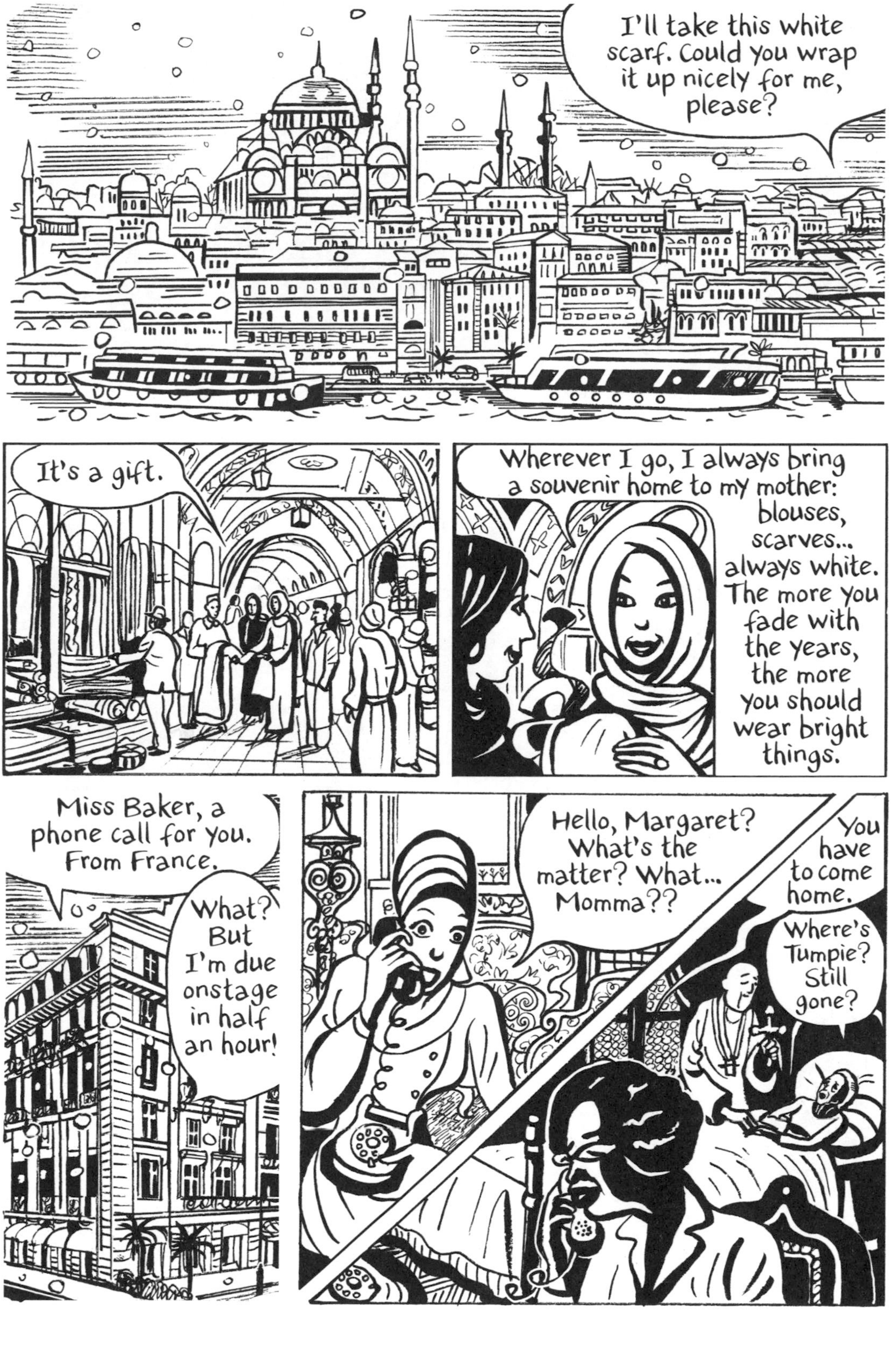
I'll take this white scarf. Could you wrap it up nicely for me, please?
It's a gift.
Wherever I go, I always bring a souvenir home to my mother: blouses, scarves... always white. The more you fade with the years, the more you should wear bright things.
Miss Baker, a phone call for you. From France.
What? But I'm due onstage in half an hour!
Hello, Margaret? What's the matter? What... Momma??
You have to come home.
Where's Tumpie? Still gone?

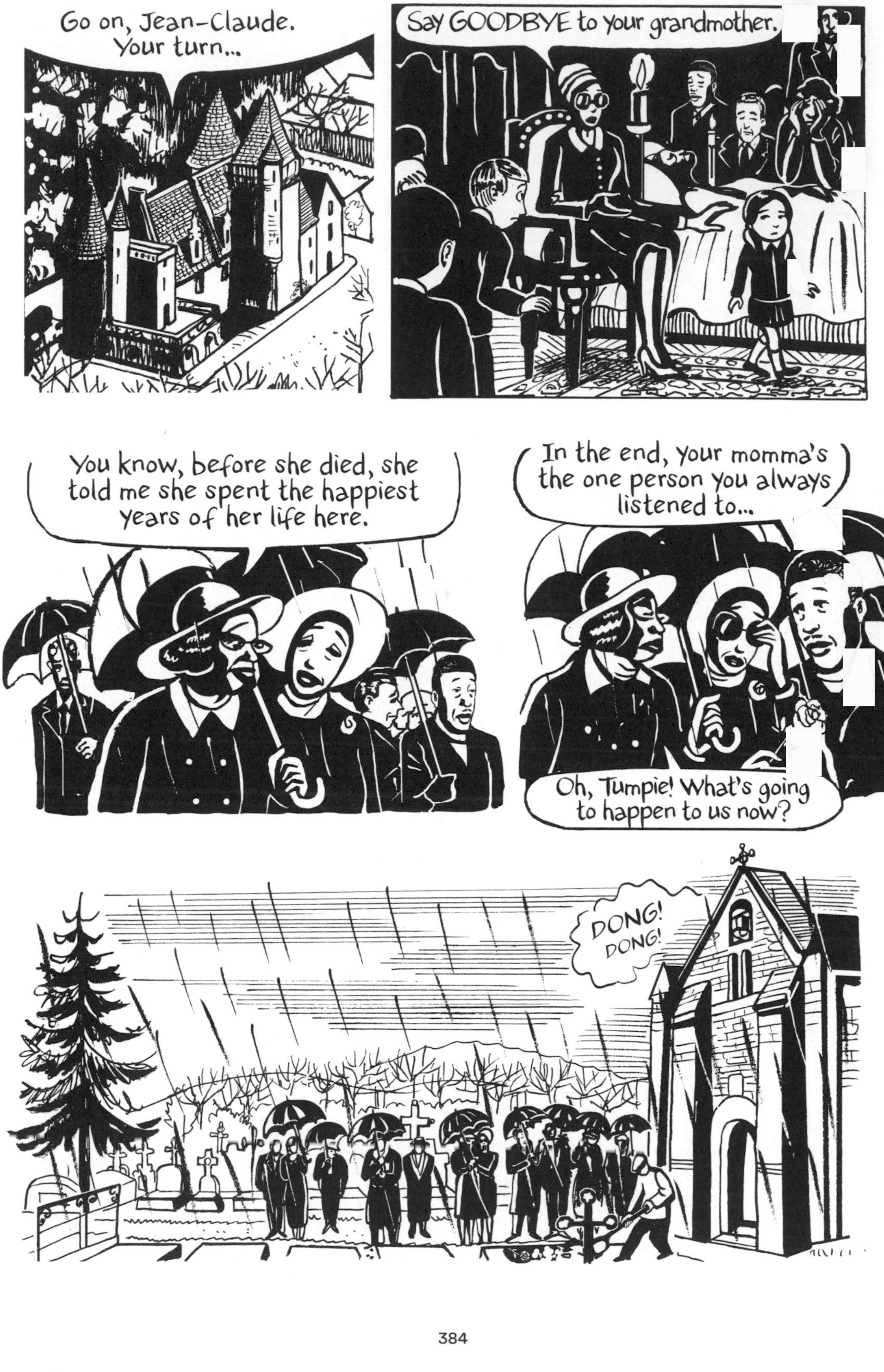
Go on, Jean-Claude. Your turn...
Say GOODBYE to your grandmother.
You know, before she died, she told me she spent the happiest years of her life here.
In the end, your momma's the one person you always listened to...
Oh, Tumpie! What's going to happen to us now?
DONG! DONG!

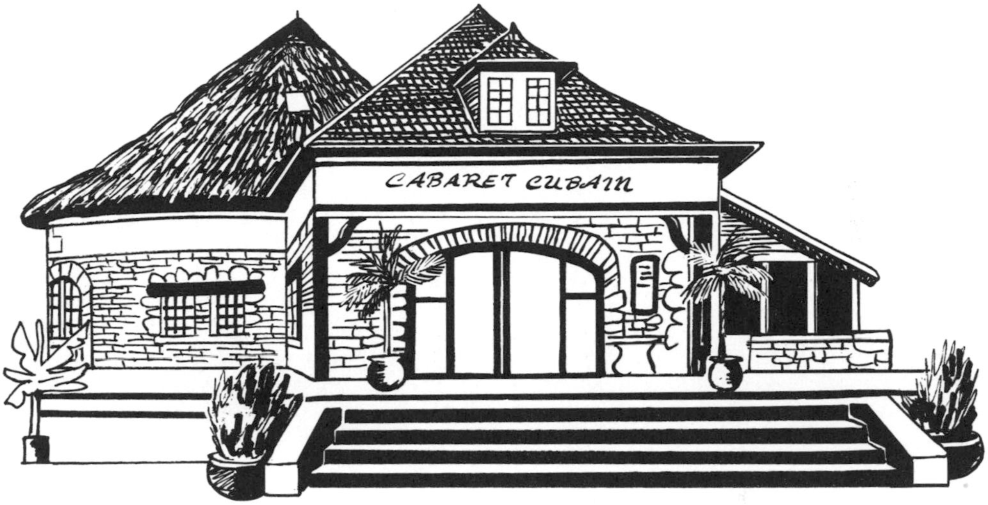
CABARET CUBAIN

1962: Cuban Cabaret, Milandes Park, Périgord, France

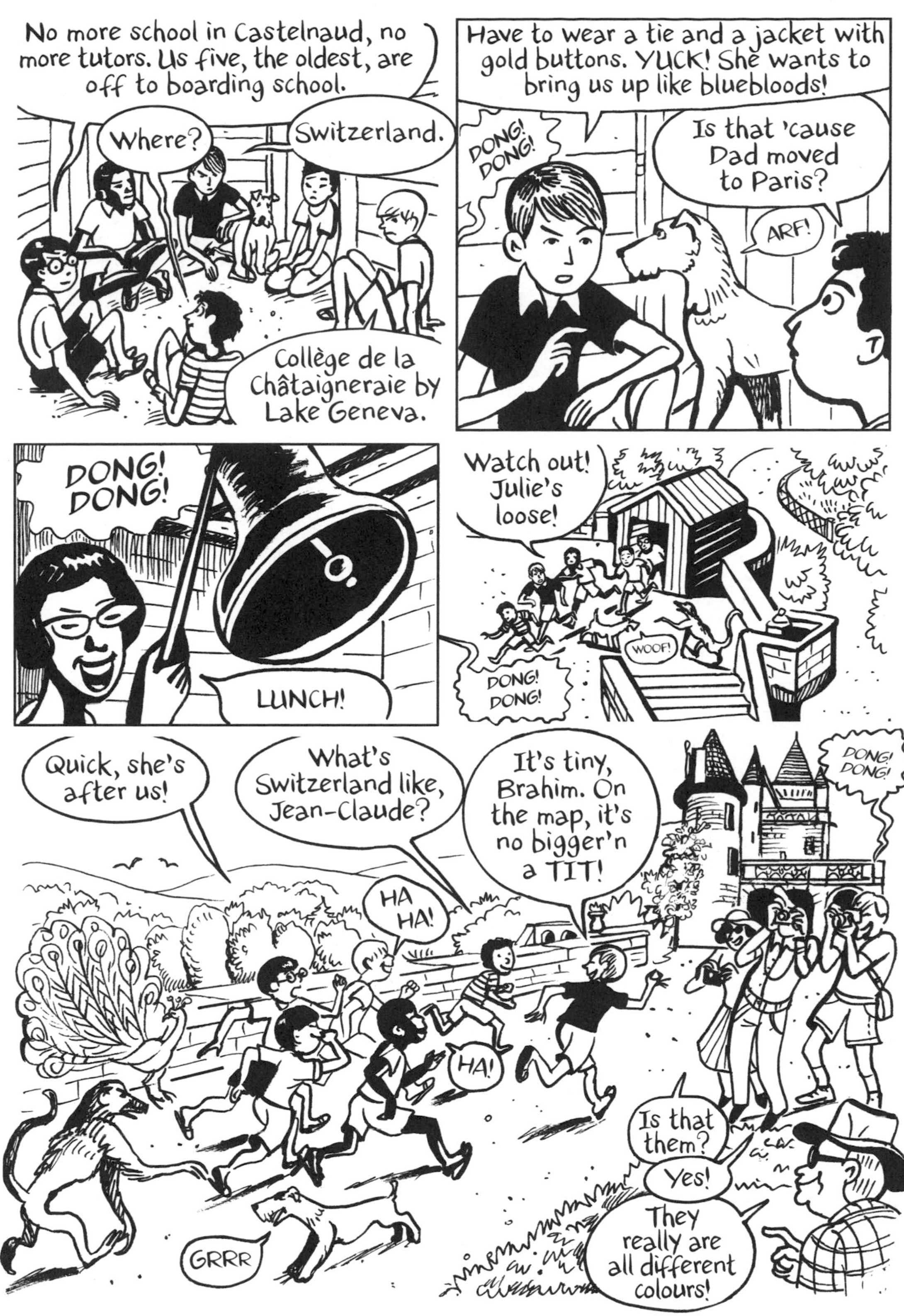
No more school in Castelnaud, no more tutors. Us five, the oldest, are off to boarding school.
Where?
Switzerland.
Collège de la Châtaigneraie by Lake Geneva.
Have to wear a tie and a jacket with gold buttons. YUCK! She wants to bring us up like bluebloods!
DONG! DONG!
Is that 'cause Dad moved to Paris?
ARF!
DONG! DONG!
LUNCH!
Watch out! Julie's loose!
WOOF!
DONG! DONG!
Quick, she's after us!
What's Switzerland like, Jean-Claude?
It's tiny, Brahim. On the map, it's no bigger'n a TIT!
DONG! DONG!
HA HA!
HA!
GRRR
Is that them?
Yes!
They really are all different colours!

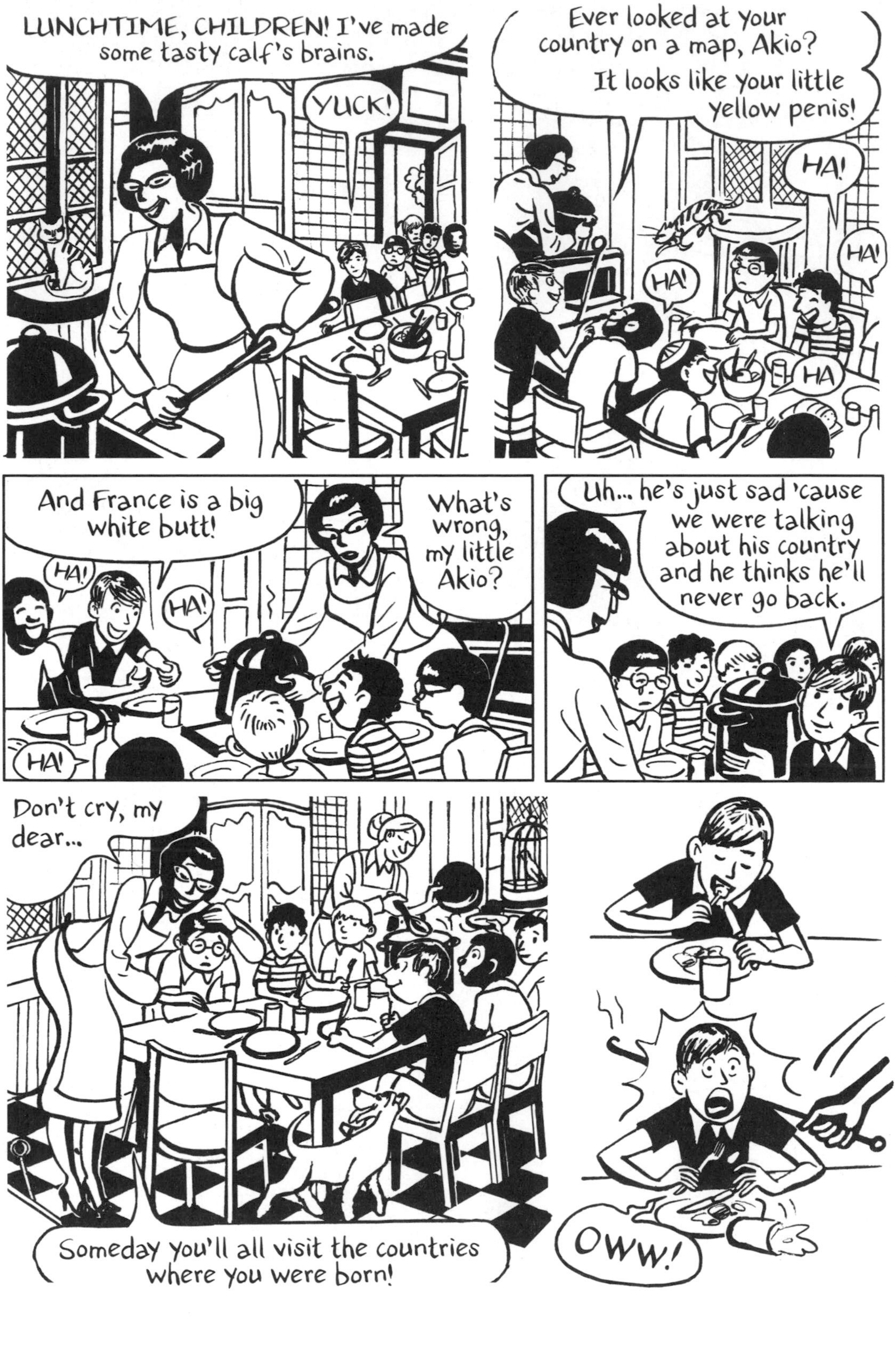
LUNCHTIME, CHILDREN! I've made some tasty calf's brains.
YUCK!
Ever looked at your country on a map, Akio?
It looks like your little yellow penis!
HA!
HA!
HA!
HA
And France is a big white butt!
HA!
HA!
HA!
What's wrong, my little Akio?
Uh... he's just sad 'cause we were talking about his country and he thinks he'll never go back.
Don't cry, my dear...
Someday you'll all visit the countries where you were born!
OWW!

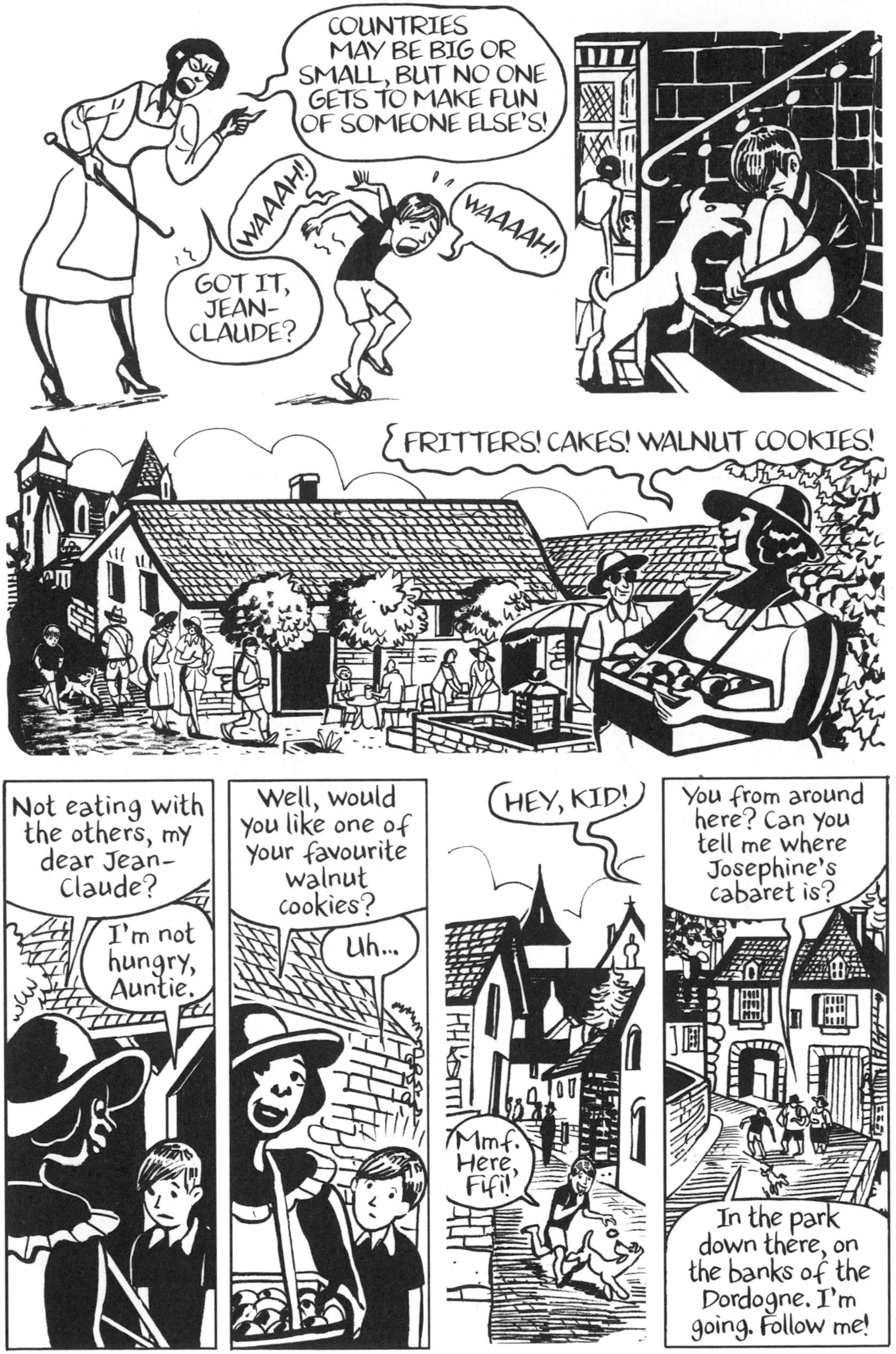
COUNTRIES MAY BE BIG OR SMALL, BUT NO ONE GETS TO MAKE FUN OF SOMEONE ELSE'S!
WAAAH!
WAAAAH!
GOT IT, JEAN-CLAUDE?
FRITTERS! CAKES! WALNUT COOKIES!
Not eating with the others, my dear Jean-Claude?
I'm not hungry, Auntie.
Well, would you like one of your favourite walnut cookies?
Uh...
HEY, KID!
Mmf. Here, Fifi!
You from around here? Can you tell me where Josephine's cabaret is?
In the park down there, on the banks of the Dordogne. I'm going. Follow me!

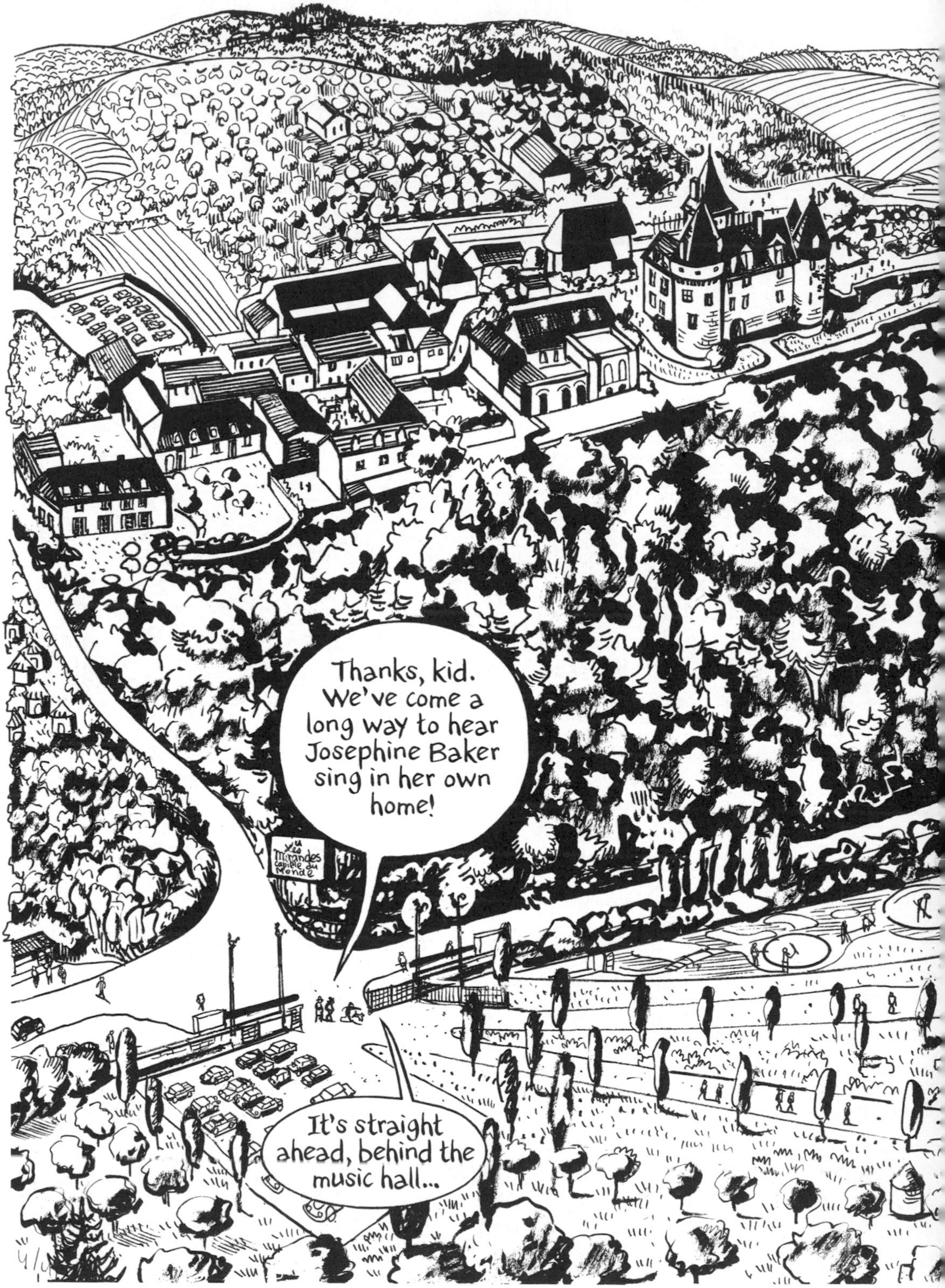
Thanks, kid. We've come a long way to hear Josephine Baker sing in her own home!
It's straight ahead, behind the music hall...

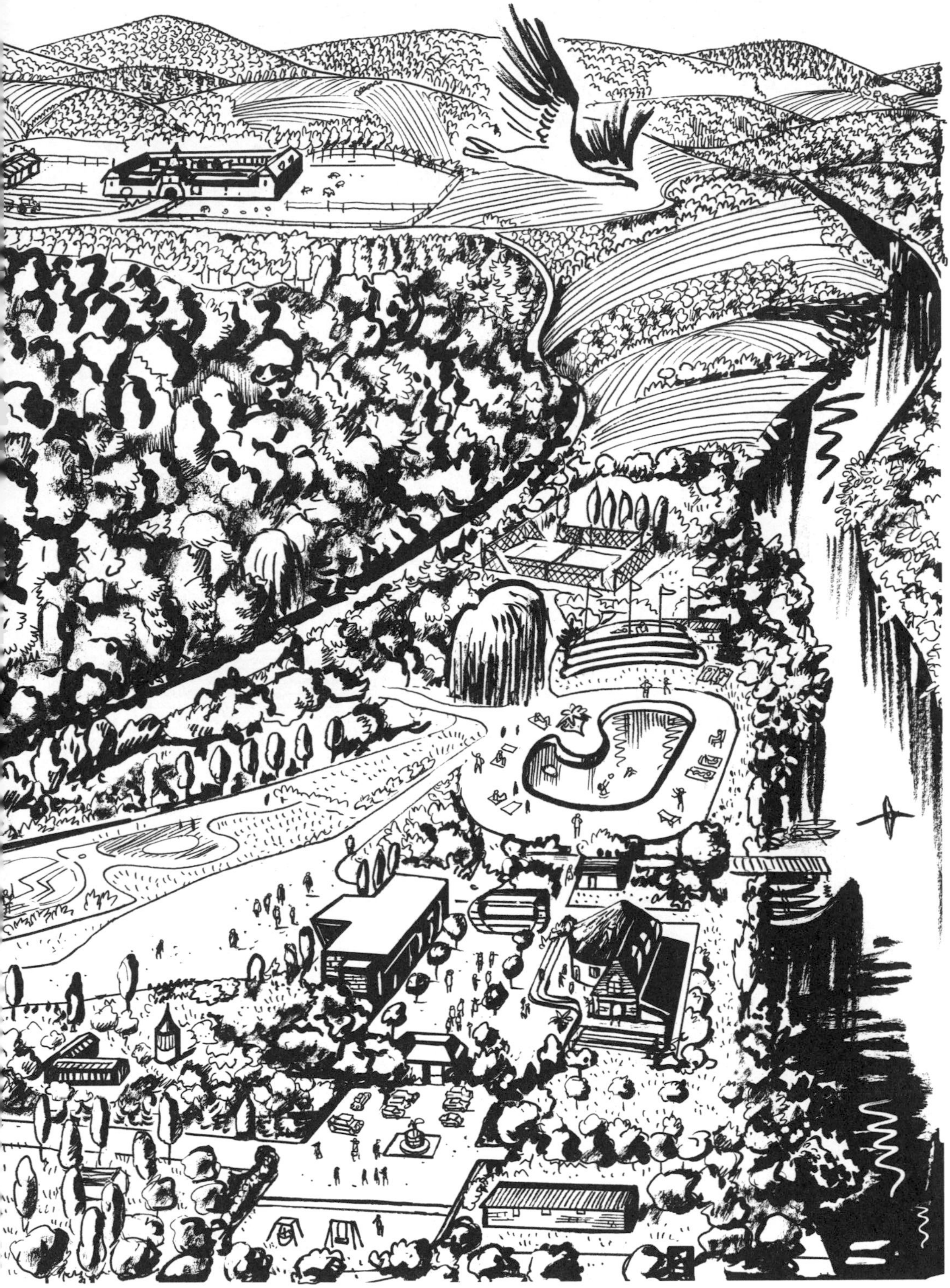

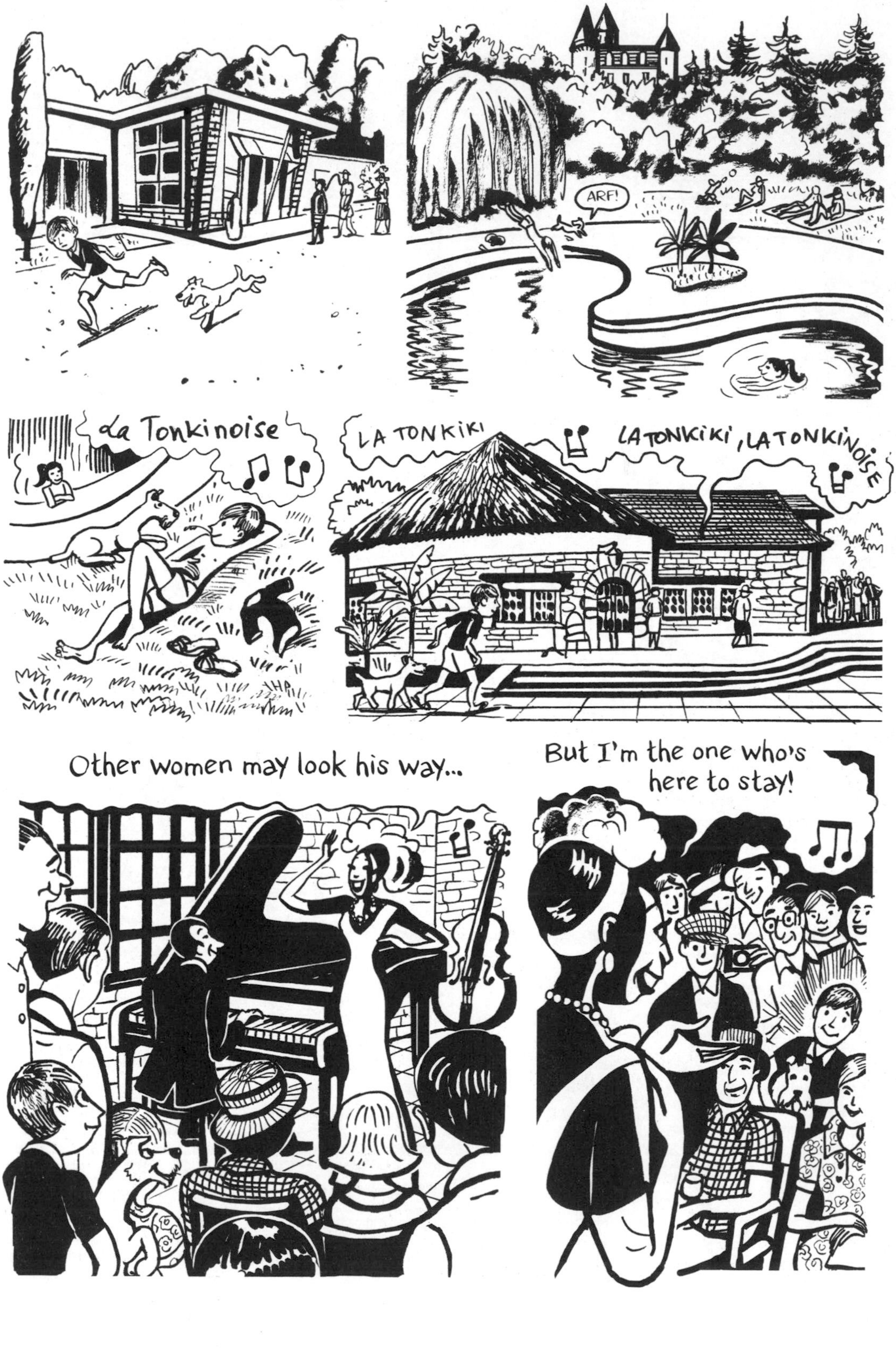
ARF!
la Tonkinoise
LA TONKIKI
LA TONKIKI, LA TONKINOISE
Other women may look his way...
But I'm the one who's here to stay!

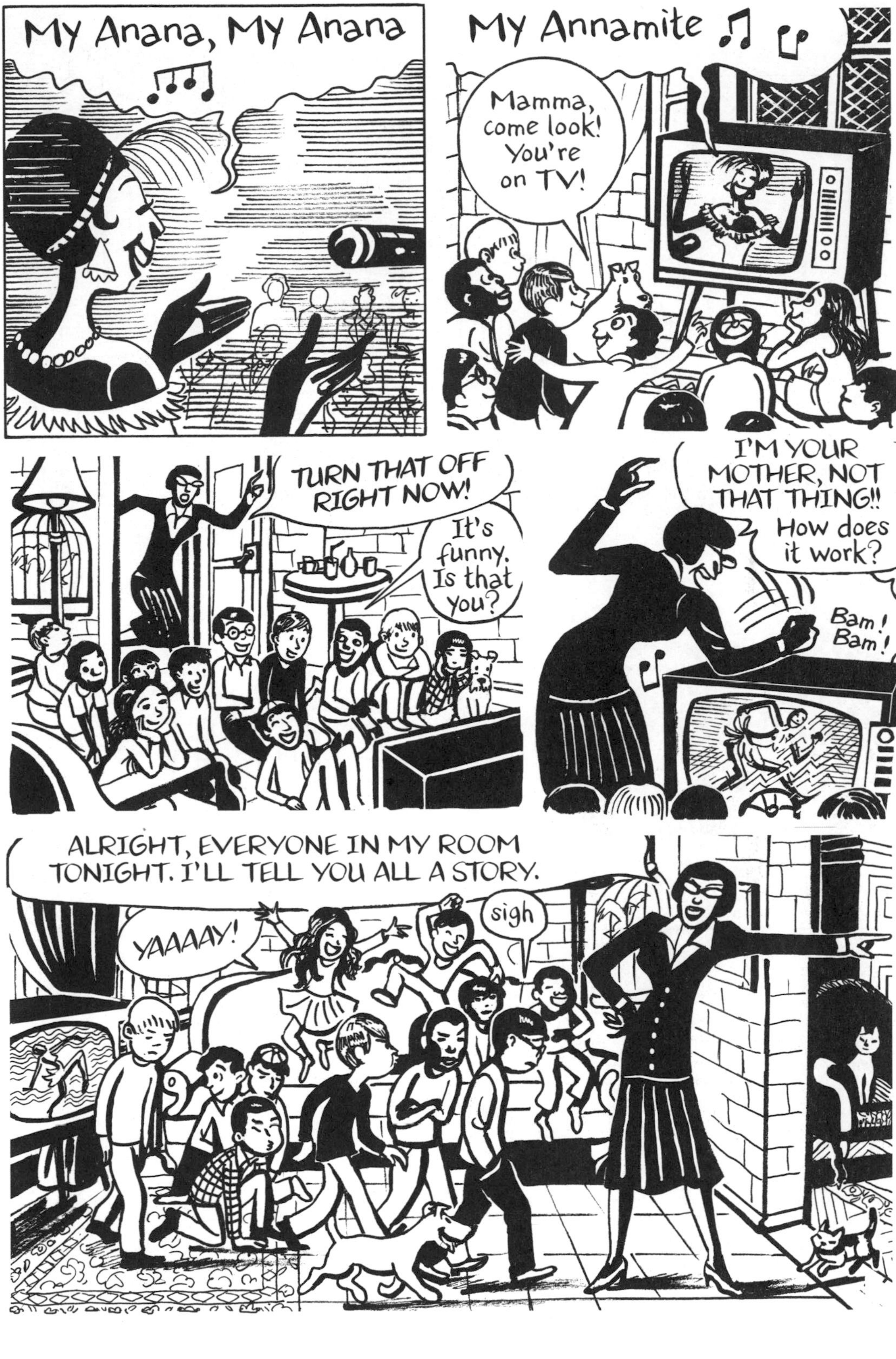
My Anana, My Anana
My Annamite
Mamma, come look! You're on TV!
TURN THAT OFF RIGHT NOW!
It's funny. Is that you?
I'M YOUR MOTHER, NOT THAT THING!!
How does it work?
Bam! Bam!
ALRIGHT, EVERYONE IN MY ROOM TONIGHT. I'LL TELL YOU ALL A STORY.
YAAAAY!
sigh

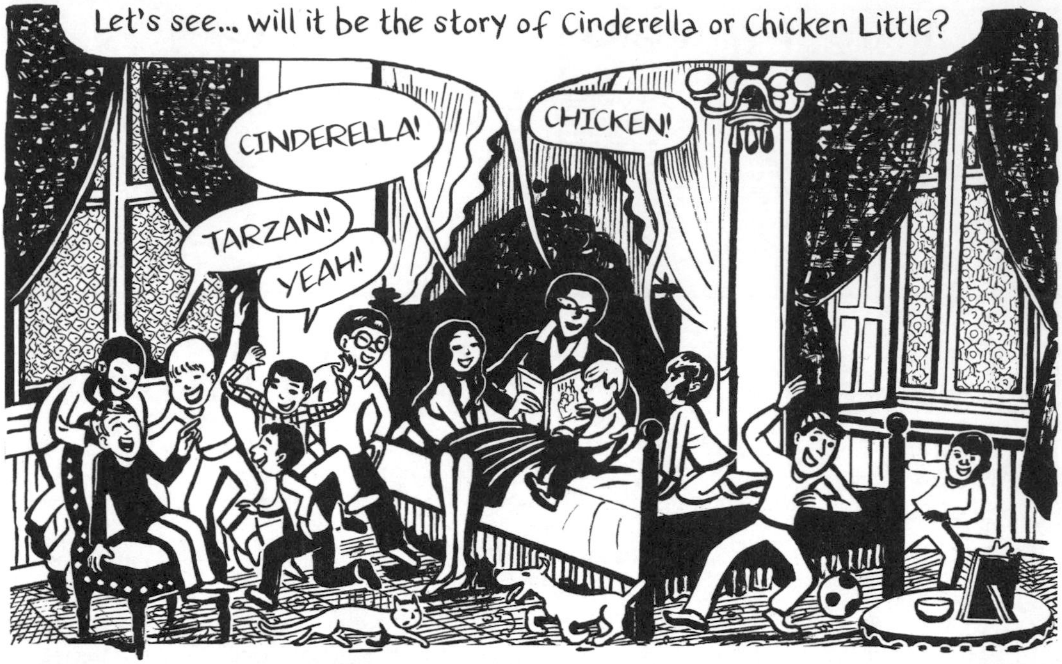
Let's see... will it be the story of Cinderella or Chicken Little?
CINDERELLA!
CHICKEN!
TARZAN!
YEAH!

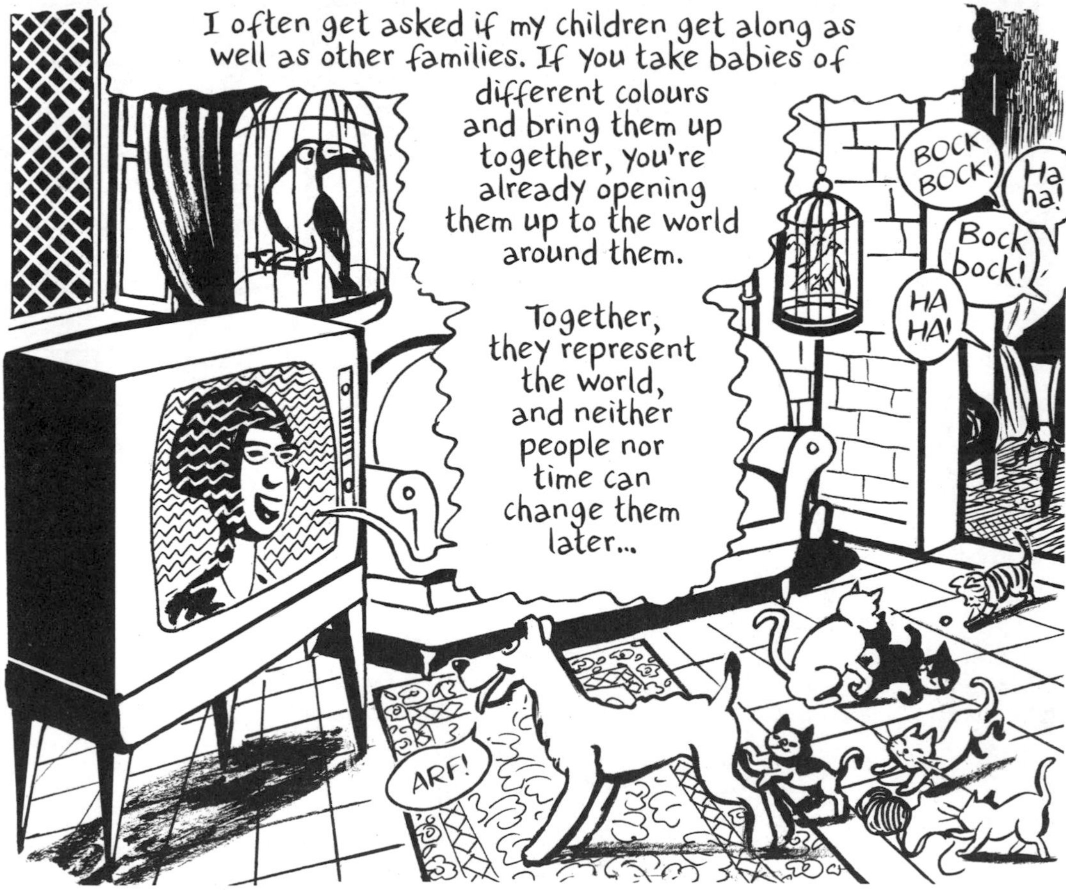
I often get asked if my children get along as well as other families. If you take babies of different colours and bring them up together, you're already opening them up to the world around them.
Together, they represent the world, and neither people nor time can change them later...
BOCK BOCK!
Ha ha!
Bock bock!
HA HA!
ARF!

1963: Lincoln Memorial, Washington DC, USA

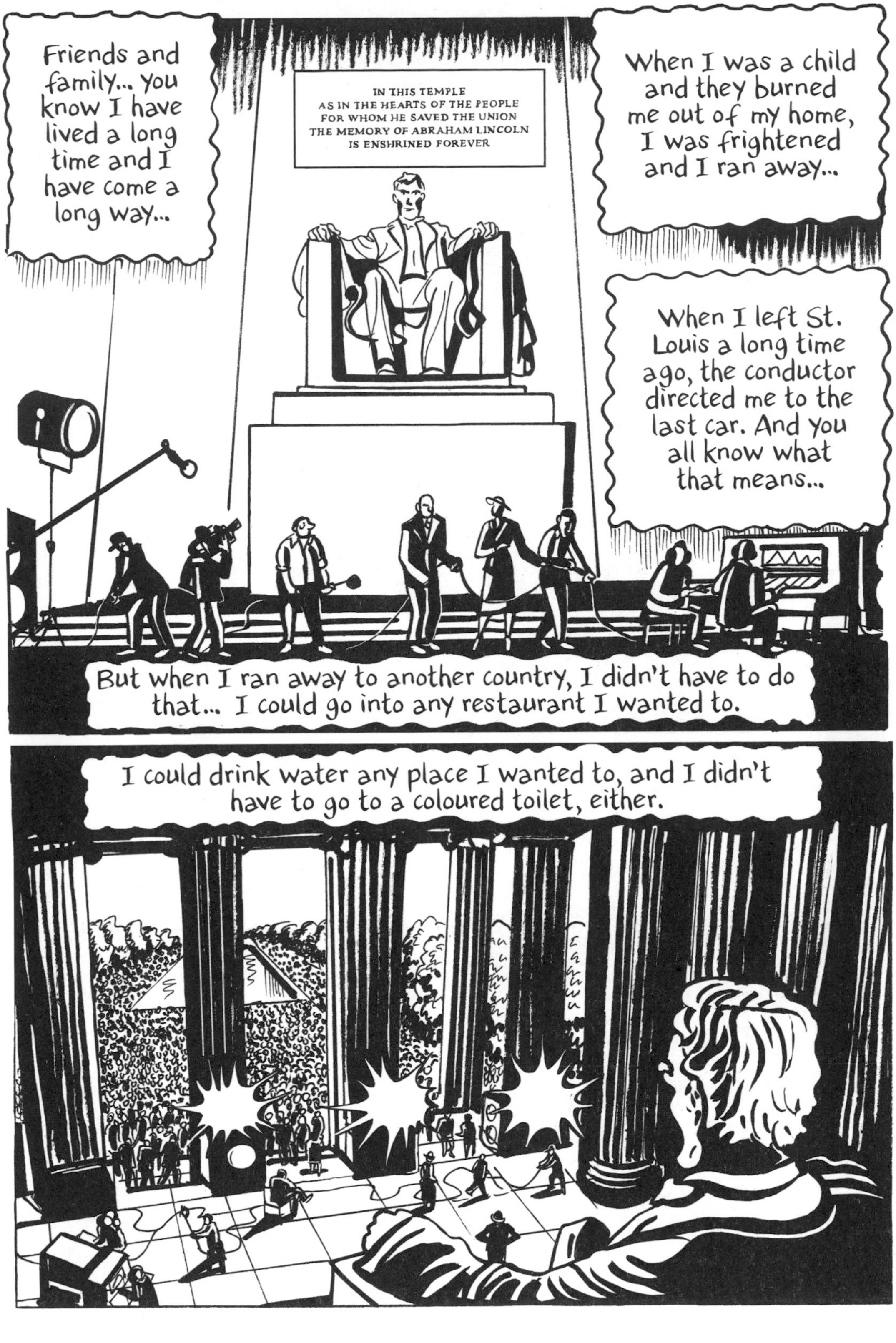
Friends and family... you know I have lived a long time and I have come a long way...
IN THIS TEMPLE AS IN THE HEARTS OF THE PEOPLE FOR WHOM HE SAVED THE UNION THE MEMORY OF ABRAHAM LINCOLN IS ENSHRINED FOREVER
When I was a child and they burned me out of my home, I was frightened and I ran away...
When I left St. Louis a long time ago, the conductor directed me to the last car. And you all know what that means...
But when I ran away to another country, I didn't have to do that... I could go into any restaurant I wanted to.
I could drink water any place I wanted to, and I didn't have to go to a coloured toilet, either.

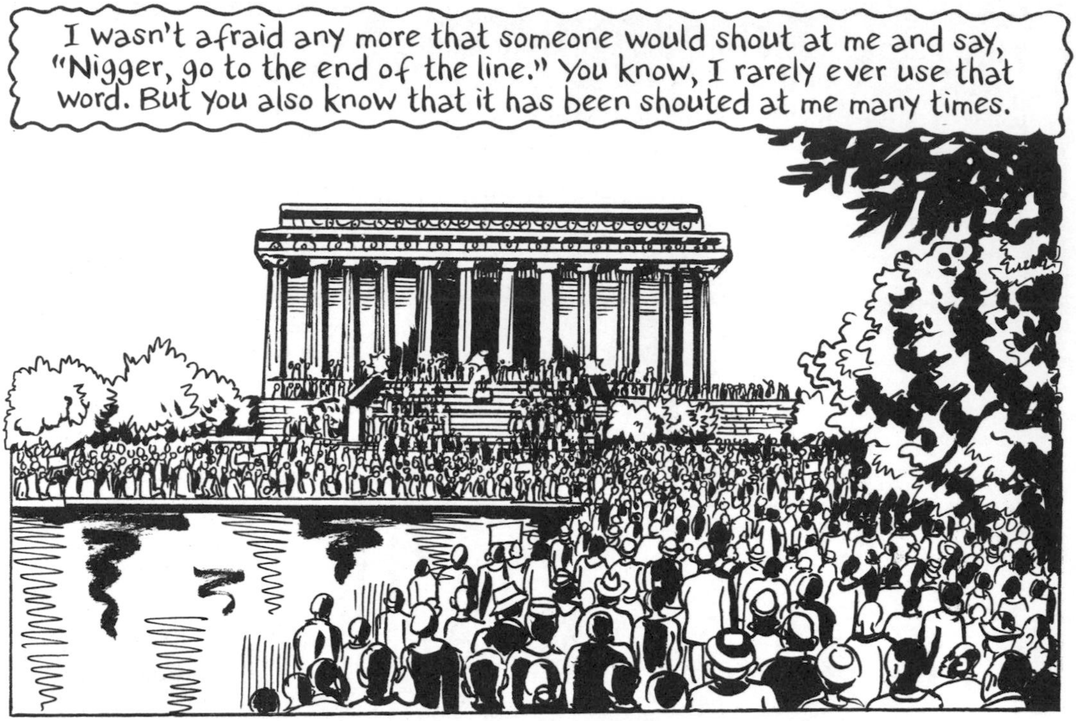
I wasn't afraid any more that someone would shout at me and say, "Nigger, go to the end of the line." You know, I rarely ever use that word. But you also know that it has been shouted at me many times.

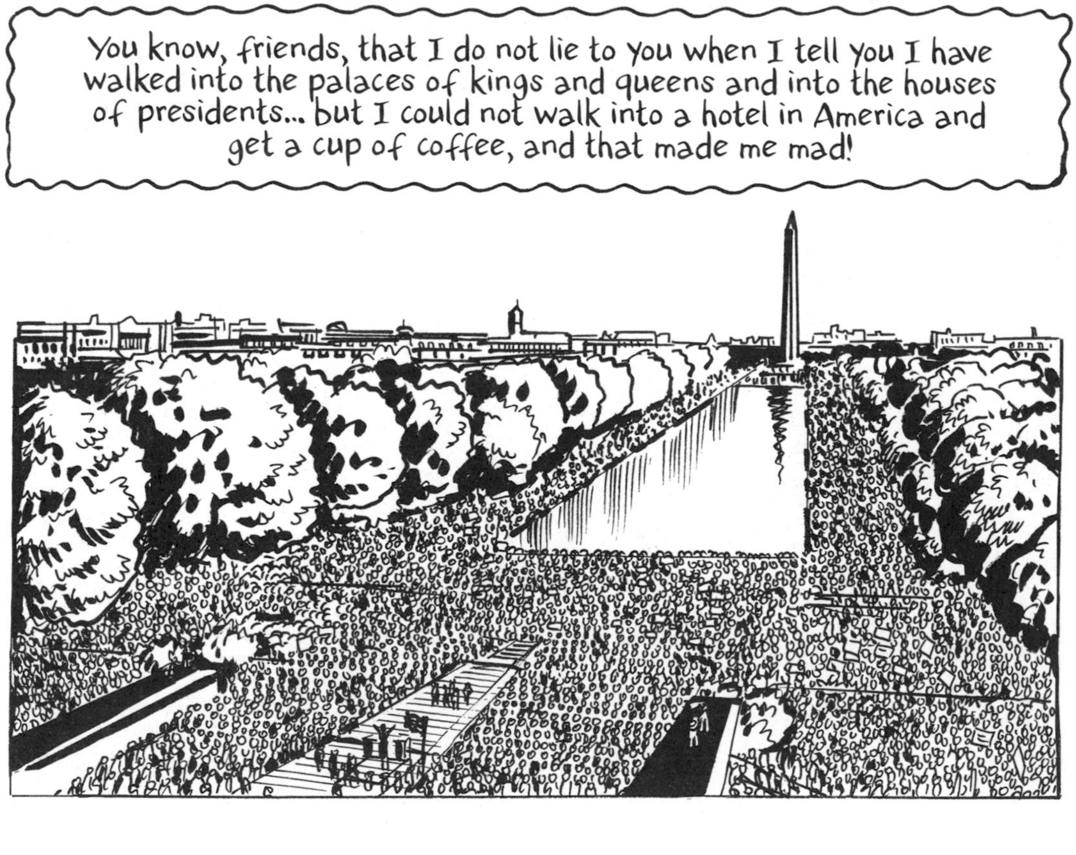
You know, friends, that I do not lie to you when I tell you I have walked into the palaces of kings and queens and into the houses of presidents... but I could not walk into a hotel in America and get a cup of coffee, and that made me mad!

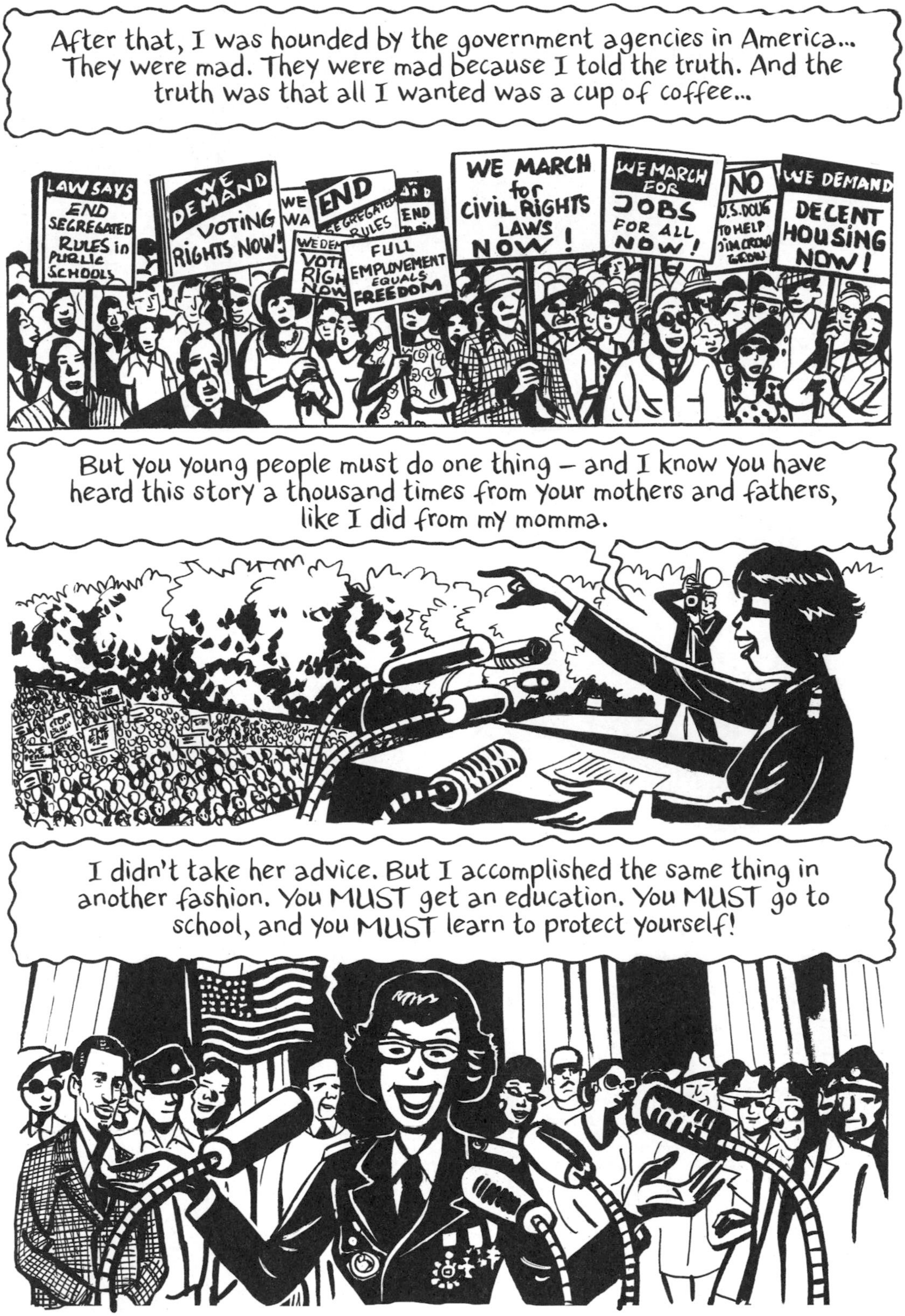
After that, I was hounded by the government agencies in America... They were mad. They were mad because I told the truth. And the truth was that all I wanted was a cup of coffee...
LAW SAYS END SEGREGATED RULES in PUBLIC SCHOOLS
WE DEMAND VOTING RIGHTS NOW!
END SEGREGATED RULES
FULL EMPLOYMENT EQUALS FREEDOM
WE MARCH for CIVIL RIGHTS LAWS NOW!
WE MARCH FOR JOBS FOR ALL NOW!
WE DEMAND DECENT HOUSING NOW!
But you young people must do one thing – and I know you have heard this story a thousand times from your mothers and fathers, like I did from my momma.
I didn't take her advice. But I accomplished the same thing in another fashion. You MUST get an education. You MUST go to school, and you MUST learn to protect yourself!

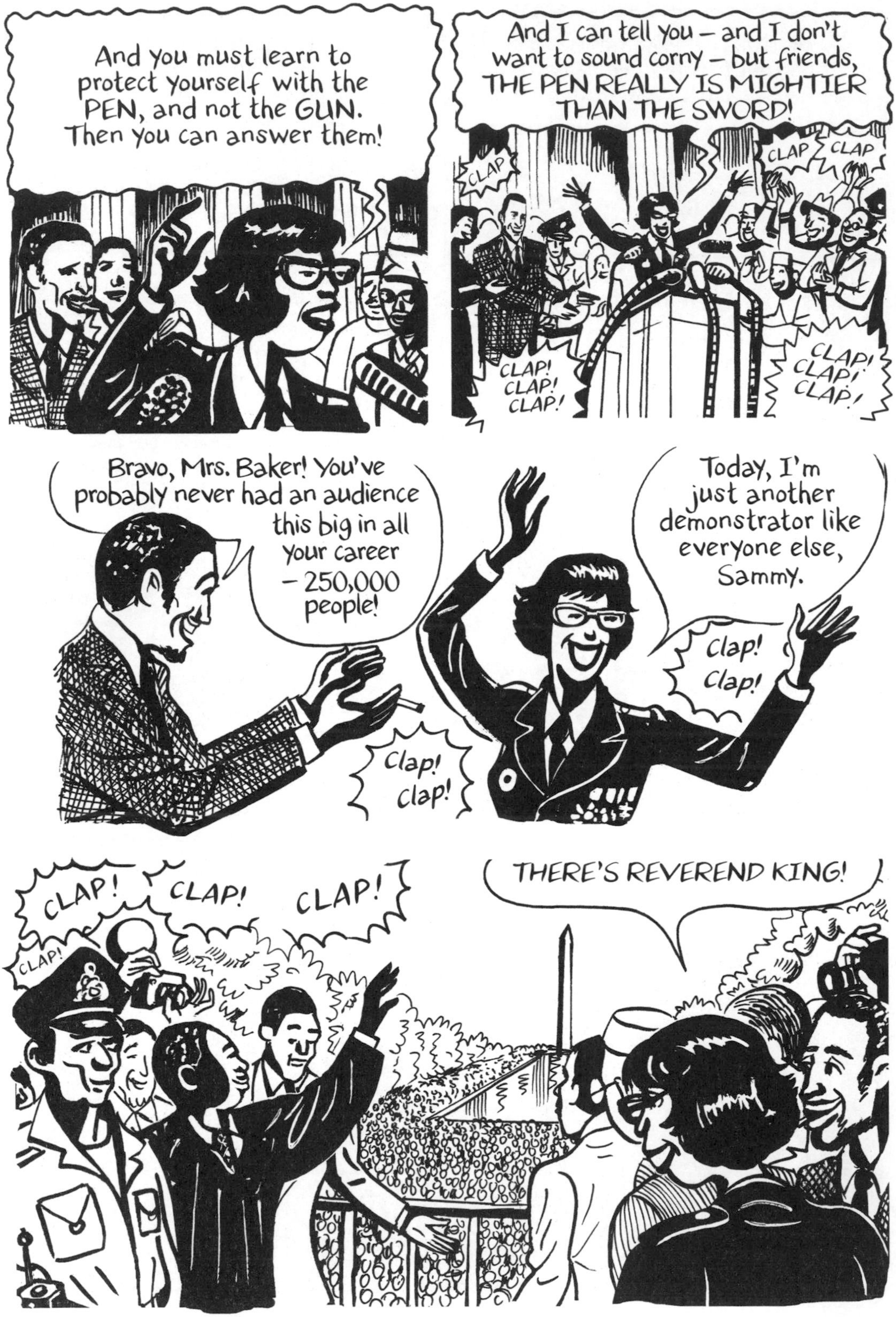
And you must learn to protect yourself with the PEN, and not the GUN. Then you can answer them!
And I can tell you – and I don't want to sound corny – but friends, THE PEN REALLY IS MIGHTIER THAN THE SWORD!
CLAP
CLAP CLAP
CLAP! CLAP! CLAP!
CLAP! CLAP! CLAP!
Bravo, Mrs. Baker! You've probably never had an audience this big in all your career – 250,000 people!
Today, I'm just another demonstrator like everyone else, Sammy.
Clap! Clap!
Clap! Clap!
CLAP! CLAP! CLAP!
CLAP!
THERE'S REVEREND KING!

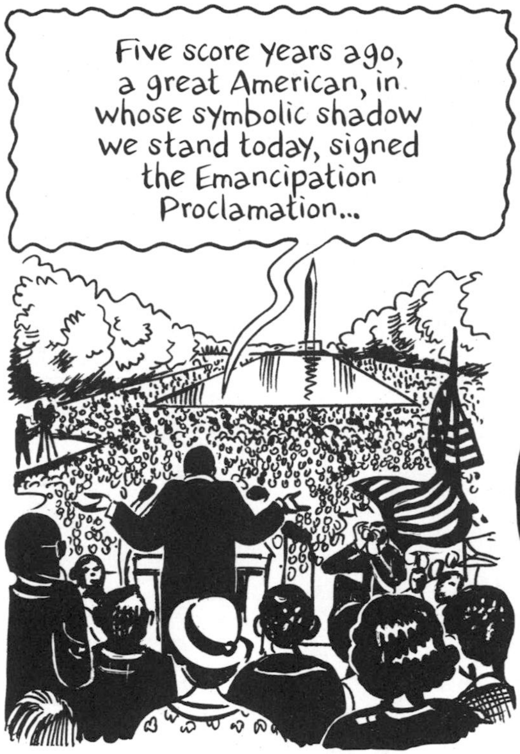
Five score years ago, a great American, in whose symbolic shadow we stand today, signed the Emancipation Proclamation...

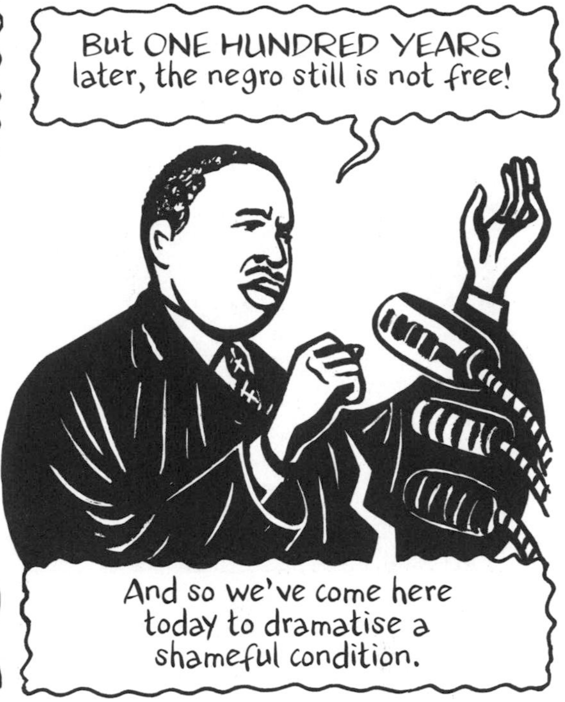
But ONE HUNDRED YEARS later, the negro still is not free!
And so we've come here today to dramatise a shameful condition.

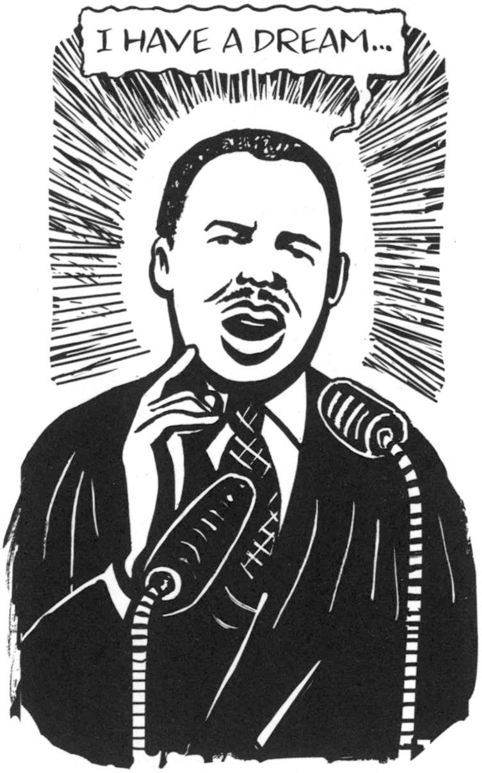
I HAVE A DREAM...

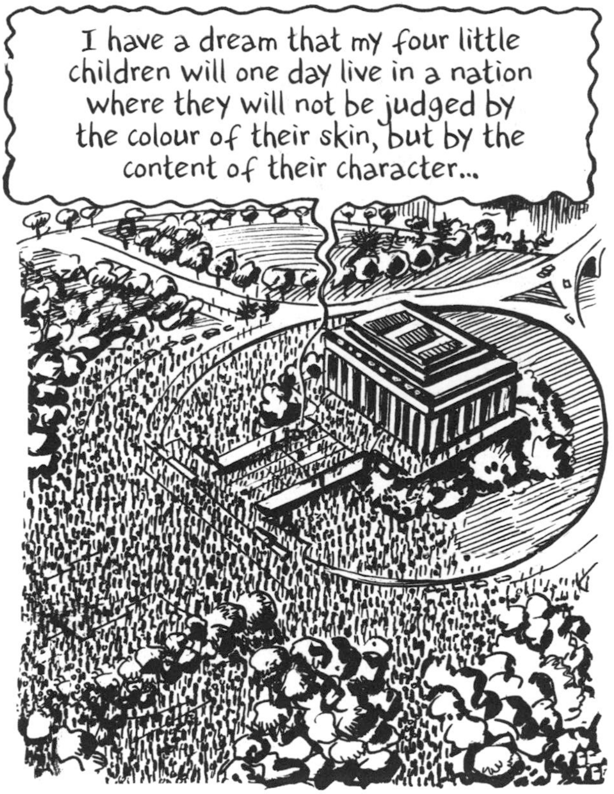
I have a dream that my four little children will one day live in a nation where they will not be judged by the colour of their skin, but by the content of their character...

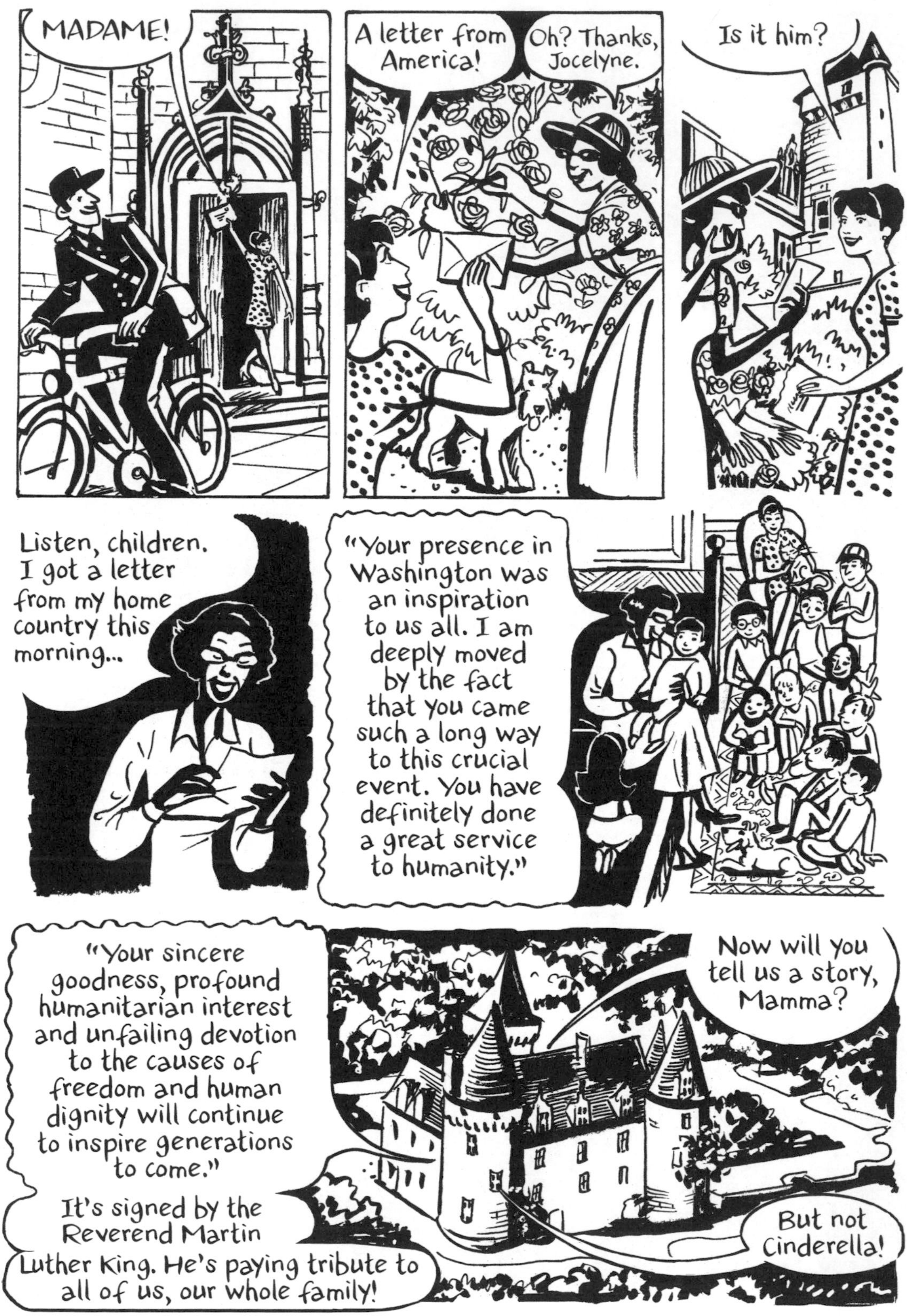
MADAME!
A letter from America!
Oh? Thanks, Jocelyne.
Is it him?
Listen, children. I got a letter from my home country this morning...
"Your presence in Washington was an inspiration to us all. I am deeply moved by the fact that you came such a long way to this crucial event. You have definitely done a great service to humanity."
"Your sincere goodness, profound humanitarian interest and unfailing devotion to the causes of freedom and human dignity will continue to inspire generations to come."
It's signed by the Reverend Martin Luther King. He's paying tribute to all of us, our whole family!
Now will you tell us a story, Mamma?
But not Cinderella!

1963: Antony, Hauts-de-Seine, France

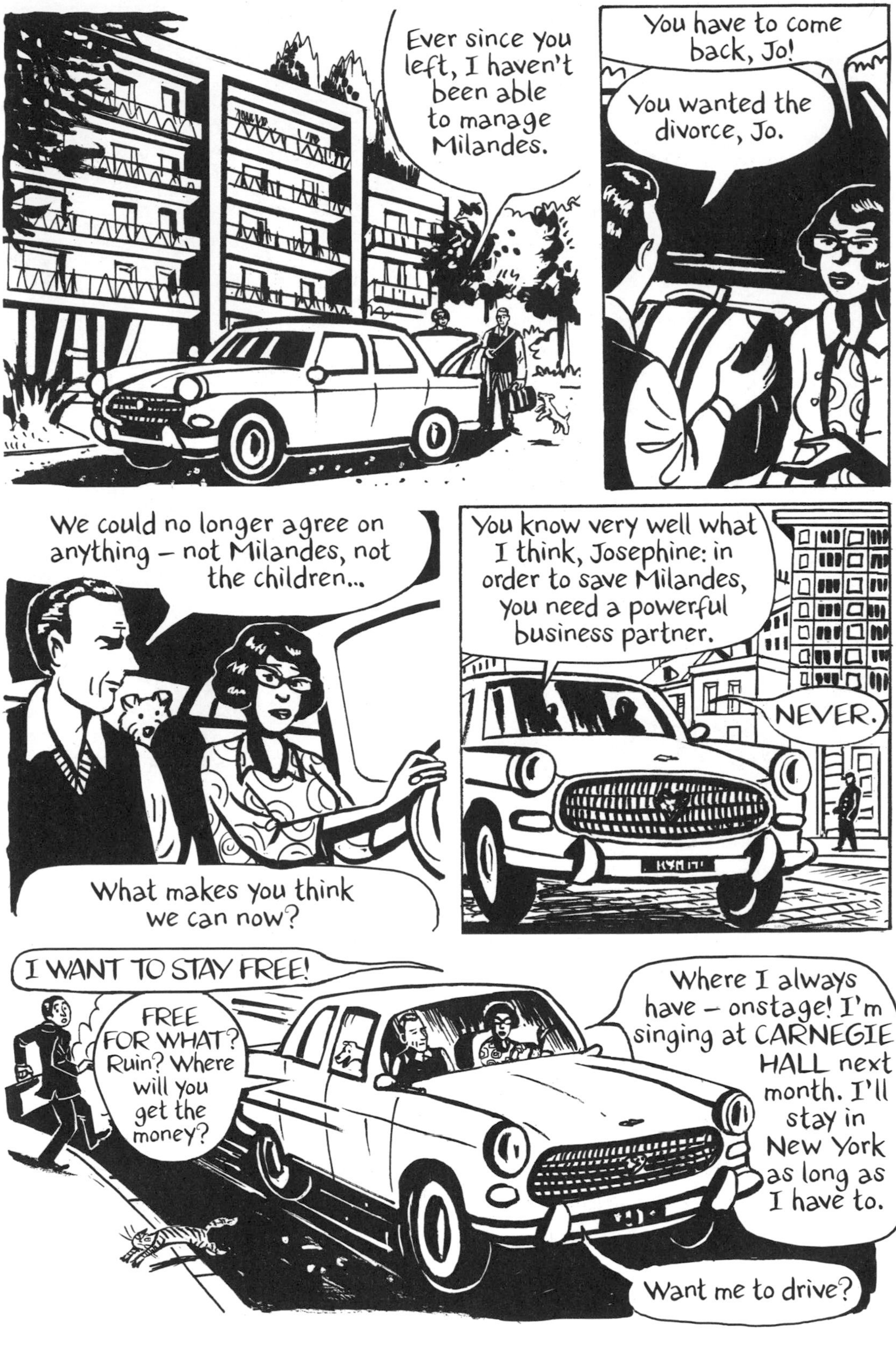

Ever since you left, I haven't been able to manage Milandes.
You have to come back, Jo!
You wanted the divorce, Jo.
We could no longer agree on anything – not Milandes, not the children...
What makes you think we can now?
You know very well what I think, Josephine: in order to save Milandes, you need a powerful business partner.
NEVER.
I WANT TO STAY FREE!
FREE FOR WHAT? Ruin? Where will you get the money?
Where I always have – onstage! I'm singing at CARNEGIE HALL next month. I'll stay in New York as long as I have to.
Want me to drive?

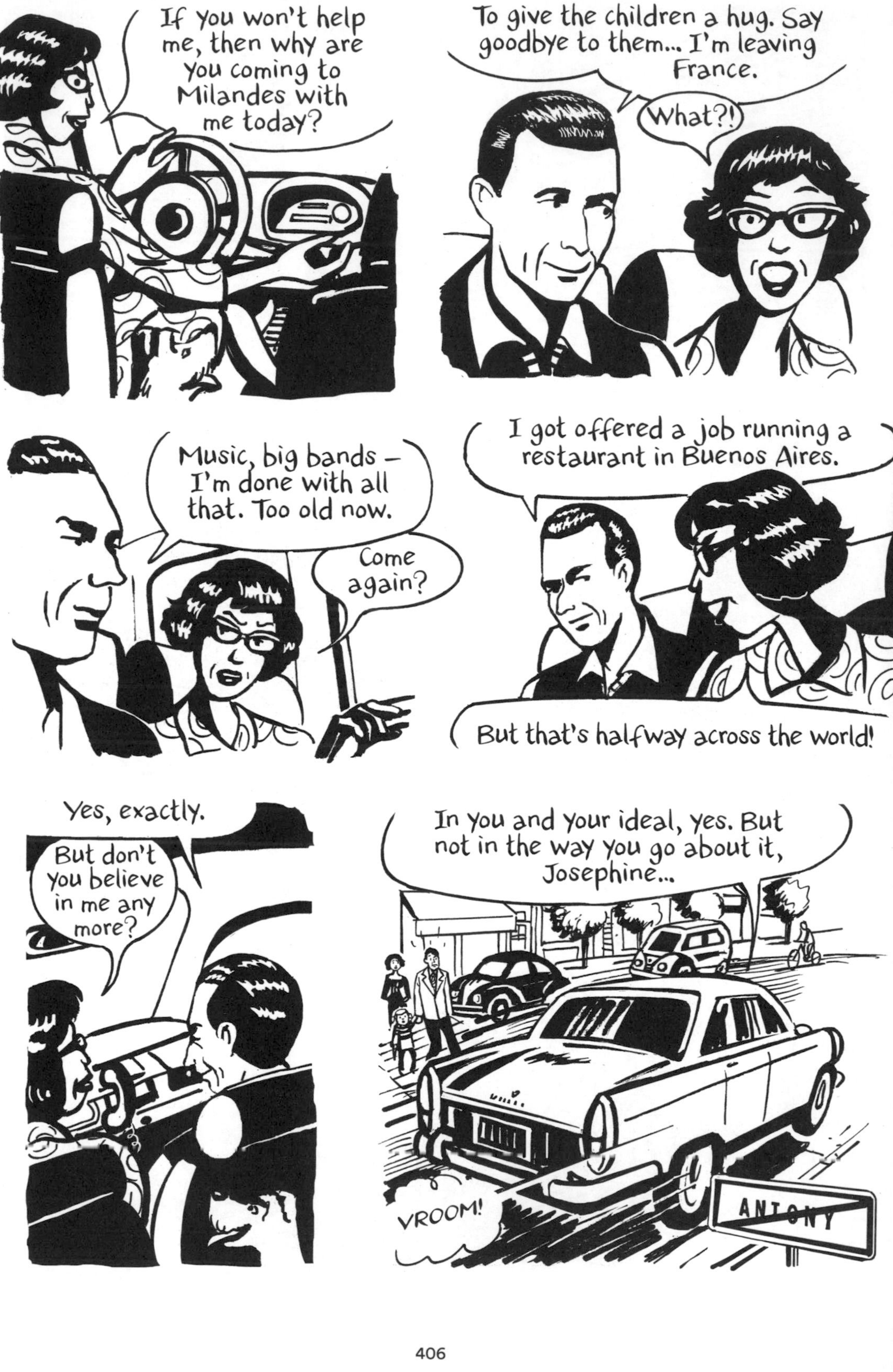
If you won't help me, then why are you coming to Milandes with me today?
To give the children a hug. Say goodbye to them... I'm leaving France.
What?!
Music, big bands – I'm done with all that. Too old now.
Come again?
I got offered a job running a restaurant in Buenos Aires.
But that's halfway across the world!
Yes, exactly.
But don't you believe in me any more?
In you and your ideal, yes. But not in the way you go about it, Josephine...
VROOM!
ANTONY

1964: Lou Tornoli Restaurant, Milandes, Périgord, France

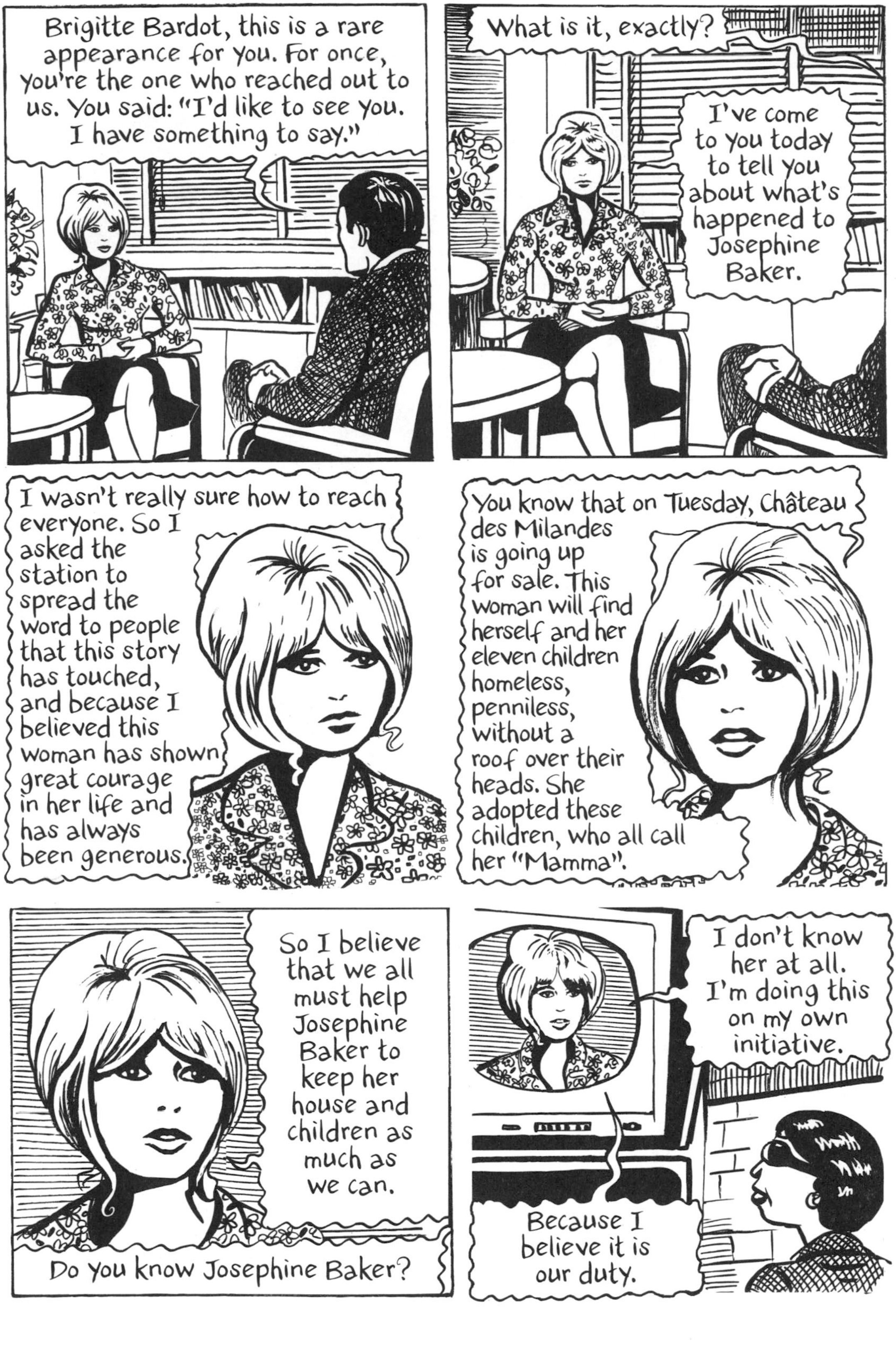

Brigitte Bardot, this is a rare appearance for you. For once, you're the one who reached out to us. You said: "I'd like to see you. I have something to say."
What is it, exactly?
I've come to you today to tell you about what's happened to Josephine Baker.
I wasn't really sure how to reach everyone. So I asked the station to spread the word to people that this story has touched, and because I believed this woman has shown great courage in her life and has always been generous.
You know that on Tuesday, Château des Milandes is going up for sale. This woman will find herself and her eleven children homeless, penniless, without a roof over their heads. She adopted these children, who all call her "Mamma".
So I believe that we all must help Josephine Baker to keep her house and children as much as we can.
Do you know Josephine Baker?
I don't know her at all. I'm doing this on my own initiative.
Because I believe it is our duty.

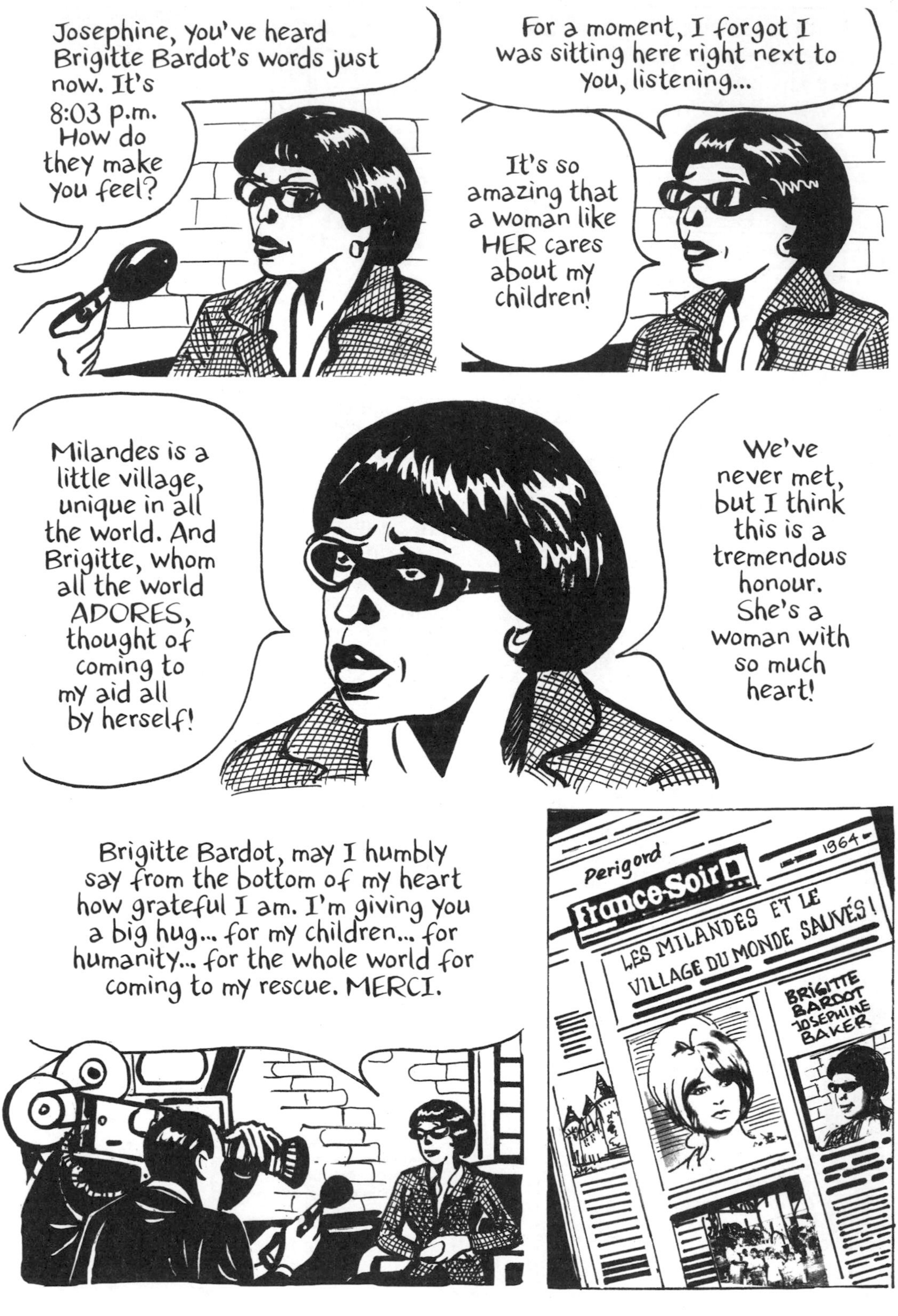
Josephine, you've heard Brigitte Bardot's words just now. It's 8:03 p.m. How do they make you feel?
For a moment, I forgot I was sitting here right next to you, listening...
It's so amazing that a woman like HER cares about my children!
Milandes is a little village, unique in all the world. And Brigitte, whom all the world ADORES, thought of coming to my aid all by herself!
We've never met, but I think this is a tremendous honour. She's a woman with so much heart!
Brigitte Bardot, may I humbly say from the bottom of my heart how grateful I am. I'm giving you a big hug... for my children... for humanity... for the whole world for coming to my rescue. MERCI.
Perigord
1964
France-Soir
LES MILANDES ET LE VILLAGE DU MONDE SAUVÉS!
BRIGITTE BARDOT JOSEPHINE BAKER

1966: Littoral Varadero, Cuba

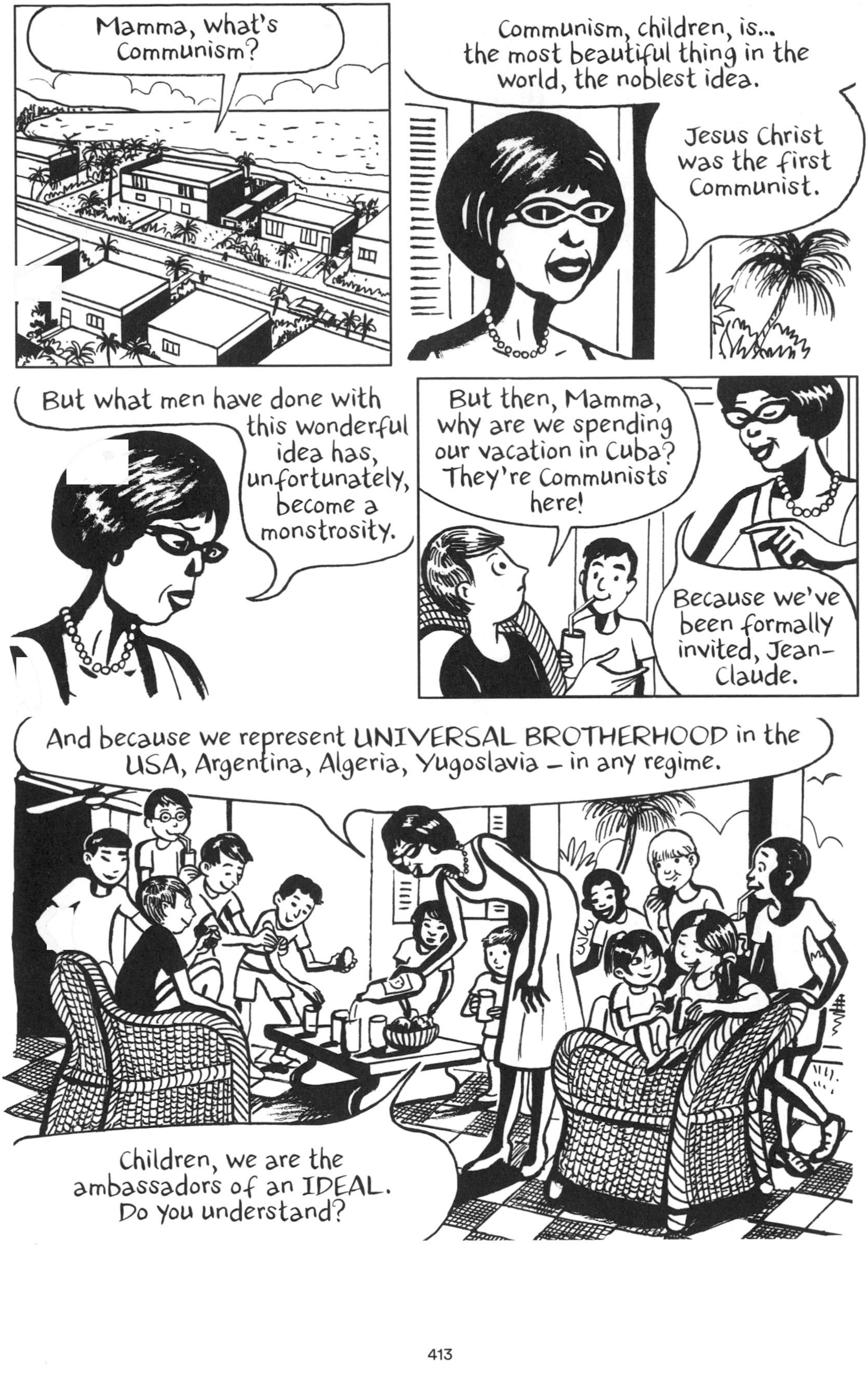
Mamma, what's Communism?
Communism, children, is... the most beautiful thing in the world, the noblest idea.
Jesus Christ was the first Communist.
But what men have done with this wonderful idea has, unfortunately, become a monstrosity.
But then, Mamma, why are we spending our vacation in Cuba? They're Communists here!
Because we've been formally invited, Jean-Claude.
And because we represent UNIVERSAL BROTHERHOOD in the USA, Argentina, Algeria, Yugoslavia – in any regime.
Children, we are the ambassadors of an IDEAL. Do you understand?

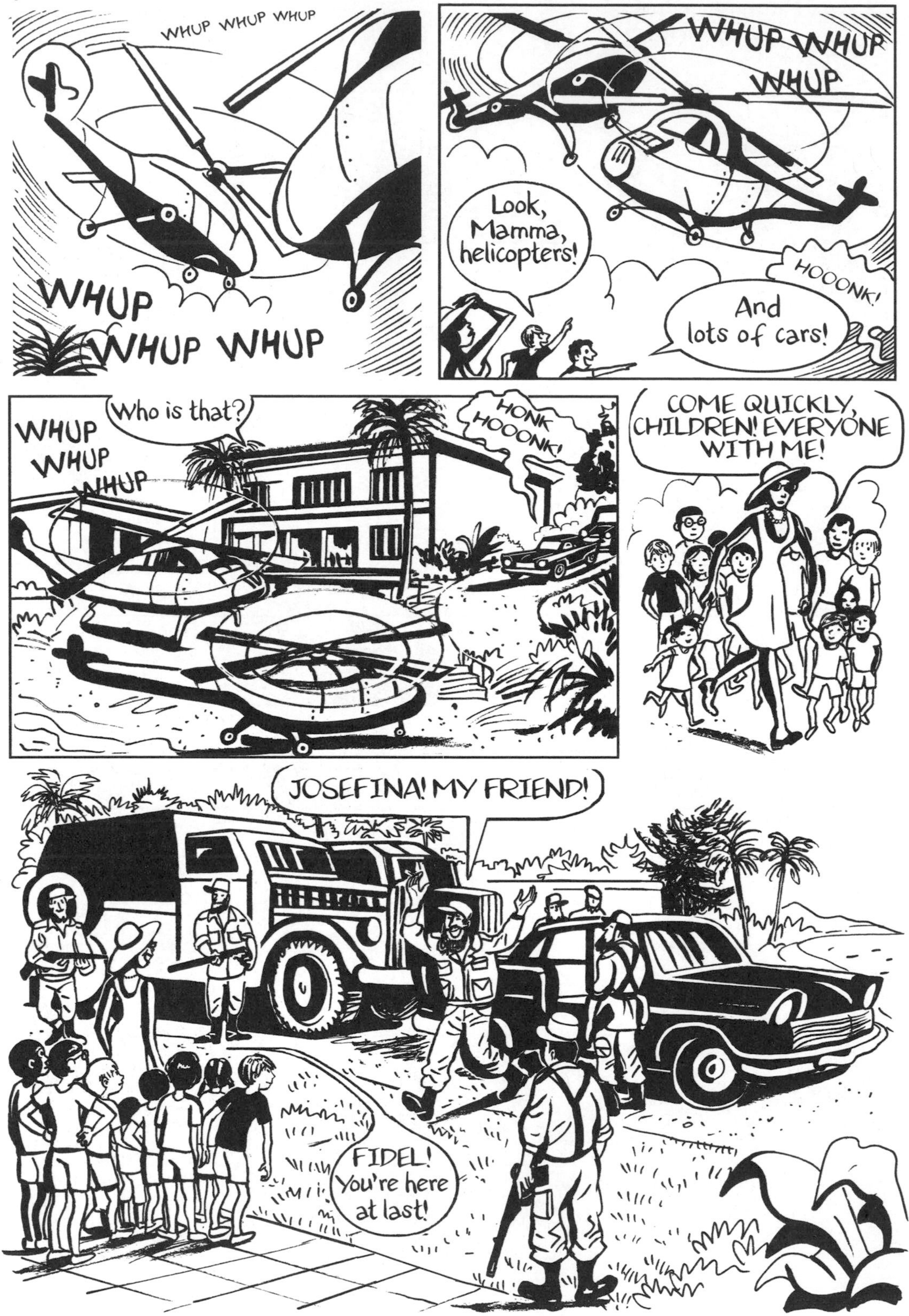
WHUP WHUP WHUP
WHUP WHUP WHUP
WHUP WHUP WHUP
Look, Mamma, helicopters!
HOOONK!
And lots of cars!
WHUP WHUP WHUP
Who is that?
HONK HOOONK!
COME QUICKLY, CHILDREN! EVERYONE WITH ME!
JOSEFINA! MY FRIEND!
FIDEL! You're here at last!

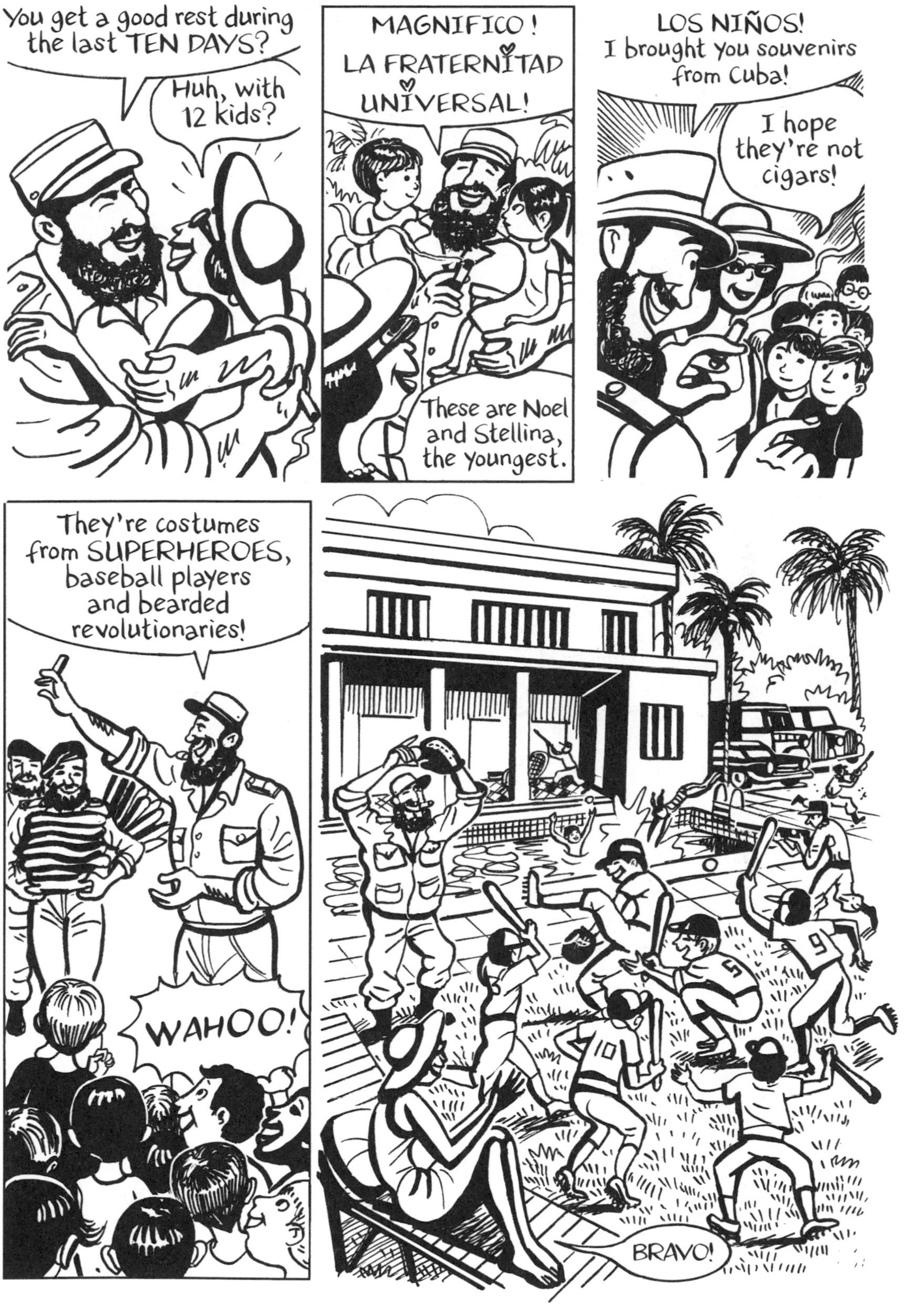
You get a good rest during the last TEN DAYS?
Huh, with 12 kids?
MAGNIFICO! LA FRATERNITAD UNIVERSAL!
These are Noel and Stellina, the youngest.
LOS NIÑOS! I brought you souvenirs from Cuba!
I hope they're not cigars!
They're costumes from SUPERHEROES, baseball players and bearded revolutionaries!
WAHOO!
BRAVO!

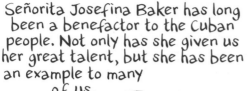

Señorita Josefina Baker has long been a benefactor to the Cuban people. Not only has she given us her great talent, but she has been an example to many of us.

Tío Fidel was still a young lawyer when I met him...

Together, we marched against Batista's dictatorship!

I was imprisoned, then deported...

I was in your wonderful country when I got the idea for a possible fraternity: whites, blacks and mulattos living here in total racial harmony.

An example for the whole world.

Josephine Baker, you are a heroine of the REVOLUCÍON!

1968: Milandes Park, Périgord, France

THIS IS MY HOUSE! MY FATHER BOUGHT MILANDES!

NOT YET! SCRAM!

That moron wised up! He's running away!

Grrr!

Akio Jarry Jangy

How about we vandalise EVERYTHING? So that son of a thief couldn't use it?

Akio Jarry Ja

Jean-Clay

Luis

One thing he'll never be able to do is erase our names!

Milandes will always be OURS!

DONG!

DONG! DONG!

DINNERTIME! Mamma's ringing the bell for the last time.

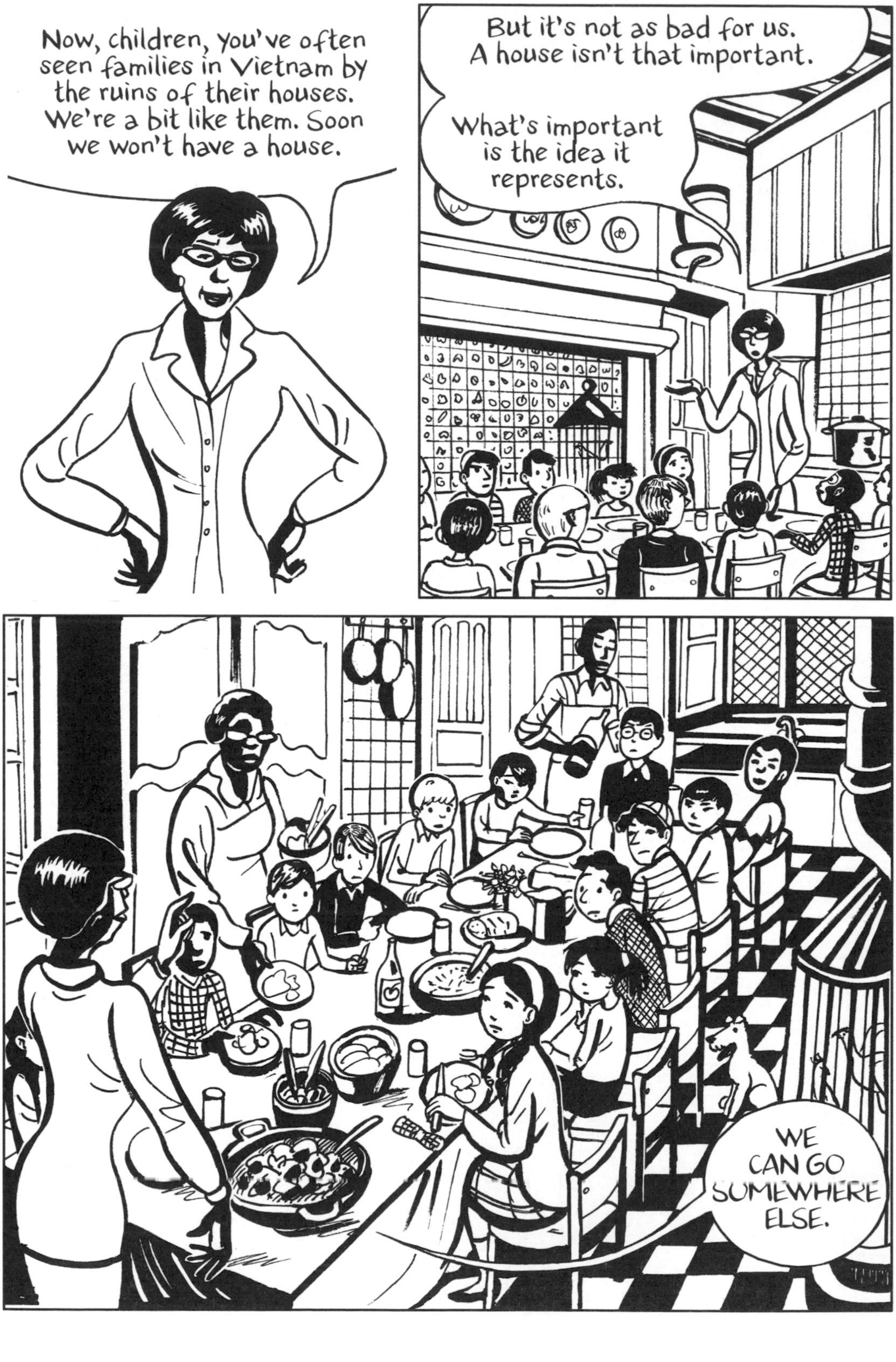
Now, children, you've often seen families in Vietnam by the ruins of their houses. We're a bit like them. Soon we won't have a house.
But it's not as bad for us. A house isn't that important.
What's important is the idea it represents.
WE CAN GO SOMEWHERE ELSE.

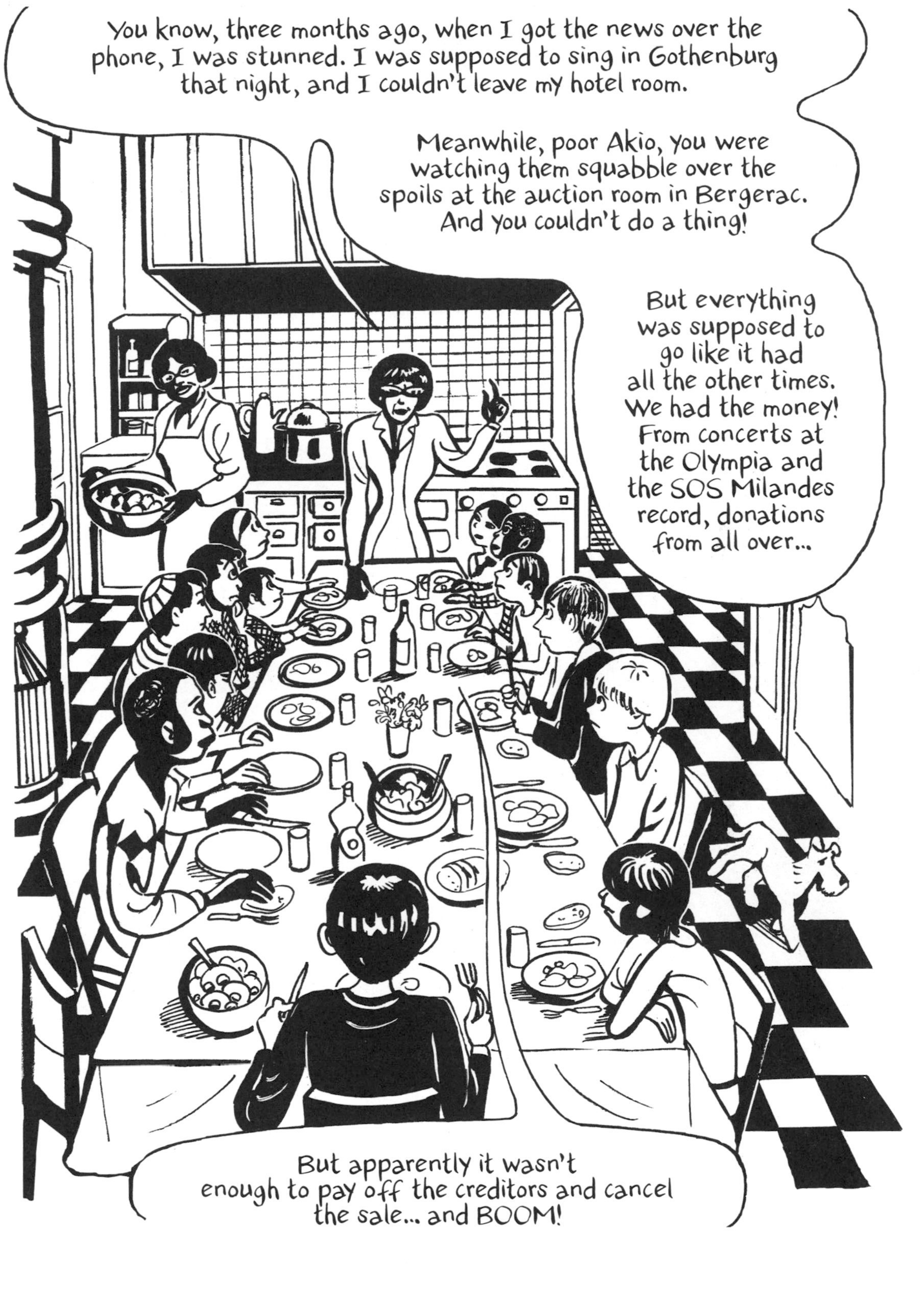
You know, three months ago, when I got the news over the phone, I was stunned. I was supposed to sing in Gothenburg that night, and I couldn't leave my hotel room.
Meanwhile, poor Akio, you were watching them squabble over the spoils at the auction room in Bergerac. And you couldn't do a thing!
But everything was supposed to go like it had all the other times. We had the money! From concerts at the Olympia and the SOS Milandes record, donations from all over...
But apparently it wasn't enough to pay off the creditors and cancel the sale... and BOOM!

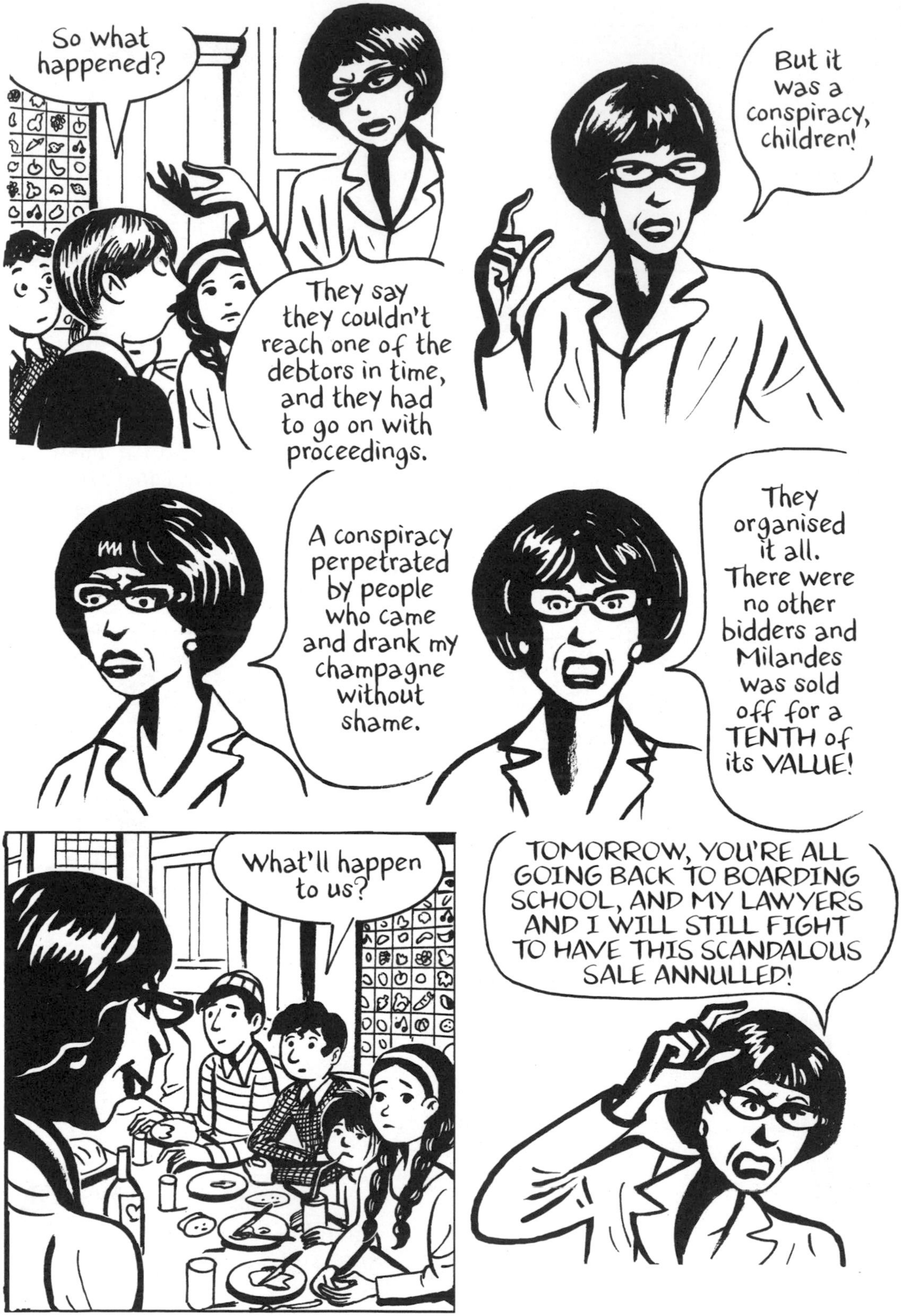
So what happened?
They say they couldn't reach one of the debtors in time, and they had to go on with proceedings.
But it was a conspiracy, children!
A conspiracy perpetrated by people who came and drank my champagne without shame.
They organised it all. There were no other bidders and Milandes was sold off for a TENTH of its VALUE!
What'll happen to us?
TOMORROW, YOU'RE ALL GOING BACK TO BOARDING SCHOOL, AND MY LAWYERS AND I WILL STILL FIGHT TO HAVE THIS SCANDALOUS SALE ANNULLED!

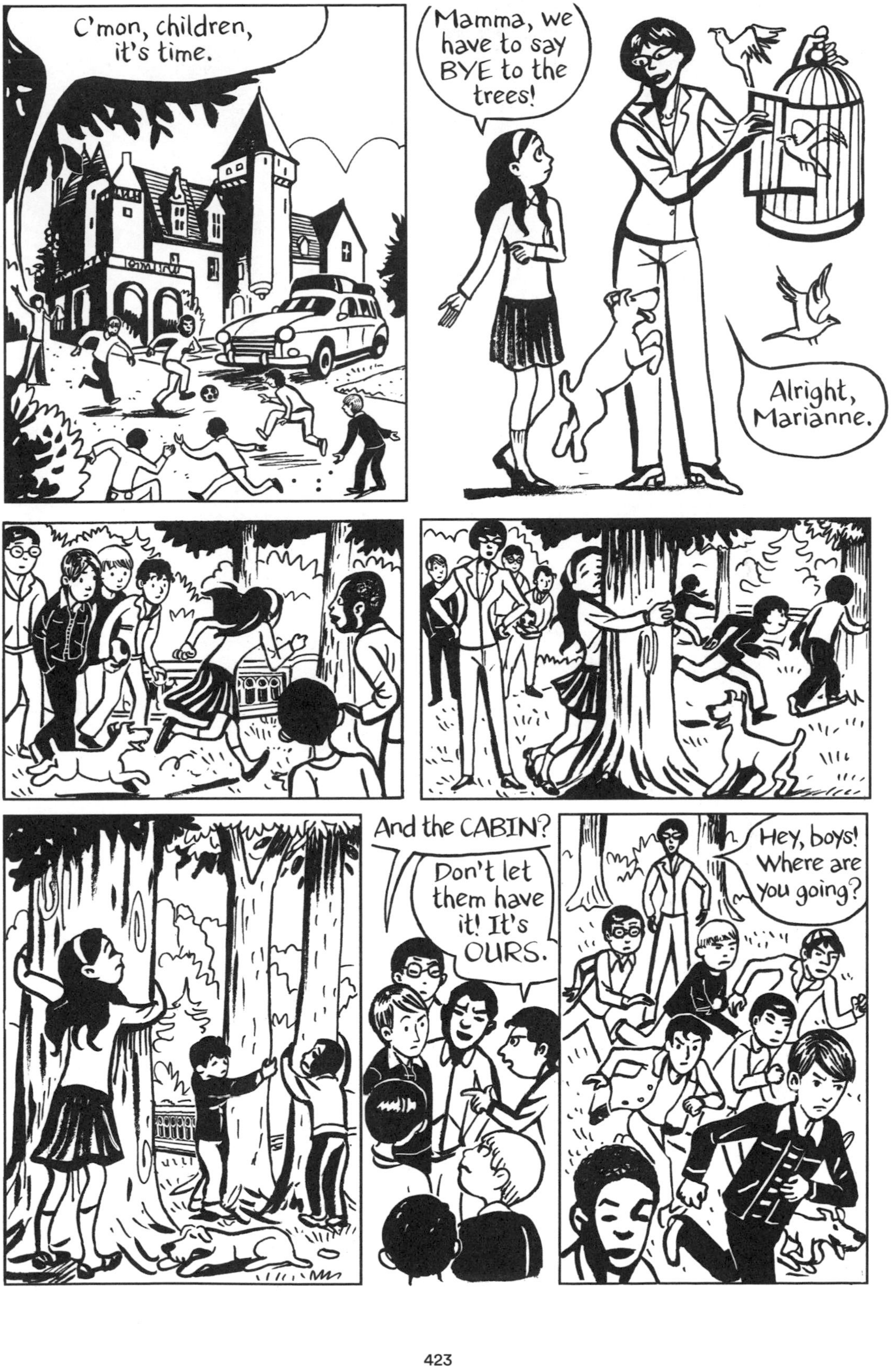
C'mon, children, it's time.
Mamma, we have to say BYE to the trees!
Alright, Marianne.
And the CABIN?
Don't let them have it! It's OURS.
Hey, boys! Where are you going?

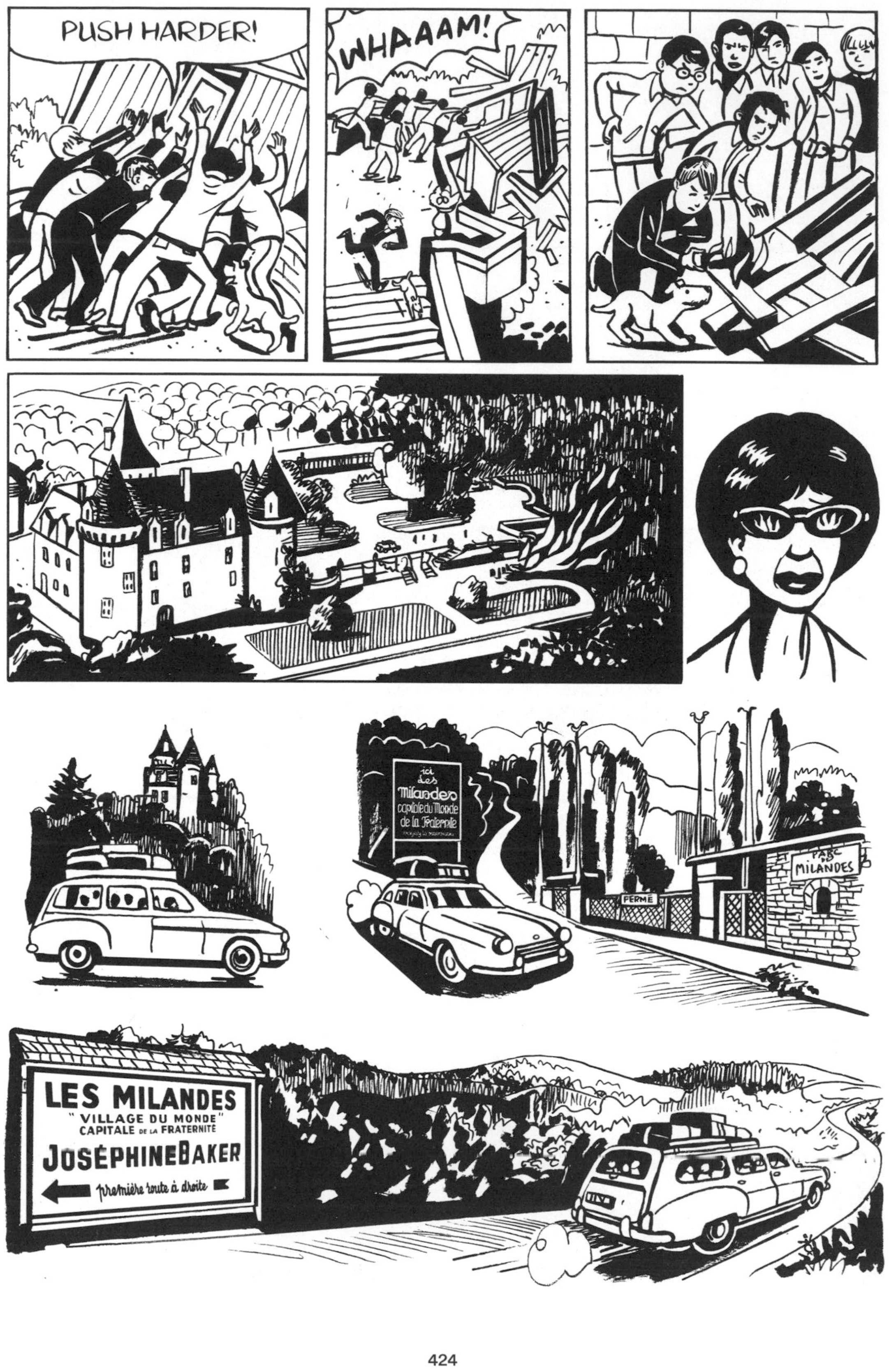
PUSH HARDER!
WHAAAM!
ici des Milandes capitale du Monde de la Fraternité
FERMÉ
ET PARC DE MILANDES
LES MILANDES
" VILLAGE DU MONDE "
CAPITALE DE LA FRATERNITÉ
JOSÉPHINE BAKER
première route à droite

1969: Villa Maryvonne, Roquebrune-Cap-Martin,
Alpes-Maritimes, France

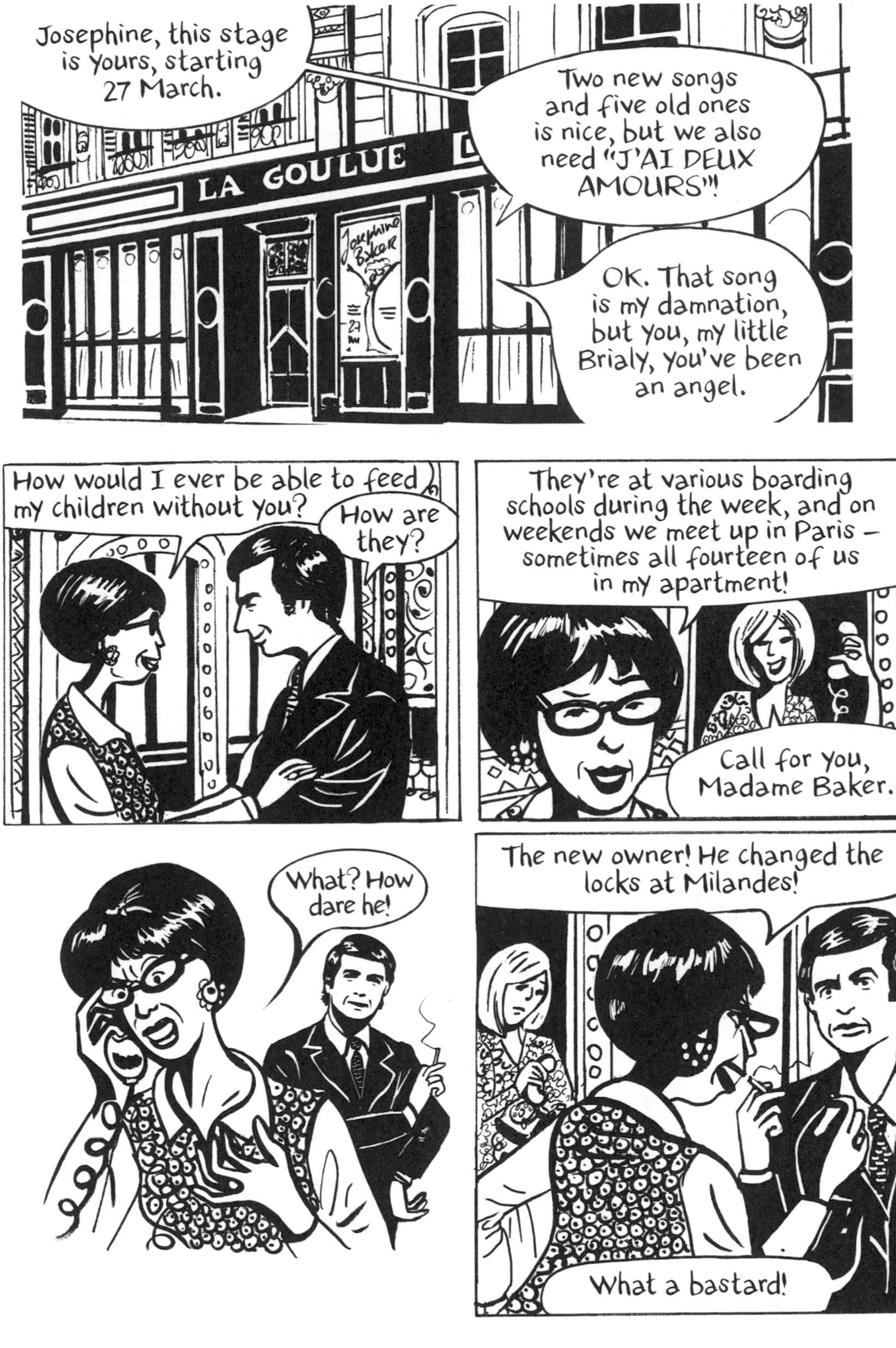

Josephine, this stage is yours, starting 27 March.
Two new songs and five old ones is nice, but we also need "J'AI DEUX AMOURS"!
LA GOULUE
Josephine Baker
27
OK. That song is my damnation, but you, my little Brialy, you've been an angel.
How would I ever be able to feed my children without you?
How are they?
They're at various boarding schools during the week, and on weekends we meet up in Paris – sometimes all fourteen of us in my apartment!
Call for you, Madame Baker.
What? How dare he!
The new owner! He changed the locks at Milandes!
What a bastard!

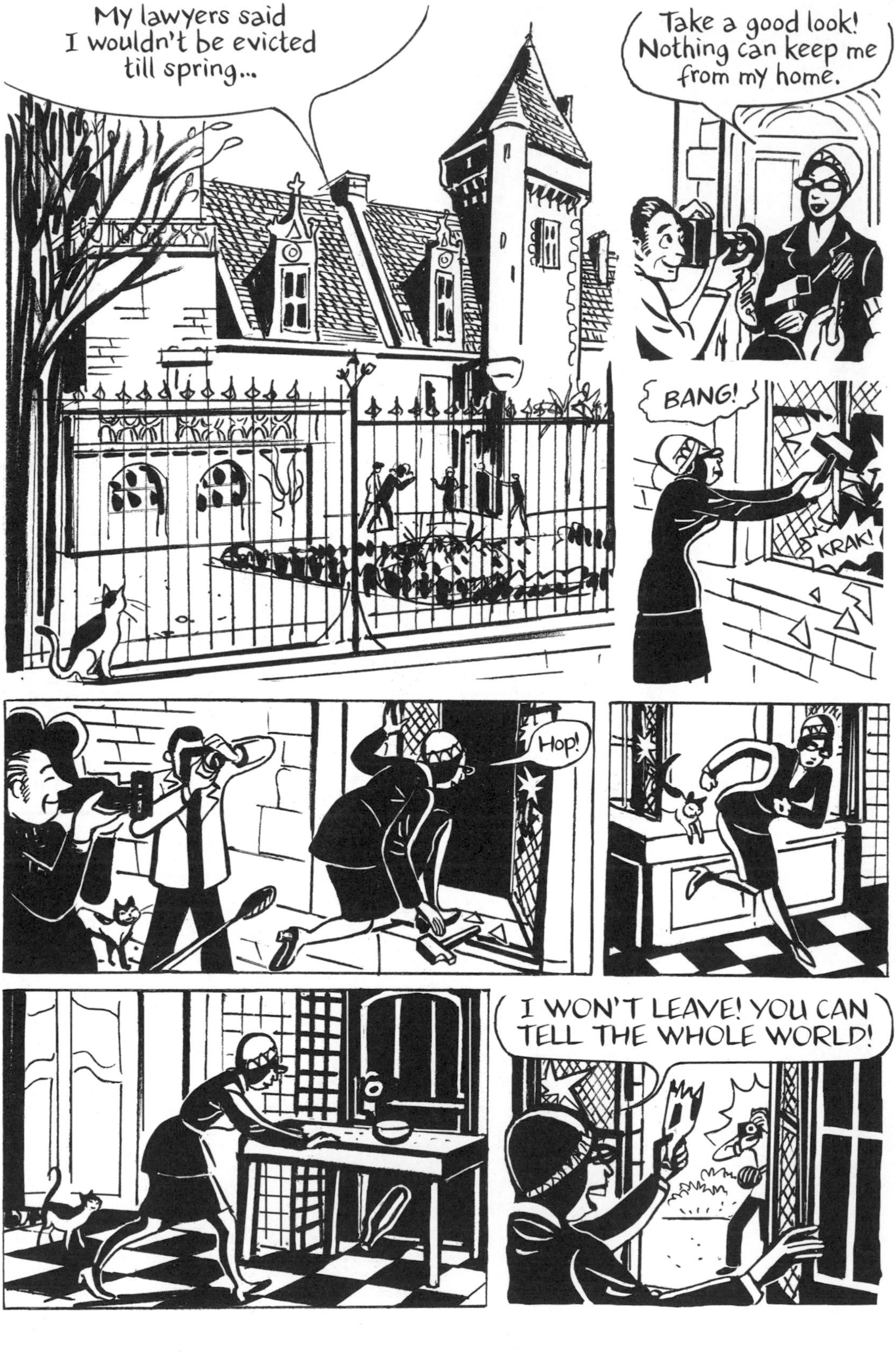
My lawyers said I wouldn't be evicted till spring...
Take a good look! Nothing can keep me from my home.
BANG!
KRAK!
Hop!
I WON'T LEAVE! YOU CAN TELL THE WHOLE WORLD!

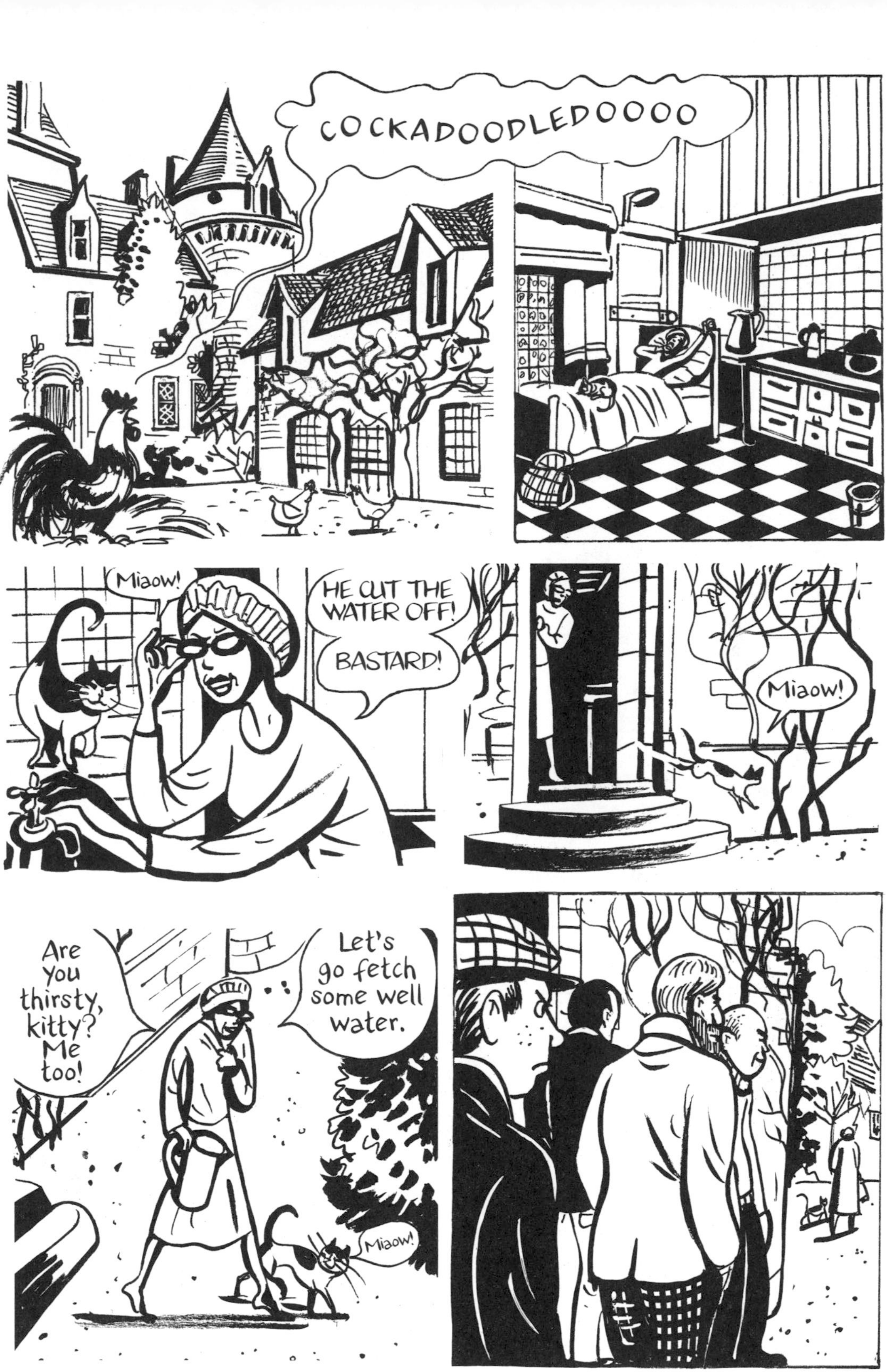
COCKADOODLEDOOOO
Miaow!
HE CUT THE WATER OFF!
BASTARD!
Miaow!
Are you thirsty, kitty? Me too!
Let's go fetch some well water.
Miaow!

GET HER!
LET ME GO!
SETTLE DOWN, YOU CRAZY OLD NIGGER!
GET OUT!

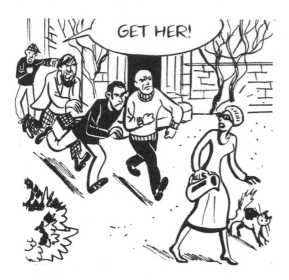

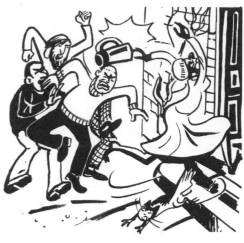

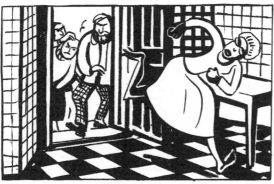

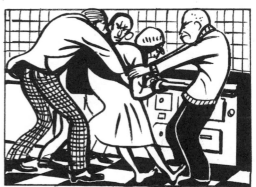

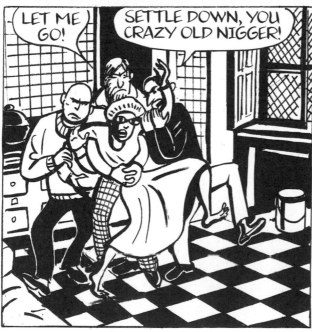

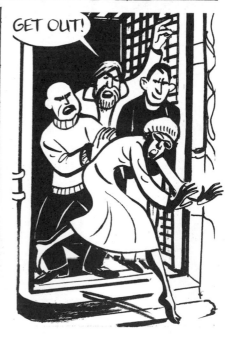

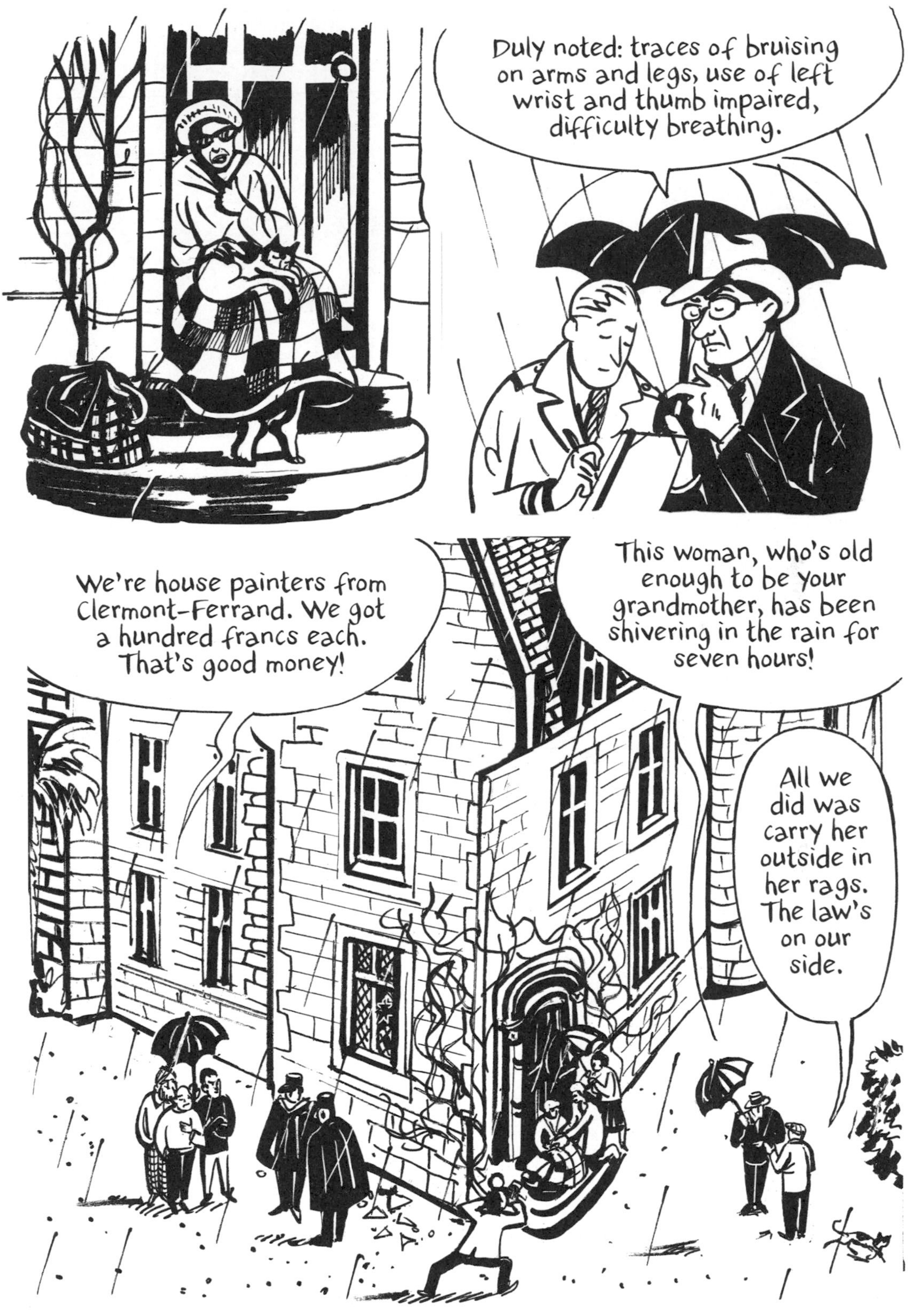
Duly noted: traces of bruising on arms and legs, use of left wrist and thumb impaired, difficulty breathing.
We're house painters from Clermont-Ferrand. We got a hundred francs each. That's good money!
This woman, who's old enough to be your grandmother, has been shivering in the rain for seven hours!
All we did was carry her outside in her rags. The law's on our side.

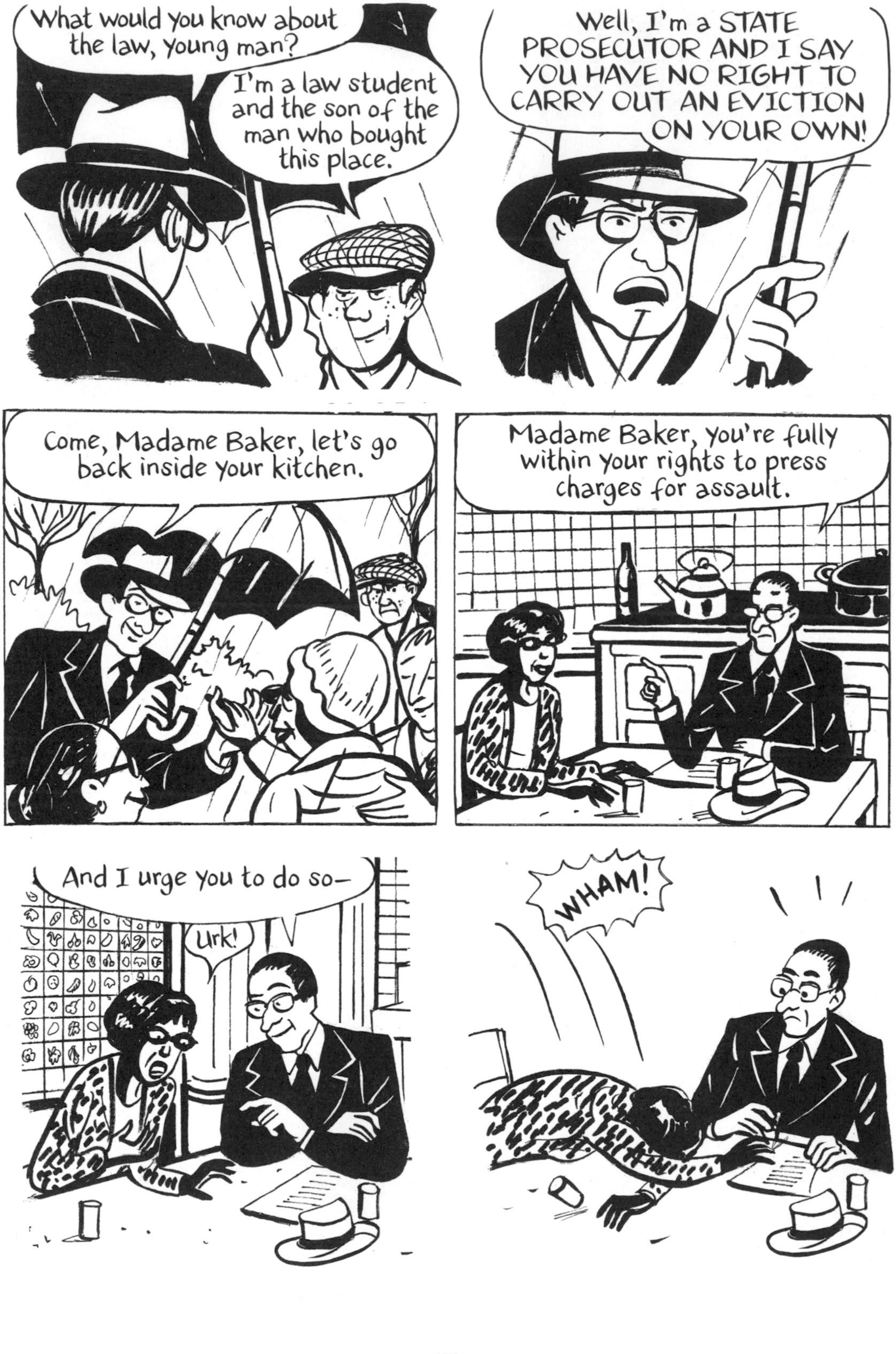
What would you know about the law, young man?
I'm a law student and the son of the man who bought this place.
Well, I'm a STATE PROSECUTOR AND I SAY YOU HAVE NO RIGHT TO CARRY OUT AN EVICTION ON YOUR OWN!
Come, Madame Baker, let's go back inside your kitchen.
Madame Baker, you're fully within your rights to press charges for assault.
And I urge you to do so—
Urk!
WHAM!

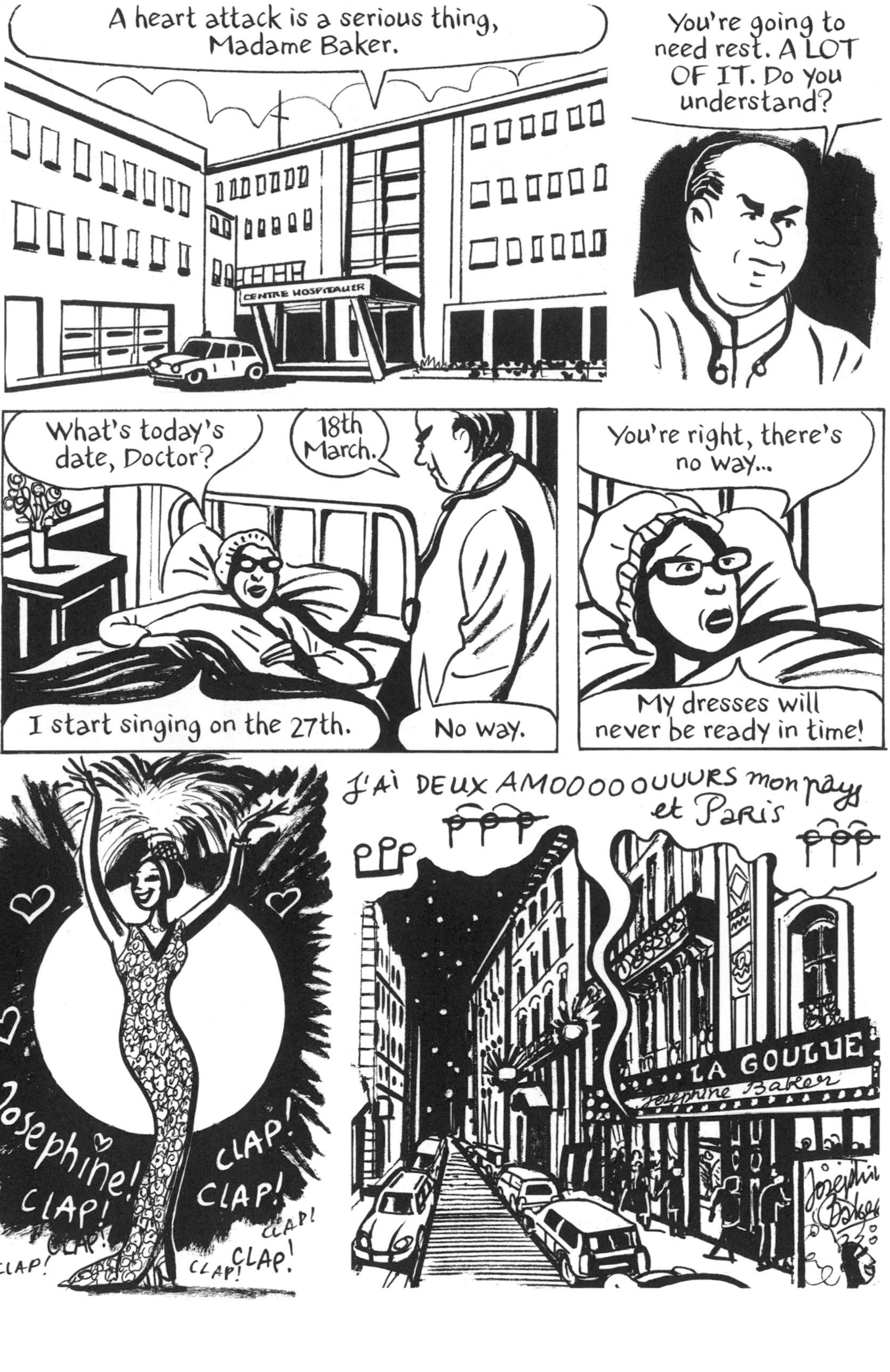
A heart attack is a serious thing, Madame Baker.
CENTRE HOSPITALIER
You're going to need rest. A LOT OF IT. Do you understand?
What's today's date, Doctor?
18th March.
I start singing on the 27th.
No way.
You're right, there's no way...
My dresses will never be ready in time!
Josephine!
CLAP!
CLAP!
CLAP!
CLAP!
CLAP!
CLAP!
CLAP!
J'AI DEUX AMOOOOOUUURS mon pays et Paris
LA GOULUE
Josephine Baker

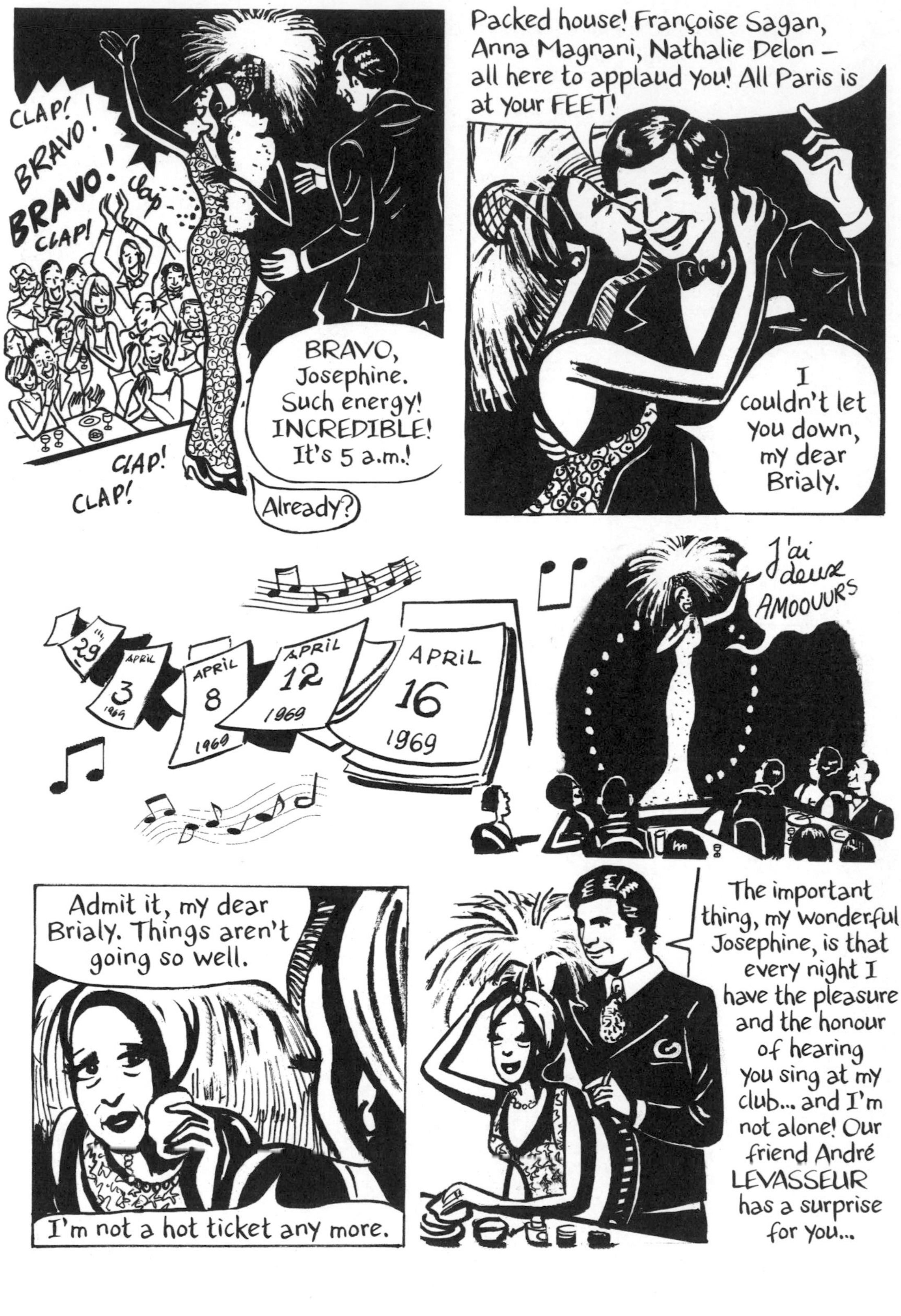
CLAP! BRAVO!
BRAVO!
CLAP!
clap
CLAP!
CLAP!
BRAVO, Josephine. Such energy! INCREDIBLE! It's 5 a.m.!
Already?
Packed house! Françoise Sagan, Anna Magnani, Nathalie Delon – all here to applaud you! All Paris is at your FEET!
I couldn't let you down, my dear Brialy.
APRIL 3 1969
APRIL 8 1969
APRIL 12 1969
APRIL 16 1969
J'ai deux AMOOUURS
Admit it, my dear Brialy. Things aren't going so well.
I'm not a hot ticket any more.
The important thing, my wonderful Josephine, is that every night I have the pleasure and the honour of hearing you sing at my club... and I'm not alone! Our friend André LEVASSEUR has a surprise for you...

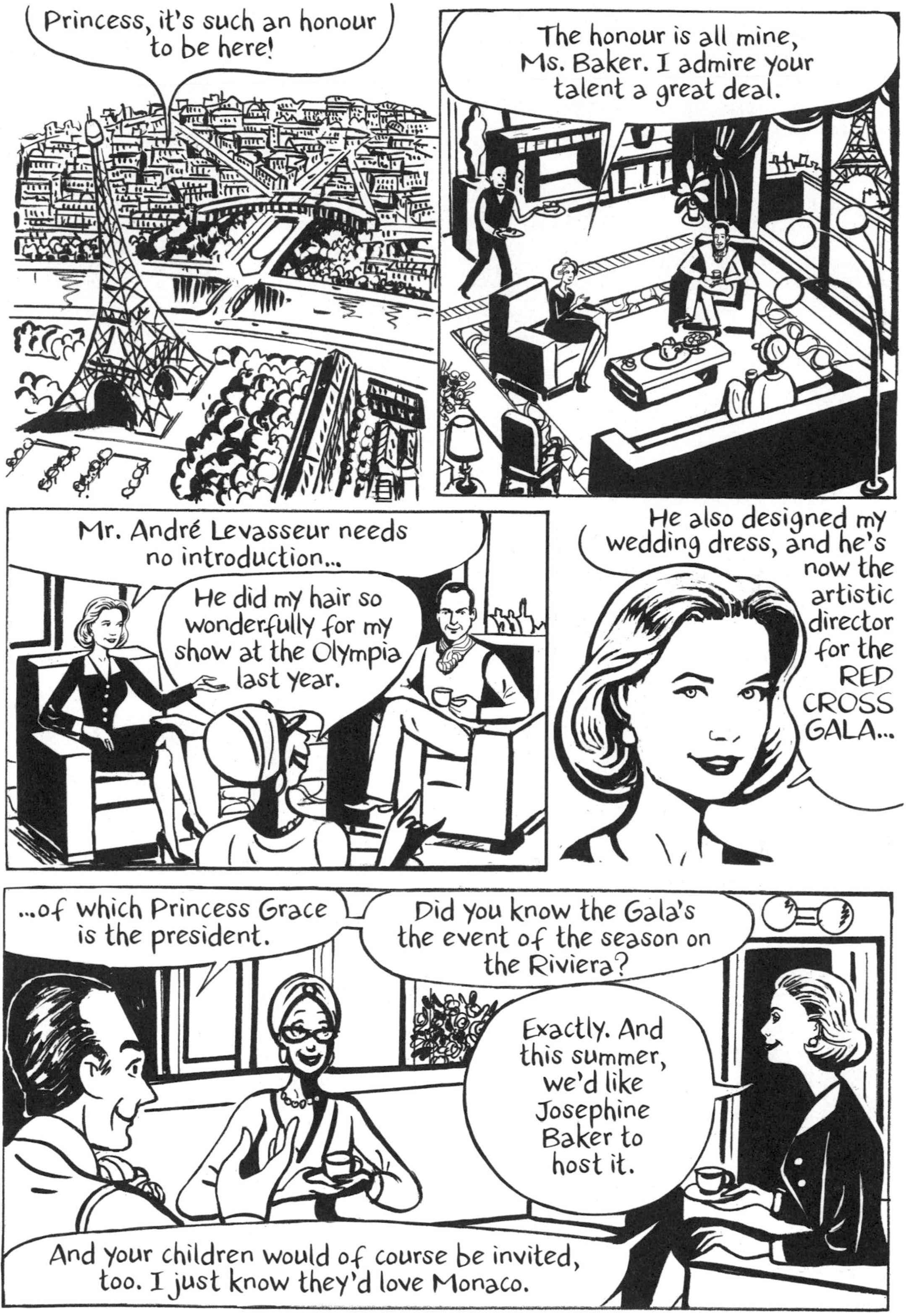
Princess, it's such an honour to be here!
The honour is all mine, Ms. Baker. I admire your talent a great deal.
Mr. André Levasseur needs no introduction...
He did my hair so wonderfully for my show at the Olympia last year.
He also designed my wedding dress, and he's now the artistic director for the RED CROSS GALA...
...of which Princess Grace is the president.
Did you know the Gala's the event of the season on the Riviera?
Exactly. And this summer, we'd like Josephine Baker to host it.
And your children would of course be invited, too. I just know they'd love Monaco.

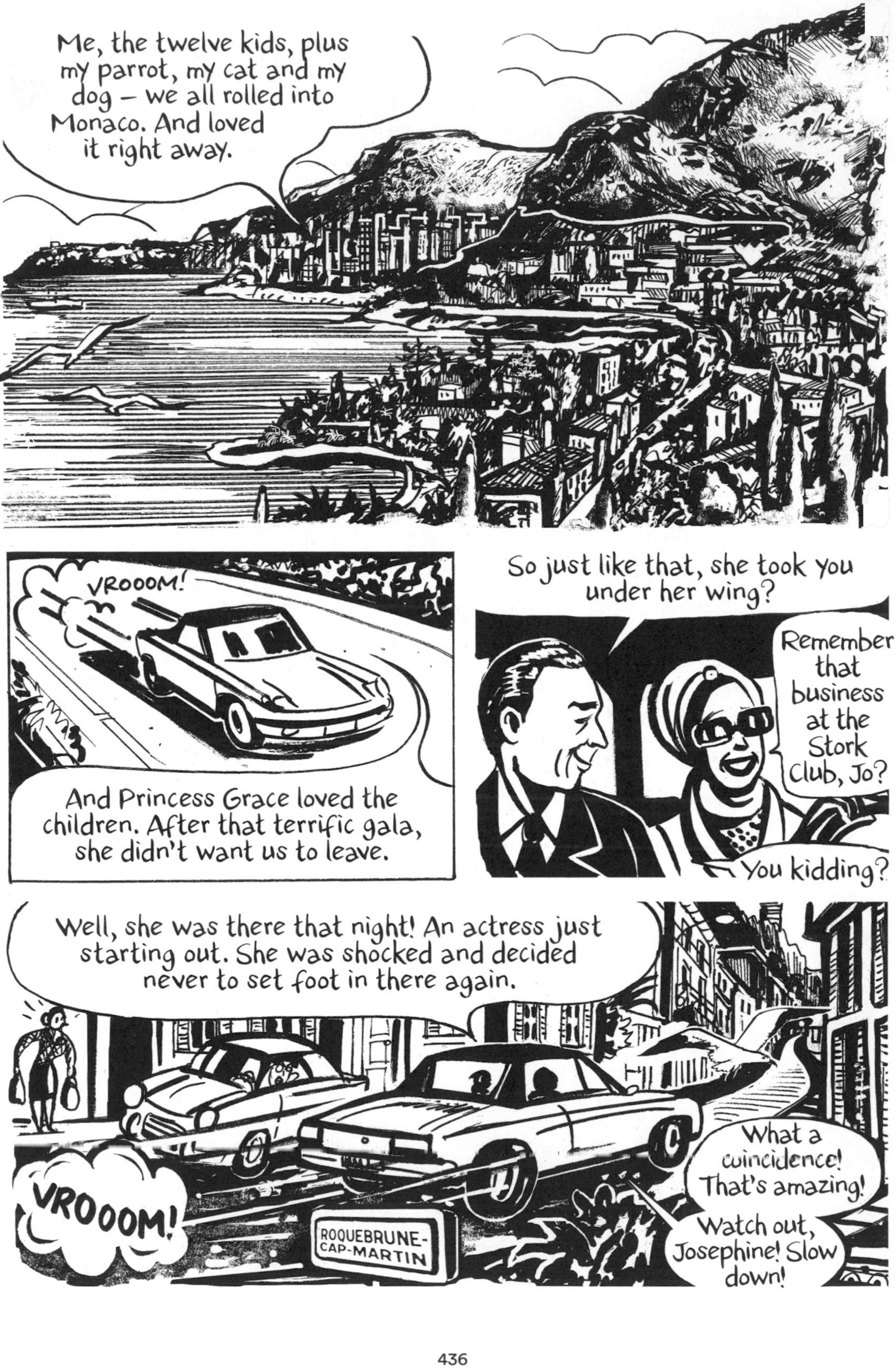
Me, the twelve kids, plus my parrot, my cat and my dog – we all rolled into Monaco. And loved it right away.
VROOOM!
And Princess Grace loved the children. After that terrific gala, she didn't want us to leave.
So just like that, she took you under her wing?
Remember that business at the Stork Club, Jo?
You kidding?
Well, she was there that night! An actress just starting out. She was shocked and decided never to set foot in there again.
What a coincidence! That's amazing!
Watch out, Josephine! Slow down!
VROOOM!
ROQUEBRUNE-CAP-MARTIN

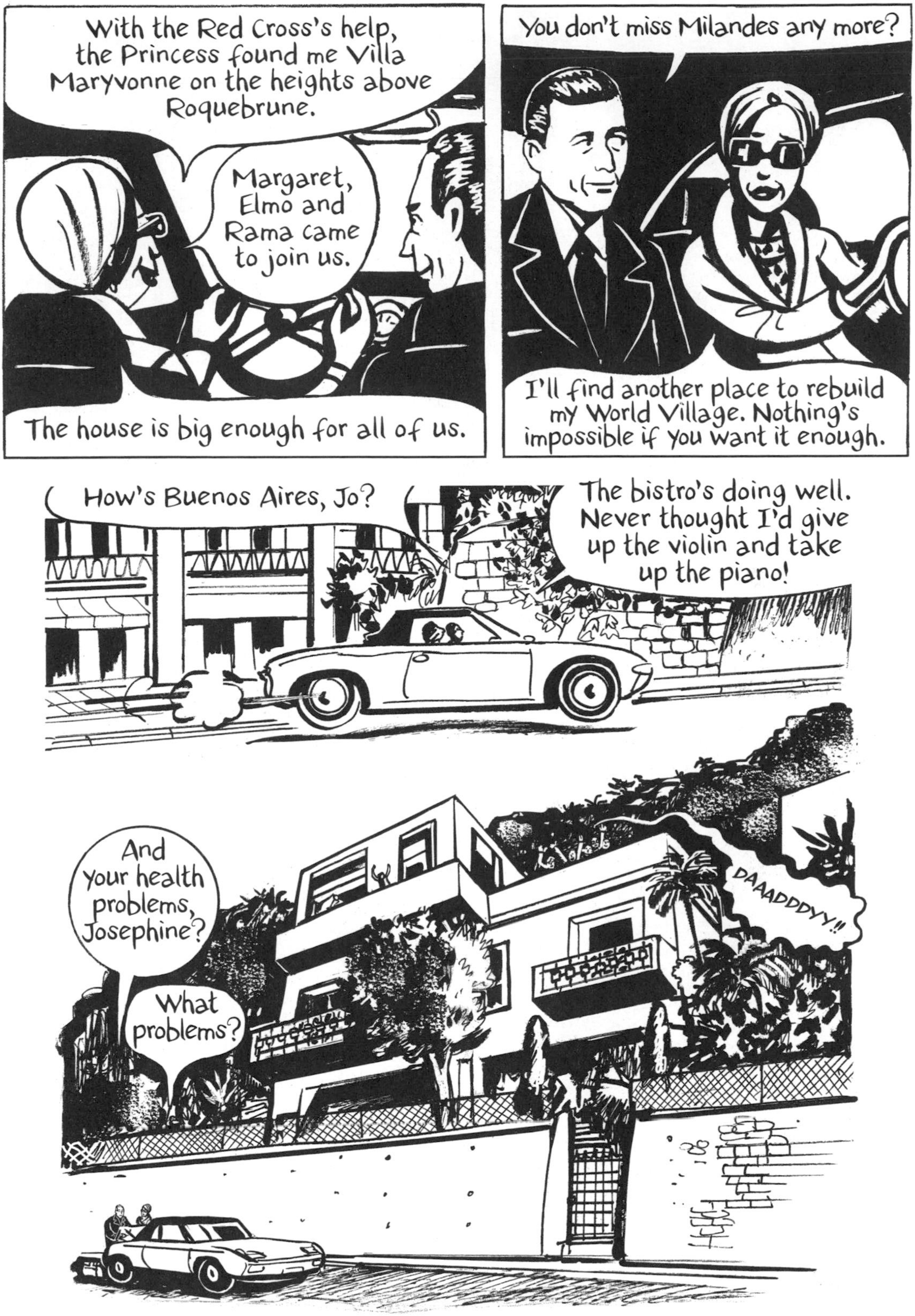
With the Red Cross's help, the Princess found me Villa Maryvonne on the heights above Roquebrune.
Margaret, Elmo and Rama came to join us.
The house is big enough for all of us.
You don't miss Milandes any more?
I'll find another place to rebuild my World Village. Nothing's impossible if you want it enough.
How's Buenos Aires, Jo?
The bistro's doing well. Never thought I'd give up the violin and take up the piano!
And your health problems, Josephine?
What problems?
DAAADDDYY!!

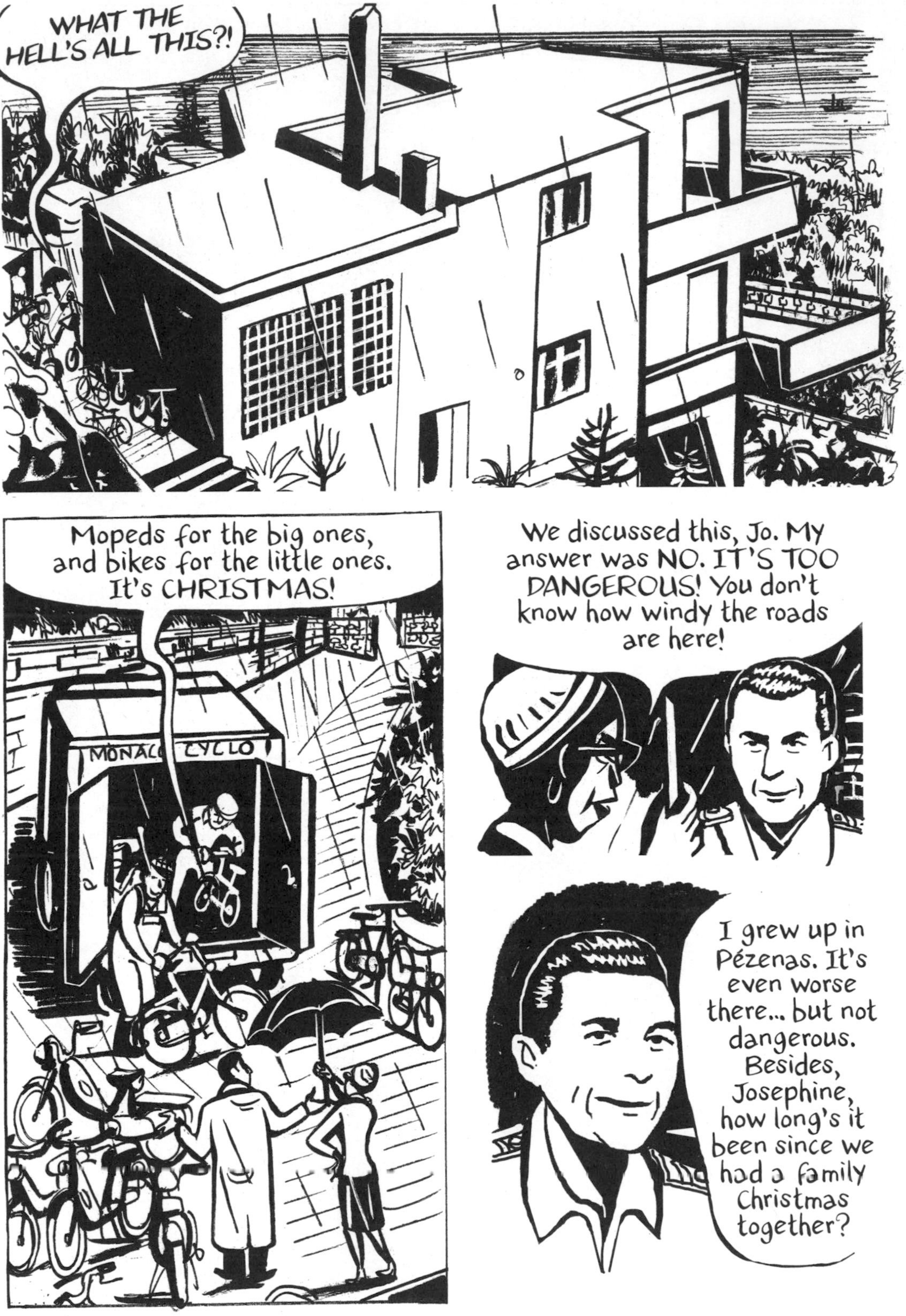

WHAT THE HELL'S ALL THIS?!
Mopeds for the big ones, and bikes for the little ones. It's CHRISTMAS!
MONACO CYCLO
We discussed this, Jo. MY answer was NO. IT'S TOO DANGEROUS! You don't know how windy the roads are here!
I grew up in Pézenas. It's even worse there... but not dangerous. Besides, Josephine, how long's it been since we had a family Christmas together?

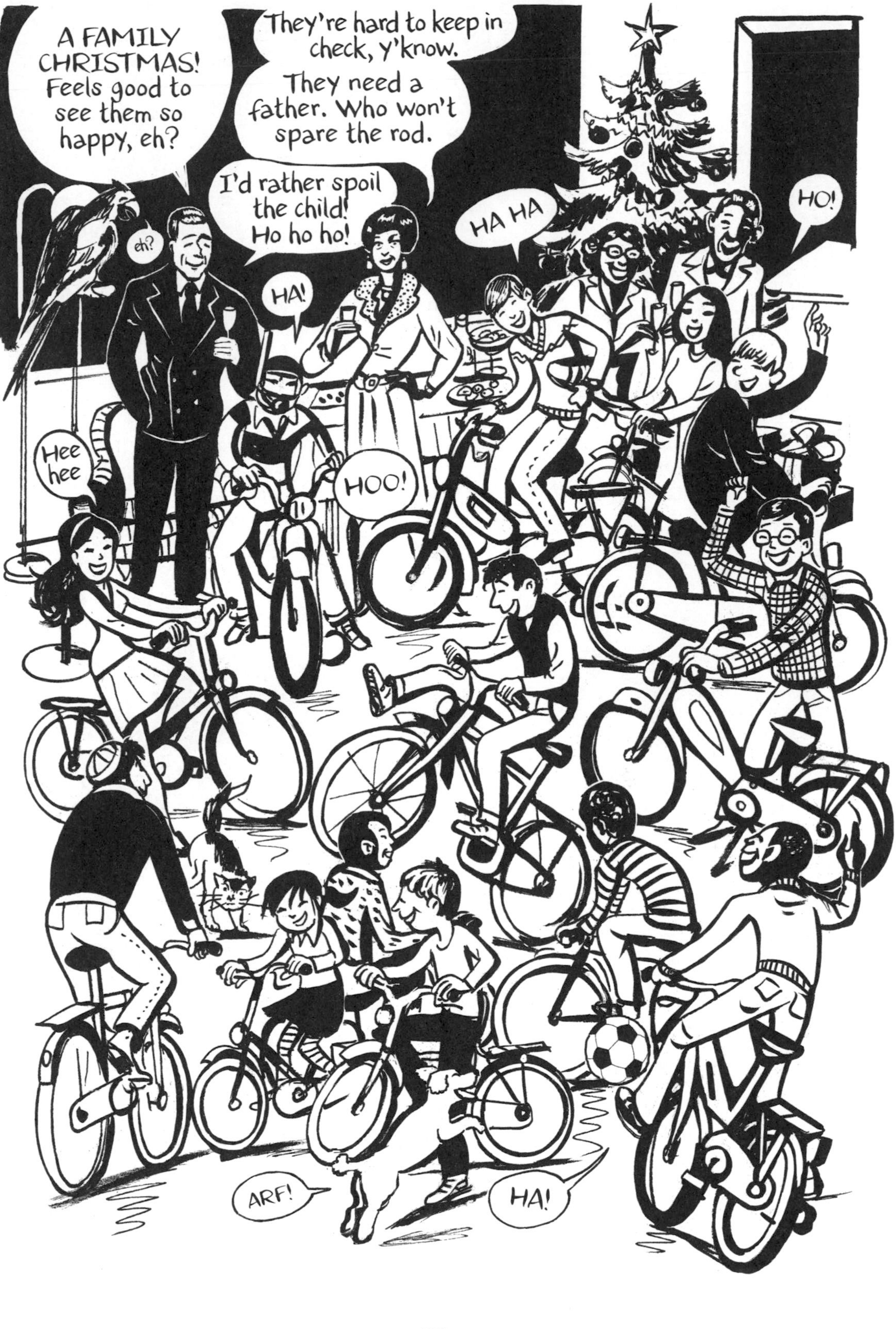
A FAMILY CHRISTMAS! Feels good to see them so happy, eh?
eh?
They're hard to keep in check, y'know.
They need a father. Who won't spare the rod.
I'd rather spoil the child! Ho ho ho!
HA HA
HO!
HA!
Hee hee
HOO!
ARF!
HA!

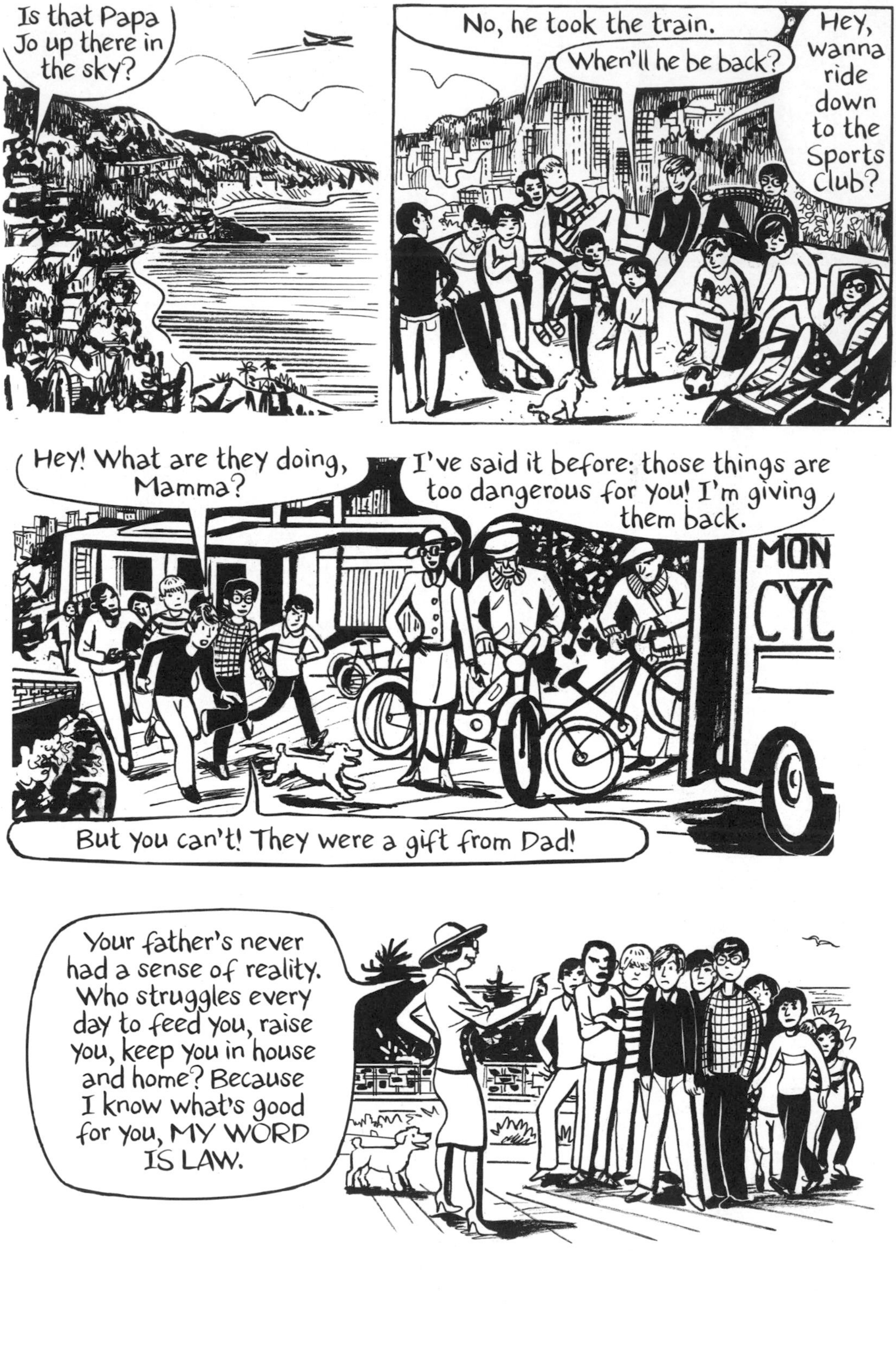
Is that Papa Jo up there in the sky?
No, he took the train.
When'll he be back?
Hey, wanna ride down to the Sports Club?
Hey! What are they doing, Mamma?
I've said it before: those things are too dangerous for you! I'm giving them back.
MON
CYC
But you can't! They were a gift from Dad!
Your father's never had a sense of reality. Who struggles every day to feed you, raise you, keep you in house and home? Because I know what's good for you, MY WORD IS LAW.

April 1975: Church of La Madeleine, Paris, France

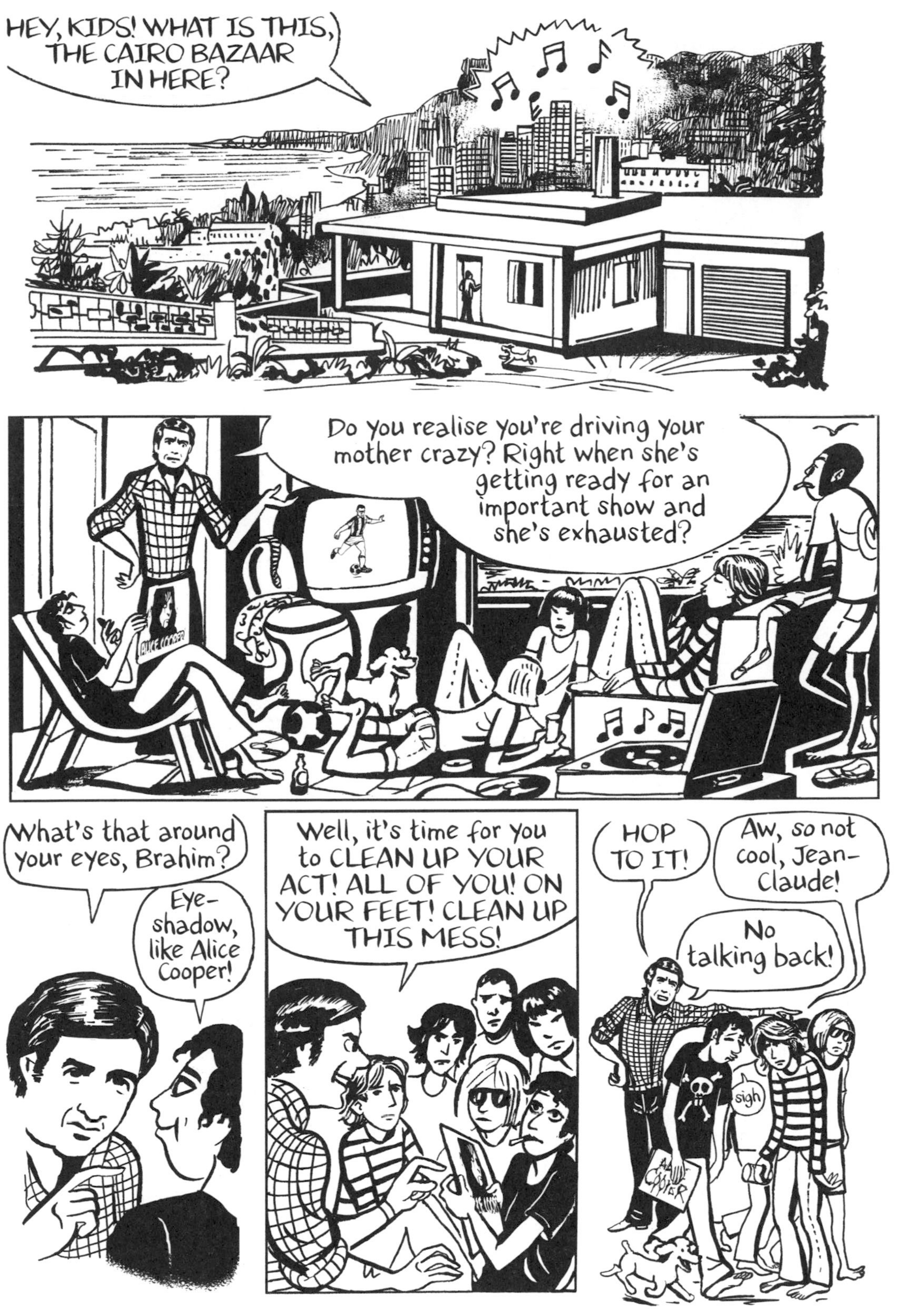
HEY, KIDS! WHAT IS THIS, THE CAIRO BAZAAR IN HERE?
Do you realise you're driving your mother crazy? Right when she's getting ready for an important show and she's exhausted?
ALICE COOPER
What's that around your eyes, Brahim?
Eye-shadow, like Alice Cooper!
Well, it's time for you to CLEAN UP YOUR ACT! ALL OF YOU! ON YOUR FEET! CLEAN UP THIS MESS!
HOP TO IT!
Aw, so not cool, Jean-Claude!
No talking back!
sigh

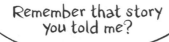
Remember that story
you told me?

When Mistinguett asked why
you wanted to adopt all those
brats, and you told her you
wanted
to set an
example?

She said
you were
crazy. "Set an
example? Are
you kidding?"

"Look how
well that worked
for Jesus. He got it
in his head that he
was going to save
the world and he
got crucified!"

Ha ha! Misty sure was good
with the
comebacks!

But she died sad
and alone.

444

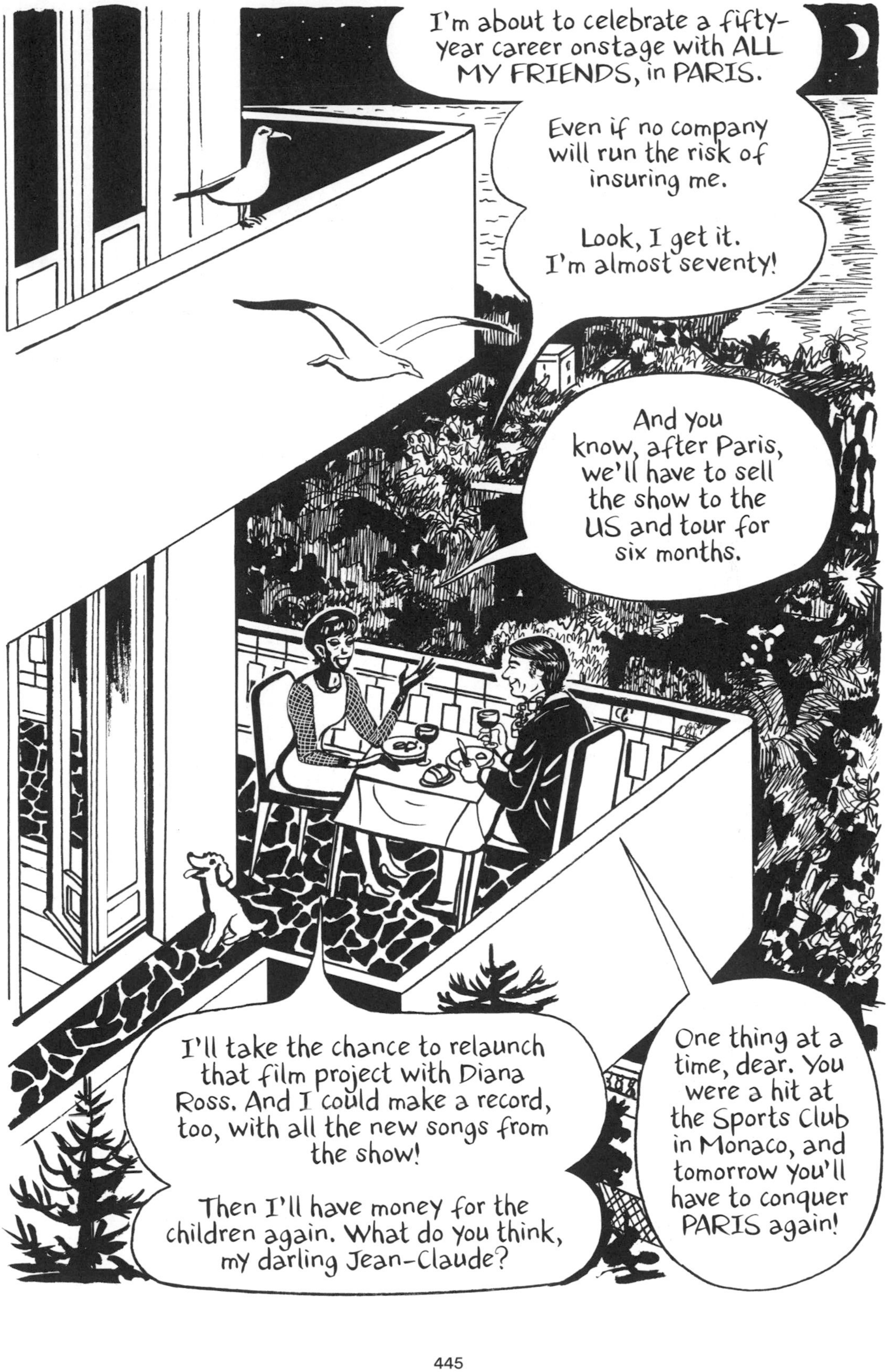
I'm about to celebrate a fifty-year career onstage with ALL MY FRIENDS, in PARIS.
Even if no company will run the risk of insuring me.
Look, I get it. I'm almost seventy!
And you know, after Paris, we'll have to sell the show to the US and tour for six months.
I'll take the chance to relaunch that film project with Diana Ross. And I could make a record, too, with all the new songs from the show!
Then I'll have money for the children again. What do you think, my darling Jean-Claude?
One thing at a time, dear. You were a hit at the Sports Club in Monaco, and tomorrow you'll have to conquer PARIS again!

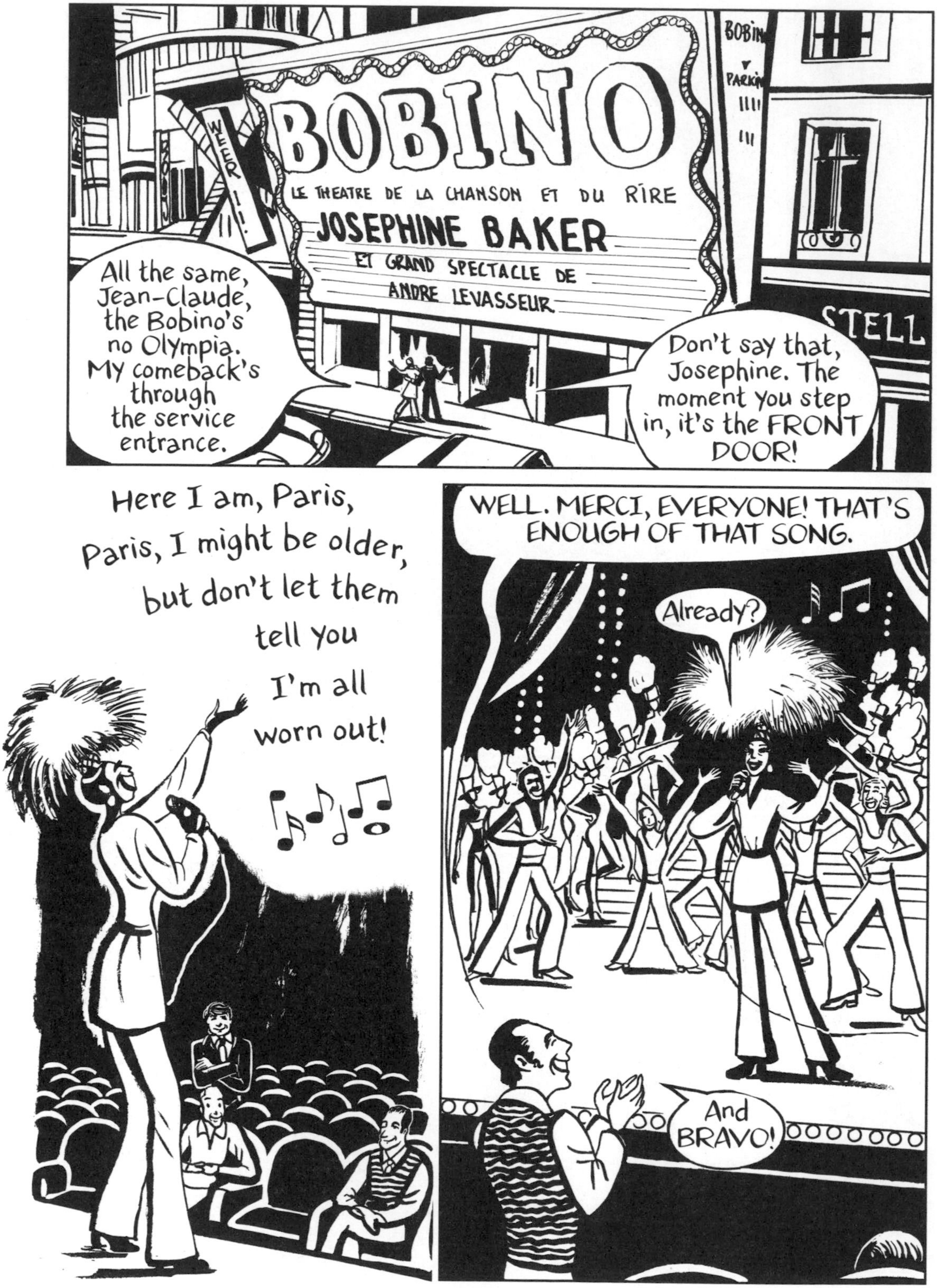
BOBINO
LE THEATRE DE LA CHANSON ET DU RIRE
JOSEPHINE BAKER
ET GRAND SPECTACLE DE
ANDRE LEVASSEUR
All the same, Jean-Claude, the Bobino's no Olympia. My comeback's through the service entrance.
Don't say that, Josephine. The moment you step in, it's the FRONT DOOR!
STELL
Here I am, Paris, Paris, I might be older, but don't let them tell you I'm all worn out!
WELL. MERCI, EVERYONE! THAT'S ENOUGH OF THAT SONG.
Already?
And BRAVO!

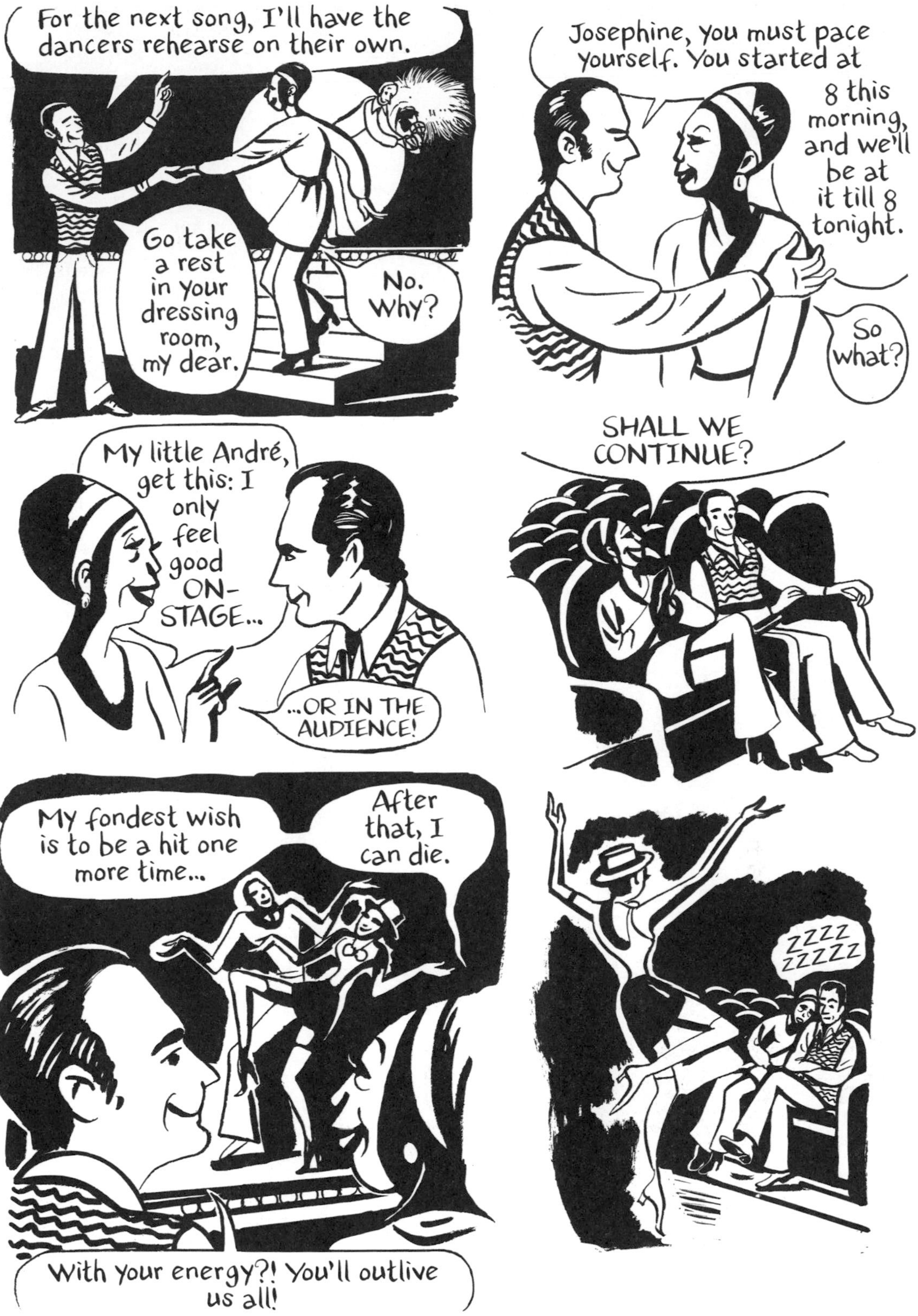
For the next song, I'll have the dancers rehearse on their own.
Go take a rest in your dressing room, my dear.
No. Why?
Josephine, you must pace yourself. You started at 8 this morning, and we'll be at it till 8 tonight.
So what?
My little André, get this: I only feel good ON-STAGE...
...OR IN THE AUDIENCE!
SHALL WE CONTINUE?
My fondest wish is to be a hit one more time...
After that, I can die.
With your energy?! You'll outlive us all!
ZZZZ ZZZZZ

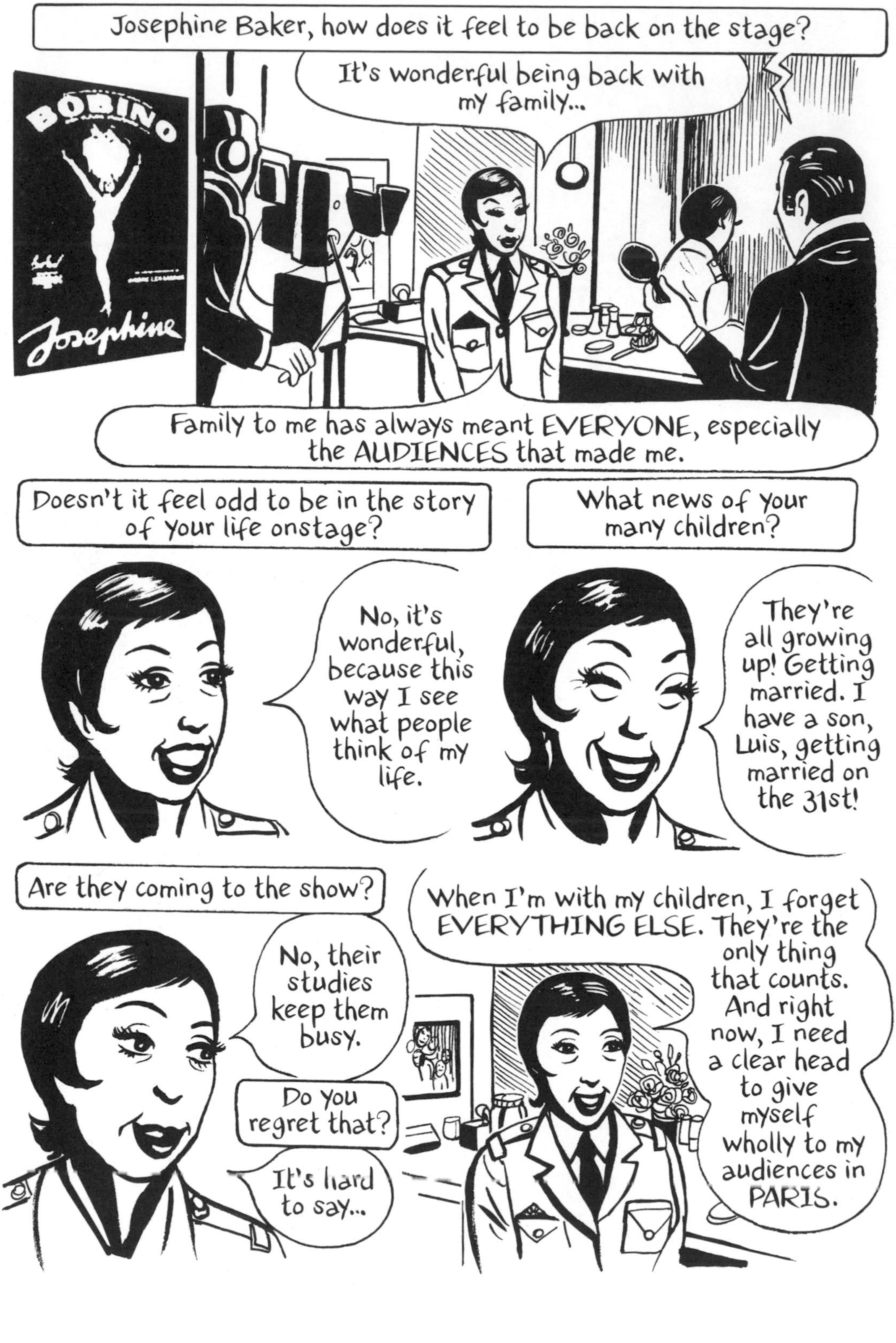
Josephine Baker, how does it feel to be back on the stage?
BOBINO
Josephine
It's wonderful being back with my family...
Family to me has always meant EVERYONE, especially the AUDIENCES that made me.
Doesn't it feel odd to be in the story of your life onstage?
No, it's wonderful, because this way I see what people think of my life.
What news of your many children?
They're all growing up! Getting married. I have a son, Luis, getting married on the 31st!
Are they coming to the show?
No, their studies keep them busy.
Do you regret that?
It's hard to say...
When I'm with my children, I forget EVERYTHING ELSE. They're the only thing that counts. And right now, I need a clear head to give myself wholly to my audiences in PARIS.

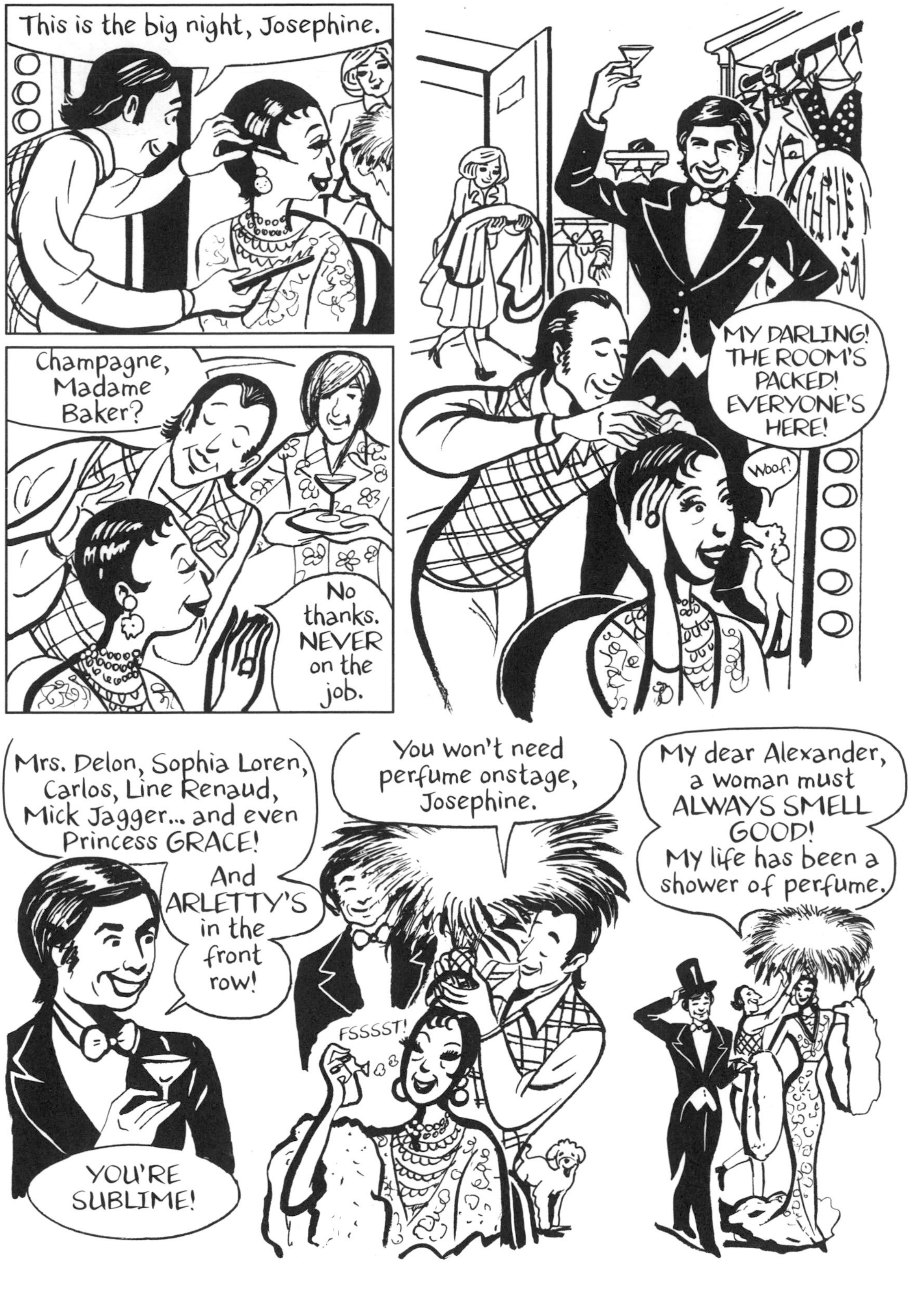

This is the big night, Josephine.
Champagne, Madame Baker?
No thanks. NEVER on the job.
MY DARLING! THE ROOM'S PACKED! EVERYONE'S HERE!
Woof!
Mrs. Delon, Sophia Loren, Carlos, Line Renaud, Mick Jagger... and even Princess GRACE!
And ARLETTY'S in the front row!
YOU'RE SUBLIME!
You won't need perfume onstage, Josephine.
FSSSST!
My dear Alexander, a woman must ALWAYS SMELL GOOD! My life has been a shower of perfume.

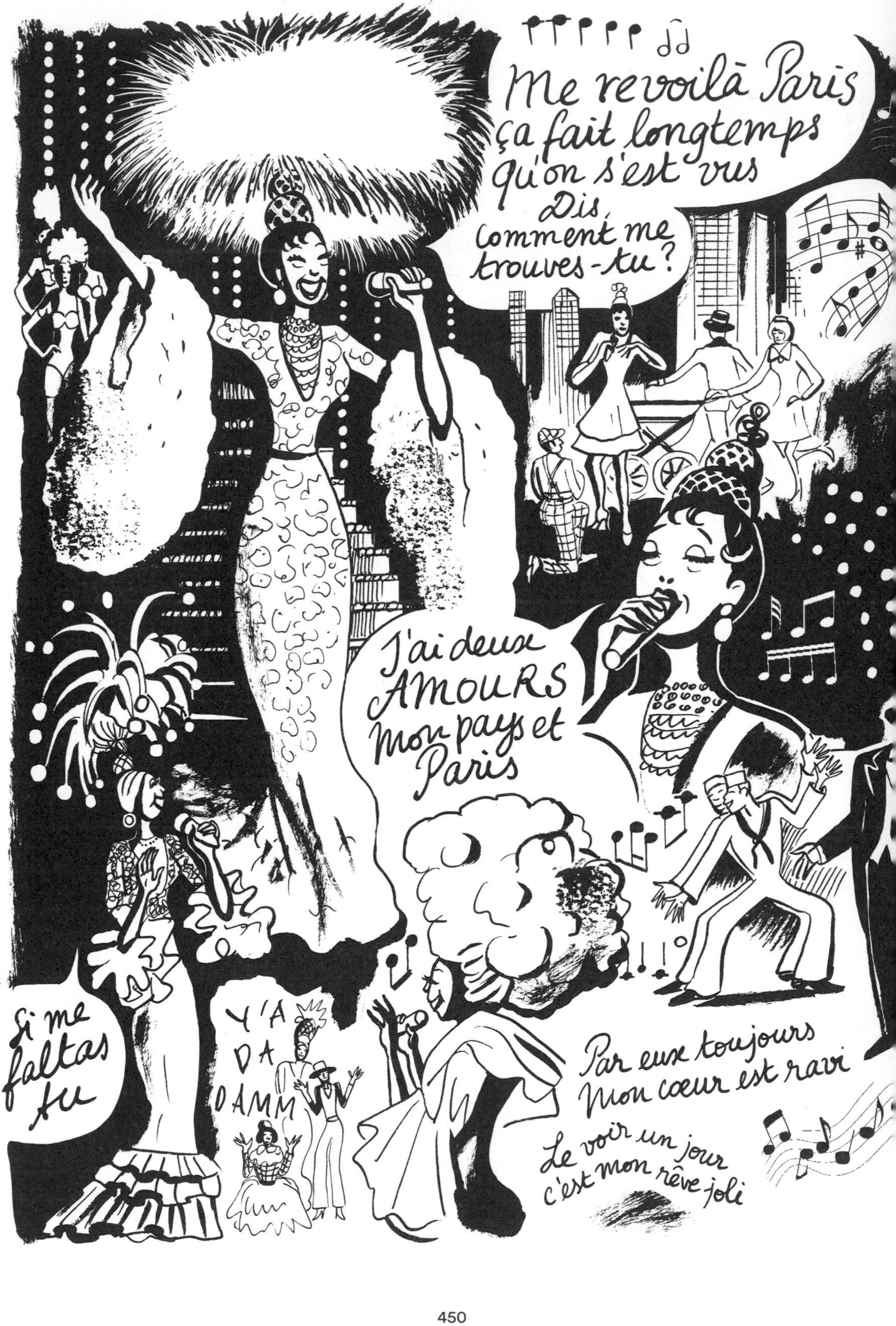
Me revoilà Paris
ça fait longtemps
qu'on s'est vus
Dis,
comment me
trouves-tu?
J'ai deux
AMOURS
Mon pays et
Paris
Si me
faltas
tu
Y'A
DA
DAMM
Par eux toujours
Mon cœur est ravi
Le voir un jour
c'est mon rêve joli

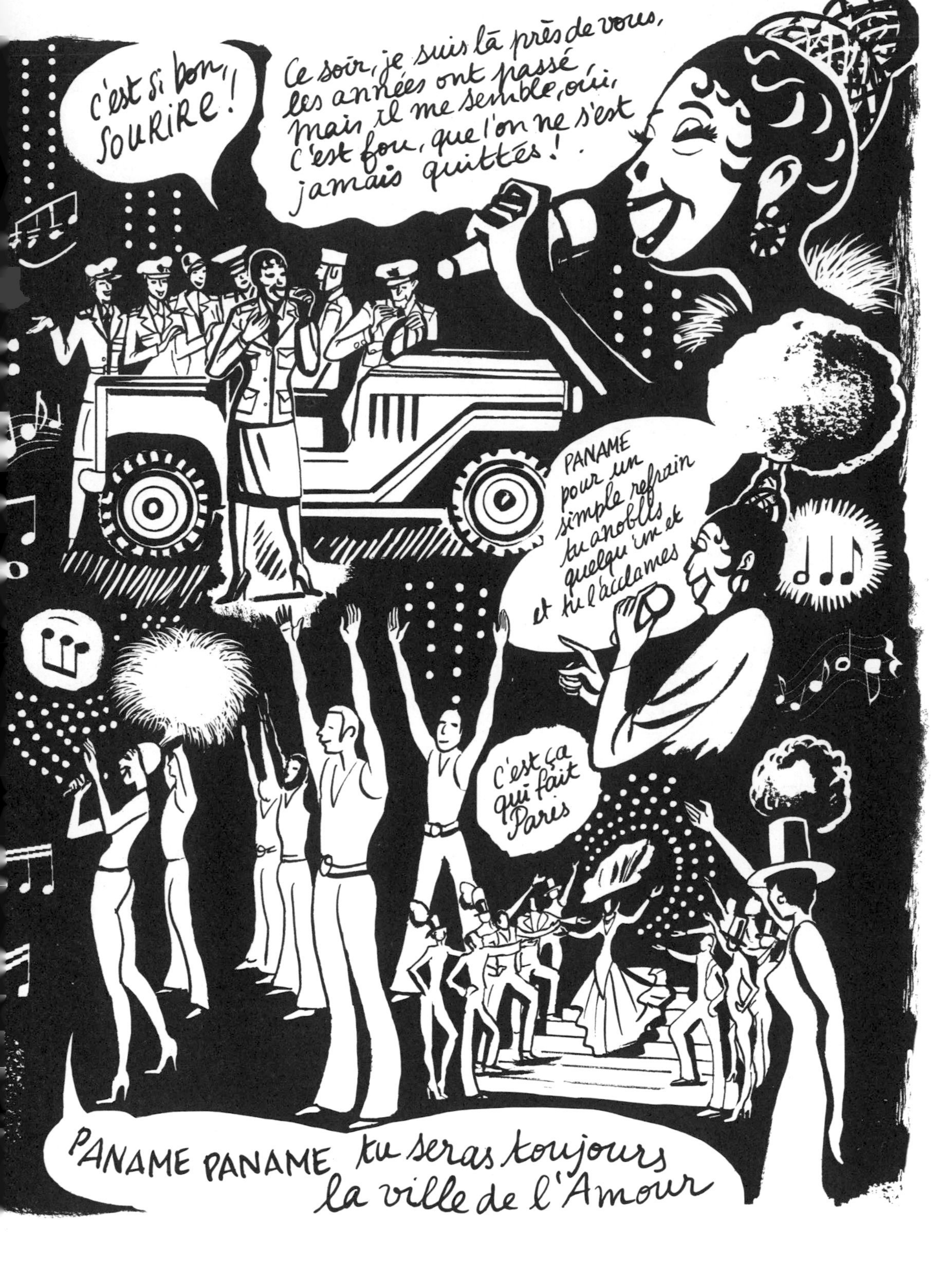
c'est si bon, SOURIRE !
Ce soir, je suis là près de vous, les années ont passé mais il me semble, oui, c'est fou, que l'on ne s'est jamais quittés !
PANAME pour un simple refrain tu anoblis quelqu'un et tu l'acclames
C'est ça qui fait Paris
PANAME PANAME tu seras toujours la ville de l'Amour

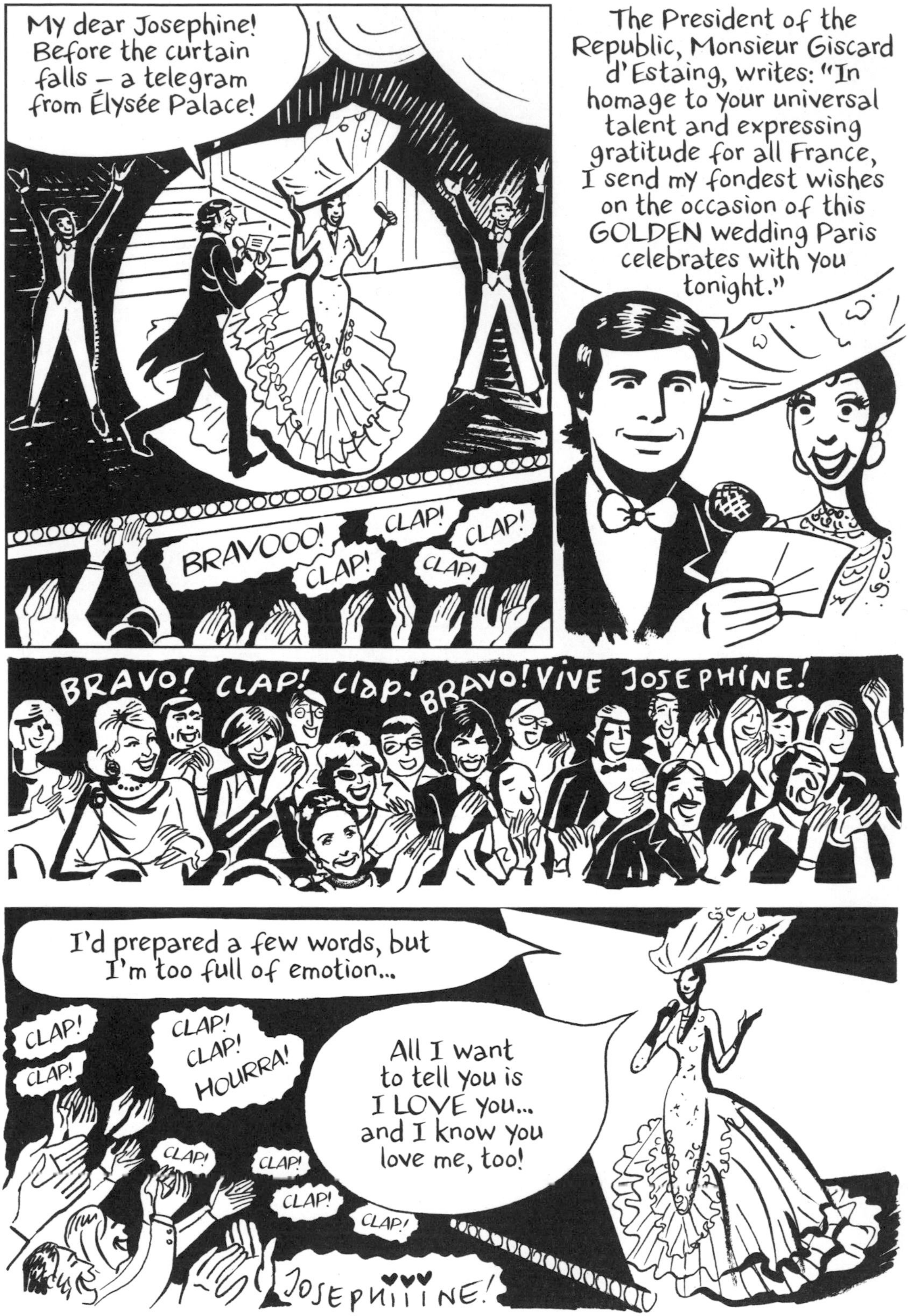
My dear Josephine! Before the curtain falls – a telegram from Élysée Palace!
The President of the Republic, Monsieur Giscard d'Estaing, writes: "In homage to your universal talent and expressing gratitude for all France, I send my fondest wishes on the occasion of this GOLDEN wedding Paris celebrates with you tonight."
BRAVOOO!
CLAP!
CLAP!
CLAP!
CLAP!
BRAVO! CLAP! Clap! BRAVO! VIVE JOSEPHINE!
I'd prepared a few words, but I'm too full of emotion...
All I want to tell you is I LOVE you... and I know you love me, too!
CLAP!
CLAP!
CLAP! CLAP! HOURRA!
CLAP!
CLAP!
CLAP!
CLAP!
JOSEPHIIINE!

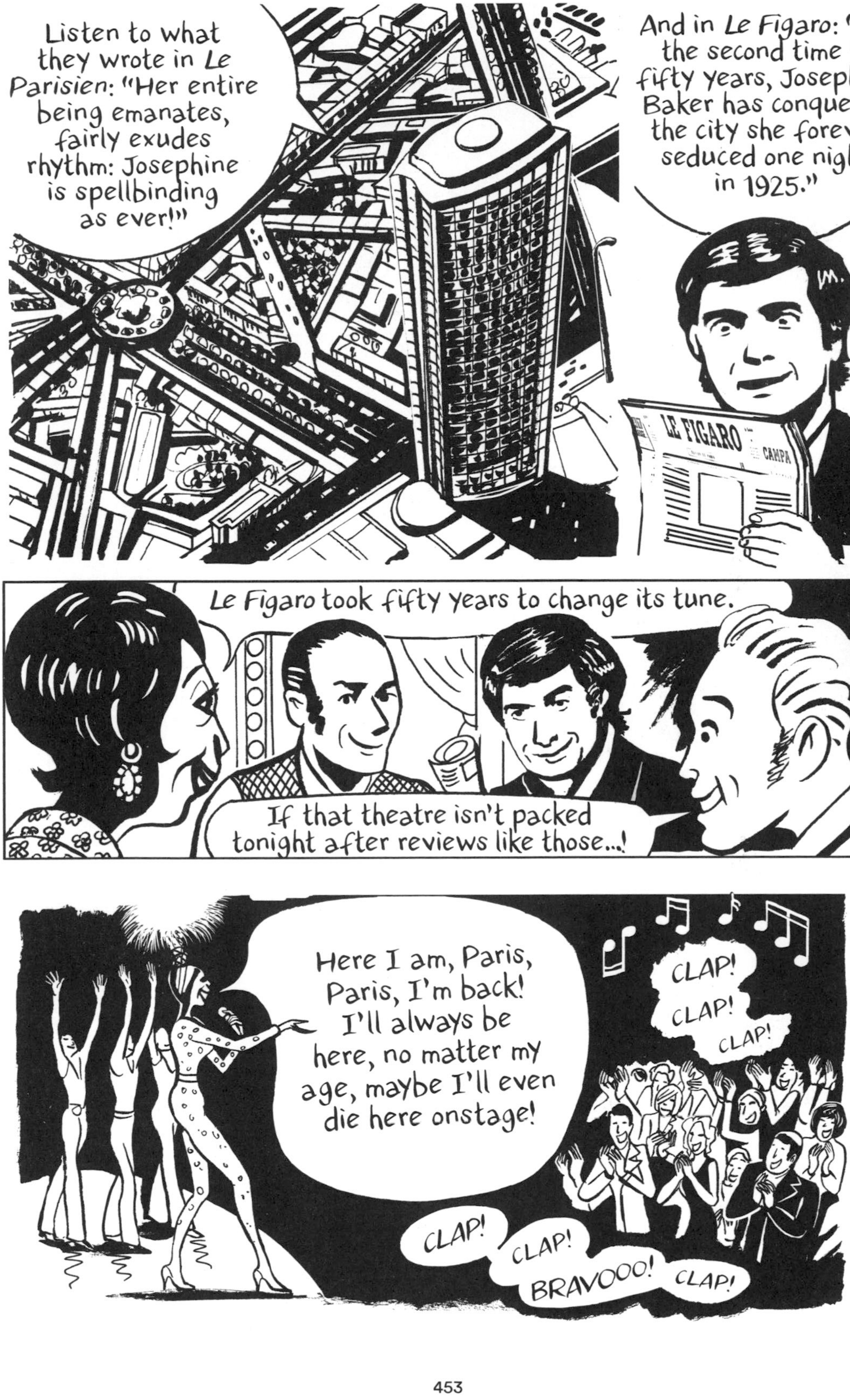
Listen to what they wrote in *Le Parisien*: "Her entire being emanates, fairly exudes rhythm: Josephine is spellbinding as ever!"
And in *Le Figaro*: "For the second time in fifty years, Josephine Baker has conquered the city she forever seduced one night in 1925."
LE FIGARO
CAMPA
Le Figaro took fifty years to change its tune.
If that theatre isn't packed tonight after reviews like those...!
Here I am, Paris, Paris, I'm back! I'll always be here, no matter my age, maybe I'll even die here onstage!
CLAP!
CLAP!
CLAP!
CLAP!
CLAP!
BRAVOOO!
CLAP!

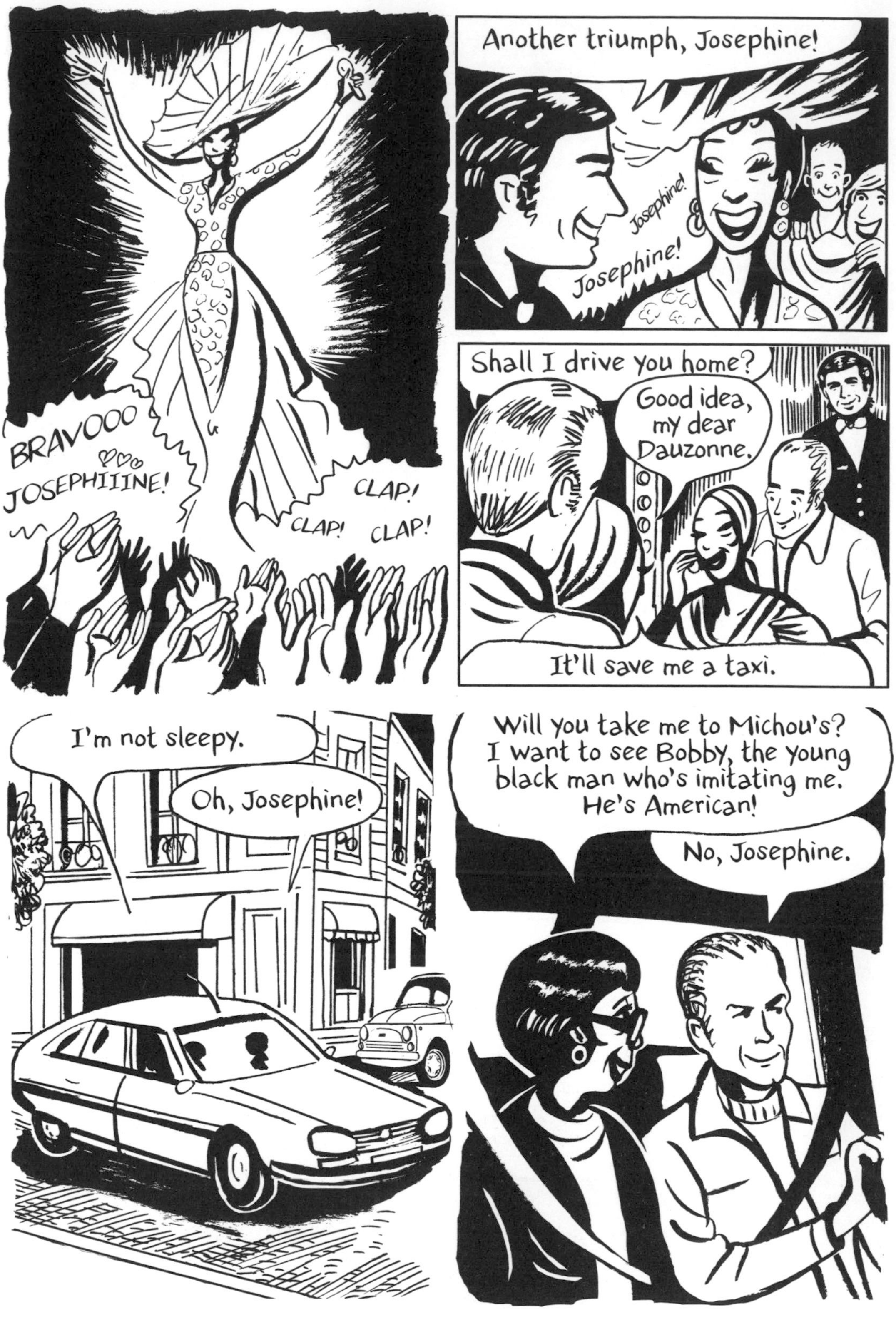
BRAVOOO
JOSEPHIIINE!
CLAP!
CLAP!
CLAP!
Another triumph, Josephine!
Josephine!
Josephine!
Shall I drive you home?
Good idea, my dear Dauzonne.
It'll save me a taxi.
I'm not sleepy.
Oh, Josephine!
Will you take me to Michou's? I want to see Bobby, the young black man who's imitating me. He's American!
No, Josephine.

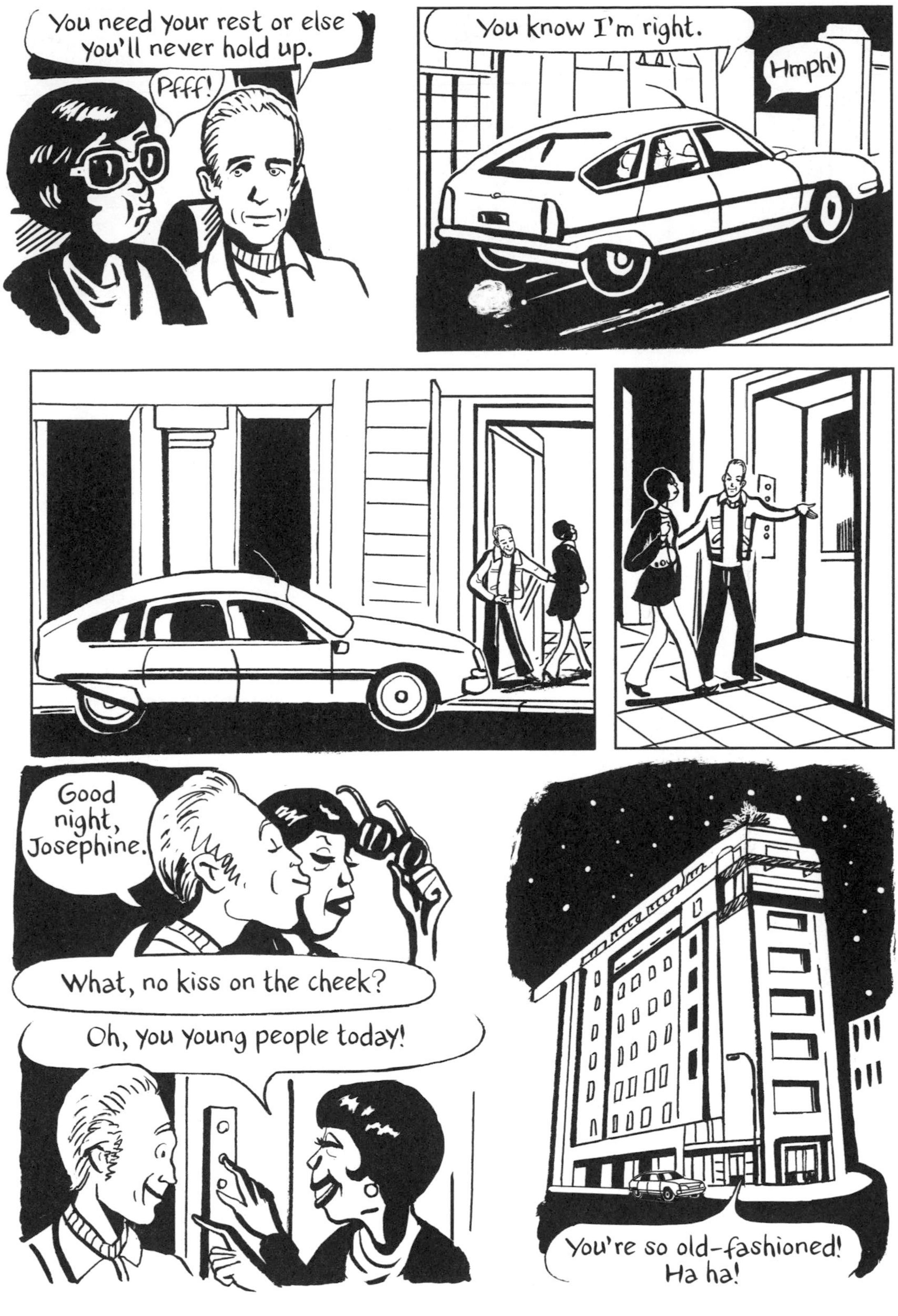
You need your rest or else you'll never hold up.
Pfff!
You know I'm right.
Hmph!
Good night, Josephine.
What, no kiss on the cheek?
Oh, you young people today!
You're so old-fashioned! Ha ha!

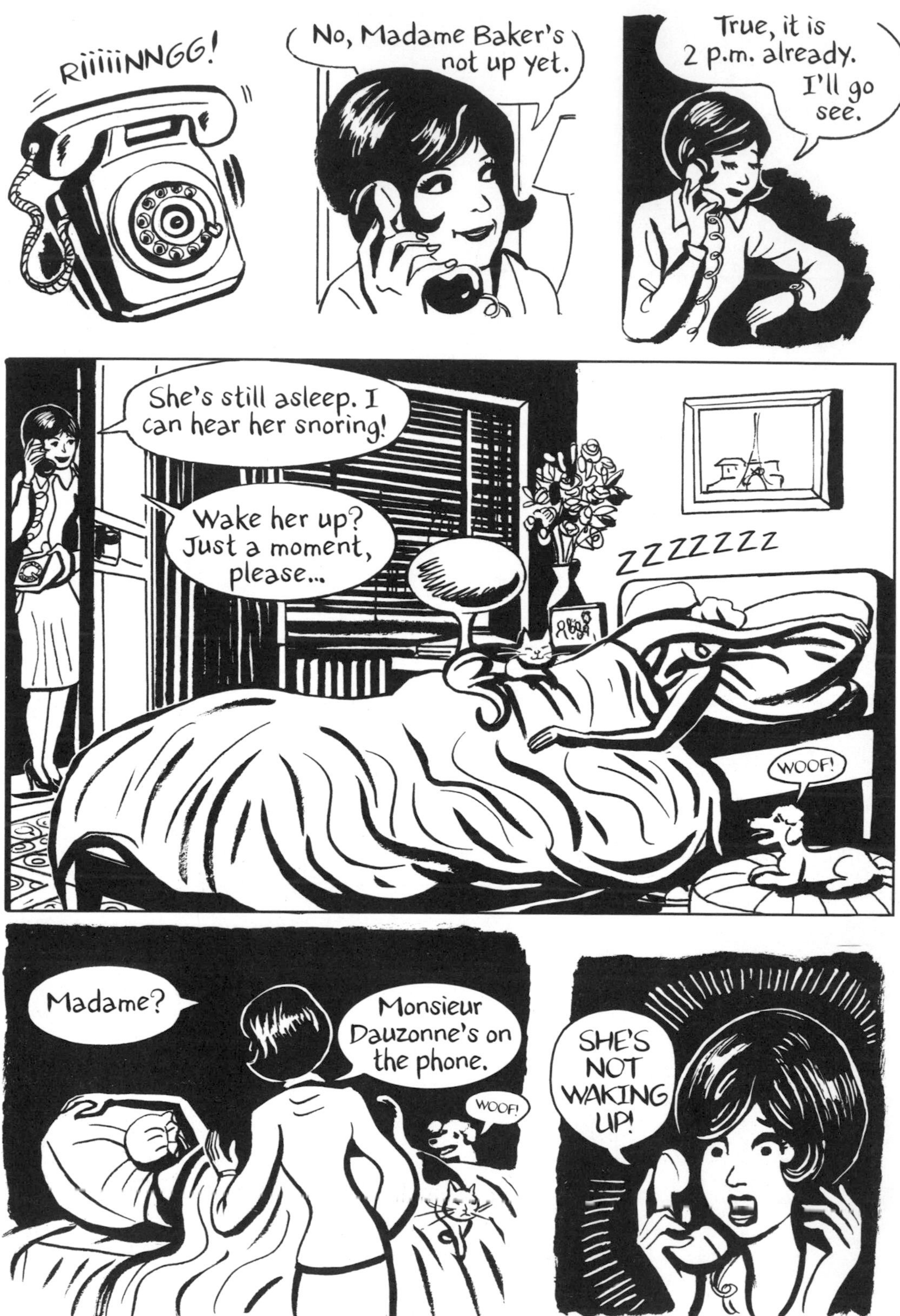
RiiiiiNNGG!
No, Madame Baker's not up yet.
True, it is 2 p.m. already. I'll go see.
She's still asleep. I can hear her snoring!
Wake her up? Just a moment, please...
ZZZZZZZ
WOOF!
Madame?
Monsieur Dauzonne's on the phone.
WOOF!
SHE'S NOT WAKING UP!

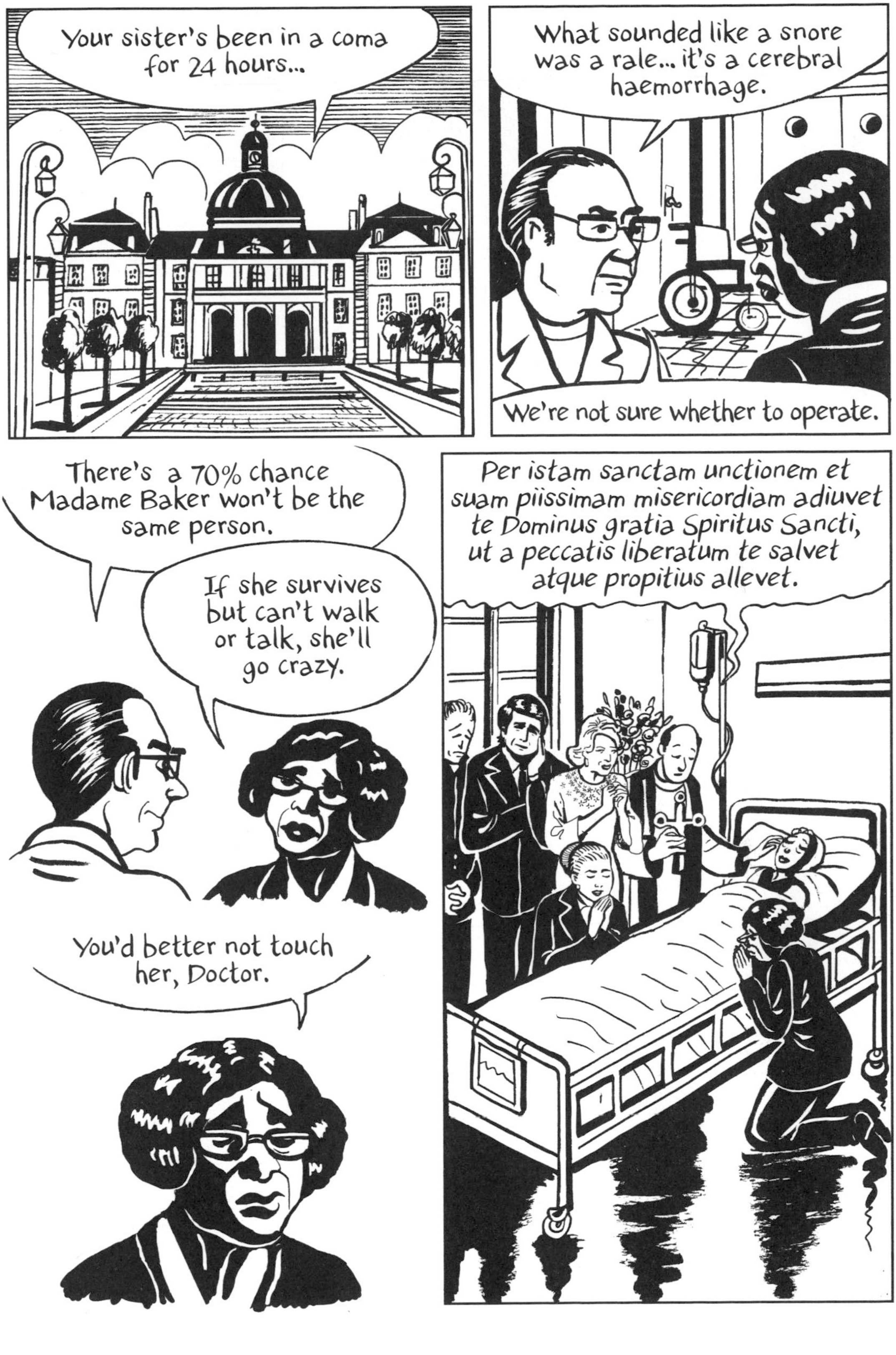
Your sister's been in a coma for 24 hours...
What sounded like a snore was a rale... it's a cerebral haemorrhage.
We're not sure whether to operate.
There's a 70% chance Madame Baker won't be the same person.
If she survives but can't walk or talk, she'll go crazy.
You'd better not touch her, Doctor.
Per istam sanctam unctionem et suam piissimam misericordiam adiuvet te Dominus gratia Spiritus Sancti, ut a peccatis liberatum te salvet atque propitius allevet.

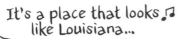
It's a place that looks ♩
like Louisiana...

Italy... ♪

Looks like
the South! ♪

Marianne?

Jean-
Claude!

What are
you doing here?
It's 6 a.m.!

Did you hear
about Mamma?

WHAT?!

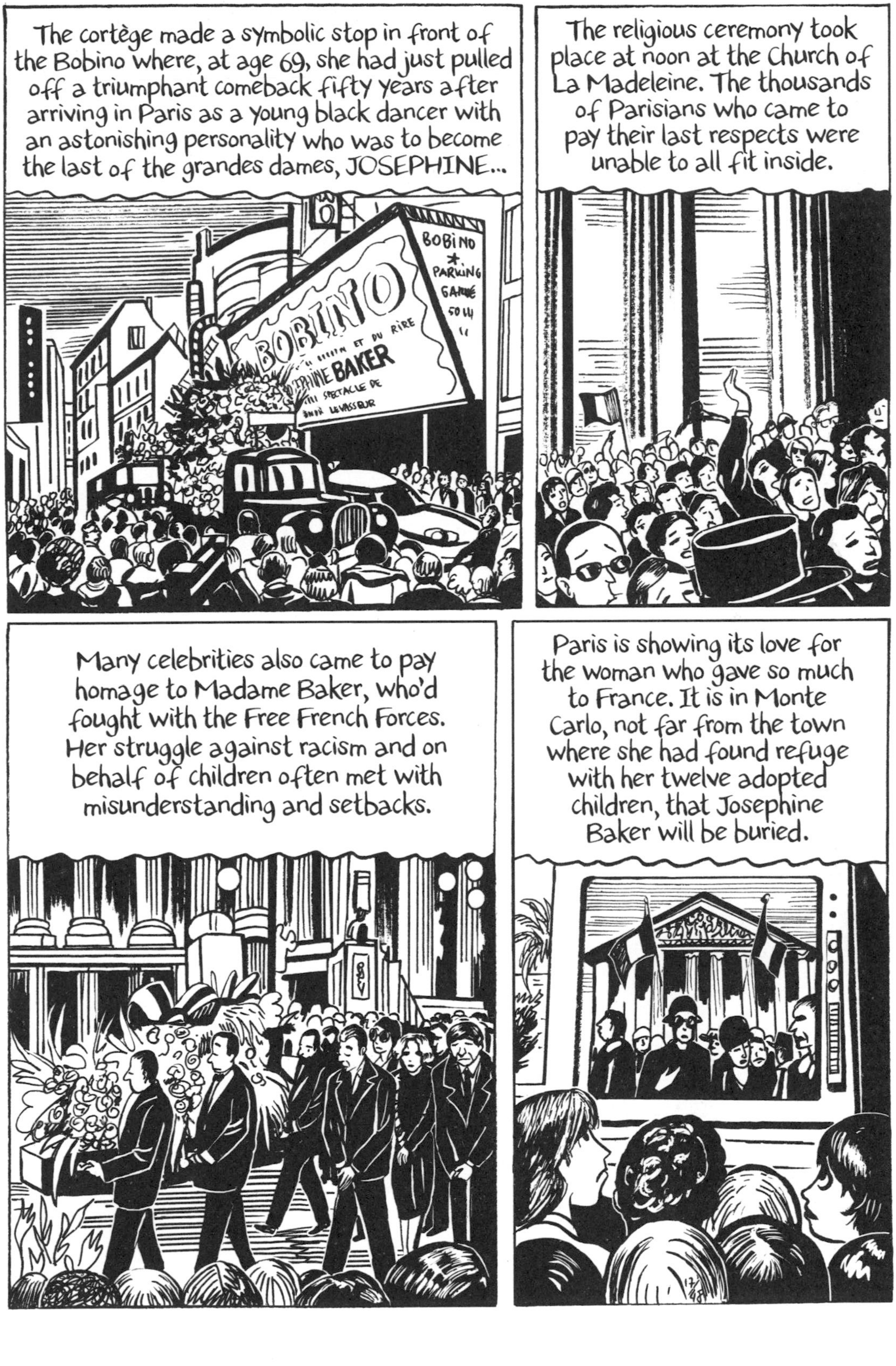
The cortège made a symbolic stop in front of the Bobino where, at age 69, she had just pulled off a triumphant comeback fifty years after arriving in Paris as a young black dancer with an astonishing personality who was to become the last of the grandes dames, JOSEPHINE...
BOBINO
BOBINO
PARKING
ET DU RIRE
BAKER
SPECTACLE DE
The religious ceremony took place at noon at the Church of La Madeleine. The thousands of Parisians who came to pay their last respects were unable to all fit inside.
Many celebrities also came to pay homage to Madame Baker, who'd fought with the Free French Forces. Her struggle against racism and on behalf of children often met with misunderstanding and setbacks.
Paris is showing its love for the woman who gave so much to France. It is in Monte Carlo, not far from the town where she had found refuge with her twelve adopted children, that Josephine Baker will be buried.

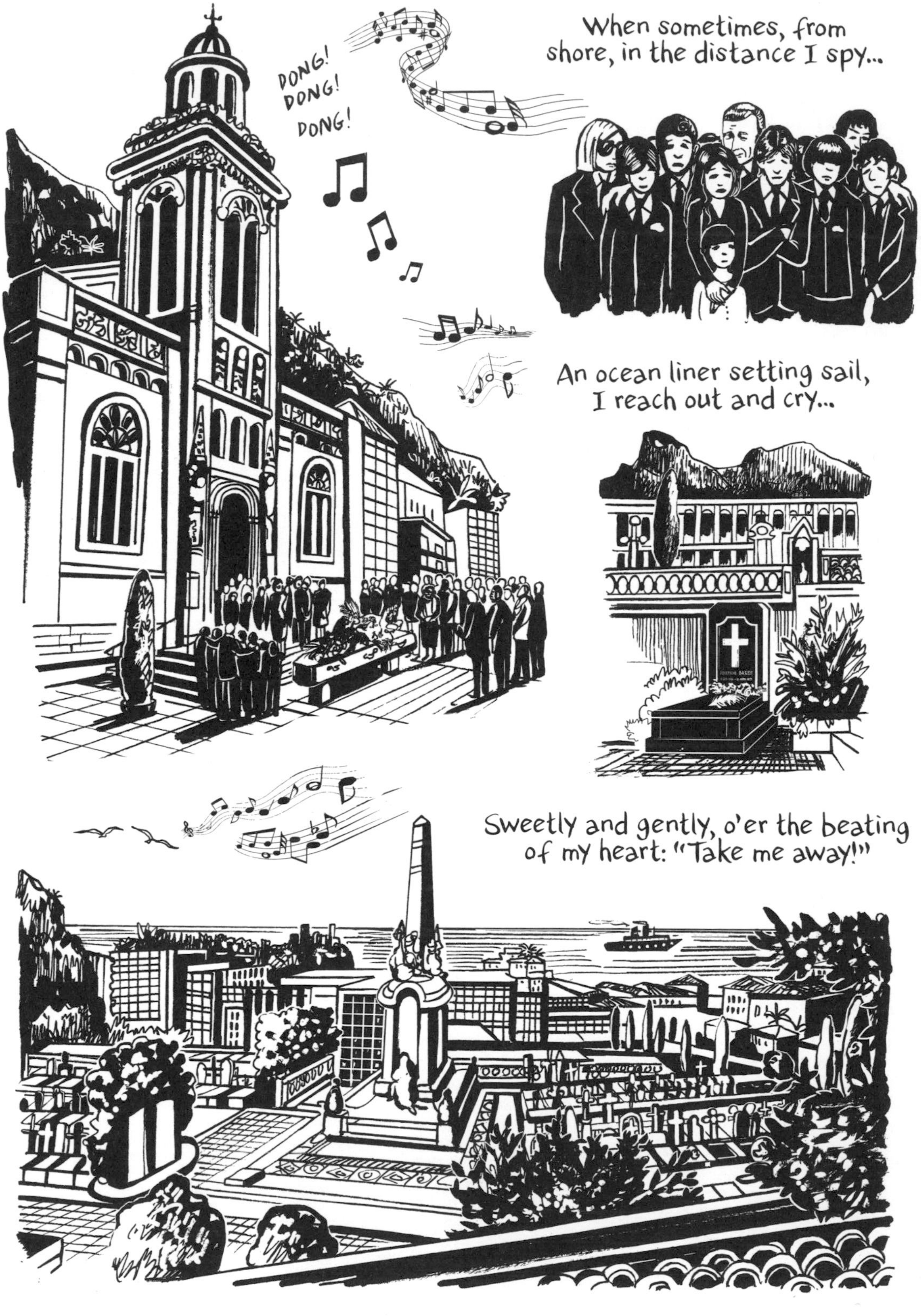
DONG!
DONG!
DONG!
When sometimes, from shore, in the distance I spy...
An ocean liner setting sail, I reach out and cry...
Sweetly and gently, o'er the beating of my heart: "Take me away!"

TIMELINE

for Josephine Baker

1906 3 June. Freda Josephine Baker is born in St. Louis, Missouri. While the maternity of Carrie McDonald is indisputable, the paternity of Eddie Carson has been brought into question by some biographers and family members.

1907 12 October. Her brother Richard is born.

1909 Carrie marries Arthur Martin, a 23-year-old coalman. Richard takes his stepfather's last name. Martin will be the father of Josephine's two sisters. One of them, Margaret, is born this same year. The family moves to 1526 Gratiot Street, south of the railroad tracks and just a few blocks from Union Station. The couple's poverty later forces them to move to Papin Street, facing the tracks.

1910 18 July. Josephine's youngest sister, Willie Mae Martin, is born.

1916 Attendance records from Dumas Elementary School show that Josephine was only present for 67 school days, preferring to watch shows at the Booker T. Washington Theatre. This year, she meets the Jones family, who teach her the rudiments of music and acting while performing at restaurants and neighbourhood festivals.

SAINT-LOUIS 1915

1917 The East St. Louis riots break out on the other side of the Mississippi. Thirty-eight African-Americans are lynched. Escaping families find refuge in the Martins' home.

1919 22 December. Josephine marries for the first time, to ironworker Willie Wells. Apart from a religious ceremony, it seems that there are no records of this marriage, which was illegal in Missouri due to the bride's age. Nevertheless, this event marked the end of Josephine's school years.

1920 November. Bob Russell's touring company takes up residency at the Booker T. Washington Theatre for two months. Russell and singer Clara Smith notice Josephine.

1921 January. In the middle of the month, Josephine appears on stage for the first time at the Booker T. Washington, in the melodrama *Twenty Minutes in Hell*. She plays the part of an angel, suspended from the rafters.
30 January. Josephine boards the last train to Memphis in the company of Bob Russell's touring company. The company performs on the circuit of the Theatre Owners Booking Association, or TOBA, which black performers nicknamed "Tough on Black Asses". Russell's troupe

passes through New Orleans before stopping in Philadelphia.
17 September. Josephine marries Willie Howard Baker, whom she met in Philadelphia.

1922 Josephine is hired for the touring company of the musical *Shuffle Along*. She stops in New Haven, Atlantic City and Massachusetts.
24 May. Josephine appears on stage in New York for the first time. To celebrate the first anniversary of the hit show *Shuffle Along*, all the companies reunite at the 63rd Street theatre.
22 July. Closing night of *Shuffle Along* on Broadway.
July–November. The touring company performs in Boston.

1923 The *Shuffle Along* troupe stops in Atlantic City in June, then spends August in Toronto – Josephine's first time leaving the US – followed by Pittsburgh and Detroit. In November, they perform at the American Theatre in St. Louis.

1924 Josephine is hired to perform in the production *In Bamville*. The premiere takes place at the Lyceum Theatre in Rochester on 10 March.
1 September. The show is renamed *The Chocolate Dandies*, and the New York premiere is held at the Colonial Theatre.

1925 25 February. *The Chocolate Dandies* plays at the American Theatre in St. Louis.
May. The New York performances come to an end. Josephine is cast in *Sam Slavin's Plantation*. She dances in the show *Tan Town Topics*.
Summer. Josephine meets Caroline Dudley Reagan.
16 September. The RMS *Berengaria*

of the Cunard Line leaves New York Harbour. Among the passengers are the cast of *La Revue Nègre* (*The Black Revue*).

22 September. At 8:30 a.m., the *Berengaria* reaches the port of Cherbourg in France. Josephine moves into the Hotel Fournet in Paris.

24 September. Preview of *La Revue Nègre* at the Théâtre des Champs-Élysées.

2 October. Opening night. Josephine appears in three dance numbers. She only sings in one, a humorous song titled "Yes Sir, That's My Baby". Kees Van Dongen paints Josephine's portrait. Piet Mondrian raves about her Charleston. Sem draws a caricature of her as a monkey.

Late November. After a triumphant and extended run at the Théâtre des Champs-Élysées, the revue moves to the Théâtre de l'Étoile.

7 December. Last Paris performance. They take the show to the Alhambra Theatre in Brussels.

31 December. Premiere at the Nelson Theatre on the Kurfürstendamm in Berlin.

1926

January. *La Revue Nègre* is onstage in Berlin.

March. Josephine returns to Paris. She begins sending $300 per month to her family in St. Louis. Premiere of *La Folie du Jour* (*Folly of the Day*) at the Folies-Bergère. In one of her numbers, Josephine wears a skirt of bananas made of leather. A camera captures the banana dance, but in the film intended for American audiences Josephine wears a white brassiere. Before the evening show, Josephine appears in tea dances at the Club des Acacias. After the show, she dances in cabarets at L'Abbaye de Thélème, the Impérial Soupers and the Milonga. Josephine moves into an apartment at 77 Avenue des Champs-Élysées, which Paul Poiret decorates. She begins adopting pets: a parrot, white mice, a monkey and a snake.

She meets Giuseppe Abatino, known as Pepito.

October. The owners of the cabaret Impérial Soupers in the Rue Pigalle rename their club the Impérial Joséphine Baker. A one-year contract is signed, but the experiment only lasts two months.

14 December. Opening night of the cabaret Chez Joséphine in the Rue Fontaine. Pepito is the manager and Dr. Gaston Prieur is the financier. Josephine tries her hand at dancing and singing by turns, from midnight till dawn. Sometimes Albert, Josephine's pink pig, shows up at the cabaret.

Late December. Josephine organises a Christmas party for the children of Paris police officers. Sculptor Alexander Calder creates his first wire sculpture portrait of Josephine. It will be exhibited two years later at the Weyhe Gallery in New York. By 1949, Calder will make five wire sculpture portraits of Josephine.

1927 Publication of *Le Tumulte Noir* (*Black Tumult*) by Paul Colin. Josephine pens the preface, with the anonymous assistance of journalist Marcel Sauvage. She meets Georges Simenon.

March. Josephine signs on to play the role of Papitou in *Siren of the Tropics*. At the Folies-Bergère, the revue *Un Vent de Folie* (*A Wind of Folly*) proves unsuccessful.

27 May. Onstage at the Folies-Bergère, Josephine announces the arrival of Lindbergh in the *Spirit of St. Louis*.

June. Josephine announces her marriage to Pepito on the day of her 21st birthday, 3 June. She claims that she has become a countess. Journalists reveal the imposture. On both sides of the Atlantic, scandal ensues.

7 June. Josephine obtains her driving licence at Porte Maillot in Paris. Josephine Baker's memoirs, recorded and adapted by Marcel Sauvage, are published in France by Éditions Kra. The book will be translated into 18 languages.

30 December. The film *Siren of the Tropics* is released in theatres.

1928 **January.** Josephine performs a farewell concert at Salle Pleyel in Paris and sings in French for the first time. Wiéner and Doucet are present.

Late January. Departure on a world tour organised by Pepito. The couple bring eleven people with them (including six white musicians) and two dogs. They also take all the records produced since 1926 (a total of 24 songs), 196 pairs of shoes, a commensurate number of dresses and furs, 141 pounds of rice powder and 3,000 postcards for Josephine's fans. She will visit 25 countries in two years. The first stop on the tour is Vienna. Municipal authorities ban her show at the Ronacher Theatre on moral grounds. Following a hearing, the premiere is allowed to take place at the Johann-Strauss Theatre on 1 March. Josephine then plays to a full house for a month. She continues to Prague.

June. Budapest, Bucharest, Zagreb.

Late June to August. Copenhagen, Oslo, Stockholm, Gothenburg.

August to September. Holland.

Winter. One-month run at the Theatre des Westens in Berlin. During this time, Pepito opens a cabaret, Chez Joséphine, at 53 Behrenstrasse. The tour continues to Dresden, Stuttgart (with two weeks at the Friedrichbau Theatre), Leipzig (at the Krystallpalast) and Hamburg (at the Hansa Theatre). The police ban Josephine's performance in Munich.

1929 **Winter.** In Budapest, Josephine reunites with Mistinguett. She spends several months in Spain: Madrid (in the snow), Barcelona, Huesca, Seville (coinciding with the Ibero-American Exposition opening in May), Pamplona, Valladolid, Malaga, San Sebastián, Oviedo, Santander, Logroño, Gijón, Zaragoza, Valencia, Córdoba and Granada.

Spring. The couple visit Pepito's family in Italy. From Genoa, they embark for Buenos Aires aboard the *Conte Verde*. In Argentina, Josephine gives 200 performances in Buenos Aires, then

LE BEAUCHÊNE ~VÉSINET ~ 1929 ~

moves on to Rosario, Córdoba and Mendoza. In Uruguay, she performs at the Urquiza Theatre in Montevideo. In Chile, she appears at the Victoria Theatre in Santiago, before going to Valparaiso. In Brazil, she makes stops in São Paulo and Rio.

20 September. *Siren of the Tropics* is released in New York. Mayor James J. Walker attends the premiere at the Lafayette Cinema on 7th Avenue. In St. Louis, the film is screened at the Booker T. Washington Theatre.

Josephine returns to France aboard the *Lutetia* with Le Corbusier, whom she met in Buenos Aires.

Josephine and Pepito purchase Le Beau-Chêne, a 30-room mansion in Le Vésinet, at 26 Avenue Clemenceau. Josephine has already acquired an apartment building on Avenue Bugeaud, in the 16th arrondissement of Paris.

1930 **January.** In Rome, Josephine is present for Pepito's mother's final days.

26 September. The Casino de Paris premieres the revue *Paris Qui Remue* (*Paris Astir*), with sets by Paul Colin. Josephine originates a song by Vincent Scotto, titled "J'ai Deux Amours". The show runs successfully for 13 months. Josephine is given Chiquita the leopard.

1931 Publication of *Mon Sang dans tes Veines* (*My Blood in your Veins*), a novel penned by Pepito based on Josephine's idea.

May. Josephine is named 'queen' of the Colonial Exposition.

13 September. Due to a terrorist attack on the Bia-Trobagy viaduct in Hungary, the *Orient Express* loses its engine and one of its cars to a precipitous fall. Twenty people die. Josephine, a surviving passenger, helps the wounded and sings to them. This information appears on several websites, with no sources attributed. This heroic event was never retold by Josephine. While it is true that she was an enthusiastic regular on the *Orient Express*, it seems that on the date in question she was scheduled to be on stage in Paris. Her show had been a hit for a solid twelve months, and would not be closing for another month. When asked about this incident, Jean-Paul Caracalla, eminent specialist of *Orient Express* mythology, mused, "That means there's yet another legend enriching *Orient Express* history!"

October. Closing night of *Paris Qui Remue* at the Casino de Paris.

1932
3 December. The revue *La Joie de Paris* opens at the Casino de Paris, with sets and a poster created by Paul Colin. Willie Mae dies following a self-induced abortion.

1933
July. Duke Ellington is invited to Le Beau-Chêne. "She showered me with presents, as if I really was somebody."

Summer. Josephine meets Jo Bouillon for the first time at the Ostend Casino in Belgium. Chiquita is sent to the Jardin d'Acclimatation in the Bois de Boulogne in Paris.

October. Josephine tours England, starting at the Prince Edward Theatre in London. After four weeks in England, her European tour continues in Iceland, Athens, Rome and Copenhagen. She goes on to Alexandria and Cairo, then Lyons.

1934
June to August. Shooting for *Zouzou* takes place in Paris and Toulon.

15 December. Dress rehearsal for Offenbach's *La Créole*. The operetta runs for six months at the Théâtre Marigny.

21 December. The film *Zouzou* is released.

1935
12 May. Closing night of *La Créole*.

25 May. Josephine goes to Tunisia to film *Princesse Tam Tam*.

She obtains her pilot's licence.

Publication of the book *Une Vie de Toutes les Couleurs* (*A Life in Every Colour*), a collection of Josephine's memories presented by André Rivollet.

October. At Le Havre, Josephine boards the *Normandie* for New York. She visits her family in St. Louis for the first time since 1921. Since then, her grandmother and stepfather have died. She makes visits to schools and to the site of the former Booker T. Washington Theatre, destroyed in 1930.

November. The film *Princesse Tam Tam* is released in France.

30 December. Preview of the *Ziegfeld Follies* at the Boston Opera House. Vincente Minelli creates the sets and costumes, Balanchine choreographs and Ira Gershwin pens the tunes. Josephine performs in three numbers: "La Conga", revived from "La Danse Sauvage", with a costume inspired by the banana skirt; "Maharanee", a sketch taking place at a Parisian racetrack, with Josephine wearing a fur-lined white dress; and "5 A.M.", with four white dancers.

1936 14 January. *Ziegfeld Follies 1936* comes to Philadelphia.
30 January. New York premiere of *Ziegfeld Follies 1936* at the Winter Garden Theatre.
8 February. The cabaret Chez Joséphine opens at the Mirage, 125 East 54th St.
26 May. Josephine returns to France aboard the *Normandie*.
September. Josephine meets Felix Marouani, who becomes her new impresario.
21 September. Pepito Abatino dies.
October. Premiere of *En Super Folies* at the Folies-Bergère, with sets and costumes designed by Michel Gyarmathy.

1937 Josephine meets Langston Hughes, who interviews her backstage at the Folies-Bergère for an American newspaper. Chez Joséphine opens in the basement of the hotel Château Frontenac on Rue François-Premier, in the spot formerly occupied by Le Gerny's, the cabaret where Edith Piaf made her debut.
Spring. Josephine meets Jean Lion.
30 November. Jean Lion and Josephine are married. Josephine begins travelling with a French passport.
18 December. Josephine begins her farewell tour in London.

1938 The farewell tour continues for three months, with stops in Tunis, Oran, Nice, Basel, Zurich, Warsaw and Berlin.
Summer. Josephine visits the Château des Milandes. According to Jo Bouillon, she was in the company of Jean Lion, but it is more likely that she was with her friend Claude Meunier, whose family owned the Meunier chocolate company.
November. After Kristallnacht, Josephine joins the International League against Racism and Anti-Semitism.

1939 The farewell tour continues with stops in Rome, Stockholm, Madrid and Berlin. Josephine meets Frida Kahlo, who has come to show her paintings in Paris at the invitation of André Breton. A 1993 biography suggests that the two women had an affair, but no sources are cited other than the author's intuition.
March to July. Josephine tours South America. Upon her return, she and Jean Lion separate.
3 September. France and England declare war on Nazi Germany. Josephine and Maurice Chevalier sing for the French army. They are also named godparents of August, the first baby elephant born in France, at the Amar Circus.
October. Josephine and Maurice Chevalier co-star in *Paris-Londres* (*Paris-London*) at the Casino de Paris. Meanwhile, Josephine begins shooting the film *Fausse Alerte* (*False Alarm*), but the war will prevent the movie from ever being completed. For the film, Vincent Scotto composes the song "Mon Coeur est un Oiseau des Îles" ("My Heart is an Island Bird") for Josephine. She debuts the song onstage at the Casino de Paris. In addition to all these activities, every Sunday afternoon Josephine sings on the radio in French and English. During this period, she sends photos to the 4,000 French soldiers with whom she corresponded as a 'war godmother'. During this period, she meets Captain Jacques Abtey of the French secret service, for whom she completes reconnaissance missions at the Italian and Japanese embassies.

1940 May. Every evening, after performing in *Paris-Londres*, Josephine visits a refugee shelter in Rue du Chevaleret in the 13th arrondissement of Paris.

June. Josephine moves into the Château des Milandes.

December. Josephine performs the opera *La Créole* at the opera house in Marseilles.

1941 **January.** Josephine travels to Algiers on the liner called *Gouverneur général de Gueydon*. She makes the journey with 28 trunks.

28 January. Arrival in Casablanca.

March. Josephine goes to Tangier, then Lisbon, where she sings and transmits secret documents to London.

April. Her divorce from Jean Lion is announced. Josephine moves to Marrakesh.

Late June. Josephine falls seriously ill with peritonitis. She is transported from Marrakesh to Casablanca, where she is treated at the Mers Sultan clinic, directed by Dr. Comte. She undergoes five operations at the clinic, including a hysterectomy.

1942 **November.** Allied landing in North Africa.

1 December. Josephine leaves the Mers Sultan clinic.

In the US, the media announce Josephine's death in Morocco. Langston Hughes writes a stirring obituary for the American press.

1943 **February.** For the first time since 1941, Josephine appears onstage. In Casablanca, she performs for African-American GIs at the opening of the Liberty Club.

In collaboration with the Red Cross, she performs a *pro bono* concert tour of American military bases in North Africa.

June. The French army – still under the command of General Giraud – refuses Josephine's musical collaboration, so she performs instead for the soldiers of the Eighth Army of the United Kingdom. Still *pro bono*, her tour continues in Tunis, Benghazi, Alexandria, Jerusalem, Haifa, Damascus and Beirut.

August. At the opera house in Algiers, Josephine sings in honour of Free France and meets General de Gaulle. His rival, General Giraud, refuses to attend. At the end of the month, the Allies agree to recognise the French Committee of National Liberation and its chief, Charles de Gaulle. From this moment until the end of the year, Josephine is finally able to perform for French troops. At the Grand Hotel in Beirut, Josephine sells the Cross of Lorraine given to her by de Gaulle, with proceeds benefiting Free France.

1944 **23 May.** Josephine is named sub-lieutenant, first-class officer of propaganda and appointed to the general staff of the French air force.

Early June. Josephine performs concerts in Corsica, then returns to Algiers.

2 October. Aboard a Liberty ship with a female unit of the air force, Josephine definitively leaves Algiers for France.

1945 Josephine and band leader Jo Bouillon meet again. She

recruits him to play for French troops stationed as far away as Germany.
28 March. At the Théâtre des Champs-Élysées – where she made her French debut 20 years earlier – Josephine participates in a gala benefiting the Free French forces in the presence of General de Gaulle. Later, she performs in London at the invitation of Winston Churchill.
September. Singing and lecture tour in Switzerland, with stops in Zurich, Basel, Lucerne and Bern.

1946 **January.** In Berlin, Josephine and Jo Bouillon perform for allied troops. Marshal Zhukov joins her in singing "La Marseillaise". The tour continues to Brussels, where Josephine reunites with Noble Sissle. He has revived the show *Shuffle Along* for American troops. Later, she continues on to Copenhagen, and in June she reaches Morocco, where she performs for the air force.
October. Though she has just undergone surgery, Josephine receives the Resistance Medal with rosette.

1947 **3 June.** In the chapel at the Château de Milandes, a wedding ceremony is celebrated for Josephine, 41, and Jo Bouillon, 39.
8 June. The deed to "Château des Milandes, village of Castelnaud-Fayrac, Dordogne" is transferred to Josephine Baker for 2.5 million francs, paid in cash. Josephine sells Le Beau-Chêne and moves out.

She tours Central and South America – Argentina, Chile, Mexico and Cuba – accompanied by Jo Bouillon. They receive a jubilant welcome.
24 December. Opening night in Boston to a chilly reception.

1948 In New York, Josephine isn't offered any bookings. She spends time with Coco Chanel and Edith Piaf. She then begins a series of articles on segregation for the daily newspaper *France-Soir*.
February. Josephine leaves America and returns home to France.
April. Josephine opens a new show at Club 48 on Rue Montaigne. Ali Khan, Rita Hayworth, Emperor Bảo Đại and Belgian Minister Paul-Henri Spaak all hear her sing. Work is done at Milandes and electricity is installed.
October. Josephine participates in a televised gala for the United Nations.
November. Carrie and Margaret move to Milandes, along with Margaret's husband, Elmo Wallace.

1949 **March.** At the Folies-Bergère, Josephine plays Josephine de Beaumarchais and Mary Stuart in the musical *Féeries et Folies* (*Fairies and Follies*).

Also this month, Jacques Abtey publishes the war memoir *La Guerre Secrète de Josephine Baker* (*Josephine Baker's Secret War*). Marcel Sauvage resumes his interviews with Josephine to complete his *Mémoires*.

At Club 48, she sings "Mon Beau Livre d'Images" ("My Beautiful Picture-Book") accompanied by a projection of

eight illustrations by Albert Dubout.
4 September. Dedication of Milandes with the opening of its first public building, "La Guinguette". 1,500 visitors are expected. By the end of the day, the count reaches 10,000.

1950
Pepito's mortal remains are transferred to the Fayrac cemetery close to Milandes. In April, Jo Bouillon's father is interred in the same cemetery.
Spring. European tour. In Rome, Pope Pious XII receives both Josephine and Jo Bouillon. The pontiff gives his blessing to her plan to adopt children "of every colour and religion". They will later be known as the "Rainbow Tribe".
Summer. Milandes opens its first hotel-restaurant, called "Lou Tornoli" ("Come again" in patois).
October. Milandes closes for the season. Josephine begins a six-month tour with Jo in Mexico and Cuba.

1951
In Miami, Josephine insists on performing for integrated audiences.
2 March. Premiere at the Strand Theatre in New York.
20 May. In honour of her combat against segregation, the National Association for the Advancement of Colored People holds "Josephine Baker Day" in Harlem.
Spring. US tour: Detroit, Washington, Atlanta, San Francisco, Los Angeles. In St. Louis, she turns down a $12,000 offer to perform at the Chase Hotel because the establishment won't allow integrated audiences.
Summer. Return to Milandes.
October. In New York, Josephine appears at the Roxy. Scandal at the Stork Club.

1952
3 February. The city of St. Louis holds a "Josephine Baker Day". She gives a free show at the Kiel Auditorium and seats her family's children in the front row.

In Mexico City, she performs at El Patio. In Las Vegas, she gives four weeks of shows at the Hotel Last Frontier (now called the New Frontier).

Her brother Richard moves to Milandes.
Autumn. On tour in Brazil, Uruguay and Argentina.
3 October. President Perón invites Josephine to the Presidential Palace in Buenos Aires. At the president's request, she spends three months participating in the social movement begun by the late Eva Perón. Josephine publicly criticises US government policy.

1953
18 February. In Cuba, Josephine gives two benefit concerts for brothers Raúl and Fidel Castro. She is arrested by the police and accused of being bankrolled by Moscow and of promoting anti-democratic activity. She is released the next day. The accusation is unfounded, but it inflames the American press.
28 December. Josephine delivers a talk for the International League against Racism and Anti-Semitism at the Maison de la Mutualité in Paris.

1954
February. Josephine visits Denmark.
April. Josephine travels to Japan. She gives 24 concerts, including several benefiting the Elizabeth Saunders Home directed by her friend Miki Sawada. Miki entrusts Josephine with two children: Yamamoto Akio and Kumura Teruya Seiji, nicknamed "Jeannot". Like their soon-to-be brothers and sisters, they will be officially adopted on 21 June 1957 at the courthouse in Sarlat, Dordogne.

29 April. After a singing tour at the Imperial Theatre in Tokyo, she meets Jiichirō Matsumoto, champion of human rights in Japan.

The tour continues in Saigon and in French military camps.

May. Return to Milandes.

September. Josephine returns from Finland with Jari, who was born in Helsinki in 1953.

1955 **March.** Josephine brings Luis back from Colombia. In the same year, Milandes becomes home to Moïse and Jean-Claude, both from the Paris region.

1956 Sale of Josephine's furnishings from the Avenue Bugeaud property in Paris.

March. The International League against Racism and Anti-Semitism holds its convention in Paris. Josephine again meets Jiichirō Matsumoto.

10 April. At the Olympia, Josephine bids farewell to the Paris stage. She has decided to perform from this point on exclusively at Milandes.

Summer. Josephine devotes herself to Milandes. She invites the poet Minou Drouet and holds a fashion show.

September. Josephine participates in the Congress of Black Writers and Artists in Paris, along with Louis Armstrong, Léopold Sédar Senghor, Richard Wright, Frantz Fanon and James Baldwin. Aimé Césaire declares, "Let the black peoples ascend the great stage of history!"

Autumn. Josephine goes on the road for a farewell tour.

1957 **9 January.** After touring North Africa, Josephine lets journalists meet her two newest children: Brahim and Marianne, both born in Algeria.

13 January. Josephine delivers an anti-racist talk at the theatre in Milandes.

May. Josephine decides to begin divorce proceedings from Jo Bouillon.

1958 One-year-old Koffi arrives from the Ivory Coast.

Jo and Jo separate for the first time. Following a ten-year hiatus from the Paris stage, Jo Bouillon forms a new orchestra. He holds a premiere at the Alhambra. The three eldest children of the Rainbow Tribe attend the show.

Josephine tours Sweden, Germany, Holland and Denmark. In Poland, she visits Auschwitz.

1959 **12 January.** Carrie passes away at Milandes.

A new arrival comes to the Rainbow Tribe: Mara, from Venezuela.

27 May. Three years after her farewell show, Josephine returns to the Olympia with the show *Paris, Mes Amours* (*Paris, My Loves*). The revue runs for nine months.

Summer. Milandes hosts performances by Jacques Brel, Louis Armstrong and students from the Paris Opera Ballet.

November. Actor Gérard Philipe invites Josephine to preside over the 30th Gala of the Union des Artistes in Paris.

1 December. Josephine initiates a young newcomer into the ways of the Casino

de Paris before her first appearance on stage. Her name is Line Renaud.

A baby of only a few months is abandoned in a trash can and discovered by a rag-and-bone man. Josephine immediately takes the baby in and names him "Noël".

1960 **17 January.** Closing night of *Paris, Mes Amours*.

Josephine and Jo Bouillon separate definitively, but he refuses to divorce until all the children have reached the legal age of 21.
March. Josephine appears at the Regal Theatre in Chicago in the American version of *Paris, Mes Amours*, which is titled *The Fabulous Josephine Baker*. She also delivers talks on racism.
4 March. Snowed in at an airport on the other side of the world, Josephine can't preside over the one-off performance of the 30th Gala of the Union des Artistes.

6 March. Josephine Baker is initiated into the New Jerusalem Masonic Lodge of the Women's Grand Lodge of France.
17 March. Opening night of *Paris, Mes Amours* at the Cirque Royal in Brussels.
April. *The Fabulous Josephine Baker* runs in Los Angeles. Later, Josephine sings at the Alcazar in San Francisco, then in the Montreal nightclub Le Faisan Bleu.
Summer. Reprise of *Paris, Mes Amours* at the Olympia in Paris.

1961 **January.** In Vienna, Josephine meets Ernst Marischka, the director of the film *Sissi*. He wants to make a film with the Rainbow Tribe. She decides not to follow through with the plan, feeling it would be too traumatic for her children.
March. Finally available for the 31st Gala of the Union des Artistes, Josephine presents a musical number with elephants.

LES MILANDES _CASTELNAUD_PERIGORD 1962_

18 August. At Milandes, Josephine receives the Legion of Honour and the Croix de Guerre from Air Force General Valin for her contribution to the French Resistance.

Present at the ceremony are former Gaullist minister Jean-Pierre Bloch, consuls from Spain, Morocco, the United States, Italy and Finland, and Gaby Morlay.

1962 **January.** Josephine gives concerts in Stockholm and brings part of the Rainbow Tribe with her.
February. Scandinavian tour.
August. At Milandes, Josephine produces and stars in *L'Arlésienne* by Georges Bizet.
September. *L'Arlésienne* comes to the Olympia in Paris to limited success.
December. Jean Nohain comes to celebrate Christmas at Milandes.

1963 **January.** An American publisher asks Langston Hughes to write Josephine's biography. The project never comes to fruition.
28 August. Josephine participates in the March on Washington for Jobs and Freedom.
14 October. In New York, Josephine performs at Carnegie Hall. After the show, she spends the rest of the night singing with Sammy Davis Jr. and Duke Ellington.
October. Still in New York, Josephine performs at the Shubert Theatre, then at the Brooks Atkinson Theatre.
November. John F. Kennedy is assassinated. Josephine, who is preparing for an American tour in 1964, visits the president while he is lying in state, to pay homage to his fight against segregation. In the same month, Jo Bouillon moves to Buenos Aires.

1964 **Winter.** Josephine returns to Broadway with *Josephine Baker and her Company*. The show is a triumphant success. She takes the show to Philadelphia.
April. Josephine returns to the Olympia with her American company.
1 June. Josephine gives a press conference. Electricity, water and phone service have been cut off at Milandes. "I need 200 million centimes to save the world's village! If I don't have the money by 9 June, this is the end of Milandes."
18 June. Stellina, of Moroccan origin, is born in Paris. She is to be the twelfth and final child of the Rainbow Tribe.
25 June. Brigitte Bardot makes an appeal on French television to help Josephine. She contributes half of the sum needed.
25 July. Josephine is incapacitated by a heart attack. She is transported to the Hôpital Boucicault in Paris.

Josephine is no longer on the rolls of the New Jerusalem Lodge.

1965 Josephine visits Guinea, Mali and Ghana. The Moroccan king Hassan II hosts her in Fez. Josephine performs in Rabat, Casablanca and Marrakesh. The Rainbow Tribe travels to Algeria.

30 August. Eddie Carson, Josephine's presumed father, dies at the age of 79.

1966 **January.** In Cuba, Josephine participates in the Tricontinental Conference. Upon returning from Havana, she is hospitalised for an intestinal blockage.
March. The court of Bergerac sets an auction date for Milandes in the month of May. Yet again, Josephine succeeds in raising the funds needed to cancel the sale.
April. Josephine attends the first World Festival of Black Arts in Dakar. She has dinner with Katherine Dunham and Langston Hughes.
July. The Rainbow Tribe travels to Cuba.
Late August. Departing from Cuba, Josephine brings her children to Buenos Aires to visit their father.
October. Moroccan tour.

1967 **Winter.** Gilbert Trigano suggests that Club Med take over the management of Milandes. Josephine does not follow through on this proposition.
   International tour in Algeria, Lebanon, the Middle East and Asia.
Summer. The Rainbow Tribe travels to Yugoslavia, where they are received by Tito.

1968 Sylvain Floirat, owner of the radio station Europe 1, offers to buy Milandes under a life annuity and by paying all of her debts, which then amounted to 46 million francs. Josephine refuses.
16 February. The court of Bergerac holds an auction for the sale of the Château at 260,000 francs, la Chartreuse at 175,000 francs, the farm and the amusement park each for 190,000 francs and 20 plots of land for 90,000 francs. A creditor ultimately annuls the auction, citing

flawed procedure: he considers the prices too low.
3 April. Josephine appears for a two-week run at the Olympia. On the occasion of her performance, Bruno Coquatrix produces an album with the record label Pathé-Marconi, titled *SOS Milandes*.
3 May. Milandes is again put up for auction. Josephine is in Gothenburg, Sweden, when she learns that her entire property has been sold. With an estimated value of 600 million centimes, the property was sold for only 91 million.
15 May. Return to the Olympia.
30 May. Josephine participates in a parade on the Champs-Élysées in support of General de Gaulle.
June. Josephine attends Robert Kennedy's funeral, accompanied by six of her children: Akio, Jeannot, Jari, Luis, Jean-Claude and Moïse. She spends much of her earnings from the Olympia on plane tickets.
29 June. Closing night at the Olympia.
4 July. Josephine suffers a stroke and receives treatment in the hospital at Périgueux.
7 October. Josephine is to be evicted from Milandes, but she takes advantage of the law against evictions in winter to obtain permission to stay until 15 March 1969.
   Over the holidays, Josephine sings in Berlin at the Schultheiss bar.

1969 **19 to 22 January.** The furnishings at Milandes are sold for 26.5 million francs, instead of the expected 40 million.
March. Eviction from Milandes.
27 March. Josephine begins a new singing tour at the cabaret La Goulue in Paris.
25 July. With her twelve children, her dog and her parrot, Josephine arrives

in Monaco to rehearse for the Red Cross Ball at the Société des Bains de Mer, on the advice of André Levasseur and Jacqueline Cartier.

Summer. Under Grace Kelly's protection, Josephine and her family move into Villa Maryvonne, perched on the cliffs of Roquebrune. The villa has five bedrooms and two bathrooms. Jo Bouillon visits for the holidays.

1970
Summer. Josephine does a cabaret tour in Italy.
October. Three-week tour in Mexico.

1971
February. Concerts in Norway.
March. Concerts in Sweden and Berlin.
April. Concerts in Brazil (Rio de Janeiro and Porto Alegre) and Argentina (Buenos Aires).

Josephine visits the Vatican for a private audience with the Pope. Akio goes with her.

1972
January. Concerts in Stockholm.

1973
May. At the Cannes film festival, Josephine meets Diana Ross. The two women dream that Diana might one day portray Josephine on the big screen.

5 to 8 June. Performances at Carnegie Hall in New York. Bricktop is the opening act. Eubie Black attends one of the performances.

July. In Copenhagen, Josephine suffers another heart attack and is hospitalised.

September. A series of concerts at the Ahmanson Theatre in Los Angeles. Gloria Swanson and Vincente Minnelli laud her performance, and Ella Fitzgerald joins her onstage for an improvisational duet.

October and November. Josephine's concerts in Detroit and San Francisco prove to be a financial failure for the producers.

31 December. Concert at the Palace Theatre in New York. On this American tour, Josephine is accompanied by Jean-Claude Rouzaud, who will later call himself "Jean-Claude Baker" and become the proprietor of Chez Joséphine, a restaurant on 42nd St. in New York from 1986 until his suicide in 2015. He is the author of a biography of the woman whom he claims – without legal grounds – to be his adoptive mother.

1974
January. Still in New York, Josephine performs at the Raffles Club and the Sherry-Netherland Hotel.

VILLA MARYVONNE — ROQUEBRUNE - 1975

April. Concert at the Beverly Hills Hotel. Audience members include Nina Simone, Eartha Kitt and Diana Ross.
July. Concerts in Japan.
8 August. At André Levasseur's request, the premiere of the show *Josephine* takes place at the Monaco Red Cross Ball, at the Monte-Carlo Sporting Club. Jean-Claude Brialy is the master of ceremonies.
Later in August. In Israel, Josephine visits Tel Aviv and Jerusalem, and meets Golda Meir.
September. Performances in Stockholm.
October. South African tour. Josephine's anti-apartheid speeches drive white audiences from the auditoriums.
November. Concerts in London.

1975 **24 March.** At the Bobino theatre in Paris, Josephine

performs a premiere for the readers of the daily newspaper *France-Soir*.
2 April. Performance for the press.
8 April. A triumphant gala performance.
10 April. Josephine falls into a coma. She is hospitalised at the Pitié-Salpêtrière Hospital in Paris.
12 April. Josephine Baker breathes her last breath at Pitié-Salpêtrière Hospital at 5.30 a.m. Line Renaud is one of the four people with her during her final moments.
15 April. A funeral service is held at La Madeleine Church in Paris. A crowd of 20,000 people gather around the church.
19 April. Josephine's body is interred in the Monaco cemetery, in the presence of Jo Bouillon and their children, as well as Margaret, Elmo and Richard.

BIOGRAPHICAL
NOTES

of main and secondary characters
in Josephine's story,
accompanied by portraits

(in order of appearance in the story)

Carrie McDonald

Born in Little Rock in 1886, Caroline was adopted by the McDonalds when she was still very young. She moved with her family to St. Louis, Missouri, when she was about ten years old. At the time, the city was undergoing a period of expansion, becoming the fourth largest in the US, big enough to host both the World's Fair and the Olympic Games in 1904. Carrie was raised primarily by her aunt on Gratiot Street. Her father was a labourer and her mother a laundrywoman. Despite her poor attendance in school, Carrie became the first in her family to learn to read and write.

From Market Street to Chestnut Street, from the brothels to the gambling dens, the sounds of ragtime could be heard from every floor. Later on, her daughter Margaret would recall: "Mama was a great success at the Sunday balls. She was unbeatable on the dance floor. She could dance with a glass of water on her head without spilling a single drop." Her boyfriend Eddie Carson was known for being an excellent dance partner. At the age of 19, Carrie was a laundrywoman like her mother, and she was pregnant. When her aunt threw her out of the house, her employer Josephine Cooper took her in. Josephine suggested that if Carrie had a girl, she should name it after her. The circumstances of Freda Josephine's birth remain a mystery. Carrie delivered her baby in a hospital for whites. According to the doctor's records, she stayed there for six weeks. Why did she choose a Germanic first name for her daughter? It was said that Carrie had worked for a German family. Who was Josephine's real father? That was a secret that Carrie would never reveal. She soon entrusted the girl to her own mother, still claiming that the father was Eddie.

Josephine had a special relationship with her grandmother. "The songs she sang as she rocked me to sleep... told of the freedom that would someday come." She had grown up on a plantation in Arkansas and had witnessed the whipping of slaves. Those memories haunted the stories that she told to her granddaughter.

Soon after the birth of her last daughter, Willie Mae, in July 1910, Carrie brought Josephine to live with her. By then, she had married Arthur Martin and had given birth to a son, Richard, and a second daughter, Margaret. One day, after Richard had been called a bastard, Carrie explained to her children: "There are no bastards in my family, you all come from the same hole!" When she later wrote her autobiography, Josephine recalled her own questions about her identity, and her mother's response: "You are all the same. Because we're all God's children. And because you are my children. The fact that your skin is lighter than Richard's, Margaret's or Willie Mae's doesn't change a thing!" Josephine was seven years old when Carrie sent her to live with the Kaisers, then with the Masons. Those experiences were not a success. Mother and daughter were in constant conflict. Twenty years later, Josephine would recall: "My mother shouted: 'Tumpie, keep it up and I'll send you to reform school!' but I never believed her, because if she did, I couldn't have stolen that coal and brought home those nickels!" When Josephine left St. Louis to seek her fortune, Carrie told Margaret: "She chose her path. It's her business."

In November 1923, Josephine returned to St. Louis with the company of *Shuffle Along*. At the American Theatre, the left side of the house was reserved for blacks. The whole family attended. Josephine stayed at the family home and left $75 for her mother.

She was in Europe for six months before finally sending word to her family that she was alive and well in Paris. She was then making her debut at the Folies-Bergère. From that time until the start of the war, she would send her mother $300 a month. She also bought a baby grand piano for her sister Willie Mae.

In 1927, Josephine granted an interview to *Amsterdam News* in which she declared that she never wanted to return to the US. She still wished to see her mother, but couldn't stand the way black artists were treated in the south. Josephine returned home anyway. When she asked her mother what had become of the money she had sent, Carrie replied: "I spent it. What did you expect?"

Following the mysterious death of Arthur, who had become mentally ill and had been placed in an asylum, in June 1936 Carrie wed Tony Hudson, 29, a Mexican mystic who spent entire nights in prayer. Carrie opened a restaurant with her daughter's financial backing. Josephine also bought her mother a little house with arched windows on West Belle Street. Carrie would later sell the property without telling her daughter. During World War II, she continued to live in St. Louis, at 4324 Garfield Avenue.

In early 1948, Josephine managed to convince her mother to come live with her at Milandes. Carrie agreed, on the condition that Margaret and her husband Elmo come with her. Carrie left her newest husband behind with no regrets.

At Milandes, the elderly African-American woman suddenly found herself the grandmother of six little boys of every colour. She became the doyenne of the Rainbow Tribe. Everyone called her Mama.

Carrie lived at Milandes for ten years. She fell ill while her daughter was touring abroad. Jo Bouillon and Margaret stayed at her bedside. Jean-Claude, her sixth grandson, would never forget the furtive caress he received on his cheek from his grandmother's dying hand. "Our grandmother lived on the second storey of the château," recalled Akio, the eldest of her grandchildren. "Every morning, we would come to her bedroom's open door and give her a kiss. One morning, the door remained closed."

Carrie passed away at the age of 73 at Château de Milandes on 12 January 1959, in Josephine's absence. She was buried a few days later at the Fayrac Cemetery in Castelnaud-la-Chapelle, with the surname Hudson, that of her forgotten husband in St. Louis.

Richard Martin

Born on 12 October 1907, Richard would never meet his real father. He ultimately took the last name of the coalman whom Carrie wed two years later. When Richard was 14, his older sister left home, never to return. The family wouldn't hear from Josephine until March 1926. She sent money home each month, but any news they heard of her came from the papers. Richard later recalled that one paper reported that Josephine was "the richest black woman in the world". "The whole family was proud. She was an exemplary woman and sister."

When he was out of work during the Great Depression, in 1929 Richard became the father of little Richard Jr.

When she returned to St. Louis in 1935, Josephine bought a truck for her little brother. During the war, already a father of six, Richard was drafted into the United States Navy, completing his service on the Great Lakes. His military pay came as a great relief.

When Josephine invited the whole family to Milandes in 1948, he was the only one to stay behind. At the time, he was managing a transport company with four trucks.

In mid-October of 1950, Josephine returned to St. Louis to try once again to convince him. "She promised me the moon and stars if I came, but I wanted to wait a little, to see what my mother and sister thought." By that time, Richard was divorced. He left behind seven children born in St. Louis.

Upon his arrival at Milandes, Josephine put Richard in charge of the brand-new Esso filling station. It was the only station for kilometres around. In summer, tens of thousands of vehicles flocked to the château, deep in rural Périgord; Richard didn't want for business. And he fell in love. On 3 June 1956, in the château's chapel, he married Marie-Louise, the village postwoman.

Richard's son Artie, having completed his military service in Germany, also came to live at Milandes with his German wife.

Upon her death in 1959, Carrie left her bible to her son. Between the pages, he found a photo of Tony Hudson. That same year, as her show triumphed at the Olympia, Josephine lost almost the entire American branch of the Rainbow Tribe. Her nephew Artie returned to the US. Richard fell in love with a young woman from Sarlat who was carrying his child, but his wife refused to divorce. Josephine was critical of the situation. Richard decided to leave.

Brother and sister wouldn't meet again until 1965. In the meantime, Richard had had three children with his new wife. He settled down some 600 kilometres from Milandes, in the town of Baillargues, where he would happily live out the rest of his life. In 1974, Richard Jr., the eldest of his children back in the US, would become the last of Josephine's American managers.

In 2016 in St. Louis, two of Richard's grandsons – one a pastor, the other retired from the military – still amiably greeted visitors on Josephine's trail. Though they had little in the way of documentation, their admiration for their aunt and her civil rights activism was sincere. They were proud that her name had been given to a boulevard in St. Louis' Midtown, even though the parking lots of St. Louis University border the street all the way to Delmas Ave, where the predominantly African-American neighbourhood begins.

Margaret Wallace

Born in 1909 in St. Louis, Margaret was one of the two daughters born to Carrie McDonald, the washerwoman, and Arthur Martin, the coalman. She was six or seven years old when she started going with Richard and Josephine on Sundays to the Booker T. Washington Theatre. There, for ten cents, they could watch shows, including films, musicals and vaudeville acts performed by black artists. Margaret later recalled that her older sister would try to recreate the magic in the basement of the house on Gratiot Street: "Grandma would lend her dresses that she would wear to play queen of the stage, making faces and strutting about. Sometimes, Richard and I would say, 'Oh no, Tumpie, not tonight!' And she would reply, 'You come in and sit down. If you walk out, I'll smack you!'"

On 30 January 1921, when Josephine took the last train to Memphis with Bob Russell's troupe, she made Margaret promise not to say anything to their mother. That night, when Carrie asked where Josephine had gone, her younger sister replied that she was staying with her friends the Joneses. Not until the next day did Margaret finally tell her mother the truth. To her great surprise, Carrie received the news calmly. According to Margaret, her older sister "had decided to take over the world".

In the early 1930s, Margaret lost her younger sister Willie Mae to a complication from her third abortion. Margaret wept for days on end.

When Josephine returned in 1935, Margaret had just married Elmo Wallace. Full of admiration, Josephine asked her, "Well, little sister, where did you find this handsome gentleman?"

In 1942, when the American media announced Josephine's death in Casablanca, Margaret rushed to announce the bad news to her mother. "No, Tumpie's not dead," her mother replied with confidence.

After a long voyage by train and boat to Le Havre, Margaret reached Milandes in 1948, with her mother and husband. The couple lodged in the large farmhouse adjoining what Josephine wished to be a model farm. There was always work at Milandes. Margaret baked and sold pastries. In summer, Elmo managed the rowboat rentals on the Dordogne. In winter, he assisted Jo Bouillon in modernising the farm.

Upon Carrie's death in 1959, Margaret was the most deeply affected: "I had lived with her my whole life." A little later, Margaret and Elmo, who until then had remained childless, adopted little Rama, born in Charleroi, Belgium.

When Josephine was hospitalised on 10 June 1975, Margaret was at Roquebrune. The next day, she boarded a plane to Paris. She was the one to make the decision not to attempt a last-minute operation that would likely have left Josephine severely disabled. With Princess Grace Kelly, Margaret prayed and sat by Josephine's bedside until her last breath, on 12 April at 5.30 a.m.

Elmo died the following year. Margaret spent the rest of her life on the French Riviera, living near her daughter. She died in 2001 at the age of 92.

Eubie Blake

James Hubert Blake was born in Baltimore on 7 February 1887, though he always claimed to have been born in 1883. Son of John and Emily – both born slaves – James, nicknamed "Hubie", then "Eubie", was their only child; his eight brothers and sisters had all died very young. As a four-year-old, the sight of an organ in a music shop left him transfixed. He took to the keys with such great virtuosity that the shopkeeper managed to convince his parents to purchase the instrument: "Your child is a genius. It would be criminal to deprive him of this gift from God." A neighbour who played the organ for the local church gave him lessons. At age 7, he switched to the piano. At age 10, he smoked his first cigarette; he would never quit. At age 15, he was playing piano in the best brothel in Baltimore. It was a secret job: "I made more money in one night than my father made in a week working as a stevedore on the Baltimore docks... I hid my earnings... I finally showed them the money. It was several hundred dollars. They no longer insisted I only play religious music."

At age 16, he composed his first song, "Sounds of Africa", which was later renamed "Charleston Rag". In 1915, his reputation as a musician and composer had already been established when he met the singer and songwriter Noble Sissle. Together, they would enjoy their greatest successes under the name Dixie Duo. When they wrote *Shuffle Along*, the first musical performed and produced entirely by African-American artists, the two musicians became legend. In Philadelphia, where the musical had become well-established, Josephine tried to join the cast of *Shuffle Along*, but Sissle's decision was final: "Too young."

With the show's success on Broadway, soon a second company was formed to tour other major American cities. This time, Josephine managed to join the cast, and she imposed her humorous style onstage.

On Broadway, *Shuffle Along* had just given its 500th performance when Sissle and Blake heard tell of the little chorus girl who was a hit with the touring company. By then, she had reached the legal age to perform in New York. "And so," Eubie Blake later said, "we had her leave the second company and we brought her to Broadway. She made us laugh till our stomachs hurt. Audiences loved her."

Before the show, Eubie was in the habit of chatting with audience members in the lobby. "Is the cross-eyed girl playing tonight?" they would ask. "They thought Jo was cross-eyed. But she was only pretending. Just like she pretended to forget the dance steps. She would do all kinds of funny things with her legs, getting mixed up, tripping, catching herself, rolling her eyes like marbles. She always danced in time, only she never did the same thing as everybody else. Folks screamed with laughter. They didn't realise she was joking around." And Eubie Blake, 36, succumbed to the charm of Josephine, 16.

Shuffle Along was still playing ten times a week, but Sissle and Blake were already working on their next project, *In Bamville*. The story took place on the last day of the Bamville fair. The company included 25 performers and three horses. Two roles were written for Josephine. "Sometimes, I was a vamp, in a silk slit gown opposite the leading man. Sometimes, I was a stupid little girl wearing oversized shoes, a dress with a big sash bow, doing my whole repertoire of funny faces." The latter role brought her more attention. Following a successful tour, the company reached New York on 1 September 1924, at which point the show was renamed *The*

Chocolate Dandies. The show ran for only three months at the Colonial Theatre. Despite the show's extravagance and the three horses on stage, the show was a financial disappointment. In total, the show – including its initial version – would run for 60 weeks. And lose $60,000.

Her reputation secured by Eubie Blake, Josephine made ready to cross the Atlantic. "She was a 'one man at a time' type of girl. We stayed together until that lady came and took her off to France," he said later.

While Josephine was enjoying success in Europe, the Sissle and Blake duo didn't survive the failure of their last production. Not until 1945 would the two men again perform together, for American troops, and then in 1969 to make a record in honour of Eubie. In the meantime, when ragtime came back into style in the 1950s, Eubie Blake would come to be considered one of the pioneers of the genre.

Josephine and Eubie would sometimes cross paths during a concert or tour; their final meeting took place at Carnegie Hall in 1973, when Eubie came to honour his former protégée.

Two years later, the musician would compose his 350th and final song, "Betty's Washboard Rag". Also in 1975, Josephine and Sissle passed away. In 1979, a musical titled *Eubie!* presented his greatest songs in a historical framework. In June 1982, he performed in public for the last time.

Eubie Blake died in New York on 12 February 1983, five days after celebrating not his 100th birthday, as he liked to claim, but his 96th.

Caroline Dudley

Born in Chicago in 1890, Caroline was the youngest of the five Dudley children. Their father, Emilius Clarke, was a renowned gynaecologist. Caroline would later say, "I spent my childhood sitting on Booker T. Washington's lap." The writer and activist, and first African-American invited to dine at the White House, was also a regular at the Dudleys' table. Passionate about music, Emilius would bring his daughters to the cabarets on State Street in Chicago, where they discovered ragtime and early jazz. The three girls were also deeply moved by their exposure to French novels and Impressionist painting. Caroline's first connection with France came about when the US entered World War I in 1917. As an auxiliary, she served coffee to soldiers leaving for the trenches.

After the war, Caroline married diplomat Daniel Joseph Reagan, with whom she had a daughter, Sophie, in 1921. When Daniel was appointed to the American Embassy in Paris, writer Gertrude Stein found them a studio apartment at 27 Rue Fleurus – across the street from her home – and arranged for a plumber to install a toilet. But it was in Washington, where the couple had lived previously, that Caroline viewed rehearsals at the Douglas Theatre, a small music hall in an African-American neighbourhood, and had the idea for a revue with an all-black cast. "That's where the little seed sprouted that would later become *La Revue Nègre*. Then it took hold of me and started to grow."

In Paris, the American made the rounds of all the theatres. She was turned away from the Casino de Paris and the Folies-Bergère. The painter Fernand Léger pointed her towards Rolf de Maré: "His theatre is a real white elephant. Just the other day, I told him, 'Bring some black people here, they're dynamite. They're the only ones who can revive your theatre...'"

De Maré financed Caroline's trip to New York. Destination: Harlem. There, she hired Will Marion Cook to write the music and advise her in the casting of her troupe. On the lookout for a female star, Cook and Caroline hit all the nightspots on Broadway. Caroline dreamed of finding a headliner like Florence Mills, but they were all too expensive for her budget. At the Plantation Club, she noticed Josephine playing the clown. "There's our star!" Caroline was 35, Josephine 19.

Caroline auditioned 40 groups before selecting the six-man band of pianist Claude Hopkins, age 22. Rehearsals took place at 232 138th Street. Dancer-choreographers Louis Douglas and his wife Marion Cook were the star couple. Maud de Forest was the lead singer. Lydia Jones, Evelyn Anderson, Bea Foote, Marguerite Ricks, Mabel Hopkins and Hazel Valentine were the chorus girls. Spencer Williams composed the music and Jack Palmer, a white lyricist, wrote songs. For the set, Caroline turned down the design offered by her friend John Dos Passos, judging it too conventional; instead she hired the young Mexican Miguel Covarrubias. On 15 September 1925, Caroline boarded the RMS *Borongaria* with all 25 members of the *Revue Nègre* troupe.

"Arrived at the station without fanfare. The artists seemed a little lost," Caroline wrote. On the programme, she was credited as producer, and her husband as director – his role was never confirmed by other records.

The premiere was held on 2 October. Fernand Léger, Kees Van Dongen,

Robert Desnos, Blaise Cendrars and Maurice Chevalier were all present. The company played to a full house: two thousand tickets were sold. Caroline suddenly became the producer of the most talked-about show in Paris.

For Caroline and all the other main players in the production, the adventure of *La Revue Nègre* ended in Berlin. Just three days after Josephine's departure, Caroline had to face the facts: "It was as though the Mississippi had dried up, after she left, our boats just wouldn't float. Josephine ran away, she was stolen from me." After briefly trying to take the runaway to court, she decided to give up. Daniel lost all of his savings in the affair; the couple divorced soon after.

In 1926, living in New York in a house with a garden in Greenwich Village, Caroline attempted to produce another African-American revue, *O Blues!*, inspired by "The Weary Blues" by Langston Hughes. Soon after, she returned to Paris. Following her father's death in 1929, her mother joined her.

On 13 January 1930, at the Place du Panthéon in Paris, the painter Jules Pascin introduced Caroline to the writer Joseph Delteil. A former Surrealist (Breton had thrown him out after the publication of his work *Jeanne d'Arc*, later adapted for the screen by Carl Dreyer), Delteil had seen *La Revue Nègre* several times in a row. He and Caroline became inseparable.

In the early 1930s, the writer's fragile health led the couple to move to the south of France, although they were in Paris in 1935 when they met Henry Miller through Caroline's older sister, who hosted a salon on Rue de Seine. A strong friendship would form between the two novelists.

In 1937, Caroline, Joseph and his sister Marie purchased La Tuilerie de Massane, a vineyard near Montpellier. Joseph's parents and sister came to live there. The cohabitation wasn't without conflict for the former coalman, his illiterate wife and their daughter-in-law, whom they called "l'Américaine".

In 1977, Delteil began work on a novel: a love story titled *Joseph et Caroline*. He would never complete it. He passed away the following year at the vineyard, a few days after their 24th anniversary.

Commenting on the success of *La Revue Nègre*, Caroline said: "I had nothing to do with it. A veritable phoenix possessed Josephine, the bird of paradise." At Carnegie Hall in 1973, Josephine dedicated her show to Caroline and invited the whole Dudley family on stage. Caroline died in Montpellier at the age of 92 in July 1982. She is buried next to Joseph in Pieusse Cemetery.

Sidney Bechet

Sidney Bechet was born on 14 May 1897 in New Orleans, Louisiana, to a Creole family. He was one of seven children. Of his father Omar, he would later say that he was "crazy about music, a peerless dancer, a lover of parties, people, life".

Sidney was six the first time he blew into a clarinet, encouraged by his mother, who would teach him the rudiments of the Louisiana Creole French still spoken there today. By the time he was 12, he was already playing with semi-professional bands. A few years later, the budding musician met a young singer from Perdido Street named Louis Armstrong.

At the age of 19, the Louisianan was making a living playing the clarinet. He soon bought his first soprano saxophone. He would become a master of these two instruments throughout his career.

Bechet travelled to Europe for the first time in 1919 and discovered Paris. In August of that year, he played for the King of England. When he was in London again two years later, a liquor-steeped love affair with a white woman of easy virtue landed him in court. Police tried to convict him of rape, but the judge simply ejected him from the country. Bechet returned to New York.

As a soprano saxophonist, Bechet joined the band of pianist Duke Ellington, who would later say of his music that it was "all soul, all from the inside". During this period, he recorded a considerable number of titles – roughly 60 – some with Louis Armstrong, Duke Ellington and the pianist Clarence Williams. Bechet decided to reinvest this financial manna in a cabaret, the Basha Club, at the corner of 155th Street and 7th Avenue in New York. The deal turned sour when his partner was implicated in a rigged gambling affair that made him an enemy of the gangster Bob Ewley. That's how Sidney met Caroline Dudley. As Will Marion Cook warned: "He might miss a show now and then, but every time he plays, [she]'ll thank the heavens."

On the day of their departure, the whole troupe was aboard, except for Sidney. "He finally showed up, very late. He's a character," Claude Hopkins recalled.

In September 1925, he was back in France with *La Revue Nègre*. In his autobiography, his memories of that period were relatively brief, amounting to about 20 lines: "Josephine and Louis [Douglas], I remember, danced the Charleston and nobody in Europe had seen that dance before, and that really started something." The following year, after Josephine's defection in Berlin, he began a tour in the USSR, and then played in Istanbul and Egypt. In 1928 and 1929, he roamed through Germany, Spain, Portugal, Belgium and France. In Paris, he played in Noble Sissle's orchestra. One December night, at 28 Rue Pigalle, he settled a fight with the banjo player Mike McKendrick with a few shots from his revolver. Three bystanders were injured. The two black musicians stood trial in February. Though the Surrealist poet Louis Aragon testified on their behalf, Bechet was sent to Fresnes prison for ten months. Upon his release, he was expelled from France. He stayed in Berlin until 1931, when he returned to New York.

In May of 1949, Bechet was invited to the Paris Jazz Fair, where his name appeared alongside Miles Davis and Charlie Parker. He was a success with French audiences. He decided to move to Paris permanently, where he played with the seven musicians in the orchestra of clarinettist and soprano saxophonist Claude Luter, whom Boris Vian vaunted in his *Manuel de Saint-Germain-des-Prés*. In 1950, they recorded "Les Oignons" ("The Onions"). The piece proved to be Bechet's first recording hit, allowing him to reach an audience of more than just jazz lovers. The previous year, he had recorded his own version of "Mon Homme" ("My Man").

In August 1951, Bechet married the German Elizabeth Zigler in Antibes. The couple moved to Grigny, in the suburbs of Paris, but soon after, Bechet met Jacqueline Peraldi and fell in love. Two years later, their son Daniel was born. Sidney moved this new family into a house in the suburb of Garches. Until his death, the musician would split his time between the two homes. Daniel became a drummer and percussionist, and would go on to play with saxophonists Dexter Gordon and Ben Webster, guitarist Larry Coryell and singer Peter Gabriel.

In 1952, Bechet played saxophone with Claude Luter's band and recorded his second most popular tune, "Petite Fleur" ("Little Flower"). The same year, Nicolas de Staël dedicated two oil paintings to him. "Les Musiciens, Souvenir de Sidney Bechet" ("The Musicians, Memory of Sidney Bechet") hangs in the Pompidou Centre in Paris.

On 28 August 1955, Sidney played a show in Mons, Belgium. He delighted the audience by playing a New Orleans version of "Doudou", a traditional song from the region. The song became a hit in Belgium, and it was soon recorded at Vogue Studios in Paris. This was to be Bechet's last international success.

On 14 May 1959, on his 62nd birthday, Sidney Bechet died in Garches of lung cancer. The following year, his recorded interviews were published in the US as the autobiography *Treat it Gentle*. Its pages are alive with the breath of the New Orleans jazzman:

"But if you have a feeling for the music, you can understand him, and that's why he keeps it so important to himself. And he's always been trying. The black man, he's been learning his way from the beginning, a way of saying something from inside himself, as far back as time, as far back as Africa, in the jungle, and the way the drums talked across the jungle, the way they filled the whole air with a sound like the blood beating inside himself."

Rolf de Maré

Born on 9 May 1888 in Stockholm, Rolf was the son of Ellen von Hallwyl and Henrik de Maré, a courtier with distant French origins. Due to his asthma, Rolf had to receive lessons from a tutor, Johnny Roosval, 22, a poor art history student. Ellen, twelve years his senior, fell in love with the young student, and the scandal made its way to the Swedish court. In 1907, the divorcee left the palace, abandoning her fortune and her son. She would become a painter, then a sculptor. Rolf was raised by his grandmother, Countess Wilhelmina von Hallwyl, one of the rare female art collectors of the early 20th century and the richest woman in the country.

In 1912, upon returning from a round-the-world trip, Rolf was swept away by an amorous passion for the painter Nils Dardel. Rolf became his patron. But as soon as he moved to Paris, Dardel plunged into alcoholism and sexual promiscuity. Nonetheless, he guided his lover, the art collector: Dufy, Laurencin, Braque, Picasso, Léger, Gris, Gauguin, Bonnard, Monet and Seurat had all entered his collection before 1914. The war brought a brutal end to all trans-European cultural exchange.

In 1919, Dardel introduced de Maré to the man who would change his life: Jean Börlin, five years his junior, a virtuoso dancer at the Royal Swedish Opera in Stockholm. In May 1909, Serge Diaghilev's Ballets Russes had, in a matter of hours, transported dance to an unrivalled level of artistic ambition: kinetic, pictorial, sensual, musical and modern. In Stockholm, Börlin dreamed of spreading his own wings, and Rolf financed his flight. In 1920, Börlin danced his first solo performance in Paris, with a piece entitled "Sculpture Nègre" ("Black Sculpture"). After this success, Rolf and Jean created the Ballets Suédois, poaching, in the process, 15 dancers from the Royal Swedish Opera – a nationwide scandal. In retaliation, the specific nature of Rolf's relationships with Dardel and Börlin were reported in the Swedish press.

In July 1920, de Maré signed a seven-year lease for the Théâtre des Champs-Élysées. On 23 October, the Ballets Suédois burst onto the Paris scene with verve. Rolf was 32, Jean 27. Jean would go on to create 23 ballets in the next four years.

De Maré also quickly became the owner of four periodicals, *La Danse-Théâtre, Comœdia illustré, Paris-Journal* and the world's first male fashion magazine, *Monsieur*, "the magazine of elegance and good manners", co-founded with fashion designer Paul Poiret. All of these would play a role in the launch of the Ballets Suédois.

Between 1921 and 1924, the stage of the Théâtre des Champs-Élysées became the venue for all kinds of innovative theatrical experimentation for the Ballets Suédois. "The antithesis of the Ballets Russes," according to Blaise Cendrars. The theatre's programming included: "Les Mariés de la tour Eiffel" ("The Brides of the Eiffel Tower") by Jean Cocteau; "L'Homme et son désir" ("Man and his Desire") by Paul Claudel; "La Création du monde" ("The Creation of the World") by Blaise Cendrars, inspired by African folktales, with music by Darius Milhaud, set and costumes by Fernand Léger; "Within the Quota", the first jazz ballet, with music by Cole Porter and a libretto by Gerald Murphy (who had been the model for Dick Diver in F. Scott Fitzgerald's *Tender is the Night*); "La Jarre" ("The Urn") by

Luigi Pirandello, with sets by Giorgio de Chirico; "Relâche" ("Release") by Francis Picabia, with music by Eric Satie, accompanied by a cinematic interlude; and "Entr'acte" by René Clair, which featured Marcel Duchamp and Man Ray playing chess on the roof of the theatre, as well as de Maré and Börlin in tuxedos.

Despite these successes, de Maré sank most of his inheritance in these productions. In 1925, he separated from his French associate, Jacques Hébertot, and closed down both the publishing group and the Ballets Suédois. He chose to focus on his theatre, whose management he had entrusted to the young André Daven.

Painter Fernand Léger was the first to suggest that Rolf produce a revue featuring African-American performers. At the same moment, the revue *Chocolate Kiddies*, with music by Duke Ellington, was a hit in Berlin, where it was being produced by singer Lottie Gee with a secessionist contingent from the company of *Chocolate Dundee*. Consequently, Rolf agreed to host Caroline Dudley's project.

In October 1926, the Swedish patron of the arts was sure that the *Revue Nègre* gamble had been a success. Josephine was pampered and promoted. She would call the theatre owner "Monsieur Rolf". She later recalled: "He came up to me, put his index finger on the top of my head (he was very tall!) and with the other hand he spun me like a top. I didn't resist, and he stopped me and in his deepest voice he said, 'You will be famous!' He seemed to believe it. So I did, too."

The programme of *La Revue Nègre* included three scenes presented by Jean Börlin. Rolf was still supporting him, but the choreographer and soloist of the Ballets Suédois was succumbing to alcohol and drugs.

After burning through the tens of millions of kronor of his inheritance, and in spite of continual assistance from his grandmother, Rolf soon had no choice but to throw in the towel. On 2 January 1927, he produced a final show, a homage to the American aviator Charles Lindbergh, who had just crossed the Atlantic.

In 1930, Börlin, 37, died in New York of a liver haemorrhage. In his hands, he held Rolf's last letter to him. Dardel died in New York, too, in 1943.

Having been unable to leave Sweden all through the war, and in spite of the recent decriminalisation of homosexuality in his country, Rolf returned to Paris in autumn 1945. In 1952, he sold a Picasso painting, *Au Lapin Agile*, for which he had paid 7,000 francs in 1914, for $40,000, then the highest price fetched by the artist's work. Three years later, he met his last partner, a 24-year-old electrician named Lars Nilsson. Rolf was 67. Rolf de Maré died while travelling in Barcelona on 28 April 1964, eleven days before his 67th birthday.

André Daven

Born Lucien André Davenport in Marseilles on 13 March 1899, the producer-to-be chose the pseudonym "André Daven" when he left for Paris to become an actor. He was 21 when he made his debut in *L'Homme du large* (*Man of the Sea*) by Marcel L'Herbier; he went on to play in five more silent films, including *La Femme de nulle part* (*The Woman from Nowhere*) by Louis Delluc. In 1923, he met Rudolph Valentino, who was on a European tour with his wife Natacha Rambova, also known as Winifred Shaughnessy. Valentino, an Italian-born former dancer turned Hollywood actor, was then the biggest male movie star in the world, due in large part to his roles in two silent feature films, *The Four Horsemen of the Apocalypse* and *The Sheik*. Women idolised him; men thought him effeminate but imitated his elegance. A friendship formed between Daven and Valentino; the star brought the young man to Hollywood to play in the film that would mark Valentino's grand return to the silver screen, *Monsieur Beaucaire*. Several of Valentino's biographers claim that he was gay and that Daven was his lover. There is no proof in support of this assertion; however, it is not impossible that Daven was the ghostwriter of both autobiographies published by Valentino in 1923. After shooting *Monsieur Beaucaire*, in 1924 Daven left California to return to Paris. Never again would he return to acting, and he became Gloria Swanson's European impresario. He also became a theatre reporter for *Monsieur*, a magazine edited by Jacques Hébertot. He was one of the young men who made up Hébertot's informal entourage – nicknamed the "Champs-Élysées Boys" by Thora Dardel, wife of Nils Dardel, who was Rolf de Maré's first great love. According to the Swedish artist's wife, Daven's beauty rivalled the great male stars of the time, John Gilbert and Rudolph Valentino.

At the beginning of 1925, Hébertot, who was not only at the helm of Rolf de Maré's four magazines but also managing the Théâtre des Champs-Élysées, was quietly pushed out by his rich associate. De Maré felt that the accounts were unclear and that, despite the success of the Ballets Suédois, he had already lost too many millions. He resumed control of the magazines and three theatres, then entrusted them to André Daven, who had just replaced the dancer Jean Börlin in his life. The magazines were soon liquidated, and Daven was able to concentrate on the three theatres. The Studio des Champs-Élysées had a modest capacity, and the Comédie des Champs-Élysées was being managed by Louis Jouvet, who had just starred in the hit film *Dr. Knock*. The main theatre, with its 2,000 seats, posed the real problem. Daven suggested transforming it into a music hall.

The high life continued on the fashionable Avenue Montaigne. De Maré drove a red Amilcar, Daven drove a white one and Louis Jouvet a blue one. "When the three of us would take off together to go have a Pernod or a *café français* at the corner of the Pont de l'Alma in the afternoon, it was a amazing spectacle," Rolf de Maré wrote.

On 22 September 1925, André Daven himself went to pick up the little company of *La Revue Nègre* at the Saint-Lazare train station: "They all spoke at once and laughed out loud. Nothing but blouses in red, green, yellow, strawberry trousers, polka dot dresses. Incredible hats – floppy hats – in cream, orange and poppy red, crowning faces of ebony, thirty pairs of astonished and joyful eyes." He brought them directly to the Théâtre des Champs-Élysées. They only had ten days to rehearse, and Daven still had no idea what to expect of the revue. He quickly came to understand that, despite the group's remarkable talents, the show was still in a very rough state, without any real artistic cohesion. A few days before the premiere, André Daven showed up in the office of Jacques-Charles, a rising-star theatre director and choreographer for Mistinguett. "My dear," Daven said to him, "they're doing two hours of tap-dancing, they'll scare everybody away. You're the only one who can pull us through." After watching a quick run-through, Charles gave the following verdict: "The mistake was trying to play Parisian! You should've been playing black." Upon Daven's suggestion, the choreographer chose Josephine to do the Charleston.

After the opening night of *La Revue Nègre*, Daven finally praised the performance: "It was the revelation of a new world, eroticism embodied in style. The naïve expression of desire, its call, its wild ardour reaching pathos. The audience was on its feet, frenzied, and gave Josephine such an ovation that she, trembling and staggered by the enthusiasm she had roused, couldn't leave the stage. We had to drop the curtain."

In 1926, André Daven married the actress Danièle Parola, and de Maré served as witness. The same year, Valentino died in New York of sudden septicaemia. 100,000 people gathered for his funeral. Sound film would make its appearance the following year – too late to hear the voice of the "Latin lover".

In 1927, when de Maré sold his theatre lease to an American investor, André stayed on as artistic director. After a few months, he chose to resign.

At the age of 28, Daven began a new life. First, he worked as a production assistant on *Monte Cristo*, directed by Henri Fescourt in 1929, and then in 1932 he began work as a producer, specialising in Franco-German co-productions. In 1934, he produced Fritz Lang's only French film, *Liliom*, followed by five Marc Allégret films between 1936 and 1938. As a refugee in the US, he worked on four Hollywood films, including two by Henry Hathaway. Upon returning to France, in 1955 he was the producer of *The Grand Maneuver* by René Clair, with Gérard Philippe. Two years later, he would produce his 16th and final film, *Cette Nuit-là* (*That Night*), by Maurice Cazeneuve, with Mylène Demongeot and Maurice Ronet, which Stanley Kubrick would cite in 1963 as one of the ten greatest films of all time. André Daven passed away in Paris on 17 November 1981 at the age of 82.

Paul Colin

Paul Colin was born on 27 June 1892 in Nancy, France. His father, an anti-clerical, "anti-German" patriot, was disappointed to see that his son didn't wish to follow in his footsteps and make a career of government. His mother pushed him to develop his artistic inclinations. Paul enrolled in the École des Beaux-Arts, an influential Paris art school, and took classes with painter Victor Prouvé, father of the future architect Jean Prouvé.

World War I took the Paris bohemian by surprise. First as an infantryman, then as a volunteer in a tank division, he would see every front, from Verdun to Villers-Cotterêts, before 1918. Once he was demobilised, he dreamed of being a painter in Paris, and made his living decorating sets until he met André Daven, artistic director of the Théâtre des Champs-Élysées.

Paul Colin's legend began with his poster for *La Revue Nègre* in 1925. Josephine and Paul would meet later: their stories became entwined during a modelling session. Paul was 33, Josephine 19. She didn't speak French, nor did he speak English. He communicated through drawing. Over the course of the revue's run in Paris, Paul launched and accompanied Josephine in Paris society. Paul was her first bodyguard, her first protector in the urbane jungle of the Continent. Though the success of *La Revue Nègre* immediately shone its light on the poster artist, Paul Colin also profited from a misunderstanding. Though he created the poster, he did not create the drawing that illustrated it. One year earlier, Miguel Covarrubias, a 21-year-old Mexican artist living in Harlem, had completed a series of drawings for *Vanity Fair*. After their publication, Caroline Dudley hired Covarrubias to create the revue's sets. Following sound professional instincts, Colin decided to maintain the graphical coherence of the set design in the poster. Three of the *Vanity Fair* drawings ended up gracing the revue's poster, which was signed by Colin.

In 1927, in honour of the publication of his portfolio *Le Tumulte Noir* (*Black Tumult*), Colin organised *Le Bal Nègre* at the Théâtre des Champs-Élysées. The poster for *Le Tumulte Noir*, even more than the one for *La Revue Nègre*, established Colin's work as being among the most modernist drawings of the day. Having integrated Covarrubias' influence, Colin seized angles and curves, inventing the jazz silhouette. His most accomplished work in this vein remains the series of 30 drawings illustrating *Les Mémoires de Joséphine Baker*, collected by Marcel Sauvage and published in the summer of 1927 by the prestigious Éditions Kra. Years later, Colin would declare to anyone who would listen, "I'm the one who invented Josephine!"

In the following 25 years, Colin would create 1,200 posters and hundreds of set designs for Fritz Lang, Henri Decoin and Julien Duvivier. He would also sign his name to the décor of some of the most famous interwar cabarets: Le Plantation, Le Tabarin and La Boule Blanche. The latter would be the venue for *Le Bal Anthropométrique*, organised in honour of the publication of a novel by his friend Georges Simenon: the first adventure of Maigret. Based near Place Pigalle in Paris, Colin opened a school where he would teach until the 1960s.

In the 1930s, Colin was everywhere. "Workdays lasting eight or ten hours would put my mind at ease about the time I lost to violins, champagne and women." The party ended in 1940. Colin would accept no commissions during the years of the Occupation, withdrawing to the secrecy of his studio to return to his primary passion: painting. In 1944, he signed the first poster of the Liberation, printed even before the shooting in the streets had come to an end. This poster would be one of his last. In 1945, at the Pavillon de Marsan, the first retrospective of his graphic work was held. He was 53. "After that exhibition, a retrospective on a past that no longer interested me, I felt a deep relief. I knew where I was; it was time to start over."

In 1957, Éditions de la Table Ronde published Paul Colin's memoir. A certain disenchantment and a profound nostalgia would mark the tone of these illustrated recollections. Of the book's 240 pages, only two are devoted to *La Revue Nègre* and Josephine. "I can still see her, frenetic, undulating, driven by the exasperated sounds of saxophones. Would her dances from South Carolina ring in a new era of civilisation, free at last of age-old fetters?"

In her 2004 book on the Paris school, Jeanine Warnod writes about Paul Colin, who had been a friend of her father, journalist André Warnod. She visited him in a retirement home for artists in Nogent-sur-Marne, where the painter had sought refuge in the 1970s. He was "ruined by years of parties, barely selling his paintings [which were] marked by an outmoded cubism," she wrote. Paul Colin, withered, unkempt, melancholic, received her in the dining room. He avoided his contemporaries, preferring to remain isolated in his room. That was where he kept all that he could salvage from the sale of his studio: a few posters from the jazz years and an easel. Paul invited his daughter's friend to view his latest paintings. "Painting, for me, is what counts. I was praised for my posters and my set designs. But I'm a painter, you understand? A painter!"

In the retirement home for artists in Nogent-sur-Marne, Paul Colin died on 18 June 1985.

Joe Alex

Though the company of *La Revue Nègre* had been rehearsing since its arrival in Paris, and though the fateful opening night was fast approaching, in early October the show was still not up to scratch. Daven and de Maré were losing hope.

Nevertheless, they hired a few black European dancers to fill out the American company. Among them were Joe Alex and the very young West Indian dancer Mathilde Darlin (nicknamed "Baby Darling" by Josephine), the future wife of the black actor Étienne Légitimus. They had 48 hours left when Daven called Jacques-Charles for help. The choreographer of Albert Willemetz's *Paris Qui Jazz* recalled: "There was certainly far too much tap-dancing, it was all impossibly monotonous, but the troupe had some excellent elements, the most wonderful willpower and an uncommon intelligence." Numbers were cut, changed or reordered. "I still needed a more voluptuous note to relieve us from all the jazz and tap-dancing. I spoke to the mulatto Joe Alex, whom I knew danced well with a partner. He assured me that one of the female dancers would be able to perform this sort of number with him: Josephine Baker."

"La Danse Sauvage" ("The Wild Dance") would change Josephine's life: "The first time I appeared before Parisian audiences, I was to perform a number that was rather... bestial. On stage, I found myself swept up in a whirlwind... I could see nothing, hear nothing, not even the orchestra, there was only the dance." Though the name of Josephine Baker was on everyone's lips from that night on, her partner's name would not make it into posterity.

Born in Recht, Belgium, on 23 February 1895, Joseph August Alexander appeared onstage in *La Belle du Far-West* in 1920, then onscreen starting in 1923. Prior to the success of *La Revue Nègre*, he had played in seven feature films, including a significant role in *Le Nègre du Rapide N° 13* (*The Negro of Express No. 13*). In a brief spurt of momentum following "La Danse Sauvage", he was credited in five films in 1926. The following year, Joe appeared again with Josephine on the set of *Siren of the Tropics*, but their names didn't appear in the same size type. In 1930, they met again at the Casino de Paris for the show *Paris qui remue* (*Paris Astir*), in which they sang a duet, "Voulez-vous de la canne à sucre?" ("Would You Like Some Sugarcane?"), a foxtrot one-step.

While he continued to pursue a career as a dancer in Paris theatres, Joe Alex also played roles in 21 feature films through 1946, though he never played a leading role. Generally pigeonholed in roles portraying servants, dancers and shoe-shiners, Joe Alex was the black silhouette in French cinema. Though his filmography includes such light fare as *Bouboule Premier* (*Bouboule the First*) by Léon Mathot, it also includes *Les Enfants du Paradis* by Marcel Carné.

In 1938, Joe Alex founded and managed the Théâtre Africain, whose company was comprised solely of black actors; the Nazi occupation put an end to his ambitions.

After 1946, there are no artistic records of the man who was Josephine's most important dance partner. He died in Berlin in June 1972 at the age of 77.

Mistinguett

The first time she heard Sidney Bechet play his version of "Mon Homme" ("My Man") in 1925, Josephine did not yet know the name of the woman who had first sung this song onstage, thanks to whom it became the greatest hit of the first half of the 20th century.

Her name was Mistinguett. Born Jeanne Florentine Bourgeois on 3 April 1875 in the town of Enghien-les-Bains, France, she grew up in Soisy-sous-Montmorency, where her parents were gatekeepers. "What we call 'vocation' is a way of narrating one's life; it's a legend, a mania for having one's story told," she would later say. Her career was forged by her will and ambition. On the train to Paris, where she would study violin, Jeanne made the acquaintance of revue artist Saint-Marcel. Taking inspiration from the hit song "La Vertinguette", he would nickname her "Miss Hélyette" before giving her the stage name "Miss Tinguette". Saint-Marcel also gave her the chance to make her debut at the Casino de Paris in 1893 with just one song – her very first: "La Môme du Casino" ("The Casino Kid").

Until World War I, Mistinguett would climb rung after rung of the music-hall ladder. By the early 1910s, at the age of 35, she had become the first lead revue dancer in Paris, to the delight of crowned heads and street gangs alike. "Being an artist is not fun and games. It's hunger, it's an occupation. You have to occupy the audience, occupy its time, have something to offer. It's a daily hunt," she wrote. Around that time, sculptor Auguste Rodin declared: "If I had to personify the muse of the music hall, I'd give her your legs, Mistinguett." It is suspected that she had many lovers and affairs: "I can't stand being courted. I don't like being touched. I am a woman who chooses." She had a son who would be raised mainly by his Brazilian father. "My principal concern was to keep pace, to avoid vacations, to sanctify my successes and my creations, to leave my beginnings behind."

In 1912, "La Miss" performed with Maurice Chevalier, a young singer 12 years her junior, whom she tried to save from his cocaine addiction. On the stage of the Folies-Bergère, they sang "La Valse renversante" ("The Wondrous Waltz"), which manifested their sensuous relationship. She was at the peak of her career and her personal life. Their separation was explosive, due in large part to their duelling egos, exacerbated by their professional rivalry. Nevertheless, Maurice Chevalier would remain, until her dying breath, the love of her life. "My work was my personal life, and my personal life was my work. There was no way out. I belonged to the audience. I had a duty to the audience. That's the reason for all of my bouts of depression. The audience is the most demanding lover."

Confronted with the jazz revolution coming from the US in the 1920s, Mistinguett was the first to bounce back, leading the revue *Paris Qui Jazz*, written by Albert Willemetz and Jacques-Charles, at the Casino de Paris. In 1925, when Josephine arrived in Paris with *La Revue Nègre*, Mistinguett did not yet have any reason to feel wary of her. Only when she came back to Paris to headline the Folies-Bergère did Mistinguett begin to see her as a rival. At the age of 40, her shapely, exposed legs had made her the queen of the European music hall; she fought to keep her title. Josephine, 20, showed her young woman's bosom: she was freer, wilder, jazzier. When Josephine made her debut at the Casino de Paris – Mistinguett's stronghold – it was war. War without truce.

In 1929, Josephine and Pepito moved to Le Beau-Chêne, only four kilometres from the house that Mistinguett had purchased for herself in 1923 in Bougival, an outbuilding of what used to be the château of the Comptesse Du Barry, Louis XV's mistress.

On 5 June 1937, the magazine *Ce Soir*, edited by Louis Aragon, organised a concert to benefit Spanish children. Picasso designed the programme's cover and Cocteau presented the performers. Among them were Josephine and Mistinguett, accompanied by Jo Bouillon's orchestra. This was surely the only time in their careers that the two singers were in the same line-up. Care was taken to ensure that the two performances were separated by an auction of paintings by Léger, Cocteau, Chagall and Colin.

During the war, Mistinguett sang for German audiences. "After the Liberation, they reprimanded me! I mean, really. And what for? I was doing my job as an artist."

Though the rivalry between the two giants of the music hall was undeniable, it is noteworthy that with the indirect exception of Paul Colin's caricature in *Le Tumulte Noir* of a Mistinguett with black skin, in none of her dictated memoirs does Josephine denigrate her elder rival. In 1949, she said: "When I'm on the verge of breaking down and I feel like giving up, I think of Mistinguett and I lift my chin. I know that you have to hold on, work hard and survive. I accept that." The assertion is perhaps not without ambiguity.

In 1954, at age 78, Mistinguett wrote a memoir, *Toute ma vie* (*My Whole Life*), published in two volumes. In it, she sketched portraits – often unflattering – of about 50 music-hall personalities, most of whom had long been forgotten. Josephine makes no appearance in the panorama, except for a dozen lines relating the searing failure of an impresario who had been ruined by one of Josephine's shows. No sooner was she mentioned than she was dismissed.

At the end of her memoir, Mistinguett evokes an evening in a nightclub in Juan-les-Pins in the early 1950s: "An old Negro with rings on his fingers lifted his instrument, and a silence fell over the young people present. At first I didn't recognise the melody he was playing. It was sad, and everyone was looking at me. The Negro, who was named Sidney Bechet, was playing 'Mon Homme'. I put on my dark glasses, but not because of the midnight sun."

Mistinguett died three years later, in 1956, in Bougival, at the age of 80.

Man Ray

September 1925. On the roof of the Théâtre des Champs-Élysées, Josephine performs the cakewalk before a photographer's lens. Behind her is the Eiffel Tower. It is her first promotional photo on French soil. In the very well-documented biography of Josephine published in 1981 by Lynn Haney, this photo is attributed to Man Ray. For a long time, her later biographers would repeat that myth. In reality, the photo was taken by Henri Manuel, 51, a fashion and celebrity photographer who, along with Man Ray and Jacques-André Boiffard, illustrated the first edition of *Nadja* by André Breton. The rights to this quintessential photograph were later entrusted to Albert Harlingue, 46, a photographer and journalist, who at his death would leave more than 70,000 images to the Roger-Viollet Agency. In reality, Man Ray's portrait of Josephine seems to have disappeared without a trace. Not even the encyclopaedic *Man Ray Portraits*, published by the Centre Pompidou in 2010, can offer any trace of this invisible portrait, though Bricktop is among the 500 personalities found in this largely unpublished trove. Agnès Vinas is the author of a book about *Les Mains libres* (*Free Hands*), a 1936 collection of poems by Paul Éluard, illustrated with drawings by Man Ray; she hypothesised that the photographer destroyed his negatives to avoid the wrath of his girlfriend, Kiki de Montparnasse. Vinas added that one of Man Ray's drawings, *Burlesque*, depicting a half-naked dancer with a black pearl, might be an allusion to his friend Josephine and to their shared destiny as American expats seeking artistic recognition in Paris. These suggestions have the merit of putting Man Ray's trajectory in perspective: the Dada painter from New York turned Parisian photographer and socialite at the height of the Roaring Twenties. There is no doubt as to whether he crossed paths with Josephine. They had mutual friends, including fashion designer Paul Poiret and poet Jean Cocteau. In 1925, when Josephine had just arrived in Paris, she first roomed in Montparnasse before moving to Montmartre. Man spoke to her in English when she was just beginning to learn French. Moreover, she would dance at the Jockey Club, Paris's premier nightclub, where the world's night owls came to mingle, and where Kiki, queen of Montparnasse, sang Robert Desnos' bawdy adaptations of popular tunes.

Man Ray's images of Kiki immortalised their relationship not only in the history of photography, but in art history as well: *Violon d'Ingres* and *Noire et Blanche* have become icons. How would he have captured his countrywoman on film? Ninety years later, the question remains.

Ernest Hemingway

Born in 1899 in Oak Park, Illinois, Ernest Hemingway first discovered Europe in uniform, when he was an ambulance driver in World War I. He returned four years later as a press correspondent and moved to Paris with his wife Hadley in January 1922. Beneath the Parisian rooftops of the Left Bank, he developed his idea of literature: "All you have to do is write one true sentence." Following a transatlantic round-trip to resign from the newspaper that had hired him, he returned to Paris in 1924, determined to write. Two years later, he published *The Sun Also Rises*, which immediately propelled him to the forefront of English-language literature.

In Montparnasse, he went to La Coupole, the Dingo Bar and the Jockey Club. The Jockey Club was the epicentre of Paris nightlife. This bar, founded by an American, served chilli con carne and featured the musical talents of Kiki, who was reputed not to wear underwear as she sang her sets. This nightclub was the first of its kind in Paris, and it attracted revellers from around the world, from Foujita to Cocteau, Mosjoukine to Pascin, Fitzgerald to Kisling.

Twenty-five years later, "Papa" Hemingway wrote to his close friend Aaron Edward Hotchner, recalling a particular night at the Jockey Club:

"Was in there one night with Don Ogden Stewart and Waldo Peirce, when the place was set on fire by the most sensational woman anybody ever saw. Or ever will. Tall, coffee skin, ebony eyes, legs of paradise, a smile to end all smiles. Very hot night but she was wearing a coat of black fur, her breasts handling the fur like it was silk. She turned her eyes on me – she was dancing with the big British gunner subaltern who had brought her – but I responded to the eyes like a hypnotic and cut in on them. The subaltern tried to shoulder me out but the girl slid off him and onto me. Everything under that fur instantly communicated with me. I introduced myself and asked her name. 'Josephine Baker,' she said. We danced nonstop for the rest of the night. She never took off her fur coat. Wasn't until the joint closed she told me she had nothing on underneath."

Literary braggadocio or visceral memory? If the writer's lines are true, they tell of the phantasmatic power Josephine held over Paris during the Roaring Twenties.

Winner of the Pulitzer Prize in 1953 and the Nobel Prize in Literature the following year, Ernest Hemingway took his own life in 1964. Three years later, a posthumous publication revealed his Lost Generation early years in Paris, with the title *A Moveable Feast*.

Harry Kessler

Count Harry Clemens Ulrich von Kessler was born on 23 May 1868 in Paris. His father was a banker from Hamburg, while his mother, whose beauty was praised by Kaiser Wilhelm I, was of Irish aristocratic descent. He was educated in Ascot and Hamburg, and then his study of law and art history took him to Bonn and Leipzig – a true European education. A wealthy patron of the arts, in 1903 he was named director of the Weimar Grand Ducal Museum, which would one day become the Bauhaus school. There, he was a promoter of French modern art. His personal collection included Gauguin (he was the first foreign buyer of the artist's work), Renoir, Seurat, Van Gogh, Bonnard, Vuillard and Maillol. A scandal involving his homosexuality, the details of which remain unclear, forced him to resign in 1907. In 1913, he founded his own publishing house, Cranach Press, which would become legendary in the world of art books due to the high quality of its publications. Kessler collaborated with the best typographers of the day, such as Emery Walker and Eric Gill.

Kessler, a well-read polyglot, knew such luminaries as Jean Cocteau, André Gide, Paul Valéry, Paul Verlaine, Thomas Mann, George Grosz, Oskar Kokoschka, Sarah Bernhardt, Edgar Degas, Henri Matisse, Edvard Munch and Serge Diaghilev, as well as a number of political figures. According to the poet W.H. Auden, he was "one of the most cosmopolitan men who ever lived".

World War I found him first on the Austro-Hungarian front, then in the Carpathians, then creating cultural propaganda in Switzerland. The experience transformed him from a warmonger into a dedicated peace activist. In 1918, Kessler began a career in diplomacy. The "Red Count" was born. After being named ambassador to Poland, he became a counsellor to Walther Rathenau, the Weimar Republic's Democratic Minister for Foreign Affairs, who was assassinated in 1924 by a small group of far-right anti-Semites. Kessler was then counsellor to Rathenau's successor, the Liberal Gustav Stresemann, future Nobel laureate.

Kessler was in Paris in 1933 when the Nazis came to power in Germany. Seven months later, Hitler paid tribute to Rathenau's assassins. The Red Count did not return to Berlin. In 1936, he published his *Souvenirs d'un Européen (Memories of a European)* with Éditions Plon. Kessler, whom Julien Green described as a "German man from the old days, courteous and learned", died in Lyons on 30 November 1937 at the age of 69. Not until 1961 would his diaries be discovered and published; they covered the period from 1918 to 1937. In 1981, his 1880–1918 diaries were published.

In his entry for 13 February 1926, the count described a party at the home of his friend, the playwright Karl Vollmöller, in Pariser Platz in Berlin. Josephine was present and engaging in sapphic play with the host's mistress, actress Ruth Landshoff. Regarding Josephine, Kessler wrote: "An enchanting creature, yet almost without sexuality. With her, one thinks of sexuality as little as at the sight of a beautiful and feral beast." With Vollmöller and the theatre director Max Reinhardt, Kessler invented a pantomime for the two women. At 5.00 a.m., the party came to an end, with the promise of completing this shared project. The next day, Kessler would dine with Albert Einstein, and no further allusion was made in his diaries to this short-lived project born of a night's revelry.

Max Reinhardt

In all of her various memoirs, Josephine mentions her February 1926 encounter in Berlin with the man who was then considered the most revolutionary theatre director of the day, Max Reinhardt. She had heard that he was an "unprecedented creator", "that he broke all the moulds of tradition, that he could play a tragedy in a circus, that he believed in theatre for the greatest number". He was captivated by Josephine. "He told me that I had a natural quality, and that was the only thing he cared about on stage: human nature. In any show, the artist is the heart and the flesh." Twenty-year-old Josephine, in turn, was fascinated by the director, 53. "Nobody had ever spoken to me of the theatre like that, and that's how I wanted to perform. 'I invite you to stay in Berlin, at the Deutsches Theater. You'll study for three years and become a great actress.' My eyes welled up..."

Maximilian Goldman was born in Baden, south of Vienna, on 9 September 1873. His father was a shopkeeper of Hungarian origin. Initially Max was inclined towards the banking sector, but attending a theatre class changed his life and his name. In 1901, he opened his first satirical cabaret, "Schall und Rauch" (Sound and Smoke). Ten years later, in London, he established his international reputation directing the play of his friend Karl Vollmöller, *The Miracle*. He directed the Deutsches Theater in Berlin from 1905 to 1930, and the Josefstadt Theater in Vienna from 1924 to 1933. In 1920, he created the Salzburg Festival with Richard Strauss.

The naturalism of his pre-war period gradually changed to expressionism over the course of the war. To his mind, the invention of modern theatre lay in machinery, in lighting, in everything that had the effect of plucking the viewer from reality to rekindle his connection to the playful and oneiric. Nevertheless, the actor remained the pivotal point of his theatre: "I believe in theatre that belongs to the actor. No longer, as in the previous decades, shall literary points of view be decisive ones... for me, the actor is the natural focal point of the theatre. He was in all the great epochs of theatre."

Reinhardt was also interested in cinema, and directed his first film in 1910. In 1935 in Hollywood, he directed an adaptation of Shakespeare's *A Midsummer Night's Dream*, with James Cagney, Mickey Rooney and Olivia de Havilland. Nazi censorship forbade the screening of the film in Germany, claiming that the director had Jewish origins. Upon the invasion of Austria in 1938, Reinhardt went into exile across the Atlantic. He opened a school on Sunset Boulevard, while continuing to pursue his career as a director. He remarried and became a naturalised citizen in 1940. He died in New York on 30 October 1943 at the age of 70.

One can only imagine what would have become of Josephine under Max Reinhardt's tutelage. Already torn between her commitments to *La Revue Nègre* and the Folies-Bergère, she would not stay long in Berlin. It was as though it were already too late for her to choose a mentor.

Ruth Landshoff

Ruth Levy was born on 19 January 1909 in Berlin. Her father Eduard was an engineer, and her mother Else Landshoff was an opera singer. Her uncle, Samuel Fischer, was a famous German publisher.

Her first onscreen appearance was in the silent film *Nosferatu* by Friedrich Wilhelm Murnau in 1922; she played the role of young Annie. That same year, she appeared briefly in Carl Theodor Dreyer's feature film *Love One Another*. Trained in Max Reinhardt's school, where she studied alongside Marlene Dietrich, Landshoff turned her attention to the theatre and performed with Reinhardt's company in Berlin, Leipzig and Vienna. In 1924, she met Karl Vollmöller, 26 years her senior, with whom she had an affair. A racing car driver, philologist, poet, novelist, translator and playwright, Vollmöller was also a member of Reinhardt's inner circle. Together, the two men achieved international notoriety with their play *The Miracle*. The play premiered in Berlin and went on to New York and London, spurring a revolution in European theatre. In 1912, the film adaptation of the play would be a worldwide success.

Though they were a generation apart, together Ruth and Karl participated in the festive and creative dynamism of the 1920s in Berlin. Oskar Kokoschka created a lithograph of Ruth intended to appear in a portfolio dedicated to five Jewish women, which remained unpublished. Among her other friends were Charlie Chaplin, André Gide and Annemarie Schwarzenback, the future travelling companion of Ella Maillart. Following a party at the home of his friend Vollmöller, Count Kessler wrote in his diary: "Reinhardt, Vollmöller and I were standing around Miss Baker and Miss Landshoff, who were embracing like a pair of beautiful young lovers."

In 1930, Ruth and Karl's relationship came to an end. The same year, Karl wrote the screenplay for *The Blue Angel*, directed by Josef von Sternberg and starring Marlene Dietrich; meanwhile, in Berlin, Ruth published her first novel, *The Many and the One*. The same year, she married Count David Yorck von Wartenburg.

In 1933, Ruth fled the Nazi regime, which had just come to power in Germany. She took refuge in France, England and Switzerland before finally moving to the US in March 1937, where she divorced her husband. In New York, she worked as a translator and then developed a career as an English-language author; she published eight books between 1939 and 1963.

When he died in 1948, Ruth was the executor of Karl's will. The playwright had also left Nazi Germany for the US. In 1941, he had penned the screenplay for *The Shanghai Gesture*, another film directed by Josef von Sternberg and starring Marlene Dietrich. In 1951, Ruth had his remains transferred to a cemetery in his native Stuttgart. On 19 January 1966, while she was performing in the play *Marat/Sade* by German playwright Peter Weiss, Ruth Landshoff died at the age of 57.

Paul Derval

Alexis Paul Pitron was born on 23 June 1880 in the 9th arrondissement of Paris. His grandfather was Hyacinthe d'Orbigny de Ferrière, who had broken with the family's military tradition to become an actor with the stage name "Derval". Twenty-five years later, his grandson adopted the pseudonym, taking it as his surname. After pursuing a career as an actor, he purchased his first small theatre, the Eden, in the suburb of Asnières; he sold it in 1918 to buy a larger one near Rue Bergère in Paris's 9th arrondissement. At the age of 38, Paul Derval became the man who would reign over the destiny of the Folies-Bergère for the next 50 years.

Inaugurated on 1 May 1869, the Folies-Bergère was the first Parisian music hall inspired by the Alhambra in London. There, crowds applauded dancers, acrobats and singers. In his painting *Un bar aux Folies-Bergère*, Édouard Manet immortalised the dandies and *filles de joie* who haunted the lobby. When he took the helm of the establishment 48 years later, Derval's first action was to throw out the current generation of courtesans. "I'm directing a theatre, not a brothel!"

In autumn 1925, he was the first to see more in Josephine than a mere dancer. He was convinced that she had the power to set Paris alight for another season. He recalled his first vision: "Right away, I went into raptures over a marvellous young woman. She was built like a Tanagra and she set the stage on fire. It was Josephine. The next day, I offered her a contract. A lively debate followed. Finally, the deal was done: Josephine Baker would be the star of our next revue." Derval began work on the production, set and costumes; Josephine, however, having left for Berlin with *La Revue Nègre*, was having trouble finding her way back to Paris. Derval wouldn't back down. First, he threatened her with a lawsuit, which impressed her not at all. Then he offered her a considerable pay raise. She would receive $5,000 per month. "The black pearl gave me a lot of grey hair," Derval would write 30 years later. But when he invited her to the Folies-Bergère, he became the one to throw the doors to the world of music hall wide open for the young artist.

For his "hyper-revue", Derval struck on the title *La Folie du jour*, which contained 13 letters. "I like Mr Derval because he's superstitious like me. I never put on my right shoe before my left. And if someone whistles in my dressing room, I throw him out. I also like him because he was an actor and he knows how to make his voice resound." "In this revue," Josephine recalled, "they had the idea to dress me with a belt of bananas! Oh, how people ridiculed this idea! And how many drawings and caricatures came out of it. Only the Devil, supposedly, could have invented such a thing." Those representations and caricatures would ultimately forge the icon of the banana dancer in the collective unconscious. It was an image that relied on fantasy more than anything: the only filmed documentation of the performance showed Josephine decked in an ample white brassiere. The genealogy of the banana skirt is unknown. Those who were closest to the event suggest that it came from the designer Paul Poiret, but Josephine preferred to name Jean Cocteau, who reportedly said: "On you, it will look very dressy."

About ten years later, despite Josephine's defection to the Casino de Paris, Derval came back into her life when he visited her in New York to persuade her to participate in his next revue. In 1937, Josephine was back at the Folies-Bergère for *En super folies* – yet again, 13 letters.

In the preceding decade, the theatre had changed. In 1928, Derval remodelled the entire interior without cancelling any shows – an operational feat that he would boast of for years to come. For the façade, he commissioned a monumental bas-relief by the Art Deco sculptor Pico. The poster for Josephine's comeback show was created by the young Hungarian artist Michel Gyarmathy. On 30 November 1937, Paul Derval served as witness to the marriage of Josephine and Jean Lion.

Josephine returned to the Folies-Bergère in 1949 for *Féeries Folies* – 13 letters. At age 43, she had ceased giving Derval grey hair. "I had to admit that Josephine had changed quite a bit and that during her last residency she was an exemplary guest, and I had nothing but praise for her."

In 1954, Derval published his memoirs, entitled *Folies-Bergère, Souvenirs de leur directeur* (*The Folies-Bergère, Recollections from the Director*). He detailed the extraordinary level of organisation required to put on a revue involving 340 people over the course of eight hours each day. It took the discipline of a drill sergeant and the psychological acuity of a lion tamer.

Paul Derval died in Paris on 15 May 1966 in the 16th arrondissement at the age of 86. A few years later, his widow would sell the Folies-Bergère to Hélène Martini, whom local legend had named "Empress of the Night". The former model had made her debut at the Folies 25 years earlier. In 1952, with her husband Henri, she had produced Josephine's show at the restaurant Les Ambassadeurs. On 7 November 1990, the façade of the Folies-Bergère was declared a national historic monument.

Bricktop

Ada Beatrice Queen Victoria Louise Virginia Smith was born on 14 August 1894 in Alderson, Virginia, to an Irish father and an African-American mother. From an early age, her red hair, inherited from her father, earned her the nickname "Bricktop". When she was 16, she began touring on the singing, dancing and vaudeville circuit. She was 20 when she found her footing in New York, forming the "Trio Panorama" with Cora Green and Florence Mills.

Bricktop arrived in Paris in 1924. At first, she danced at the Music Box and the Grand Duc, a cabaret where drinks were served by none other than the future poet of the Harlem Renaissance, Langston Hughes. Later, Bricktop began working at Chez Florence, a cabaret owned by the American Florence Jones. "There were artists who went to Europe, but not many, and hardly any black people. I barely knew where Paris was, and I didn't speak a word of French, but I had travelled to quite a few American cities and it seemed to me that Paris couldn't be much different." For Bricktop, Paris in the Roaring Twenties was "magnifique". There was already an American presence. John Steinbeck showered her with yellow roses, and it has been said that she was the inspiration for Cole Porter's "Miss Otis Regrets". She was the first to bring the Charleston to Paris, and she taught the dance to F. Scott and Zelda Fitzgerald, Ernest Hemingway and the Prince of Wales. But Josephine was to be the real promoter of the Charleston a year later. Bricktop was on tour in Barcelona when *La Revue Nègre* opened in Paris. When she returned to Paris, Josephine had already become the new idol. "I saw her one day on the Champs-Élysées, you couldn't get within 300 metres of her."

Bricktop opened a cabaret bearing her name in Montmartre. Around the same time, she became a close friend of Josephine, who was 12 years her junior. She bore witness to the craze stirred up by the young woman: "All the great designers wanted to do her wardrobe. Her apartment was right next to my nightclub. One day, I went to visit her, and there was a mountain of dresses heaped on the floor. I asked her why she didn't hang them up. 'No point in bothering, Brickie, tomorrow they'll take these away and bring me another pile.'" The arrival of Pepito would put a strain on their relationship.

Except for the period from 1939 to 1944, "the Doyenne of Café Society" would run her cabaret Chez Bricktop continuously until 1961. She was 66 when she decided to retire to her homeland: "I'm tired of spending the whole night on my feet."

The last time she saw Josephine was in 1973, when she made her comeback at Carnegie Hall in New York. Bricktop performed the opening act and introduced her friend of 50 years.

Bricktop continued to sing in New York into the 1980s, and she appeared in Woody Allen's film *Zelig*.

She died on 1 February 1984 at the age of 89, after spending the day on the phone, chatting with friends.

Pepito

Giuseppe Abatino was the youngest of four, born on 10 November 1898 to Sicilian parents: his father was an infantry colonel and his mother came from a cultured, bourgeois family. Pepito spoke French, English and German.

Josephine and Pepito met at Joe Zelli's Royal Box, a club in Montmartre. A former second lieutenant in the Italian army, he was on vacation in Paris and staying with his cousin Zito, an artist and friend of Josephine. Standing 1.65 metres tall, he wore high heels and a tattered tailcoat, but he was a marvellous tango dancer. Despite his reputation as a gigolo, Josephine fell for him. This may have had a little to do with his resemblance to actor Adolphe Menjou (Hollywood's faux Frenchman), of whom Josephine was a fan. He had "eyes at once gay and serious behind his monocle, his mouth ironic but tender", Josephine said. At the end of his vacation, Pepito went back to Rome, but he soon returned, determined to be her lover and manager. Josephine would later explain: "At last, I had someone to help me fight my battles."

Pepito took it upon himself to educate Josephine. He hired a down-and-out countess to teach her good manners. His first brilliant idea was to have her open her own cabaret, Chez Josephine, with money from one of her admirers. Though he could never claim Josephine's exclusivity as a lover, he took on a role in her life that nobody else ever would: Pygmalion. "In the world of the theatre, each time a man manages his wife's business, people say he's a pimp. I think it's funny... No, what is heavy for me is his jealousy. Meanwhile, I have the best manager in Paris."

One night when he was feeling jealous after Noble Sissle came to visit Josephine backstage, Pepito asked his wife why she hadn't married "a person of colour". Josephine retorted, "It's the person I care about, not the colour." It was an old lesson imparted by Eubie Blake, Sissle's former partner.

With the purchase of Le Beau-Chêne in the suburb of Vésinet, Pepito provided Josephine with a luxurious setting that was just the right size (outsized extravagance would come later with Milandes): she had room enough to house all the animals and friends she desired.

As her agent, Pepito was quick to sing Josephine's praises to the likes of Delage automobiles, Piast cigarettes and Réard knitwear. But the best deal he ever landed – and the most profitable – was with Bakerfix, whose Paul Colin-designed jars sold by the millions, earning the couple royalties for years. The part of the story that often gets left out was that Josephine's regular use of Bakerfix burned her hair to a crisp.

Pepito was everywhere at once. In 1934, he had one of his great epiphanies as Josephine's manager. For the first time, she was playing the leading role in an operetta, *La Créole*, and she was shooting her first sound film, *Zouzou*. Pepito was particularly invested in the film, and had written the concept himself. It was a tailor-made role: the irresistible rise to fame of a young creole music hall starlet. The romantic male lead, Jean Gabin, is Zouzou's adopted brother; the two have an ambiguous relationship. After reading the script, Josephine wondered why they didn't marry at the end. Pepito's reply was as good as a declaration of faith: "Zouzou the star belongs to her art. Just like you." Pepito was a man who wished to make his fictions realities.

In the spring of 1935, Pepito sojourned across the Atlantic to prepare Josephine's grand return to the US. He signed a rather favourable contract with Lee Shubert, director of the *Ziegfried Follies*, guaranteeing Josephine first-class travel accommodations, $1,500 per week, permission to perform in a cabaret and her name on its own line in the show's programme. In early October 1935, before boarding the *Normandie* for New York, Josephine publicly praised Italy's invasion of Ethiopia, claiming that Emperor Haile Selassie "enslaved his people". A few years earlier, however, Mussolini's blackshirts had protested at the Black Pearl's visit to their country. With his superior people skills, Pepito managed to smooth over those difficulties. Josephine's pro-Mussolini declaration would haunt her all her life, in spite of her later retractions. Nevertheless, her brief alliance with the fascist regime later gave her access to the Italian diplomatic authorities, which she spied on for the French.

In New York, their collaboration came to an end. Pepito returned to France alone, probably in early 1936. Upon his arrival in Paris, he wrote to his friend Miki Sawada: "The affair between Josephine and myself will soon be terminated, based on our mutual agreement, and we will live our lives separately." Pepito wouldn't have time for that. After his return, Arys Nissotti, producer of *Zouzou*, noticed that his friend's complexion had turned yellowish and that he was complaining of stomach pain. He sent him to the doctor, who diagnosed advanced-stage liver cancer. They decided not to inform Pepito. On 12 September 1936, the illness took his life.

After his death, the imbroglio of their affairs – real estate, jewellery, Bakerfix royalties and a music publishing company – resulted in Pepito's sister inheriting part of the fortune. Josephine was philosophical in accepting the arrangement, saying that his sister was "his only family". "Without Pepito, Le Beau-Chêne was an empty shell."

She attended the funeral alongside Pepito's latest conquest, "a beautiful redhead from the Folies", but Josephine played the role of widow.

In the 1950s, Josephine decided to have the body of her former Pygmalion transferred to a cemetery near Milandes.

Georges Simenon

Josephine Baker and Georges Simenon: theirs was a love affair straight out of a novel, but history was quick to smooth over the asymmetries of their chronology. At the time of their liaison – which even inspired a book – Josephine was the unrivalled star of the European stage, while Georges Simenon was a nobody. Or rather, he was Christian Brulls, Germain d'Antibes, Georges-Martin Georges and Georges Sim, all pseudonyms for one novelist churning out book after book of popular fiction.

Born in Liège on 13 February 1903, the son of an accountant and a shop employee (the terrible Henriette, who didn't hide her preference for his younger brother, Christian), Georges Joseph Christian Simenon learned to read at the age of 3. He was 16 when he began his working life as a reporter-at-large at the *Gazette de Liège*; over the next four years, he would write more than 1,000 articles. The paper's conservative Catholic editorial line was detectable in a handful of those pieces, tending toward anti-union, anti-Dadaist and even anti-Semitic sentiments.

Simenon first arrived in Paris in 1922, and then returned to Liège in 1923 to marry Tigy in March of that year. The couple immediately moved back to Paris for good.

Simenon submitted his early work to Colette, who was then the literary editor for *Le Matin*. She called him "mon petit Sim" ("my little Sim") and advised him to write "simple stories, not literature". She published the young hopeful's first texts in September 1923. In 1924, Simenon ventured into popular fiction with *Le Roman d'une dactylo* (*The Typist's Story*), written over the course of a morning on the terrace of a Paris café. "I thought, I can't start out writing a real novel, first I have to learn the trade." His apprenticeship spanned almost 200 novels and 1,000 short stories published under 27 different pseudonyms by 1931. He worked at a pace of up to 24 typed pages per day. This new financial means allowed the couple to move to the elegant Place des Vosges in the summer of 1924.

Paul Colin introduced Georges and Josephine. In the Simenons' apartment – an artist's loft ahead of its time – Colin's stylised portrait of Josephine hung over the bar.

Most of Simenon's biographers are rather vague regarding the timeline of George and Josephine's affair, vacillating between 1925 and 1929 without offering many details. They were very young: Georges was 24 and Josephine 21. Journalist Marcel Sauvage, author of *Mémoires de Josephine Baker*, explained that he and Georges shared the role of Josephine's secretary for a few months: "She had asked me to help her. 'You'll take care of the daytime. At night, it'll be Sim'." It was the era of Chez Josephine, the cabaret that Pepito opened for her in 1926. This makes it likely that the liaison between the dancer and the budding novelist occurred no earlier than the end of 1926 or the beginning of 1927. In that year, among a bevy of other books, the writer used the rather transparent pseudonym Georges Sim to publish a romance novel entitled *Defense d'aimer* (*Loving Prohibited*), the story of a journalist who falls in love with an American music-hall dancer.

In his autobiographical *Mémoires intimes*, Simenon wrote that at the time of their break-up, he fled to Île d'Aix "to try to forget her". This flight took place in 1927. He then wrote a novel published in the newspaper *Paris-Soir* entitled *Dolorosa*.

Not until 1931 did Georges Simenon's name appear on the cover of a novel, *Le Pendu de Saint-Pholien (The Hanged Man of Saint-Pholien)*, the first of Inspector Maigret's investigations. It was the first of 200 novels published under the author's real name; he categorised the Maigret novels as "semi-literary" and the rest as "hard novels", using his idiosyncratic terminology. He was 29 at the time. From that moment on, Simenon fascinated intellectuals, who tried to comprehend his literary enigma. In 1941, André Gide called him "a genius novelist". German philosopher Hermann von Keyserling used more paradoxical terms: he was "a genius imbecile".

Jo and Sim met again in 1951. On 3 June, Josephine performed in Hartford, Connecticut. Then living in Lakeville, Connecticut, Simenon attended the concert with his new wife, Denise. The next day, Jo and Jo came to visit them. They spent the night and left the next day. Dolores James, Simenon's African-American housekeeper, was fascinated by Josephine: "She did whatever she wanted with folks, with a snap of her fingers. I adored her! Over here, it's the opposite: only whites get to snap their fingers!" Dolores also noted that Georges and Josephine dominated the conversation and that neither Jo nor Denise seemed to exist. In a 1984 *New York Times* interview, Simenon, 80, claimed: "We were ready to marry, but I was poor at the time... I did not want to be Mr Baker. So I went for six months to a small island... to forget."

With Denise, Georges had three children: Marie-Jo, John and Pierre. In 1972, at the age of 69, Simenon gave up fiction, but not storytelling. He published 21 autobiographical volumes in dictated form. Two years later, he gave up the comfort of his luxurious home in Épalinges, Switzerland, to move into a tiny house in Lausanne with his final partner, Teresa – a former housekeeper.

His last years were darkened by the suicide of his daughter Marie-Jo. Georges Simenon died on 4 September 1989 at the age of 86.

Tigy

Georges Simenon was 17 and a half when he met Tigy, 20, at a New Year's party at his parents' house in 1920. The young journalist at the *Gazette de Liège* hung out with art students, and Régine Renchon was studying painting at the fine arts academy in Liège. She had already been featured in art shows, and her name was in the air. Georges didn't like the name Régine and decided to call her "Tigy", "a word that doesn't mean anything". The nickname stuck.

In 1922, Tigy and her father saw Georges to the train station in Liège. He was leaving for Paris. He would go by himself, but it was a dream they shared. "When you're young, provincial or Belgian," Tigy would later say, "Paris is inherently attractive. Paris consecrates artists." He wrote her as many as 14 letters per day. "The most romantic sentences I ever wrote in my life, I think," the novelist would say 50 years later.

In March 1923, Georges came back for her. First, they married. Georges bought a tuxedo on credit and Régine was baptised at her future mother-in-law's request. In Paris at last, they move to Rue Faubourg-Saint-Honoré, at the end of a cul-de-sac. Later on, they would rent a two-room, ground-floor apartment on Place des Vosges.

One wrote, the other painted. They made a pact. They had three years; if one of them caught a big break, the other would quit. Tigy showed her work on the street, in Place Constantin-Pecqueur, at the "daub fair" where paintings hung from the trees. One day, Tigy said to Georges, "You look so tense! Go sit in a café. You're scaring the customers..." He sat on a café terrace on Rue Caulaincourt and spent the morning writing his first mainstream novel, *Le Roman d'une dactylo* (*The Typist's Story*), which would be his humble entry into the world of literature. Tigy also met with success. One day, she sold two paintings for 1,800 francs. The couple decided to use the money to spend a few months on the island of Porquerolles. They would return to the island in 1933, and made regular visits until 1939.

The revenue from Georges' novels allowed the couple to rent an apartment on the second floor of the same building on Place des Vosges. They kept the ground-floor apartment as Tigy's studio.

For their new apartment, they commissioned furniture by the avant-garde interior designer Dim, whom they had discovered at a *salon* for decorative arts. Frequent visitors to their home were Foujita, Marcel Vertès and sometimes Josephine in person, the novelist recalled, adding: "At three in the morning: a number of naked bodies, others reclining on black velvet pillows, where they would spend the rest of the night. At six in the morning, I sat down at my typewriter to write my 24 pages for the day." "It was always a bit of a bash," Tigy would say 50 years later. "Of course, there was that adventure with Josephine Baker, I'll have to get used to the idea..." Not until she read her ex-husband's *Mémoires intimes* in 1981 did Tigy learn of his affair with Josephine. Simenon explained: "Tigy's jealousy was intransigent, and she had announced to me that the day she learned I was cheating on her she would kill herself. For 20 years, I lived with that threat over my head." He added: "I had to lie." Much later, in a published dialogue with director Federico Fellini, the Belgian novelist said that he had had sexual relations with 10,000 women over his lifetime. "He was joking…" Tigy responded. It took her 22 years to discover her husband's chronic infidelity, when she caught him in the act with Boule, the housekeeper from Normandy whom they had hired in the late 1920s, and who had, since then, received a daily visit from the man of the house. Tigy commanded Georges to choose between them; instead, the peculiar arrangement persisted.

Following the break-up with Josephine in 1927, Georges sought refuge on Île d'Aix. There, Tigy would paint her most melancholic portrait of her husband. Since Georges had become the first to make a living as an artist, they kept their pact: Tigy's paintings would never leave her studio.

In the 1930s, they travelled the world. "For years, Tigy and I would alternately explore frigid and torrid climates, crossing the equator several times on several oceans, discovering each of the five continents. What was our destination? Where were we going? Everywhere. Nowhere."

Marc Simenon was born on 19 April 1939 in Uccle, a suburb of Brussels. Tigy was 39. To her son and, later, her grandchildren, she was known as "Mamiche". After the war, Georges, Tigy and Marc crossed the Atlantic to live in the US.

In 1950, the unthinkable occurred. Georges decided to divorce. He loved another: his secretary, Denise, with whom he would have three children. The divorce was finalised in Reno, Texas. Their marriage lasted 26 years, two months and 29 days. Georges saw to it that Tigy would live near his residence so that he could continue to see his son regularly. Once Marc had grown up, and had hired Boule to take care of his own children, Tigy left America to live alone in Nieul-sur-Mer, among her portraits of Georges and the table at which he used to write. She passed away on 22 July 1985 at Porquerolles, in the arms of Marc's wife, actress Mylène Demongeot, who had this to say to a friend of Tigy's: "Mamiche was a woman of infinite dignity and discretion. I knew her for 18 years and not once, or only very rarely, did a bitter or vengeful statement escape her lips. She was a sensational woman."

Four years after her death, when reproductions of Tigy's paintings were finally revealed to the public, Jacques de Decker of the Académie Royale in Brussels wrote in *Le Soir*: "Her talent as a painter was evident. In a very Art Deco style, with a well-defined sense for colour and a predilection for the flat hues and geometric forms that structured her realism, Régine Renchon evidenced a singular disposition." In that regard, her portraits of Georges from the 1920s and 1930s form a more penetrating depiction of the man's solemnity than any other perspective from that period.

Colette

In 1927, when Josephine welcomed Colette to her cabaret, the former was 21 and the latter 54. Born Sidonie-Gabrielle Colette in 1873, daughter of a military officer and a feminist, the young woman from Burgundy would become "la grande Colette", a major personality on the Paris literary scene. From *Claudine at School* in 1900 to *The Last of Chéri* in 1926, Colette published 20 novels and built a respected oeuvre that found a wide readership. Colette was also a newspaperwoman. As the literary editor of *Le Matin*, she published Georges Simenon's first short stories.

In 1927, Colette had just moved to the Palais-Royal. Two years previously, she had met Maurice Goudeket, age 36. Theirs would be Colette's third marriage, following Willy, the literary slave driver who had helped Colette to discover her own talents, and Henry de Jouvenel, with whom she had a daughter, nicknamed "Bel-Gazou".

Colette herself had had a dancing career at the Folies-Bergère, the Moulin Rouge and the Bataclan. She remained passionate about the music hall, which she wrote about for the paper. She adored Josephine, whom she called her "little brown daughter". One evening, she gave Josephine a copy of *L'Envers du music-hall* (*The Underside of the Music Hall*). In the novel, Colette tells of her own experiences as a travelling performer in pre-war France, when the 20th century still resembled the 16th. Colette and Josephine's camaraderie came in part from their shared experience as nude dancers. In 1907, at the Moulin Rouge, in the dance "Rêve d'Égypte" ("Dream of Egypt"), Colette played the role of a mummy whose bandages were slowly unravelled in a sapphic performance by her partner, Mathilde de Morny, until she was practically nude. Garbage was thrown onstage to the sound of hisses; the audience cried scandal and called the police. The performance was banned and Colette's "sulphurous" reputation was sealed.

Josephine would hold on to a letter from Colette, which she had written, she explained, "on very old paper, which I've kept for so long it has yellowed". She continued: "These sentimental pages are only appreciated by sensitive souls, children and poets. That's why I'm leaving this paper in your hands."

In 1936, during a rehearsal for the revue *En super folies* at the Folies-Bergère, Colette came to visit Josephine. For the show's premiere, Colette wrote: "Paris will go to the Folies to see Josephine Baker, nude on stage, demonstrating how to dance in the nude with modesty."

Neither woman shied away from a love life combining heterosexual and homosexual encounters. Some have suggested that they may have had a liaison of their own. Neither Josephine nor Colette ever discussed this subject. The suggestion appears for the first time in a 1993 biography published in the US, supported only by the intuition of the biographer, who called Josephine his "adoptive mother". He claimed to have an aptitude for detecting which of her many friends had also been her lovers. Rumour or not, the story seems too rooted in fantasy to be recorded as fact in the present biography, romantic though the idea may be.

Colette passed away in the arms of Maurice Goudeket on 3 August 1954 at the age of 81.

Maurice Dekobra

Maurice Tessier was born on 26 May 1885 in Paris. His father, Anatole, was a salesman in the silk industry. Jeanne, his mother, gave piano lessons. She transmitted her love of reading to her only son, introducing him to the works of Walter Scott and Fenimore Cooper. At the age of 17, he decided to become a writer and set off to live in Berlin, where he began a career in journalism. When he was 23, Maurice adopted his pseudonym after visiting a fortune-teller who read his fortune in the entwined form of two cobras. In 1918, having served as an interpreter in the war, he was a lieutenant when he was demobilised at the age of 33. Between 1918 and 1925, he published 16 novels, which met different fates: his fifth book came close to winning the prestigious Goncourt Prize; his fifteenth sold 500,000 copies; at the age of 40, he published his all-time bestseller, *La Madone des sleepings* (*The Madonna of the Sleeper Cars*). "Liberated as she was in her moral contingencies, she lived her life in accordance with her desires and the unpredictable impulses of her ever-aroused imagination." Thus he described his character Lady Diana, as though echoing the secret aspirations of a generation of women who had experienced a hard-working and patriotic brand of liberation during the war, only to be resubmerged under the leaden weight of a society dominated by male power and desire. She plumbed the brand-new realms of psychoanalysis and revolutionary socialism. Maurice Dekobra pioneered a new literary genre: what the French called the "cosmopolitan novel" was deemed "escapist literature" in the US. He became one of the wealthiest writers on the planet.

In 1927, when the novelist tried his hand at screenwriting for Josephine's first silent picture, *Siren of the Tropics*, he had no experience writing for film, but his last three novels had been adapted for the screen at Paramount – all within the space of a year – giving his name special weight when it came to attracting talent and financial backers.

The formulaic and cliché-ridden screenplay did not do justice to Dekobra's talent for storytelling. Later on, Josephine said that she "hated" the result. It was a disappointing experience that would not often appear on his résumé. Nevertheless, the novelist would later return to the Hollywood film industry to seek refuge when France was under Nazi occupation. He would draw from the experience to write *La Madone à Hollywood* after the war. Meanwhile, in France, his bestseller *Macao, l'Enfer du jeu* (*Macao, Gambling Hell*) was being adapted by Jean Delannoy, featuring Eric von Stroheim and Mireille Balin.

Maurice Dekobra died on 1 June 1973 at the age of 88, having sold more than 90 million copies of his 98 titles worldwide. Not long before, the lifelong bachelor had burned all of the personal papers that might have elucidated his private life. His last novel, published the previous year, was entitled *La Madone des Boeings*.

Henri Étiévant

What does Henri Étiévant have to do with this story?

Born on 13 March 1870 in the 18th arrondissement of Paris, he began his career onstage at the Théâtre Libre, where he had been hired by André Antoine. Later, he joined the companies of the Œuvre and Odéon theatres. He performed all over Europe. He was already 38 years old the first time he played an onscreen role that was noteworthy enough to remain in the annals of cinema, in 1908. Over the next five years, he would act in 54 films, including five with Camille de Morlhon. In 1911, he got behind the camera to direct his first film, *La Fin d'un joueur* (*A Gambler's End*). In 1914, he directed four films for Vitascope in Berlin with his partner, Thea Sandten. War would bring an end to their cosmopolitan love affair, and to the director's budding career. He left for the front. He returned to film in 1920, and by 1924 had made nine more films, including four starring Charles Vanel.

Étiévant was 57 when he joined the production of *Siren of the Tropics*. Josephine was 22. They were from different worlds; hers was the world of nightlife. It is possible that Étiévant was attached to the project as a sort of professional guarantee, ensuring that the project would be completed on budget and on time. Mario Nalpas seems to have been on board primarily to reassure Josephine and to guide the wild young star through the realities of a film set.

Following *Siren of the Tropics*, Étiévant would work on two more films, including one with Mario Nalpas; the advent of sound film meant the end of his career. He appeared in front of the camera in a handful of films from the 1930s, including those of his friend Julien Duvivier, whom he had known at the beginning of his career. Étiévant's daughter Yvette, born in New York in 1922, would become an actress as well. Onstage, she took part in the first productions of *The Maids* by Jean Genet, as well as José-André Lacour's *L'Année du bac*. Onscreen, she appeared in over 50 films, working with Robert Bresson, Alain Resnais, Henri Verneuil, Julien Duvivier, Georges Franju and Robert Hossein. Her father wouldn't live to see her in her most popular television role as the wife in *L'Homme du Picardie*, a 1968 series about a boatman and his family. Henri Étiévant passed away in obscurity on 9 August 1953 at the age of 83.

Mario Nalpas

It is not impossible that *Siren of the Tropics* first took shape in a conversation between Pepito and Mario Nalpas at Chez Joséphine. Mario and his brother Alex were friends of the couple. Their father, Louis Nalpas, helped define the role of the film producer in France. Born in the Greek community in Smyrna, Turkey, he produced his first film in 1911. He launched the careers of directors Abel Gance, Germain Dulac and Louis Deluc, and he founded Victorine Studios in Nice. Director Henri Fescourt called him a "business poet". Louis Nalpas set a high bar for his two sons.

After working as a film distributor in Brazil, Alex Nalpas began producing films in France, credited with about ten titles by the 1930s. In 1927, he produced the rudimentary music-hall film *La Revue des revues*, which features two numbers with Josephine, who dances brilliantly and with ease in front of the camera. Meanwhile, Mario Nalpas edited Henri Fescourt's 1922 film *Mathias Sandorf*, produced by his father Louis. Mario directed his first film in 1924; two years later, when he directed his second film, *La Fin de Monte-Carlo*, he was backed by veteran Henri Étiévant.

In her memoirs published in 1927, Josephine said that the project was presented to her by "the intermediary": Alex, perhaps. The idea of bringing together Maurice Dekobra and Josephine Baker – the two jewels of a certain cosmopolitan trend – no doubt came from Mario.

Siren of the Tropics was filmed at Studios Éclair in Épinay, a northern suburb of Paris. On the neighbouring set, Gaston Ravel was directing *Madame Récamier*. In the refreshment room, the two casts mingled: black actors in rags alongside young marquis in noble regalia. "Under brand new yellow straw huts, we watched princesses led to the scaffold... I danced the Charleston while they guillotined." Accustomed as she was to freedom of movement, Josephine did not like the constraints of the film set. She had to perform within a square outlined in chalk on the floor. If she stepped out of bounds, she was out of focus. But the worst was the harsh lighting that dazzled her all day. It took several weeks after she finished shooting for her sleep to return to normal, undisturbed by flashes of light. She would say of the experience: "They didn't understand anything... They neglected to study, to take into account my nature."

Though *Siren of the Tropics* was the beginning of the end of Étiévant's career, it marked the beginning for Mario Nalpas. The following year, he made his solo directorial debut with *Monte-Carlo*, the sequel to *La Fin de Monte-Carlo*. But in 1928, following his fifth feature film, *La Symphonie pathétique*, again co-directed by Étiévant, Mario gave up directing films. In the early 1930s, he was in charge of production for two films, one of which was *The Charm of Seville*, the last film produced by Louis Nalpas. The father left the film industry in 1932, and it seems that the sons stopped working at the same moment.

Luis Buñuel

Born on 2 February 1900 in Calanda, Spain, Luis Buñuel grew up in Zaragoza. His family was solidly bourgeois, and Luis endured education in a Jesuit institution until the age of 15. He was 19 when he moved to Madrid, where he developed friendships with Salvador Dalí and Federico García Lorca. He was 25 when he moved to Paris and dared to cross swords with the arts, in both words and images.

In Paris, Luis watched movies, rhapsodising over Sergei Eisenstein's *Battleship Potemkin* and *The Last Laugh* by F.W. Murnau, but Fritz Lang's films *Metropolis* and *Destiny* were a revelation to Buñuel: he wanted to make movies. Initially he took acting classes with Jean Epstein, who would hire him as an assistant director on his film *Mauprat*. During the shooting of this film, the young newcomer became friends with cameraman Albert Duverger, who introduced him to a pair of filmmakers, Étiévant and Nalpas, who were looking for an assistant for their next film, *Siren of the Tropics*. The young Spaniard was hired. "That film is not one of the best memories of my life," he would later admit to screenwriter Jean-Claude Carrière. It was the first time the 27-year-old came anywhere near a music-hall star. "The starlet's caprices to me seemed intolerable. Once, when she was expected to be on the set and ready to begin shooting at 9 a.m., she arrived at 5 p.m., slammed the door on her way into her dressing room and started smashing all her make-up vials. Somebody enquired about the reasons for the outburst. The answer: 'She thinks her dog may be sick'."

In Josephine's defence, at the time of the shooting, she was also performing in a show at the Folies-Bergère, and then dancing at her own cabaret until dawn. When she showed up on set at 9 a.m., she had only slept three hours.

After the scene with the broken vials, Luis Buñuel approached the film's male lead, Pierre Batcheff, who later recalled: "I told him, 'That's cinema.' And he replied brusquely: 'That's your cinema, not mine.' I couldn't help but agree. We became excellent friends."

Two years later, at Studio des Ursulines, Luis Buñuel claimed his place in cinema history with his short film *Un Chien Andalou* (*An Andalusian Dog*), produced with money given to him by his mother. Batcheff was in front of the camera, Duverger behind. Compatriot and co-writer Salvador Dalí poured tar into the eyes of stuffed donkeys. At the film's premiere, hosted by Man Ray and Louis Aragon, audience members included André Breton, Paul Éluard, Tristan Tzara, Jean Arp and nearly all of the Surrealists, as well as Picasso, Le Corbusier, Cocteau and Kiki de Montparnasse. Buñuel would long remember their "extended applause".

Luis Buñuel died in Mexico 54 years later, at the age of 83. In the meantime, he had directed 34 films in France, the US and Mexico. Not only did he garner awards from Cannes, Hollywood and Venice, but he also wrote an entire chapter of cinematic history.

Pierre Batcheff

Piotr Bacev (according to historians) or Benjamin Batcheff (according to his death certificate) was born a Russian national in Harbin, Manchuria, on 23 June 1901 (according to historians) or 1907 (according to his death certificate). His father was a professor of languages. The Chinese city of his birth was then defining itself as a modern urban hub under Russian influence, situated on an extension of the Trans-Siberian railway.

There are no records of the exact date of the young actor's arrival in Paris, but by the early 1920s, the Russian Revolution had already caused a major influx of Russian talent on to the French cinematic landscape. This was true of creators as well as actors; silent film did not require knowledge of the local language. In 1925, Pierre married film editor Denise Piazza.

In 1927, when he met Josephine and shared top billing with her in *Siren of the Tropics*, Batcheff had only been working in the business for four years; nevertheless, he had already appeared in 14 films and had worked with a diverse group of filmmakers, including Jean Epstein, Marcel L'Herbier, Gaston Ravel, Raymond Bernard and Abel Gance. Having become a popular leading man in French cinema of the day, he was offered a new character to play in this film: a fop. He detested it.

In the years following *Siren of the Tropics*, he acted in about 15 more films; paradoxically, it was his role in a short experimental film that would earn Batcheff a place in cinematic history. In 1929, he agreed to participate in the first film by young Luis Buñuel, whom he had met on the set of *Siren of the Tropics*. *Un Chien Andalou* would be recognised as a hallmark of Surrealism.

Batcheff was exasperated with French cinema, which had relegated him to the role of romantic male lead. Then he met a small group of up-and-coming directors, brothers Jacques and Pierre Prévert and Marcel Carné, with whom he developed a screenplay tailored for him in the hopes of creating a comical and lyrical character *à la* Buster Keaton. Jacques and Simone Prévert moved in with Denise and Pierre Batcheff at 3 Square de Robiac. Marcel Carné considered the resulting screenplay one of Prévert's best: *Émile-Émile* was definitively laid to rest by the writer after his actor friend's sudden death.

Pierre Batcheff died on the night of 11 April 1932 in his apartment in the 7th arrondissement of Paris. A few hours later, he was supposed to sign a contract that would have been very important for his career. The circumstances of his death remain obscure. The most commonly cited version is suicide: he was alleged to have died of an overdose of sleeping pills. The version offered by the press in the days following the star's death mentioned the initial autopsy report. According to this document, the actor had suffered a heart attack from a drug overdose – most likely cocaine. A few days earlier, Pierre Batcheff had invited his friend Jacques Prévert to accompany him to Père-Lachaise Cemetery.

Robert Mallet-Stevens

Born in 1886 in Paris, Robert Mallet-Stevens came from the sort of enlightened bourgeois family that knew how to appreciate Impressionism right from the start. His uncle, the Belgian financier Adolphe Stoclet, built Stoclet Palace in Brussels, a masterwork by architect Josef Hoffman, member of the Vienna Secession. Mallet-Stevens would write of this Klimt-decorated palace that it was "the first Modern building". Naturally, once the young architect graduated in 1906, he drew his influences from Vienna – Hoffman, of course, but also Adolf Loos.

Mallet-Stevens' work only spanned the two decades of the interwar period. Some of his buildings are considered monuments in the history of architecture, including Villa Paul Poiret, which would remain unfinished due to the fashion designer's insolvency, and Villa Noailles, the interior of which was created by the most avant-garde designers of the day (Eileen Gray, Sonia Delaunay, Marcel Breuer, Jean Prouvé, Djo-Bourgeois and Francis Jourdain) and which was immortalised by Man Ray's film *The Mysteries of the Château of Dice*. In Paris, the Modernist imagination was captured by two of his creations: Rue Mallet-Stevens, which is lined with mansions designed by the architect, and Villa Cavrois à Croix, which is considered to be his masterpiece.

For Mallet-Stevens, there was no hierarchy among art forms; he was also passionate about film. Not only did he write about the subject, but he also created several film sets: between 1920 and 1928, he designed at least 20. He worked with many filmmakers – Raymond Bernard, Pierre-Gilles Veber, Jacques Riven, Jean Renoir and Henri Diamant-Berger – but his collaboration with Marcel L'Herbier on *L'Inhumaine* would usher him into film history. "A film set, if it is to be a good set, must 'act'. Be it Realist, Expressionist, Modern or antique, it must play a role."

Siren of the Tropics was the last film he worked on as a set designer. Not only did he create all of the interior sets, but the exterior scenes were also filmed on the street bearing his name, where construction had started the previous year. His artistry would cease to grace the silver screen when sound film came to the fore. If this was a matter of cause and effect, the explanation is most likely that the sudden change brought about a swift shift in personnel; numerous silent film directors were pushed aside by this technological revolution.

During the Occupation, Mallet-Stevens went into hiding in the south of France to protect his wife, Alice Khan, who was Jewish. He died in 1945 at the age of 58, and his architectural *oeuvre* was quickly forgotten. Not until the 1980s would his reputation be revived and his buildings saved from the ravages of abandonment. In the 2000s, Villa Noailles and Villa Cavrois received a complete restoration.

Adolf Loos

Born in Brünn in the Austro-Hungarian Empire (in what is today Brno, Czech Republic), Adolf Loos was orphaned at the age of seven but went on to pursue studies in Vienna and Dresden before embarking for the US, where he lived in Chicago, then New York. In 1896, he returned to Vienna. Drawing inspiration from the Chicago School, the architect began defending an absolute sobriety of line and a rejection of all ornamentation. He thus took up an opposing stance to the Vienna Secession, judging their credo, which aligned with Art Nouveau, too decorative.

In 1908, he published his most famous theoretical work, *Ornament and Crime*, which was translated into French and published in Le Corbusier's journal *L'Esprit nouveau* in the early 1920s. "The principle of beauty results from the principle of economy, and the principle of economy results from the principle of utility, which relies upon human need. The practical is beautiful." Loos' theory was a forerunner of modern architecture, and would influence Bauhaus as well as Constructivism. His theories stemmed from one principle: "Only a very small part of architecture belongs to art: the tomb and the monument. Everything else that fulfils a function is to be excluded from the domain of art."

Putting his words into practice, opposite the Imperial Palace in Vienna he constructed a building whose façade caused a scandal due to its extreme simplicity.

In 1923, he was invited to the *Salon d'Automne* in Paris, where his popularity was growing among the avant-garde. In 1925, the Romanian author Tristan Tzara, one of the founders of Dadaism, and his wife, the Swedish artist Greta Knutson, asked him to design the house they wished to build on a lot abutting Avenue Junot in Montmartre.

Josephine Baker was on tour in Vienna when she met Alfred Loos for the first time. The architect would later recall that she was dissatisfied with the work she had commissioned from a French architect. "I couldn't contain myself. 'What, you didn't come to me straight away? Don't you know that I can design the best plans in the world for you?' [...] I designed a plan for Josephine [...] I regard it as one of my best." In 1928, the Viennese architect designed a building intended to replace the one that Josephine owned on Avenue Bugeaud in Paris. An alternating pattern of black and white marble was to cover the façade and gables. Though it was never built, the zebra-striped house that Loos imagined for Josephine has entered architectural legend.

Adolf Loos died on 23 August 1933, a few months after Hitler came to power in Germany and a few months before the start of the Austrian Civil War. Just in time to celebrate his lifelong campaign: "After a thirty-year combat, I have emerged victorious. I have freed humanity from superfluous ornament. 'Ornament' used to qualify what was 'beautiful'. Today, thanks to my life's work, it is a qualifier for what is 'inferior'."

Le Corbusier

Josephine and Corbusier met in November 1929. Since that spring, with Pepito by her side, Josephine had been crisscrossing South America on her first tour of the continent. In Uruguay, Chile, Argentina and Brazil, she had had triumphant success. In Buenos Aires, she gave nearly 200 performances. Le Corbusier was on tour as well, delivering a series of talks over the course of which the Swiss architect would reinvent urbanism and architecture. Though he had built fewer buildings than he would have liked – in 20 years, a dozen mansions and a handful of apartment buildings – his theoretical vision for cities had already changed the course of the history of architecture.

On 14 November, they departed Buenos Aires on the ocean liner *Giulio Cesare*, heading for Sao Paulo; they travelled together for five days: "A simple man and gay; we have become friends. I amuse him with my little songs, which I sing for him as we walk around the bridge." "She wants to show white people the greatness of the Negroes. From head to foot, this woman is nothing but candour and simplicity," Le Corbusier wrote to his mother, his ultimate confidante. "After the 'intelligent' women of Buenos Aires society, I recognise truth here. Josephine reminds me of Yvonne. They have the same conception of life." Yvonne was a model from Monaco.

In Sao Paolo, and then in Rio, Le Corbusier attended Josephine's performances. He was moved to tears. Soon, she began singing for him without witnesses. They quickly began toying with an architectural project. Pepito had suggested tearing down her building on Avenue Bugeaud to make room for Le Corbusier to design a mansion. But Josephine was more interested in a project for the orphans of the world: "His architecture of the future seems so intelligent: on the ground, gardens for pedestrians, and the cars up in the air on elevated highways [...] But he also says 'the city is made for men, and not the contrary, Josephine!'"

On 9 December, the *Lutetia* left Rio for Bordeaux. Aboard the ocean liner were Josephine, Pepito and Le Corbusier, having co-ordinated their return voyage to Europe. Of the twelve days they spent together during the crossing, there remain the colour sketches of Josephine, posing nude, signed by the architect who had always regarded himself as a painter, as well as two photos taken at the celebration for the crossing of the Equator. Le Corbusier had dressed up like Josephine. "He's irresistibly funny. Oh! Monsieur Le Corbusier, what a shame you're an architect! You'd have made such a good partner!"

On 21 December, the *Lutetia* docked in Bordeaux. Other lives awaited the dancer and the architect. Yvonne Gallis and Charles-Édouard Jeanneret-Gris, known as "Le Corbusier", married in 1931. His masterworks were yet to come: the Radiant Cities, the Open Hand Monument, Notre Dame du Haut and the Headquarters of the United Nations. He died on 27 August 1965 at the age of 77, near his seaside house in Roquebrune-Cap-Martin, certain that he had been the most influential architect of the century.

Henri Varna

Henri Eugène Vantard was born in Marseilles in 1887. He began his acting career in his native city using the pseudonym "Varna" – far less remarkable than his real last name, which means "braggart" in French. In 1908, when Varna was 21, he went to Paris. A jack-of-all-trades, he acted in films for Louis Feuillade and sang onstage at the Bataclan. In 1912, in a casino in the coastal town of Cayeux-sur-Mer, his life changed forever when he met the impresario Oscar Dufrenne. They would become lovers. Twelve years his senior, Dufrenne brought Varna along on all of his adventures, first as his assistant and then as his associate. Oscar managed the business; Henri managed the artists. In 1914, they decided to conquer Paris, becoming the artistic directors and then the owners of the Concert Mayol until 1933. They also managed Le Palace starting in 1923, the Bataclan and the Théâtre des Bouffes du Nord from 1927 to 1932, and Les Ambassadeurs and the Moncey Music Hall. In 1924, they began the ambitious construction of the Théâtre de l'Empire on Avenue Wagram, which they sold in 1931 to the financier Alexandre Stavisky, a legendary crook whose violent murder was never solved. Meanwhile, in 1929, they purchased the Casino de Paris. There, Henri Varna directed his first revue, starring Mistinguett. He would go on to do 20 more revues in this theatre.

After watching his local newsvendor sell two copies of Josephine Baker's souvenir programme from the Folies-Bergère while complaining that he never had enough, Dufrenne suggested to his partner that they produce a show starring Baker. Though Dufrenne thought that the American performer had a "little voice", he knew a good business move when he saw one. For Josephine and Pepito, the invitation to perform at the Casino de Paris was just one more step in their ascendance to glory. Replacing Mistinguett on the venue's esteemed grand staircase was no small victory. "Varna guided me and boosted my confidence, all the while giving me freedom," Josephine recalled.

It was Varna's idea to give his new star a male leopard, acquired from the Hagenbeck menagerie in Hamburg and curiously dubbed "Chiquita". "It will be marvellous publicity. You can take him everywhere with you," Varna said to her. Indeed, their very first outing together on the Champs-Élysées gathered a crowd of several hundred onlookers. Chiquita participated in one of the scenes in the show *Ounawa*. He was also featured on the poster created by Zig. Chiquita proved to be a first-rate publicity stunt, but the song "J'ai deux amours" ("My Two Loves"), co-written by Varna with music by Vincent Scotto, proved to be more than just a hit: it went down in history as Josephine's anthem.

After a successful 13-month run, Mistinguett resumed her place on stage in October 1931. Then in 1932, Josephine returned to the Casino de Paris with *La Joie de Paris* (*The Joy of Paris*).

The next year, near midnight on 25 September 1933, a tragedy shook Paris: Oscar Dufrenne was found murdered in his office at Le Palace. After being hit 26 times with a billiard cue, he was suffocated underneath a rug. A sailor he had met in the theatre's gallery had been seen following him into his office. Investigators did not immediately understand the nature of the relationship the producer may have had with this stranger. Oscar Dufrenne, 58, was a public man: a radical socialist city councilman for the 10th arrondissement, general councillor for the Seine department of France, *Chevalier* of the Legion of Honour, president of the theatre director's union, arbitrator at the trade tribunal and patron of several charities. The scandal finally broke when Dufrenne's personal secretary, an ex-lover who was jealous of his relationship with the singer Jean Sablon, revealed his boss's love life. The press leapt at the story, spreading wild rumours and hypotheses. Dozens of sailors and prostitutes were interrogated. At last, an arrest was made: Paul Laborie, former sailor, Parisian gigolo, nicknamed "Paulo les belles dents" ("Paulo Pretty Teeth"). The circus-like trial acquitted Paulo, who was convicted a year later of robbery and was imprisoned for ten years. The police would never solve the mystery.

And so, at the age of 48, Henri found himself alone at the helm of a Parisian nightlife empire. In late October 1939, Varna produced a new revue at the Casino de Paris with the very *à propos* title *Paris-Londres* (*Paris-London*), featuring Josephine Baker, Maurice Chevalier and his wife, the Romanian Jewish singer Nita Raya. Josephine debuted the number "Mon coeur est un oiseau des îles" ("My Heart is an Island Bird"), composed by Vincent Scotto. Varna's idea was to create a show that would be entertaining for British as well as French soldiers. Success was assured.

Varna continued working all through the Occupation, transforming the Théâtre Mogador into a temple to the operetta, all while remaining the director of the Casino de Paris, Le Palace and the Théâtre de la Renaissance. In later decades, he cast Line Renaud as the star of some of his revues at the Casino de Paris. He asked Josephine to advise the newcomer, who would never forget her kindness.

Henri Varna retired in 1966 and died of a heart attack three years later, at the age of 82.

When she heard the news of his death, Josephine was at La Goulue, where she was then performing. The restaurant-cabaret owned by Jean-Claude Brialy was then under the direction of Jacques Collard, who would go on to receive several Molière Awards for his theatrical adaptations. He was with Josephine, aged 63. "I think she was deeply moved. Part of her youth died with him."

Vincent Scotto

Vincent Scotto was born on 21 April 1874 in Marseilles. His parents were from the island of Procida, in the Gulf of Naples. Vincent began composing songs by ear on his guitar when he was very young; not until he was 32 years old, at the end of many long years of singing his compositions in relative obscurity, did he finally achieve success. In 1905, he composed the music for "La Petite Tonkinoise". The comedian and singer known as Polin included the song in his repertoire the following year. It became a hit. A dozen more singers performed the song, including Maurice Chevalier and Mistinguett. Paris suddenly opened its arms to the musician from Marseilles. From that moment on, Scotto only played his songs for the famous performers who would sing them.

One day in 1930, in a doorway opening on to Rue de la Chaussée d'Antin in Paris, he composed the song "J'ai deux amours" ("My Two Loves") for Josephine. It would be the signature song for the show *Paris qui remue* (*Paris Astir*), the new revue by Henri Varna at the Casino de Paris. Josephine would recall the first time she heard the song in Varna's office: "I started to murmur, *J'ai deux amours, mon pays et Paris...*' ['I have two loves, my country and Paris'] as I leaned against the piano. I could feel that that song would be mine, it expressed so well what I was thinking." "And on the evening of the premiere," Scotto recalled, "Josephine was sensational when she articulated it in her pretty voice with its crystalline notes. It was a revelation, because until that moment, she had only sung exotic melodies, dressed in a grass skirt or a bunch of bananas."

"La Petite Tonkinoise" was the other great Scotto song to enter Josephine's repertoire; her version would become the most famous.

In his *Souvenirs de Paris* (*Memories of Paris*), published in Toulouse in 1947, Vincent Scotto devoted a chapter to Josephine. At the time of his writing, Josephine was still singing for soldiers. Scotto wrote: "I knew that beyond her duties as a soldier, she was contributing her time to several charities, paying for her own costumes, travel and substantial orchestra from her own pocket. Without flinching, she sunk a fortune – her own. And when I talked to her about saving for the future, she said, 'Monsieur Scotto, France gave me everything, now it's my turn to give everything for France'."

"J'ai deux amours" would remain the most emblematic song in Josephine's repertoire for the next 45 years. For audiences, not hearing Josephine sing "J'ai deux amours" was like not hearing her at all – the tyranny of the smash hit. Nevertheless, it was said that Josephine still enjoyed singing the song, allowing herself every modulation possible. She sang it so much that it became a way for her to make light of herself.

Vincent Scotto died on 15 November 1952 in Paris, at the age of 78. Five years earlier, Marcel Pagnol wrote to him: "My dear Vincent, when you go, you'll leave one or two hundred songs, your own feelings, your own ideas, which will go on benefiting people who have not yet been born." Scotto composed 4,000 songs, 200 film scores and 60 operettas.

Erich Maria Remarque

Erich Paul Remark was born on 22 June 1898 in Osnabrück, Germany; he had distant French ancestors who bore the name Remarque. He was drafted into the German army in 1916 when he was 18 years old, and he was sent to the Western Front the following year. In late June, his unit was assigned to the front in Flanders. In July, Remark was wounded by grenade shards in his neck, leg and hand – "only light wounds," he would say. Nevertheless, he stayed in hospital until October 1918. When he returned to civilian life the following year, he was an elementary school teacher until he published his first novel in 1920, *The Dream Room*. The book was a commercial failure, which led him to turn to journalism in 1922. In 1924, he adopted the pseudonym Erich Maria Remarque. Under that name, he published *All Quiet on the Western Front* in 1929. This pacifist novel, which describes his experience of the war, became an immediate international bestseller. By the end of the year, a million copies had been sold in German and half a million in English. The next year, Hollywood took notice and Lewis Milestone directed a feature film adaptation. The film would receive two Oscars, but it was banned in Germany under pressure from riots organised by the Nazi Joseph Goebbels. Hitler's future propaganda minister condemned Remarque's work as defeatist.

Remarque may have first met Josephine in Berlin around 1926. They met again in Paris around the end of 1930 or the beginning of 1931, while she was enjoying the success of *Paris qui remue* at the Casino de Paris. Remarque was among the revellers invited to celebrate with her in her dressing room. He was also regularly invited to Le Beau-Chêne, where he may have crossed paths with Duke Ellington and Luigi Pirandello.

Marcel Sauvage recalled a luncheon at Le Beau-Chêne. All the guests, including Erich Maria Remarque, had arrived, but there was no sign of Josephine. Sauvage went up to her room. "I can't get up," she said, "I'm tired. Tell them to wait for me and to start lunch if they're hungry." When she finally appeared, she was wearing silk pyjamas.

In 1933, the Nazis came to power and Remarque became a target of harassment. He moved to Switzerland. He was stripped of his German citizenship and his books were burned. He left Europe for the US in 1939 and didn't return until 1948. Back in Germany, his sister Elfried was convicted of defeatism and beheaded by the Nazis in 1943. The refugee in America was embraced by Hollywood and by a handful of actresses. He had a complicated love affair with Marlene Dietrich, whom he nicknamed "the Puma".

In 1958, he married the Hollywood actress Paulette Goddard. At the beginning of the 1960s, the couple returned definitively to Europe.

The novelist passed away in Locarno, Switzerland, on 25 September 1970, at the age of 72. He had published 11 novels and had lived his entire life with a suitcase within reach: "I always keep a bag packed in case I suddenly need to escape."

Albert Willemetz

"With all your African colonies, why are there so few Negro actors on the French stage?" To Josephine's question, the playwrights of the 1930s had no answer, though they agreed with her – and yet, nobody offered her a role. Not until 1935 did a theatre director dig into the repertoire to find a suitable role for her. That shrewd man was Albert Willemetz, director of the Théâtre des Bouffes-Parisiens and one of the masters of French operetta.

Born in Paris on St. Valentine's Day in 1887, Albert Willemetz was the son of an insurer from Montmartre and an aristocrat from Auvergne. At school in the posh suburb of Neuilly, Albert met Sacha Guitry, who would become his friend and lifelong accomplice. Even then, Guitry noticed his brilliant classmate's talents: "With incredible skill, he would modify the lyrics of popular songs and mischievously sneak in the names of our teachers, to comic effect." When Albert was 13, his parents took him to see *Carmen*; he was dazzled and a vocation was born. "First, make a living!" his father commanded. In 1907, Albert joined the Ministry of the Interior; he was appointed deputy secretary for the Central Commission for Mandatory Assistance of the Elderly, Infirm and Invalid. The same year, he had his first theatrical success with the revue *En cinq sec!* Albert struck a balance in his life between these two seemingly antithetical worlds: he had as many professional successes in the one career as in the other. He married Thérèse Despras in 1911. In 1914, he was exempted from military service due to heart trouble, and in 1918, he became Secretary to Prime Minister Georges Clemenceau. One day when Albert was in a depression – Thérèse had tuberculosis and would not live through the following year – Clemenceau said, "Willemetz, *dans la vie faut pas s'en faire*" ("in life, it's best not to fret"). On 12 November 1918, right after Armistice Day, his second operetta, *Phi-Phi*, afforded the librettist his first great triumph onstage at the Bouffes-Parisiens. His music career took flight.

Between 1913 and 1956, he wrote nearly 200 revues, operettas and musicals, many of which became hits. He came to be known as the inventor of the modern operetta. Albert wrote his lyrics over the score, whereas tradition dictated that the music be composed after the operetta's libretto had been written. This simple but offbeat approach gave Willemetz's songwriting its singular dynamic. The songwriter insisted on using the English term "lyrics" to designate the fruit of his labours, and he was the first to sense that jazz would be the prevailing sound of the post-war period, offering that sound to revue audiences with *Paris Qui Jazz*.

It was only a small step from operetta lyrics to music-hall songs, and once more Willemetz crossed that threshold with brio. Within a few decades, he had written over 3,000 songs, many of which were tailored for a particular singer. He wrote for many of the most popular French singers of the day, including Maurice Chevalier, Arletty, Bourvil, Fernandel, Michel Simon, Jean Gabin, Barbara and Léo Ferré. "The popularity of a song is as inexplicable as the success of a perfume. The notes are in the air." In 1920, he wrote his first standard, Mistinguett's "Mon Homme". It would become her favourite. Thirty years later, Billie Holiday and Barbra Streisand would continue to sing it. For Maurice Chevalier, Willemetz wrote the lines that would become as emblematic as the singer's boater hat: "In life, it's best not to fret! As for me, I never do." He would become the only president of SACEM (a French society similar to ASCAP) who did not read music. "When it's a danceable tune, the legs remember."

In 1928, Willemetz was able to purchase the Théâtre des Bouffes-Parisiens, the theatre which, since the time of Jacques Offenbach's direction starting in 1855, had been devoted to the operetta. He would remain its director for the next 30 years.

Jean Gabin owed his film career to Willemetz. He had signed Gabin for a two-year contract at the Bouffes-Parisiens, but had not planned roles for him in any of the upcoming productions. Rather than paying him to do nothing, he suggested that Gabin try to find another job. "Listen, my dear Gabinos, if you find something, don't hesitate – take it," the theatre boss said bluntly. Soon after, producer Adolphe Osso offered Gabin a role in a film: "At first, I was furious and terribly disappointed by Willemetz's attitude, then I said to myself, 'Go for the movie business, and see what happens!'" the actor said.

Five years later, in 1935, the two men met again on a film set. Willemetz had just co-written the screenplay of a musical film, *Zouzou*. Gabin was starring opposite Josephine Baker. Willemetz would have a profound influence on Josephine's career, but not via his screenplay. That same year, he asked her to make the riskiest bet of her professional life. Willemetz, a regular at Chez Joséphine, was convinced that she had what it would take to leave the music hall for the theatre. "I've got it!" he said one day, "Josephine will play Offenbach's *La Créole*!" Willemetz adapted the libretto, included some new songs – samba, cha-cha-cha – and tailor-made a role for Josephine. "I couldn't wait to perform at the Bouffes-Parisiens, my first 'real' theatre." She went on to say: "At last I would play to a family audience, without my feathers and spangles." Willemetz explained to Josephine that when Offenbach first produced *La Créole* at the Bouffes-Parisiens, the theatre had been in a different location, which housed the present-day Théâtre Marigny. That was where their production of *La Créole* would be staged in December 1935. Arletty, Sacha Guitry, Simone Simon, Eddie Cantor and Pierre Lazareff all came to applaud Josephine. The operetta was a hit.

Willemetz and Josephine would toy with other projects which never came to fruition; she had had her operetta experience, but she never made it part of her regular practice.

Albert Willemetz died in Marnes-la-Coquette on 7 October 1964, at the age of 77.

"We're quick to forget / These little regrets / Everything will work out! / In life, it's best not to fret…"

Sacha Guitry

In 1934, at the Théâtre des Bouffes-Parisiens, rehearsals took place for Jacques Offenbach's operetta *La Créole*, whose leading role had been entirely rewritten for Josephine. Despite the joy she felt to finally have a role as a real actress on the stage of a historic theatre, the rehearsals proved to be hellish. That "damned script" to learn and memorise! Josephine was a sprinter, used to the short duration of a song. An operetta was a marathon. She would start to tremble whenever she heard "Josephine! Places, please!" She would say, "I just can't seem to cram that script into my head... Oh, I'll never make it!" and Sacha Guitry was there to reply, "Of course you can, mademoiselle!" Albert Willemetz's best friend agreed without hesitation to come to Josephine's aid.

Sacha was born on 21 February 1885 in Saint Petersburg, where his father, actor Lucien Guitry, had signed a nine-year contract. His first name came from his godfather, Tsar Alexander III. He wrote his first text for the theatre in 1902. His father then gave him an opportunity to perform onstage, but a romantic rivalry (it was said of both father and son that they were ladies' men) would leave them estranged for a decade.

Sacha was two years older than Albert. They had been fast friends since their school days. Of "Tino", Sacha would say: "He's a friend who can boast that he has never paid me an impromptu visit – in reality, I'm always expecting him." Their bond was also an artistic one: together, they would pen seven revues. It was not by chance that the main character of one of Guitry's first films lived on "Rue Albert-Willemetz." In the same year, Albert served as witness at the marriage of Sacha and Jacqueline Delubac, his third wife. Surprising and unpredictable Sacha! Albert would later recall how, for eight days, his childhood friend had owned the Manet painting *Un bar aux Folies-Bergère*. The art dealer Bernheim had installed the painting in his house, ready to exchange it for paintings by Renoir, Sisley and Monet. Sacha returned the painting definitively to the dealer, and the legendary work went on to grace the walls of the Tate Gallery.

The first time Sacha went to help Tino prepare Josephine for her role, she accepted his authority without discussion: "Albert was telling the truth when he said that Guitry thought it was an excellent idea to cast me in Offenbach's *Créole*! Albert and Sacha have been close friends for years. They were in the same religious institution, and Albert has endless stories about 'that bum Sacha'. Four years ago, Pepito and I were at the Théâtre de la Madeleine to see [Guitry's] *Et vive le théâtre!* (*And Long Live the Theatre!*). There was a fantastic scene about critics. And I thought to myself, he's brave."

When Josephine, 29, felt like she'd never manage, Guitry replied, "Of course you can do it, mademoiselle. You have the makings of a fine comedienne because you're completely natural." His unmistakable voice was the one to appease her and guide her as she learned the craft. Every time he came to visit, he would take her aside: "He, better than anyone, taught me the art of the theatre. Onstage, be as you are in life. In life, observe with the theatre in mind. And laugh at the critics." She would retain all her lessons from Sacha Guitry.

Soon after the liberation of Paris, Sacha was thrown into jail. Albert bent over backwards to obtain his friend's release. Sacha had continued his artistic activities under the Occupation. The American magazine *Life* even published a list in 1942 of French artists who deserved the firing squad: Sacha was mentioned alongside Mistinguett, Maurice Chevalier, Marcel Pagnol and André Derain. When he was released from prison two months later – without ever being brought to trial – the two men quarrelled over a trifle. According to Albert's granddaughter: "Sacha had such a habit of sharing everything with Albert, he was so used to seeing him involved in everything, by his side in all the same struggles, the same events, the same moments of glory, joy or difficulty, he simply couldn't tolerate that he hadn't gone to prison with him." Albert said of the incident: "Sacha stayed angry at his father and brother for 15 years. If he's cross with me today, that means that I've become part of the family." They would reunite ten years later, on the pretext that Sacha wished to do a screen adaptation of *Florestan Premier*, which they had written together. And pretext it was. Sacha suffered from polyneuritis and was very ill; he had had 22 teeth extracted and required three morphine injections per day to tolerate the pain. Albert came to him. When he walked through Sacha's large salon, he was gripped with emotion: "It's not a lively place any more. It's a museum. No more cigarettes burning in the ashtray." Sacha awaited him in his small bedroom. They met again as though it was the first time, 60 years earlier in school. Since then, Sacha Guitry had written 124 plays and directed 36 films – of which 17 were adaptations of his own plays. With few exceptions, he had acted in all of his productions. "A complete *auteur*," François Truffaut would say of him, restoring his cinematic legacy, which had been underestimated in its day.

So that his friend could write his screenplay, Albert petitioned authors' societies and lenders, and finally raised two million francs. Twenty million remained unpaid. On 20 July 1956, Sacha quoted to Albert a phrase from Michel de Montaigne celebrating the author's friendship with Étienne de la Boétie: "If you press me to say why I loved him, I can say no more than it was because he was he, and I was I." Sacha added, "At this moment, my dear Tino, I know just how right Montaigne was." Four days later, Sacha died. Albert wrote: "It feels as though my heart, which loved him so, shall stop as well. All of a sudden, life has ceased to be interesting to me."

Marc Allégret

The father of Marc Allégret, pastor Élie Allégret, had been tutor to André Gide; for that reason, when Marc was born on 22 December 1900 in Basel, he also entered the world of the man whom he would soon call "Uncle André". An intense relationship quickly formed between the two men. André was captivated by Marc's beauty and sensitivity; Marc, in turn, was fascinated by his mentor's mind and sensibility. On a trip to England in June 1918, they became lovers. The following year, the writer began work on a novel that he would only finish in 1925: a book for Marc. "It was for him, to win his attention and esteem, that I wrote *The Counterfeiters*," Gide wrote in his journal. But during that period, Marc's sexuality strayed towards women. While listlessly attending political science classes, he organised artistic soirées that allowed him to interact with Picasso, Cocteau and Man Ray, whom he asked for technical training in photography. Thus was born his passion for images. Uncle André offered to travel with him to Africa, giving him an immediate opportunity to apply the American photographer's teachings. Not only did he bring home still photographs, but also a feature-length documentary, *Voyage au Congo*, which was produced by Pierre Braunberger, edited by Denise Batcheff and screened at the Théâtre du Vieux-Colombier in Paris in 1927. This was a defining moment: Marc would be a director. He learned short subject and documentary film technique, then directed his first feature film in 1930, *Le Blanc et le Noir* (*The White and the Black*), serving as a last-minute replacement for director Robert Florey. He was subject to constant oversight from the writer, Sacha Guitry; the playwright had initially vilified cinema, but later embraced it as a means of ensuring that his plays would endure. Allégret became a director at the very beginning of the sound film era, and immediately came to understand cinema's newest dimension. One generation replaces another.

When the screenplay for *Zouzou* landed on his desk in 1934, Marc Allégret had already directed six feature films. These included the hit *Lake of Ladies*, written by Colette and introducing his then-lover actress Simone Simon; and *Mam'zelle Nitouche*, which led him to film scenes in a music hall – a milieu that had fascinated him since his earliest Parisian escapades. The cast of *Zouzou* also came from the world of the music hall. The film's financier, Arys Nissotti, produced music hall shows; he had first met Josephine and Pepito when he organised concerts at his casino in Tunis in 1928. Pepito wrote the film's concept: the metamorphosis of a simple Creole woman into a great music-hall star. Carlo Rim and Albert Willemetz wrote the script; music played an important role in the production, with compositions and arrangements by Vincent Scotto and Georges Van Parys. Josephine was accompanied onscreen by Jean Gabin, Viviane Romance, Pierre Larquey and Joë Alex. Denise Batchoff was the editor. The film was shot from June to August, in Paris and Toulon.

The director came away from the experience with fond memories of Josephine. "In every scene we asked her to play, she incorporated the full strength of her original nature. What a joy for a director to see an artist who doesn't hide her personality when she enters a new situation, who brings her personal talents and charms to a script." Josephine enjoyed retelling this anecdote from the film: "Oh! The scene with the bird that I freed from its cage... I wanted to play it again and again, each time I thought to myself, I'm granting this bird its freedom... But the little bird didn't want to leave! He was happy where he was! And Mr. Marc Allégret was getting impatient. Cinema is a land of realities, where every minute costs more than it does elsewhere."

In 1937, Marc married actress Nadine Vogel, daughter of publisher Lucien Vogel and granddaughter of artist Herman Vogel. Uncle André attended the ceremony and wept. The next day, he wrote of Marc, who had remained his friend: "Deep down, he is like his father, he never has time to face himself, he escapes from himself in his work..."

In 40 years as a filmmaker, Marc directed 40 feature films. For generations of aspiring actors, his film *The Curtain Rises* would remain a cult classic. Directed in 1938, the film featured Louis Jouvet as the director of a conservatory. Among the students were Bernard Blier, Claude Dauphin and Odette Joyeux.

Even more than his films, Allégret's cinematic legacy lies in his reputation as a discoverer of new talents. His films debuted many great French actors, including Fernandel, Raimu, Michèle Morgan, Jean-Louis Barrault, Gérard Philippe, Jean-Pierre Aumont, Louis Jourdan, Micheline Presle, Danièle Delorme, Mylène Demongeot and Brigitte Bardot, whom he discovered in the wake of his young assistant, Roger Vadim.

In 1950, Allégret halted his headlong rush through film history long enough to turn his camera toward André Gide. He wouldn't finish editing *Avec André Gide* (*With André Gide*) until two years later, after the writer's death in 1951. Marc was deeply affected by the author's passing.

One generation replaces another. Edged out by the directors of the French New Wave, in the 1960s Allégret devoted himself to documentary filmmaking. In 1970, however, he made his way back to fiction with *Le Bal du comte d'Orgel*, screened on the opening night of the Cannes Film Festival. He died three years later on 3 November. His name is still associated with the silver screen thanks to Catherine Allégret, daughter of Marc's youngest brother, filmmaker Yves Allégret, and actress Simone Signoret. The next generation of performers would not carry on the Allégret name, however: Catherine's son, Benjamin Castaldi, a French television personality, kept the last name of his father, actor Jean-Pierre Castaldi.

Jean Gabin

Josephine: "*Zouzou* is a story that Pepito wrote just for me. I think it's a good role, because it's true and sincere." It was the story of a little Creole laundress who becomes a star of the Parisian music hall, with Jean Gabin playing the leading male role opposite her.

Born on 17 May 1904 in Paris, Jean-Alexis Moncorgé was the son of Ferdinand, an operetta actor whose stage name was Gabin, and Hélène Petit, a cabaret singer. By 1922, when he was 18, his father was tired of seeing him take on a series of odd jobs; he insisted that his son accept a minor role on the stage of the Folies-Bergère. His career didn't really take off until 1928, when Mistinguett noticed him. She hired him to perform in her chorus; later, he sang duets with her at the Moulin Rouge. The following year, at the Théâtre des Bouffes-Parisiens, Gabin secured his place in show business by playing the romantic male lead in the operetta *Flossie*, with lyrics written by Albert Willemetz. In 1930, he acted in his first feature film, *Chacun sa chance* (*To Each his Chance*). The advent of sound film brutally obliterated a generation of silent-film pioneers. Gabin, with his light eyes and rugged nonchalance, was there to pick up the baton. In 1935, when he was approached to play Josephine's adopted brother, he had already appeared in 15 films. He was 30.

"I've always liked Jean Gabin. He's speaks so naturally that it's hard to tell if he's speaking in character or not. And when he says to me, 'Comely as you are, I don't know why you should be afraid!', I have to wonder if he's reciting a line written by Mr Willemetz for *Zouzou*, or if he's encouraging me, Josephine."

The films that made Gabin a legend of the pre-war French screen would all come after *Zouzou*. Before 1939, he was in *La Bandera*, *La Belle Équipe* and *Pépé le Moko* by Julien Duvivier; *The Lower Depths*, *La Grande Illusion* and *La Bête humaine* by Jean Renoir; and *Port of Shadows* and *Le jour se lève* by Marcel Carné and Jacques Prévert. His career was interrupted by the war, his Hollywood exile with Marlene Dietrich and his voluntary service with the Free French forces in 1943.

Upon his return to France, the star had grown heavier and his hair had gone grey. Not until the mid-1950s would he find his place in post-war film legend, becoming one of the four 20th-century French actors to draw the biggest crowds to the cinemas – he had probably more than 200 million viewers over his lifetime. His films from this period include *Four Bags Full* by Claude Autant-Lara, *The Sicilian Clan* by Henri Verneuil, *Razzia* by Henri Decoin, *Le Pacha* by Georges Lautner, *Inspector Maigret* by Jean Delannoy and *Le Chat* by Pierre Granier-Deferre. When he passed away on 15 November 1976 at the age of 72, Jean Gabin had been in 95 films. Critic Michel Cournot would write in the French newspaper *Le Nouvel Observateur* that Gabin's best role had been the one he played in *Zouzou*.

Luigi Pirandello

In the early 1930s, when playwright Luigi Pirandello was a regular visitor to Le Beau-Chêne and its famous proprietor, he was fleeing the torment of recent heartache. The author of *Six Characters in Search of an Author* had always been unlucky in love.

He was born on 28 June 1867 in Agrigento, Sicily, to a wealthy bourgeois family. His father had been a "redshirt" in support of Giuseppe Garibaldi, and had fought for Italian unification. Being less partial to physical action, young Luigi wrote his earliest poems at age 13, and published his first short story four years later. He was in love with his cousin, and planned on marrying her and consequently entering the family business. But at the age of 20 he had a change of heart and left for Rome, where two years later he published his first book of poetry. He continued his studies at the University of Bonn and emerged with a PhD in philosophy.

Back in Sicily, the young man of 27 married Maria Antonietta Portulano, daughter of his father's associate. It was an arranged marriage with a substantial dowry. The couple had three children. They lived in Rome, where Pirandello taught for 24 years. Some observers have surmised that the admiration of his female students was in part to blame for Maria's jealousy, which developed into clinical paranoia. He shunned definitive diagnosis, choosing instead to live in domestic hell for over 17 years, before finally allowing her to be committed.

While his body of work includes 237 short stories, eight novels, essays and poetry, posterity has mainly upheld his plays. He came to the genre late in life, in his fifties; it was a "parenthesis", in his words. *Six Characters in Search of an Author* is a subversive *mise en abîme* calling into question all the rules of theatre. It was a flop when it was first produced in Rome, but it went on to become a hit in Milan, then on stages across Europe and the Americas. In 1925, he received support from the Mussolini regime, which allowed him to form his own theatre troupe. He fell in love with the young actress Marta Abba. Both of these paths were abruptly curtailed in 1928.

Following two years of voluntary exile in Berlin, Pirandello moved to Paris. His reputation preceded him. In 1922, Charles Dullin had directed *The Pleasure of Honesty*; the next year, Georges Pitoëff gave Parisian audiences *Six Characters in Search of an Author*. Pirandello often came to Le Beau-Chêne. He explained to Josephine that their frequent encounters had allowed him to study her in detail; he was planning on writing a play about her and *for* her. Josephine introduced Marcel Sauvage to Pirandello; Sauvage would later recall that Josephine used to call the playwright "Papa".

In December 1934, Luigi Pirandello received the Nobel Prize in Literature for his "bold renewal" of the dramatic form. Suffering from a weak heart, he died two years later at the age of 69, while he was in the middle of writing a screenplay and a play for the stage. Josephine was a momentary muse, but she never became a Pirandellian heroine.

Jean Lion

Jean Lion was born in 1910 in the 15th arrondissement of Paris to Ernestine Levy and Maurice Lion, a livestock trader.

In 1935, when he was only 25, he formed a sugar trading company with two associates, setting up offices on Rue Matignon in Paris. Contrary to legend, he was not a billionaire; however, he did have the means to acquire American cars and an aeroplane. His main pleasures were planes, horses, hunting and women.

Their shared taste for horses led Josephine and Jean to get hitched. They were married on 30 November 1937 in Crèvecoeur-le-Grand, the village where the groom then lived. According to Albert Ribac, one of his associates, "Jean had political ambitions and he thought Josephine's popularity might be useful." Their union permitted Josephine to acquire French citizenship.

After their wedding, Jean held on to his own apartment but moved into Le Beau-Chêne with his parents. Witnesses agree that the newlyweds hardly agreed on anything. Even when Jean visited his wife in Rio during her South American tour, their reunion ended with a domestic dispute.

In early 1940, Jean Lion was seriously wounded. His friend Albert brought Josephine to visit him. Moved, she called him "my hero".

In the summer of 1940, he came to Milandes, where his parents had already taken refuge. Jacques Abtey made it possible for Josephine to obtain exit visas for the entire Lion-Levy family. In April 1941, their divorce was finalised. Nonetheless, Jean came to visit Josephine when she was hospitalised in Casablanca, probably near the end of 1942. He had fought with the French army in Tunisia, and would receive the Croix de Guerre. Despite her fatigue, Josephine made it a point of pride to put on make-up and jewellery for his visit.

Jean Lion, Officer of the Legion of Honour and recipient of the medal of the Order of Liberation, died of Asian flu in Paris in 1958 at the age of 48. In a letter, Josephine said of him: "The dead are forever part of the family."

Jacques Abtey

Born in Alsace in 1906, army officer Jacques Abtey was assigned to the counter-intelligence service of the army's general staff, more commonly known as the "Deuxième Bureau" ("Second office"). Chronically understaffed, there were only about ten officers available three years later to confront the infamous "fifth column" of German agents that had infiltrated behind French lines. One of Abtey's "honourable correspondents", Daniel Marouani, informed him that celebrity Josephine Baker – who could get into any embassy in Paris – would be a perfect addition to the Deuxième Bureau. The army captain didn't hesitate to contact her. Their first meeting was at Le Beau-Chêne in September 1939. "When I met Captain Abtey, I was surprised," Josephine wrote. "The Deuxième Bureau evoked for me, maybe because of its name, some pen-pusher, but instead I saw an energetic, athletic man of my own age."

A week later, the singer brought the officer precious reconnaissance gleaned from an attaché at the Italian Embassy. "Her progress in the specialisations in which she received my instruction were so consistent, and came about so rapidly, that I couldn't help but see the exceptional qualities that she possessed." A few months later came the German invasion, a devastating defeat. Jacques Abtey heard General de Gaulle's "appeal". He made his decision. On his way to England, he stopped at Milandes – which he always called "Mirandes" – to visit his former honourable correspondent. According to the officer's later account, he and Josephine were lovers for almost the entire duration of the war.

Josephine, too, chose to engage in the Free France movement, and to head to London. But ultimately the Free France covert intelligence division preferred to send both Josephine and Abtey to North Africa. Abtey managed to pose as her secretary, Monsieur Hébert. In their luggage, they carried precious reconnaissance given to them by one of Abtey's former superiors. From that point on, it was understood "that Josephine Baker and myself were considered to be soldiers in the service of Free France". Their first important mission was to transport secret documents into Portugal by way of Tangier; Josephine had to complete this operation by herself, as Abtey/Hébert had been unable to obtain a visa. When Josephine fell seriously ill in Marrakesh in 1941, Abtey had her transported to a hospital in Casablanca. Until the Allied disembarkation in Morocco in 1942, he would spend much of his time at his friend's bedside; her room in the clinic at Mers-Sultan thus became a secret meeting place for Moroccans and French Gaullists with the American vice consul.

Jacques was also present when Josephine came to Algiers (after singing for British and American troops) to meet General de Gaulle for the first time. All the while, she had been using her talents in the service of French troops.

"Moroccans, Muslims, Arabs that Josephine and I have met along the roads that led us from Marrakesh to Agadir, from Agadir to Fez and Tlemcen, from Algiers to Tunis, Tripoli, Benghazi, Alexandria, from Cairo to Jerusalem, Jaffa, Haifa, Damascus, Beirut; you have shown us your souls, and we have seen that they are beautiful." The captain could not say the same of all the French people exiled in North Africa and the Middle East. A power struggle had begun between Gaullists and Giraudists; the former were supported by the British, while the latter were supported by the Americans. Abtey and his boss at the Special Services division were left on the sidelines. After the Allies disembarked in France and reluctantly recognised de Gaulle's authority, the slight to the captain was finally set right. In 1945, he was appointed to the General Staff of General Schmitt in Marseilles. In December, he went on leave and returned to Paris, where he saw Josephine. She was wearing her blue air force coat, and she asked him to help her fill a car with 200 kilograms of veal that she had just purchased by pawning her own jewellery so that she could provide food to the needy on the outskirts of Paris. She also intended to have a ton of coal delivered to them. She had found it in the cellar of her building on Avenue Bugeaud. "That coal belongs to me," she said to the captain. "My property manager bought it with the rent money. The people living in that building are rich and they'll do what they have to do if they want their rooms heated!"

In late March 1946, upon returning from Germany where she had performed for French troops at her own expense, Josephine asked her friend "Jack" to go with her to Milandes. A few months later, having been promoted to major, Abtey married a young woman named Jacqueline Ceiller de la Barre. Josephine held a reception for them to celebrate the event. A year later, it was Josephine's turn to be married. Naturally, the Abtey couple were in attendance.

In 1948, Major Jacques Abtey published *La Guerre secrète de Joséphine Baker* (*Josephine Baker's Secret War*), in which he gave a detailed account of their covert activities between 1939 and 1944. In 1967, he joined Frigate Captain Fritz Unterberg-Gibhart, who had been his German counterpart in counter-intelligence, to publish *Deuxième Bureau contre Abwehr*, wherein the two former adversaries recounted both sides of their secret wartime games of strategy. Jacques Abtey died in 1998.

An auction in Paris in 2015 revealed for the first time a drawing of the Château de Milandes in pencil and sanguine, signed J. Brad, alias Abtey.

Mohammed Menebhi

When Josephine arrived in Marrakesh in 1941, Morocco had been a French protectorate since 1912. She expected to be greeted by the city's pasha, Thami El-Glaoui, whom she had known before the war and had already visited. But in light of the current political situation, the pasha entrusted her into the care of his brother-in-law, Moulay Larbi, who in turn called upon the assistance of another brother-in-law, Mohammed Menebhi, son of a former ambassador to the court at St. James' Palace. Menebhi owned a house in the medina of Marrakesh, where Josephine stayed with her pets and Captain Abtey. The officer would later say of their host: "He was a magnificent individual. He had a noble soul, and he gave his heart to the Gaullist cause." Josephine would write that he was "marvellous".

When she was hospitalised in Casablanca in 1942, Menebhi came to visit his friend, bringing her favourite dish, chicken tagine with lemon. Nineteen months later, when she was finally able to leave the Mers-Sultan clinic, she went directly to stay with Menebhi to convalesce. This time, he opened his palace doors to her – one of the most beautiful homes in the imperial city, built on 2,000 square metres in the 19th century by Mehdi Menebhi, War Minister for Sultan Moulay Abdelaziz. Josephine befriended her host's three daughters, who came to call her "Tata Jo" ("Auntie Jo"). "I loved her like a big sister," Hagdoush later said. "My father invited her to dine with him, and she lived in a different world than the other women, my father's wives and concubines." Donald Wyatt, an African-American army major and friend of Josephine, said that Menebhi had explained to him that "in Moroccan society, the role of women was to serve men, to give them pleasure and children, but Josephine didn't fall under these restrictions".

In 1943, to reciprocate an invitation from the American Consulate in Marrakesh, Menebhi held a party intended to promote friendship among peoples. The guests were French, British and American. The latter group included black officers. But following the cocktail hour, a white American officer declared that he had never sat at the same table as a "negro". Menebhi was ready to throw out the racists, but Josephine held him back. Later, Wyatt recalled: "When the dancers arrived, he formed the couples, only choosing black officers, while the white officers sat there watching us. The slight was apparent. Josephine thought that she had never seen such an intelligent move."

In 1947, Mohammed Menebhi was present at Milandes for Josephine's wedding. Ten years later, the singer invited him to the château again, but at that time he was a ruined man; Morocco's independence had been costly for leading families close to the French.

Dar Mnebhi, the family's former palace, was long abandoned. It was finally restored in the 1990s and today houses the Museum of Marrakesh.

Charles de Gaulle

Josephine did not hear Charles de Gaulle's appeal on 18 June. Jacques Abtey was the one to make her aware of the existence of General de Gaulle, the man who decided to continue fighting in the name of Free France. In the summer of 1940, for Josephine and for the majority of French people, the man speaking from London was a total unknown.

Born on 22 November 1890 to a bourgeois, monarchist, Catholic family, Charles de Gaulle was the son of professor Henri de Gaulle. An avid reader of Jules Verne, when he was 16 he wrote a science-fiction tale set in 1930, at the end of a conflict with Germany, in which "General de Gaulle" defeated the enemy at the head of the French army.

On 30 September 1909, Charles was accepted into the Saint-Cyr military academy. He was later nicknamed "le Connétable" ("the Constable"). In 1910, he published a short story, "Le Secret du spahi: la Fille de l'agha" ("The Secret of the Spahi: the Agha's Daughter") in *Le Journal des voyages*. He volunteered for the prestigious 33rd Infantry Regiment (which had gained renown at Austerlitz) under the command of Colonel Philippe Pétain, 56. The two men took an immediate liking to one another.

Between the summer of 1914 and the autumn of 1915, Le Connétable was wounded three times. Promoted to captain, he was under Pétain's orders when he was imprisoned at Verdun.

In 1924, his first book of military theory was published: *The Enemy's House Divided*. He was Marshal Pétain's protégé throughout the 1920s, saying of him that he was "a great man". He took up the pen once again, this time as a ghostwriter, composing Pétain's speeches and a work of military history. The two men kept their distance after Pétain asked somebody else to rewrite de Gaulle's manuscript *Le Soldat* (*The Soldier*). Nevertheless, in 1932, de Gaulle dedicated *The Edge of the Sword* to Pétain. Two years later, the soldier-author published his major work, *The Army of the Future*, wherein he advised and defended the use of tanks within independent armoured units. France's high command, including Pétain, disputed Le Connétable's point of view; meanwhile, British and German military minds – including General Guderian – displayed some appreciation for his ideas. Léon Blum admitted that had the colonel's advice been followed, "disaster would have been averted, the war itself perhaps avoided".

In 1938, Pétain and de Gaulle had a falling-out when de Gaulle published the text of *Le Soldat* under the title *France and Her Army*. Though de Gaulle had written the text in its entirety, Pétain considered himself to be at the text's core. "If force is required to construct a state, by the same token the warrior's effort has value only by virtue of politics." De Gaulle or Pétain?

One year later, war broke out with Germany. Guderian and his armoured vehicles destroyed everything in their path. At the head of his armoured division, de Gaulle, who came to be nicknamed "Colonel Motors", couldn't hold back the Nazi panzers. At the end of May, he was temporarily appointed brigadier general. In early June, Prime Minister Paul Reynaud appointed him Under-Secretary for War. While Deputy Prime Minister Pétain was in favour of signing an armistice, de

Gaulle wanted to fight to the end. On 9 June, he was in London, meeting Winston Churchill for the first time; they took a liking to one another. Eleven days later, the rupture was definitive. Pétain sentenced Charles de Gaulle to death. It was de Gaulle's turn to become a storybook hero of France.

Josephine met the general for the first time at the Algiers opera on 13 August 1943. At that time, his command of the Free French forces was still disputed. President Franklin D. Roosevelt saw in de Gaulle the makings of a dictator, and preferred the Vichyist general Henri Giraud. Prime Minister Churchill, deeply irritated by his protégé's intransigence, inflexibility and lack of gratitude, turned his back on him as well. Yet the Allies had to acknowledge his officers' bravery (including Leclerc, de Lattre and Kœnig) and his legitimacy in the eyes of the French Forces of the Interior (including Communists); this, ultimately, forced them to view de Gaulle as their sole interlocutor when he reached Paris on 25 August 1944. Pétain was sentenced to death a year later, but was immediately pardoned by de Gaulle.

In the meantime, on 23 May 1944, Commander Abtey conferred on Josephine the grade of air force sub-lieutenant. On 5 October 1946, she also received the Resistance Medal, though she had to wait until 1957 to be received into the Legion of Honour. She also received the Croix de Guerre and the Free France Voluntary Services Commemorative Medal.

There has been a persistent rumour (diffused by one of her American biographers as well as some Gaullist circles) that Josephine and General de Gaulle had been intimately involved. There is nothing to support this rumour. Might they have met during the Roaring Twenties? In 1927, Charles, then a husband and father, was commander of a unit on the Rhine. In 1929, he was in Beirut and Syria. It is true that on 12 May 1940 he had his quarters in Vésinet, the suburb where Le Beau-Chêne was located, as this was where his armoured division was assembled for a few days. During this time, Josephine was running back and forth between the Casino de Paris and the refugee shelter on Rue Chevaleret. On 3 June 1951, when General de Gaulle visited Milandes, he did not go unnoticed. His presence may have raised the suspicions of some observers; however, at the time the lady of the house was on tour in the US.

No other official meeting between the two legendary personalities was ever documented, with the exception of a reception in 1960 at the US Embassy in honour of General de Gaulle, where Josephine – in sub-lieutenant regalia – was introduced to President Eisenhower. It is unquestionable, however, that once he was back in power, President de Gaulle tried to help save Milandes. Josephine responded: "I made some mistakes and there is no need for France to pay for my mistakes." In May of 1968, with her oldest son Akio, Josephine marched in a parade on the Champs-Élysées in support of the Gaullist regime. "I know that I angered some people by marching for de Gaulle. Too bad. It's a shame that France does not have a cult of loyalty."

Jo Bouillon

From the town of Pézenas, in the Hérault region of France, Jean Bouillon taught violin at the Montpellier Conservatory. His three sons all obtained the First Prize in violin at the Paris Conservatory. George died in a gas attack during World War I, but as early as 1915 Gabriel began to perform for Marcel Proust and Reynaldo Hahn before pursuing an international career as a violinist. Joseph ("Jo"), the youngest of the Bouillon boys, born on 3 May 1908, decided to turn his back on classical music and made a bee-line for jazz and pop. The violinist was first hired by the Gaumont Orchestra in Paris, but in 1936, at the age of 28, he started his own 15-piece big band. The Orchestre Jo Bouillon would count singer George Guératy among its personnel. One evening, he accompanied Madame Josephine Baker for the length of one concert on the Belgian coast. She arrived so late that there was no time to rehearse before they went in front of the audience. "I thought she was haughty," he admitted to his eldest son twenty years later. Jo also played with Mistinguett and Maurice Chevalier, his music-hall mentor. The orchestra would travel across France and Belgium, performing in auditoriums and casinos, until 1939, when geopolitics forced him to stop his career.

In 1940, Jo Bouillon was drafted into the 225th Infantry Regiment. He played in the military band conducted by his friend Pierre Guillermin. When he was demobilised, Bouillon formed another big band with Guillermin at the piano. In 1942, he played at the Circus Medrano and accompanied the group Les Compagnons de la Chanson at the cabaret Les Boeufs sur le Toit. "Towards the end of the Occupation," Guillermin explained years later, "we were forced to work for the Germans, under the threat of being deported to the concentration camps." Thus, Jo Bouillon's orchestra played every day on the airwaves of Radio-Paris, a collaborationist radio station. After Liberation, one of the members of the Free French Purge Committee suggested to Josephine, who was looking for a band, that she contact Jo Bouillon. This time, things went well: "I have never met a woman who made me think of a torrent, a wildfire and a nightingale all at once." The meeting with Josephine and her offer to play for the French army allowed him to easily slip through the cracks of the Purge, and to witness first hand the end of the hostilities. "We arrived in cities where the ruins were still smouldering and the blood hadn't dried. Josephine never looked away, never took a step back. She just gritted her teeth."

In 1947, when Josephine married Jo, she knew that the artist was bisexual and scoffed at the bafflement displayed by some of her friends. She knew that Jo would make a good husband and a good father. "I married an Amazon," Jo wrote. The newlyweds went straight into a six-month tour of South America with 21 musicians. But Jo and Jo had more ambitious plans. They wanted to open the Milandes estate to the public and give birth to the Rainbow Tribe. "Josephine never put her rifle down, always at war with the hydra of racism," Jo said.

At Milandes, the bandleader turned into a one-man band. And father of a large family. While Jo managed Milandes, Josephine held the purse strings, and she had a tendency to loosen them without knowing how much was inside. The couple clashed over the estate's management, as well as the number of adopted children. In 1957, an initial separation weakened the relationship. Josephine demanded a divorce; Jo refused, wanting to keep all his rights as father of the children who bore his surname. No divorce "as long as there's an underage child".

In 1963, after one last family Christmas, Jo left Europe for Argentina, arriving in Buenos Aires on the day of the JFK assassination. In the chic downtown neighbourhood of Palermo, he would spend the next two decades running a French gourmet restaurant, Le Bistro.

Jo left behind him eleven children for whom he would always be "Papa". But once Jo had left, Josephine began to lose her footing: how could she earn enough money through concert dates, all while managing an immense estate that required her full-time presence? Until the end of her reign at Milandes, the singer would fall prey to all kinds of crooks and profiteers.

In 1966, the jazz violinist Stéphane Grappelli, a close friend of Jo, visited Josephine at Milandes. She wanted news of her exiled husband. "I could sense that she really adored him," the musician said.

In the early 1970s, Jo was joined by his fourth son, Jari from Finland. He had been studying hotel management in Switzerland; what better teacher than his own father to guide him in his new vocation? At Josephine's death in 1975, Jo was surprised to discover that he was her sole beneficiary. He brought the youngest of the Rainbow Tribe to Argentina. In 1976, with the help of journalist Jacqueline Cartier, he amassed all the notes, fragments of autobiography, letters and unfinished manuscripts that Josephine had left behind. Rounded out with his own memories and their children's accounts, *Josephine* was published by Éditions Robert Laffont. The book is part autobiography, part polyphonic biography. In the introduction, Jo wrote, "Josephine the star [...] Heroic Josephine [...] Josephine the militant [...] Maternal Josephine [...] I had known them all, a collection of lives in one."

Jo Bouillon died in Buenos Aires on 9 July 1984, at the age of 76. According to his youngest daughter, Stellina, Joseph had never forgotten Josephine: "He died loving her."

Bessie Allison Buchanan

If Charles and Evelyn Allison had stayed in Virginia and not migrated to New York, Bessie wouldn't have been born in 1902 in Harlem, where all of America's rhythms collide. At 19, she starred in the most groundbreaking revue on Broadway, *Shuffle Along*, in 1921. Two years later, Josephine would join the company. The two women's friendship extended back to those years spent honing their craft.

In 1929, Bessie married Charlie Buchanan, manager of the Savoy Ballroom, and gave up her acting career to become involved in social and civic activities. Her first foray into political life was in 1949, when she was invited to join the campaign for Herbert Lehman, Democratic candidate for Senate. Lehman won, and Bessie developed a taste for politics. She understood that there lay the pull necessary to change laws and the chance to be the voice of her community.

When Josephine came to Harlem in May 1951 to be honoured by the NAACP for her contribution in the struggle against segregation on Josephine Baker Day, she also reunited with her friend Bessie, with whom she shared long conversations. They were not only old friends reminiscing about their youthful indiscretions, but were first and foremost two women heavily involved in a common cause: the full emancipation of their community. On 20 May, sitting side by side in a Cadillac that drove by the crowd of thousands of people wearing "Welcome, Josephine Baker" badges, the two women looked radiant. They became inseparable.

A few months later, in October 1951, when Josephine made her entrance at the Stork Club, she was accompanied by two friends from France, the opera singer Roger Rico and his wife. Rico, from Oran, was performing in a successful Broadway musical. Her old friend Bessie joined them as well. The Stork Club was the centre of society life in New York. It was a place where the worlds of media, business and entertainment all came together. It was the place to be seen. This wouldn't prove difficult for Josephine and Bessie, as they were the only two black women present.

When their steaks had yet to arrive an hour after ordering, tension mounted. "Rico's wife begged me to leave to avoid a more obvious slight," Josephine later said. Bessie Buchanan retorted that the situation was scandalous, and that the NAACP should be alerted. She wanted to call Walter White, the NAACP secretary. She wanted to ask him to send a bailiff to confirm that they had refused to serve her. When a "tiny little steak" finally arrived, Roger Rico had already paid for the meal, protesting out loud in his deep voice.

The next day, newspapers picked up the story. The day after, at 7 p.m., banner-wielding members of the NAACP blocked the entrance of the Stork Club for an hour.

A few days later, the son of the Pasha of Marrakesh was also refused admittance to the Stork Club. The owner of the establishment, Sherman Billingsley, admitted to the press that he was obliged to exclude a certain type of client that the majority of his regular customers judged undesirable.

As a point of principle, Josephine, backed by her friend Bessie, was deeply justified in going after the Stork Club; in practice, however, what should have been a victory turned into a disaster. That night at the Stork Club, she saw the reporter

Walter Winchell. The next day in the press, she reproached him for not helping her. He defended himself by saying that he had left before the scandal broke. Against everyone's advice, Josephine didn't let it go. By attacking Winchell, who had thus far been a staunch supporter of the singer and of the African-American civil rights movement, she was uselessly risking media suicide. At the age of 57, the Jewish reporter from New York had specialised in hunting down Nazis (he was the first to denounce Adolf Hitler on the American airwaves), Communists (he supported Senator McCarthy and his witch hunt) and racists all of "clans". His monthly show was broadcast simultaneously on the airwaves and on the ABC television network. His audience and influence were far greater than that of a touring black singer. The controversy mounted. Winchell retaliated. When he called her a "fascist", an "anti-Semite" and a "former collaborator under the Nazi occupation", Josephine tried in vain to bring him to justice for libel, but the damage had already been done. One immediate consequence was the sudden cancellation of a film contract. When winter arrived, Josephine returned to Milandes.

In 1954, against her husband's advice, Bessie made a bid for the Democratic nomination for the seat for Harlem's 12th district in the New York State Assembly. She won by an overwhelming majority in November 1954, against the African-American Republican candidate, Lucille Pickett. She was the first black woman to be part of the Assembly and became a national figure. She was re-elected three times, holding her position for eight years between 1955 and 1962. Hailed as the "First Lady of Harlem", she proposed more than 150 bills to the legislature, mostly in the areas of racial segregation, education and social services. "I've always tried to introduce the kind of bills which would most vitally help the people in my district."

In 1963, the former Cotton Club dancer joined the New York State Commission of Human Rights. At the age of 66, she retired from political life but still remained an active member of the black community in Harlem. She died in 1980 at the age of 78.

Grace Kelly

The only thing missing from the story of Josephine Baker was a real princess. Grace Kelly would play that role in 1968. After being kicked out of Milandes, Josephine couldn't fight any more. She was 62, her twelve children were scattered among various boarding schools and came to visit her on the weekends in her tiny apartment in Paris. She sang every night at La Goulue, a cabaret run by Jean-Claude Brialy, a long-time fan. But each night, the room grew a little emptier. Then came the miracle of the princess. At the suggestion of her artistic director, André Levasseur, she hired Josephine Baker for the Red Cross gala in Monaco, an organisation she presided over. The children were invited, too. Moved by her courage and resilience, the princess helped Josephine and her Rainbow Tribe to move into Villa Maryvonne in Roquebrune-Cap-Martin. This would be the final home of the former queen of Milandes.

The first encounter between the two women – unbeknownst to Josephine – was back in May 1951. "It was at the Stork Club, when the 'incident' occurred. I didn't know who Josephine Baker was back then. My date had to tell me. I thought she was so brave, facing that scandal the way she did… Me, I was so shy! Back then, I was just a little actress that no one had ever heard of, I would have been happy to crawl into a hole. And I remember asking myself at that moment: would I have been so brave?"

Grace was then 22. She was the daughter of a powerful entrepreneur in the masonry business in Philadelphia, a womaniser who wasn't the most attentive of fathers. Grace turned to acting, without her parents' consent but with the help of her uncle George Kelly, a successful playwright. She moved to New York at the age of 18 to study theatre. She quickly began modelling for companies such as Coca-Cola and Colgate, performing onstage and appearing in a few television shows. In March 1951, she featured in her first Hollywood production, *14 Hours*, directed by Henry Hathaway. At the time of the Stork Club incident, she was back on the East Coast, where she was alternating between television and theatre, looking for her breakout role. She seemed to have found it the following year with *High Noon*, a western directed by Fred Zinnemann, starring Gary Cooper. But it was John Ford's *Mogambo*, shot in Africa and starring Gary Cooper and Ava Gardner – who would become a life-long friend – that made Grace Kelly a star, earning her an Oscar nomination for Best Supporting Actress. British filmmaker Alfred Hitchcock would then turn her into a film icon in 1953 by casting her in *Dial M for Murder*, co-starring Ray Milland. Her rise was almost perfect, but in 1954 it was Grace's turn to face a scandal. Would she be brave enough?

Like Josephine, Grace was said to have had many lovers – some confirmed by her mother who, on the eve of her daughter's wedding, named Gary Cooper and Clark Gable – but it was an affair that took place in 1953 between her and Ray Milland, whom she idolised and who was 24 years her senior, that nearly destroyed her career. After a 22-year marriage – one of Hollywood's most durable – the actor had no choice but to divorce. Grace came under attack by the press, which called her a "home-wrecker". A scandal of this magnitude could very well have shut her out of the studios, which she claimed to "hate". Her father sent her a public relations consultant. She set up a press conference where she admitted her mistakes. Grace was absolved; Ray Milland went back to his wife. The actress returned to the studios. For a little while.

Contrary to the legend spread by Paramount, it wasn't during the shooting of Alfred Hitchcock's *To Catch a Thief* that Prince Rainier of Monaco met Grace Kelly, but a year later, during the 1955 Cannes Film Festival. Their engagement was announced on 6 January 1956 in New York. Grace made one last film with Frank Sinatra, Bring Crosby and Louis Armstrong – *High Society* – before giving up acting after eleven films, three Golden Globes and an Oscar. She was married on 19 April 1956 in the Monaco cathedral. Produced by MGM, the "Wedding of the Century" was broadcast live by Eurovision and watched by 30 million people around the world. The event ended her career on a majestic note.

In 1957, when her daughter Caroline was born, the princess received a signed copy of *La Tribu arc-en-ciel* (*The Rainbow Tribe*), a children's book published by Josephine earlier that year. From that moment, the two women began a correspondence. Josephine's appearance at the Sporting Club in Monaco in 1968 dazzled Grace: "Like the rest of the audience, I was amazed by her beauty and by the courage that it all represented." When Josephine decided to settle with the Rainbow Tribe on the cliffs of Roquebrune, Grace was there once again: "The prince and I lent her the money that she needed for the down payment and I called upon the executive committee to provide the rest." Josephine insisted on paying back her debt. Six months prior to her death, Josephine had paid off the house.

In 1976, one year after Josephine's death, Jo Bouillon was a guest at the princess's Paris apartment. They talked about her as a mother and a performer: "We thought the same thing: that the family unit is the foundation of a society and the reason why a sick society must be cured. I also deeply admired her as a performer. She was unique." She added: "There are people who never die."

On 13 September 1982, Grace Kelly suffered a stroke while driving her Rover. She drove off a winding road in Cap-d'Ail and crashed 40 metres below. She died the next day.

Miki Sawada

Born in Oiso, Japan in 1901, Miki was the eldest daughter of Baron Iwasaki and the granddaughter of Yataro Iwasaki, the founder of Mitsubishi, a major Japanese industrial conglomerate. Miki's father, a diplomat, led the Mitsubishi Empire until World War II.

Surrounded by three older brothers and two little sisters, the very active young girl studied English with Umeko Tsuda, founder of the women's university Tsuda College, who dedicated her life to the education of women.

At the age of 20, Miki married the diplomat Renzo Sawada and converted to Christianity. Renzo would become an ambassador and the Vice-Minister for Foreign Affairs. Being the wife of a diplomat, she travelled the world: Argentina, Beijing, London, Paris and New York. Thanks to her ability to speak English and her engaging personality, she blended in with international pre-war high society. In 1931, Miki Sawada met Josephine Baker in Paris, where her husband was assigned. It was during a society party that she heard the performer talk about her monthly visits to the needy. Intrigued, the Japanese woman asked if she could come with her. "Why don't you want to keep the beautiful image of Paris as you know it?" Josephine asked her. Miki Sawada insisted. Three weeks later, the Japanese woman accompanied the American to the slums of Paris. She parked her car in front of a building and opened her packed trunk: "Each package was tied with a ribbon of a different colour to identify the contents: medicine, clothes, food, toys. It brought tears to my eyes to see Josephine picking up the little ones, stroking their hair. She wasn't doing it for effect." This was at a time when Miki was full of spiritual questioning about the meaning of life.

World War II destroyed Miki's life, taking her youngest son with it. After the war, the Mitsubishi dynasty's assets were taken away. Horrified by the number of abandoned children who were persecuted for having a Japanese woman for a mother and a soldier from the West for a father, Miki welcomed a great number of them into her own home.

In 1954, Miki Sawada played host to Josephine Baker in Japan. Despite harassment from Americans, she came to sing and to see Miki. The two friends went to the Hiroshima Peace Memorial, but most importantly, they visited the orphanage that Miki had founded with the sale of her last remaining assets and donations from a former British governess, Elizabeth Saunders, in whose honour the foundation was named. That day in May 1954, Miki entrusted Josephine with two of the children. Their fathers were Westerners and their mothers were Japanese. They were Akio and Jeannot. Nearly 150 other children at the orphanage were adopted by American parents. Meanwhile, Renzo Sawada was exculpated and became the Japanese ambassador to the United Nations.

When, in the late 1960s, Josephine sent Akio and Jeannot to Japan for a year in order for them to explore the land they came from, Miki would watch over them. In 1973, the two women reunited one last time at Carnegie Hall, where Josephine paid tribute to her Japanese friend.

Miki Sawada passed away in Spain in 1980, at the age of 79. She is still honoured in Oiso, her hometown, where a museum was named after her, displaying her precious and unique collection of Kakure Kirishitan artefacts, the founding traces of Christianity in Japan.

Akio Bouillon

When Josephine came back from her trip to Japan in 1954, she wasn't alone: her first two adopted children were with her. The elder, Yamamoto Akio, was born in 1952 and the younger, Kimura Teruya Seiji, renamed "Jeannot" by his new mother, was born in 1953. Akio was introduced as Korean and Jeannot as Japanese. They both came from the Elizabeth Saunders Home, an orphanage for mixed race children under the supervision of Miki Sawada. Josephine had come for the younger child; his mother, an orphanage employee, had just passed away. "When she came to see Jeannot, I was already walking," Akio said 62 years later. "And I don't why, I was drawn to her, I clung to her skirt, I followed her everywhere. Every time she visited, I was there and I followed her. She got used to my presence and decided to take me with her."

Thus the Rainbow Tribe was founded in 1954. Ten other children would join the Tribe by 1964, and Akio would be a big brother to all of them. "My father gave me the responsibility of being the eldest. I had to be a good example and take a lot of things on the chin. I never had a childhood; I was the buffer between the children and the parents. It was a strict, old school, pre-war type of upbringing, but my father never mistreated me; instead he'd tell me what I did wrong. Every day, he would make the rounds of all the estate's activities. From the age of five, I would accompany him in his daily routine with Rosalie and Sweet, Mom's poodle and Dad's cocker spaniel."

The father of the Tribe may have dwelled at Milandes, but that wasn't the case for the mother, who was often away but eminently present. "My mom had inherited the pugnacity of her African-American ancestors: 'nothing is impossible if you want it.' She forged my character. That's how I was raised. I was also given a taste for non-conformity and the bohemian life."

In 1963, when his parents separated and his father left for Argentina, 11-year-old Akio was devastated. "Dad told me: 'I'm leaving the family in your hands.'" Five years later, the eldest brother of the Rainbow Tribe witnessed first hand Josephine's properties being auctioned off at the Court of Bergerac, while she was performing in Sweden. Akio accompanied Mr Dirand, "the loyal and faithful manager of the estate". They waited for Bruno Coquatrix, who had come to deliver a cheque for 400,000 francs, earned from the Olympia concerts and the live album released soon after. Only 300,000 francs were needed to prevent the château from being sold, but all the other properties were lost: amusement park, farm, hotel, restaurant and museum. "And Bruno Coquatrix never came," Akio recalled. "The château was sold, like everything else, at a third of its actual value. When we went outside, we found the impresario smoking a cigar, standing on the sidewalk. He had arrived late and hadn't even come in, letting the auction happen as planned. Mr. Dirand was furious. I think that Bruno Coquatrix had intentionally arrived late. Mom had worked very hard for that money and he saw that château as a huge money pit. She would risk losing everything again, it was prolonging the inevitable. Maybe he believed that he was saving her from herself."

For the longest time, Akio believed that he was Korean. In the early 1970s, when they first moved to Monaco, he had just completed high school and his mother offered to send him to university in Japan; Akio began to question his origins: "But

Mom, it's a well-known fact that Koreans and Japanese are hostile towards each other. I'm going to have trouble with the Japanese!" "Don't worry about it. You are Japanese. You were born in Japan!" This revelation was confirmed a few months later by Miki Sawada when she hosted the two Bouillon brothers in her country. "I asked Miki: 'If I had been Korean, would I have been accepted in this country?' She answered me with a smile: 'You know, Japanese people didn't tolerate mixed race Japanese, much less Koreans...' When she came back with Jeannot and me, Mom couldn't justify the concept of the Rainbow Tribe if we both came from the same country. The Korean War was in full effect. So I became Korean! A little white lie..." In Tokyo, Akio studied the language of his true ancestors for a year and a half at the St. Joseph School.

When he came back to France, the young man studied at a Swiss boarding school with the hope of being accepted at Sciences Po in Paris. "It was very difficult for Mom to pay for it. The following summer, in Monaco, I decided to stop and go to work. I got a job in a bank, Mom was furious."

In early 1975, Akio crossed the Atlantic to join his father in Buenos Aires. "I always missed him," Akio said. Josephine passed away just a few months later. The eldest son didn't attend her funeral and remained in Argentina for another six years before going back to France. He would return ten years later to be with Jo during his final moments and to bring his body back to the Monaco cemetery to be buried near the other Jo.

He was more than 50 years old when, thanks to an interview in a Japanese newspaper, Akio learned how he came to be an orphan. "It was raining in the city of Yokohama. It happened in September 1952. A young girl of 12 or 13 was working at a kiosk. A woman suddenly came in, soaking wet, carrying a two-month-old baby in her arms. She asked: 'I'm going to get an umbrella, can you watch my baby?' The young woman went out into the rain and never came back."

In 2016, at the age of 64, Akio Bouillon has not forgotten what he learned from his parents and from his mother's ongoing struggle. "Today, it's up to us, her children, to do the job: perpetuate her message of brotherly love."

Jean-Claude Bouillon-Baker

In 1955, when Josephine came to get Jean-Claude at the Saint-Vincent-de-Paul orphanage, she already had four young boys. Jean-Claude was the first French one. Born on 23 December 1953 in the 15th arrondissement of Paris at the Boucicaut hospital, he was immediately abandoned by his biological mother and became a ward of the state. Jean-Claude would learn later in life, while looking at his file at the social security office, that Josephine had seen a picture of him before choosing him. But in December 1955, she was stuck in Sweden, where her show was a huge hit, and couldn't come to pick up the boy still known administratively as "Philippe". She begged the child welfare services not to give him to somebody else before her return.

Along with Moïse, who was adopted at the same moment, Jean-Claude arrived at Milandes on 21 December 1955. "I was two years old, minus two days, to be precise. Mom didn't want me to spend another birthday in the orphanage. Our very first photo together: I'm sitting on her lap, in front a cake with two candles." Château life with the Tribe had begun.

The first clouds appeared on the horizon when Jo and Jo, Mom and Dad, separated in the 1960s. This was when Jean-Claude became a "problem child". He began alternating between posh boarding schools and disciplinarian ones, with the occasional expulsion.

When his mother died, 13 years later, Jean-Claude dropped out of high school. "Then Dad put me in a boarding school in Cannes and I failed the graduation exam at the age of 19!" Yet, after two years of studying at the university of Paris-VIII, he got a diploma in film studies. He had finally found his vocation. In 1979, he became a production manager for documentaries. In 1997, his daughter Clara was born, and in 2001, his son Joseph, named after his father.

In 2012, under the name "Bouillon-Baker", Jean-Claude published a book about his personal experience of the Rainbow Tribe, *Un château sur la Lune* (*A Castle on the Moon*), subtitled "Le Rêve brisé de Joséphine" ("Josephine's Broken Dream"). In March 2013, he contacted Catel Muller, convinced that his mother "would have enjoyed being drawn" by her, and infected her with his enthusiasm for Josephine.

Since then, Jean-Claude has attempted to discover his origins. "In my mythology, my biological mother was a Breton prostitute. I wanted her to have extenuating circumstances; I'm moved by the idea of a prostitute with a heart of gold!" She turned out to have been a fatherless 19-year-old, born on France's northern coast, who had already become a mother at the age of 17 and was incapable of taking responsibility for a second infant, even though the child welfare services had asked her to several times.

"A wall went up between us, built by the 'amnesia of an emotional shock'. I would never learn about my father. I say this without cruelty or cynicism, but I don't think I got short-changed: an exceptional mother, an enchanting father, a family life like none other... This little ward of the state was touched by the fairies of destiny."

Brahim-Brian Bouillon-Baker

"The story of Marianne and me, rescued as toddlers from the Palestro massacre, was something that my mom made up," Brian discovered many years after Josephine's passing. Though it appeared that his biological parents were the collateral victims of fighting between Algerian and French soldiers, it was in Orléansville – later called El-Asnam – that Slim the orphan was found. A ward of the state under the name "Jacques", he was in an orphanage in Algiers when Josephine came to visit, looking to adopt a little girl. "All the babies were asleep, except me. When she came close to me, I smiled at her and her heart melted. Especially when she learned that we were born on the same day: 3 June! Thus, I was named Brahim, which she and Aunty always pronounced 'Brian'!" This seventh child of the Rainbow Tribe would work with a tutor who attempted to teach him the precepts of Islam, as well as a little Arabic, but he was a young man of his time and place: a fan of Brian Jones, Bryan Ferry and especially Brian De Palma.

Brahim-Brian lost his mother two months before he graduated from high school. After completing his military service, Brian hesitated between a career as a sports journalist and an actor. Jo Bouillon introduced his son to friends working for the daily sports paper, *L'Equipe*, where Brian first started working as a freelancer while studying at the Perimony Drama School on Jean-Claude Brialy's advice. In the summer of 1977, Grace Kelly helped him find an agent. He started landing small and medium roles on French television: *Les Cinq Dernières Minutes, Papa Poule, Hôtel de police, Médecins de nuit* and *Series Rose*. His film career began under the direction of Polish filmmaker Walerian Borowczyk. "Back then, for an actor of my skin colour, the range of parts available was still pretty limited: an immigrant, an Emir, an Iranian terrorist..."

At the beginning of the 1980s, Peter Brook introduced him to Ellen Stewart, the founder of *La MaMa Theatre*, a famous Off-Off-Broadway company. Brian did two shows before Borowczyk called him back to France to shoot two pictures which would never be made. With his acting career stalling in Paris, "B-B-B" became a receptionist at the Hôtel du Cygne, where a client, a young man of mixed race with bleached hair, tried to get closer to him. Brian rejected the advances of one Thierry Paulin, who would turn out to be the most vicious French serial killer of the decade.

Knowing full well that the time was not yet ripe for an Arab actor to become a movie star, Brian started working in the closed circle of voice acting. At the same time, he resumed writing for newspapers, including *France Football* and *L'Echo des savanes*. In 2006, in honour of his mother's centennial, he published *Le Regard d'un fils*, followed in 2008 by the documentary *L'Autre Joséphine*, directed by Philip Judith-Gozlin, which took him from St. Louis to Monaco. It was around that time that he met Sabine. Fate brought them together: in 1963, she was introduced to Josephine Baker in the Olympia dressing room. Because the little blonde girl was born the same year as Brian, the mother of the Rainbow Tribe declared, "they should be betrothed!" Five decades after that prediction, Sabine and Brain were finally married.

Jocelyne Coffre

"Josephine Baker is looking for a secretary who can speak English and Spanish fluently." In 1962, when 17-year-old Jocelyne in Bordeaux saw this job offer at her secretarial school, she didn't have to think twice. The next day, she was with her mother on the train to Milandes. Josephine, 56 and severe, received the young applicant, who admitted that her English was fairly basic and her Spanish almost non-existent. She was touched by her candour – the young lady "dreamed of travelling the world" – and so she offered to take her on for a three-month trial period. Their collaboration would last two and a half years.

"She had me take dictation for a great many letters. She had me write in English, particularly to Martin Luther King. In the beginning, she told me all the time that I 'lacked experience'. One day I said to her: 'Madame, I give you my youth; give me your experience.' From that day on, she never reproved me for my lack of experience. After that, when she introduced me, she would say: 'This is Miss Coffre, a "coffer" of kindness.'"

Over the next two years, young Jocelyne travelled all over the world: Mexico, Peru, Uruguay, Argentina, Brazil, Sweden, Denmark, Germany and Switzerland. They travelled together, just the two of them, but accompanied by 20 suitcases packed with costumes and musical scores. Jocelyne's typewriter was always close at hand. On the plane, Josephine kept dictating to her. Sometimes, she fell asleep for a few minutes and then resumed where she left off. The other passengers complained that the tapping of the typewriter kept them awake.

Except for when Josephine was on stage, they were together constantly. When staying in a hotel, they always shared the same room. "She had a fabulous body. The colour of her skin, the length of her thighs, it was beautiful! I'll feel inadequate for the rest of my life!" However, Jocelyne was living her dream of travelling the world. In Montevideo, a famous hairdresser cut her childish pigtails. In Berlin, she bore witness to the alcohol-fuelled reunion between Josephine and Duke Ellington. In Copenhagen, she wept as she listened to Josephine's speech about brotherhood. In Gothenburg, Josephine needed laundry detergent and sent Jocelyne to get some, without a penny in her pocket and without knowing a word of Swedish. "'Just do it!' she told me. What I feared most was getting lost. Josephine knew that I had no sense of direction. I found a supermarket, the first I saw. I took a box of detergent and, in broken English, asked them to send the bill to the hotel. I knew the Swedish word for 'thank you'. I said 'thank you' a thousand times and I left with my box of detergent. And when I came back, Josephine could not believe her eyes. She said, 'My dear, you can do whatever you want in this life, you'll always succeed!'"

One day, in 1964, for personal reasons, Jocelyne had to leave Josephine. They remained in correspondence. Years later, having become a bailiff, Jocelyne, in turn, would become responsible for five employees: "Josephine taught me to handle my secretaries' 'little screw-ups' with a smile!"

Martin Luther King

On 27 August 1963, Coretta and her husband Martin Luther King Jr. arrived from Atlanta to participate in what they hoped would be the largest peaceful gathering in their long battle against segregation: the March on Washington for Jobs and Freedom. All night, in his hotel room, Martin kept honing his speech. He wanted to talk about the "bad cheque" given to black people, a reference to Abraham Lincoln's Emancipation Proclamation whose centenary had been celebrated that year.

Born in 1929, Martin had become a pastor in 1954, in Montgomery, Alabama. The previous year, he had married Coretta Scott, with whom he would have four children. The year after, he was catapulted to the forefront of the civil rights movement. On 1 December 1955, when Rosa Parks was arrested for refusing to give up her seat to a white man on a bus in Montgomery, the 26-year-old pastor called for a boycott of the bus company. For 382 days, the 400,000 black people living in the city pooled together to make sure that they could get around without having to use public transport. During that time, the Kings' home was bombed and the pastor himself was beaten and arrested. The boycott ended with the Supreme Court outlawing segregation in public places. A herald of non-violent resistance was born.

In the spring of 1963 in Birmingham, racial tensions reached an all-time high. In this city, where 35% of the population was black, local authorities enforced what was the harshest segregation to be found in America. "The colossus of segregation," as Martin Luther King called it. In the public sphere as well as the private sphere, most jobs could not be held by black people, except for labour in steel factories. Protests would begin with boycotts, soon followed by marches and non-violent sit-ins. Tensions were rising. Images of police dogs unleashed on black children were seen around the world. Martin Luther King was arrested and put in prison. Behind bars, he used newspaper margins and squares of toilet paper to write his first major text, "Letter from Birmingham Jail". "I am in Birmingham because injustice is here," he wrote, before quoting St. Augustine: "an unjust law is no law at all." President John F. Kennedy phoned Coretta: "I just want you to know that we are doing everything we can." Eight days later, Martin was released. A federal mediator was appointed, the mayor resigned and the chief of police was fired. African-Americans were finally allowed into public places. The Kennedy administration lost no time in proposing a series of anti-segregation laws to Congress. Coretta made a suggestion to her husband: "People all over the nation have been so aroused by the impact of Birmingham that you should call a massive march on Washington to further dramatise the need for legislation to completely integrate the black man into American society. I believe a hundred thousand people would come to the nation's capital at your invitation."

On the morning of 28 August, it was announced on television that only 25,000 protesters would participate in the event. "Sad and defeated", the Kings left their hotel, only to find 250,000 people waiting for them outside. "They had come by plane, train, bus, automobile, some by bicycle and a few by foot, from all parts of the nation. Almost a fourth of that enormous crowd was white. It was a beautiful sight," recalled Coretta.

Wearing her highly decorated dress uniform, Josephine landed in Washington on 28 August 1963. On that day, it wasn't the singer who took the mic, but the activist. She talked for no more than eight minutes, the same amount of time given to the other speakers. Martin Luther King spoke last. He, too, had a time limit. "Martin was tremendously moved," wrote his wife. He delivered a finely honed speech, which started off with the notion of the "bad cheque". "And so, we've come to cash this cheque," Luther King said with resolve. "We refuse to believe that the bank of justice is bankrupt." When he finished his speech by repeating "now" four times, the entire crowd joined in chanting that word. It was the turning point. "Their response lifted Martin in a surge of emotion to new heights of inspiration," Coretta recalled. "Abandoning his written speech, forgetting time, he spoke from his heart, his voice soaring magnificently out over that great crowd and over to all the world." The reverend dreamed out loud.

In November, Josephine received a letter signed by Martin Luther King. "This is just a brief note to express my deepest gratitude to you for all of your kind expressions of support. We were all inspired by your presence at the March on Washington. I am deeply moved by the fact that you would fly such a long distance to participate in that momentous event. We were further inspired that you returned to the States to do a benefit for the civil rights organisations." A few days later, JFK was killed in Dallas. But his political commitment did not die with him. In July 1964, Congress passed the Civil Rights Act, which forbade discrimination on the basis of race in accessing public facilities, hiring, promoting, firing, setting wages, housing and education. In October of the same year, King obtained the Nobel Peace Prize. But his fight wasn't over yet. In 1967, he took a stand against the Vietnam War, but on 4 April 1968, while in Memphis to show his support for the black sanitation workers' strike, he was shot dead while standing on a balcony at the Lorraine Motel. Martin Luther King Jr. was 39. He never saw his dream for America become reality.

Sammy Davis Jr.

On a golf course somewhere in the US, a white man approached Sammy Davis Jr. and asked him: "What's your handicap?" The singer/dancer/musician/actor answered: "I'm black, I'm blind in one eye and I'm Jewish. Don't you think that's enough?" The entertainer was always credited with that line, though he himself denied it. Still, he recognised that being the punchline of a joke was a sign of great notoriety.

Born in Harlem in 1925 to Elvera Sanchez and Sammy Davis Sr. – both dancers – Junior began honing his craft as an artist at the age of three by following his father on tour, before spreading his own wings. The world of show business had long shielded the young man from day-to-day racism, something he experienced for the first time at the age of 18 when he joined the army. "That was when I realised that my father had protected me up to that point. He had hoped that I'd be able to escape the slurs and the hate." During that period, Sammy Davis Jr. became involved in the civil rights movement. "My talent was a weapon, a strength, a way of defending myself. It was the only means I had for trying to make the people around me think."

He danced, sang, played drums and vibes. Sammy was already an accomplished performer when, at the age of 29, he recorded his first successful album in 1954, *Starring Sammy Davis Jr.* That same year, he lost an eye in a car accident on Route 66. During his convalescence, he converted to Judaism. Five year later, Frank Sinatra invited him to join the "Rat Pack" – whose core members included two other singers, Dean Martin and Peter Lawford. Though their headquarters was the Sands Hotel in Las Vegas, they performed in venues all over the country, starred in Hollywood films and recorded albums. The Rat Pack – so named by Lauren Bacall after Humphrey Bogart came home from a bender with Frank Sinatra – would dazzle America till the end of the 1960s. The counter-culture put an end to the reign of tuxedo-clad crooners.

In 1960, Sammy Davis Jr. sent shock waves through the segregated US by marrying Swedish actress May Britt. Interracial marriages were then forbidden in 31 states. From that moment, he refused to perform in segregated venues.

In 1963, during the March on Washington, he was with Sidney Poitier – another African-American star of the day – to welcome Josephine Baker on the steps of the Lincoln Memorial. He called her "Madame Béker", using a French accent.

Sammy and Josephine would meet again a decade later on the Côte d'Azur. The entertainer had come to sing on the stage of the Sporting Club in Monaco, but on the night of the gala, following a dispute with the organisers, Sammy refused to leave his yacht. Living next door, Josephine filled in for him at the last minute; a favour that Princess Grace Kelly would never forget.

After a decline in health due, according to him, to excessive drinking and various drugs, Sammy Davis Jr. died in Beverly Hills in 1990 at the age of 64.

Brigitte Bardot

On 4 June 1964, Brigitte Bardot contacted the French national broadcasting agency: she had something to say on the air. The number one celebrity of France's prosperous post-war era had spent the last eight years dodging the paparazzi wherever she went; French television seized the opportunity to get her in front of the camera. Bardot wasn't there to talk about herself, however, but to bring people's attention to the plight of Josephine and the Rainbow Tribe. Since the beginning of the year, the pressure exerted by various creditors had become more than Josephine could handle. At the château, water and electricity had been cut off. All of the furniture, as well as the farming and restaurant equipment, would soon be auctioned off. On 1 June, Josephine held a press conference: "This time, I'm crying for help!" Brigitte Bardot answered the call.

The actress would turn 30 in a few months, and she was at the height of her fame. Bardot was born in 1934; her film career began in 1952, at the age of 18. She learned to perfect her craft under the direction of Sacha Guitry, René Clair and Marc Allégret. But it was her husband and mentor, Roger Vadim, who turned her into a movie star by casting her when she was 24 in his first feature film, *And God Created Woman*. The character, in combination with the actress's natural screen presence, turned her into a model of modernity and rebellion for an entire generation. According to feminist Benoîte Groult, Brigitte Bardot gave women of every nationality and walk of life the desire to free themselves from the constraints of male-dominated society. During the next eight years, until 1964, she starred in over a dozen films, some of which became classics: *In Case of Adversity*, directed by Claude Autant-Lara, based on the novel by Georges Simenon and co-starring Jean Gabin; *The Truth*, directed by Henri-Georges Clouzot; *A Very Private Affair*, directed by Louis Malle; and *Contempt*, directed by Jean-Luc Godard, based on a novel by Alberto Moravia. In 1964, when Brigitte made a plea for Josephine, people listened. Thirty years later, she said she was still "moved, deeply moved by the severe distress inflicted on this amazing, generous woman who had made an indelible mark on that sensational era [...] and who cared passionately about giving, adopting, saving and uniting in brotherly love all the people of this world". The actress found it "unfair" that those dreams should be sold to the highest bidder. Her miraculous call to action spread around the world and helped Josephine to raise enough money to keep Milandes.

In 1973, at the age 39, after starring in over 47 films, the greatest French actress of the second half of the 20th century abandoned her career. She decided instead to focus on saving baby seals with her animal rights foundation. Her first major battle for the protection of baby seals turned her once again into a media target, only this time it was all for a good cause. She would never veer from her course.

In correspondence with Catel Muller, Brigitte Bardot said that she had given Josephine Baker one million francs, half of the total needed. Oddly enough, it appears that the two women never met in person.

Fidel Castro

On 29 December 1965, Josephine set foot on the tarmac of the Havana airport with writers Alberto Moravia and Mario Vargas Llosa. A crowd of Cuban admirers welcomed her, crying: "Bienvenido, Josefina!" The story of Josephine and Cuba is something of a love affair.

In October 1950 and January 1952, she sang in Havana, where she had already garnered fame. Not until February 1953 would she cross paths with two young nationalist activists, the Castro brothers – Raul and Fidel – who had already cheered her from their seats in the audience during her previous visits. In mid-February, during a protest, a young student was killed by the dictator Batista's police force. After her show, the singer attended his wake along with the Castro brothers and decided to offer the proceeds of two of her performances to the brothers' political movement. Born in 1926, Fidel Castro was the illegitimate son of an illiterate Galician immigrant turned prosperous landowner and his cook. Fidel was a young lawyer who had just received a degree in social sciences. Raul was his shadow.

A few days later, the singer was arrested by the Cuban military intelligence agency. She was questioned about her Communist sympathies and a mug shot was taken of her holding a placard showing the number "0000492". Josephine left Cuba a few days after her release and vowed never to set foot in the country again as long as Batista was in power. Five months later, on 26 July, Fidel led a failed armed insurrection. He was sent to prison for fifteen years.

When Josephine returned to Cuba in 1965, she had kept her word: Batista had fallen from power. He had since been overthrown by Fidel Castro. Sentenced to prison in 1953, the young revolutionary was pardoned two years later and chose exile in Mexico. There, along with his brother Raul and the Argentinian doctor Ernesto Guevara, he created the 26th of July Movement and organised a revolutionary invasion of Cuba in December 1956. Batista's armies were waiting for them. Of the 82 freedom fighters, only 16 survived, including Guevara and the Castro brothers. The survivors found refuge in the Sierra Maestra mountains, where they organised guerrilla forces with US government support. In 1959, after joining forces with other guerrilla movements, Castro and his *barbudos* entered Havana on 8 January and seized control, still with the blessing of the US. Castro was appointed Prime Minister a month later, and began to implement a series of reforms centred on the nationalisation of banks, industries and land. Soon enough, US corporations and their interests came under attack. A year later, the former ally became their worst enemy. A power struggle ensued, resulting in the cessation of all commercial transactions between North America and Cuba. The regime that Castro first labelled "Socialist", then "Marxist-Leninist" and finally "Communist" turned to its big brother, Russia. In April 1961, the invasion of Cuban exiles armed by the CIA in the Bay of Pigs turned into a military disaster that the rest of the world viewed as a humiliation for the US. A year and a half later, in October 1962, the installation of Russian missiles on Cuban soil – only 145 kilometres from Miami – was considered by the US as a blatant act of aggression. The missile crisis led the world to the brink of nuclear war. The threat was averted when Khrushchev and Kennedy came to an agreement.

In 1965, the Cold War continued, with the world divided into Eastern and Western blocs. But the mid-1960s also saw the emergence of post-colonial and pro-Communist movements on the three continents often ignored by geopolitics: Latin America, Africa and Asia. In Cuba in January 1966, the Tricontinental was formed, a coalition of anti-imperialist forces from these three continents.

At the instigation of Ahmed Ben Bella (Algeria), Mehdi Ben Barka (Tunisia), Salvador Allende (Chile), Hô Chi Minh (Vietnam) and Che Guevara (Cuba), delegates from 82 countries – including rival siblings Russia and China – came together in Havana. Josephine received a very official invitation from the Cuban Embassy in Paris, as a salute to her involvement in the fight against racial segregation. But she was also there to sing. The so-called "Lider Maximo" came to listen to her at the Teatro Garcia Lorca. She was greeted with cheers on Plaza de la Revolución and listened to the interminable speech Castro made on the occasion. "The Tricontinental," she said to the Cuban press, "is an amazing thing, with all these people of different countries, languages, skin colours. I consider myself extremely lucky to sing in front of such an audience. The whole human race united as one family."

Josephine stayed on the 24th floor of the Habana Libre Hotel, along with the delegations. It was said: "The higher your room is in this 25-storey hotel, the closer you are to the court" – Fidel's renowned suite was situated on the top floor. As it happened, in the room next to Josephine's was Frenchman Régis Debray, 25, who would become Che's travelling companion in Bolivia.

Writer Roger Faligot revealed in 2013 that during a private interview with Fidel, Josephine alerted him to an assassination plot to be carried out during the conference. She was no doubt relaying a message given to her by French intelligence. Indeed, several assassination attempts against Castro were thwarted during the conference. Josephine would later be named lieutenant of the Revolutionary Armed Forces.

Six months later, Josephine returned to Cuba for the summer. This time, she was accompanied by the entire Rainbow Tribe. They later recalled attending a speech delivered by "Uncle Fidel". The man harangued the crowd in Spanish for six hours straight, under the Cuban sun.

In 1967, after Che's assassination, Josephine sent a letter to Fidel informing him that she mourned with Cuba.

Fidel Castro died on 25 November 2016.

Jean-Claude Brialy

It was no coincidence that Jean-Claude Brialy ended up being the last of Josephine Baker's fairy godmothers. The son of a French officer stationed in Germany, young Jean-Claude discovered the music hall for the first time in 1949 thanks to his aunt, the Parisian of the family, when she took him to see a revue starring Josephine at the Folies-Bergère. "I was absolutely dazzled," he would write five decades later. "Seeing how excited I was, how I clapped and cheered, my aunt was the first to know and support my calling for show business."

Born in Algeria in 1933, Jean-Claude was nine when he crossed the Mediterranean to live in France. He left his childhood behind him; so began the long, dark tunnel of life in the barracks. "My parents had decided to raise me like it was the 1880s." Cinema and amateur theatre were his only escape – two passions that his father and mother strongly disapproved of. At the age of 18, having just graduated from school, a headstrong and rebellious Jean-Claude told his father that he intended to move to Paris, where he would study at the Conservatoire de Paris. *Entrée des artistes*, a film featuring his idol Louis Jouvet as a stern teacher, was a major factor in this emotional and romantic decision.

"My father asked me to do my military service first. After that, I would be of legal age and I could do whatever I wanted."

It just so happened that Jean-Claude was assigned to the Army Film and Photographic Unit in Baden-Baden, where the undisciplined young man had a chance to play the clown. Specifically, in a short film entitled *Chiffonard et Bonaloy*, he played the role of an undisciplined draftee named Chiffonard. The film happened to be directed by a young Pierre Lhomme, who would go on to become a master cinematographer. His friend Pierre was from Paris; when they were on leave, he would invite Jean-Claude to spend time in the capital. There, he introduced him to his group of friends, young folk who talked about films all night, haunted movie theatres all day and had begun to share their strong opinions about film in the pages of *Les Cahiers du cinema*. Their names were Jean-Luc Godard, Claude Chabrol, François Truffaut, Alain Cavalier and Jacques Rivette. Jean-Claude was always the "funny one". He became the actor of the group. "I was their pet, their entertainment, their little night (and day) music." When Rivette, Rohmer, Godard and Truffaut began shooting their first short films in 1956, it was only natural that Brialy's name ended up in the credits of each. He had to wait a few years, however, to make his first appearance in front of mainstream audiences, when he starred in Claude Chabrol's first two feature films, *Le Beau Serge* (1958) and *Les Cousins* (1959), which turned him into one of the most iconic actors of the French New Wave.

When Jean-Claude Brialy first crossed paths with Josephine Baker near the end of 1960, he was already an established actor. Although his career as a leading man was short-lived, he was top-billed in over 60 of the more than 100 films comprising his CV. Godard's *A Woman is a Woman*, Truffaut's *The Bride Wore Black*, Allégret's *Le Bal du comte d'Oregel* and Rohmer's *Claire's Knee* were among the first productions that he starred in during the initial decade of his career. In 1968, on the Île Saint-Louis in Paris, he purchased an old corner café, which he renamed L'Orangerie. There, it was not uncommon to see the likes of Prince Rainier, Grace Kelly, Liza Minnelli, Yves Saint-Laurent, Woody Allen, Marlon Brando, Anouk Aimée, Steven Spielberg, Robert De Niro, Jack Nicholson, Jacques Chazot and Arletty.

One day in January of 1969, while reading *Paris Match*, the actor learned that Josephine had been expelled from Milandes: "I was outraged by the fact that they would treat this woman like a thief." That evening, a man came up to his table at L'Orangerie. He claimed to have recently acquired a cabaret and asked the actor to handle the programming. Brialy was about to decline the offer, but then: "Suddenly, I remembered... and I thought: 'Why not... Josephine Baker?'" Jean-Claude managed to reach her at her hotel in Stockholm. "Why are you helping me?" the 64-year-old singer asked. "Because I believe in signs, and that you are on my path." On 27 March, Josephine began her singing engagement at La Goulue. "Josephine sang with a powerful voice and unbelievable energy, considering her health."

The next summer, Brialy sat front-row in Monaco, applauding his friend's comeback. "She would write me these four-page letters nearly every day, to talk about her life in Monaco."

In 1974, Princess Grace asked Josephine to headline a revue to be held at the Monte Carlo Casino. Jean-Claude was also involved in the event: "We went to work and came up with a series of scenes depicting the important moments in her life and career. I did the transitions between numbers. The revue was a smash hit, despite the jaded audience."

Meanwhile, at the Bobino, Jean-Claude was still present, presiding as a witty and respectful MC. "The show was a triumph till the end of its run. Josephine was glowing, but it took its toll on her. Every day I would tell her to rest, to save her strength, but she was running herself ragged and wouldn't listen to me."

He was the first, along with André Levasseur, to rush to her bedside when Josephine was hospitalised after she fell into the coma from which she never awoke. When Grace Kelly joined them, she asked: "What can I do, Jean-Claude?" "Madame, I believe that Josephine wished to be buried in Monte Carlo, she was happy there," the actor replied. Later, he would write: "Josephine had never spoken to me about it, but I truly believe that she would have wanted to be buried in the principality."

Thirty-two years later, on 30 May 2007, Jean-Claude Brialy, 74, died of jaw cancer, an illness which he had kept hidden from those close to him.

Akio, Jeannot, Luis et Jari

THE RAINBOW TRIBE
by Jean-Claude Bouillon-Baker

"The Rainbow Tribe": the name my mother chose for us under the world's curious gaze. Our Tribe resembled a large tree rooted in the rich Périgord soil, instantly recognisable thanks to its foliage of hands and faces of children of every colour… foliage that would not fade or change for more than 15 years.

People came from all over France and beyond to see with their own eyes and touch with their own hands the legend promulgated by the media. A garden blossoming with children, and a rather singular head gardener: a woman who stood tall with unshakeable elegance under all circumstances. She would proclaim to everyone willing to listen – and everyone, in every language, wanted to hear it from her mouth – that she and her husband, the man with the conductor's wand, had planted this tree, unique in all the world… the Tree of Universal Brotherhood. But this gardener, with her rich voice and coffee skin, also knew when to be a mother hen, watching over her strange and multi-coloured brood, protecting it from intrusive voyeurism.

She was a magician in the land of "Jacquou le Croquant", a Cinderella recreating the dashed dreams of her own childhood, which had been full of shouting, injustice and racial and social stigma… The "Rainbow Tribe", a "Cinderella story", a "Noah's Ark" for outcasts and orphans… Everything at Milandes was metaphor, and everything was real…

When we entered this world, there was always a war raging somewhere… a conflict flaring up and sorting human beings into two categories: the living and the dead. From that chaos, my mother pulled the members of her Tribe. Some were orphans of war in Korea and Algeria. Others were the victims of abandonment – intentional or not, poverty was always implicated. Long-term remuneration, a secret agreement between our mother and the biological one, would seal the fates of some. None of us had a happy beginning.

How did that round table of children always manage to turn in harmony, in spite of all the latent atavisms that might revive from one day to the next? By making them all live together from infancy, having them fraternise from their earliest years, by impressing an idea deep into the malleable material of their

Jean-Claude, Moïse, Brahim et Marianne

young minds and hearts – though they might not look alike, they would come to resemble one another – until it was so! That was Mom's daily credo, her absolute certainty in the face of all the scepticism, smirks and sarcasm...

Apart from the devastating fact that she could not bear children herself, I like to imagine that she was also inspired by the many skin tones in her own family: Margaret, Richard and Willie Mae were not all of the same dark hue. To dare to do such a thing, she must have felt the weight of an incredible empathy for humankind in general... and for the innocent and vulnerable in particular.

We never lived like nobles. Ostentation and superiority complexes were banished from our childhood. So was making fun of the defenceless... My backside still remembers that lesson! Of course, there were attempts at posh schooling; our mother had long ago become "proper", groomed by her early years in Paris and turned into a devout converted Catholic with age. Having hardly gone to school herself, she harboured a sort of "Old France" reverence for fine institutions: she blindly trusted teachers, whose omnipotence over the human mind sometimes resembled a surgeon's domination over the human body.

Liberté, égalité, fraternité – freedom, equality, fraternity – are the watchwords for all of our experiences in those years and for everything that survives her. The freedom to explore the countryside's every nook and cranny, in every season... to swim across the Dordogne (I would've drowned, if it hadn't been for my brother Luis' bravery and sang-froid, thus sparing my mother the pain of burying a child)... to live in the treetops... to skirt the château's machicolations 30 metres above ground... to sit at table with young chimpanzees... to stage mock battles with the heavy 18th-century swords that lined the grand spiral staircase...

All equal in Mom's love and overflowing tenderness, in Dad's Cartesian wisdom and paternal fidelity, despite the ocean that separated us. All equal in the eyes of a wonderful fairy-tale princess, Grace Kelly... in the eyes of Castro,

Koffi, Mara, Noël et Stellina

Boumediene and Tito, who welcomed the Tribe. Spiritual equals, kneeling before Pope Paul VI, who blessed all the monotheistic religions of the world, assembled in one family at the Vatican. Equal, above all, among one other... in a perfect, reciprocal equality that fortified the racial tolerance we all were bathed in...

Do they get together? Moreover, do they still love each other? Children have grown up into husbands, wives, single adults, fathers and mothers, grandfathers and grandmothers (19 children and grandchildren at the time of writing). Despite the distance, from Buenos Aires to New York, from New York to Paris, from Paris to Monaco, from Monaco to Venice – though they live far away and work in different fields, they come together whenever they can. Their unaltered affection is tempered in the steel of a true brotherhood, the mysterious force that binds survivors and refugees. In the depths of the river of childhood remains that changeless gem: the potential for another kind of love, given at Milandes, by an exceptional woman. Nothing can uproot the great multiracial tree that she germinated... not the deterioration of intellectual integrity that lies in wait for everyone, nor the threat of the coming era.

P.S. Josephine, one of the nine granddaughters of Josephine, was married on 4 June 2016, at Milandes, in the château's chapel, 69 years after her grandmother... the grandmother who was about to turn 69 at the time of her death... the grandmother who was torn away from her precious Milandes... in 1969! A tangle of little signs and symbols, showing that maybe, somehow, the legend of Josephine at Milandes continues...

BIBLIOGRAPHY

Josephine authored four books in her lifetime: two autobiographies, one novel and a children's picture-book. One year after her passing, Jo Bouillon edited a collection of memories and accounts. These works were the primary sources for understanding her character.

Les Mémoires de Joséphine Baker, collected by Marcel Sauvage, illustrated Paul Colin (Kra, 1927, expanded second edition 1949).
Mon sang dans tes veines, Pépito Abatino, Félix de la Camara, based on an idea by Josephine Baker, illustrated by Georges de Pogédaïeff (Isis, 1931).
Une vie de toutes les couleurs, Josephine Baker and André Rivollet (Arthaud, 1935).
La Tribu arc-en-ciel, Josephine Baker, Jo Bouillon, illustrated by Piet Worm (Mulder & Zoon, 1957).
Josephine, Josephine Baker, Jo Bouillon and Jacqueline Cartier (Robert Laffont, 1976).

Two of Josephine Baker's sons also published memoirs of their childhood in the Rainbow Tribe:

Bouillon-Baker, Brian, *Joséphine Baker, le regard d'un fils*, with Gilles Trochard, preface by Dee Dee Bridgewater (Patrick Robin, 2006).
Bouillon-Baker, Jean-Claude, *Un château sur la Lune*, preface by Henry-Jean Servat (Hors Collection, 2012).

Abtey, Jacques, *La Guerre secrète de Joséphine Baker*, preface by Charles de Gaulle (Siboney, 1947).
Allen, James, Als, Hilton and Litwack, Leon F., *Without Sanctuary, Lynching Photography in America* (Twin Palms Publishers, 2000).

Bachollet, Raymond, Debost, Jean-Barthélemi, Lelieur, Anne-Claude and Peyrière, Marie-Christine, *Négripub, l'image des noirs dans la publicité* (Somogy, 1994).
Baker, Jean-Claude and Chase, Chris, *Josephine, the Hungry Heart* (Cooper Square Press, 1993).
Bardot, Brigitte, *Initiales B.B.* (Grasset, 1996).
Barnichon, Gilles, Hillion, Daniel and Watin-Augouard, Luc, *Cunard, les majestés de l'Atlantique et leurs concurrents* (Babouji/MDV-Maîtres du Vent, 2009).
Bechet, Daniel, *Sidney Bechet, mon père* (Alphée, 2009).
Besse, François and Kressmann, Mathilde (editors), *Paris Années folles, 100 photos de légende* (Parigramme, 2014).
Besson, Jean-Louis, "Max Reinhardt, le réel et le rêve au théâtre" in *L'Ère de la mise en scène* (CNDP, 2005).
Blanche, Jacques-Émile, *De Gauguin à La Revue nègre* (Émile-Paul Frères, 1928).
Bodin, Thierry (editor), *Catalogue Lettres & Manuscrits autographes* (Ader Nordmann, 2015).
Bonini, Emmanuel, *La Véritable Joséphine Baker* (Pygmalion, 2000).
Bonini, Emmanuel, *Joséphine Baker, 100 images pour une légende* (La Lauze, 2001).
Bonnal, Jean-Claude, *Joséphine Baker et le village des enfants du monde en Périgord*, preface by Line Renaud (PLB, 1992).
Brialy, Jean-Claude, *Le Ruisseau des singes* (Robert Laffont, 2000).

Brialy, Jean-Claude, *J'ai oublié de vous dire...* (XO, 2004).
Bréon, Emmanuel and Rivoirard, Philippe (editors), *1925, Quand l'Art déco séduit le monde* (Norma, 2013).
Brieu, Christian, Ikor, Laurent and Viguier, Jean-Michel, *Joinville le cinéma, le temps des studios* (Ramsay, 1985).
Brunelin, André, *Gabin*, préface de Dominique Gabin (Robert Laffont, 1987).
Buñuel, Luis (with Carrière, Jean-Claude), *Mon dernier soupir* (Robert Laffont, 1982).

Chaigne-Oudin, Anne-Lucie, *La France dans les jeux d'influences en Syrie et au Liban, 1940-1946* (L'Harmattan, 2009).
Chevalier, Maurice, *Ma route et mes chansons, Londres, Hollywood, Paris, Vol. 2* (Julliard, 1948).
Cinqualbre, Olivier (editor), *Robert Mallet-Stevens, architecte (1886-1945)* (Centre Pompidou, 2005).
Clairet, Marcel and Patard, Frédéric (editors), *Cherbourg, port du Titanic et des transatlantiques* (La Presse de la Manche, 2011).
Colette, *L'Envers du music-hall* (Flammarion, 1913).
Colin, Gerty, *Maurice Chevalier, une route semée d'étoiles* (Presses de la Cité, 1982).
Colin, Gerty, *Jean Gabin* (Presses de la Cité, 1983).
Colin, Paul, *Joséphine Baker et la Revue nègre, lithographies du Tumulte noir*, preface by Karen C.C. Dalton and H.L. Gates (La Martinière, 1998).
Colin, Paul, *La Croûte* (La Table Ronde, 1957).
Cullas, Philippe, *Maurice Dekobra, gentleman entre deux mondes* (Séguier, 2002).
Collective work, *Art Deco Fashion* (Pepin Press, 2007).
Collective work, *Harlem, a Century in Images* (Studio Museum in Harlem/Skira Rizzoli Publishing, 2010).

Corre, Anne-Marie, *Le Roman de Marrakech* (Perrin, 2012).

Covarrubias, Miguel, *Negro Drawings* (Knopf, 1927).

Crémieux-Brilhac, Jean-Louis, *La France libre* (Gallimard, 1996).

Crozet, René, *Annales de géographie 1936* (volume 45, no. 256).

Debray, Régis, *La Guérilla du Che* (Le Seuil, 1974).

Debray, Régis, *Loués soient nos seigneurs* (Gallimard, 1996).

Derval, Paul, *Folies Bergère*, preface by Maurice Chevalier (Paris, 1954).

De Wailly, Henri, *Liban, Syrie: le mandat* (Perrin, 2010).

Dufresne, Claude, *Tout ce que Mistinguett m'a dit* (Michel Lafon, 2005).

Dumas, Pierre, *Le Maroc* (Arthaud, 1931).

El-Dahdah, Farès and Atkinson, Stephen, *The Joséphine Baker House: for Loos's Pleasure* (MIT Press, 1995).

English, T.J., *La Cité sauvage, New York, 1963-1973* (La Table Ronde, 2012).

Fabre, Geneviève and O'Meally, Robert, *History and Memory in African-American Culture* (Oxford University Press, 1994).

Faligot, Roger, *Tricontinentale* (La Découverte, 2013).

Faligot, Roger, "Joséphine Baker, notre agent à La Havane" (*Vanity Fair*, 2014).

Feininger, Andreas, *New York in the Forties* (Dover Books, 1978).

Gordon, Mel, *Voluptuous Panic: The Erotic World of Weimar Berlin* (Feral House, 2006).

Hageney, Wolfgang, *Paris 1928-1929* (Belvédère, 1985).

Haney, Lynn, *Josephine Baker* (JC Lattès, 1981).

Harris, Nini, *Downtown St. Louis*, preface by Charlie Brennan (Reedy Press, 2015).

Hippenmeyer, Jean-Roland, *Sidney Bechet* (Tribune éditions, 1980).

Houssiau, Bernard J., *Marc Allégret, découvreur de stars*, preface by Roger Vadim (Cabédita, 1994).

Houssin-Dreyfuss, Sarah (editor), *Paul Poiret, couturier-parfumeur* (Somogy, 2013).

Hughes, Langston, *The Big Sea* (Knopf, 1940).

Kastner, Carolyn, *Miguel Covarrubias, Drawing a Cosmopolitan Line* (Georgia O'Keeffe Museum/ University of Texas Press, 2014).

Kessler, Harry, *Cahiers 1918–1937* (Grasset, 1972).

Kessler, Harry, *Journey to the Abyss: The Diaries of Count Harry Kessler, 1880–1918* (Laird Easton, Knopf, 2012).

King, Coretta Scott, *My Life with Martin Luther King Jr.* (Holt, Reinhart and Winston, 1969).

King Jr., Martin Luther, *I Have a Dream* (public domain).

Kisch, John Duke, *Separate Cinema*, preface by Henry Gates Jr. and afterword by Spike Lee (Reel Art Press, 2014).

Klüver, Billy and Martin, Julie, *Kiki et Montparnasse, 1900-1930* (Flammarion, 1989).

Lacassin, Francis, *Conversations avec Simenon* (La Sirène, 1990).

Lahs-Gonzales, Olivia, *Josephine Baker: Image and Icon* (Reedy Press, 2006).

Lamming, Clive, *Larousse des trains et des chemins de fer*, preface by Louis Gallois (Larousse, 2005).

Leigh, Wendy, *Grace Kelly* (Nouveau Monde, 2007).

Lesacher, Alain-François, Sclaresky, Monique and Champollion, Hervé, *Paris hier & aujourd'hui* (Ouest-France, 2000).

Miller, Henry and Bellon, Denise, *Mejores no hay! (Un voyage en Espagne)* (Finitude, 2012).

Mirande, Yves, *Souvenirs*, illustrations by Sem (Librairie Arthème Fayard, 1952).

Mistinguett, *Toute ma vie* (2 volumes, Julliard, 1954).

Mohrt, Michel and Feinstein, Guy, *Paquebots, le temps des traversées* (Maritimes et d'outre-mer, 1980).

Montesi, Albert and Deposki, Richard, *Central West End St. Louis* (Arcadia Publishing, 2000).

Montesi, Albert and Deposki, Richard, *Downtown St. Louis* (Arcadia Publishing, 2001).

Montesi, Albert and Deposki, Richard, *St. Louis Union Station* (Arcadia Publishing, 2002).

Morris, Ronald L., *Wait Until Dark: Jazz & the Underworld, 1880–1940*, preface by Jacques B. Hess (Bowling Green University Poplar Press, 1980).

O'Connor, Patrick and Hammond, Bryan, *Josephine Baker*, preface by Elisabeth Welch (Little, Brown and Company, 1988).

Onana, Charles, *Joséphine Baker contre Hitler* (Duboiris, 2006).

Peacock, John, *La Mode du XXe siècle*, preface by Christian Lacroix (Thames & Hudson, 2003).

Pétry, Claude, *Paul Colin et les spectacles* (Musée des Beaux-Arts de Nancy, 1994).

Poiret, Paul, *En habillant l'époque* (Grasset, 1930).

Poirier, René and Lehideux, Patrick, *L'Automobile et son histoire* (Gründ, 1956).

Préjean, Patrick, *Albert Préjean*, preface by Christian-Jaque (Candeau, 1979).

Ray, Man, *Portraits, Paris-Hollywood-Paris* (Centre Pompidou, 2010).

Rebillard, Éric and Powrie, Phil, *Pierre Batcheff and Stardom in 1920s French Cinema* (Edinburgh University Press, 2009).

Retnani, Abdelkader, *Tanger années 20* (La Croisée des chemins, 2010).

Ruffin, Frances E. and Marchesi, Stephen, *Martin Luther King Jr. and the March on Washington* (Penguin Books, 2001).

Rim, Carlo, *Mémoires d'une vieille vague* (Gallimard, 1961).

Ross, Alex, *Diary of an Aesthete* (The New Yorker, 2012).

Roueff, Olivier, *Jazz, les échelles du plaisir* (La Dispute, 2013).

Roussel, Éric, *Charles de Gaulle, 1890-1945* (Gallimard, 2002).

Sachs, Maurice, *Au temps du Bœuf sur le toit* (Grasset, 1987).

Schroeder, Alan, *Ragtime Tumpie*, illustrations by Bernie Fuchs (Little, Brown and Company, 1989).

Scotto, Vincent, *Souvenirs de Paris* (S.T.A.E.L., 1947).

Seeling, Charlotte, *La Mode au siècle des créateurs* (Könemann Verlag, 2000).

Sim, Georges (aka Georges Simenon), *Défense d'aimer* (Ferenczi & Fils, 1927).

Simenon, Georges, *Mémoires intimes* (Presses de la Cité, 1981).

Slaoui, Abderrahman, *L'Affiche orientaliste* (Malika, 2010).

Tafersiti Zarouila, Rachid, *Tanger, réalités d'un mythe* (Zarouila, 1998).

Tetley, Gary, *Images from the Architecture of Theodore Carl Link* (Landmarks Association of St. Louis, 2009).

Tims, Hilton, *Erich Maria Remarque, le dernier romantique* (Les Belles Lettres, 2014).

Toft, Carolyn Hewes, Overby, Osmund and Pettus, Robert C., *Laclede's Landing* (Landmarks Association of St. Louis, 1977).

Vignaud, Roger, *Vincent Scotto, l'homme aux 4,000 chansons* (Autres Temps, 2006).

Ware, Chris (editor), *The Rag-Time Ephemeralist* (The Acme Novelty Library, Fantagraphics Books, 1999-2002).

Warnod, Jeanine, *L'École de Paris* (Arcadia/Musée du Montparnasse, 2004).

Weill, Alain and Rennert, Jack, *Paul Colin, affichiste* (Denoël, 1989).

Willemetz, Albert, *Dans mon rétroviseur* (La Table Ronde, 1967).

Willemetz, Jacqueline, *Albert Willemetz, le prince des Années folles* (Michalon, 1995).

Wood, Ean, *La Folie Joséphine Baker* (Le Serpent à plumes, 2001).

FILMOGRAPHY

La Revue des revues, silent film by Joe Francis, 1927, 103 min. Script: Clément Vautel and Joe Francis. Production: Alex Nalpas. Restored by the Danish Film Institute and Lobster Films in 2005.

La Sirène des tropiques, silent film by Henry Étiévant and Mario Nalpas, 1927, 86 min. Script: Maurice Dekobra. Sets: Robert Mallet-Stevens. With Pierre Batcheff, Régina Dalthy, Georges Melchior and Régina Thomas. Restored by Lobster Films in 2006.

Zouzou, film by Marc Allégret, 1934, 85 min. Script: Pepito Abatino, Carlo Rim and Albert Willemetz. Music: Vincent Scotto and Georges Van Parys. Editing: Denise Batcheff. With Jean Gabin, Pierre Larquey and Viviane Romance.

Princesse Tam Tam, film by Edmond T. Gréville, 1935. 77 min. Script: Pepito Abatino and Yves Mirande. Sets: Lazare Meerson and Alexandre Trauner. With Albert Préjean and Viviane Romance.